THE HISTORY
OF SOUTHERN
LITERATURE

THE HISTORY
OF SOUTHERN
LITERATURE

General Editor

LOUIS D. RUBIN, JR.

Senior Editors

BLYDEN JACKSON

RAYBURN S. MOORE

LEWIS P. SIMPSON

THOMAS DANIEL YOUNG

Associate Editor

MARY ANN WIMSATT

Managing Editor

ROBERT L. PHILLIPS

Louisiana State University Press
Baton Rouge and London

Copyright © 1985 by Louisiana State University Press
All rights reserved
Manufactured in the United States of America

Designer: Albert Crochet
Typeface: Linotron Sabon
Typesetter: G & S Typesetters, Inc.

LIBRARY OF CONGRESS CATALOGING IN PUBLICATION DATA
Main entry under title:

The History of Southern literature.

   Includes index.
   1. American literature—Southern States—History
and criticism.   2. Southern States in literature.
I. Rubin, Louis Decimus, 1923–
PS261.H53   1985   810'.9'975   85-10183
ISBN 0-8071-1251-8 (cloth)
ISBN 0-8071-1643-2 (paper)

Louisiana Paperback Edition, 1990
99 98 97 96 95 94 93 92 91 90   5 4 3 2 1

This book is dedicated
to the memory of
C. HUGH HOLMAN
by its editors
who were also his friends
and who remain his beneficiaries

Contents

CONTENTS

xi

Acknowledgments

MANY PEOPLE helped in the creation and production of *The History of Southern Literature*, and we should like to express our gratitude. Thanks to Florence Blakely, Mary Canada, Emerson Ford, Elvin Strowd, and Mattie Russell of the William R. Perkins Library, Duke University; Robert M. Willingham, Jr., of the Ilah Dunlap Little Library, University of Georgia; E. L. Inabinett and Alan Stokes of the South Caroliniana Library, University of South Carolina; to Miriam J. Shillingsburg and James E. Kibler, Jr., for their careful reading of portions of the manuscript and their detailed, cautionary advice; to Nelle Smither for valuable bibliographical information; to Ann Burroughs for research assistance; to Florence Whitmire, Virginia Seaquist, Cheryl Shows, and Mary Anne Benoist for typing and proofreading; to Heidi Bullock and Kieran Quinlan for invaluable editorial assistance; to Margaret B. Moore for various scholarly courtesies; to W. Coburn Freer and William J. Payne of the University of Georgia for released time; to Peter Shillingsburg of the Department of English at Mississippi State University and Brenda Bridges for the many hours spent teaching editors and typists to use the computer; and to Russell Kegley and Edwin Ellis of the Department of Computer Science and the staff at the Computing Center at Mississippi State.

The generous support received from the National Endowment for the Humanities and from the Hillsdale Fund has made this project possible, and the efforts of the Office of Graduate Studies and Research, the Business Office, the Department of English, especially Joseph E. Milosh and Priscilla Ammerman and the staff of the *Mississippi Quarterly*, at Mississippi State University have been indispensable in managing the grants we received.

For thirty years and more the Louisiana State University Press has been the leading scholarly publisher in the field of Southern history and literature, so it was no more than fitting that, once the idea for a history of that literature had been proposed, the venture became a joint enterprise of the Society for the Study of Southern Literature and the Louisiana State University Press. To Beverly Jarrett, executive editor and associate director, the editors of this book are indebted for guidance and encouragement from the outset. It is her book just as much as ours. To Shannon Sandifer, editor, we are grateful for copy editing of the manuscript in a fashion that has been both meticulous and intelligent.

No statement of acknowledgments or indebtedness would be complete without saying that the specific idea of this history was Mary Ann Wimsatt's; as the then-president of the Society for the Study of Southern Literature, it was Dr. Wimsatt who proposed the venture. Once it was under way, she and Robert L. Phillips worked long and hard to coordinate the planning. Dr. Phillips as managing editor handled the formidable task of keeping the enterprise on track and on schedule, seeing to the preparation of the computer script, and otherwise doing the immense amount of labor that translated an idea into a reality.

THE HISTORY
OF SOUTHERN
LITERATURE

Introduction

This book offers an account of the principal developments in the history of Southern literature from its beginnings up to the present time, and characterizes the writings of those authors who have played significant parts in creating it. The collective work of a number of scholars, the book will, we hope, be useful to anyone wishing to learn the more important facts about a particular Southern writer or group of writers, the literature of a particular time or locale in Southern history, or the relationships between the writings of one time and place and those of another. In short, it tells the story of the South's literature.

Not since the early 1950s has there been published a book that attempted to present, within the pages of a single volume, a history of the literature of the American South from its earliest days onward. The late Jay B. Hubbell's monumental *The South in American Literature, 1607–1900* was reasonably complete, insofar as the state of scholarship in Southern literature then permitted, up through the period of the Civil War; the chapters for the period 1865 to 1900 were more in the nature of a summary. But since it appeared—in part because it appeared—far more has come to light about the earlier literature, in particular for the colonial period. The same is true for the literature of the years following 1865.

Considerably more pages in this book are devoted to the writings of the twentieth century than to those of earlier periods. This is as it should be. Far more Southern writing has appeared in the present century than in all the previous years combined. Moreover, from a qualitative standpoint, the principal importance of much of the earlier literature lies in the extent to which it contributes to the development of the literary imagination that would flower in the twentieth-century Southern Literary Renascence.

For the literature of the years since the close of World War II, there are chapters and subchapters about individual authors and groups of authors, with less effort made to shape such discussions into overall units. The reasons for this, we trust, will become obvious upon reflection. The sorting-out process of time has not yet produced an agreed-upon canon of important and less-important writings; to attempt to arrive at and enforce such a canon would be premature. All of us are familiar with otherwise valuable literary histories that have sought to treat recent writers and writings with the same kind of conceptualized forms and patterning as were appropriate for earlier work; in almost all instances, the passing of only a decade or two has caused such undertakings to seem not merely confusing but frequently absurd. So it seemed wiser for us to attempt no such overall shaping for the more recent literature, but instead to ask good scholars to write accounts of good writers, and to trust the common concerns and emphases of the time and place to provide most of the congruence. For the student interested in learning about recent Southern literature, we felt this approach would prove more useful, and less likely to grow swiftly out of date.

It would have been easier, and far more tidy, to have included only brief mention of recent writings, and in effect to have concluded this history of Southern literature at or about the year 1950. To have done so, however, would in our judgment have rendered the book considerably less useful to the larger body of readers. For the very recent authors, however, who have done almost all of their publishing during the last decade or so, and whose careers are still very much open to change and development, we commissioned brief summarizing essays. Here it seemed best to select contributors with special competence in the most recent work and to leave the choices and emphases to them.

When, as a committee of the Society for the Study of Southern Literature, we first began work, the editors had no assurance that any financial help whatever would be forthcoming. Chapters were commissioned with the hope, but not the guarantee, of modest recompense. Fortunately, a small but distinguished foundation, the Hillsdale Fund of Greensboro, North Carolina, responded to our importunities with a grant that would cover at least the considerable costs of preparing the material for publication. Somewhat later the National Endowment for the Humanities, that ever-sympathetic champion of the cause of the beleaguered written word in our time, came through with a larger grant that provided stipends for contributors and editors, released time and secretarial and computer help for the managing editor, necessary editorial travel, and various other needs. We are rather proud, however, of the fact that our scholarly colleagues were willing to take on their assignments when no recompense could be offered. (And, if the skeptic will consider the implications of that fact, he or she will understand why it is possible, in the 1980s, to speak with some assurance of the continuing existence of a Southern literature.)

In a work such as this one, especially for the later chapters, it has been necessary to make judgmental choices about inclusions. Our choices will not satisfy everyone entirely, but no choices would; perhaps no choices should. But given the human limitations of our collective editorial wisdom and the practical limitation of space available, we believe that we have been thorough and reasonably objective.

Originally we had planned to have each chapter of the history followed by a brief bibliography of available scholarship on the subject. What we soon found was that no single format for listing scholarship would serve the diverse needs of various kinds of chapters. So we decided, after much soul-searching, that if we wanted to produce a one-volume history of Southern literature, all bibliographical information would have to be omitted. There is available, after all, a wealth of bibliographical work, both generally and for individual authors; and the annual bibliographical checklist of the Society for the Study of Southern Literature, published each spring in *Mississippi Quarterly*, provides ample annotation for new scholarship. M. Thomas Inge's essay "The Study of Southern Literature," appended to this book, offers a guide to just where such scholarship is available.

It ought to be noted that this book came into being during the first several years of the ninth decade of the twentieth century—which is to say, a quarter-century following the *Brown* vs. *Board of Education* decision, and more than a half-century after the publication of *I'll Take My Stand: The South and the Agrarian Tradition*. All five of its senior editors were born in the South of the 1910s and 1920s, grew up during the 1920s and 1930s, and did their graduate study during the 1940s and 1950s. They were born and grew up, that is, in a South that was still economically impoverished, rurally dominated, in politics monolithically Democratic, and racially segregated. All of them knew what it was to see some few white-bearded old men wearing uniforms of grey, and other white-bearded old men who had once been slaves. All of them grew up and pursued their academic careers in a South that was rapidly becoming industrialized and urbanized, achieving an economic prosperity far beyond the experience of earlier generations, moving decisively toward a two-party political system, and escaping at last from the crippling, stultifying burden of two centuries of legalized, institutionalized racial discrimination.

In terms of literary history, the senior editors of this history grew up while the leading figures of the Southern Renascence were writing and publishing the books that placed the onetime Sahara of the Bozart at the very center of American literary creativity (though not close to the center of the reading, reviewing, and marketing of that literature). They were roughly the contemporaries of what has been called the "second generation" of the writers of the Renascence, who began publishing their stories and poems in the 1940s and 1950s. They were to varying degrees acquainted with many of the writers of both generations, sometimes closely.

Just as the political, social, and economic developments in the twentieth-century South had the effect of placing the region in a less defensive and less isolated position *vis-à-vis* American life as a whole, so the distinguished achievement of twentieth-century Southern literature, read and admired as it was on several continents, made its study a considerably less provincial and chauvinistic enterprise than had once been true.

Here it is necessary to keep in mind the history of scholarship in Southern literature. It was in the 1830s and 1840s, as the sectional conflict between North and South began to take on serious proportions, that the idea of a "Southern" literature came into being as a thing distinct from American literature as a whole. Subsequent developments —the heated-up slavery controversy, secession, military defeat, Reconstruction, widespread and enduring poverty, a colonial economic dependency upon the Northeast, pervasive segregation in almost every aspect of daily life, one-crop agriculture and a political and social order still dominated by its rural components—not only intensified the sense of the South as being set apart from and, for the white community, united against the rest of the nation, but gave to the literary imagination, and to those who studied it, a powerful sense of regional identity and sectional mission. Thus it was not until the 1890s that a scholarship began to emerge that could be importantly critical of aspects of Southern society.

After the First World War, as the literary Renascence came into flower, there developed a major rift between "scholarship," which was essentially historical and mainly devoted to the earlier literature, and "criticism," which was principally concerned with the literature of modernism. The poet-critics of Vanderbilt University were prime movers in the so-called New Criticism, which though by no means anti- or even ahistorical, focused its attention upon the text of the literary work rather than its biographical or historical correlations. Yet at the same time it was these critics, and their students and allies, who were the first to recognize the importance of such writers as Faulkner. And it was they who identified the literature of the Southern Renascence as a culmination of the region's literary and cultural history, rather than some bizarre modernist deviation from it. It was they who could perceive that the stories and poems of the modern Southerners not only depicted but

4

embodied the powerful currents of change, and of resistance to change, that have so strikingly and sometimes so violently characterized the social experience of the twentieth-century South.

When the modernist split between historical scholarship and criticism began to be healed, as began happening in the 1940s and 1950s, the way was clear for the development of a body of scholarship concerning the literature of the South that could be historically informed, critically sophisticated, and, since it was free of much of the excessive regional defensiveness of earlier generations, no longer constrained to explain away or gloss over any and all shortcomings, either in the literature itself or in the society out of which it grew.

From the outset, the editors of this volume planned a racially integrated history, which would chronicle the writings of black and white authors, but at the same time recognized essential differences in the community heritage, since to ignore those differences would produce a distorted view of the literature. Except in the earlier chapters, when necessarily there was very little black literature in the South, white and black authors are discussed throughout interchangeably, in separate chapters and subchapters. In addition to writing several chapters himself, Blyden Jackson has also contributed sequences to certain other chapters that develop the role of black authors in the literary scene being chronicled.

That literature may usefully be viewed in terms of its historical unfolding, its changing relationships to a changing time and place, is not universally acknowledged in contemporary critical thought. That American literature can be importantly considered in terms of its regional origins is likewise by no means a general assumption among scholars of that literature any more. Why, such a scholar might ask, should the "Southern" identity of either an author or a work be regarded as significant? What has American literature to do with preserving the sectional allegiances of the mid-nineteenth century?

To such questions, the editors for and contributors to this book would respond that the Southern identity is important because it is. Whether it ought or ought not to be is irrelevant. The facts are that there existed in the past, and there continues to exist today, an entity within American society known as the South, and that for better or for worse the habit of viewing one's experience in terms of one's relationship to that entity is still a meaningful characteristic of both writers and readers who are or have been part of it. The historical circumstances that gave rise to that way of thinking and feeling have been greatly modified. Yet in the year 1984, as this history is being prepared for the printer, to consider writers and their writings as Southern still involves considerably more than merely a geographical grouping. History, as a mode for viewing one's experience and one's identity, remains a striking characteristic of the Southern literary imagination, black and white.

Had this book been planned only five years earlier than it was, at least three scholars, all of them longtime associates and friends of the present editors, would have played prominent roles in its shaping and editing. The late Richard Beale Davis, Arlin Turner, and C. Hugh Holman were among the leading scholars of Southern literature of the past quarter-century. With the present editors they were instrumental in forming the Society for the Study of Southern Literature, whose project this book is. Much of what appears in the pages of this history bears the imprint of their thinking. To one of them the book is dedicated. To C. Hugh Holman, and to Richard Beale Davis and Arlin Turner as well, go our thanks for labors well performed.

LDR

PART I

COLONIAL AND ANTEBELLUM SOUTHERN LITERATURE

 1607–1860

LEWIS P. SIMPSON

Introduction to Part I

In the first chapter of this initial section of *The History of Southern Literature*, J. Leo Lemay quotes a graphic passage from Arthur Barlow's account of the exploring expedition that immediately preceded the first attempt at the settlement of Virginia. Nearing the shore of the new land, the members of the party—aboard a vessel that was in all probability reeking with the stench of the long Atlantic crossing—smelled the land breeze and were transported into the very midst of a "delicate garden, abounding with all kinds of odoriferous flower." They landed to walk on the ground of "the first creation," where existence demanded no "toil or labor." Thus long before there was an identifiable South, the poetry of a promotion tract prophesied the South as both an emotional entity and a geographical place. In the years immediately following, in spite of the fact that the first attempts to colonize the Virginia wilderness ended in the unknown disaster that befell the Lost Colony and the despair that overcame the Roanoke group, the history of the South yet to come into self-conscious existence began to assume the literary image of a transaction between pastoral dream and historical reality. The emergence of this image may be viewed as a part of a larger transaction that has been at the center of the American literary portrayal of the origin and destiny of the nation as a whole. But an understanding of American literary history demands the recovery of the particular Southern version of the transactional image, now being eclipsed by the image of a continental South extending from California to Virginia and called the Sun Belt. Perhaps we should say that an attempt to comprehend our literary history—or for that matter American history in general—requires the effort to penetrate the meaning in antebellum America of the Southern as opposed to the New England (or, more broadly, the Northern) version of the great American transaction between dream and reality. In this implicit relationship, the drama of each transaction rested on the confidence of those who shaped it that they knew the truth of the Republic. For the North the truth embraced

9

the indivisibility of the Union and, with increasing intensity in the decade before the Civil War, the abolition of slavery as the condition of a free and equal society. For the South the truth enfolded the idea of the sovereignty of state and section over the national power and, ultimately, the concept of a great slave society as the rational basis of freedom and equality. In deciding by means of a catastrophic bloodletting that the nation could not be separated and that slavery would be abolished, the Americans did not destroy but with tragic irony fulfilled the necessary relationship, the cultural symbiosis, between the Southern and New England colonies that had been created in the common shedding of revolutionary blood. The destruction of the Confederacy and the Reconstruction of the South in effect brought into existence the second American Republic. This Republic rests on the mystical notion—slow to be accepted in the South and still not shared by all Southerners—that the nation finds its symbol of unity not in the blood of the American Revolution but in the redeeming power of the blood that was shed in fratricidal conflict. In recent years we have seen "Dixie" abandoned, while even white Southerners accept "The Battle Hymn of the Republic" as a second national anthem.

The complexities of the antebellum literary and intellectual negotiation between the South and New England—to be sure, the entire symbiotic relationship of the sections—had its inception in the colonial beginnings. In contrast to the religious motive present in the colonial enterprises that in the sixteenth and seventeenth centuries went out from the metropolis of Europe to the trans-Atlantic frontiers—a motive vividly proclaimed in the theocentric vision of the writers of the New England migration—the intention of the Virginia promoters, though hardly divorced from a religious impulse, implied the secularization of the colonizing movement. Through nuance, if not in any overt way, the vision of the possibilities of Virginia suggests its connection with the secular critique of man and God, nature and society that by the Elizabethan Age was engaged in the final deconstruction of the medieval world and the institution of modernity. In fact, the modern mind was heralded in the poetry of Captain John Smith's contemporaries, notably Shakespeare, and attained its first definitive formulation in another contemporary, Sir Francis Bacon. While Smith, at least as he depicted himself, was cast in the mold of heroic knighthood, he was a type of modern conqueror, not simply treading the ground of Virginia but planting it. He anticipated Bacon's advice in his essay on plantations (1626) to discover the secrets of nature in new places and exploit their utility for man. Conscious of himself, he once put it, as both an "actor" and a "relator," Smith was aware that the printing press was a prime instrument of a new age, not only as the means of a drastic extension of literacy, but as an integral part of an unprecedented subjectification of man's knowledge of what he knows and how he knows it—of a complete movement of world and self into mind. In a profound sense the secularization of the colonial enterprise equated the movement to the New World and the movement of man and his world, of existence, into the human mind. This equation, expressed in tone and manner, in the writings of Smith, Robert Beverley, and William Byrd, differentiates the writing in the chief Southern colony, Virginia, from writing in the major New England colony, Massachusetts, where the process of secularization, far from being synonymous with the first settlement, worked itself out slowly in an intricate drama that can be traced from John Winthrop at the commencement to John Adams at the end of the colonial period. This drama held the literary promise that would flower in the nineteenth century in Emerson and Hawthorne, whereas the intellectual and literary situation in early Virginia held the expectation that flowered in the revolutionary movement, especially in Thomas Jefferson's succinct summation of the political, and not less the literary, consequence of the transference of world and self into mind—the Declaration of Independence.

Although evangelical Christianity became a widespread influence in the nineteenth-century South, the Southern literary intelligence remained essentially secular in character. Because of his reservations about slavery, Jefferson became suspect to later Southern men of letters. But the inclination to depose Jefferson as a model political philosopher in favor of John C. Calhoun involved only a shift in attention from the multifaceted rationalism of the full Enlightenment to a more austere and legalistic rationalism. Bacon, Newton, and Locke, Jefferson's holy trinity, remained key figures in the Southern intellectual pantheon, and the rational mind remained the proper model of society. Romanticism in the South did not assume the form of an Emersonian disdain for eighteenth-century formalism, but took the shape of nostalgic lament for a presumed loss of an undefined order. In Poe the sense of loss is accompanied, as in "The Fall of the House of Usher," with a desperate fear of the destructive force of the irrational. Symptomatic of this fear no doubt was the attraction of Southern men of letters to the idea of the South as a model of civilization. Potentially the highly charged ironies, the poignant inner drama, of life in the antebellum South provided a great poetic and novelistic subject, but it was in New England, not in the South, that a literary renaissance occurred. Save in Poe, who spent a good deal of his career outside the South, the Southern literary mind, following the political mind, closed itself around the slavery issue and suppressed the ironic dimensions of Southern subject matter. (There was no black literary expression in the antebellum South. Slaves were generally not permitted by law to learn to read and write, and masters were forbidden to teach them. The few black writers who emerged before the Civil War in one way or another got beyond Southern boundaries; as explained in the chapter on antebellum fiction, the first novel by an American black was written and published in London.) The one area of the Southern literary expression, save for Poe's works, that is accorded genuine respect today is that of humor. Considered by contemporary Southerners to be a subliterary form, the humorous writings of the Old South (especially of the Old Southwest: Georgia, Alabama, Mississippi, Tennessee, Arkansas) now seem to be a substantial literary achievement. Although very restricted in setting and scope, this body of writing— which begins with William Byrd's account of the backwoods North Carolinians and ends with George Washington Harris' creation of the Tennessean Sut Lovingood—brings into play the multiple ironies of the pastoral dream of the South in the context of historical reality. As the second American Republic began its course in history, the inheritor of the Southern school of humorists, Mark Twain, made the comic interpretation of life in the South germane to the whole literary vision of the American negotiation between dream and history.

J. A. LEO LEMAY

The Beginnings

American, and Southern, literature began when Sir Walter Ralegh
sent four major expeditions to Virginia, which was then defined
as that "part of the World, which is between the Florida and the Cape
Breton" (now Georgia through Nova Scotia). First came Arthur Barlow's exploring party in 1584; second, the colonizing expedition under
Ralph Lane in 1585; third, the colonizing party, the Lost Colony, under
John White in 1587; and last, a supply party in 1590. The third expedition is famous in American legend and literature for the birth of Virginia Dare—"because this child was the first Christian born in Virginia
she was named Virginia"—and for its mysterious disappearance. The
Lost Colony left only the word CROATOAN carved on a post. But the first
and especially the second expedition left significant literature. Arthur
Barlow's account of the 1584 exploration portrayed America as paradise. When the sailors reached shoal water, they smelled the sweet air,
"so strong a smell, as if we had been in the midst of some delicate garden, abounding with all kinds of odoriferous flower." Exploring the
land they found an abundance, "as in the first creation, without toil or
labor." Although Barlow mentioned the fighting waged by some Amerindians against other tribes, he stressed their friendly behavior. They
were "most gentle, loving, and faithful, void of all guile, and treason,
and such as lived after the manner of the golden age." He thought them
the most "kind and loving people in the world," glad to trade valuable
furs for trinkets.

Such was the dream. Ralegh used Barlow's account to promote his
colonizing expedition in 1585, the first English attempt to found a permanent settlement in what is now the United States. The colonists knew
little of fishing or farming, expecting to enjoy the natural abundance of
the Garden of Eden that was Virginia—and expecting to be fed by the
"kind and loving" Indians in exchange for trinkets. They settled at
Roanoke because it was close to Florida, near which the Spanish gal-
leons, freighted with gold and silver, passed on their way from the New

13

World to Spain. But Roanoke lacked a good harbor; after losing part of their provisions when a boat overturned, the colonists nearly starved. When Sir Francis Drake came by in June, 1586, they gave up and returned with him to England. But Thomas Hariot and John White had gained valuable experience in America.

Although the 1585–1586 colonizing attempt had failed miserably, Ralegh still wanted to colonize and backed John White's plan to send out families and farmers and artisans, persons who expected to work to create a self-sufficient American plantation. Ralegh asked Hariot to write a pamphlet that would counteract the stories, brought back by some colonists, of near starvation, Indian treachery, and miserable heat. Hariot's *A Briefe and True Report of the New-Found Land of Virginia* (1588) accounted for America's bad image, described the possibilities for marketing American commodities (stressing the availability of lumber), told of the natural foods and plants and wildlife in America, and concluded with a good discussion of "the nature and manners of the people." Although Hariot assured his readers that the Amerindians were "not to be feared," he claimed that, if necessary, they could easily be defeated in war. Hariot's pamphlet was a great success. Richard Hakluyt reprinted it the following year in his "prose epic of the modern English nation," *The Principal Navigations, Voyages, Traffiques, and Discoveries of the English Nation.* In 1590, Théodore de Bry began his great series of publications entitled *America* by issuing Hariot's *Briefe and True Report* in German, Latin, French, and English, embellished with de Bry's engravings of John White's drawings. These engravings not only became the first widely distributed portraits of eastern seaboard Amerindians and native American flora and fauna, but they also changed English and European perceptions of their own ancestors. Henceforth, Europeans viewed their progenitors as versions of the American Indian. Thus the Amerindian influenced European ideas of civilization's development.

When Hariot wrote *A Briefe and True Report,* he could not have known that the expedition setting out under John White would become the Lost Colony. Those colonists, including eighty-five men, sixteen women, and eleven children, were the only emigrants before the 1620 Pilgrim Fathers to include a large portion of families. They intended to settle within the Chesapeake Bay area, probably near the mouth of the James River, where they knew from their exploring forays of 1585 and 1586 that good harbors and fertile lands existed. But the mariners had booty on their minds and dumped the planters at Roanoke. When John White left in August, 1587, to return to England for supplies, the colonists intended to abandon Roanoke and move to the Chesapeake region. No one can be positive what happened to them. But the evidence suggests that they did move and that they made an alliance with a small tribe called the Chesapeake Indians. They left a few men with the friendly Indians on Croatoan, an island now part of Cape Hatteras, south of Roanoke, well-known to White and to the sailors. The men were probably supposed to lead the supply ships to the main settlement on the Chesapeake. But the guides were no longer at Croatoan when White finally managed to return. And in late April, 1607, when three English ships sailed into the Chesapeake Bay, Powhatan killed the remaining "Lost Colonists," along with their Indian allies. That, at least, is what Powhatan told Smith, what the London Company wrote to its governor Sir Thomas Gates in 1609, and what William Strachey wrote in his *Historie of Travaile into Virginia Britannia* (1612). But there are inconsistencies among these accounts, and the mystery of the Lost Colony may never be definitively solved.

The successful English colonization of America began on May 24, 1607, when the planters sent over by the Virginia Company of London landed at Jamestown. But for more than a decade, failure seemed probable. The earliest leaders, always excepting Captain John Smith, could not cope with frontier conditions. Some died, some tried to abandon the colony, and all of them continually bickered. The first starving and seasoning time, the summer of 1607, reduced the "first planters" from 105 to 38. (The earliest Americans called themselves planters, by which they did not mean farmers but the planters of a new civilization.) When the apolitical Captain John Smith was finally elected president of the council in September, 1608, he changed the colony's failing tendency, but after he left in October, 1609, things fell apart. That winter without Smith became the terrible starving time, and the few settlers remaining alive in June, 1610, were actually sailing down the James River, abandoning the attempt to settle America, when they encountered Lord De La Warr bringing a new supply of settlers. The success of the English colonization in America remained doubtful until 1618, when the Virginia Company finally introduced the headright system, whereby each immigrant to America, or the person who paid for his passage, was granted fifty acres of land. That policy, together with John Rolfe's discovery that tobacco could furnish a successful crop for English sale, seemingly assured Virginia's future. But one more crisis threatened to ruin the settlement: the Indian massacre of the whites in 1622, followed by a final starving time (June, 1622, to September, 1623). But by 1624, when King James dissolved the Virginia Company, Virginia had become home for a number of individuals. And by 1633, they had achieved identity as Virginians.

Throughout the years 1607 through 1624, the Virginia Company attempted to lure settlers to America. Like every colony, Virginia began with a spate of promotion tracts. The literature emphasized the natural bounty of nature, especially the abundance of fish, fowl, and game, healthful climate, fertile soil and available land (which the Virginia Company always promised to parcel out at a future date), easy prospects of wealth, the excitement of new adventure, the certainty of creating an estate and rising in the social hierarchy, the local Indians' friendliness, the glory of converting the heathens to Christianity, and the grandeur of adding new dominions to the British empire. Colonization was not just a worthy enterprise for God and country; it promised adventure, glory, and gold. Every major setback and every new disaster prompted apologies, explanations, and new exhortations, which could take the form of news reports, sermons, ballads, prose arguments, or verse compliments. Promotion tracts appeared in every decade and dominated seventeenth-century Southern literature; the major single theme of American literature, the American dream, flows directly from them. The typical subject matter of the tracts carried over into most other early American genres. Accounts of exploration, tales of personal adventure, scientific nature reports, and the histories of the colonies almost all became, at least in part, promotional. Nearly all the major early American writings, from the works by Captain John Smith and William Bradford to Cotton Mather's *Magnalia Christi Americana*, William Byrd's *History of the Dividing Line*, Benjamin Franklin's *Autobiography*, Crèvecoeur's *Letters from an American Farmer*, and Jefferson's *Notes on the State of Virginia*, either are promotional or have the promotion of America as a major theme. Although the ostensible audience was English or European, emigrants especially read the tracts—and so did the Americans. The genre was inescapable for several reasons. Promotional literature was the primary literature about America; it was local; and it was abundant. Promotional literature defined America and what it meant to be an American, and it replied to the widespread negative images of the New World and its settlers.

Virginia, "the mother of all our plantations" as Captain John Smith called it, had and needed more promotional material than any other colony. Besides the broadsides and brief pamphlets published by the Virginia Company, translations of American materials by Richard Hakluyt and Pierre Erondelle (both in 1609) appeared; Robert Johnson (1609 and 1612), Lord De La Warr (1611), William Strachey (1612), and Edward Waterhouse (1622) all wrote tracts concerning Virginia. In addition to Michael Drayton's great ode "To the Virginian Voyage," poems appeared by Richard Rich (1610) and Christopher Brook (1622), and the anonymous ballads *The Laste Newes from Virginia* (1611, no copy known) and *Good News from Virginia* (1624) appeared as well as others on the Virginia lottery (1612), and on the massacre (1622, no copy known). Sermons by William Symonds, Robert Gray, Daniel Price (all in 1609), William Crashaw (1610), Alexander Whitaker (1613), Patrick Copland (1622), and John Donne (1622) celebrated the colony of Virginia. Numerous other sermons incidentally praised the enterprise, including ones by Richard Crakanthorpe, George Benson, and Robert Tynly in 1609 alone. In addition, Captain John Smith wrote eight books concerning America, Samuel Purchas published his great compilation *Hakluytus Posthumus, or Purchas his Pilgrimes* (1625), and numerous colonists sent back manuscript letters and accounts of Virginia. Not all of these writers claimed that Virginia was an "earthly Paradise" (Johnson, 1609), but most of them thought colonization would increase England's empire, serve God, reduce English overpopulation, and make the emigrant rich. Perhaps Edward Waterhouse, writing after the Indian massacre of the whites in 1622, advanced the most infamous reason. He thought settlers should come to America to kill the Indians in order to conserve the wildlife!

The most notable later promotion tracts are William Bullock's *Virginia Impartially Examined* (1649) and John Hammond's *Leah and Rachel; or, The Two Fruitfull Sisters, Virginia and Maryland* (1656). Hammond had lived for twenty-one years in the Chesapeake area, fled to England because his life was in danger, but returned as soon as he could. He writes that he loves America, "that sweet, that rich, that large country," and resents the slurs on it. Although it is "not such a Lubberland as the Fiction of the Land of Ease is reported to be, nor such a *Utopian* as *Sr. Thomas Moore* hath related to be found out," America is the land of opportunity, where poor people who work hard will succeed. "Some from being wool-hoppers and of as mean and meaner imployment in England have there grown great merchants, and attained to the most eminent advancements of the country afforded." He describes in detail the miserable poverty of England's poor, calling their lives pitiful and expressing his surprise that people could manage to survive in such conditions. "And yet it were dangerous to advise these wretches to better their conditions" by emigration, "for fear of the cry of *spirit, a spirit*." Let the English, if they must, live in misery; he is returning to America, the "Country in which I desire to spend the remnant of my days, in which I covet to make my grave."

When George Calvert, first Lord Baltimore, decided to create his feudal Catholic colony on the northern Chesapeake, he enlisted the aid of the Jesuits. Andrew White (1579–1656), an English Jesuit and former professor of theology and prefect of studies at various European

Jesuit seminaries, had become Calvert's friend during one of his several English missions. White volunteered to spread Catholicism among the American Indians. Since Catholicism was prohibited in England, Cecil Calvert, who succeeded his father as Lord Baltimore in 1633, could not openly proclaim that he wanted to create a Catholic colony, so he argued for religious toleration in Maryland. White wrote, and Cecil Calvert revised, the first Maryland colonization tract, *A Declaration of the Lord Baltimore's Plantation in Mary-land* (1633), which promised two thousand acres of land to immigrants who brought over good equipment and five servants. The Calverts appealed not to England's poor but to the wealthy gentry who had servants and wanted a landed estate. Further, everyone knew by word of mouth that the appeal was especially to Catholic gentlemen. As Thomas Cornwallis, one of the first colonists and a younger son of a wealthy Catholic family, said, "Security of conscience was the first condition I expected from this [the Maryland] government." Although some of the Jesuits, like the devout Andrew White, expected to convert Indians, the Jesuit order invested heavily in the colonization attempt because Maryland was to become a Catholic barony. In writing the promotion tract, White, echoing Captain John Smith, said he knew "all men are not so noble-minded . . . but commonly Pleasure, wealth and honour" lure them, not the conversion of Indians. So White told about Maryland's abundant fish, furs, and timber, pointed out that tobacco grew well there, and listed the various native foods. White's portrait of the corn harvests echoed Hesiod's account of the Elysian Fields where the fertile soil yielded three harvests a year.

And so off they sailed, a few Catholic gentlemen, two Jesuits, and nearly ten times as many servants, mainly Protestants. White's second Maryland colonization tract, *A Relation of the Successfull Beginnings* (1634) narrates the events between the colonists' arrival in the Chesapeake Bay on March 3 and the date that White sent off his account, May 27, 1634. During those eleven weeks the colonists explored the area, made contact with several Indian tribes, settled at St. Mary's where they built a fort mounted with cannons, and planted a variety of crops. White has a knack for interesting detail. When a small boat overturned, the servant women lost "much linnen," and White ruefully added, "among the rest I lost the best of mine, which is a very main loss in these parts." He records the Indians' astonishment at seeing the *Ark*, a ship of nearly four hundred tons; they called it a canoe and wondered "where so great a tree grew that made it, conceiving it to be made of one piece, as their Canoes are." The sound of the cannon also amazed them: "When we shoot, our Bow-strings give a twang that's heard but a little way off: But do you not hear what cracks their Bow-strings give?"

White's final promotion tract, *A Relation of Maryland* (1635), is longer and more formal, with chapters devoted to such topics as a description of the country and its commodities, and is distinguished by a fine chapter on the Indians. White criticizes the callous attitude of Smith and such New England authors as William Wood, whose "only point of pollicy . . . is, to destroy the Indians, or to drive them out of the Country, without which, it is not to be hoped that they can be secure." But White lived among them and came to know and like them. He claims that "by kind and fair usage, the Natives are not only become peaceable, but also friendly, and have upon all occasions performed as many friendly Offices to the English in Maryland and New England, as any neighbor or friend uses to do in the most Civil parts of Christendom." He implies that the whites should adopt some of the Indian customs, since the settlers are strangers in the Indian country. He disgustedly concludes, "It is much more Prudence, and Charity, to Civilize, and make them Christians, then to kill, rob, and hunt them from place to place, as you would do a wolf."

George Alsop wrote Maryland's best later promotion tract, *A Character of the Province of Mary-Land* (1666), altogether the most extraordinary literary achievement in the genre. The author, a devout Anglican of yeoman background (his father was a tailor and his older brother a joiner), had a literary reputation among his peers. As a young man of twenty-two, Alsop precipitously indentured himself to four years' service as a servant in Maryland. But he was obviously educated and met with comparatively easy work, probably as a clerk. Alsop adopts the persona of a madcap wit, rash and energetic, who exists in a "world-turned-upside-down," where Puritans have seized power, executed the king, and created confusion. And so he is off to the New World. Promotion tracts usually invited scoffing and satire, but Alsop forestalled such reactions by using a self-conscious style that burlesques itself. Alsop writes an excessive prose—exuberant, energetic, and always active, full of hyperboles and farfetched figures of speech. It undercuts anyone who would ridicule it, for the scoffer would thereby prove himself a fool who did not recognize that Alsop was deliberately overstating his case and mocking himself.

> The Trees, Plants, Fruits, Flowers, and Roots that grow here in Maryland, are the only Emblems or Hieroglyphicks of our Adamitical or Primitive situation, as well for their variety as odoriferous smells, together with their vertures, according to their several effects, kinds and properties, which still bear the Effigies of Innocency according to their original Grafts; which by their dumb vegetable Oratory, each hour speaks to the Inhabitant in silent acts, That they need not look for any other Terrestrial Paradise, to suspend or

tire their curosity upon, while she is extant. For within her doth dwell so much of variety, so much of natural plenty, that there is not any thing that is or may be rare, but it inhabits within this plentious soil.

Throughout his tract, Alsop counters in various ways the criticisms against America and against promotional literature, even while he burlesques the usual approach of the promotion writers. He directs his own satire, however, primarily at the evils of English society, in which merchants and tradesmen must constantly "catch, snatch, and undervalue one another, to get a little work, or a customer; which when they have attained by their lowbuilt and sneaking circumventings, it stands upon so flashy, mutable, and transitory a foundation that the best of his hopes is commonly extinguished before the poor under-valued Tradesman is warm in the enjoyment of his customer." Although his self-conscious style contains a note of parody, there can finally be no doubt that Alsop seriously makes his pitch. Nature itself, not the madcap persona, invites the reader to emigrate to America—*"Dwell here, live plentifully, and be rich."*

Although a few tracts celebrated Carolina before Charles II granted the colony to several proprietors in 1663, its promotion really began then. The first important Carolina promotion tract, William Hilton's *A Relation of a Discovery lately made on the Coast of Florida* (1664), featured a detailed description of the Cape Fear area of North Carolina and listed inducements for prospective colonists. The anonymous pamphlet *A Brief Description of the Province of Carolina* (1664), probably by Robert Horne, promised 100 acres for every person who paid for his own transportation. By 1669 the headright was increased to 150 acres. In March of 1669 or 1670, the first of five versions of *The Fundamental Constitutions of Carolina*, written by Anthony Ashley Cooper, first earl of Shaftesbury, one of Carolina's eight proprietors, and by his secretary John Locke, appeared. Theoretical political documents, such as the *Fundamental Constitutions*, are common staples of early American literature, but Carolina's is probably the most famous seventeenth-century document, not because of its democratic tendencies or theoretical advances, for it was nearly as conservative as the reactionary *Charter of Maryland*, but because John Locke, that great innovator of modern thought, had a major hand in writing and revising it. In 1682 three noteworthy Carolina promotion tracts appeared: Thomas Ash's *Carolina*, mentioning corn whiskey for the first time; Robert Ferguson's *Present State of Carolina*, containing valuable details on the local Indians; and Samuel Wilson's *Account of the Province of Carolina*, stressing the easy life resulting from the warm climate. John Crafford's *New and Most Exact Account* (1683) offered reasons for thinking that the Indians were descended from the Israelites; and the anonymous *Carolina Described* (1684) reprinted materials from the best previous descriptions and offered new terms for the emigrants.

The continual stream of American promotional literature called forth numerous oral and written satires. Although such satires occur in a great variety of literary genres, the general category may be called antipromotional. Americans from the seventeenth to the twentieth centuries have chafed at the criticism, slander, and contempt, and American literature often reflects, usually resents, and always is conscious of the English and European attitudes toward America and Americans. Generally ignored, overlooked, or downplayed, antipromotional writings constitute an extraordinarily important and influential corpus of literature.

The reasons for the existence of antipromotional literature are literary, historical, and social. The overblown accounts of America as a land of milk and honey naturally drew lubberland satires in the tradition of "The Land of Cockaign," portraying America as a fool's paradise and mocking persons who could believe such exaggerations. The playwrights of the seventeenth century especially cast slurs on the Edenic reports of American life. Thus the fool Seagull in *Eastward hoe!* (1605), by George Chapman, John Marston, and Ben Jonson, believes that "gold is more plentiful ther [in Virginia] then copper is with us," that the climate is temperate and that Virginia naturally abounds with "all sorts of excellent viands: wild boar is as common there as our tamest bacon is here; venison as mutton."

In addition to satires inspired by literary traditions, three actual practices gave Virginia and later overseas colonies a bad name. First, because labor in America was scarce and expensive, colonial agents lured persons to sign on as indentured servants for the price of their transportation. Such persons, condemned to a four- or seven-year servitude, often were sold to hard taskmasters and bitterly regretted their indentures. Second, some English youths and maidens were kidnapped for American service. The shortage of women caused the Virginia Company to send over "young maids to make wives" for the planters. Since the price paid for women in Virginia more than covered their transportation, and since few young women volunteered, kidnapping could be profitable. In 1618 some forty young women fled the parish of Ottery in Somerset for fear of Owen Evans, a kidnapper active in the area. And third, convicted felons were sometimes shipped to America, giving rise to the categorization of Americans as convicts.

Although the latter two practices were uncommon, they did exist. As early as October 17, 1614, the Spanish ambassador to England reported that Virginia "is in such bad repute that not a human being can be found to go there." He said that thieves, condemned to death, were offered the possibility of being shipped to Virginia, but they "replied at once, decidedly and with one accord, that they would much rather die on the gallows here, and quickly, than to die slowly so many deaths as was the case in Virginia."

Those three practices resulted in a popular literature (including ballads, chapbooks, rogue literature, and plays) featuring the misery of American life and the contemptible status of those who emigrated. In Philip Massinger's *The City Madam* (1632), Virginians are described as "Condemned wretches, Forfeited to the law," and as

> Strumpets and bawds,
> For the abomination of their life,
> Spewed out of their own country.

Quite a few ballads deal with kidnapping. Most of them survive in unique copies from later printings, but internal evidence, and in a few cases the entries in the Stationers' Company registers, dates them from the seventeenth century. Examples include *A Net for a Night Raven* (*ca.* 1660); *The Woman Outwitted . . . Sold . . . to Virginia* (rpr. *ca.* 1709); *The Kid-Napper Trapan'd* (1675); *The Trapan'd Welchmen Sold to Virginia* (1688); *Constancy Lamented . . . Sold to Virginia* (*ca.* 1695) and its sequel *Love Overthon . . . Sold to Virginia* (*ca.* 1695), which still survives in the Southern oral tradition as a folk song; *The Trappan'd Maiden* (rpr. *ca.* 1709); and *The Dumb Maid: or The Young Gallant Trappan'd* (n.d.).

Ballads and chapbooks dealing with rogues and transported criminals—a popular motif used splendidly by Daniel Defoe in *Moll Flanders* and *Colonel Jack*—were also common. Perhaps the most popular was a song, dating from the 1660s, which survives in six eighteenth-century editions. *The Unhappy Transported Felon* tells the story of James Revel, who was "forced to drudge and slave" for fourteen miserable years in Virginia "amongst tobacco plants." Ebenezer Cook echoed this ballad and another in *The Sot-Weed Factor* (1708). Another seventeenth-century ballad concerning transported felons, *The Lads of Virginia* (n.d.), is known only from a deteriorated nineteenth-century printing. Richard Head's best-selling picaresque fiction *The English Rogue* (1665) features many low-life scenes, including transporting felons to Virginia and kidnapping. An actual transported felon with the appropriate surname Hellier was sent to Virginia, where he worked on a plantation named Hard Labour. There he murdered his master, mistress, and a maid before he was captured and executed. His *Vain Prodigal Life and Tragical Penitent Death* appeared in chapbook form in 1678 and 1680. Throughout the seventeenth century and beyond, the English had some basis for their contempt for America and Americans. Dr. Samuel Johnson echoed a common English attitude when he said of the Americans, "They are a race of convicts and ought to be thankful for anything we allow them short of hanging."

English and European perception of the breakdown of traditional values on the American frontier also inspired contempt for America. As early as 1618, John Pory reported to his English patron, Sir Dudley Carleton, that "our cowkeeper here of James city on Sundays goes accoutered all in fresh flaming silk; and a wife of one that in England had professed the black art, not of a scholar, but of a collier of Croydon, wears her rough beaver hat with a fair pearl hatband, and a silken suit thereto correspondent." Pory's scorn of and amusement at the nouveau-riche drips from his pen—and he knew that his patron would be aghast not only at such airs by peasants, but also at their ability to afford dress supposedly suited only for the gentry and aristocracy. The examples of success, so appealing to the ordinary people and so often cited by the promotion writers, wherein wool hoppers or cow keepers rise from rags to riches, seemed an abomination to those Englishmen who placed great value upon the status quo and upon the traditional hierarchy. To them, America represented social barbarianism, and Americans were a rude, uncultivated people. Even those few Americans who were not only well-educated and wealthy but also aristocratic found themselves subjected to condescension and scorn by their English contemporaries. And American literature, from the earliest promotion tracts to the twentieth century, reveals how Americans responded.

Of course numerous minor genres, including sermons and meditative religious poetry (for example, *A Song of Sion* [1662] by John Grave), occur in seventeenth-century Southern literature. But prose narratives of shipwrecks and explorations are a continuing staple. The classic shipwreck account is William Strachey's "A Reportory of the Wreck and Redemption of Sir Thomas Gates, Knight," written in 1610 about the shipwreck of the *Sea Venture*, the command ship carrying Gates and Sir George Somers to Virginia. Although the account was not published until Purchas included it in *Purchas his Pilgrimes*, it circulated widely in manuscript, and Shakespeare evidently read it and reflects it in *The Tempest* (written 1611). Henry Norwood's "A Voyage to Virginia" in 1649 tells a tale of incredible hardship and of cannibalism, incidentally revealing that the author was nearly as indefatigable as Captain John Smith. And the Reverend Jonathan Dickinson's *God's Protecting Prov-*

idence (1699), telling of his Florida shipwreck and adventures among the Indians, became a best seller in England and America. Accounts of travels into the American interior include Edward Bland's *The Discovery of New Brittaine* (1651), describing an exploring trip to the Southwest that reached the upper branches of the Roanoke River, in what is now North Carolina; John Lederer's *The Discoveries of John Lederer* (1672), recounting expeditions to the Blue Ridge Mountains in 1669 and 1670, from which heights Lederer saw the Shenandoah Valley and the Appalachian Mountains in the distance; and the story of an exploration across the Allegheny Mountains and into West Virginia by Robert Fallam and Thomas Batts in 1671. Such narratives characterize early American literature and, in the hands of Strachey, Norwood, and Dickinson, are written with skill and artistry.

An extraordinary event in the latter part of the seventeenth century produced its own literature. In 1676, Nathaniel Bacon, Jr., a member of the Virginia Council, led volunteers against the Indians attacking the frontiers. When Governor William Berkeley declared Bacon a traitor, several skirmishes followed in which the traitor and his followers easily bested the government. But Bacon's death on October 18, 1676, deprived the rebellion of its leader, enabling Berkeley to capture the other rebels. These actions caused a spate of English publications, all basically expressing puzzlement over how and why Bacon could have so successfully opposed established authority. But if the question interested English readers, it fascinated seventeenth-century Virginian and later American historians and raised the specter of American revolt against England. No one quite understood how or why the Indian war turned into a rebellion. Thomas Mathew, who took part in it, tried to explain it a generation later ("The Beginning, Progress, and Conclusion of Bacon's Rebellion"), but Mathew feebly put the blame for the rebellion on Richard Lawrence, an Oxford graduate. His explanation did nothing to clear up the puzzle, either for Mathew or later historians. Although Mathew failed in his primary purpose, he vividly recorded several scenes and anecdotes, including Charles II's supposed judgment on the actions of Governor Berkeley: "That old fool has hang'd more men in that naked country than he had done for the Murther of his Father."

The most interesting account, and the best literature of late seventeenth-century Virginia, is John Cotton's "A History of Bacon's and Ingram's Rebellion," often called the Burwell Papers because the manuscript was in the possession of the Burwell family by the late eighteenth century. Cotton masks his fascination with the significance of Bacon's Rebellion beneath a flippant persona that scorns both parties. But the narrator's wit, irony, and ridicule are continuously undercut by the seriousness of the actions, the oppression and avariciousness of the government, the cowardice of Berkeley's followers, and the severity of Berkeley's revenge.

To be sure, neither John Cotton nor any other seventeenth-century Virginia historian would commit treason to justify Bacon's actions. Cotton portrays Bacon and his followers as giddy fools doomed to fail. Although his mock-heroic, scurrilous tone toward the entire history allows Cotton not to be labeled a traitor, his underlying sympathies at first lie with Bacon and the rebels rather than with an oppressive government. His underlying attitude is also revealed by the two famous elegies incorporated within the manuscript. Although the first elegy was supposedly written by a Bacon supporter and the second, which replies to the first, by an opponent, both are undoubtedly by John Cotton; and in this case, excellence is the test of authorial sympathy. The first is the better poem.

> Bacon's Epitaph, made by his Man
> Death why so cruel! what, no other way
> To manifest thy spleen, but thus to slay
> Our hopes of safety, liberty, our all
> Which, through thy tyranny, with him must fall
> To its late Chaos?

Liberty and *safety* are key terms in the poem—and evidently in Bacon's appeal to his contemporary Virginians. Cotton implies that the basic reasons underlying the rebellion are political. Although many issues becloud the picture, later writers can hardly help but view, as the revolutionary generation did, Bacon's rebellion as an anticipation of the American Revolution.

Much seventeenth-century Southern literature has perished in war and disaster and more has been lost by the normal ravages of carelessness and time, but a great deal of early Southern literature is still extant, little of which has been well-edited or thoroughly studied.

J. A. LEO LEMAY

Captain John Smith

The major mythic hero of the Middle Ages and Renaissance—and later, as numerous chapbooks, ballads, and Sir Walter Scott's novels testify—was the chivalric knight, whose heroic combats often occurred in tournaments with the aristocracy and gentry looking on. America's indigenous heroes have been the Indian fighters, frontiersmen, and gun-fighters, such as John Mason, Thomas Church, Daniel Gookin, John Lovewell, Thomas Cresap, and Robert Rogers in the colonial period, and Daniel Boone, Davy Crockett, Kit Carson, Wild Bill Hickok, Wyatt Earp, and Buffalo Bill Cody in later times. Captain John Smith fulfills the heroic roles of the Renaissance and the colonial period, and his biography illustrates the changing nature of heroic action. Before sailing for Jamestown in 1607, Smith fought in various European wars, finally serving as commander of a Christian company against the "infidels." In 1602 in Transylvania, now part of Hungary, Smith, as the champion of the Christian army, killed the Turkish champions in three separate tournaments. Each confrontation took place in a large arena, "the Ramparts all beset with fair Dames, and men in Arms," the champions striding out to a flourish of music, their pages leading their horses and bearing their lances, pistols, battleaxes, and swords. The ritualistic pageantry ended in a grisly battle, with the survivor raising the helmet of his dead opponent and cutting off his head.

Smith lived by his personal motto: *vincere est vivere*, "to conquer is to live." (His motto, an adaptation of the common *vincere vel more*, "To conquer or to die," is the earliest indication of his literary talents.) No Englishman among his contemporaries, not even that chivalric figure of the age, Sir Philip Sidney, achieved the reputation in deed or battle of the indomitable Captain John Smith. Then he went off to the wilderness of America. There in 1607 he became "Nantaquoud," the most feared Indian fighter of his day. Powhatan himself testified that "if a twig but break, every one cry there comes" Nantaquoud! In Europe, when severely wounded in battle and presumed dead, Smith was rescued by pillagers and sold as a slave in Turkey. He killed his master there and made his way alone across northern Turkey and southern Russia, to emerge almost miraculously in Christian Europe. In America, when his companions were slain by an overwhelmingly superior force and when he himself, after killing at least two Indians and wounding others, gradually retreated into a swamp where the bog finally imprisoned him, Captain John Smith was saved at first by his magical display of a compass and his explanation of cosmography and later by the intervention of Pocahontas, to emerge alive, again almost miraculously, some four weeks later at Jamestown.

His life was charmed. But, like Caesar—and the comparison occurred to him—Smith is almost as well known for his writings as for his actions. Smith became a writer because he was an explorer. But he found he had a flair for writing, a greater devotion to colonization than any English contemporary, and an urge to commit his knowledge and experience to the permanency of print. His first publication, sent from Jamestown in 1608 as a letter to a friend, described the earliest explorations and the Jamestown settlement. Although addressed to an individual, such letters were meant for wide circulation. Smith probably expected his friend Richard Hakluyt (1552–1616), the editor of exploration accounts, to use it in a future edition of his *Principal Navigations*. The separate publication of *A True Relation of such occurrences and accidents of noate as hath hapned in Virginia* (1608) no doubt surprised and pleased Smith. It was the first printed English account written in a permanent colony. Although not published by the London Company, Smith's *True Relation* was evidently edited to downplay the Indians' hostility and the constant bickering among the factions within the council. Smith skims over the first starving time during the summer of 1607, when "the living were scarce able to bury the dead" but he gives many passages of graphic description: "As yet we had no houses to cover us, our Tents were rotten, and our cabins worse then naught: our best commodity was Iron which we made into little chisels. The president['s], and Captaine *Martir's* sickness, constrained me to be Cape Marchant, and yet to spare no pains in making houses for the company; who notwithstanding our misery, little ceased their malice, grudging, and muttering." The no-nonsense, brusque, ironic, impatient, feisty, courageous, passionate, noble, vainglorious, and absolutely independent personality of the professional soldier/author comes through every page. Smith respected hard work and loathed laziness. *A True Relation* contains numerous passages of high adventure related in tantalizingly brief snippets.

After being severely burned in an accident (since Smith tells us that the accidental firing of "his powder bag . . . tore his flesh from his body and thigh 9. or 10. inches square, in a most pitiful manner," we must suspect that his genitals were severely damaged) and after the 1609 reorganization of the Virginia Company left him with a severely reduced role, Smith returned to England to seek the most expert medical help, to justify himself in person against the slanders circulating against him, and to change the organization and policies of the Virginia Company. He certainly failed in the last two efforts. But in England, he wrote his second book, *A Map of Virginia* (1612), featuring the first of his two great American maps. William P. Cumming characterizes Smith's map of the Chesapeake area as the "most accurate and detailed map of any comparable area on the North Atlantic coast of America until the last quarter of the century." The book itself is well-organized, in two parts, with the first part written entirely by Smith. Although Smith no doubt hoped to win a renewed position for himself with the Virginia Company, he was too independent and too democratic for the company. He repeatedly condemns the settlers who are unaware of the labor and sacrifice demanded by a new colony. Although his unhesitating discrimination between the upper class and the commonality of the Indians testifies to his typical Renaissance and seventeenth-century acceptance of degrees of social hierarchy, as do the various lists of persons automatically categorized by their social status, he repeatedly reveals a democratic tendency. "The labor of 30 of the best only, preserved in Christianity, by their industry, the idle livers of near 200 of the rest." In Smith's scale of values, the achievers, who were not usually the gentlemen, are really the best.

The second part of *A Map of Virginia,* entitled *The Proceedings of the English Colony in Virginia,* chronicled events from 1606 to 1612. Although it was supposedly taken from the writings of Thomas Studly, Anas Todkill, Walter Russell, and "other diligent observers," Smith obviously wrote much of it and revised the whole. The Reverend William Simmonds further revised the account. Howard Mumford Jones hypothesizes convincingly that Simmonds probably provided the excellent structure of the book (the division into twelve chapters), but contrary to Jones, it seems likely that Smith himself wrote the fifteen set speeches. They are certainly based upon actual speeches, and Smith earlier and later wrote comparable rhetorical pieces. Although the colony's success was still in doubt, Smith and other survivors already took pride in being the first planters and looked forward to future successes. The *Proceedings* narrated the devious maneuverings of the Indians and whites. The Indians, coached by Powhatan, constantly tried to maneuver the whites into a defenseless position in which they could be slaughtered with impunity; and the whites, led by Smith, attempted to get the Indians to raise corn and other crops to support the settlers. These constant rituals of deceit are broken by bouts of violence. But the presence of the Indians calls into question the bases and nature of civilization. Smith's various complex appreciations of different cultures point to a continuing major intellectual subject of early American literature.

Like the Massachusetts Puritans, Smith was little attracted by visions of a peaceful kingdom or of the idyllic life, yet he could not resist an occasional romantic portrait of a sensual primitive utopia. Smith vividly portrays the masque staged by the Indian maidens when he and an advance party came to Powhatan's camp bearing gifts. The Indians had prepared a large fire "in a fair plain field" when suddenly "amongst the woods was heard . . . a hideous noise and shrieking." Then:

> 30 young women came naked out of the woods (only covered behind and before with a few green leaves), their bodies all painted, some white, some red, some black, some partie colour; but every one different. Their leader had a fair pair of stag's horns on her head, and an otter skin at her girdle, another at her arm, a quiver of arrows at her back, and bow and arrows in her hand. The next, in her hand a sword; another, a club; another, a potstick: all horn[e]d alike. The rest, every one with their several devises. These fiends, with most hellish cries and shouts rushing from amongst the trees, cast themselves in a ring about the fire, singing and dancing with excellent ill variety, oft falling into their infernal passions, and then solemnly again to sing and dance. Having spent near an hour in this maskarado, as they entered, in like manner departed.

Smith's third book, *A Description of New England* (1616), gave New England its name, presented the first accurate map of its coast, projected its economic possibilities as a center for fishing, lumbering, and shipbuilding, and contained his earliest full formulation of the American dream.

> Who can desire more content, that hath small means: or but only his merit to advance his fortune, then to tread, and plant that ground he hath purchased by the hazard of his life? If he have but the taste of virtue and magnanimitie, what to such a mind can be more pleasant, than planting and building a foundation for his Posterity got from the rude earth, by God's blessing and his own industry, without prejudice to any? If he have any grain of faith or zeal in Religion, what can he do less hurtful to any: or more agreeable to God, then to seek to convert those poor Savages to know Christ, and humanity whose labors with discretion will triple requite thy charge and pains? What so truely suites with honour and honesty as the discovering things unknown, erecting Townes, peopling Countries, informing the ignorant, reforming things unjust, teaching virtue; and gain to our Native mothercountrie a kingdom to attend her: find employment for those that are idle,

because they know not what to do; so far from wronging any, as to cause Posterity to remember thee; and remembering thee, ever honour that remembrance with praise?

And yet, Smith is also a realist. He knows that wealth is the great lure. "For, I am not so simple to think, that ever any other motive than wealth will ever erect there a Commonweale." He says that the hope of "gain will make them affect that, which Religion, Charity, and the Common good cannot."

The book also reveals Smith's own mature self-image. His American experiences and thorough commitment to America transformed him from soldier to explorer, from major of a regiment to governor of a plantation, and from a superior military strategist to a major mapmaker. With *A Description of New England,* Smith becomes the grand promoter of American colonization. Here too, he first gives his own ideal genealogy. What Columbus, Cortez, Pizzaro, de Soto, and Magellan have done for Portugal añd Spain, he has done, and is doing, for England. He argues that major past civilizations rose to greatness under the leadership of men who, adventurous in youth, used the judgment and wisdom gained through experience to guide their countries to prosperity. So too, the downfall of civilizations resulted from excessive indulgence and laziness, lack of experience, a disregard for honor and true merit, and a desire for personal gain. Such, he implies, is the present state of England. But America poses an alternative "for men that have great spirits and small means."

In 1624 Smith published his major work, *The Generall Historie of Virginia, New England, and the Summer Isles . . . from their first beginning An. 1584 to this present 1624.* He uses the relations of previous persons, sometimes valuably explaining them, usually shortening and tightening them, and occasionally expanding them. He especially revised his own earlier accounts of the Jamestown settlement and early explorations. Although he had omitted or abbreviated the various Indian skirmishes in *The True Relation* (1608) and in *The Map of Virginia* (1612), he presented them at length in the *Generall Historie.* His most famous addition tells of his rescue by Pocahontas, to which he had alluded several times before. The *Generall Historie* describes what happened when the captive John Smith was brought before the assembled Indians and Powhatan.

> At his entrance before the King, all the people gave a great shout. The Queen of *Appamatuck* was appointed to bring him water to wash his hands, and another brought him a bunch of feathers, instead of a Towell to dry them: having feasted him after their best barbarous manner they could, a

long consultation was held, but the conclusion was, two great stones were brought before *Powhatan:* then as many as could laid hands on him, dragged him to them, and thereon laid his head, and being ready with their clubs, to beat out his brain, *Pocahontas* the King's dearest daughter, when no entreaty could prevail, got his head in her arms, and laid her own up on his to save him from death: whereat the Emperour was contented he should live.

What is one to make of the incident? Perhaps Smith, whom the Indians knew to be a *Werowance* (a leader), was being adopted into the tribe. If so, the ceremony was a ritual, and Pocahontas had been selected previously as his sponsor. Although Smith was good with languages and had already picked up some Algonkian, he evidently did not know that the ceremony was a rite of initiation—if it was. Or perhaps the Indians actually had decided to kill Smith before Pocahontas exercised her prerogative as the chief's daughter to save him. That was what Smith believed, and it may be so. One may even doubt that the event actually happened. No other white person was present, leaving Smith, once again, as the only witness to an incredible tale. Besides, his earliest account of his captivity (*A True Relation*) says that when he finally met Powhatan the chief kindly assured him of "his friendship and my liberty within four days." If the first report is true, can the second one also be?

Even if Powhatan did use Smith "with all the kindness he could devise," the ritual of adoption certainly could have taken place. Indian relations after Smith's release, as recounted in both *A True Relation* and in *A Map of Virginia*, demonstrate that Powhatan, Pocahontas, and John Smith all behaved as if a special relationship existed between Smith and Pocahontas. Powhatan sent her to Jamestown to deliver his apologies and secure the release of captured Indians. Smith writes that for Pocahontas only did he allow the captives to go free. Moreover, although no other whites were present, Pocahontas was there. When she went to England, Smith wrote a letter to Queen Anne describing how she had saved his life at the risk of her own. Although Pocahontas died in childbirth in 1616 at the end of her stay in England, she must have spoken to her husband, John Rolfe, about her experiences with Smith. If Smith lied about Pocahontas' saving his life, it is most surprising that neither Pocahontas, nor Rolfe, nor any other Indian who had been present and later learned to speak Algonkian, ever called Smith a liar. And if anyone ever called him a liar in private, we may be certain that such a tale would have been recorded by a contemporary. Further, if any contemporary ever questioned the validity of the tale, Smith would have replied in print to the charge.

Although the evidence generally testifies that Smith told the truth as he knew it, we do lack definitive proof that Pocahontas saved him. But if

Pocahontas did not save him, if he did not defeat three Turkish champions successively in single combat, if he did not kill his master when a slave in Turkey and make his way across the desert to Russia, or if he did not escape from French pirates by setting off alone in a small boat at night during a tempest that wrecked the pirates' ship, then he possessed an extraordinarily fertile imagination, a Defoe-like realistic genius, and a feeling for archetypes comparable to Homer. If his tales are his own imaginative creation, then he is a greater writer of fiction than anyone has ever suspected.

In 1626 Smith wrote a small treatise entitled *An Accidence, or the Pathway to Experience* (1626), which he revised and expanded as *A Sea Grammar* (1627). Smith's penultimate publication was his *True Travels* (1630), which unfortunately only dealt with his pre-Virginia experiences, no doubt because his later adventures were all chronicled in his American publications. Smith's eighth and last book, *Advertisements for the Unexperienced Planters of New England, or Anywhere* (1631) not only contains several graphic passages on Virginia, but indicates that even at the very end of his life, Smith still hoped to return to America "to live and die among you . . . and to make *Virginia* and *New England,* my heirs, executors, administrators and assignees."

Long before the publication of *Advertisements* in 1631, John Smith was a confirmed writer, even projecting another work, which would have told of the evolution of shipbuilding and seamanship, the rise of sea power, the major battles at sea, and the achievements of the great sea explorers from ancient times to Smith's own day. He died on June 21, 1631, too feeble to sign his will. Although he spent only three years in Virginia and several additional months exploring the New England coast, Smith is America's first important author. He wrote the first book from a permanent English settlement in America. He was the first person to say that he loved America and that America was his most significant experience. He wrote the first full formulation of the American dream. His statements on the possibilities of life in America are adumbrated in his first two books, given grand rhetorical expression in his third one, and repeated and elaborated in several later works. He also introduced significant Amerindian relationships into English literature. On one hand, the idyllic dream of love between different races and cultures underlies his accounts of Pocahontas, and on the other, the threat of warfare and genocide darkens the encounters between Powhatan and Smith. Smith thus repeatedly and memorably deals with later major themes of American literature. Last, he was the first good writer to devote himself to America, his greatest subject. He constantly grew better as a writer, becoming more artful in his use of grand rhetorical prose.

He is often an inspiring and thoughtful writer in treating such subjects as history, geography, the aspirations of life, and the vanity of existence. His noble sententiae are especially striking, and none more than his definition of history. "History is the memory of time, the life of the dead, and the happiness of the living."

ROBERT D. ARNER

Literature in the Eighteenth-Century Colonial South

With the single exception of William Byrd of Westover, Southern writers of the six or seven decades before the war for independence have been entirely overshadowed by writers of the revolutionary generation. Yet the literary achievement of the prerevolutionary period is significant both in its own right and for its cumulative revelation of what Lewis P. Simpson has recently called the "secularization of spirituality in the planting colonies," a "progressive subjectification of history in the individual consciousness" that Simpson finds to be the central phenomenon of postmedieval Western civilization and that in America reaches its grandest expression in the political prose of Thomas Jefferson (See *The Brazen Face of History: Studies in the Literary Consciousness in America* [Baton Rouge, 1980], 89–92). This is not to suggest that the mind of the early South is in any sense obsessively, unimaginatively, or self-consciously monolithic in the way the New England mind was once thought to be. Indeed, one characteristic of Southern literature of the early and middle eighteenth century is the diversity of forms, themes, and genres it exhibits, not even excluding early excursions into the novel by Arthur Blackamore, who wrote both *The Perfidious Brethren*, which is set in Virginia, and *Luck at Last* in the 1720s, and Thomas Atwood Digges, whose *Adventures of Alonzo* (1776) is often cited as the first novel by an American. The range of literary interests and the intellectual vigor displayed by prerevolutionary Southern authors fully justify Richard Beale Davis' claim that it was indeed a golden age of Southern writing.

Ancient laws of primogeniture, to say nothing of simple courtesy to a time-honored critical convention, require that any survey of Southern literature begin with the literature of Virginia. Almost as well established is the convention of beginning with Virginia's histories, in some ways the cousins-german of the promotional literature of earlier generations. For example, one of the premier works of the period, *The History and Present State of Virginia* (1705) by Robert Beverley (*ca.* 1673–

34

1722), surely originates in a crisis of misinformation and misunderstanding about Virginia—mere travelers' tales, Beverley called them—that impelled him to set the record straight and sometimes drove him to exact comic vengeance through humorous hyperbole: frogs, the bane of every visitor to Virginia who ever tried to get a good night's sleep, become enormous, a bountiful blessing—so large, Beverley avers, that "six *French-Men* might have made a comfortable Meal" of the carcass of a single one of them. (For native Virginians, the joke would take on an extra dimension once the Abbé Raynal had published his conclusions that animal life diminished in the New World.)

Beverley extols the rivers and natural abundance of Virginia, though he also criticizes the laziness of Virginians themselves, who a century after Captain Smith's experiences still expect to take their ease in Eden. He saves his sharpest commentary for a series of royal governors—only Alexander Spotswood escapes unscathed—whose ignorance of Virginia and the Virginian's fierce love of liberty has had disastrous consequences, impeding the progress of the colony. Beverley repeatedly opposes the laws of nature, represented most often by idealizations of the Indians, to the written laws of Englishmen, which signify for him only entrapment in history and the compelling of one generation to live by the limitations and mistakes of their ancestors.

For modern readers, one of the tragic paradoxes of *The History and Present State of Virginia* is Beverley's defense of slavery in a book otherwise characterized by an uncompromising defense of liberty and the rights of Englishmen living in America, a position that Beverley shares with Thomas Jefferson. Since Beverley relied quite heavily on other sources for his *History*, and since no close textual analysis separating his writing from the works of others has yet been undertaken, praise for his prose style may be a bit premature, but there can be no doubt that his book remains a major literary document on its own merits as well as the most important precursor, both in theme and image, of Jefferson's *Notes on the State of Virginia*.

Unlike Robert Beverley, who declares himself an Indian and writes from the point of view of a Virginian throughout, Hugh Jones (1692–1760) adopts the point of view of a sophisticated Englishman in *The Present State of Virginia* (1724). Although perhaps not as self-consciously selected nor as consistently maintained as Beverley's rhetorical self, Jones's voice lends special authority to the claim that of all England's North American colonies only Virginia may "be justly esteemed the happy retreat of true Britons and true churchmen," since Jones can make that assertion without laying himself open to the charge of provincial patriotism. The rhetorical stance also permits Jones to combat effectively the slanderous tales about uncouth Virginians by speaking as a Londoner and reminding his readers that Londoners display the same attitude toward citizens of Bristol and other English cities, snobbish prejudices that are patently unfair. In actuality, he says, the "habits, life, customs, computations, etc. of the Virginians are much the same as about London," a wistful hyperbole that is, however, central to the purposes of his narrative, which is to promote Virginia as a civilized, culturally sophisticated place, "one of the most valuable gems in the crown of Great Britain." Written in a graceful and occasionally witty prose, Jones's *Present State of Virginia* does more than defend the Old Dominion from her detractors and provide information about life in the plantation; it also contributes to the developing myth of the gracious, urbane Cavalier Virginian and of a life founded on the best precepts of reason and a fondness for rural virtues and simple pleasures—the epitome of the golden mean.

The *Present State of Virginia and the College*, written mainly by Commissary James Blair (*ca.* 1655–1743) with help from Edward Chilton (d. 1707) and Henry Hartwell (d. 1699), has a history of intrigue perhaps more fascinating than any single story it unfolds. Written in 1697 and presented to England's Board of Trade on October 20 of that year, the *Present State* apparently profited from the contributions of the philosopher John Locke, who had a hand in more than one colonial enterprise. Its purposes were to inform the Board of Trade of problems in Virginia and to propose solutions to those problems, which from Blair's point of view at the time included the replacement of Governor Sir Edmund Andros by Francis Nicholson. Blair, referred to as the "Kingmaker of Virginia," was successful in his proposal, then quarreled bitterly with Nicholson and secured his removal and that of his successor, Alexander Spotswood, as well. Unpublished until 1727, the *Present State* was brought out by Blair probably in support of his lobby for a liquor tax bill to underwrite the salaries of clergymen, an enterprise in which he was again successful. The history itself is highly critical of Andros but retains some favorable commentary on Nicholson, evidence that Blair probably permitted his immediate propagandistic needs to override an editorial policy that otherwise would almost certainly have omitted any praise of Nicholson.

One final historical narrative of significance is William Stith's *History of the First Discovery and Settlement of Virginia* (1747), which carries its story through 1724, the same year as Hugh Jones's *Present State*. Stith (1707–1755) has none of the stylistic graces of his predecessors, but his political principles, which even more clearly than Beverley's are against English governmental policies that stifle the rights of Virginians, reflect a Whig perspective in Stith's use of the familiar images and vocabulary of Whig politicians. George Yeardley saves the struggling Jamestown settlement, for example, by restoring to the people "their Birthright, the Enjoyment of *British* Liberty." In classic Whig fashion, Stith sets the "native Right" of the people against "the Oppression and Tyranny of Governors" in his historical drama. Although billed as an objective account relying on the documents of early settlers for its information, Stith's history is actually one of the earliest American histories (Cotton Mather's *Magnalia Christi Americana* of 1702 is perhaps its most illustrious predecessor) to seek to legitimize the principles of the present by imposing those principles on an interpretation of the past, thereby appearing to make the present a matter of historical inevitability. As Richard Beale Davis has pointed out, Stith's *History* also articulates many of the principles of the revolutionary generation.

Stith's book was published by the Williamsburg printer William Parks, whose presence in Virginia and, especially, whose establishment of the *Virginia Gazette* in 1736 insured that other forms of literature besides history would flourish in the Old Dominion. Parks and his successors, William Hunter, Joseph Royle, Alexander Purdie, and John Dixon, actively encouraged local literary culture, particularly poetry and the essay, by publishing short works on pages that might otherwise have been blank during slack seasons for news from abroad. Indeed, the best early eighteenth-century pre-Parks poem, Arthur Blackamore's "Expeditio Ultramontana" (*ca.* 1716), eventually found its way to one of Parks's papers, the *Maryland Gazette*, in a translation by George Seagood (d. 1724).

The poem, printed in 1729, recounts the adventures of Governor Alexander Spotswood and the Knights of the Golden Horseshoe in their exploration of the Blue Ridge Mountains and discovery of the Shenandoah River, which Spotswood promptly renamed the Euphrates (luckily the Indian name survived). Blackamore (*ca.* 1679–*ca.* 1723), a tutor at the College of William and Mary who was finally dismissed for excessive drinking and sent back to England in 1717, combined in his poems just the right mixture of classical allusion, biblical reference, romantic adventure, and patriotic imperialism to raise Spotswood's expedition from a minor event in Virginia history to a symbol of the Virginian's contemplation of and confrontation with the West, the frontier. Surely, for instance, the poem provided William Byrd, at whose home Blackamore was a frequent visitor, with some useful ideas for transforming his journal of the dividing line into the excellent literary performances of

The Secret History of the Line and *The History of the Dividing Line*, though the influence seems as much one of attitudes and general literary strategy as of specific allusions and images.

The establishment of Parks's printing press in Virginia was heralded, appropriately enough, by the publication of John Markland's *Typographia: An Ode, on Printing* (1730), which appeared in the same year that Parks began operations in Williamsburg. Inscribed to Governor William Gooch, *Typographia* is perhaps the earliest American poem to identify the productions of the printing press with the fecundity of the womb of time and, through classical allusion, to make "the sexuality of modern history" its covert theme, uniting writer, publisher, and reader in an "intimate historical transaction" (to borrow yet another concept and several phrases from Lewis Simpson). The poem also anticipates dozens of other American encomiums to the press as the principal agent of liberty and learning, from Franklin's comical account in Dogood Paper No. IV to Barlow's enthusiastic pronunciamentos in *The Columbiad* to George Washington Cutter's mindless panegyric, "The Press" (1857), one object of Herman Melville's devastating scorn in Chapter 30 of *The Confidence-Man*.

Still, whatever role the press was eventually to play in fostering an unfounded and even dangerous American optimism in the early eighteenth century, the Williamsburg press soon justified Markland's enthusiasm by printing the "Monitor" essays in the *Virginia Gazette*, a collection of twenty-two short pieces (only sixteen survive) probably written by the students or faculty of William and Mary or possibly by someone like Benjamin Waller. The essays imitated the format of the *Spectator* and *Tatler*, but contained enough new and native material to mark their originality. The same year that the "Monitor" helped to launch the *Gazette*, William Dawson published his *Poems on Several Occasions by a Gentleman of Virginia* (1736), a pleasant collection of light verses addressed to ladies by a poet ultimately to become commissary and the president of William and Mary. In 1737 appeared an anonymous elegy "On the Death of the Hon. Sir John Randolph, Knt.," probably the most distinguished elegy written in the colonial South.

The work of Joseph Dumbleton (possibly a pseudonym), associated mainly with the *South-Carolina Gazette* but represented in Parks's paper by "The Paper Mill" (*Virginia Gazette*, 1744), is in a different vein altogether; a comic treatment of the symbolic union of sexuality and printing that John Markland had already treated seriously, "The Paper Mill" finds in Parks's call for used linen and silk to help make paper the amusing prospect that

> *Delia*'s Smock, which, rent and whole,
> No Man durst finger for his Soul;
> Turn'd to *Gazette*, now all the Town,
> May take it up, or smooth it down.

Parks somehow missed the poems of Charles Hansford, a blacksmith whose major work was written between 1749 and 1752 but remained unpublished until 1961; his poems include "Of Body and Soul," a meditative verse; "My Country's Worth," a patriotic verse; and "Barzillai," a vivid description of the perils of whalemen and an indictment of the follies of contemporary fashion.

Two years after Parks's death in 1750, William Hunter published the most important book of verse to be written in colonial Virginia, Samuel Davies' *Miscellaneous Poems* (1752). Davies (1723–1761), easily the most outstanding figure in the history of religion in midcentury Virginia, was a Presbyterian preacher of considerable education and power, as his extant sermons show, and a fervent patriot. He denounced cowardice not only from his pulpit ("The Curse of Cowardice," preached May 8, 1758; published 1841), but also from the pages of the *Gazette*, in which appeared his "Virginia Centinel" essays in 1756 through 1757, during the darkest days of the French and Indian War. The famous "Centinel No. 10" attacks George Washington and the Virginia Regiment that accompanied Edward Braddock on his ill-starred expedition into western Pennsylvania, and until the recent researches of J. A. Leo Lemay (who also attributes the series to Davies) was the only essay of the series believed to be extant.

As a poet, Davies writes primarily (and predictably) religious verse, including elegies and epitaphs, though he occasionally indulges in genteel verse for the ladies or in patriotic and propagandistic poetry, as in his most famous poem "*On the barbarities of the* French, *and their savage allies and proselytes, on the frontiers of* Virginia" (1757). With the exception of such verses, which exploit melodramatic and sensational images in order to inspire outrage in the hearts of Virginians, Davies' poetry tends toward conventional religious themes, chaste diction, biblical allusions, and a sparing use of imagery.

The same frontier turmoil that led Davies to criticize Washington and Virginia's soldiers also helped to inspire a lengthy and anonymous satire, "Dinwiddianae," which charged that Lieutenant Governor Robert Dinwiddie, out of cowardice and stupidity, had mismanaged the war against the French and the Indians. The satire is even more directly aimed at the "pistole fee," a levy Dinwiddie attempted to impose on patents for all newly acquired land. Although the third part of the manuscript copy surviving as BR[OCK] 74 in the Huntington Library purports to be "The third edition Published at the Reque[st] of the People 1757," the satire circulated only in manuscript and was not published until 1967, when Richard Beale Davis edited it for the Transactions of the American Philosophical Society. The author of this satire was probably John Mercer, though other names, including Richard Bland, Landon Carter, George Wythe, Benjamin Waller, and Peyton Randolph, have been suggested. The author, using the pseudonym of Benjamin Brown Coat, A.M., addresses Virginia as a "Forsaken, helpless, hopeless land" victimized by a "Witless, heartless, helpless band, / Kings, Judges, Generals, apeing . . ." and draws repeatedly on Shakespeare, Swift, Pope, Butler, Cervantes, and others in mounting one of the strongest attacks against a royal official to be found prior to the literature of the Revolution.

Published with "Dinwiddianae" in Davies' "Colonial Virginia Satirist" is a bitter satire directed against the hypocritical piety and money-grubbing greed of the Virginia planters. Almost certainly by James Reid, an indentured schoolmaster at Thomas Claiborne's Sweet Hall in King William County, and entitled "The Religion of the Bible and Religion of K[ing] W[illiam] County Compared," it is dated 1769 and forms a stark contrast with the piety preached and exemplified in the sermons of Samuel Davies and in other accounts of religion in the early South, notably Hermon Husband's *Some Remarks on Religion* (written 1750, published 1761) about religion in North Carolina. Reid's characterization of a King William County gentleman needs also to be set next to Hugh Jones's earlier portrait of a typical Virginian, for there is little resemblance between the two: a "King William County Gentleman . . . attends worship only to make bargains, hear and rehearse news, fix horse races & cock matches, and learns if there are any barbacued Hogs to be offered in sacrifice Gratis to satisfy a voracious appetite." Money "gilds over all his stupidities, and although an Ass covered over with gold is still an Ass, yet in King William County a fool covered with the same metal, changes his nature, and commences a GENTLEMAN." In Reid's indictment, one hears again the same criticism of Virginia that was leveled against it in the seventeenth century, namely, that it is a place where the social order is remarkable for its instability, where social climbing is normal behavior and all the old distinctions of birth and breeding are lost.

The most accomplished satirist of colonial Virginia, Robert Bolling, Jr. (1738–1775), of Chellowe Plantation, Buckingham County, would surely have been excluded from James Reid's fulminations, for there was no better blood south of the line than the Buckingham County Bollings. A direct descendant of Pocahontas and John Rolfe, Bolling brings us to the very eve of the Revolution in Virginia, writing with amused detachment about the inoculation riots in Norfolk, Virginia, in which party politics surely played a part, and with more concern though still a degree of amusement about local efforts to boycott goods taxed by Britain. From the perspective of literary history, perhaps Bolling's most important poem is "Neanthe" (*ca.* 1768), recently edited by J. A. Leo Lemay, which contains practically all the ingredients of Southern humor most scholars would have us believe did not appear until fifty or seventy-five years later (including the gruesome fight to the finish, grotesque sexual jokes, and the mockery of the outsider). A number of other poems, such as his satire on the bailment of Colonel John Chiswell (1766), are almost as important. During the early and middle 1760s, Bolling dominated the pages of London's *Imperial Magazine* and the *Virginia Gazette*, though nearly as many or more of his poems do not appear to have been published at all and remain largely unread in the manuscript collections at Colonial Williamsburg, the Virginia Historical Society, and the Henry E. Huntington Library. Not until his numerous and important poems have become part of the story will there be an accurate accounting of the range and value of the prerevolutionary literature of Virginia.

As in Virginia, in Maryland the name of William Parks is intimately connected with nearly all early literary activity. Parks, whose press at Annapolis antedates his establishment in Williamsburg by several years, was brought to Maryland as public printer by Thomas Bordley in the spring of 1726. Bordley himself had already made an important contribution to the political literature of the province with his "Epistolar Preface" to *The Charter of Maryland, Together with the Debates and Proceedings of the . . . Assembly . . . 1722, 1723, and 1724* (1725), in which he lamented that "the Character of a great Commoner, so much esteemed in *England*," seemed altogether unknown in the province because the public had previously not had access to the laws and the proceedings of the assembly. In less than a year after his arrival, Parks would have the sad task of printing "An Elogy On the Death of Thomas Bordley" (1726) written by Ebenezer Cook, the first wholly belletristic work published in the South.

With the founding of the *Maryland Gazette* in 1726, Parks offered an outlet for local talent and soon began receiving contributions from Cook, Richard Lewis, and other Maryland writers. Parks's most important publication during these early years, however, was Daniel Dulany, Sr.'s *The Rights of the Inhabitants of Maryland, to the Benefit of English*

Laws (1728), a restrained, effective plea against the Proprietary contention that English laws were not automatically in force in America. In one form or another, the dispute would reverberate throughout the halls of nearly all colonial assemblies, finally culminating in Jefferson's *Summary View of the Rights of British America* (1774) as the last major colonial plea for equal treatment under British law.

In Ebenezer Cook (1667?–post-1732) and Richard Lewis (1700?–1734), the province of Maryland lays claim to the two best poets of the early South. Cook is best remembered for *The Sot-Weed Factor* (1708), revised and published as the "third edition" (no second edition is known to have been printed) by William Parks as part of *The Maryland Muse* in 1731. The other poem in *The Maryland Muse*, also by Cook, was "The History of Colonel Nathaniel Bacon's Rebellion in Virginia." Recounting the misadventures of a self-important greenhorn who comes to Maryland as a tobacco merchant expecting to take advantage of the credulity of the inhabitants but who ends up being duped himself, *The Sot-Weed Factor* is arguably the single best poem written in America before the American Renaissance, and certainly one of the best satires any American writer has yet produced. It uses frontier America as a device for exploding the pretentiousness and preconceptions of the sot-weed factor, and in turn uses the pretentiousness and preconceptions as a way of exposing life in the province of Maryland to be a ridiculous parody of civilization, achieving thereby a complex irony approaching that of many modern masterpieces of so-called black humor.

Cook is less successful in his "History of Bacon's Rebellion," largely because the speaker himself is not an integral character in the action as in *The Sot-Weed Factor*. But in the annals of colonial literature the poem is still an important one, as well as a major literary treatment of an important event in colonial history, anticipating the American's ambiguous relationship to his own past as either a subject for ironic skepticism (Irving's *History of New York*, Melville's *Israel Potter, et al.*) or romantic hyperbole, as in a multitude of historical romances. A third long poem, *Sot-weed Redivivus* (1730), comments on the economic woes of Maryland, particularly the single-crop system, the lack of currency, and the plague of absentee landlords, revealing in the process Cook's commitment to the land of his adoption. In addition to the elegy on Bordley referred to earlier, Cook also wrote elegies on Nicholas Lowe (1728), William Lock (1732), and Benedict Leonard Calvert (1732), performing the role of public poet competently if not spectacularly.

If Ebenezer Cook had any rival for the semiserious title of Poet Laureate of Maryland, it was the much younger Richard Lewis, who wrote polished and regular iambic pentameter verses in contrast to Cook's rough hudibrastics. Combining lyricism with a love of nature and a touch of preromantic melancholy elevated toward philosophy by sentimental and deistical piety, Lewis produced his best work in "Description of the Spring, A Journey from Patapsco to Annapolis, April 4, 1730," in which the cycle of the day suggests the cycle of the seasons and the stages of one's life. The journey is magnified into a commonplace but still effective analogy for the poet's progress toward his ultimate goal, the Heavenly City. Lewis' earliest extant poem is a competent translation of Edward Holdsworth's popular Latin poem *Muscipula*, which Lewis rendered as *The Mouse Trap; or the Battle of the Cambrians and Mice* (1728) and used as an occasion for paying playful tribute to his own Welsh ancestry.

One of Lewis' most ambitious poems, "*To Mr.* Samuel Hastings (*Shipwright* of Philadelphia) on his launching the Maryland-Merchant . . . ," appeared in the *Maryland Gazette* in 1729. Largely a progress piece on the history of shipbuilding, the verses implicitly predict that ships such as the *Maryland-Merchant*, eventually constituting the kind of local commercial fleet that Cook had advocated in *Sot-weed Redivivus*, will rescue Maryland's economy. "Food for Criticks," which survives only in the *New England Weekly Journal* and the *Pennsylvania Gazette*, was probably written in 1731 and contains some of Lewis' most effective descriptions of American nature, including a catalog of game fish probably derived from Pope's *Windsor Forest*.

Although Lewis wrote numerous other poems, including elegies on Benedict Leonard Calvert (1732) and Captain Charles Calvert (1734) and "Congratulatory Verses" celebrating Thomas Penn's arrival in Pennsylvania (1732), his other most important poem is *A Rhapsody* (1732), like "Journey," a poem that finds in nature an occasion to meditate upon the brevity of man's life and the purposes for which he is designed by the Creator. "Be my Life crown'd with Peace, to Thee resign'd" writes Lewis, "Blest with Content, and with a tranquil Mind. . . . May I, with Decency submit to Fate, / And find myself in a more happy State."

Lewis died in March of 1734, but his memory, like Cook's, remained green among the Maryland poets of the next generation. The Reverend Thomas Cradock, himself a poet of some importance, remembered Lewis in "The Maryland Divine" (an imitation of Virgil's fourth eclogue) as a "poor, unhappy Bard" who was still read with delight. Although some of Cradock's sermons, such as "A Merry Hart, or Innocent Mirth not Inconsistent with Religion" (1747), have historical importance and may help to explain why, sixty years later, Washington Irving insisted upon referring to "Merry-Land" in his *History of New York*, Cradock's most important contribution to colonial Southern literature is "Maryland Eclogues In Imitation of Virgil's By Jonathan Spritly, Esq." (post–1744), which satirizes corrupt clergy, the apparently increasing practice of miscegenation among slaveholding planters, the evils of excessive drinking, the alarming spread of infidelity in the province, the colonists' cheating of Indians in land transactions, and other vices and follies—all with a distinctly regional and local flavor despite a universality of motive.

The most original and important writing produced in midcentury Maryland came from two later immigrants, the Scotchman Dr. Alexander Hamilton (1712–1756) and the Irishman James Sterling (1701–1763), who came to Annapolis in 1739 and 1737, respectively, and entered immediately into the cultural life of the provincial capital. With William Parks's final removal to Williamsburg and the cessation of the *Maryland Gazette,* the province needed a new printer, and when Jonas Green arrived from Philadelphia in 1738, yet another central figure in the cultural history of the province and, like Hamilton, a future member of the Tuesday Club had appeared in the small city. In 1745, Green resuscitated the *Maryland Gazette,* apparently with assurances from Hamilton, Sterling, Dr. Adam Thomson ("Philo-Muses"), and others that they would regularly contribute original compositions.

Nevertheless, with the exception of the so-called "Quevedo" essay (1748), a lighthearted look at authors currently flourishing in "this our Woodland Country," Hamilton's best work remained unpublished. His *Itinerarium* (1744), of which there is still no readily available modern edition, besides being an invaluable resource for cultural historians, is a classic piece of American humor, containing a wealth of amusing vignettes and ironic observations about colonial customs in settlements and cities as diverse as Annapolis and Boston. The "History of the Ancient and Honourable Tuesday Club" (1754), about the club Hamilton founded in 1745 which left its mark on similar Southern societies for at least a century, still awaits a modern edition, though portions of it, including the first sustained piece of drama criticism written in America, have been described and edited by J. A. Leo Lemay and Robert Micklus. There is absolutely no reason to quarrel with Lemay's assessment that Hamilton deserves to "rank as a major American writer of neoclassic prose."

James Sterling is another matter, since most of his writing, including a good proportion of material eventually published in America, had been completed before he came to Maryland and was refurbished for American publication. Major exceptions are "The Sixteenth Ode of Horace's *Second Book,* Imitated, and Inscribed to His Excellency Samuel Ogle, Esq.," which appeared in the *Maryland Gazette* on March 31,

1747, and especially the long *Epistle to the Hon. Arthur Dobbs, Esq.* (1752), written in Ireland but clearly owing its inspiration to experiences in America and Sterling's commercial interest in the discovery of the fabled Northwest Passage; moreover, Sterling indites his verses, he claims, as a "tuneful Savage," plainly an effort to establish an American persona. Sterling also delivered the opening sermon to a special meeting of the legislature called on December 13, 1754, to raise money for the defense of Maryland's frontiers in the French and Indian War. Like Samuel Davies' sermons on the same subject, it is a mixture of anti-French polemic and patriotic exhortation.

Occasional essays and verses continued to appear in the *Maryland Gazette* and other colonial journals and newspapers, the most important of which are the poem "On the Invention of Letters" (1758) and other timely pieces like "The Patriot" (1758), as well as the long "Pastoral, *To his Excellency* George Thomas" (1758), which had evidently been written in 1744 to commemorate the death of Alexander Pope and was now refashioned for Sterling's new purposes. Although not a member of the Tuesday Club, Sterling attended meetings on two occasions and, like Hamilton and several other Marylanders who were members—Thomas Bacon is perhaps the most prominent next to Green and Hamilton—left his impress on Maryland culture.

Compared with Virginia and Maryland, the three remaining Southern colonies of North and South Carolina and Georgia have left little evidence of literary culture. With only the small settlements of New Bern and Wilmington, North Carolina lacked the sense of literary community—one might even call it a sense of literary heritage—that was part of the cultural milieu of Virginia and Maryland. Although James Davis began the *North Carolina Gazette* in 1751 and continued publication until 1759, too few issues survive to draw any conclusions regarding its local contributions save that its general context does not appear to have been as belletristic as its Virginia and Maryland counterparts. In 1764, Davis tried again with the *North Carolina Magazine,* which became the *North Carolina Gazette* again in 1768, but no local writers dominate its pages as Cook, Lewis, and Hamilton did the *Maryland Gazette.* Even Governor Thomas Burke, a practicing poet and one of Robert Bolling's favorite literary antagonists in Virginia, wrote relatively little after he moved to North Carolina. The major literary production of the colony during the prerevolutionary period remained John Lawson's *History of North Carolina* (1708; entitled *A New Voyage to Carolina* in 1709), though Mark Catesby's *Natural History of Carolina, Florida, and the Bahama Islands* (1731–1743) is a superior piece of natural history and runs a close second on the score of literary value as well. It is indicative of North Carolina's slow development that Lawson's *New Voyage,* written more than a century after the settlement at Jamestown, should be largely promotional in intention and mainly devoted to natural history and descriptions of the Indians.

The case was somewhat different in South Carolina, largely because of the growing cosmopolitanism of the port of Charleston and the *South-Carolina Gazette* of Thomas Whitmarsh. A competitor of Eleazor Phillips, Jr.'s *South-Carolina Weekly Journal* (of which no known copies are extant), the *Gazette* passed to Lewis Timothy upon Whitmarsh's death in 1733 and, under the editorship of Timothy and his wife Elizabeth, eventually attracted contributions from Joseph Dumbleton, whose very popular "A Rhapsody on Rum" appeared in 1749, and other writers dwelling in the colony. About the same time that the "Monitor" essays were appearing in Parks's *Virginia Gazette,* the *South-Carolina Gazette* featured the much shorter-lived (only three essays are extant) but equally playful "Meddlers Club Papers," which among other things jestingly comments upon sexual license in the seacoast city. The leading poet of South Carolina during this period is probably Dr. James Kirkpatrick (earlier Kilpatrick), author of *The Nonpareil* and *The Sea-Piece* (1750), the first of which gracefully praises the beauty of the woman to whom it is inscribed, a Miss Townsend or Townshend, in praising also the beauty of the bird she keeps as her "cheerful Captive." Another South Carolina poet, Rowland Rugeley, also flourished in the middle of the eighteenth century and published his best-known work, the bawdy *Story of Aeneas and Dido Burlesqued,* in 1774.

Of the *Georgia Gazette,* founded by James Johnston in 1763, next to nothing is known. The youngest of the colonies, Georgia had produced but one noteworthy piece of writing by the eve of the Revolution, Patrick Tailfer, Hugh Anderson, and David Douglas' *True and Historical Narrative of the Colony of Georgia in America* (1741), with its mocking dedication to "James Oglethorpe, Esq." and his wise policy of protecting his settlers from the vices of luxury by "entailing a more than primitive poverty upon us." Written in imitation of Swift, the dedication rhetorically assumes that Oglethorpe actually aims at the collapse of his colony and congratulates him for having almost achieved that end. As biting a satire as almost any penned in colonial America, the *True and Historical Narrative* exploits the principles of decorum for the purposes of a cynical humor that would remain one of the hallmarks of Southern literature.

J. A. Leo Lemay's appendix to the *Bibliographical Guide to the Study of Southern Writers* (1969) lists more than fifty early Southern authors not included in this survey. Despite the abundance of literary activity, however, the eighteenth-century South appears to have been as alien to its contemporaries as it has been to modern critics. In 1771, the editors of the first edition of the *Encyclopedia Britannica* located Virginia for their readers as "one of the British American colonies, situated between seventy-four and eighty degrees west long. and between thirty-six and thirty-nine degrees of north lat.," as if the land were, like Antarctica of the present day, entirely uninhabited. To be sure, readers could learn a bit about American geography: Virginia was "bounded by the river Patowmack, which separates it from Maryland, on the north; by the Atlantic-ocean, on the east; by Carolina, on the south, and may be extended as far westward as we think fit."

In that asyntactical final phrase lie embedded both the sense of propriety and political realism, the "fitness" of pushing too far and too fast into inhospitable and disputed terrain, and the self-confident, imperialistic promise out of which much of the literature of the prerevolutionary South was generated. Marked as well by a growing self-awareness and regional pride, attitudes nourished in part by both internal and external political pressures and by a sense of a shared literary and intellectual heritage, Southern literature of the early and middle eighteenth century presents rich and varied opportunities for continuing study of the sources of the Southern imagination.

ROBERT BAIN

William Byrd of Westover

The richness and variety of William Byrd of Westover's works have made him the most important Southern writer before Jefferson, Poe, and Simms. Byrd's character sketches and literary exercises, his letters, his three secret diaries (first published in the 1940s and 1950s), and his four prose works—*The History of the Dividing Line Betwixt Virginia and North Carolina Run in the Year of Our Lord 1728, A Progress to the Mines in the Year 1732*, and *A Journey to the Land of Eden Anno 1733*, all first published in 1841, and *The Secret History of the Line*, first published in 1929—have earned him the reputation as a major colonial American author as well as the preeminent writer of the colonial South.

Because Byrd's life and writings invite cultural-historical criticism as well as literary criticism, the distinctions between the two often blur and account for quite different readings of the man and his work. Commentators have compared Byrd's works favorably with those of such authors as Franklin, Irving, Swift, and especially Samuel Pepys. They have credited Byrd with beginning "the Southwestern tradition" in American literature; they have read his works as epitomizing the "gaiety and greed" of the colonial Virginia enterprise; they have viewed Byrd as an atypical Virginian and as the archetypal Southern aristocrat of the Golden Age; they have seen in Byrd's prose the creation of the mythic Southern cavalier; they have portrayed his life and works as evidence of his divided consciousness of himself as both Englishman and American; they have argued that Byrd, before Jefferson, is a Southern pastoral writer whose works illustrate that Negro slavery was the serpent making the Southern Eden an uneasy country and different from any other in Western culture. Critics have described his works as epic, mock-epic, pastoral, satire, romance, comic, and humorous. They have called his major prose works travel literature, frontier narratives, diaries, Southwest humor, and propaganda. They have praised Byrd as one of the best American classicists of his day and have marveled at his library of more than 3,600 volumes. They have discussed him as an amateur naturalist and physician. Summing up Byrd's reputation, Richard Beale Davis noted: "As writer and man William Byrd has been labelled belated Restoration cavalier and satirist, Queen Anne wit, pamphleteer, promoter, American Pepys, virtuoso, travel writer, and historian. He is most of these things in some degree, and more." More he is.

Byrd's education prepared him well for running a plantation, for political leadership, and for authorship. Born March 28, 1674, he was the son of William Byrd I, a migrant London goldsmith who inherited Virginia land and who parlayed his plantations and his Indian trading into a sizable fortune. When William Byrd II was seven years old, his father sent him to school in England; there he received the usual classical education and became a compulsive reader. He then studied business in Holland and London, and law at the Middle Temple, being admitted to the bar in April of 1695. Through the influence of his mentor Sir Robert Southwell, he was elected to the Royal Society on April 29, 1696. In London, Byrd enjoyed the social life and befriended literary and learned men.

Returning to Virginia briefly in 1696, he was elected to the House of Burgesses, but went back to England before serving his term. During that London residence, he wrote witty letters to "Facetia" (Lady Elizabeth Cromwell) and some character sketches, notably his autobiographical "Inamorato L'Oiseaux." Byrd returned to Virginia in 1705 to inherit his father's 26,000-acre estate; he was also appointed the colony's receiver general, a lucrative post, and married Lucy Parke, daughter of Colonel Daniel Parke, on May 4, 1706. On September 12, 1709, Byrd became a member of the powerful Virginia Council, a position he held until his death.

Business and politics sent Byrd again to England in 1715, where his wife Lucy died of smallpox on November 21, 1716. Within weeks he was writing passionate letters to "Sabina," a young heiress named Mary Smith. That suit failed. He published some light verses addressed to ladies in *Tunbrigalia* (1719) and a pamphlet, *A Discourse Concerning the Plague, with Some Preservatives Against It by a Lover of Mankind* (1721). After a brief visit to Virginia in 1720–1721, Byrd returned to England in the fall of 1721 to court several ladies and finally to marry Maria Taylor, a twenty-five-year-old heiress, in May of 1724. In need of money for his growing family, he returned to Virginia in the spring of 1726.

Byrd's most productive years—both as a writer and, despite heavy debts, as an empire builder—followed his return to Virginia. One of three Virginia commissioners appointed in 1727 to settle a boundary dispute with North Carolina, Byrd and his delegation met the North Carolinians in March of 1728 to run the line. Beginning at Currituck Inlet, they surveyed the line until April 8 and continued from September 20 through November 22, traveling 241 miles from the sea to the Appalachian foothills. The North Carolinians and one Virginia commissioner abandoned the survey in October, leaving Byrd and his Virginians to complete the task. From that experience came *The History of the Dividing Line* and *The Secret History of the Line*. Byrd also bought 20,000 acres of western Carolina land for two hundred dollars; in these years he more than doubled his land holdings. He built in 1730–1731 the house that still stands at Westover. He visited in 1732 with former Governor Alexander Spotswood at Germanna to learn about iron mining and smelting; *A Progress to the Mines* describes his journey. He visited his western lands in 1733 and laid out the towns of Richmond and Petersburg; from that adventure came *A Journey to the Land of Eden*. Plagued by debts, he considered selling Westover in 1735–1736 and spent much energy in his later years trying to find settlers for his western lands. Samuel Jenner, an agent in Bern, Switzerland, published *Neu-gefundes Eden* (1737), a promotion tract to lure the Swiss to the New Eden. Although Byrd may have written notes for this work, most information comes from John Lawson's *New Voyage to Carolina* (1709). When Byrd died on August 26, 1744, he had paid off his debts and owned 179,440 acres. He also had in manuscript the four prose narratives that would bring him literary fame.

None of Byrd's lesser works would entitle him to eminence as a Southern writer. His *Philosophical Transactions* (1697) about an albino Negro boy is negligible; critics disagree about whether his *Discourse Concerning the Plague* (1721), which recommends tobacco as the principal preventive, is a serious scientific work or a satire. His brief *Description of the Dismal Swamp and a Proposal to Drain the Swamp* (1789, 1837, 1922) echoes the dividing-line histories. The verses in *Tunbrigalia* (1719), written to entertain friends at Tunbridge Wells, are witty, but ephemeral. His legal and state papers are important historically, but have little literary value. His unpublished commonplace book, owned by the Virginia Historical Society, contains his judgments about his reading as well as sententiae copied from his reading. His translation of "The Ephesian Matron" from Petronius' *Satyricon* is the best of these short works. But Byrd's character sketches, literary exercises, letters, diaries, and four prose works comprise a sizable and impressive achievement for a man busy with planting and politics.

Although Pierre Mirambaud and Richard Beale Davis have written sensibly about the character sketches and literary exercises, these works have not yet received their due. Whether the characters imitate Theophrastan models or are based on individuals whom Byrd knew, the best ones have vigor and often psychological and moral insight. In "Dr. Glysterio," thought to be a portrait of Samuel Garth, Byrd captures in about five hundred words the character of a madcap eccentric. Dr. Glysterio is "a Physician at the Coffee house, a Poet at the colledge, a sloven at court, a Beau in the country, & a mad man every where." A "notorious skimmer of the sciences" unable to "spare time from his amusements . . . to penetrate beyond the surface and terms of things," Dr. Glysterio flits through life unabashed, filling "at once his purse and the Bills of Mortality." Byrd creates in "Dr. Glysterio" an amusing posturer whose dilettantism is dangerous.

He sketches in "Cavaliero Sapiente," a portrait of Sir Robert Southwell, the good and gracious man. He praises Sapiente for his "sound & vigorous mind," for practicing religion "in all her charms," and for possessing "Zeal without bitterness, Devotion without hypocrisy, and charity without ostentation." The "Friend, and favorite of mankind," Sapiente has served his country well without compromising admirable values. These dozen or so sketches, written before his return from England in the 1720s, and those in his letters illustrate Byrd's deftness at drawing character and foreshadow his lively portraits in *Secret History*.

"Inamorato L'Oiseaux," Byrd's self-portrait written before 1705 and sent in a letter to "Minionet" in 1723, depicts the enamored bird as a man who learned of love before he learned of good and evil. He says, "Tis well he had not a twin-sister as Osyris had, for without doubt like him he wou'd have amouretted with her in his mothers belly." In love, he was a foolish figure, but he "never interlop't with anothers wife or mistress, but dealt altogether where the Trade was open & free for all Adventurers." He believes "that without Ladys, a schollar is a Pedant, a philosopher a Cynick, all morality is morose, & all behaviour either too Formal or too licentious." Despite his weakness for women, Byrd "thinks himself as firmly bound by his Word as by his hand & seal, and wou'd be as much asham'd to be put in mind of one, as to be sue'd for the other." Byrd exaggerates some of his qualities, but sketches himself with an "essential truthfulness," according to Richard Beale Davis.

Among Byrd's other literary exercises is "The Female Creed," a bawdy listing of women's foibles and superstitions. His poem "Upon a Fart," a parody of Anne Finch's "Upon a Sigh," is a witty blast.

Byrd's letters, collected for the first time in Marion Tinling's *The Correspondence of the Three William Byrds of Westover, Virginia, 1684–1776* (2 vols., 1977), have been a rich source of information about the colonial South and their author. His oft-quoted letter to the earl of Orrery (July 5, 1726) presents, according to Robert D. Arner and others, a succinct "definition of the myth of the Old South" as Virgilian pastoral. In that letter Byrd describes himself as living "like one of the patriarchs" with "my flocks and herds, my bondmen and bondwomen, and every sort of trade amongst my own servants, so that I live in a kind of independence on every one but Providence." Yet in a letter to the earl of Egmont (July 12, 1736) he considers putting an end to "this unchristian traffick of makeing merchandize of our fellow creatures" because the slaves "blow up the pride, & ruin the industry of our white people" and because the increasing number of slaves creates "the necessity of being severe." Byrd's analysis of slavery anticipates Jefferson's judgment fifty years later. His letters touch upon most of the issues of his day.

Letters to ladies he courted and to kinfolk reveal a more private and playful man. His letters to ladies (Facetia, Charmante, Minionet, Fidelia, and others) show that in matters of the heart Byrd could be both witty and foolish. Letters to kinfolk include comic anecdotes, characters, and sometimes bawdy tales. He writes to Jane Pratt Taylor (October 10, 1735) the story of an "Italian bono roba" who tries unsuccessfully to enlarge her breasts with an ingenious device. The letters also record Byrd's constant struggle to pay his debts and build his empire.

When Byrd's three secret diaries appeared, scholars called him an American Pepys. But Byrd is not an American Pepys. Unlike Pepys, who wrote personal essays about his day's activities, Byrd simply records in formulaic entries what happened each day, seldom commenting on the meaning of those events. Kept in a seventeenth-century shorthand, the diaries were for Byrd's eyes only and often record intimate details of his private life. A typical entry looks like the one for May 4, 1711.

> I rose at 6'oclock and read two chapters in Hebrew and some Greek in Lucian. I said my prayers and ate boiled milk for breakfast. I danced my dance. The weather was very cold. I sent G-r-l with a letter to Colonel Hill which came from Mr. Perry concerning his ship. Nurse sent for her things which were delivered. I settled some accounts. My sick people were better, thank God Almighty. My sister Duke and Colonel Eppes came and stayed to dinner. I ate pork and peas for dinner. In the afternoon my sister went home and the Colonel went away and then I went and read some law till evening. Then I took a walk about the plantation to see how everything was but my wife stayed at home and was melancholy. I said my prayers and had good health, good thoughts, and good humor, thank God Almighty. I gave my wife a flourish.

Agreeing that the diaries have little literary merit, critics have described the entries as repetitive, formulaic, dull, drab, banal, and monotonous; the diaries are, however, historically significant. Ross Pudaloff has argued recently that keeping the diaries gave Byrd a grip on life by creating for himself in language a sense of order and control.

Within these formulaic and almost incantatory entries, there is much variety. Of the three diaries, *The Secret Diary of William Byrd of Westover, 1709–1712* (1941) and *The London Diary (1717–1721) and Other Writings* (1958) present the liveliest and most revealing accounts. Entries in *Another Secret Diary of William Byrd of Westover, 1739–1741, with Letters and Literary Exercises, 1696–1726* (1942) are briefer and less informative. In the diaries, he records his reading in Hebrew, Greek, Latin, French, Italian, Dutch, and English, and in law, medicine, physics, mathematics, geometry, and religion, though he seldom gives titles and authors. As a farmer, he charts the weather, seasons, plantings, and harvests. He writes of his hospitality to legions of visitors and of such social doings as dances, card playing, and gambling. Always conscious of his place in the social and political hierarchy, he enjoys special courtesies and acknowledgments from the governors. He even considers a friend's advice about bribing his way to the governorship of Virginia.

Preoccupied with his health and diet, he dwells on his physical condition—even the number of stools he has when sick. As an amateur physician, he prescribes "vomits" and other remedies for his servants and neighbors. He settles accounts, conducts public and private business, and writes many letters. He puzzles over dreams and occult signs. A religiously enlightened man, he says his prayers almost every day, attends church faithfully, writes his religious creed, and reads sermons. He dances his dance, a physical exercise. He weeps occasionally when Lucy is melancholy, and on his thirty-sixth birthday, he laments that he has achieved so little. He disciplines servants and slaves, having them whipped occasionally and once making a child drink a "pint of piss" for bed-wetting. He keeps score of his lovemaking with Lucy and others (he "rogers" them or gives them a "flourish") and notes when he has "manual uncleanness" or "uncleanness" with a woman, evidently references to masturbation. After Lucy died, he whores in London, picking up women, taking them to a bagnio, and sometimes rogering them two or three times. Even in his sixties, he "played the fool" with Sally, Marjorie, or F-r-b-y. Despite the repetitions and formulaic qualities, the diaries—prepared and annotated by Louis B. Wright, Maude H. Woodfin, and Marion Tinling—give more information about colonial Virginia life than any other single set of documents available.

Composition dates of *History* and *Secret History* remain uncertain. During the expedition, Byrd probably kept a shorthand journal, now lost; from that journal he wrote in 1728 and 1729 two official reports to

England. The best guess is that he began work on the histories in 1732 and that *Secret History* is the earlier version. He wrote to Peter Collinson on July 18, 1736, that he was hanging on to "my history of the line" because he had resolved "never to venture any thing unfinisht out of my hands." References in *History* to an electrical storm in 1736 and to George Whitefield's preaching (1738 in America) indicate that Byrd may have been revising as late as 1738 or 1740. No solid evidence exists for dating *A Progress* and *A Journey*.

That *Secret History* and *History* are two distinct books based on the same experience but intended for different audiences is evident throughout both texts. *Secret History* is a Southern American book for a Southern American audience; *History* is a Southern American book for a British audience. Although Byrd did not plan to publish *Secret History*, he circulated the manuscript among friends. He fills it with characters familiar to many Southerners, aims his satire at individuals as well as groups, and gives fewer explanations than he does in *History* (for example, in *History* he explains what a tomahawk is). The satire of *History* is more general because a British audience would be unfamiliar with its targets; it also contains more information about plant and animal life and about providing for a frontier expedition, perhaps for promotional purposes. In the *History* he also relies more heavily on biblical and classical allusions to make the unfamiliar known to his readers and sometimes compares American scenes with British scenes for the same reason. Although the books are quite different, they do, as Percy G. Adams notes, complement each other.

Byrd peoples *Secret History*, which is half as long as *History*, with lively characters on a jolly outing. He draws the North Carolina commissioners as bumbling incompetents, giving them fictional names to match their intellectual and social status: Jumble, Shoebrush, Plausible, and Puzzlecause. These hoggish men, representing their "porcivorous country," arrive at Currituck Inlet much better provided for their bellies than for business. Byrd satirizes these characters for their small-mindedness and social pretensions. In the Virginia delegation are Meanwell, Astrolabe, Dr. Humdrum, and Firebrand, the latter of whom is the champion of self-interest and chaos and who is Byrd's chief protagonist. Byrd portrays himself as Steddy, the man who holds the company together and who, as John Seelye notes, completes the mission in "His Majesty's Service." These characters provide the book's conflict and comedy and give Byrd's narrative much of its vitality.

But Byrd sketches other characters as well. Besides the portraits of pork-eating poor whites, Byrd draws a number of characters who anticipate later fictional creations. Byrd's most famous portrait is that of Ned

Bearskin, the Saponi Indian guide and hunter, who gives a detailed account of his religion. Byrd calls the Saponi guide our "honest Indian Bearskin" and portrays him much as Cooper does Chingachgook. Byrd's thumbnail sketch of Old Captain Hix, who joins the party for a few days, anticipates Cooper's Natty Bumppo. An experienced frontiersman, the white-haired Captain Hix at three score and ten shoots as straight as the younger men, keeps pace with men half his years, and entertains the company with a trading song. In the character of Orion, a mathematics teacher at the College of William and Mary, Byrd draws the tenderfoot having trouble coping with the wilds. In young Robin Hix, Byrd portrays the independent yeoman who refuses to carry Orion's "greatcoat" in the march through Dismal Swamp. Admiring Robin, Byrd sees the justice in his refusal. His character of Epaphroditus Bainton, a sixty-year-old hunter and guide, suggests the fictional Daniel Boone, though Bainton has little of Boone's nobility.

Besides the central conflict between Steddy and Firebrand, Byrd records bear stories, Indian lore, bawdy tales of the company's conduct with frontier maids, and the story of the company's founding of the "Order of Maosti, signifying in the Saponi language a turkey's beard." The badge of the order carries a Latin motto celebrating the turkey that supplies meat to the adventurers. Byrd also satirizes the saints of New England who sell rum the Virginians call "Kill-Devil." Throughout the narrative, Steddy commands.

Because Byrd had in mind for *History* a British audience and London publication, he changed his book radically. He dropped the characters' fictional names, de-emphasized the personal conflicts, deleted letters exchanged by the commissioners, omitted Steddy's four harangues to the company, and shifted the focus of his satire from individuals to groups, mainly the Lubberlanders of North Carolina. He also omitted the thumbnail sketches of Bainton, Old Captain Hix, and others, but retained that of Ned Bearskin.

To "cover this dry skeleton, and make it ["my journal"] appear more to advantage," Byrd added much to his *History* (William Byrd to Peter Collinson, July 5, 1737, in Marion Tinling [ed.], *The Correspondence of the Three William Byrds of Westover, Virginia, 1684–1776* [2 vols.; Charlottesville, Va., 1977], II, 523–24. "My Journal" is evidently a reference to a manuscript version of one of the histories). Preserving the chronological order of *Secret History*, he fleshed out his narrative by writing a prefatory "history" of the colony to place the boundary dispute in context. He expanded his descriptions of Norfolk and of the landscape in general, and he wrote more about plant life, especially rattlesnake root and his favorite herb—ginseng. He added lore about possums, polecats, panthers, rattlesnakes, alligators, and squirrels; some of these tales are tall ones. Toward the end of the book, he wrote about how future expeditions should provision themselves and about his vision of the wild, but bountiful, landscape settled and civilized. Some additions came from Byrd's reading as well as from his journal of running the line.

North Carolina continues to receive the bite of Byrd's satire in *History*. Describing that colony as "Lubberland" because of nature's plenty and the people's laziness, Byrd calls the North Carolinians pagans and infidels who "pay no tribute, either to God or to Caesar" and who "keep so many Sabbaths every week, that their disregard of the seventh day has no manner of cruelty in it, either to servants or cattle." The men make their women do all the work and are "slothful in everything but getting of children." The colony's chief business is raising hogs because it requires no effort. Eating so much pork fills the people "full of gross humors" and makes them look so syphilitic that a man with a nose cannot hold "any place of profit in the province." A lawless haven for "runaway slaves, . . . debtors and criminals," North Carolina encourages a democratic spirit that allows everyone to do "what seems best in his own eyes." Byrd is glad to return to the "Christendom" of Tidewater Virginia after his adventure in Lubberland. Midway through *History*, Byrd's satire on North Carolina diminishes and the book becomes a natural history and narrative of a frontier expedition.

Byrd wrote *A Progress to the Mines* and *A Journey to the Land of Eden*, both much shorter narratives, in the style and spirit of *History*, but he sustains neither of these as artfully as he does in the longer works. As Richard Beale Davis notes, *A Journey* is really an appendix or afterword to *History*. But among his Southern contemporaries who wrote—Robert Beverley, John Lawson, James Blair, Hugh Jones—William Byrd of Westover attempted more and achieved more as a citizen of the republic of letters.

LEWIS P. SIMPSON

The Ideology of Revolution

A ny brief attempt to describe the literature and the literary sensibility of the revolutionary period in the Southern states must center in Virginia, a focal point of the Revolution, and particularly in the thought and writings of Thomas Jefferson. This lawyer, statesman, and man of letters, who was also a planter and a slave master, not only defined the ideology of freedom that unified the Revolution for the nation and proclaimed it to the world; by dramatic implication he discovered the special character of the ideology in Virginia (and the other Southern states) and intimated the eventual rise of the separatist South, if not quite the civil conflict of unprecedented ferocity that would destroy the first American Republic.

The fundamental revolutionary writings by Jefferson are merely four in number and of no great size in body. In chronological order they are: *A Summary View of the Rights of British America* (1774); the Declaration of Independence (1776); "A Bill for Establishing Religious Freedom" (1777); and Jefferson's only book, *Notes on the State of Virginia* (first authorized edition, 1787). Although emanating from a mind fostered by the culture of a small slave society on the colonial margin of eighteenth-century Europe, these works may be viewed in sum as constituting a climactic expression of the world historical secularity that had been in process of formation in Western civilization for three or four centuries. Essentially this process consisted in the radical displacement of a transcendent reference for either natural or social order—the medieval cosmology, the heavenly city of the Christians, the ideal republic of the philosophers—by the subjectification or internalization of nature and history. Seeking to expand its "knowledge of Causes, and secret motions of things," to "enlarge the bounds of Human Empire to the effecting of all things possible," as Sir Francis Bacon put it in the *New Atlantis*, the human mind began to inquire not only into nature but into the nature of man: his physiology and society, and especially his mentality. Discovering its seemingly limitless capacity for planning and

57

retrospection, for contrivance and analysis, the mind suggested itself as the source and model of natural and social order. By the time Giovanni Battista Vico made that plain in *The New Science* (1744)—"the world of civil society has certainly been made by men and . . . its principles are therefore to be found within the modifications of our own human mind"—the movement of reality into mind (ironically often considered to be a process of objectifying knowledge) had become the determining force of modern history. Jefferson's writings are the works of a mind engaged in inventing a civil order that would be called the Great Experiment, a society testing whether or not the expression of freedom and equality, as evolved in the modifications of the human mind, is the true principle of man's nature in society. Yet Jefferson's writings are at the same time the works of a mind that, though it conceived slavery to be wrong in moral principle, could never find, save in conjectural possibility, a way to end its involvement in the practice of slavery. All his long life the author of the Declaration of Independence remained a slave master, participating in a social system in which the enslavement of one human being by another was the major means of order. In the inability of a modern man of letters like Jefferson to terminate his role as slave master lies the chief key to the history of literature in the antebellum Southern states.

The appearance of the modern man of letters had been announced on Easter Sunday, 1341, when Petrarch stood in the Senate House on Rome's Capitoline Hill to be crowned with a laurel wreath and to deliver a coronation oration (the text from Virgil's *Georgics*, not from the Bible), in which he explained that, employing a "genius" granted from above, he had a vocation to tell stories that were "veils of truths physical, moral, and historical," doing so "in the stable and enduring style of a true man of letters." As Alvin B. Kernan has said in recreating the coronation scene, Petrarch assumed the role of "a poetic savior," reborn at Easter, who by "means of his 'divinely given energy' and the power of his art would restore and combine both the Christian Eden and the pagan Golden Age" (Alvin B. Kernan, *The Imaginary Library: An Essay on Literature and Society* [Princeton, N.J., 1982]). Petrarch prophesied the man of letters as secular Christ. Three hundred years later the prophecy was fulfilled in Bacon, who, though scrupulous in his token acknowledgment of the Christian mystery, announced the appearance of the modern man of letters as complete secularist. The power of the poetic mind, as suggested by Petrarch, to secularize the image of the state as a restored Rome in the midst of a lapsing Christendom was contiguous with the far more radical power of the scientific mind as suggested by Bacon. In the now destroyed Christendom, Bacon, in whom the "style of the true man of letters" and the style of the scientist were still one, created the state in the image of the New Atlantis. Meanwhile the quest to unite truth and secular letters had created a new dominion in the Western orders of existence: the homeland of the man of letters, a realm additional to the interrelated realms of church and state, a third realm, a republic (or commonwealth) of letters.

Although the movement out of England to the Atlantic seaboard often bore the character of a reaction against the motives of modernity as represented by the man of letters and the third realm, the migration had a strong affinity with the movement of man and nature into mind. No specific situation is more illustrative of that affinity than the settlement of Virginia. The Elizabethans who first came to Virginia, Perry Miller argued, had a strong religious motivation. But lacking the religious cohesiveness of the Puritans who were shortly to arrive in New England, the Virginians little resisted the possibilities of the wealth to be gained by producing and marketing the newly popular weed called tobacco. Pursuing an opportunistic attitude, they were by the end of the seventeenth century—when the New Englanders were advocating a heroic millennialism and had scarcely yet begun to temper their pervasive religiosity—wholly committed to a quest for wealth and were making a society decidedly secular in its intellectual tone. In the Virginia cerebation (to use a term employed by Richard Beale Davis), the tone had been sounded even at the beginning of the Virginia colony in the writings of Captain John Smith. Taking on a complex resonance in the works of Robert Beverley and William Byrd II, the tone became definitive in Thomas Jefferson. Jefferson embodies the transformation of the writer from an actor-relator like Smith, who acts in the old heroic style but with a marked degree of self-consciousness writes and publishes an account of his acts, into the modern man of letters, who is attuned to mind as the model of society and is wholly self-conscious about writing as a historical act. With increasing force Jefferson understood his function as a man of letters to be the making and carrying out of history. His increased understanding marks the difference between *A Summary View of the Rights of British America* and the manifesto of mind two years later, the Declaration of Independence. The Declaration subordinates specific grievances against the Crown, such as taxation without representation, to the supreme issue of the Revolution, the efficacy of mind as the source and model of history, as opposed to a transcendent reference for order decreed by God, the patriarchal and hierarchical system of monarchy. The classic case for monarchy was made by Jonathan Boucher, Anglican priest and Virginia Tory, in *A View of the Causes and Consequences of the American Revolution*. In this book (not published until 1797), a series of sermons preached between 1763 and 1775, Boucher assumes that "men were clearly formed for society" and the government of society was "the original intention of God, who never decrees the end, without also decreeing the means." Even if not expressly set forth, Boucher says, the means are clearly pronounced in the Bible.

> For, we are not to judge the Scriptures of God, as we do of some other writings; and so, where no express precepts appear, hastily to conclude that none are given. On the contrary, in commenting on the Scriptures, we are frequently called upon to find out the precept from the practice. Taking this rule, then, for our direction . . . we find, that, copying after the fair model of heaven itself, wherein there was government even among the angels, the families of the earth were subjected to rulers, at first set over them by God; *for, there is no power, but of God; the powers that be are ordained of God.* The first father was the first king; and if (according to the rule just laid down) the law may be inferred from the practice, it was thus that all government originated; and monarchy is its ancient form.

Presenting in highly charged poetic summary the British critique of the patriarchal origin of government advanced by John Locke and others, the Declaration of Independence reverses the traditionalist mode of discovering the precepts of order in practices instituted by God. But in deriving the precepts of order from the human reason as justification of the Revolution, the Declaration does not assert an all-embracing repudiation of the authority of ancient practices. For one thing, while it may imply the abrogation of the church-state relationship in the self-evident truths it proclaims, the Declaration fails to make any explicit statement to this effect. For another thing, it is very nearly silent about the existence of the ancient institution of slavery in a nation that would guarantee the reasonable right of each individual to "life, liberty, and the pursuit of happiness." The Declaration refers to slavery only in the oblique charge that the king has committed the atrocity of "exciting domestic insurrection among us." The specific historical event behind the accusation was an appeal in 1775 by the governor of Virginia, Lord Dunmore, for slaves to rise against their masters. In its original form the reference is fuller and more graphic, denouncing the king for having "waged cruel war against human nature itself" by enslaving unoffending Africans, trafficking in them, and then encouraging them to turn on their masters, "thus paying off former crimes committed against the LIBERTIES of one people, with crimes he urges them to commit against the LIVES of another." But the Continental Congress modified this accusation, probably because it suspected that Jefferson was employing a literary strategy to denounce slavery rather than the king.

The omission of the issue of the separation of church and state from the Declaration of Independence—when Jefferson considered this divorcement to be absolutely necessary for the attainment of freedom—and the near omission of the slavery issue—a far more perplexing but central issue for Jefferson—reminds us how inadequately the Declaration describes the relationship of mind to the historical society in which its author lived and wrote. This relationship is described more adequately in the *Notes on the State of Virginia*. Written in 1781–1782, this work consists of responses to a series of questions proposed by François de Marbois, secretary of the French legation in Philadelphia during the revolutionary years, to several prominent members of the Continental Congress. Asked on behalf of the French government, which had become considerably involved in the Revolution and was more and more concerned about its outcome, Marbois' questions were designed to obtain concrete information about the various American states. One set of questions went to Joseph Jones, a member of the Virginia delegation, who transmitted them to Jefferson, believing him to be a more capable respondent. Then governor of Virginia, Jefferson took on the task of answering the French queries with enthusiasm. As he embarked on it, however, the fortunes of war turned heavily against the revolutionists. Benedict Arnold invaded Virginia, forcing the evacuation of the capital city of Richmond. Other disastrous events followed, and Jefferson, threatened with an official investigation of his conduct in office, retired from the governorship. In that dark time, made darker by the illness of his wife and the death of an infant daughter, Jefferson, living in a state of refuge at his country retreat, Poplar Forest, filled his days with hard work on what would become *Notes on Virginia*. He finished his work in late 1781 and sent the results to Marbois. But hardly satisfied with what he had been able to accomplish, Jefferson revised and expanded the manuscript during the next two years. Thereafter he brought out in France a small private edition of his work to which he affixed the simple title it has borne ever since. Later, having become involved in an unsatisfactory French translation, Jefferson made arrangements with the London printer John Stockdale for the publication in 1787 of what he regarded as a definitive text.

More than any other work of the revolutionary age, Jefferson's *Notes on Virginia* represents the inner drama of his role as revolutionary statesman and man of letters—as an American representative of the intellect of the Enlightenment struggling to assimilate history to his desire for and his will to order, and coming up against the deep uncertainties and vexations accompanying the contradictory motives of the self's desiring and willing. Bracketed by an initial chapter answering a query about the exact limits and boundaries of Virginia (which in the book is both Jefferson's native place and, symbolically, the new nation) and a final chapter responding to a query about histories and documents pertaining to Virginia's "affairs present or antient," *Notes on Virginia* gives the superficial impression of being factual and analytical. But the book is in spirit more poem than scientific treatise.

In its effort to conform nature, man, and society to mind, *Notes* develops the image of Jefferson implied in the Declaration of Independence, the man of letters as carrier of history. Through implication the book reveals the complexity this role assumes when the man of letters, conceiving himself to bear the dynamic principle of freedom, confronts the disposition not only of society but of rationality itself to justify the practice of various forms of slavery, among those being slavery to the expedient needs of the state, slavery to religion, and slavery to the institution of slavery itself. At times—notably in the chapter on the constitution of Virginia and in the chapters dealing with laws, religion, and manners—Jefferson's *Notes* constitutes a disturbing gloss on the Declaration of Independence.

The discussion of the Virginia constitution in the *Notes*, for instance, concludes with a meditation on the appalling proposal before the Virginia assembly in 1776 to imitate the practice of the Roman republic when faced with an emergency by setting up a dictatorship. This idea, Jefferson declares, could only have been utterly repugnant to one "who did not mean to expend his blood and substance for the wretched purpose of changing this master for that." Jefferson gives more attention in *Notes* to another fear of enslavement. Strongly related to his dismay over the prospect that the Revolution might end in the replacement of one tyrant with another was the fear (expressed in Query XVII) that in spite of their willingness to lavish "their lives and fortunes for the establishment of their civil freedom," the revolutionists may be willing to remain in "religious slavery." Although the constitutional convention of 1776 in Virginia had passed a declaration of rights affirming that it is "a truth, and a natural right, that the exercise of religion should be free," the government had not fully implemented freedom of religion in statutory law. This must be done, Jefferson says. Even though the "spirit of the times" is such that the people of the country will not approve "an execution for heresy, or a three years imprisonment for not comprehending the mysteries of the Trinity," the times will change.

> Our rulers will become corrupt, our people careless. A single zealot may commence persecutor, and better men be his victims. It can never be too often repeated, that the time for fixing every essential right on a legal basis is while our rulers are honest, and ourselves united. From the conclusion of this

war we shall be going down hill. It will not then be necessary to resort every moment to the people for support. They will be forgotten, and their rights disregarded. They will forget themselves, but in the sole faculty of making money, and will never think of uniting to effect a due respect for their rights. The shackles, therefore, which shall not be knocked off at the conclusion of this war, will remain on us long, will be made heavier and heavier, till our rights shall revive or expire in a convulsion.

In 1786, about four years after the conclusion of the war and two after the final revisions on *Notes on Virginia*, Jefferson's lengthy effort to strike the shackles of religious authority in Virginia was successful. The Virginia assembly (influenced heavily by James Madison) passed the "Bill for Establishing Religious Freedom" Jefferson had drawn up in 1777. The action was momentous. Not only did it allow freedom of opinion about religion, marking the formal disestablishment of the joint authority of church and state; it recognized, as never before in history, the authority of the man of letters and the literary polity. Through Jefferson, Madison, and other statesmen who were men of letters, the realm of secular letters had not only asserted its coexistence with the church but had, it would seem, completed the task it had begun with the Declaration of Independence: the creation of a modern secular state in the image of the rational, lettered, free mind.

But any assurance Jefferson may have felt about the new nation as a symbol of the free mind was undercut by a fear less definable and, under the historical circumstances, less possible of alleviation than his fears about revolutionary America becoming enslaved to a dictator or a postrevolutionary America becoming enslaved to religious bigotry. Jefferson's fear was that he himself and other makers of the Revolution were enslaved to the historically existent slavery system in their world. The chapter on laws in *Notes on Virginia* (Query XIV) takes up the problem not of British subjects as slaves of the king but its logical sequel: the relationship between Americans and their chattels—the relationship between masters who have freed themselves from their master the king and should fulfill their commitment to freedom by emancipating their own slaves. Jefferson's approach to the problem is premised on the conviction that, while the slaves must be freed, the freedmen, for reasons that are political, physical, and moral, cannot be incorporated into the society in which they have lived as slaves. The political reason is that whites and Negroes could not live in a state of freedom and equality without engaging in a disastrous war of extermination—an inevitable outcome decreed by differences "fixed in nature" : a difference in color, which gives a "superior Beauty" to the white race; and, still more significantly, a difference in mental capacity, which renders Negroes inferior in the faculties of reason and imagination, if not in the faculty of memory. Unlike the slaves of ancient Rome, who were the same color as the masters and frequently were well educated, slaves in America cannot be assimilated "without staining the blood" of the masters. Whereas in Rome "emancipation required but one effort," a second, "unknown to history," is necessary in America. "When freed, he [the slave] is to be removed beyond the reach of mixture." Considering the enormous difficulties that would have faced any wholesale colonization project, the necessity of emancipation was effectively countered by the means necessary to achieve it. The educated mind of the slave master could not really cope with the problem of how to free his illiterate slaves, yet he must find a way. How desperate the dilemma could become emerges in *Notes on Virginia* when Jefferson, turning his attention in the eighteenth query to the seemingly unportentous matter of customs and manners in the state, suddenly and unexpectedly heightens its character. Under the influence of slavery, the master, he says, becomes morally inferior to his slaves. In what is undoubtedly the best-known passage in *Notes* Jefferson portrays the "whole commerce between master and slave" as "a perpetual exercise of the most boisterous passions, the most unremitting despotism" on the part of the master and "degrading submissions" on the part of the slave. The consequences of the slavery system, while so bad for the slave that he may well want to refrain from perpetuating his condition by fathering children, is far worse for the master, whose moral character is utterly corrupted by the despotic passions and the habitual indolence consequent upon having others labor for him. The only solution to a situation so depraved as that existing in the society of Virginia is a visitation of God's justice, an extermination of the masters by the slaves. Either this dire event or "total emancipation" must occur.

In the light of the known facts about the lives of the Virginia slave masters, including most obviously the life of Jefferson himself, the account of their character in Query XVIII of *Notes on Virginia* is not credible. But it is not false. It is a deliberate fiction. "Considering history as a moral exercise, her lessons would be too infrequent if confined to real life," Jefferson said in justification of his fondness for Laurence Sterne. Although presumably without direct awareness of what he was doing, he followed that dictum in the eighteenth query. Anxiously probing the meaning of slavery as an institution of his society, he invented a dramatic situation symbolizing a complex tension between the precept that slavery is morally wrong and the pragmatic historical experience of the world the slaveholders had made. It was because of their experience that they could inaugurate a desperate war to secure their freedom from bondage to a monarch but, in declaring their cause to a "candid world," make no mention of emancipating those they held in perpetual bondage. Their experience had taught them that in the practical realization of the ideal of freedom slavery could be an indispensable support. In *American Slavery / American Freedom: The Ordeal of Colonial Virginia* (1975), Edmund S. Morgan has convincingly suggested the thesis that Virginia planters, large and small, abandoned indentured labor and established slavery as their labor system because it enabled them to solve the threat presented by a class of poor landless whites that would grow ever larger as servants were released from their bonds and, as Bacon's Rebellion (1676) had already indicated, could overwhelm them. "In the republican way of thinking as Americans inherited it from England [Morgan says], slavery occupied a critical, if ambiguous, position; it was the primary evil that men sought to avoid for society as a whole by curbing monarchs and establishing republics. But it was also the solution to one of society's most serious problems, the problem of the poor. Virginians could outdo English republicans as well as New England ones, partly because they had achieved a society in which most of the poor were enslaved." It was logical for the Virginia assembly in 1780 to enhance the commitment to republican liberty by rewarding soldiers engaged in the struggle for freedom with three hundred acres of land and a slave.

At almost the same time this action was taken, Jefferson, in a revelatory moment of great psychic and poetic intensity (which as far as one can tell from his writings would not be repeated), made vividly articulate a monstrous moral irony: the slaveholders, who had staked their lives, their fortunes, and their sacred honor on the overthrow of what they conceived as their political enslavement, were themselves enslaved by a subtle power greater than that of the British Empire. They were enslaved by their own slaves. It is rather amazing how cogently in a symbolic fiction, the eighteenth query of *Notes on Virginia*, Jefferson anticipates the analysis of mastery and bondage in Hegel's *Phenomenology of Mind*, published over twenty-five years later (1807). In *The Problem of Slavery in the Age of Revolution, 1770–1823* (Ithaca, N.Y., 1975), David Brion Davis observes that Hegel's argument that the "slavish consciousness" is an "object which embodies the 'truth' of the 'master's certainty of himself'" is integral with an intricate Hegelian dialectic of

> dependence and independence, of losing and finding one's identity in another consciousness. . . . Even to outsiders, his [the master's] identity consists of being a master who consumes the produce of his slave's work. Accordingly, the master is incapable of transcending his own position, for which he risked his life and for which he could lose his life, should the slave decide on a

second match of strength. The master is trapped by his own power, which he can only seek to maintain. He cannot achieve the true autonomy that can come only from the recognition by another consciousness that he regards as worthy of such recognition. The condition of omnipotent lordship, then, becomes the reverse of what it wants to be: dependent, static, and unessential.

Although American masters had not acquired their chattels by means of direct capture—had inherited them or bought them on the domestic or world slave markets—in owning them they put their lives at risk of a rebellion, the most feared event in the Southern states. In his pre-Hegelian depiction of the master-slave relationship, Jefferson sees a slave rebellion as virtually foreordained. He expresses the hope that the slaves (whom he strikingly accords the status of citizens), their spirit rising, and the masters, their meanness of spirit abating, somehow will come into a mutuality of freedom, leading to an act of total emancipation by the masters. But this possibility appears to be slight. Any hope of its becoming actuality seems to be connected with the ostensible subject of the eighteenth query, bad manners. Better manners on the part of the masters would allow for the rising spirit of the slaves and make possible their eventual freedom. Yet Jefferson is hardly urging an improvement of manners. Underlying his vision of the slave society of Virginia is the sensitivity to the subjective mode of modern society that Hegel shows when he interprets the ancient relationship of masters and slaves as basically subsisting in the radical dependency of the master—who must count on his recognition by his slave for his very existence—and the potentially radical freedom of the slave, who recognizes his own identity when he wills not to recognize his master's. In such an emphasis on the will of the self the symbolism of slavery and freedom is reversed. In its ultimate meaning Query XVIII of *Notes on Virginia* may be a quite ominous interpretation of the Declaration of Independence. Jefferson may suggest that the fundamental impulse of the American Revolution, far from being the assertion of the freedom of the mind, is the assertion of the identity of the modern self. Jefferson may suggest that the self, seeking its identity, uses the rational mind as an instrument to end its captivity to, its suppression in, the old hierarchical order, but rejects all rational constructs, obeying only the need to exist in its own image; that the self, expressing its will to self-dominion through the illiterate slave as well as through the man of letters, is capable of any act of violence required by its will to identity—of committing in the name of the will to freedom any act necessary to fulfill the will to identity.

Developing the symbolic fiction of the slave master sunk in his rage and indolence, Jefferson rendered highly dubious the image of the slave master as man of letters. That must be the reason why in the nineteenth query of *Notes on Virginia* ("The present state of manufactures, commerce, interior and exterior trade?") he turned his poetic power to the creation of a counterfiction, that of the yeoman on his self-subsistent farm as the model figure of American society. In his portrayal of the farmer, Jefferson gives him no slave for his service in the Revolution. He envisions him as having an exemplary freedom from the mob of the poor, but this comes from the unprecedented opportunity in America for the individual to find, through personally possessing and laboring in a small tract of the earth, a self-identity that is synonymous with freedom. Jefferson's pastoral invention of the yeoman farmer as the embodiment of the ideology of freedom was more relevant to the literary imagination in the nonslaveholding parts of the new nation than it was to the man of letters in the South. Southern men of letters in the age after Jefferson were doomed to condemn the poet-prophet for his reckless statements about slavery; and equating freedom of mind as the great principle of social order with the ancient practice of slavery, they were to see the practice as principle. They were to try to invent a slave society that would be a symbol of mind.

LEWIS LEARY

1776–1815

"With us the dawn of literary achievement is, I fear, very far removed," wrote St. George Tucker of Williamsburg in 1796.
"Mr. Jefferson is the only man in this country who has yet entered the
public lists, and had Mr. Jefferson been unable to print his own work at
his own expense, it would probably have mouldered in the dust of his
closet."

Tucker was thinking of Jefferson's *Notes on the State of Virginia*, privately published in London twelve years before, a volume sometimes
remembered as the new nation's first masterwork, admired for its stand
against slavery, its championship of the Indian, and its carefully documented proofs that plants, animals, and even people flourished quite as
well in the New World as anywhere else. He took no account of Jefferson's public writing on policy, nor of the writings of George Mason,
author of Virginia's Bill of Rights, Richard Henry Lee (1732–1794)
who opposed slavery of every kind, Patrick Henry (1736–1799) whose
fiery speech before the Virginia legislature in March, 1775, had inspired
thousands to prefer death to loss of liberty, or James Madison
(1751–1836) whose contributions to *The Federalist* had done much to
insure stability to the new national constitution. These men performed
patriotic duties. They supplied a literature of power that insures them a
place in the history of American thought. In times that tried men's souls
what else was appropriate? Madison, who as a collegian at Princeton
before the war had joined his classmates Hugh Henry Brackenridge and
Philip Freneau in writing light satirical verse, two years after graduation
decided that "poetry, wit, criticism, romances, plays, &c. . . . deserve
but a small portion of a mortal's mind, and something more substantial,
more durable, and more profitable, befits a riper age."

Almost alone among his Virginia contemporaries, Bermuda-born St.
George Tucker (1750–1827) quietly followed a belletristic way, writing
hundreds of verses, most of which he tucked away among his papers,
many of which he circulated in handwritten copies among his friends.

Only occasionally did he publish, and then mainly patriotic things, like *Liberty, A Poem on the Independence of America*, which appeared in 1788, some five years after it had been written. During the spring and summer of 1793 he contributed a series of anti-Federalist satires, "Probationary Odes of Jonathan Pindar," to Philip Freneau's *National Gazette* in Philadelphia, gathering them into a volume three years later. He published a saucy letter to Jedidiah Morse who in his *American Geography* had said some slighting things about the manners of the people of Williamsburg, and he wrote with some heat on the shortcomings of Jay's Treaty. After consultation with friends in Virginia, Pennsylvania, and New England, he presented in 1796 *A Dissertation on Slavery* in which he advocated gradual abolition. He occasionally published admonitory letters to public officials, and in 1805 presented a five-volume American adaptation of Blackstone's *Commentaries*. But most characteristic of his temperament were his lyrics, informal essays, and plays, including a spirited political farce, *Up & Ride, or the Borough of Brooklyn*; a dramatized satire on western land speculation, *The Wheel of Fortune*; and a musical comedy, *The Times, or the Patriots Roused*. Most of these remain unpublished among his papers at Williamsburg.

Tucker wrote to please himself, his family, and his friends—including his brother-in-law Theodoric Bland and his neighbor William McClurg, both closet poets also. Bland was the author of a long celebration of the Battle of Lexington, all but sixteen stanzas of it lost, which includes such stirring, memorable lines as, "Shall Brunswick's line, exalted high / . . . See hapless freedom prostrate lie?" The fame of McClurg rests almost entirely on "The Belles of Williamsburg," a jaunty *jeu d'esprit* that Tucker did much to extend and preserve. Although some of his verse has recently been collected, Southern literary scholarship has not yet caught up with St. George Tucker.

His neighbors in Mecklenburg County, the Munfords, father and son, have finally fared better. Robert Munford (*ca.* 1737–1783) published nothing during his lifetime, but in 1798, fourteen years after his death, his son William put together in Petersburg *A Collection of Poems and Plays by the Late Colonel Robert Munford*, which contained a deft translation of the first book of Ovid's *Metamorphoses*, a long humorous poem entitled "The Ram," done in the manner of Butler's *Hudibras*, several shorter poems, imitative but of unusual merit, and two plays. *The Candidates; or the Humors of a Virginia Election*, written in 1770, is a rowdy farce about the political ambitions of such people as Mr. Wou'dbe, Mr. Strutabout, Mr. Smallhopes, and a worthy man named Mr. Worthy. It was not publicly performed until 1945, but its composition in 1770 gives it precedence by seventeen years over Royall Tyler's

The Contrast, which has long been called the first American comedy, and which also had as its hero a worthy man named Worthy.

A better play, written by Munford in 1776, is *The Patriots, a Comedy in Five Acts*, first publicly performed on its bicentennial in 1976. It contrasts the moderation of patriotic gentlefolk like Mr. Meanwell and Mr. Trueman to the raucous, false patriotic stir caused by troublemakers like Colonel Strut, Mr. Thunderbolt, and Mr. Tackabout. The action is conventional, including an apparently ill-starred love affair between Mr. Trueman and the fair young Mira, whose father is a Tory. Many of the best things in *The Patriots* are its songs, some written in parody of contemporary patriotic verse but better done than most of the verse they parody, others written with firm comic rhythmic control, like the lines:

> We'll drink our own liquor—our brandy from peaches;
> A fig for the British—they may all buss our breaches,
> Those blood sucking, beer-drinking puppies retreat
> But our peach brandy fellows can never be beat.

The younger Munford (1775–1825) was not so easy a poet. In 1798, he presented his own *Poems and Compositions in Prose on Several Occasions*, which was coolly received. He later wrote much newspaper verse, including cutting anti-Federalist satires. Prominent in law and politics, he spent his leisure hours in a translation of the *Iliad* that was not published until 1845, twenty-one years after its author's death. Equally unsuccessful was St. George Tucker's brother Nathaniel (1784–1851), a Virginian only by virtue of his poem *The Bermudian* having been published in Williamsburg in 1773. Trapped during the Revolution in Edinburgh where he had gone to study medicine and in England where he established a small practice, in 1784 he sent his brother the manuscript of a long patriotic masque called *Columbinus*, suggesting to St. George that it be presented to the Congress as a national play, to be ceremoniously performed on every Fourth of July. It was not, nor was it published until 1976.

But in literature, as in much besides, Virginia led the way. War-torn Georgia produced little. John Joachim Zubly (1724–1781), who had represented that colony in the Continental Congress, in 1775 had published a forthright pamphlet, *The Law of Liberty*, in which he insisted that "Americans are no idiots" and "appear determined not to be slaves," but that the "idea of separation between America and Great Britain is so big with so many and such horrid evils, that every friend to both must shudder at the thought," was soon banished as a Tory, returning only when the British occupied Savannah in 1779, and then died two years later, better remembered for streets named in his honor than for literary accomplishments. Georgia recovered slowly from its war wounds. It invited reform. Young men from Yale, like Abiel Holmes and Jedidiah Morse, settled briefly there to inculcate New England ways. Joel Barlow's Connecticut brother-in-law, Abraham Baldwin, moved there permanently in 1784, became active in politics and was a principal force in the establishment of a system of higher education throughout the state, bringing his college mate Josiah Meigs to Georgia as president of its new Franklin College. But there was little of literary culture. Henri Placide or some other theatrical entrepreneur occasionally passed through with a troupe on its way north from the West Indies to more profitable stands in Philadelphia or New York, but seldom seem to have lingered long. Even the newspapers of Georgia were short-lived, most of them managed by imported or itinerant journeymen. But Georgia finally produced a playwright when in August, 1809, the *Georgia Gazette* advertised for sale *The Mysterious Father, a Tragedy in Five Acts* by William Bullock Maxwell, a young man who three years later went insane, and a year after that died of tuberculosis at the age of twenty-seven.

South Carolina did better. Charleston was known not only as the commercial capital of the South, but as a city that prided itself on its cultural activities, its theater and concerts and open-air gardens, balls and dancing assemblies, racetracks and cockpits. Hector St. John Crèvecoeur, who visited there just before the Revolution, found its inhabitants "the gayest in America." But war had wounded Charleston. As the British left, returning exiled leaders like the Pinckneys, the Laurenses, and the Rutledges were busied with affairs that left little time for literature. But the St. Cecilia Society provided quiet evenings of music, and Harmony Hall was available for theatrical and other public entertainment. Charleston remained a hospitable place, known for the charm of its ladies and the urbane ease of its gentlemen. "Plays, concerts, and assemblies amuse the town," said one visitor from England, and "visiting, entertainments, and parties of amusement are the pleasures of the country." There was reading in plenty as the Charleston Library Society reopened its doors, but literature was in short supply. Much of it came to Charleston by accretion, supplied by new residents from the North or by visitors from overseas.

Among them was Aedanus Burke, Irish-born, but trained in law in Virginia, who came to South Carolina in the mid-1770s and served during the Revolution in its militia. His *Considerations on the Order of the Cincinnati* in 1783 created large interest, not only throughout the United States but in Europe, where it was translated into French by Mirabeau, and from that translation rendered into German for further dissemination. An ardent democrat and through most of his life a successful though testy jurist, Burke was known both for his Irish wit and for his irascible Irish temper. A more judicious person was Dr. David Ramsay (1749–1815), a Pennsylvanian educated at Princeton, who came to Charleston in 1773 and there married, as his third wife, a daughter of Henry Laurens. Called on to deliver the oration "On the Advantages of Independence" on July 5, 1778, he anticipated some aspects of American romanticism by suggesting that his countrymen "pierce the veil cast over mankind by artificial refinements" by revealing and recording "all the avenues to the heart, through study and understanding of human nature as it really is." Literature and the arts, true religion, empire, and riches, he said, "are now fixing their long and favorite abode in this new western world." Ramsay's own contributions to the literary resurgence of the New World were extensive but modest: *A History of the Revolution in South Carolina* in 1785, the longer *History of the American Revolution* in 1789, *Life of George Washington* in 1807, and *History of South Carolina* in 1809, none of them particularly original in content or comment, but all committed to the proposition that the "study of eloquence and Belles Lettres" in America was becoming more serious than it had ever been before.

Polemicists thrived in South Carolina, but of poets there were few, and these imported. Philip Freneau of New Jersey, scudding up and down the Atlantic coast as the captain of trading vessels, dropped off verses for publication in Charleston newspapers whenever his ship touched in at that port. His best-known lyric, "The Wild Honey Suckle," derived from his observations in the outlying lowlands of Charleston, and his "Log Town Cabin," portraying the unpleasantness of Southern frontier living, both appeared first in Charleston periodicals. And his brother Peter Freneau, who settled in Charleston soon after the war as a printer and politician, provided deft translations from French classics to the *City Gazette*, which he edited with distinction for many years. Even more prolific was young Dr. Joseph Brown Ladd of Rhode Island, a cousin to the young lady who would become Ralph Waldo Emerson's mother. Ladd came to Charleston in the late fall of 1784 and almost immediately began to flood its newspapers with poems over the signature of Aroeut. He wrote patiotic songs, sentimental lyrics, and pondering philosophic inquiries. A chameleon rhymer, he wrote under the influence of Goethe, Ossian, Collins, Milton, and the Old Testament prophets. He casually dropped such prestigious names as Fenelon, Voltaire, Locke, Newton, Bacon, and Plato. He postured as translating with equal ease from Hebrew, Greek, Latin, German, and French. No such public display of learning had appeared in Charleston before. When a volume of *The Poems of Aroeut* appeared early in 1786, it was a social if not a financial success. Among its more than two hundred subscribers were Moultries, Pinckneys, Draytons, and Rutledges. But not nine months later the twenty-two-year-old poet was dead, killed in a duel with another newcomer from Rhode Island.

Equally prominent in Charleston periodicals a few years later was John Davis, a visitor from England who in 1798 and 1799 kept up a running poetical exchange with Lucas George, an Irish instructor at the College of Charleston where Davis also briefly taught. Their verse was light and inconsequential, hardly worth preserving, though Davis collected portions of his into a slim volume entitled *Poems Written at Coosahatchie* in 1800. But each of these young men soon left South Carolina, George to become finally a schoolmaster on Long Island, and Davis for continued literary adventures in Virginia and further north, as recorded in his *Travels of Four Years and a Half in the United States of America* in 1800, a well-packed storehouse of information and opinion. Davis may be best remembered for being the first to record in fiction the story of Pocahontas, first as an anecdote in his novel *The Farmer of New Jersey* in 1800, then as a novelette, *Captain Smith and Pocahontas*, in 1805, and finally as a full-length novel, *The First Settlers of Virginia*, also in 1805. In *Walter Kennedy, an American Tale* in 1808, he was among the first to attempt the dialect of the Southern black.

Davis was anticipated in Virginia as a writer of fiction by Samuel Reif, presumably of Richmond, who in 1797 had published in Philadelphia a sentimental epistolary romance called *Infidelity, or the Victims of Sentiment*. What happened, happened in Pennsylvania, but it might have happened anywhere among high-strung people of sentiment who like to expose their wounds and talk about them. And in verse he was succeeded by William Maxwell of Norfolk, who went to Yale where he became a literary protégé of its president, Timothy Dwight, to whom in 1812 he dedicated his collected work *Poems*, asking with some chagrin, "Why should he write in these prosaic times, / When few, if any, care a fig for rhymes?" But South Carolina produced little during this period, except occasional verse in the *Charleston Courier* contributed by William Crafts (1787–1826), the Harvard-educated son of a former Boston merchant who published *The Raciad and Other Occasional Poems* in 1810, and ten years later the long poem *Sullivan's Island* that made many readers think of Alexander Pope's *Windsor Forest*. Not until 1813 when Washington Allston (1779–1843), also Harvard-educated and who studied painting in England where he struck up a friendship with Coleridge and the Wordsworths, published in London his *Sylphs of the Seasons* did South Carolina produce a literary artist who, as his friends said, "put to rest the calumny that America has never produced a poet." Although Allston's quick rhymes may now seem to cloy, he did consider literature, like painting, an art worth strenuous endeavor.

North Carolina, though its libraries were active and its newspapers filled with borrowed verse, provided few claimants to literary fame. Perhaps chief among them was Irish-born Thomas Burke (*ca.* 1747–1783), its representative in 1776 to the Continental Congress, and its governor from 1781 till his death two years later at the age of thirty-six. For Burke, poetry was play; its end was, he said, to please, or sometimes to tease, without rancor or high seriousness. He praised "Bacchus, God of wine and mirth," and he praised Venus also, and sometimes Mars in patriotic wartime verse and light political satire. Some of his verses appeared in the *Virginia Gazette* and the *State Gazette of North Carolina*; one poetical exchange with a lively Pennsylvania girl found a place in the prestigious *Gentleman's Magazine* in London, but most of what he wrote remained in manuscript until published in 1961.

Also briefly a North Carolinian, William Hill Brown of Boston, then not yet widely known as the author of *The Power of Sympathy* (1789), now remembered as America's first novel, had written plays and had contributed generously to New England periodicals, notably in a series of versified fables. In North Carolina he added to those fables with "The Lion and the Terrapin" and with other verse and prose in the *North Carolina Journal* at Halifax, including a long and spirited endorsement of the proposed new University of North Carolina. Hardly more than a year after his arrival, he caught a fever from which he died in September, 1793.*

Perhaps North Carolina's chief claim to literary remembrance is that in 1814 Dr. Charles Caldwell went north to Philadelphia for two years to edit its distinguished literary periodical, the *Port-Folio*. He was succeeded in that post by John Hall from Maryland, a state which during this period had more writers born than flourishing within its boundaries. It had Charles Carroll (1737–1832) of Carrollton, who was active in printed discussion of how the new nation should be managed. But some of its more prominent early controversialists had turned Tory, like Daniel Dulany (1722–1797) who spoke his mind forcefully and then in exile remained silent, and Jonathan Boucher (1738–1804) who

---

* Two novels, apparently by the wife of the state printer, Joseph Gales, who had come to North Carolina from Philadelphia, are advertised in the Raleigh *Register* on April 29, 1805, as just published and for sale at one dollar each. They are listed as *Lady Emma Melcombe and Her Family* (1784?) and *Matilda Berkely, or Family Anecdotes* (1804?). No copies of either have been discovered.

in England in 1797 published the proloyalist *View of the Causes and Consequence of the American Revolution*, but whose spirited *Reminiscences of an American Loyalist* remained unpublished until 1925. The poems of Francis Scott Key (1779–1843), a native of Pipe-Creek in western Maryland, were not collected until after his death, but late in life, in 1834, he published *The Power of Literature and Its Connection with Religion*, a prose work that might have been forgotten had it not been written by the person who twenty years before had watched bombs bursting in air across the Chesapeake and produced a national anthem written to the rhythm of the popular British drinking song, "To Anacreon in Heaven." Certainly the words of no song, written in the North or in the South, have been repeated more often, with more various accent, than those of his "The Star-Spangled Banner."

Like South Carolina, Virginia also depended, though to a lesser degree, on imported writers. Perhaps chief among them was the Irish firebrand John Daly Burk (*ca.* 1775–1808), who fled there in 1799, a fugitive from charges of sedition resulting from his brief editorship, as successor to Philip Freneau, of the outspoken *Time-Piece* in New York. He settled first as a schoolmaster in Arundel County, but by 1801 had made his way to Petersburg where he became prominent in political and literary circles. He was already an author of some renown, whose play, *Bunker Hill, or the Death of General Warren*, published two years before, had become a set piece, appropriate for patriotic occasions, whose *Female Patriotism, or the Death of Joan D'Arc* had played successfully in New York in 1798, and whose *History of the Late War in Ireland* a year later had provided a rallying cry for friends of liberty everywhere. In Petersburg his historical drama *Oberon, or the Siege of Mexico* was performed in 1802, and five years later his *Bethlem Gabor, Lord of Transylvania* was presented there by the Thespian Society of which Burk had become an active member. Meanwhile he had been preparing *History of Virginia*, the first three volumes of which appeared from 1801 to 1804, the fourth completed by other hands after his death. With a fellow Irish poet, John McGreery, he planned to publish a collection of Irish airs supplied with original American lyrics. Although the collection did not appear until 1824, and then severely truncated, Burk's introduction to it was printed in the *Richmond Enquirer* on May 27, 1808. But by that time the jaunty Irish litterateur was dead, the victim in his early thirties of a duel fought six weeks before on Fleets Hill, just outside of Petersburg.

But Virginia also had writers of her own, or nearly her own, whose influence extended beyond her borders. Perhaps of most lasting fame is Mason Locke Weems (1759–1825), the nineteenth child of David

Weems of Arundel County, Maryland. In his early teens the boy was sent abroad to study medicine in London and Edinburgh, and served briefly on a British ship of war before returning in 1776 to America, where records of his activities are wanting until 1782 when he was off to Europe again, this time for ordination as an Anglican priest. From 1784 to 1789, he was rector of All Hallows in his native county. By 1794 he was an itinerant bookseller for Mathew Carey of Philadelphia, and the next year married Frances Ewell of Dumfries, Virginia. In Dumfries he is said to have occasionally conducted services in the church attended by George Washington. But most of his life, up to that time and after, is legend. What is known is that he traveled assiduously through the Southern states, preaching, fiddling, and exhorting, peddling such books as, he said, would "dulcify and exalt human nature."

Many of the books were of his own making, with such catchy titles as *Hymen's Recruiting Sergeant, God's Revenge against Murder, God's Revenge against Gambling, God's Revenge against Adultery, The Effects of Drunkenness,* and *The Bad Wife's Looking Glass.* But none did as well as his *Life of Washington,* which seems first to have appeared as a pamphlet called "The Beauties of Washington," probably issued before the death in December, 1799, of the president. By the beginning of the next year, Weems had revised and lengthened it, for, as he wrote, "Millions are gasping to read something about him," and "I am very nearly prim'd and cock'd for 'em." And indeed he was. For some time he had tried to peddle volumes of John Marshall's cumbersome five-volume biography that appeared from 1804 to 1809, but it was too long and too expensive for most of Weems's country clients; so in 1805 he expanded his own brief history of Washington's life, adding to it the now famous fable of the cherry tree and young Washington's inability to tell a lie. That was what his customers wanted, and it sold well—more than forty editions before Weems's death in 1825, and an uncounted number of editions since. "Parson" Weems believed that American heroes should be hallowed and "the beauties and beatitudes of the Republic" kept clear before the people's eyes. He wrote the popular *Life of Marion* in 1810, *Life of Franklin* in 1815, and *Life of Penn* in 1822, but none of them have had the duration or influence of his *Life of Washington* which, like John Smith's story of Pocahontas, created an American legend, read and revered far beyond the borders of the South.

Also traveling through the backcountry regions was Paul Henkel, a Lutheran missionary who roamed the Shenandoah Valley preaching principles of sound Christian morality, who in his *Kurzer Zeitvertrieb* warned maidens that

> There's much in life to harm you.
> In marriage have a spacial care
> Lest worthless rascals charm you

and who in a "Mirror for Brandy-Lovers" pled to all people, "I pray you therefore stop and think, / Before you taste another drink." But back-country was backcountry, and the sometimes bibulous sentimental rhymes of Giles Julap of Chotank, Virginia, in *The Glosser; a Poem in Two Books* in 1802 can perhaps be excused because their author was reputed to be a gentleman of more than ordinary convivial habits. But interest was growing in newly settled frontier lands. The *Travels through North and South Carolina, Georgia, East and West Florida* by the Philadelphian William Bartram (1739–1823) in 1791 introduced readers to the dangers and beauties of largely untraveled territories far more successfully than did the pedestrian *A Topographical Description of the Western Territory of North America* presented in London a year later, by Gilbert Imlay (*ca.* 1754–1828), an adventurer from New Jersey. John Filson (*ca.* 1747–1788), also from New Jersey, in *The Discovery, Settlement, and Present State of Kentucke* in 1784 introduced "The Adventures of Col. Daniel Boon" to a public eager for homespun derring-do, and Daniel Bryan, of Rockingham County in Virginia, a distant relative of Boone, prettied these adventures into lackluster blank verse in his *The Mountain Muse* in 1813, a praiseworthy but unsuccessful attempt at a frontier epic.

More down to earth were the raucous rhymes of Thomas Johnson (*fl.* 1789–1799), who in *The Kentucky Miscellany* in 1794 wrote doggerel reminders of roughhouse tavern brawls, admitting that, for himself, when "My spirits . . . begin to shrink, / I rise to take another drink," but who proved himself a solid good citizen by offering four years later *Every Man His Own Doctor; or, The Poor Man's Family Physician*, which described the "plain safe, and easy means to cure themselves from most disorders incident to this climate, . . . the medicine being the growth of the country and about almost every man's plantation." Beside these leather-stocking fine remedies, the *Festoons of Fancy* with which the young Kentucky attorney William Littell (1768–1824) in 1814 celebrated "flow'ry vales, and verdant trees" and the false coquetry of frontier maidens, and who wrote in prose of "love and delicacy," seem vapid indeed. Richmond could have done as well, or Charleston. In fact, Richmond did, in the effusive *Notes of an American Lyre* published by Judith Lomax in 1813, and the "moral miniature painting" in verse of Richard Dabney's (1787–1825) *Poems, Original and Translated*, two years later. By 1815, Davy Crockett, many adventures behind him, had not yet become a frontier justice of the peace.

Perhaps presently best remembered among Virginia writers is William Wirt (1772–1834). Like Weems, he was the youngest child of a first-generation emigrant Maryland family, who at the age of twenty came to Virginia, where his wit, convivial humor, and practical common sense allowed him to rise to some affluence and much prestige as an attorney in Norfolk and Richmond, a clerk of the House of Delegates, chancellor of the district court in Williamsburg, in 1817 attorney general of the United States, and in 1832 an unsuccessful candidate for the presidency. Early in his career, he had asked St. George Tucker whether being known as a man of letters would injure his reputation as a lawyer, and received from the older man the answer that, yes, it very well might. As a result of that advice, or perhaps because of his own innate, canny German-Swiss intelligence, almost everything that William Wirt wrote was anonymous or pseudonymous. Only his *Sketches of the Life and Character of Patrick Henry*, over which he had worked for twelve years before it was published in 1817, appeared with his name on its title page. He planned to follow it with other lives of patriot heroes, through which, he said, he hoped to "earn money and fame." But by this time, Wirt's literary career was over. Politics seemed to be, and perhaps was, the more effective means to those ends.

Wirt was a sensible man who, like Tucker, had married well and made the most of that and other connections. Although in correspondence he could be jaunty, a man among men, swinging without restraint in caricature or humorous riposte, almost everything that he published was tightened to observations that could amuse or instruct without raising hackles in response. This was particularly true of the series of essays that he contributed in August and September, 1803, to the Richmond *Virginia Argus,* which later in that year were collected into a volume called *Letters of the British Spy,* and by 1832 had run through twelve popular editions. Modeled, at least in title, on Montesquieu's *Les Lettres Persanes* (1721) and Goldsmith's *Citizen of the World; or Letters from a Chinese Philosopher* (1760), which had already produced models for Philip Freneau and Peter Markoe in Philadelphia, it purported to consist of "letters written by a young Englishman of rank, during a visit to the United States in 1803, to a member of the British Parliament," the letters having been discovered hidden away "in the bedchamber of a boarding-house in a seaport town of Virginia." They tell of a residence of upwards to six months in Richmond, and of the strange people and strange notions he encountered there. He speaks of the inequality of land distribution among Virginians, Southern eloquence and the decline of Southern influence in national politics, representative idiosyncratic Virginians, fossils found on the banks of the James River, injustices of the white man to the Indian (including a brief reference to Pocahontas), and he wondered what the ghost of Captain John Smith would think of the Virginia of 1803. He commended education and eloquence and care taken in writing clearly. Little that he wrote should have disturbed any reader, though some of it did; and even less invited enthusiastic response. But the essays were popular, reprinted, excerpted from, or imitated up and down the Atlantic coast. Wirt himself was perhaps their best critic; they "bespeak," he said, "a man rather frolicksome and sprightly than thoughtful and penetrating."

During the next two years, Wirt contributed with nine other members of the loosely formed Rainbow Association a series of essays to the *Richmond Enquirer*, the first ten of which were collected in 1804 as *The Rainbow: First Series*, a volume that sold so badly that no second series appeared (Jay B. Hubbell, "William Wirt and the Familiar Essay in Virginia," *William and Mary Quarterly*, 2nd ser., XXIII [April, 1943], 142–44, identifies other members of the Rainbow Association as James Ogilvie, George Tucker, Thomas Ritchie, George Hay, Meriwether and Skelton Jones, Peyton Randolph, and John and Henry Brockenbrough. Wirt's contributions have not been positively identified, though Joseph C. Robert, "William Wirt, Virginian," *Virginia Magazine of History and Biography*, LXXX [October, 1972], 408n, attributes to him one early in the series on the emancipation of women, and another, on November 18, 1804, on the value of combining fancy with argument in oratory). After that Wirt's pen was idle for ten years, except in lively correspondence with such friends as St. George Tucker, whom he encouraged to contribute to a continuation of the *Rainbow*, and with whom he exchanged snippets of verse and jovial good cheer. In 1811 he commenced another series of essays in the *Enquirer*, which he called "The Sylph," but its contents were not satisfactory nor its title appropriate, so he put it aside for another series called "The Old Bachelor," designed "virtuously to instruct . . . innocently to amuse." He called on friends for contributions and they responded, but much of the series was his own, speaking of education, manners, gambling, and the all-usurping desire among Virginians for public office (Contributors to the series are said to have included Louis Girardin, Dabney and Frank Carr, George Tucker, Richard Parker, and David Watson, most of whose contributions can be identified because they are addressed "To the Old Bachelor." Some dozen "To the Old Bachelor" essays by St. George Tucker are found in manuscript among the Tucker-Coleman Papers at the College of William and Mary, but none has been identified as appearing whole or in part in "The Old Bachelor" series. See Joseph C. Robert, "William Wirt, Virginian," 427n). Never had Wirt's wit seemed livelier as he attempted now, he said, "to awaken the taste of the people for literary attainments." But what he meant as good-natured raillery was taken by some readers as personal attack. Wirt wrote, he said, "in the hope of doing good—but my essays dropped, dropped into the world like stones into a millpond," making small ripples that circled briefly, and then disappeared. But collected into a volume in 1814, *The Old Bachelor* did well, and should have. It contained some of the most effective writing of its kind to appear in the United States before Washington Irving's *Sketch Book* half a dozen years later.

Meanwhile, Wirt had written a play called "The Haunted Pavilion, *alias* The Path of Pleasure," encouraged by St. George Tucker who provided it with a prologue and an epilogue. It was a comedy of political intrigue and, like Robert Munford's *The Patriots,* the thwarted but finally triumphant love between the son of one faction and the daughter of another. Plans were made for its presentation at the Richmond theater, but when on December 26, 1811, that theater was destroyed by fire, it was offered to managers in New York and Philadelphia who rejected it, one giving as his reason that the action of the play was laid so near Philadelphia that "there could be nothing of dramatic illusion in scenes so familiar."

During the War of 1812, Wirt pressed Tucker to complete his own drama, "The Times, or the Patriots Roused," in order to put Yankee Federalists in their place, and he encouraged his friend in Williamsburg to write a new satirical *M'Fingal* to satirize "the infamous Tory meeting at Hartford" which then threatened to disunite the country. For "poetry, wit, criticism, romances, plays, &c." did indeed "deserve but a small portion of a mortal's mind." In the young nation "something more substantial, more durable, and profitable" was certainly needed. William Wirt never quite understood, as perhaps St. George Tucker did, that the substantial, endurable, and ultimately profitable in literature need not be delivered with bludgeon strokes, but can be rapier thrusts of grace and precision. Neither Wirt nor few of his contemporaries might have understood why the moral tracts and legend-producing small incidents of Mason Locke Weems and John Davis' exuberant outsider's view of American life survive more sturdily than his own well-meaning exercises in correction.

CRAIG WERNER

The Old South, 1815–1840

Literature written in the South around 1815 shared most of the basic concerns of that written in the North. By 1840 the increasing divergence of economic, political, and social conditions had created a specifically Southern literature reflecting the distinctive concerns and attitudes that were to survive as constituting elements of Southern literature in later eras. A complex concern with slavery generated numerous white defenses of Southern culture and sectional autonomy, distinctive Afro-American forms including slave narratives and a complex folk literature, and a romantic plantation tradition in fiction. Southern romanticism, developing out of Cooper, Byron, and Scott, differed sharply from the philosophical romanticism of Northern writers in its emphasis on the mythic elements of history rather than the metaphysical dilemmas that fascinated the transcendentalists. Although few major figures wrote during the period—Edgar Allan Poe and William Gilmore Simms are the only exceptions—a number of talented lyricists, romancers, and essayists contributed to the development of a uniquely Southern sensibility.

A growing consciousness of the South as a distinct region, reflected in the titles of periodicals such as the *Southern Literary Messenger* (founded 1834), the *Southern Review* (founded 1828), and the *Southern Literary Gazette* (founded 1828), accompanied the political polarization sparked by the issues of slavery, states' rights, and tariff policy. Between 1815 and 1840, the sectional alignment of the United States shifted, gradually and incompletely, from East-West to North-South. During the Monroe administration, commentators spoke with conviction of an "Era of Good Feelings" predicated on the development of a unified American culture distinct from that of England. The Missouri Compromise of 1820 suggested, at least momentarily, the possibility that the divisive political potential of slavery could be handled without open conflict. Returns from the presidential election of 1824 provide little evidence that Virginia perceived its interests to be more closely aligned with those of Mississippi than with those of Pennsylvania. By

1832, however, the South had united strongly (if, on the part of the seaboard areas, somewhat grudgingly) behind Andrew Jackson in opposition to Henry Clay's "American System," which was widely interpreted as an attempt to advance Northern manufacturing interests at the expense of the South. Subsequent events of the 1830s shattered all hope of diminishing sectional animosities. The Nat Turner slave rebellion of 1831 destroyed the movement toward voluntary emancipation in Virginia. A year later the nullification controversy, marking the transition of John Calhoun from nationalist to sectionalist, highlighted the political and economic issues that would force the sections farther and farther apart until the Civil War.

The primary source of these political tensions, which had profound literary implications, lay in the emergence of cotton as the primary focus of the Southern economy. In addition to its reliance on low tariffs and cheap labor, the cotton economy encouraged the development of the typical Southern pattern of sparsely settled regions organized into isolated farms or large plantations that modeled themselves loosely on what they imagined to be the pattern of English country estates. Perhaps the most important literary consequence of this pattern of social organization concerns education. Throughout the antebellum period, public schooling was almost unknown in the South, especially in the rural areas. Despite the emphasis placed on education by Southern leaders such as Thomas Jefferson, most white Southerners were educated by tutors in "old-field" schools, or in academies supported by tuition payments and staffed by teachers of widely varying capability. Although the educational system of the Old South often involved classical subjects in addition to the basics of mathematics and literacy, most observers reported an extremely erratic, and generally low, level of achievement. Academies for girls also offered instruction in reading and writing but they concentrated primarily on "refined" subjects such as French, piano-playing, and painting. Limited almost entirely to whites and upper- or middle-class children, the educational system precluded the development of a large literary audience in the sparsely populated South. As late as 1830 nearly one-third of the Southern adult population remained illiterate.

While the basic educational system languished, Southern colleges and universities provided a substantially better opportunity for the region's literary and political leaders, who attended Southern institutions as readily as those of New England. Most of the Southern colleges operating in 1815 were supported by religious denominations, especially the Presbyterians (Hampden-Sydney, East Tennessee, Washington—later Washington and Lee—and Transylvania) and the Episcopalians (William and Mary, St. John's, the College of Charleston). Several church-related schools, notably Transylvania (in Lexington, Kentucky), received substantial state aid; East Tennessee eventually evolved into the University of Tennessee. The close relationship between church and state in education helped maintain colleges in the face of declining enrollments (William and Mary had only eleven students in 1824), but it also subjected them to pressure from the conservative religious movement that spread through the South beginning in the 1820s. Despite the widespread acceptance of deism among educated Southerners early in the century, by 1827 the Presbyterian clergy was able to force the theologically liberal Horace Holley out of the presidency of Transylvania. Nevertheless, several Southern colleges compared quite favorably with their Northern counterparts in both the classical and the professional areas of study. The University of Virginia, founded 1825, probably ranked as the second best university in the United States, surpassed only by Harvard. With its international faculty, extensive curriculum, and Jeffersonian educational philosophy, the University of Virginia exercised a decidedly cosmopolitan influence on Southern culture throughout the 1830s. Among the notable scholars of the Old South were William Munford, the first American translator of the *Iliad* (published in 1846, nearly twenty years after his death); Wilkins Tannehill, whose *Sketches of the History of Literature, from the Earliest Period to the Revival of Letters in the Fifteenth Century* (1827) demonstrates an extensive knowledge of the classics; Francis Walker Gilmer, whose *Sketches of American Orators* (1816) reflects the importance of oral forms in Southern and American culture; and George Tucker, who taught philosophy, economics, and literature at the University of Virginia.

Most students at the Southern universities intended to practice law or medicine, and viewed literature primarily as a gentleman's avocation. The literary communities that developed in Baltimore around John Pendleton Kennedy, in Lexington (sometimes called the "Athens of the West"), and especially in Charleston around Hugh Swinton Legaré and William Gilmore Simms consisted largely of lawyers who met to discuss political and literary issues and published their writing in various newspapers and magazines, many of them quite ephemeral. As sectional tensions heightened, these periodicals took on an increasingly Southern character, reflecting a widespread dissatisfaction with Northern publishers, who nonetheless continued to dominate the book-publishing business without serious competition. Southern periodicals such as *Niles' Weekly Register* of Baltimore (founded 1811), the *Southern Review* of Charleston (supported by Legaré and Stephen Elliott) and the *Southern Literary Messenger* of Richmond published the work of nearly every significant antebellum Southern writer, but never developed any aesthetic (as contrasted with political) position distinct from those of the Northern periodicals. The *Messenger*, which employed Poe from 1835 to 1837, flourished until the Civil War, attracting contributions from Northern literary figures such as James Russell Lowell and Lydia Huntley Sigourney. In addition to these publishing activities, the urban literary circles, which included numerous members with fine personal libraries, supported groups such as the Library Society of Richmond and the Charleston Library Society. Both public and private collections typically emphasized English and classical writing but also included works by Americans such as James Fenimore Cooper and the New Englander William Ellery Channing, who was one of many to come under attack as the political situation worsened in the 1840s and 1850s.

The forces that led to Southern repudiation of the North can be traced through the changing emphasis of political writing of the period. During the 1810s and 1820s, statesmen-writers such as Jefferson, William Wirt, John Marshall, and John Taylor continued to advance the vision of a unified America typical of the colonial and revolutionary periods. Even the young John Calhoun echoed their sentiments. By the 1830s, however, Calhoun's sectionalist speeches both reflected and helped create the widespread shift in the tone of political discourse. Despite his contact with Jefferson and Madison, George Tucker, University of Virginia professor, editor of the *Virginia Literary Museum* (founded 1829) and minor novelist, emphasized the South's particular needs in his numerous books, such as *Essays on Various Subjects of Taste, Morals, and National Policy* (1822) and *The Life of Thomas Jefferson* (1837). Albert Pike, who was born in Boston but moved to the Southwest in 1831 and became an active proslavery spokesman, adopted a more extreme sectionalist position and eventually served as a Confederate general. Before becoming the editor of the *Arkansas Advocate* in 1835, Pike composed his *Prose Sketches and Poems, Written in the Western Country* (1834), which includes descriptions of frontier life similar to those of the early Southwestern humorists. While Pike and others vigorously defended the slave system, several attacks on the institution appeared, notably *David Walker's Appeal, in Four Articles; Together with a Preamble to the Coloured Citizens of the World, but in Particular, and Very Expressly, to Those of the United States of America* (1829). Written by David Walker, a freeborn black raised in Wilmington, North Carolina, *Appeal* calls for violent slave uprisings and anticipates the abolitionist emphasis on slavery as an immoral institution inviting the wrath of God. Especially after the events chronicled in *The Confessions of Nat Turner* (1831), an account of one of the bloodiest slave revolts in United States history written by Virginia lawyer Thomas R. Gray after interviewing Turner in his cell, the racial situation deteriorated rapidly and many Southern periodicals thereafter began to exclude all antislavery sentiments.

In addition to their political interests, some of the urban literary circles supported theater groups that, despite intermittent opposition from Puritanical clergymen, broadened the region's cultural perspective. Productions of classic British plays, especially by Shakespeare and the eighteenth-century comic playwrights, exerted a significant influence over the characters created in the fiction of Simms, Kennedy, and other romancers. Relatively few Southern playwrights enjoyed literary or popular success, however, and none of their plays survive as anything other than historical curiosities. Throughout the entire period, Southern drama closely resembled that written in the North, emphasizing nationalistic themes, and historical events. George Washington Parke Custis wrote numerous plays on American themes including *The Indian Prophecy* (1827), *The Eighth of January* (1834), a celebration of the Battle of New Orleans, and *Pocahontas, or The Settlers of Virginia*, which capitalized on the widespread popular interest in the legend and was extremely popular when produced at the National Theatre of Washington in 1836. Most of the notable playwrights of the Old South, however, lived and worked in Charleston, where Simms, Isaac Harby, William Ioor, and John Blake White wrote on a variety of topical and romantic themes. Harby, whose dramatic criticism was included in an 1829 collection of his work, demonstrated his commitment to democratic principles and his concern with the practical problems of dramatic structure in *The Gordian Knot* (1810) and *Alberti* (1819). Similarly, Ioor's *Independence; or Which Do You Like Best, the Peer, or the Farmer* (1805) and White's *The Triumph of Liberty* (published 1819) celebrate the democratic values of Jefferson and Jackson respectively. Outside of Charleston, Southern theater emphasized performance much more strongly than dramatic writing. James Caldwell, an actor born in England, founded several theaters in the lower South, most notably the St. Charles Theater of New Orleans (1835). Traveling companies such as that managed by Sol Smith toured the South throughout the first half of the century, performing melodramas and farces more frequently than the classics.

More important to the long-range development of Southern literature than the formal playhouses were the minstrel shows, which began to appear in the 1830s. Combining elements of the popular theater with musical adaptations of slave songs "composed" by white minstrels such as Thomas D. Rice, these shows helped fix the black stereotypes so important to the plantation tradition in fiction. Equally importantly, however, they testified to a white fascination with Afro-American culture that could not be expressed directly, given the dominant racial beliefs of the Old South. Among the first important demonstrations of popular culture's ability to contribute to cultural pluralism, the minstrel shows drew freely on the extensive body of Afro-American oral expression that has proved a rich source of material for Southern writers of both races. Although the first major collection of Afro-American folk literature, *Slave Songs of the United States*, edited by William Francis Allen, Charles Pickard Ware, and Lucy McKim Garrison, was not published until 1867, most of its sources indicate that the real dawning of interest in Afro-American culture took place several decades earlier. Although the Native American tribes of the South also possessed a distinct oral literature, it exerted little influence on the written literature of the region until much later.

The 1820s and 1830s also saw the first examples of writing in formal genres by Southern blacks. Some of this writing appeared as poetry. Vastly more significant, both for Southern and American (as well as Afro-American) literature were the slave narratives, a small flood of which were published between 1830 and the Civil War. All tended to be abolitionist tracts, purportedly by bondsmen who had fled the South. The heavy hand of a white antislavery editor to whom the narrative had been "dictated" was easily perceptible in a number of them. What may well be the best of them, however, were written by their announced authors. Of these, increasingly informed opinion regards as finest of all Frederick Douglass's *Narrative* (1845), in which the abolitionist polemics ingratiatingly accompany an absorbing personal history. Other narratives of note were written by, among others, William Wells Brown (1848), America's first black novelist; Henry Bibb (1849); James W. C. Pennington (1849), the "Fugitive Blacksmith"; Josiah Henson (1849, 1858, and 1879), the not altogether proven prototype for Harriet Beecher Stowe's "Uncle Tom"; Henry "Box" Brown (1851), who actually escaped from his master in a box; Samuel Ringgold Ward (1855); and William and Ellen Craft (1860). As a class the antebellum slave narratives sold well, partly because in a day when popular literature flourished on sensationalism and sentimentality the slave narratives presented a goodly measure of both. Yet, a strong element in the success of the slave narratives was their sympathetic representation of a subculture, largely through an effective resort to a picaresque mode of fiction. In virtually each of its distinctive features the antebellum slave narrative has affected all black American literature subsequent to it.

A second "invisible" literary tradition—that of Southern women—

also began to assume its outline during the 1830s. Southern women such as Eliza Wilkinson, whose *Letters* (published 1839) provides an account of the British invasion of Charleston in 1779, frequently wrote letters and diaries that offer valuable insight into both major historical events and the everyday conditions of Southern life. Few of these women wrote in generic forms, however, and the region's leading periodicals published very little writing by Southern women prior to 1840.

One important exception to the pattern of unpublished women was Caroline Howard Gilman, who was born in Boston but lived and worked in Charleston throughout her adult life. In addition to founding a children's magazine, the *Rose Bud* (later the adult *Southern Rose*) in 1832, Gilman wrote numerous stories, poems, and novels, including *Recollections of a Housekeeper* (1834) and *Recollections of a Southern Matron* (1837). The latter, sentimental and didactic like most Northern women's fiction of the era, focuses on the experience of a plantation girl growing into womanhood, the first Southern fiction on the theme that would become a standard feature of the tradition. Along with her dramatic poem "Mary Anna Gibbes, the Young Heroine of Stono, S.C." (1837), an account of a girl's heroic actions during the Revolution, Gilman's novels establish her as the single most important predecessor of the numerous women who began publishing in the South during the 1840s and 1850s.

Most literature of the Old South, however, was written by the white upper- or middle-class males connected with the literary circles of Charleston, Richmond, Baltimore, and Lexington. Like their counterparts in Philadelphia, New York, and Boston, these writers read and emulated the works of English romantic writers, particularly Byron, Thomas Moore, and Walter Scott. While regional tastes and style were generally similar in 1815 when James Fenimore Cooper was adapting Scott's style of historical romance to specifically American conditions, by 1840 clear differences had appeared between Northern and Southern romanticism. To a large extent, these differences reflect the social and political pressures that encouraged Southerners to develop a romantic view of plantation life and discouraged the philosophical/theological speculation evident in New England transcendentalism.

The one unquestionably major writer of the Old South, Edgar Allan Poe, both contributed to and transcended the attitudes of his contemporaries. Although Poe defended his native region's institutions and encouraged the work of many Southern writers through favorable reviews, his poems and stories rarely confront social issues. Poe's psychological vision of evil, rooted in the Gothic tradition and frequently tinged with comic irony, aligns him more strongly with Hawthorne and continental romanticism than with Kennedy or Simms. Certain of Poe's works, notably "The Fall of the House of Usher," "The Murders in the Rue Morgue," and *The Narrative of Arthur Gordon Pym, of Nantucket* (1838), can be seen as repressed allegories concerning the anxiety, guilt, and fear emanating from slavery. At best such interpretations cast an interesting sidelight on the sources of Poe's images of torment, incest, and madness; at worst, they distract attention from the imaginative landscape Poe actually created for his psychological and aesthetic speculations.

The only other writer of the era with a strong claim to lasting significance, William Gilmore Simms contrasts sharply with Poe and seems much more typical of his place and time. Moving from a nationalistic opposition to nullification in the early 1830s to an active defense of slavery in the 1850s, Simms's political beliefs parallel the changing Southern consensus. Appropriately, Simms's novels, obviously derivative of Scott and Cooper but nonetheless important examples of the genre of the historical romance, treat both national and sectional themes. These related, but increasingly distinct, interests permeate the two substantial series of novels Simms worked on throughout his career: the Revolutionary War romances, beginning with *The Partisan: A Tale of the Revolution* (1835), and the border romances, beginning with *Guy Rivers: A Tale of Georgia* (1834). *The Yemassee* (1835), perhaps his finest novel and one of the better Southern examinations of the multiracial heritage of the region, combines elements of both the Revolutionary and the border romances in its description of the Carolina Indian conflicts of the eighteenth century.

The reputations of Poe and Simms rest primarily on their fiction, but both also composed lyric poetry that typifies that of the Old South in its emphasis on the picturesque elements of romanticism. Poe's psychic landscapes such as "The Haunted Palace" and "The City in the Sea" and Simms's evocative "The Edge of the Swamp" clearly share an underlying sensibility with Southern lyricists such as Edward Coote Pinkney, Richard Henry Wilde, and Thomas Holley Chivers. Most of these lyricists wrote poetry only as a sideline to their professions and were unconcerned with developing rigorous philosophical or aesthetic stances. Nonetheless, many showed technical proficiency while working in lyrical, and on occasion narrative, modes. Wilde, who was born in Dublin, and Pinkney, who was born in London and died at age twenty-five, were probably the most talented after Poe. Wilde's "Lament of the Captive," a hauntingly musical lyric, evokes the Byronic image of the isolated individual wandering amid scenes of natural beauty. Similarly, Pinkney echoes the Byronic sensibility in poems such as "The Voyager's Song," which expresses a yearning for a "sublunary paradise" where love and beauty will be protected from "*human* transiency." The real strength of Pinkney's poems, however, reflects his ability to create a verbal music resembling that of the Cavalier poets. Even the titles of his best poems— "Serenade," "The Widow's Song," "A Picture Song," and several titled simply "Song"—suggest their suitability for musical setting. One of the few Old South lyricists who was not also a lawyer, Chivers shared Poe's and Pinkney's concern with the music of poetry. In fact, Chivers' friendship with Poe led to charges of plagiarism in the 1850s. Nonetheless, Chivers' eleven volumes of poetry and drama include enough polished work and their prefaces state his critical positions clearly enough to support the contention that the influence between him and Poe was to some degree reciprocal.

Given the concern with the music of poetry evident in the works of Poe, Pinkney, Wilde, and Chivers, it is not surprising that many lyrics of the Old South are better known as songs than as poems; Francis Scott Key's "The Star-Spangled Banner" is of course the most famous, but others such as Samuel Henry Dickson's "I Sigh for the Land of the Cypress and the Pine" also enjoyed popular success in their time. Several minor poets of the Old South worth noting are the painter Washington Allston (*The Sylphs of the Seasons, with Other Poems*, 1813), Philip Pendleton Cooke (best known for "Florence Vane" and "Life in the Autumn Woods"), William Crafts (best known for "The Raciad," a poem on life in Charleston written in the manner of Pope), and William Maxwell, whose work resembles that of the Connecticut Wits more closely than that of his Southern contemporaries. One intriguing, if aesthetically undistinguished, departure from the typical Southern lyric was Daniel Bryan's *The Mountain Muse: Comprising The Adventures of Daniel Boone; and The Power of Virtuous and Refined Beauty* (1813), an attempt to create an American epic, notable primarily for its moving evocations of the landscape of Kentucky.

The fiction writers of the Old South shared the poets' preference for romantic literature, modeling their historical romances on the work of Scott and Cooper. Simms's introduction to *The Yemassee* provides an accurate description of the romance as it developed in his own works and in those of William A. Caruthers and John Pendleton Kennedy. Arguing that the romance should be clearly distinguished from the domestic novel, Simms declares that "it does not confine itself to what is known, or even what is probable . . . it hurries . . . through crowding and exacting events." Caruthers' *The Cavaliers of Virginia* (1834–1835) and *The Knights of the Horse-Shoe* (1845), and Kennedy's *Horse-Shoe Robinson* (1835) and *Rob of the Bowl* (1838) differ from Hawthorne's romances in their lack of explicit concern with psychology and aesthetics, and certainly correspond to Simms's definition. The first literary treatment of Bacon's Rebellion of 1676, *The Cavaliers of Virginia* includes a multitude of events rendered even less "probable" than the historical material would dictate by Caruthers' reliance on a transparent Gothic plot. Nonetheless, Caruthers' treatment of several Gothic motifs partially compensates for the book's structural and stylistic deficiencies. In addition to presenting the cavalier myth of Southern ancestry in exceptionally clear form, *The Cavaliers of Virginia* manipulates the motifs of hidden guilt and ancestral sin in a manner that suggests the cultural thesis and antithesis explored in depth by later writers such as George Washington Cable and William Faulkner.

Kennedy's two romances recast events and legends drawn from the Revolutionary War era and set in the upper South. Kennedy surpasses Caruthers in his ability to create memorable characters; in *Rob of the Bowl*, for example, he places familiar Shakespearean types in an American setting to enliven a well-crafted plot. Both Kennedy and Caruthers, like most of their contemporaries North and South, suffered from their failure to create a style appropriate to their American materials, relying on elevated diction or on a dialect derived more directly from the comic stage than from their linguistic surroundings. Despite this shortcoming, the works of both Caruthers and Kennedy stand apart from formulaic Gothic romances such as Allston's *Monaldi: A Tale* (1841) and fictional essays such as Tucker's *The Valley of Shenandoah, or, Memoirs of the Graysons* (1824).

While Caruthers' and Kennedy's historical romances unquestionably represent the dominant tendency in Southern fiction during the 1830s, their books with contemporary settings identify the basic concerns that separate Southern from Northern fiction during the remainder of the antebellum period. Caruthers' epistolary novel *The Kentuckian in New York* (1834) contrasts life in the North and South, taking a conciliatory stance on most divisive issues. Caruthers notes the disparity between economic and social conditions in the manufacturing North and the agricultural South but refuses to condemn the character of Northerners. Similarly, he defends the paternalistic slavery of Virginia while condemning the cruelties that he associates with slavery in South Carolina. Despite these efforts to increase sectional harmony, however, *The Kentuckian in New York* realistically portrays the numerous sources of discord that forced the South into increasingly defensive positions.

Kennedy's *Swallow Barn* (1832), despite its pastoral surface, provides even clearer evidence of the divergence of North and South. A leisurely description of life on a Virginia plantation, the novel is the first major work of the plantation tradition. Kennedy populates his Old Dominion with comic eccentrics, cultured gentlemen, gracious ladies, and contented childlike slaves. Although he concerns himself much more directly with picturesque local legends than with political issues, Kennedy implicitly defends slavery as an institution beneficial for both races. Far more significant as cultural myth than as aesthetic creation, *Swallow Barn* can be seen legitimately as the first major statement in the literary battle over the image of slavery that includes works as disparate as *Uncle Tom's Cabin, Uncle Remus, His Songs and Sayings, The Conjure Woman, The Clansman, Gone with the Wind*, and *Roots*.

Kennedy cast *Swallow Barn* in the form of a traveler's report, capitalizing on the interest in Southern and Southwestern ways reflected in the vogue of travel books such as New York native James Kirke Paulding's *Letters from the South* (1817) and Joseph Holt Ingraham's *The South-West, by a Yankee* (1835). In addition, Southwestern humorists, many of them journalists, willingly fed the national appetite for sketches set in the frontier areas of Kentucky, Tennessee, Georgia, Alabama, Mississippi, and Arkansas. *A Narrative of the Life of David Crockett, of the State of Tennessee* (1834), composed by Crockett and Thomas Chilton and far more valuable as a source of tall tales than as historical biography, helped fix the image of the uncultured but insightful backwoodsman in the American imagination. The first important literary collection of Southwestern humor, Augustus Baldwin Longstreet's *Georgia Scenes, Characters, Incidents, Etc. in the First Half Century of the Republic* (1835), earned substantial popular acclaim while contributing to the image of a raucous lower South quite different from Kennedy's cultured seaboard. Perhaps the most important contribution of humorists like Longstreet to the Southern tradition lay in their use of a vernacular style less stilted than that of the romancers and lyricists.

If the Old South produced relatively few writers of lasting importance, it nevertheless occupies a crucial position in the cultural history of the United States. For the first time, Southern writers developed concerns clearly distinct from those of their Northern contemporaries, generating a romantic tradition based on historical mythology rather than philosophical speculation. Many of the constitutive elements of later Southern literature—the plantation tradition, Southwestern vernacular humor, the Afro-American narrative of ascent—first assume during the 1820s and 1830s the forms so important to writers such as Mark Twain, William Faulkner, and Richard Wright. By 1840 Southerners who a quarter-century before would have seen themselves as part of a nationalistic American mainstream were consciously creating and defining the characteristics that gave their region a literary identity clearly its own.

MARY ANN WIMSATT

Antebellum Fiction

Antebellum Americans, especially in the South, relished the popular romance as it had developed from the mid-eighteenth century onward, given great impetus by the historical novels of Walter Scott; and it is to the romance tradition and its several offshoots, Gothic, sentimental, and domestic, that we may trace the main features of the fiction produced between 1830 and 1870. That fiction employs, with ingenuity and gusto, the motifs of romance in all ages—the mysterious births, concealed parentage, separated lovers, kidnappings, robberies, and shipwrecks, as well as the general emphasis on tribulations-preceding-rewards that are the stock-in-trade of the genre and of the Western myths from which it ultimately descends. Antebellum popular romance, more particularly, is action-packed, ornately descriptive, moralistic, fond of dabbling in the irrational or the bizarre, and openly, persistently symbolic. Whether it has a historical or contemporary setting, it exists within a framework of orthodox religious values that bolsters its firm divisions between right and wrong or good and evil, as well as its marked tendency toward providential or wish-fulfillment endings. The resulting stylized format of this fiction, which twentieth-century readers tend to deplore, expresses political, social, and moral attitudes of the public in a manner highly agreeable to a nineteenth-century middle-class readership thirsty for confirmation of its value systems and its own hegemony of taste. Hence the literary statement of the nineteenth-century writer about the meaning of the past for the present or the direction of contemporary life is more likely than that of his twentieth-century counterpart to be reflected in forms where private attitudes are deliberately subordinated to public views and where procedures are conventionalized to a sometimes surprising degree.

The climate for fiction, and hence the texture of fiction itself, changed during the course of the antebellum period, largely because of unstable economic conditions, developments in the book market, and steady expansion of the reading public. The 1830s saw the establishment of the historical romance as the dominant form for prose fiction in the country at large; all the major Southern antebellum authors tried their hands at this mode. Late in the decade, however, the panic of 1837, by curtailing the market for long novels, effectively sounded the knell for historical fiction of the Scott and Cooper type, though established writers continued to work in the form until after the Civil War. Appearing in the 1840s, partly in response to the changing book market, were cheap paperbound novels, mammoth weekly newspapers in which current British and American fiction was serialized, annuals, gift books, and numerous, sometimes short-lived periodicals—all of which resulted in several species of subliterature and in the marked decline in literary taste that James D. Hart in *The Popular Book* (1950) has noted. By the 1850s, long fiction was back on its feet, though shakily, but the market continued to move away from the dignified historical romances of the earlier era. In that decade, sometimes called the "feminine fifties," emerged both men and women writers whose prodigious output for the pulp trade eclipsed the reputation and the sales of Cooper, Hawthorne, and Simms, as Hawthorne in particular was wont to complain. The market for long fiction, indeed for literature in general, was again disrupted by the Civil War; afterwards, as literary taste shifted toward realism and publishing houses like T. B. Peterson specialized in floods of cheaply issued books, fiction further altered its course.

But the authors of the early antebellum period felt themselves secure in the exploration of historical subjects. The most notable of these authors—John Pendleton Kennedy, Nathaniel Beverley Tucker, William Alexander Caruthers, and John Esten Cooke—are linked by a thoroughgoing pride in the South, a concern for political issues, particularly slavery and secession, and a patriotic devotion to Virginia and its cavalier legend. All except Cooke began their literary careers in the 1830s and had quit writing long fiction by the end of the 1840s; Cooke, who belongs to a slightly later period, inherited from his predecessors the vision of a shining cavalier past that he wove into a series of works set in Virginia. Cooke was talented, but of this group, Kennedy (1795–1870) was the one best equipped to make Simms look to his laurels had Kennedy chosen seriously to pursue a professional literary career. That he did not choose to, preferring instead to involve himself in state and national politics and in the lively cultural life of Baltimore, is to some extent a measure of the man and an indication of his genial, public-spirited temperament. Throughout his life his family circumstances, his residence in the border state of Maryland, and his tranquil disposition would color his literary endeavors and his political views.

Born in Baltimore to an Irish immigrant father in the merchant business and a mother from a tidewater Virginia clan, Kennedy studied law, dabbled in literature with the Addisonian *Red Book* (1819–1820), and then commenced writing in earnest with *Swallow Barn* (1832), his first and in many ways his best book. It reveals his grounding in Washington Irving and the eighteenth-century British essayists, and perhaps the influence of William Wirt's *Letters of the British Spy* (1803) which, like Kennedy's volume, portrays the reaction of a Northern visitor to the South. In Kennedy's words, "a rivulet of story wandering through a broad field of episode," *Swallow Barn* shows his sympathetic, judicious appraisal of Virginia institutions and customs, ranging over such diverse topics as the history and resolution of the boundary dispute between neighboring property owners, comic devil-doings in the inset "Mike Brown" yarn, and an earnest discussion of slavery. Kennedy concludes, through his characters and in accents familiar to the times, that slavery, though morally wrong, must be dealt with by the South without Northern interference. For readers content to move at Kennedy's leisurely pace, *Swallow Barn* represents the author at his best—rambling, charming, and desultory. Both by inclination and talent he was apparently more suited to imaginative excursions in the essay form than to the historical fiction he was next to write.

Yet his two historical novels, *Horse-Shoe Robinson* (1835) and *Rob of the Bowl* (1838) have substantial merits, though these may be dimmed for twentieth-century readers by Kennedy's prolixity and his tendency to digression. Set in Virginia and South Carolina, the two states that had suffered most from the Revolution in the South, *Horse-Shoe Robinson*, like Simms's Revolutionary War romances of the same decade, uses military history for its framing action, which culminates in the battle of King's Mountain. Making patrician characters and their opponents symbolize aspects of the historical situation, Kennedy mirrors the divisions caused by war in the various political stances of the Lindsay family, in standard fashion pitting the British villain St. Jermyn (masquerading as Tyrrel) and his servant James Curry against the partisan hero Arthur Butler and his companion Horse-Shoe. That Kennedy, like Simms, knew and relished Southern backwoods humor is shown through the character and speech of Horse-Shoe, who uses terms like "obstrepolous" and "flusterification" and boasts, "My name is Brimstone, I am first cousin to Belzebub."

If in his first two books Kennedy paid tribute to his mother's native state, in his third one he traced some elements in the colonial history of his own. *Rob of the Bowl: A Legend of St. Inigoe's*, set in the extreme southeastern portions of coastal Maryland, is a more unusual if finally a less successful venture into historical fiction than is *Horse-Shoe Robin-*

son. In it Kennedy treats the Roman Catholic/Protestant clashes of 1681 as they affect the families of the proprietary Charles Calvert and his collector of the port Anthony Warden; threading in and out of this account is the tale of the title character, Robert Swale, who has lost both legs and must walk with their stumps in a trencher or bowl. Like Cooper in *Lionel Lincoln* (1825), Kennedy includes a story of mysterious parentage that is resolved when Rob turns out to be the father of the young hero, Albert Verheyden; like Simms in *The Yemassee* (1835), he makes pirates the main villains of the piece and the particular enemies of Albert and his sweetheart Blanche Warden. After *Rob,* Kennedy returned to portraits of nineteenth-century life and to Irving as a model in *Quodlibet* (1840), an anecdotal account by the pretentious Solomon Secondthoughts that pillories Jacksonian democracy somewhat as Irving had pilloried Jeffersonianism in *A History of New York.*

Among Kennedy's notable nonfiction works bearing on Southern matters are his two-volume biography of William Wirt (1849), his pamphlet *The Border States* (1860), and his pseudonymously-issued *Mr. Ambrose's Letters on the Rebellion,* published serially during 1863 and 1864. Here Kennedy, who in 1852 to 1853 had been secretary of the navy and hence aware of Union interests, forcefully argues that states have no right to secede and that the real motive for secession was not slavery but the South's desire for national political domination.

Very different from Kennedy's reasoned stand on political issues was the embittered sectionalism of Beverley Tucker (1784–1851), the author of three novels—*George Balcombe* (1836), *The Partisan Leader* (1836), and *Gertrude* (serialized 1844–1845)—along with several political treatises. Of patrician family, Tucker was the son of St. George Tucker and the half brother, through his mother's first marriage, of John Randolph of Roanoke, who schooled him in political matters. As a federal judge, he spent about seventeen years, from 1815 or 1816 to 1833, in Missouri, where *George Balcombe* is partially set. A frontier romance of the sort Simms and R. M. Bird were writing, it uses the familiar romance device of a missing will as a hook on which hang diverting scenes of Missouri backwoodsmen, thugs, Indians, and swindlers.

Returning to Virginia, in 1834 Tucker accepted appointment to the College of William and Mary, where his views on states' rights and slavery were influenced by those of the chancellor, the eloquent Thomas Dew. Those views are expressed in *The Partisan Leader: A Tale of the Future,* the best known of Tucker's novels and one which attracted considerable attention in its time. Issued under the pseudonym Edward William Sidney with a spurious date of 1856 on its title page, it purports to describe events in 1849, including Martin Van Buren's election to an unprecedented fourth term and the formation of a successful Southern confederacy. Although the book is less a novel than a protracted political screed approaching allegory, it follows standard fictional practices of the time in having its leading characters symbolize different social or political positions and mating or separating them accordingly. It speaks strongly against wrongs the North dealt the South through the tariff, paints a fervent picture of slave-master loyalties, portrays the situation of Virginia divided between allegiance to the Union and sympathy for the Confederacy, and depicts armed conflicts, in which colorful Virginia mountain men take part, between Union and militia troops. Tucker enthusiastically viewed the volume as "the first *Bulletin* of that gallant contest, in which Virginia achieved her independence; lifted the soiled banner of her sovereignty from the dust, and once more vindicated her proud motto . . . SIC SEMPER TYRANNIS! AMEN. SO MOTE IT BE."

Like Tucker, William Alexander Caruthers (1802–1846) was a loyal Virginian, though a son of the mountain region rather than the tidewater; trained as a physician, he lived in various places in the North and South but used Virginia as the main setting of his three novels—*The Kentuckian in New York* (1834), *The Cavaliers of Virginia* (Vol. I, 1834; Vol. II, 1835), and *The Knights of the Horseshoe* (1845). Unlike Tucker, he disliked slavery and, especially through *The Kentuckian*, tried to promote intersectional goodwill while capitalizing on current literary trends. The book, which has a contemporary setting, is partly straight narrative and partly epistolary. It uses a journey structure into which are incorporated several love stories involving Southerners traveling north and a Northerner who goes south; and it includes a number of travelogue descriptions of Northern and Southern scenery. Its title character, Montgomery Damon, a boisterous Kentuckian who accompanies two Virginia aristocrats to New York, is modeled on Davy Crockett as filtered through James Kirke Paulding's Nimrod Wildfire, a chief character in *The Lion of the West* (1831). Caruthers had seen the revised version of the play—significantly retitled *The Kentuckian, or A Trip to New York*—when he was living in New York.

Jay B. Hubbell calls *The Kentuckian in New York* "a mixture of the sentimental, the lachrymose, and the Gothic"—but it is scarcely more so than *The Cavaliers of Virginia*, Caruthers' first attempt at the historical mode and, according to Curtis Carroll Davis, the book that fueled the cavalier legend in fiction. Its ostensible subject is Bacon's Rebellion of 1676 against the royal governor Sir William Berkeley; but its actual emphasis throughout much of the narrative is on the violent melodramatic ordeals, heavily seasoned with the Gothic, to which Nathaniel Bacon and his fiancée are subjected, brought about in part by the decrees of "The Recluse," a huge and somber figure who, like Hawthorne's Grey Champion, is one of the regicide judges seeking solitude in America.

Caruthers's final novel, *The Knights of the Horseshoe*—called "The Knights of the Golden Horse-Shoe" in the serialized version—is generally considered his best book on the basis of its sprightly style and coherent, clever plotting. Like *The Cavaliers*, it uses colonial Virginia history—in this case, Governor Alexander Spotswood's expedition across the Blue Ridge Mountains into the Valley of Virginia—as a background for several complicated love stories, punctuating the whole with episodes of murder, treason, and Indian fighting. Among historical novelists of the period, North and South, Caruthers is noteworthy for his lively prose, a refreshing change from the ponderosities of Simms or Cooper, his use (sometimes overuse) of varied kinds of narrative material, and his ability to shift from playful to melodramatic or lachrymose manner as his need requires.

Artistically, John Esten Cooke (1830–1886) was the beneficiary of these several attempts to glorify Virginia in fiction, a debt he acknowledged by his history of Virginia (1883) and by his unrelenting work in historical romance after the form had reached its zenith and begun its decline. A cousin of John Pendleton Kennedy, the younger brother of Philip Pendleton Cooke, and devoted friend and admirer of Simms, he was the most talented of the novelists whose careers span the antebellum and early postbellum eras. Descended on both sides from distinguished Virginia families, he was born in Winchester but spent much of his early life at his mother's plantation in the Shenandoah Valley. The family moved to Richmond when Cooke was ten, and unable to attend the University of Virginia, while studying law he attached himself to the *Southern Literary Messenger* and its editor John R. Thompson, turning out in profusion poems and other items for the journal. It was probably his long association with the *Messenger* that accounts for the marked element of "magazine fiction" in his writing—easy charm, superficial grace, and rosy, romantic pictures of Virginia living.

In an autobiographical sketch, Cooke claimed that he was "a *Virginian*, a *monarchist*, what is called a cavalier by blood and strain and feeling," insisting "I believe that any merit of my writing . . . will be found in the fact that I am *Virginian* and *Cavalier*." He furthermore claimed that in fiction his aim had been "to paint the Virginia phase of American society, to do for the Old Dominion what Cooper has done for the Indians, Simms for the Revolutionary drama in South Carolina, Irving for the Dutch Knickerbockers, and Hawthorne for the weird Puritan life of New England." Taken together, these statements suggest the derivation and the dominant cast of his books. His first novel, *Leather Stocking and Silk* (1854), an attempt to paint early nineteenth-century life in Martinsburg in northern Virginia (now West Virginia), is an obvious outgrowth of the short fiction he had published in the *Messenger* and in *Harper's*. It traces through several generations the fortunes of families connected with the town and the nearby mountains, looking to Cooper for its title and some traits in a leading figure (hunter John Myers) and to Irving for its breezy manner and its picture of a mock-supernatural prank.

The two novels generally considered Cooke's best—*The Virginia Comedians* (1854) and its sequel *Henry St. John, Gentleman* (1859)—treat tidewater Virginia on the eve of the Revolution. Both use the device, dear to Irving and to eighteenth-century British writers, of memoirs edited from manuscript, a ruse that allows Cooke to mingle comments in his own voice with quotations from his ostensible source. *The Virginia Comedians*, a brisk but uneven blend of history and romance, depicts, in Cooke's words, "the curiously graded Virginia society" of the late colonial era, represented by the patrician Cavalier clans of the Effinghams and Lees, by stalwart plainer people such as Charles and Ralph Waters and (at the historical level) Patrick Henry, and by various dialect-speaking low figures who furnish comic relief. Although purportedly about Patrick Henry's efforts to integrate colonial-political elements before the approaching military conflict, the book, as its title hints, is more directly concerned with a troupe of actors in Williamsburg and the abortive passion of Champ Effingham for the troupe's leading lady, Beatrice Hallam, who prudently marries Charles Waters instead.

Henry St. John continues Cooke's emphasis on the mixture of social elements in Virginia culture by making the title character, who shifts from loyalism to patriotism during the story, a descendant of Champ Effingham and a great-grandson of Pocahontas. It is less successful than its predecessor in uniting history and fiction, as it tends to alternate between long disquisitions on the Revolution by Patrick Henry and other characters and equally long love passages between Henry St. John and a heroine with the ultraromantic name of Bonnybel Vane, who furnished the title *Miss Bonnybel* for a later edition of the novel.

Cooke served throughout the Civil War with the Army of Northern Virginia; his seven books about the war develop the Cavalier legend in the service of the Lost Cause. Among the more notable of these books are his biographies of Stonewall Jackson (1863) and Robert E. Lee (1871) and his novels corresponding to those biographies, *Surry of Eagle's-Nest* (1866) and its sequel *Mohun* (1869), which treat military developments from 1861 through 1865, chiefly in Virginia, and which lovingly describe Jackson, Lee, Jeb Stuart, James Longstreet, and other Confederate officers. Both *Surry* and *Mohun* continue the ruse of the edited manuscript that Cooke had used in *The Virginia Comedians* and *Henry St. John*, and both profit from Cooke's firsthand experiences in some of the military events he describes; but both unfortunately show the faults that had marred his earlier books and would mar his later ones—an inability to integrate historical and fictive material or to fashion orderly plots and subplots, together with a willingness to cater to popular taste evidenced in his tendency to desert story lines in order to serve up romantic pictures of battles and military leaders.

In charm, sprightliness, and easy grace, Cooke's other books, ranging from *Pretty Mrs. Gaston* (1874) to *The Virginia Bohemians* (1880) and *My Lady Pokahontas* (1885), resemble the local color of Louisiana that George Washington Cable and Grace King were beginning to produce. But as Cooke himself knew, he was born too late for the vogue of historical romance that he insisted on cultivating, and forced to earn money by his pen, he wrote too much, too hastily, and too superficially to rival Simms or Kennedy at their best.

Alongside the historical novels that tried to portray with some dignity important events in the country's past that shaped its nineteenth-century condition, there developed in the 1830s and 1840s a more lurid strain of fiction in which historical trappings function chiefly as an excuse for the exploration of violent criminal or sexual passions. Emphasizing improbable melodramatic elements that in earlier fiction had been subordinate to weightier matters, this strain makes melodrama the main business of the tale. Such is the case in the novels and stories of Joseph Holt Ingraham (1809–1860), whose books, though little known today, were nineteenth-century best sellers outranking better books by more established authors, owing largely to Ingraham's ability to work in different modes of popular writing ranging from travel sketches to historical romance, topical treatments of antebellum life, and vast novels on biblical themes. Ingraham, in fact, provides an instructive contrast to the more famous writers of the era. Kennedy, Caruthers, and Cooke, though they might chafe at the restrictions imposed by their genre or their readers, all wrote more or less in service to established social, political, and religious positions, depicting episodes from American history in a manner that echoed the nation's public interpretation of its past. Ingraham seized upon what has been called the "dark underside" of romance increasingly visible in the genre since the eighteenth century, and at the beginning of his career turned out sensational volumes on historical subjects that barely escape being sordid. (Longfellow, supposedly quoting Ingraham, called them "the worst novels ever written.")

A native of Massachusetts, Ingraham migrated to Mississippi in 1831, producing *The South-West, by a Yankee* (1835), a series of travel essays, as a memorial to his experience. He then published, in swift succession, *Lafitte; or The Pirate of the Gulf* (1836), *Burton; or, The Sieges* (1838), and *Captain Kyd; or, The Wizard of the Sea* (1839), historical novels using a thin thread of fact in elaborately embroidered fictional episodes recalling Gothic romances like *The Monk* as well as the more respectable fiction of Walter Scott. All three works focus on the crime-and-seduction sequences central to Gothic fiction; all use the figure of the Byronic hero-villain socially exiled yet capable of good deeds and yearning to repent; and despite their flagrant, probability-violating scenes, all exist within the value matrix formed by popular religion and supported by the social fabric. *Lafitte* treats the well-known privateer who helped American forces in the War of 1812 (Jacob Blanck, *Bibliography of American Literature* [New Haven, 1963], IV, 460, says Ingraham may have plagiarized *Lafitte* from the manuscript of a Cambridge graduate. Evidence exists for an 1828 edition of the novel subtitled *The Baratian Chief*); *Burton* is a fictionalized account of episodes from Aaron Burr's life; and *Captain Kyd*, the least integrated and most lurid of the three, portrays the fortunes of a noble seventeenth-century Irish family improbably transplanted to America. Influenced equally by Scott and Monk Lewis, *Captain Kyd* blends extremely detailed descriptions of Irish customs with sensational accounts of piracy, robbery, murder, and witchcraft. After *The Quadroone* (1841), set in New Orleans, Ingraham, sensing that money was to be made through magazine fiction, turned out narratives like *The Dancing Feather* (1841) for periodicals at a furious pace.

Then in the early 1850s, the purveyor of semisalacious lore suddenly and dramatically changed his course. He became an Episcopal minister and produced several best-selling novels based on biblical subjects—*The Prince of the House of David* (1855), *The Pillar of Fire* (1859), *The Throne of David* (1860)—that foreshadowed the vogue for biblical narrative in the postbellum era. His switch from pulp to religious fiction is less surprising than it seems, for religion, chiefly Roman Catholicism, had formed a colorful undercurrent in his earlier books whose pirates, called "demoniacs," and innocent, pious characters are secular versions of the figures who play major roles in his late works. One of his last books, *The Sunny South* (1860), a series of travel letters purportedly written by a Northern governess in the South, unites the vein he had opened in *The South-West* with the epistolary form of his late novels to produce a volume that, on the eve of the Civil War, spoke forthrightly for the individuality and charm of Southern culture.

If Ingraham veered in the course of his life from the dark to the bright sides of the romance tradition, Emma Dorothy Eliza Nevitte Southworth (1819–1899) and Caroline Lee Whiting Hentz (1800–1856) kept their forays into Gothic domains firmly within what Leslie Fiedler calls the white or antiseptic formulas of popular writing. Mrs. E. D. E. N. Southworth, who was born in Virginia, set many of her novels in that state and in Maryland, where her ancestors had lived. In 1849, separated from her husband and forced to support herself and two young children, she began to write, serializing her first novel, *Retribution*, in the Washington, D.C., *National Era*. Many of her later works first saw print in the *Era* or the *Saturday Evening Post* and, after 1857, in the New York *Ledger*, run by Robert Bonner.

Among Southworth's most popular books after *Retribution* were *The Curse of Clifton* (1852, other editions titled *Fallen Pride* and *The Mountain-Girl's Love*); *The Hidden Hand* (1859, also called *Capitola's Triumph*); and *Ishmael* (1863) and its sequel *Self-Raised* (1864), both based loosely on the life of William Wirt and originally serialized as a single work with the title *Self-Made*. There is a strong element of juvenile literature in these and other Southworth volumes, in which children are sometimes prominent figures. Thus *Vivia* (1856) traces the fortunes of three counterpointed heroines from childhood through education to maturity, meanwhile interweaving a tale, straight from Gothic romance, of lovers secretly married, wickedly separated, and serving in Roman Catholic orders before being finally, chastely reunited. *Ishmael*, which opens with an unhappy version of the Cinderella legend, focuses heavily on the incredible goodness and ability of the boy Ishmael, who rises through wit and pluck to fame. Byronic heroines appear in *Ishmael* and *The Curse of Clifton*, one appropriating "the ambition of Lucifer," the other declaiming, "I ask no leave of earth or Heaven for what I do!" Beneath her melodramatic plots, which even a contemporary woman writer of her breed stigmatized as "possibility-scorning," Southworth stresses such traditional virtues as honesty, purity, trust, and love; she repeatedly warns against secret marriages and other forms of deception practiced on parental or guardian figures. And like Ingraham, she seasons her writing with homely humor based on dialect-speaking characters, blacks and whites, from the lower class.

The ten novels of Caroline Lee Hentz are more even in texture, somewhat less crammed with incident, and slightly less sensational than Southworth's, though they too run the gamut of melodrama standard to the pulp trade. Born in Massachusetts, Hentz lived in several parts of the South and West after her marriage to a French immigrant, whom she assisted in running and teaching at various girls' schools. After early success with *Aunt Patty's Scrap Bag* (1846) and *The Mob Cap; and Other Tales* (1850), she produced her first novel, *Linda; or, The Young Pilot of the Belle Creole* (1850), which treats a young, dutiful Louisiana plantation heiress, her weak-willed father, her unkind stepmother, and her contrasted suitors, Roland Lee and Robert Graham (who lent his name to the sequel to *Linda* published in 1855). Through such figures as Graham, Claudia in *The Planter's Northern Bride* (1851), and the title character of *Ernest Linwood* (1856), Hentz displays the corroding effects of passion unchecked by reasoned restraint.

The Planter's Northern Bride, which remains Hentz's best-known book through its status as the answer to *Uncle Tom's Cabin*, like Caruthers' *Kentuckian in New York* tries to soothe the sectional prejudice by showing Southerners traveling in the North and Northerners in the South, while like *The Partisan Leader* it imprints nearly every page with impassioned propaganda for the Southern cause. Centering on the magnanimous Southern planter Russell Moreland and his New England bride Eulalia, it contrasts an honorable and a flagitious abolitionist, paints an abortive slave uprising, discourses lengthily and, to mid-twentieth-century ears, offensively on the innate inferiority of the Negro, and in phrases typical of the times excoriates the economic system that bred the Northern "wage-slave" and the wretched seamstresses of Britain. For all its emphasis on the saintly Eulalia, this book, like *Marcus Warland* (1852), has male figures in the foreground. But in *Eoline; or, Magnolia Vale* (1852) and *Helen and Arthur* (1853), Hentz emphasizes sturdy, independent single women as well as rebellious younger heroines who eventually come around to sensible points of view.

In contrast to Ingraham, Southworth, and Hentz, whose novels were aimed more or less at adults, Francis Robert Goulding (1810–1881), a minister and native of Georgia, wrote his several books for the juvenile market. After *Little Josephine* (1844), composed for the American Sunday School Union, he published in 1852 his most popular work, *Robert and Harold; or, The Young Marooners on the Florida Coast*, which went through many reprintings. It contains characterizations of educated, responsible parents, a good deal of interesting naturalist and medical lore, and a Robinson Crusoe plot in which children accidentally shipwrecked are forced to live by their always-ethical wits. As their subtitles indicate, the Woodruff stories, including *Sapelo; or, Child Life in the Tide Waters* (1888), *Nacoochee; or, Boy-Life from Home* (1871), and *Sal-o-quah; or, Boy-Life Among the Cherokees* (1870), trace children's progress from home through school into semi-independent adolescence sprinkled with Indian adventures. In their emphasis on childish pranks and on children forced to live without consistent adult supervision yet abiding by their parents' values, Goulding's works form an interesting contrast to *Tom Sawyer* and *Huckleberry Finn*.

Two developments in the 1840s, the increasing popularity of travel writing and the spread of periodical literature, made possible the careers of David Hunter Strother (1816–1888) and Joseph Addison Turner (1826–1868), whose literary production, though markedly slimmer than that of their more important contemporaries, tells a good bit about conditions for authors near the end of the antebellum era. A native of Virginia and a relative of John Pendleton Kennedy, Strother was fortunate in being able to illustrate the several travel pieces he wrote in the 1850s for *Harper's Magazine*. Those were *Virginia Illustrated, North Carolina Illustrated, A Winter in the South*, and *A Summer in New England*. His fondness for travel, his ability for both art and writing, and a meeting with Washington Irving led him to adopt the pen name Porte Crayon for his work. When published in book form (1857), the five parts of *Virginia Illustrated*, which appeared in *Harper's* during 1854 and 1856, incorporated Strother's earlier account of "A Visit to the Virginia Canaan," a tale of an expedition into the Blackwater Falls area of Virginia. Influenced by British and American travel narratives, *Virginia Illustrated* recalls Smollett and Sterne in its use of a story thread for its travel adventures, its sharp portrayals of the travelers, and its bantering presentation of scenery and character. As Strother's chief chronicler Cecil D. Eby remarks, the work also resembles Southern humor in its persistent realism and its comic portraits of a farmstead romance and a boasting backwoodsman. *North Carolina Illustrated*, a less interesting piece, shows typical Virginia snobbery, as Eby notes, toward the Old North State. Strother served with Union forces during the Civil War, and afterward refused to return to the pleasantries of his earlier writing, preferring instead, though with little success, to entice his *Harper's* public into a serious examination of the war through a series of personal recollections.

The Georgia planter Joseph Addison Turner is remembered chiefly for his encouragement and support of Joel Chandler Harris, whom as a youth he helped educate in literature, printing, and publishing. But in his own right he was something of a minor litterateur, editing and writing for several Southern periodicals—among them *Turner's Monthly* (1848), *Plantation: A Southern Quarterly Journal* (1860), and *Countryman* (1862–1866), in which his poem in heroic couplets, "The Old

Plantation," appeared. The *Countryman* shows the continuing influence of eighteenth-century Britain on Southern magazines, for Turner consciously modeled it on the *Spectator*, the *Tatler*, and the *Rambler*. He assiduously sought, as Simms had done before him, to "contribute . . . to the creation of a separate and distinct Southern literature." But he was even less successful than Simms had been in stimulating that literature through periodical publication.

Of somewhat special interest in antebellum Southern fiction, if only because of their color, are the two black writers William Wells Brown (1814?–1884) and Martin R. Delany (1812–1885). Both are historically important in Afro-American literature.

Brown was born in the Kentucky bluegrass in or near the town of Lexington, but was taken by his owner to Missouri in 1816. A pronounced octoroon, he claimed at least once (erroneously, it seems) to have been a grandson, through his mother, of Daniel Boone. From 1827 until the very end of 1833, under three successive owners, Brown's home was in St. Louis. On New Year's Day in 1834, stealing away from a river steamer belonging to his last owner and docked at Cincinnati, he began a walk that propelled him, suspicious of everyone he saw, entirely across the state of Ohio in the dead of winter to a relatively secure haven in Cleveland. Within the next quarter of a century he became justly famous as a lecturer for both the abolitionists and the crusaders for temperance (who were often, as in his case, alternately each). For the last twenty-four years of his life, however, he practiced medicine in Boston, Massachusetts.

In the *Narrative of William Wells Brown, a Fugitive Slave, Written by Himself* (1847), Brown wrote one of the best and most widely circulated of all slave narratives. The title of his *The Anti-Slavery Harp: A Collection of Songs for Anti-Slavery Meetings* (1848) speaks for itself. His play, *The Escape: or, A Leap for Freedom: A Drama in Five Acts* (1858), is credited with being the first play by a black American writer. In 1849 Brown had gone abroad. He stayed abroad, principally in the British Isles, largely because of the harsh provisions against fugitive slaves included in the Compromise of 1850. In London he assembled and had printed a collection of his own letters, *Three Years in Europe; or, Places I Have Seen and People I Have Met* (1852), the first book of travels by an American fugitive slave to be published in England. Attesting to his perennial interest in black history are four works: *St. Domingo: Its Revolution and Its Patriots* (1854); *The Black Man, His Antecedents, His Genius, and His Achievements* (1863); *The Negro in the American Rebellion* (1867); and *The Rising Son; or The Antecedents and Advancement of the Colored Race* (1873). Even so, the feat that uniquely distinguishes him is his authorship of *Clotel* (1853), written in London and issued to the world by a London printer, but still the first novel ever published by an American black.

Four versions of *Clotel* exist: the original version; *Miralda; or, The Beautiful Quadroon: A Romance of American Slavery, Founded on Fact* (1861), which ran as a serial of sixteen installments in the *Weekly Anglo-African* from December 1, 1860, through March 16, 1861; *Clotelle: A Tale of the Southern States* (1864); and *Clotelle; or, The Colored Heroine: A Tale of the Southern States* (1867). Essentially, all four versions repeat the same story. Yet they differ considerably in detail, as they do in the spelling of the name Clotel. The original version, significantly subtitled *The President's Daughter*, explicitly attributes to Thomas Jefferson a liaison with his attractive light-skinned slave Currer, by whom he has two daughters of surpassing beauty, Clotel and Althesa. All three of these fair creatures, after the death of their aging second owner, are auctioned off in Richmond. Subsequently, with a profusion of melodramatic incident and no lack of abolitionist polemic, the novel pursues each of them to a dire and woeful demise. Currer and Althesa both perish of the yellow fever—the mother in Natchez, the daughter in New Orleans. Clotel, barely thwarting the professional slave catchers closing in on her, plunges deliberately into what becomes her watery grave from a bridge across the Potomac, within sight and almost within sound of the Capitol at Washington. A much happier fate awaits Clotel's daughter and only child, Mary. As the novel ends, she, the beneficiary of an amazing series of possibly even more amazing coincidences, marries in France the one man she has long loved dearly. It was for complicity in the handsome fugitive slave's escape that Mary was sold into slavery in the Deep South.

In its repetition of basic characteristics of the slave narrative as a form, no less than in the racial protest that virtually informs its every line, *Clotel* belongs very much to Afro-American literature. Yet it belongs also, if not more, to all Southern and all American literature. Its *weltanschauung* is quite thoroughly and unselfconsciously that of a person raised in America, especially in the American South. And despite its bitter, unceasing denunciation of the huge majority of white Americans who then indulged in racism, it espouses integration, not black separatism.

Martin R. Delany, as black of complexion as Brown was white, was born free in Charles Town, near Harper's Ferry, in what is now West Virginia (abolitionist John Brown was hanged at Charles Town). Delany, at the age of nine, was taken by his mother to live in Chambersburg, Pennsylvania, primarily because Chambersburg was "free." At nineteen, a youth taking charge of his own life, he trudged on foot across the Allegheny ridge to Pittsburgh, where he spent his early manhood and married the half-Irish daughter of a son of the prosperous black entrepreneur "Daddy Ben" Richards. Restless and searching, Delany practiced as a physician and surgeon (adept at the cupping and bleeding still reputable in orthodox attempts at healing before the Civil War), published newspapers, studied medicine for a semester at Harvard (he was denied further matriculation because of his color), visited Africa, emigrated with his wife and children to Canada, returned with his family to the United States, received (near the end of the Civil War) a major's commission in the Union army, and spent almost all of the last twenty years of his life in South Carolina, far from the family he had managed before then to keep with him. He died, reunited with this family, in Wilberforce, Ohio.

Delany was one of the very few Negro leaders of his day who championed the Negro's return to Africa. In his *The Condition, Elevation, Emigration, and Destiny of the Colored People of the United States Politically Considered* (1852), he emphasized the fatuity, as he conceived it, of the American Negro's failure to leave America and go back to Africa. Black pride was a sentiment about which Delany felt strongly and most positively. It is the sentiment that pervades his last book, *Principia of Ethnology: The Origin of Races and Color with an Archeological Compendium of Ethiopian and Egyptian Civilization* (1879). And it is the sentiment that colors, and dignifies, with the darkest of sable hues, the manly, well-featured, highly intelligent protagonist of Delany's only novel, *Blake; or, The Huts of America* (1859). Fittingly, in his every action this paragon of virtue in ebony exemplifies not simply black pride but also black leadership of the most enlightened and sincerest (hence, militant and separatist) kind.

In the beginning of the novel, Blake is introduced as the slave Henry Holland who, when his slave "wife" is sold away from him to Cuba, takes unauthorized leave of his master, whom he hates monumentally, and travels through the South organizing a secret network of blacks sworn to participate, given the proper summons, in a general insurrection of America's slaves. Next he goes to Cuba, resumes his true identity as Blake, recovers and legally marries his "wife." He is, incidentally, a native Cuban—named, in Spanish, Carolus Henrico Blacus—and a cousin to the black Cuban poet and patriot, Placido. Blake's story, as given in his novel (some six chapters of which are not extant), concludes with Blake, a true heroic slave, deeply involved in the capacity of commander-in-chief with another secret network of blacks sworn to the overthrow of slavery, albeit not in America, but in Cuba.

As *Clotel* speaks for integration, so *Blake* advocates black separatism. Also, only David Walker's *Appeal* (1829) antedates *Blake* as a fiery expression of black militancy. Delany had reacted with resolution and great courage to an action of the Supreme Court of Pennsylvania which, in 1838, declared that Negroes could not be citizens of the state. He made, in the very next year, an excursion into the South as far as Texas prospecting for land that Negroes could settle on terms amenable to his concepts of their humanity. This excursion, to some extent, underlies *Blake*. It did not make *Blake* less American than *Clotel*. After all, the same American environment conditioned similarly both Delany and Brown. But it did make *Blake*, of the two novels, much the more political. For Delany, a combative pragmatist, was constitutionally disinclined to accept, as did Brown and other Garrisonians, any hypothesis that American slavery could be demolished by moral suasion. However love might affect men, in Delany's view the lust for power tended always to exercise on human behavior a stronger influence. And so *Blake* is not only about right and wrong. It is also about power and powerlessness, only one of which, Delany obviously believed, could ever, for minorities, be right.

MARY ANN WIMSATT

William Gilmore Simms

For energy, charm, productivity, commitment to a literary vocation, and also for the relative mediocrity of all but a handful of his works, William Gilmore Simms (1806–1870) has few peers in American literature. Aware of his importance in literary history but uncertain how to determine the ultimate value of his writing, critics have struggled for more than a century to define the place of this ambitious, engaging author in the American literary canon, to quiet the restless ghost of Gilmore Simms with its disturbing complaint that it had left all its better works undone. The problem of reading, let alone assessing, Simms's immense body of work has proved insurmountable for all but his most dedicated students, and the records of those who, like Trent and Hubbell, have persisted are tributes more to perseverance than adept appraisal.

Yet Simms, rather than Poe, is the representative antebellum Southern man of letters whose career bespeaks poignantly the dilemma of the professional author in America. From the 1830s until the Civil War, he dominated the literature and spoke for the intellectual life of the section. Hence a comprehensive picture of his writing—poetry, drama, fiction, and criticism—helps make clear the literary and cultural conditions of his region and the extent to which he drew upon it in his work. The qualities that have distinguished Southern literature from its inception are present, at almost every point, in Simms: a keen awareness of time and the past; a strong sense of place; an effort to render characters and events in concrete, particularized detail; and a fond perception, which informs his pronouncements on agriculture, slavery, frontier expansion, and secession, of the South as a distinctive civilization. Approached sympathetically, this intense and dedicated author provides valuable indexes to the concerns of his era and region.

Simms began his career as a poet, and it was through his poetry that he originally hoped to win lasting literary fame. His first poem published in book form—*Monody, on the Death of General Charles*

Cotesworth Pinckney (1825)—looks forward to his later work in its devotion to the Southern past, its tribute to a Carolina Revolutionary War hero, and its awareness of literary convention. Likewise, the very different *Atalantis* (1832), a fanciful story of the sea that combines passages in dramatic form with graceful lyrics, shows his discriminating use of tradition in its deliberate echoes of Shakespeare and Milton. Among the more important of his numerous volumes after *Atalantis* are *Southern Passages and Pictures* (1839), a group of descriptive and meditative poems; *Areytos: or, Songs of the South* (1846), lively musical lyrics embodying, as he says, "the supposed warmth of a Southern temperament"; *The Cassique of Accabee* (1849), perhaps his most important poem on an Indian subject; and the two-volume collection *Poems Descriptive, Dramatic, Legendary and Contemplative* (1853), assembled for the Uniform Edition of his works and in a sense the capstone of his poetic career.

In *The Poetry of William Gilmore Simms: An Introduction and Bibliography* (1979), James E. Kibler, Jr., the chief student of Simms's verse, notes justly that "Simms's poetic talents were not narrow, and he brought to much of his poetry the same creative energy which characterizes his best prose." As Kibler also notes, many of Simms's poems show his link to persistent Southern literary and cultural concerns—a dislike of industrialism and materialism, a desire for continuity among generations, a sense of the past and history, and a tendency to experiment with literary technique. Adept at many forms, Simms uses rhyme royal, ottava rima, the Spenserian stanza, blank verse, the sonnet, and the ballad in his numerous volumes. As in his fiction, he treats national, patriotic, or timely topics—the War of 1812 and the Revolution in such poems as "New Orleans," "Benedict Arnold," and "Major André"; Indians in "The Last of the Yemassee" and "The Green Corn Dance"; the Southern frontier in "The Texian Hunter" and "The Western Emigrants"; and nature in "To the Evening Star," "To a Winter Flower," "First Day of Spring," and "Apostrophe to Ocean."

Bryant's presence is strong in Simms's nature poetry, as is Byron's in his satiric verse and some love lyrics. Thus the general situation, the cadences, and the philosophical reflections of the narrator in "To a Bird at Sea" recall "To a Waterfowl," while the tone and rhythm of "When We Two Parted" undoubtedly influenced Simms's poem beginning "Destined to sever / Thrice hapless, for years." And the author of *Don Juan* hovers over *Donna Florida* (1843), as a single stanza suggests:

> I want a Muse, as Byron did a hero;
> None of your frowsy dames of classic ages,
> Cold, marble damsels, always below zero,

Forever 'mongst the chronicles and sages,
But one who would not shrink from a *bolero*,
Did we require to have one in our pages;
Who'd laugh, or sing, or dance, when I request her,
Nor wait for the certificate from Nestor.

While some of Simms's poetry is glib or imitative, it exhibits ingenuity and technical skill beyond what is usually ascribed to him; and all of it is spirited. In particular, his treatment of such standard personifications as Fortune, Folly, Love and Time (whom he irreverently calls an "old codger") shows a winning playfulness. As James Kibler claims, Simms's poetry in all its aspects deserves closer scrutiny than it has yet received.

Simms's work in drama is similarly ambitious and engaging, if ultimately less successful than his verse. Such sketches as "Caius Marius" and "The Death of Cleopatra" show the nineteenth century's love of lofty subjects from foreign history, together with the painfully stilted diction such subjects usually evoked. Particularly interesting are Simms's full-length plays with contemporary settings—*Norman Maurice* (1851), a melodrama of love and politics, and *Michael Bonham* (1852), a treatment of the Texas war for independence that stars Davy Crockett as a major figure. "Benedict Arnold," a work begun in the 1830s and serialized in the 1860s, reflects Simms's enduring concern with Revolutionary War topics of the kind that he abundantly explored in history, biography, and fiction.

Although his plays and poetry are beginning to draw critical attention, the average academic reader still knows Simms chiefly through his fiction, and it is in his novels and tales that he made perhaps his most substantial contribution to Southern literary traditions. Emerging into a field already tilled by Scott and Cooper, he set the standard for a generation of Southern novelists. In so doing, he described the South in its historical and cultural diversity: his major fiction derives from his experiences in two Southern regions that twentieth-century scholarly studies distinguish—the coastal, low country, plantation, or tidewater area of his childhood and maturity, and the frontier or backwoods expanses of the Gulf South that he explored in the 1820s and 1830s and the Appalachian Mountain South in which he traveled in the 1840s. These regions, historically disparate though linked by emigration patterns and to some extent by climate and geography, gave rise to the two major branches of his fiction—historical tales and romances set in the Carolina low country and border and mountain fictions taking place in the backwoods South. The main works in each of these branches reveal the Southern sectional differences that Simms knew from experience and from his reading of history; and they also demonstrate his commitment to two dominant and contending nineteenth-century literary forms, realism and romance.

Born in Charleston and living much of his life in or near it, Simms was steeped in low-country traditions. He expresses his vision of low-country culture in works published from near the beginning to almost the end of his career—*The Yemassee* (1835), the Revolutionary War romances (1825–1841, 1851–1867) save for *Joscelyn* and *The Scout*; the novelettes *Castle Dismal* (1844), *Maize in Milk* (1847), and *The Golden Christmas* (1852); the short novel *Paddy McGann* (1863); and the colonial romance *The Cassique of Kiawah* (1859). In the long works, seen in terms of their time of setting, he traces the development of the coastal region from the founding of the Carolina colony in the late seventeenth century through the Indian wars and the Revolution. In the novelettes he surveys various aspects of nineteenth-century plantation culture, *Castle Dismal, Maize in Milk*, and *The Golden Christmas* taking place near midcentury, the framing narrative of *Paddy McGann* set during the Civil War. All his long fiction laid in the low country is historical; the shorter works, which reflect values and procedures established by the novels, view the customs and traditions of antebellum society from perspectives that Carolina history affords.

For most of these volumes, Simms employs the structures and conventions of romance as he had learned them from Malory, Shakespeare, Spenser, Sidney, and especially from his master Walter Scott, whose format for popular fiction he adapted to the conditions of the coastal and border South. The key to Simms's fiction is in its assimilation of romance structures once associated with aristocratic literature to popular or bourgeois modes, a process that had existed in the novel ever since the spread of literacy and print in the mid-eighteenth century had made fiction the staple fare of a mass reading public. Nurtured on realism, our century has been slow to heed Simms's insistence that his works are romances. Yet all his long novels, like Scott's and Cooper's, employ the central elements of romance as twentieth-century literary theorists describe it. They express the ideals of the ruling class, in Simms's case the planting class of the colonial and antebellum South; they dramatize the conflicts of these ideals with forces threatening them by a two-sided or dialectic structure revealed most obviously through their main narratives, symbolic constructions in which attractive heroes and heroines representing the ideals battle opponents representing the anti-ideals; they resolve this conflict through persistently happy endings in which heroes defeat enemies and marry heroines; and they use as perhaps their most characteristic setting the natural domain represented in its pastoral dimension by the plantation and in its wilder aspect by the forests from which Carolina estates were carved.

Simms's low-country novels also exhibit an enveloping or a framing action grounded in history that is the particular source of the romance symbolism and the wellspring of the time perspective, an element that develops out of the passage of time between his era and the period he is depicting. By means of the time perspective, he imposes the interpretation of his age upon the events of the past and ratifies the verdicts that history had already rendered.

Thus, in a typical Revolutionary War romance such as *Katharine Walton* (1854), Simms pits partisan officer Robert Singleton and his fiancée Katharine against crafty, villainous Nesbitt Balfour, British commandant of Charleston, echoing this configuration in his subplot—in which Singleton's friend, the British officer John Proctor, and Katharine's friend, the loyalist Ella Monckton, battle and defeat Balfour's creature, Major Vaughan. The situation in the love story echoes the situation at the framing level where, through Simms's spirited references to historical action completed, partisans likewise defeat their enemies and free their country of foreign threat. Hence, the structure and resolution of Simms's generic Revolutionary War romance love plot, the most nearly "ideal" of such narratives in his fiction, mirror what he saw as the ideal resolution of the revolutionary cause.

Comparable structural conventions distinguish Simms's novels of Spanish and Spanish-American history, *Pelayo* (1838), *The Damsel of Darien* (1839), *Count Julian* (1845), and *Vasconselos* (1853). And, except for the framing action, they also govern his four border romances, *Guy Rivers* (1834), *Richard Hurdis* (1838), *Border Beagles* (1840), and *Helen Halsey* (1845)—together with books connected to them in setting or theme, like *Confession* (1841) and, to a lesser extent, *Beauchampe* (1842) and *Charlemont* (1856), a retelling of the famous Kentucky tragedy of the 1820s. The four main border romances naturally reflect the travels of Simms's young manhood; but they also reflect his acquaintance with the spectacular exploits of John A. Murrell, the sinister "Reverend Devil" and "Great Western Land Pirate" who with his henchmen terrorized the Old Southwest near the time Simms went there. In these books, Simms grafts his own youthful experiences upon the standard literary pattern of the journey, here undertaken by a young man from the older South who, making his way westward, falls into the hands of and finally helps to destroy a gang of criminals modeled on the Murrell thugs. The dialectic structure of these volumes, which have a loosely contemporary rather than a historical setting, issues from the clash between law and crime, or more broadly, between the ordered society of the civilized plantation South and the anarchistic criminal elements flourishing on the frontier. The fact that the conflict in each volume is resolved by forces representing the civilized South communicates Simms's view, expressed in letters and speeches as well as in fiction, that the institutions of this region must serve as models for those of its newer neighbor.

Simms developed the typical format for his long fiction in the 1830s, at the height of the romance's popularity in America, and had literary conditions continued as he anticipated, he would have had little need to modify his procedures. The 1840s, however, worked some changes in the market for novels that had lasting consequences for his career. The panic of 1837, which resulted in a badly depressed financial climate for long fiction, the development of new printing methods that made cheaply bound books economically profitable, and the habit, widespread before international copyright protection, of pirating the works of English authors in mammoth weekly newspapers all made Simms's relatively costly two-volume novels unfeasible. Therefore, in the decade that should have seen the maturation of his talent and the solidifying of his literary reputation, he was forced away from his central field into varied and occasionally trivial projects that gave his career a decidedly miscellaneous turn. The works he produced in the 1840s included more poetry, like *Lays of the Palmetto* (1848) and *Sabbath Lyrics* (1849); a history (1840) and a geography (1843) of South Carolina; an edition of the Shakespeare apocrypha (1848); and a collection of essays in two volumes, *Views and Reviews in American Literature, History and Fiction* (1845), which constitutes perhaps his most significant work in criticism. A document in the Young America–Knickerbocker battles, it argues vigorously for a native literature based on American history and landscape and comments sweepingly on Cortez, Cooper, Mrs. Trollope, Benedict Arnold, and the Southern frontier.

Probably Simms's most important literary productions of this busy decade are his tales and novelettes, published first in magazines or in inexpensive paper covers rather than in hardback form. Since the 1820s, various Southern periodicals had furnished him convenient outlets for his stories, and he had already built up a substantial body of short fiction, collected in three volumes during the 1830s—*The Book of My Lady* (1833), *Martin Faber, the Story of a Criminal; and Other Tales* (1837), and *Carl Werner* (1838)—before he turned to the Indian and backwoods subjects of *The Wigwam and the Cabin* (1845), in some ways a coda to his border romances. After this collection, Simms's only significant assemblages of short stories were *Southward Ho!* (1854), which reprints a number of early pieces awkwardly spliced to a framing narrative, and *The Lily and the Totem* (1850), a series of lightly fictionalized historical narratives about the Huguenots in Florida.

Simms's short fiction, in general, is more diverse in subject and techniques than are his novels, and more in debt to European, especially German, sources. In short fiction he felt fairly free to experiment with satire, fantasy, whimsy, fairy lore, the dream vision, the supernatural, and what he was fond of terming "diablerie." "Logoochie," "The Cherokee Embassage," and "The Arm-Chair of Tustenuggee" are comic treatments of Indian life, while "Oakatibbe" is a tragic one; "Caloya" is a fairly straightforward (and for Simms's age shocking) portrayal of Indian-and-Negro sexual relationships; "The Lazy Crow" is a humorous story of Negro superstitions; "Carl Werner," "Conrade Weickhoff," and "Grayling" are fairly creditable ghost stories; and "Ponce de Leon," perhaps Simms's best tale, is a deftly humorous rendition of Spanish legend in which the aged explorer, rejuvenated by the magic fountain, spurns the superannuated coquette who had once spurned him.

Meanwhile, Simms's enforced occupation, in those "begging times for authordom," of what he called the "editorial *fauteuil*" of the *Magnolia*, the *Southern and Western*, and the *Southern Quarterly Review* necessarily exposed him to recent developments in British and American writing, which he diligently and sometimes lengthily reviewed. As a result of that exposure, he turned his gaze to a subject that had long attracted him, Southern or Southwestern humor—hitting its stride in the 1840s with works like William Elliott's *Carolina Sports*, Hooper's *Adventures of Simon Suggs*, and Thompson's *Major Jones's Courtship*—and also to what he had once disparagingly called "social life" fiction or the novel of manners. Both of these modes were to form important influences on his mature writing; for both he found abundant material in antebellum Southern culture; and through both, contemporary varieties of realism made their way into his fiction.

Low-country society, particularly Charleston, with its elegant, caste-conscious aristocracy gave Simms plenty of targets for satire. Typically enough, biographical as well as cultural influences lay behind his mature excursions into the novel of manners. Long at odds with Charleston for its neglect of letters and its thirst for the "fashionable and foolish," in a series of works published near midcentury, notably *Charleston, and Her Satirists* (1848) and *Father Abbot* (1849), he lampoons the city's tendency to "drowse in the lap of vanity." Expanding on this vision, in novels and novelettes of the 1850s he leavens his customary romance format with saucy portraits of fashionable follies. *The Golden Christmas*, his first full-scale employment of the manners method, pokes gentle fun at stately Madam Girardin, swollen with ancestral pride as she strolls down Charleston's King Street, greeting only those with impeccable family lineage; *Katharine Walton* pits callous, frivolous loyalist socialites against upright, sober patriot leaders; *Eutaw* (1856) shows the abortive love of Nelly Floyd, a quintessential romance character, for wealthy Sherrod Nelson, a loyalist officer who is tainted by the vices of fashionable life; and *The Cassique of Kiawah*, perhaps Simms's best novel, locates the roots of contemporary Charleston's decline in the vanities of the seventeenth-century city. In these works, Simms's mockery of patrician pretensions connects him to a persistent strain in Southern letters, from the urbane satires of William Byrd to the trenchant social comedies of Ellen Glasgow, and shows the congeniality of the tidewater South for the novel of manners.

If the foibles of low-country aristocrats encouraged Simms to infuse "social life" realism into his romances, rural Carolina and the Gulf and mountain South laid the groundwork for his semihumorous portraits of plainer people. In the border romances, with their pictures of strolling actors and bragging backwoodsmen, he had already flirted with the kind of Southern humor that centers on humble life; by the 1850s, with this humor firmly established in the national literary marketplace, he was ready to employ it in earnest. For *As Good as a Comedy* (1852), a novelette that appeared in the Library of Humorous American Works, he fashioned a framing narrative that shows nine travelers packed snugly into a stagecoach—in standard fashion contrasting the stilted language of the narrator with the rich dialect of the central character, "a broth of a boy in the shape of a huge Tennessean" who supplies the material for the central tale. It is a yarn of comic doings in middle Georgia, filled with activities made popular by Augustus Baldwin Longstreet and William Tappan Thompson—a horse race, a gander pulling, a country circus, and numerous bouts of drinking.

More obviously than *As Good*, the short novel *Paddy McGann*, serialized in 1863, signals Simms's move into the humorists' camp. It too has a framing story, in which gentlemanly planters speaking typically genteel-planter language consort with the Irish backwoodsman of the title, who boasts that he was "nursed on whiskey, weaned on whiskey, and vaccinated with whiskey." Paddy's fondness for the bottle makes him equally fond of the tall tale, and he tells his skeptical listeners increasingly extravagant yarns of an enchanted gun, a witch doctor who tries to remove the spell, haunted woods, deer that cannot be killed, and a semicomic demon that lives in a stump and intermittently menaces Paddy.

From *Paddy McGann* it is but a short step to Simms's masterworks of backwoods humor, "How Sharp Snaffles Got His Capital and His Wife" and "Bald-Head Bill Bauldy," two long tall tales that record his experiences in the 1840s with professional Appalachian mountain hunters and their Saturday night "Lying Camp," where he heard the stories in oral form. "Sharp Snaffles" (1870) blends the quiet details of the backwoods courtship yarn with the freewheeling fantasy of the hunt, while "Bill Bauldy" (unpublished until 1974), a wild story of undersea adventures among alligators, combines the ancient literary form of the dream vision with a parodic version of the Indian captivity narrative. Even *Voltmeier* (serialized 1869), a long and serious mountain romance whose central plot recalls the plots of the border novels, uses backwoods humor in its picture of the villain Richard Gorham, "jest as cunning a Yankee sarpent as ever skinned his shadow to git something for the Sunday market." So the late 1860s find Simms, somewhat belatedly, working a vein that the humorists had mined successfully nearly twenty years before. Had he seen fit to open it sooner, we might rank him today alongside Longstreet, Harris, and Hooper for his robust comic talent.

Like other antebellum authors, Simms energetically involved himself in politics; and as the Civil War approached, his activities as a spokesman for slavery and secession intensified. His lecture tour of the North during 1856 was ruined by his spirited defense of South Carolina's role in the Revolution against Northern criticism springing from the contemporary sectional conflict, and his essay in *The Pro-Slavery Argument* (1852) launches an equally spirited defense of the "peculiar institution." The war itself, the harbinger of a new economic and literary climate, virtually closed his career. His letters of the 1860s paint a pathetic picture of the aging author struggling to provide for his family and rebuild his reputation by peddling old tales and fabricating new ones. Once the most promising of Southern writers, in the last years of his life, enfeebled by incessant drains on his energy and probably suffering from cancer, he ground out several works, among them *Joscelyn* (1867) and *The Cub of the Panther* (1869), which were serialized in short-lived Southern periodicals. He died on June 11, 1870, in Charleston.

From Henry James and William Dean Howells onward, readers who crave more subtle kinds of realism than Simms produced have poked fun at his fiction without stopping to consider the demands of the romance tradition in which he worked and his particular contributions to it. However outmoded his procedure may seem to modern eyes, his romance framework, with its emphasis on the time perspective, is a fundamental part of his total literary statement. Through it he continues the symbolism intrinsic to romance while asserting what he describes in *Views and Reviews* as the direction, the purpose, and the moral tendency of history. In his fiction, essays, orations, and historical studies about the Revolutionary War, as C. Hugh Holman demonstrates, he expands and makes vivid our sense of that conflict while rebuking Northern readers eager to play down the South's role in it; he also creates the memorable figure of Captain Porgy and some equally memorable grotesques such as Ned or "Goggle" Blonay and the "mean-sperrited" Blodgits, who are part of a persistent strain in Southern writing. In his border romances, he sketches realistic pictures of the flashiness and chicanery of the flush times, while adding perceptibly to our stock of humorous backwoods types. In his mountain fiction, as Miriam Shillingsburg and Charles S. Watson show, he anticipates the local colorists of a later generation in the imaginative use he makes of Appalachian subjects. And in his poetry, as James E. Kibler claims, he warrants comparison with such established American romantic writers as William Cullen Bryant, his longtime mentor and friend.

There remains the perennial problem of the flaws in his writing, perhaps particularly in his fiction—its careless construction, digressiveness, and prolixity. For these elements the harried author is responsible; yet, found also in Scott and Cooper, they are flaws of the popular fiction, and especially historical fiction, of his era. Keenly sensitive to the reception of his writing, throughout his life Simms complained that South Carolina neglected it, and him. Exaggerated though his claim may be, the state, and the South, however well they served him in certain ways, also hindered the full development of his artistic abilities. Little concerned with letters and lacking major publishing centers, the South set no great value on the literary vocation; hence it fostered no climate in which literary talent could prosper and afforded Simms no models of successful writers whose example might have stimulated and challenged him. So when he claimed, in the epitaph composed (though not used) for his tombstone, that despite unceasing labors he had left all his better works undone, he had, as he probably realized, not only his own deficiencies to blame. In a very real sense, he was also a victim of what Poe once called the "literary supineness" of the South.

RAYBURN S. MOORE

Antebellum Poetry

<hr>

As Albert Pike indicated in *Prose Sketches and Poems* in 1834, the situation of poetry in the antebellum South was not very propitious.

> Alas! to him,
> Whose eye and heart must soon or late grow dim,
> Toiling with poverty, or evils worse,
> This gift of poetry is but a curse,
> Unfitting it amid the world to brood
> And toil and jostle for a livelihood.
> The feverish passion of the soul hath been
> My bane.

In 1830 few books of poems by Southerners had been published or favorably noticed, and Pike, a native of Massachusetts who had gone to Arkansas, was well aware of this fact. Edward Coote Pinkney had published *Rodolph* (1823) and *Poems* (1825), but as Poe observed later, Pinkney's reputation as a poet suffered because he was a Southerner. Poe himself had published in 1827 and 1829 two volumes that had barely been noticed, and a third, *Poems* (1831), containing such lyrics as "To Helen," "Lenore," and others, was reviewed by only a few Northern periodicals. Nor had William Gilmore Simms's poetry received any better reception in the South. He had published five volumes by 1832 to a generally lukewarm local response. Indeed, readers frequently responded more favorably to such fugitive poems as Francis Scott Key's "The Star-Spangled Banner" (1814), Richard Henry Wilde's "The Lament of the Captive" (1815?), and, later, Poe's "The Raven" (1845) and Theodore O'Hara's "The Bivouac of the Dead" (1848).

The plight of Southern poetry of this period is not much different from that of Northern poetry. Philip Freneau had been publishing poems since before the American Revolution, but whatever audience he had possessed disappeared long before his last collection appeared in

1815. William Cullen Bryant's first book of poems appeared in 1821 and was well received, but realizing the limitations of a career as poet, he took an editorial position with the New York *Evening Post* in 1825, where he remained until his death in 1878. Even as popular as Henry Wadsworth Longfellow's poetry eventually became, he did not feel free to leave teaching until 1854 after the financial success of *Evangeline* (1847) and the prospective popularity of *Hiawatha* (1855).

The situation, then, could hardly deteriorate much in the ensuing three decades before the Civil War. What happened was that more poems and poets appeared, not necessarily better ones. Clearly, few Southern poets made their livings by writing poetry during this period. Pike himself taught, edited newspapers, and became an attorney; Pinkney served with the United States Navy and subsequently devoted himself to journalism and the law; Wilde early took to the law and politics; and O'Hara tried teaching, journalism, and military service. Only Simms, Poe, Thomas Holley Chivers, and George Moses Horton of this generation of Southern litterateurs concentrated on writing, and they assuredly discovered that poetry would not pay. Aside from occasional poetic composition in the 1840s, Poe turned chiefly to fiction, editing, and criticism after 1831, and Simms, though he continued to write poems throughout his career, focused after 1833 on fiction, editing, history, and other genres for his literary livelihood. Chivers and Horton were special cases. Chivers had independent means and could afford to pay for the publication of his own books. Horton (1797–1883), though he migrated to Philadelphia after the Civil War, spent most of his adult life as a sort of living legend, providing himself with subsistence from poetry (often acrostics) that he sold to students at the University of North Carolina in Chapel Hill. He was a lyricist of perhaps astonishing range and virtuosity, producing *Hope of Liberty* (1829), *Poetical Works of George M. Horton* (1845), *The Colored Bard of North Carolina* (1845), and *Naked Genius* (1865).

To scan the achievement of Southern poets during 1830 to 1860, then, is to consider primarily the accomplishments of Thomas Holley Chivers, Alexander Beaufort Meek, Philip Pendleton Cooke, and James Mathewes Legaré. Others like John R. Thompson, Henry Timrod, and Paul Hamilton Hayne who began publishing before the Civil War made their chief contributions during the war and thereafter. The major figures, Simms and Poe, are discussed elsewhere. A special class of Southern antebellum poets cannot be named. They were the anonymous slaves who wrought out of their humble lives and their Christian faith the moving texts of the Negro spirituals.

Assuredly, the work of William J. Grayson, Daniel Alexander Payne,

Mirabeau B. Lamar, Albert Pike, and Theodore O'Hara should also be mentioned. Grayson (1788–1863), South Carolina lawyer, journalist, politician, and occasional poet, published in *The Hireling and The Slave* (1856) a strong attack on the industrial system and a defense of slavery—not "the best system of labor, but . . . best for the Negro and this country." Horton (1797?–1883?), on the other hand, showed what a Negro poet could do by selling poems to students at the University of North Carolina and eventually publishing three volumes: *The Hope of Liberty* (1829), *Poetical Works* (1845), and *Naked Genius* (1865). Payne (1811–1893), a free Charlestonian by birth who went north in 1835, where he became a Methodist bishop and the most eminent Negro clergyman of his time, wrote careful lyrics in the manner of Alexander Pope. His "The Mournful Lute or The Preceptor's Farewell" lamented his departure from South Carolina. His *Pleasures and Other Miscellaneous Poems* appeared in Baltimore in 1850.

A Georgian turned Texan, Lamar (1798–1859) was an important military and political figure in the Southwest (he succeeded Sam Houston as president of Texas) who counted among his literary friends Wilde and Meek and whose only contemporaneous collection, *Verse Memorials* (1857), contains many "spontaneous effusions" composed for ladies' albums, a tradition to which Wilde, Pinkney, Poe, and other Southern poets frequently contributed. A more serious poet was Pike, a New Englander who spent much of his life editing newspapers and practicing law in Little Rock, New Orleans, Memphis, and, later, Washington, D.C. His best work, "Hymns to the Gods," appeared in part in *Blackwood's* in June, 1839, and later in full in *Nugae* (1854), a collection of pieces privately printed in Philadelphia for family and friends. A later poem, "To Isadore" (1843, subsequently "The Widowed Heart"), may have influenced "The Raven." The reputation of O'Hara, on the other hand, is based upon one poem, "The Bivouac of the Dead" (1848), surely one of the best-known elegies in American literature. Just as surely, *Les Cenelles* (1845) may be the most curious of all the volumes of antebellum Southern verse. It is America's first anthology of Negro poetry. The contributors to it were all near-white free New Orleanians: Armand Lanusse (1812–1867), Victor Sejour (1817–1874), Nelson Debrosses (n.d.), and Nicol Riquet (n.d.). They wrote only in French.

Altogether the work of these minor bards is derivative and characteristically Southern in the general sense that much of the verse is written for the ear, indeed is closely related to song in its stress on verbal melody and harmony. Dryden and Pope may be heard in Grayson's work as well as Payne's, the Cavalier poets in Lamar's, and Keats, Shelley, and Byron in Pike's and, except for Keats, in Horton's. The work of these poets may also suggest a certain Southernness in that it is the contribution of professional men—lawyers, soldiers, teachers, journalists—who seldom devoted themselves to poetry and were rarely paid for their efforts. Horton, admittedly, is an exception in that he did seek to sell his verse for pay and that some of his work was written, like Grayson's, in behalf of a political cause, though hardly the same one.

More consequential writers—Chivers, Meek, Cooke, and Legaré—contributed to the bulk of poetry published during the period if not always to the quality. Chivers, a native of Washington County, Georgia, who took a degree in medicine at Transylvania University but practiced rarely, devoted himself to poetry and literature and published, mostly at his own expense, eleven volumes of verse and drama, beginning with *The Path of Sorrow* (1832) and continuing with, among others, *Conrad and Eudora* (1834), *Nacoochee* (1837), *The Lost Pleiad, and Other Poems* (1845), *Eonchs of Ruby* (1851), *Virginalia* (1853), *Memoralia* (1853), and ending with *The Sons of Usna* (1858). His poems, generally, were not written "for the Public," as he admitted in 1856, but "as a felicitous outpouring of that oversoul of passion, which if suffered to remain dammed up, would effectually damn me to utter distraction." Nor were the critics favorable to such an "outpouring" as Chivers' poems display. Even such friendly critics as Simms and Poe warned him of certain excesses. Simms urged him in 1852 to give up Poe "as a model and as a guide," and Poe had pointed out in 1845 that Chivers was "writing *not* to mankind, but solely to himself."

Chivers' critical notions and his practice are difficult to compress and summarize. His approach, contrary to that of other Southern poets with the possible occasional exception of Poe, was transcendental in nature. In a letter to Poe in 1840, he asked:

What is Revelation but Transcendentalism? It is the effect of inspiration. What then is inspiration, if it is not a power given to the soul to recognize the beautiful of a truth, which is transcendent in its nature, when compared with other truths? We may convey the idea of a heavenly truth by an earthly one—that is, we may make an earthly truth the representative of a truth beyond expression. . . . This shows that language has a higher office than to manifest the relations which subsist between us and the external world—although our knowledge comes therefrom. We may express the existence of a truth which is beyond expression.

Poetry, he maintained in the preface to *Nacoochee* (1837), "is the power given by God to man of manifesting . . . the wise relations that subsist between him and God." It is the "soul of [man's] nature, whereby, from communing with the beauties of this earth, he is capable of giving birth to other beings brighter than himself." Later, in *Memoralia* (1853), he added that poetry "consists in a perfect unition of . . . Passion and Art—a pure body united to a pure soul," and characterized poets as "the *Revelators of the Divine Idea through the Beautiful*."

Chivers' poetry reflects these ideas and others in a melange of metrical pattern and verbal melody. His verse frequently but by no means always sounds like Poe's, for he has his own ideas and diction and presumably influenced Poe almost as much as Poe influenced him.* He made much of "the originality of Art" and wrote Simms in 1852 that he did not, "like other Americans, steal the old English forms and send [his] imitations forth . . . as *something* achieved." The often anthologized "Apollo" (1853) illustrates something of Chivers' originality in form and language and offers a brief example of his transcendental thought, nebulous at times though it may be. Other frequently quoted lyrics—"Isadore" (1841), "Rosalie Lee" (1853), and "To Allegra Florence in Heaven" (1842)—are printed to show, as in the first two pieces, Chivers' influence on or debt to Poe and to demonstrate in the latter the unevenness of his verse and the lack of critical insight. More attention needs to be given to such verse as "Railroad Song" (1851), "Corn Song" (1853), and to other efforts that reveal his interest in Negro and Indian topics, language, rhythm, and melody. Some efforts have been made to encourage such understanding by Parks, Hubbell, and, lately, by Charles Lombard (1979), but much yet remains to be done.

Despite his interest in Southern experience, diction, and music, and the relationship of his verse to Poe's, Chivers remains something of an anomaly. He never quite managed to control his experiments or to discipline his wayward talents or to mold an aesthetic that would free and serve the poetic spirit within him. C. Hugh Holman's conclusion in 1970 is still close to the mark: Chivers "did with limited success what Poe did with genius."

Unlike Chivers, Alexander Beaufort Meek (1814–1865) did not devote himself fully to literature. A native of South Carolina who grew up in Alabama and attended the University of Georgia and the University of Alabama, Meek subsequently practiced law, became a probate judge,

---

* The question of this influence is too complex to be resolved here; indeed, it has not yet been satisfactorily resolved in the full-scale treatments devoted to it. Nevertheless, for discussion, see S. Foster Damon, *Thomas Holley Chivers: Friend of Poe* (New York, 1930); Charles H. Watts II, *Thomas Holley Chivers: His Literary Career and His Poetry* (Athens, Ga., 1956); Edd Winfield Parks (ed.), *Southern Poets* (New York, 1936), xciv–cii; Richard Beale Davis (ed.), Introduction to *Chivers' Life of Poe* (1952); Jay B. Hubbell, *The South in American Literature, 1607–1900* (Durham, N.C., 1954), 550–59; and Charles M. Lombard, *Thomas Holley Chivers* (Boston, 1979).

served as assistant secretary of the treasury in Washington, edited a newspaper in Mobile and a literary magazine in Tuscaloosa, spoke at various functions, and wrote history and poetry. Is it any wonder, then, that several of Meek's Southern contemporaries complained that he "gave too much to society; too much to partisan politics; too much to inferior considerations." At the same time, Meek knew very well that few cultured Southerners took literature seriously as a means of life or livelihood and frequently regarded, as he put it, "poetry and nonsense . . . as convertible terms." Still, he expressed his literary views forthrightly in the essays "Southern Literature" (1839) and "Americanism in Literature" (1844), and in the preface to his *Songs and Poems of the South* (1857) where he maintained that the "poetry of a country should be a faithful expression of its physical and moral characteristics," that its "imagery should be drawn from the indigenous objects of the region," and that its "sentiments" should "naturally arise" from "its climate, its institutions, habits of life, and social condition." He produced two books of poetry upon these principles: the aforementioned *Songs and Poems of the South*, the only collection of his verse—but a popular one—that ran through four editions in 1857, and *The Red Eagle* (1855), a long narrative poem on the Indian and the early history of the Southwest.

Meek is remembered now for a few pieces of occasional verse—"The Mocking-Bird," "The Death of Richard Henry Wilde," and "The Fated City"—and a few other lyrics in *Songs and Poems*—"The Stone Mountain," "The Capitol by Moonlight," and elegies on Clay, Webster, and Jackson. In addition, *The Red Eagle*, subtitled *A Poem of the South*, is not only a narrative of some power but also an eloquent account of the Creek War of 1813, of William Weatherford (Red Eagle) and his exploits, and of Andrew Jackson that, according to Meek, adheres "strictly to historical truth, even in details" and whose dedication to Simms not only reinforces its historical context but also invokes Simms's interest in the border South. As a whole, Meek's poetic achievement hardly challenges that of Chivers, erratic as that was, or that of Cooke or Legaré for that matter, but in *Red Eagle* Meek contributed something that few other nineteenth-century Southern poets (Simms and Hayne are possible exceptions) accomplished—the completion of a reasonably successful long narrative poem.

Generally speaking, Chivers and Meek finished their careers—each was over fifty when he died and had had a fair opportunity to experiment with topics and techniques. That is not the case, however, with Cooke and Legaré, each of whom in his own way may be characterized as an "inheritor of unfulfilled renown." It is true that neither writer devoted himself to literature, as Chivers had, but neither, on the other hand, lived to reach thirty-six.

Cooke (1816–1850), the elder brother of John Esten Cooke and a cousin of John Pendleton Kennedy, was a member of a distinguished Virginia family and a graduate of Princeton who studied law with his father, John Rogers Cooke, and practiced desultorily. He also farmed unsuccessfully, hunted avidly, studied seriously Chaucer, Spenser, and the romantic poets, and contributed his early verse to *Knickerbocker Magazine* and the *Southern Literary Messenger*. He was among the first to recognize Poe's genius, and Poe returned the compliment, selecting "Florence Vane" for publication in *Burton's Gentleman's Magazine* in March, 1840, and noting in 1841 that Cooke had written "some of the finest poetry of which America can boast." "Florence Vane," despite its subsequent collection in *Froissart's Ballads*, became one of the most widely reprinted fugitive lyrics by a Southerner in the nineteenth century and, consequently, Cooke's best-known poem. Reportedly written to describe his youthful affection for and rejection by his cousin Mary Evelina Hunter Dandridge, "Florence Vane," with its sentimentality, its melancholy, its music, and its echo of Catullus, may serve as a model for Southern love poetry of the period. Its last stanza anticipates Housman's "With Rue My Heart is Laden" in diction and form if not in idea:

> The lilies of the valley
> By young graves weep,
> The pansies love to dally
> Where maidens sleep;
> May their bloom, in beauty vieing,
> Never wane
> Where thine earthly part is lying,
> Florence Vane!

Froissart's Ballads (1847), however, is Cooke's most important contribution to Southern poetry, for in this volume he includes narrative poems (only three of which are based upon Froissart) that are, according to Cooke, actually modeled upon John G. Lockhart's *Ancient Spanish Ballads* (1823) and collects a number of lyrics denominated "Miscellaneous," including, among others, "Florence Vane"; "Life in the Autumn Woods" (1843), Cooke's best nature poem; and "The Mountains" (1845), a piece praised by Poe. The narratives are ballads, as Cooke admitted, only "by courtesy of the most liberal interpretation of the word." But at least two—"Geoffrey Tetenoire" and "The Master of Bolton"—are of his own invention, and display skill in the art of storytelling (though traces of Scott and Macaulay may be noted). These narratives remind one that Cooke would soon compose prose sketches and tales for the *Messenger*, at least one of which, "The Chevalier Merlin" (1849–1850), deals with similar materials, uses parallel techniques, and is, as Poe observes, "Less a novel than a poem." Disappointed by the financial failure of *Froissart's Ballads*, Cooke, as Poe had earlier, turned to prose fiction in 1848, but before he could firmly establish himself with the public as an author of romances, he died as a result of a hunting accident in January, 1850, at the age of thirty-three, his "career too soon ended," as John D. Allen concluded in 1942. "If he had lived," Hubbell observed twelve years later, "he would have written better stories and poems."

Several points made about Cooke apply as well to James Mathewes Legaré (1823–1859), also a member of a distinguished family, a student of the law, and a poet who turned to fiction when his poems failed to pay. Legaré was a third cousin, once removed, of Hugh Swinton Legaré (1797–1843), one of the editors of the *Southern Review* (because of his literary position dubbed by some the Dr. Johnson of Charleston) and a leading legal mind and public servant who eventually became attorney general of the United States (1841–1843). Young Legaré attended the College of Charleston and St. Mary's College in Baltimore and studied law with James Louis Petigru, another important Carolina lawyer as well as a staunch Unionist and close friend of H. S. Legaré. Instead of devoting himself to the practice of law, Legaré started publishing poems in 1843 in the *Rambler*, the *Orion*, the *Southern and Western Monthly Magazine and Review* (Simms' magazine), the *Literary World*, the *Southern Literary Gazette*, and the *Southern Literary Messenger*. By 1845 he had composed enough poems for a book, but Carey and Hart, publishers in Philadelphia, rejected the manuscript of *Orta-Undis, and Other Poems* which was not published until May, 1848, after Legaré had paid William Ticknor and Company in Boston for an edition of five hundred copies. Legaré was not satisfied with the collection, as he indicated to Longfellow in April, 1850 (among other things, he was unhappy with the Latin title), and planned a second volume, but was never able to find a publisher.

The reviewers liked the book better than the poet did, but there was little public response. Legaré turned to fiction, painting, and invention, eventually discovering a fiber he called "Plastic-Cotton" from which he formed various pieces of furniture. The author of "On the Death of a Kinsman" (1843), "Flowers in Ashes" (1847), "Tallulah" (1848), "Haw-Blossoms" (1848), "Last Gift" (1848), "To Jasmine in December" (1848), and "Thanatokallos" (1849) deserves better, and more recent critics have sought to give Legaré his due as a poet. Beginning with Ludwig Lewisohn in 1903, continuing with Parks in 1930, Hubbell in 1954, Holman in 1970, and culminating with Curtis Carroll Davis in 1971 (Davis' first article had appeared in 1944), Legaré has begun to come into his own. If Davis is a bit excessive in his conclusion that at his best Legaré is "appreciably better than Paul Hamilton Hayne and certainly the equal of Henry Timrod and Edward C. Pinkney," then Hubbell is closer to the mark with his observation that Legaré's poems "reveal a more careful and competent workmanship than those of all but three or four of his Southern contemporaries," and Holman is on the mark with his characterization of Legaré as "one of the authentic lyric voices of the antebellum South."

As a whole, the poetry of 1830 to 1860 seldom breaks the mold of British tradition, but the Southern love of sound, of eloquence, of music, of the inexhaustible voice talking, reading, orating, chanting, singing, may be heard from Wilde to Legaré and beyond, and the melodies and harmonies of these sometime poets fix themselves in the memories of readers and hearers until "Florence Vane," "To Allegra Florence," and "The Bivouac of the Dead," as well as "The Lament of the Captive," "A Health," "To Helen," "The Raven," or "Annabel Lee," reverberate not so much in the mind as in the ear. Poetry of this period, then, is not about ideas, meter-making arguments as Emerson maintains, but about song, or as Poe expresses it, "Music, the most entrancing of the Poetic moods."

ROBERT D. JACOBS

Edgar Allan Poe

Edgar Poe (1809–1849) has had the bizarre fate of being one of the most famous nineteenth-century American writers, but the one least admired by critics writing in English. On the popular level he has for generations been taken as the prototypical poet (a role he relished), but during the twentieth century his short fiction has received more critical attention than his poems. In his own time he was notorious for his slashing literary critiques, but since his criticism was chiefly in the ephemeral mode of book reviews, modern attention has been focused on a few theoretical statements he made in two key reviews (of Longfellow's *Ballads* and Hawthorne's *Twice-Told Tales*) and three essays ("The Philosophy of Composition," "The Rationale of Verse," and "The Poetic Principle"). Consequently he has been viewed as a rhetorician who set such strict methodological limits for the composition of fiction and poetry that he diminished both genres into formulaic exercises. Nevertheless Poe played an important historical role as a literary critic, for he helped free American literature from the burdens of overt didacticism and a narrowly conceived nationalism.

From his very birth Poe was influenced by the international. His mother, Elizabeth Arnold Poe, was the daughter of a British actress transplanted to the United States and was a stage performer herself from the age of nine. His father, David Poe, Jr., of Baltimore, defied his family in order to go on the stage. Since the nativist tradition in the American theater scarcely existed at the time, the repertoire of Poe's parents was made up of foreign plays, and for the first three years of his life Edgar Poe, living in close quarters with his parents, absorbed sights and sounds that if not always foreign were certainly not native American.

The flavor of the international still blended with Poe's experience when, after his mother's death on December 8, 1811, in Richmond, Virginia, he was taken into the home of John Allan, a young Richmond businessman; Allan was a Scot who did not arrive in the United States until he was fifteen and whose relatives, with whom he maintained close ties, were mostly in Scotland. Poe's foster mother, Frances Valentine Allan, was his respectable Virginia connection, and probably Poe would have been more firmly shaped by the mold of Virginia had not the Allans in 1815 taken him to England, where for five years Allan would attempt to establish a London branch of his mercantile firm, Ellis and Allan. During the impressionable years between six and eleven Edgar Poe was an English schoolboy, and he was to remember his experiences so well that nearly twenty years later he incorporated the scene and regimen of the Manor House School and the name of the headmaster, the Reverend John Bransby, in his tale "William Wilson."

When the Allans returned to Virginia in 1820 and Poe was sent to private schools in Richmond, his cultural dislocation was apparent. An orphan, a child of the theater dependent on the charity of the Allans, Edgar Poe was just a bit foreign and not quite respectable; his knowledge that his mother's profession was considered morally suspect haunted Poe for the rest of his life, and it was especially disquieting for an insecure adolescent. Poe was by no means an outcast, but he lacked the easy social identity of the born-and-bred Virginians who were his school-mates. He rarely invited his friends to his home, where he was increasingly involved in temperamental clashes with John Allan. Poe's foster father thought him sullen and ungrateful, while Poe resisted efforts to force him into the configuration of a business apprentice. He even wrote a poem in 1825 ("O, Tempora! O, Mores!") about a Richmond clerk, a "frisky counter-hopper," as if to show his contempt not only for the man but also for trade in general. Some fifteen years later Poe would satirize the businessman as a type in a burlesque called "Peter Pendulum."

When Allan sent Poe to the new University of Virginia in 1826, he allowed the seventeen-year-old youth barely enough money to cover initial expenses. This parsimony was probably a disciplinary measure, but Poe was a Virginian in pride if in little else (his early poems parade his pride as well as his feeling of difference). He would have the appearance and life-style of a gentleman in spite of John Allan; he bought expensive clothes on credit and ran up large gambling debts. At the end of the term Allan refused to pay the debts and brought Poe home in disgrace.

In Richmond in early 1827 the conflict between Allan's cultural imperatives—the Scots in Richmond were business-oriented—and Poe's personal inclinations intensified. Allan and Poe quarreled frequently, and Poe kept to his room much of the time and wrote verses, an activity considered in Virginia to be a graceful accomplishment but not a serious pursuit for a nearly grown man. Edgar Poe was serious about his poems, however. When after a final bitter quarrel with Allan in March, 1827,

Poe left Richmond for Boston, he carried with him a thin sheaf of verses that he managed to have published under the title *Tamerlane and Other Poems*. On the paper cover of the little book was the attribution "By a Bostonian," which may have been an oblique kind of homeseeking. After all, he had been born in Boston, though his parents had left that city while he was still an infant. Shamed in Richmond, Poe would entreat the city of his birth, placing before its urban populace the treasures of his heart and mind that Richmond, in the person of John Allan, had rejected. Surely Boston, the intellectual center of the nation, would be interested in a talented new poet. Unfortunately almost no one noticed Poe's little book.

Had the Bostonians read Poe's verses they would have discovered a spirit of alienation expressing itself in conventional romantic postures. The young poet had learned from Byron to raise personal feelings to significance by attributing them to magnified characters. Poe's own choice of noble surrogate was Tamerlane, a fourteenth-century Mongol conqueror; and the theme of his title poem, stated in prefatory remarks, was the "folly of even *risking* the best feelings of the heart at the shrine of Ambition." Thus Poe, presenting himself as an archromantic, refuted Allan's monitory lectures and the conventional wisdom of the time. The shorter poems of the book develop as persona the visionary child beloved by the romantics, the sensitive loner who preferred the glory of his imagination to the squalor of mundane reality. Having always felt his difference, Poe was now parading it.

With this publication at the age of eighteen Poe began his career as a writer, but it would be several years before he could pursue it professionally. Meanwhile, masking his identity under the transparent pseudonym Edgar A. Perry, he joined the United States Army on May 26, 1827. For nearly two years, spent mostly at Fort Moultrie in the harbor of Charleston, South Carolina, Private Perry performed competently the duties of clerk in H Company of the 1st Artillery; but the army was only an interlude for Edgar Poe. With a second book of poems in manuscript he was ready to leave the service by December, 1828, and solicited his foster father's help in obtaining a discharge. (Allan was considered Poe's legal guardian.) At Allan's request, which was based on Poe's promise to attend the United States Military Academy, Edgar Perry, having been promoted to sergeant major, was discharged from the army on April 15, 1829. Soon he surfaced in Baltimore, looking for a publisher and finding one. Hatch and Dunning brought out *Al Aaraaf, Tamerlane, and Minor Poems* in December, 1829. There was a distinct maturation in the twenty-one-year-old poet: his best work is no longer in the mode of the Byronic confessional, and he engages quasi-philosophical themes—the withering of the imagination under the assault of scientific truth seeking and the celebration of beauty as a divine attribute. Already Poe was developing his aesthetic credo.

Poe's brief stay at West Point—June, 1830, to February, 1831—was apparently devoted to the writing of poems. When he had a third manuscript ready for book publication, he deliberately invited court-martial, since he knew that Allan as his guardian would never consent to his resignation from the cadet corps. Court-martialed and found guilty of neglect of duty, Poe left West Point for New York City on February 19, 1831. His manuscript would be published in April by Elam Bliss as *Poems by Edgar A. Poe*, second edition. By listing the work as the second edition he suppressed his first book, *Tamerlane and Other Poems*. Some of Poe's best poems were in the 1831 edition, including "To Helen," "Israfel," and "The City in the Sea." But then as now poets could not live by their art and Poe had to support himself.

Soon Poe left New York for Baltimore, where he was to find a home with his paternal aunt, Mrs. Maria Clemm, and her young daughter, Virginia, whom later he was to marry. It was in Baltimore during the early 1830s that Poe out of necessity discovered the literary mode at which he would be most successful. He began writing short fiction, which could find a market in magazines, newspapers, and gift books; at first he imitated (or burlesqued) the tales he had read in popular magazines such as *Blackwood's Edinburgh Monthly*, but soon he was to find his own voice. His tale "MS Found in a Bottle" won the first prize of fifty dollars in a contest staged by the *Baltimore Saturday Visiter*. More important, the contest gained him the attention of John Pendleton Kennedy, one of the judges. Kennedy put the young author in touch with T. W. White, a printer in Richmond, Virginia, who in 1834 began publishing the *Southern Literary Messenger* with the avowed purpose of awakening the South from its intellectual lethargy.

It was with the *Messenger* that Poe began his professional career. For the first time he was able to publish his own tales and poems with some freedom. But what gained him almost instant notoriety after he became assistant editor of the journal was his book reviews, a few of which were done in the spirit of the British quarterlies that used broad sarcasm and even ridicule against aspiring authors. Americans were not used to such tactics in their own magazines. A beginning American literature, struggling to establish itself in competition with the mature literature of England, was supposed to be encouraged by American critics, not tomahawked (as the current phrase had it) by savage reviewers. T. W. White was alarmed by Poe's slashing reviews, particularly by his review of *Norman Leslie*, a novel by a New York editor, Theodore S. Fay. Then too, he was jealous of Poe's assumption of authority on his magazine, and he disapproved of Poe's occasional lapses from sobriety. In January, 1837, Poe was forced to resign from the *Messenger*. Unfortunately that situation became a pattern. Poe's aggressive journalism disturbed timid publishers, and he himself was intolerant of employers who did not share his vision of a superb literary journal that would be an arbiter of taste throughout the country. For the rest of his life Poe would struggle to found his own magazine that would exhibit his own high standards, but for the next few years he would have to work for others.

In May of 1836 Poe had married his cousin Virginia Clemm, who was not yet fourteen at the date of her wedding, so when he went to New York in February, 1837, he took with him a wife and mother-in-law. His one accomplishment during a year in New York was the publication of his short novel, *The Narrative of Arthur Gordon Pym*, which was brought out by Harper and Brothers in July, 1838. The book was an attempt to profit from the current vogue of travel literature, but as usual with Poe it was an excursion into the fantastic recounted with a Defoe-like verisimilitude. Some reviewers, taken in by Poe's device of having pretended to edit the manuscript of the traveler Pym, treated the novel as a real-life adventure.

It was to Philadelphia that Poe moved his family in summer, 1838. This was to be his home for the next six years. From June 1, 1839, until June 1, 1840, he worked for *Burton's Gentleman's Magazine*, and from February, 1841, until April, 1842, he was assistant editor of *Graham's Magazine*. During this period Poe published some of his finest tales and matured as a critic, writing for *Graham's* the reviews of Longfellow's *Ballads* and Hawthorne's *Twice-Told Tales* that expressed his theory of poetry and of short fiction. He was also able to bring out a collection of his own short tales, *Tales of the Grotesque and Arabesque* (1840). His greatest ambition during this period, however, was to publish his own journal. In 1840 he printed a prospectus of the "Penn Magazine," but could not find backing. Eventually he changed the title of the prospective journal to "The Stylus," but it was never to be published, though Poe tried every expedient at his disposal.

Without a job in Philadelphia after 1842, Poe and his family existed on his scanty earnings as a free-lance journalist until the spring of 1844, when once more he moved to New York, then as now the greatest publishing center of the nation. The New York years between 1844 and 1849 were for Poe a time of poverty and personal tragedy, even though he was to achieve his greatest popularity with the publication of "The Raven" (1845) and was to become known to such luminaries as Robert Browning in England and Charles Baudelaire in France. His wife, Virginia, already suffering from tuberculosis, was to decline slowly until her death in January, 1847, at a cottage Poe had rented in Fordham (then a country village), in May, 1846. Much of Poe's energy in New York was spent in wrangling with other authors, including a lawsuit for libel against Thomas Dunn English, but he was able to bring out twelve of his tales in book form in July of 1845 and *The Raven and Other Poems* in November. At last, in October, 1845, Poe became owner of a literary weekly—not the grand monthly journal that he had hoped for, but a struggling little newspaper called the *Broadway Journal*, for which he paid fifty dollars in borrowed money. Without operating capital, though Poe tried to borrow from everyone he knew, he was able to maintain the journal for only a little over two months, until January, 1846.

After the death of his wife in January, 1847, Poe was in a state of collapse for several months. Even so he was able to work on a cosmological treatise he called *Eureka*, which was published in 1848. All of the speculative ideas he had previously published in the guise of fiction ("The Colloquy of Monos and Una" and "Mesmeric Revelation") were now gathered together in a lengthy essay that advances Poe's theories about the origin and end of the universe, the essential nature of God and the nature of man as God's creation. Like his admired Coleridge, who rested his literary theory upon a philosophical base, Edgar Poe attempted to draw together the scattered threads of his thought into a consistent pattern. In some measure he succeeded. The same year Poe made a trip back to his childhood home, Richmond, hoping to arouse interest in the magazine project he had never abandoned. In July of 1849 he went back to Richmond for the same purpose. Upon his return trip to New York in late September he stopped in Baltimore, where on October 3 he was found on the streets critically ill. He was taken to Washington College Hospital and died on Sunday, October 7. The cause of his death is still speculative. It was to be many years before reliable accounts of Poe's life were available. Ironically he had named as his literary executor the Reverend Rufus Wilmot Griswold, a sometime minister and literary anthologist who hated Poe. Griswold forged passages in Poe's letters to support an interpretation of the poet's character in a "Memoir" that exaggerated his faults and minimized his virtues. Griswold, who published the first edition of Poe's works, gave the dead writer an unsavory reputation that lasted until the twentieth century, though Poe's defenders, chief among whom was his English biographer, John Henry Ingram, did much to refute Griswold's charges in the half-century after Poe's death. It remained for Arthur Hobson Quinn to demonstrate in his *Edgar Allan Poe: A Critical Biography* (1941) how

Griswold's forgeries had distorted Poe's letters. Poe's personal reputation has been rescued from slander, but his significance as a literary figure is still open to debate.

Unquestionably Poe's literary work is very uneven, ranging from scurrilous ethnic humor in "A Tale of Jerusalem" to the superb control of tone and language in "The Fall of the House of Usher." It should be remembered, however, that he had to spend much of his creative energy on journalistic trivia simply to earn a living. During a professional career of nearly eighteen years he commanded a regular salary for little more than four years. When he had no editorial post, his annual income was at most a few hundred dollars and usually much less. He could often sell inferior work for much more than his best brought him; for instance, "The Balloon Hoax," a journalistic trick, was sold for fifty dollars, while his admired detective story, "The Purloined Letter," brought him only twelve. Considering the precarious nature of his journalistic vocation, it is not surprising that Poe was rarely at his best and that his talent is less substantially demonstrated by works than that of his great contemporaries, Hawthorne and Melville. Even so, Poe's contribution to our literary history is extensive.

Poe's achievement as a writer lies in three areas: criticism, short fiction, and poetry, examined here in that order. His significance as a critic was much greater in his own time than today, for he made it a matter of principle, whenever he had an editorial voice on a magazine, to try to raise American literary standards by introducing an analytic and judgmental method in book reviewing, by insisting upon literary rather than moral criteria for evaluation, and by arguing that art should be international as opposed to the current strain of literary nationalism. The world was the only proper theater for the literary *histrio*, Poe always insisted. By force of circumstances a book reviewer instead of a literary theorist such as Coleridge, Poe in some of his book reviews adopted the caustic methods of the literary quarterlies of Great Britain, but he wrote relatively few such reviews. In his most characteristic critiques he used traditional rhetorical principles to evaluate the language and metrics of poems, while insisting upon the aesthetic as opposed to the didactic end of poetry in general. His chief technical criterion for both the poem and the short tale was what he called the "unity of effect." Every word should assist in bringing about a preconceived effect on the reader's feelings, and both the poem and the short tale should be limited in length so that the intensity of the effect would not be diminished. Poe's stringent limits for the length and subject matter of a poem are now considered an eccentricity, but by demanding a tight plot structure and functional detail in short fiction he helped bring about the carefully plotted stories that reached the height of their popularity more than half a century ago. The short stories of today, however, are looser in form than Poe would have countenanced. Finally, by analyzing the work itself rather than discussing at length the life and ideas of the author (see Poe's "Exordium," 1842), he was in some degree anticipative of a certain trend in twentieth-century criticism, the New Criticism of the 1940s and 1950s.

Poe was the best short-story writer of his time in America, though his two published collections of short tales earned him more fame than money. More than any other writer of the time, Poe helped create the genre of the short story. He was a master at using atmosphere, recently called "mood-invested space," to create a unity of tone; and he succeeded in turning the hackneyed tale of terror into explorations of the human psyche under conditions of intolerable stress with an intensity not achieved by others who exploited the Gothic. On the other hand, his comic tales, what he called his "grotesques," with their word play, exaggerated characters and absurd plots, were more appealing in his own time than they are today. Poe wrote few detective stories, but his detective hero, C. Auguste Dupin, with his nameless companion who served as narrator, was the model for A. Conan Doyle's Sherlock Holmes and Dr. Watson and half a dozen other analytical detectives. Poe's arabesques, such as "The Fall of the House of Usher" and "Ligeia," have inspired a number of modern writers of fantasy as well as a series of films that bear little resemblance to Poe's original stories. It is clear that Poe's work has continued to have an appeal, even when distorted by modern adapters.

In his poetry Poe was insistently contemporaneous. His poems bore a family resemblance to those published in the journals of his day, and the chief literary influences on his verse were the poets of the recent past: Byron, Moore, Shelley, Keats, and Coleridge. Even his celebrated dictum from "The Philosophy of Composition," that the death of a beautiful woman was the most poetic subject in the world, may have resulted from his observation of the great number of laments for the departed published in newspapers and magazines. Poe's friends Philip Pendleton Cooke of Virginia and Thomas Holley Chivers of Georgia both published lyrics on dead women much in the manner of Poe. Mark Twain would satirize this obituary poetry in Huck Finn's account of the poems of Emmeline Grangerford. But Poe's own elegiac poems far surpassed those of his contemporaries in melody and rhythm, even though his subjects were conventional.

Entirely unconventional, however, was his symbolic use of landscape to suggest states of being, as in "The City in the Sea," "The Valley of

Unrest," and "Dreamland." Poe's use of imaginary scenes to correspond to psychic phenomena appealed to the French poets Baudelaire, Mallarmé, and Valéry; and his lifelong argument for the value of aesthetic experience and the value of the poem in creating that experience anticipated the aestheticism not only of the French but also of the modern American poet Wallace Stevens. Although few twentieth-century poets writing in English have acknowledged the influence of Poe, many, such as T. S. Eliot, have been influenced by the French symbolists, who themselves were indebted to Poe. Inescapably Poe's verse is part of our literary heritage.

A question sometimes debated is Poe's place in the literature of the South. Certainly he was for his time the best writer of poems and short tales claiming the South as home. His only rival, William Gilmore Simms of Charleston, South Carolina, was primarily a novelist. Unlike Simms, Beverley Tucker, and others, Poe was not a Southern apologist. Although he sometimes vilified the transcendentalists of Boston, he rarely fell into the defensive posture against abolitionist criticism that Simms and Tucker adopted. Poe's politics, what he had, were Southern Whig, but except for occasional thrusts against Jacksonian democracy, his writings showed little concern for political affairs. Reviewing Poe in the context of Southern literature, one may say correctly that he wrote on topics common to Southern poets, but with a tone and a range of symbolic reference all his own. His insistent lyricism was congenial to the Southern temperament, but probably his penchant for the brief lyric derived from the early German romantics rather than the Cavalier tradition so honored in the South.

Obviously many paradoxes mark the life and works of Edgar Poe. He professed to be a Virginian, but he was never quite at home in the South. He maintained, during a period of intense literary nationalism, that art by its very nature was international. At a time when poetry was justified in terms of explicit moral value, Poe asserted that the didactic was out of place in poems. Finally, though he is the poet still most familiar to American school children, he has found his greatest admirers in France among a sophisticated audience of poets and literary critics. The French have been equally attracted to his short fiction, yet the influence of his short stories has been greater on the writers of popular detective and fantasy fiction than on the creative elite. Born in Boston and reared in Virginia, Edgar Poe has become a citizen of the world, a status he would have considered entirely appropriate.

MARY ANN WIMSATT and ROBERT L. PHILLIPS

Antebellum Humor

W illiam Trotter Porter (1809–1858), in his introduction to *The Big Bear of Arkansas* (1845), claimed the tales he had collected in the volume showed "a new vein of literature . . . opened in this country." Although Porter dated the opening 1829, the year that *Skinner's Sporting Magazine* began publication, the antecedents of Southern humor (in our century widely and perhaps inaccurately labeled Southwestern humor) can be found as early as the seventeenth and eighteenth centuries in the work of George Alsop, Robert Bolling, and William Byrd II of Westover. Bolling, as Leo Lemay has shown, creates a humorously repulsive Southern colonial grotesque in his hudibrastic poem "Neanthe," while Byrd's urbane observations on several subjects, like the rustic Lubberlander life he found in North Carolina, anticipate the aloofly genteel attitude of a number of commentators from the early nineteenth century onward toward rough-and-tumble Southern country living. Generally lawyers, journalists, or farmers by professions, these commentators, who wrote in regional and national newpapers like the New Orleans *Picayune* or the New York *Spirit of the Times*, had often read the best of the eighteenth-century British writers, including Pope, Addison, Steele, Fielding, and Smollett. They were also influenced, though the fact is less widely recognized, by such nineteenth-century British authors of sporting material as Robert Smith Surtees (1805–1864) and Pierce Egan (1772–1849). Surtees' tales of the inimitable cockney fox hunter John Jarrocks resemble much Southern humor in their sly wit and their blending of the polite and colloquial voices, while Egan, whose encyclopedic interest in all forms of sport issued in a steady flow of publications, perhaps influences the genre most directly through his *Life in London* (1824), which merged with *Bell's Life in London*, a periodical that formed the leading model for the *Spirit of the Times* (1831–1856).

The humor that grew steadily in the South from the colonial period onward was by no means a solely Southern phenomenon. New England had its Down East comedy in such characters as Brother Jonathan, Jack Downing, Jo Strickland, and their kin abounding. The rural portions of the country in their inevitable contact with civilization spawned the humor that existed in the North, South, and Midwest. Keelboatmen, yellow-blossoms-of-the-forest, and gentlemanly observers became national stereotypes; hunting and racing, favorite topics of the humorists, were national pastimes. And it was chiefly through the influence of a Vermonter transplanted to New York—William T. Porter, the genial, gregarious editor of the *Spirit* and tireless devotee of comic and sport writing—that the Southern branch of American humor blossomed.

Porter's primary interest was in racing, and the *Spirit*, whose character changed somewhat during its long run, was originally designed as an outlet for racing and other sporting news. In the late 1830s, after the paper had attained large national circulation, Porter made two tours of the South, cementing his ties with sportsmen who were in many cases also authors and planters whose support he needed for his journal. His travels, concentrated in the parts of the South linked by the Ohio-Mississippi river systems and in such racing centers as Louisville and New Orleans, laid the groundwork for his friendships with writers of the Gulf South in the next decade, and hence prepared for the increasing appearance of these writers in the *Spirit*. While Porter visited Columbia and Charleston on his return to New York and used substantial material from the Southeast in his paper, his main connections, both in person and through the *Spirit*, were with the Deep South and the sizable group of writers who flourished there.

The 1830s saw the first significant fruits of Southern humor with the publication of important books by Augustus Baldwin Longstreet, Davy Crockett, and C. F. M. Noland. Longstreet's *Georgia Scenes* (1835) is usually credited with being the first major collection of humor, Southern style. Although written without Porter's help or influence, Longstreet's sketches demonstrate, as does the *Spirit*, the crucial role of newspapers in bringing rural backwoods humor before the public. Longstreet (1790–1870) apparently wrote these tales in hopes of stimulating interest in the newspapers he edited, the Milledgeville *Southern Recorder* and the Augusta *States-Rights' Sentinel*. He had come to journalism by an indirect route. Born in Georgia to parents of Northern stock, after attending law school in Litchfield, Connecticut, he was involved in law and politics in Georgia before he began editing the papers in which the "Georgia Scenes" first appeared. To these sketches of backcountry life he brought a sharp ear for dialect, an interest in regional peculiarities, and a solid grounding in such writers as Washington Irving, Parson Weems, Addison, and Steele. *Georgia Scenes* is thus the heir of the genteel tradition in both British and American letters and of the vernacular tradition developing in America through Weems, Crockett, Northern writers such as Seba Smith, and oral, newspaper, and almanac humor. Its many-stranded derivation shows up in its considerable variety of material, ranging from satiric social commentary in "The Song" and "The Ball" to vivid pictures of rustic activities in "The Shooting Match," "The Horse Swap," and "The Dance." Its sketches are channeled through Abraham Baldwin and Lyman Hall, two narrators whom Longstreet had invented for the newspaper series and named for early Georgia patriots, hoping thereby to keep his authorship of the sketches secret.

Longstreet uses Hall and Baldwin to develop the series of contrasts that lies near the heart of the book—between past and present, between country and village life, and between vernacular and genteel speakers. Generally—and here the roots of the eighteenth-century traditions are apparent—Longstreet criticizes excesses in both town and rural living, often using plain people who exemplify the best qualities as standards by which rude brawls or silly sophistications may be judged. He is less consistent in his choice of present over past, or, despite a virtual platoon of critics who favor his dialect over his genteel style, in the preference he shows one or the other language level. His narrative voice, in which an earthy vernacular challenges but is usually held in check by polite elevated language, shows his overriding if occasionally conflicting concerns with public morality and with uninhibited, violent behavior. Thus in several sketches—notably "Georgia Theatrics," "The Fight," and "The Turf"—Hall with his prissy, fussy tone is a vehicle for Longstreet's moral judgments, however extravagant these may seem to modern ears or however much at odds they may be with the main thrust of the tale. At the end of "The Fight," for example, in a moralizing coda that annoys twentieth-century readers but probably represents Longstreet's view, Hall thanks "the Christian religion . . . schools, colleges, and benevolent associations" for helping to subdue the finger-biting and eye-gouging he has just described. Such contrasts function to demonstrate the complicated moral and cultural situation existing in northern Georgia at the time Longstreet wrote the sketches, referred to in his wish to describe both speech and behavior that were rapidly passing away.

Longstreet's second series of "Georgia Scenes" published in Simms's *Magnolia* (1842–1843) shows the literary fame his book had brought him, but it also shows his dwindling interest in fiction. Written after he had turned from law and editing to preaching and had begun his long career as proslavery polemicist and college president, the series is disappointing to admirers of the earlier volume, though in its parody of trivial small-town concerns it foreshadows Mark Twain's sharp portraits of village life. His single novel, *Master William Mitten* (1864), a gloomy tale of a good boy gone wrong, is a moralistic piece that Mark Twain, if he knew it, must have hated.

Gentlemanly narrators like those Longstreet had created did not have the field to themselves in humor. Rustics resembling the people Hall and Baldwin describe—sometimes a countryman fearful of "book larnin'," sometimes a backwoods braggart or "ring-tailed roarer"—spoke in their own voices, on the stage and in print. The roarer's origins, like those of his crafty counterpart, the Yankee, are obscure, lying perhaps in the collective fear, pride, and courage of the people who set out into and across the Appalachians to render the wilderness subject to their own purposes. Walter Blair and Hamlin Hill in *America's Humor* (1978) have described the development of the roarer figure in popular culture, particularly his appearance on the stage, where, after taking shape through such characters as Oppossum in Alphonso Wetmore's *The Pedlar* (1821), he burst into full bloom as Nimrod Wildfire in James Kirke Paulding's *The Lion of the West*, which opened in New York in 1831. Wildfire, the boastful backwoodsman from Kentucky, was popularly identified with David Crockett (1786–1836), the most famous of all the real or legendary roarers. In fact, when the actor James Hackett brought the play (revised and retitled *The Kentuckian*) to Washington in 1833, Crockett sat in the front row and after the performance exchanged bows with Hackett.

Frontiersman Crockett, half-realistic, half-fantastic, was engendered by the collective imagination of the country, incorporating elements from rural Pennsylvania, Ohio, Kentucky, and Tennessee. The "real" Davy, born in east Tennessee, was elected to the state legislature in 1821 and to the United States House of Representatives in 1827. Returned to Congress in 1829, he was defeated in 1831 and reelected in 1833. A homesteader and hunter, a spinner of tall tales, a master of frontier wit and gamesmanship, and the hero of the Alamo, Crockett was fiercely independent but poorly educated. Some elements based on actual circumstances went into the making of the legendary Davy; but that figure was the product of considerable backwoods mythmaking efforts as well. The bibliographical tangle created by the volumes ascribed to Crockett has proved both challenging and vexing to his fans (and they are legion), but thanks to the careful researches of Franklin Meine, Walter Blair, Richard Hauck, James Shackford, and Stanley Folmsbee, we can now speak with some confidence about Crockett as author and as folk demigod.

As a hero Davy stands tall in the national pantheon; as an author of Southern literature David's position is somewhat less imposing. Although many works were attributed to him, he actually wrote very little, as Hauck's *Crockett: A Bio-Bibliography* (1982) makes clear. According to Hauck, Crockett probably supplied Mathew St. Clair Clarke with information included in *The Life and Adventures of Colonel David Crockett of West Tennessee* (1833; later editions were titled *Sketches and Eccentricities of Col. David Crockett . . .*). It may have been his disappointment with Clarke's book that led Crockett to seek the help of Thomas Chilton to write *A Narrative of the Life of David Crockett of the State of Tennessee* (1834; annotated edition, 1973). Other books, including *An Account of Colonel Crockett's Tour to the North and Down East* (1835), *The Life of Martin Van Buren . . .* (1835), and *Col. Crockett's Exploits and Adventures in Texas . . .* (1836), have little authenticity though they may contribute to the legendary character. The many tales about him that were circulated in newspapers, the *Spirit of the Times*, and the Crockett almanacs that were published between 1835 and 1856, however, did more than the books did to create "Davy."

Although politics and the sophistication of the editor Chilton, a Kentuckian, affect the tone, Crockett's character and his skill as a storyteller emerge in language and event to make the *Narrative* a superb autobiography. Disaffection for Andrew Jackson, for example, caused Crockett to alter some of the facts of his participation in the Creek War; it was more convenient for a potential nominee of the Whig party to claim to have enlisted for sixty days in Jackson's army rather than the ninety that Crockett actually served. Chilton's diction, as Shackford and Folmsbee have pointed out, is sometimes intrusive. Nevertheless, tales of "Noah's freshes" that destroyed his property, of the many "wild *varments*" he hunted, of cliffs that go "slap-right straight down," and of his angry father whose "steam was high enough to burst his boilers" appear in language that seems to be Crockett's own, a language characterized by aphorisms, metaphor, and hyperbole that became characteristic of Southern humor.

The early Crockett almanacs, particularly those of the Nashville series, 1835–1838, which Franklin Meine has edited, were designed to capitalize on Crockett's popularity and contained sketches taken from *The Life and Adventures* and the *Narrative*. Almost from the beginning, however, the mythical Davy appears in boasts of the half-horse, half-alligator, yellow-blossom-of-the-forest variety, and in the hunting tales that grow bigger than life. Soon one finds the Davy who, far removed from the halls of Congress and the Alamo, can walk up Daybreak Hill, unfreeze the earth from universal wastes, and walk home "with a piece of sunrise in [his] pocket."

Aside from Longstreet and Crockett, perhaps the most significant humorist appearing in the 1830s was C. F. M. Noland (*ca.* 1810–1858), who late in the decade began sending his N. of Arkansas and Pete Whetstone letters to the *Spirit*, for which he continued to write throughout Porter's editorship of the paper. Noland, who was born in Virginia, after flunking out of West Point had moved to the raw and bustling border territory of Arkansas at the behest of his father, who sought a rigorous discipline for his son. It seems likely, however, as Lorne Fienberg suggests, that his discipline produced pressures on Noland's self-styled hot and wayward temperament that underlie the division between N. and Pete—one a gentlemanly author of sporting epistles whose character ostensibly resembles Noland's, the other a saucy backwoodsman and sometime clown who is in certain respects the comic obverse and alter ego of both Noland and N. These personae, together with a third one, Jim Cole, reveal Noland's involvement in both the genteel and the roughshod elements of Arkansas backwoods living—the great zest with which, according to a contemporary, Alfred W. Arrington, "he shoots a bullet, or a bon-mot; and wields the pen or the bowie knife with the same . . . energetic fury of manner."

Both the N. and the Pete letters are rambling and desultory, allowing Noland to treat a wide array of topics—politics, racing, and, particularly in the Whetstone series, peddler yarns, gambling, opera, drama, frolics, fighting, and country games. Noland's employment of the Pete persona lets him smuggle into the *Spirit* a fair amount of commentary on political issues, like Van Buren and the United States Bank, whose direct treatment Porter had banned. The early Whetstone letters center on activities in Arkansas, but as the series develops, like Seba Smith Noland takes his country character on a tour of such "sivilized" places as Louisville, Trenton, and New York, in time-honored fashion having his shrewd commentator on Arkansas affairs turn yokel before such city amenities as "opery" and pickles.

Near the end of this lively decade, the panic of 1837, which affected so many phases of antebellum life, worked some changes in the publishing industry that had far-reaching consequences for humor. Among other things, it deflated the market for long fiction while raising the stock of shorter, more miscellaneous works, including humor, which increasingly appeared in book form and hence reached a wider reading public than it had reached through newspapers and magazines. Particularly important for humor in the 1840s were several events occurring near the same time and presided over by Porter in conjunction with the Philadelphia firm of Carey and Hart, whose operations greatly affected the fortunes of Southern authors. In 1845 the publishers, who had earlier shown a taste for comedy by publishing *A Narrative of the Life of*

David Crockett and Joseph Neal's *Charcoal Sketches* (1837), asked Porter to cull some tales from the *Spirit* for an anthology of Southern stories. The results were *The Big Bear of Arkansas* (1845) and *A Quarter Race in Kentucky* (1846), which, containing tales by Northern and Midwestern as well as Southern writers, helped establish humor as a staple in the nation's literary fare.

Probably sensing they had struck a rich vein, in 1846 Carey and Hart began, perhaps with Porter's advice, the Library of Humorous American Works, the series of paperbound volumes that until the 1880s disseminated the work of some of America's most notable comic writers in book form and kept the better collections in almost constant circulation. Among the volumes issued or reissued by Carey and Hart or their successors, notably T. B. Peterson, were Sol Smith's *Theatrical Apprenticeship*, Dennis Corcoran's *Pickings from the Picayune*, Porter's *A Quarter Race in Kentucky*, W. T. Thompson's *Major Jones's Courtship*, John Robb's *Streaks of Squatter Life*, Joseph Field's *The Drama in Pokerville*, J. J. Hooper's *Some Adventures of Captain Simon Suggs*, T. B. Thorpe's *The Mysteries of the Backwoods*, Joseph Cobb's *Mississippi Scenes*, T. A. Burke's edition of *Polly Peablossom's Wedding*, and H. C. Lewis' *Odd Leaves from the Life of a Louisiana Swamp Doctor*.

Of these volumes, *Major Jones's Courtship* (1843) by Georgia's William Tappan Thompson (1812–1882) became one of the most popular books in the genre. Thompson was born in Ravenna, Ohio, and had worked in Florida before moving to Georgia. There, like his friend and mentor Longstreet, he engaged in journalism, writing first for the Macon *Family Companion* and then for the Madison *Southern Miscellany* the dialect letters that would eventually become *Major Jones's Courtship*. The original version of the book, containing sixteen letters with an appended sketch, was issued by C. R. Hanleiter as a subscription premium for the *Miscellany*. The following year Carey and Hart brought out an expanded version containing twenty-six letters; they reissued the volume, again expanded, in the Library of Humorous American Works during 1847. *Courtship* went through nearly thirty printings before 1900, the 1872 Appleton edition containing previously uncollected material (T. B. Peterson, in a move that has caused much bibliographical confusion, combined thirteen sketches from the Appleton edition with another sketch and in 1879 issued the resulting volume as *Rancy Cottem's Courtship*).

For *Major Jones's Courtship* and *Major Jones's Sketches of Travel* (1847), Thompson employed as spokesman and central figure a prosperous, plainspoken middle-class farmer who, like Seba Smith's Jack Downing and Noland's Pete Whetstone, functions both as homespun philosopher and as country bumpkin during travels in the city. Resembling domestic romances shaped for a feminine reading market, the first of these volumes takes its characters through courtship, marriage, and (in the expanded versions) family life, while highlighting such rural customs as candy pulling and a militia muster. The second, which grew out of Thompson's contributions to Park Benjamin's *Western Continent*, finds "the Maje" journeying from Georgia to the North, a device that allows Thompson to praise Southern virtues, take swipes at "bobolitionists," and comment on issues of the day. In *Chronicles of Pineville* (1845), a series of stories about the "genus '*Cracker*'" featuring pranks and pratfalls in rural Georgia, Thompson leaned too heavily on Longstreet for his model, and the result is a volume whose fortunes have been considerably less enduring than those of the genial Major Jones.

Meanwhile, as if spurred by Porter's volumes, anthologies of humorous stories proliferated, especially in the decade of the 1850s; among noteworthy ones are T. A. Burke's edition of *Polly Peablossom's Wedding* (1851); S. P. Avery's *The Harp of a Thousand Strings* (1858); Thomas Chandler Haliburton's *Traits of American Humor* (1852, 3 vols.) and *Americans at Home* (1854, 3 vols.); William E. Burton's *Cyclopedia of Wit and Humor* (1858); and an anonymous *American Wit and Humor* (1859). These and kindred volumes are particularly valuable in that they contain tales by a number of accomplished yarnspinners who never published collections of their own but who merit brief attention here. William C. Hall, Alexander McNutt, P. B. January, Thomas Kirkman, Hamilton C. Jones, and John B. Lamar are simply a few of the many authors, some of whom can be identified only by pseudonyms, whose sketches appear in these books. William C. Hall's five "Yazoo" tales that feature Mike Hooter, bear hunter and Methodist zealot, are among the best in the genre. Hall's Mike, according to John Q. Anderson, was based on the character of a fairly substantial farmer of the region who took exception to finding himself on the pages of the *Spirit* narrating tales about how his daughter used a sausage for a bustle and how an ingenious Yazoo bear can unload his hunters' weapons.

Another Mississippian, Governor Alexander McNutt, known to Porter's subscribers as the Turkey Runner, achieved some fame for his hunting stories set in the Yazoo Delta featuring Jim and Chunkey, who were champions of the liquor barrel as well as the forest and creek. P. B. January, writing as Obediah Oilstone in the *Spirit*, was best known for "That Big Dog Fight at Myers's," a story about how a drunken man, Iron Tooth, bested Myers' watch dog in a fair dog fight. Thomas Kirkman's "A Quarter Race in Kentucky," published in the *Spirit* in 1836, became the title sketch for Porter's second compilation; in another story by Kirkman, "Jones's Fight," a somewhat distinguished Kentucky colonel returns to his hometown tavern and reports how in an eye-gouging, finger-biting fracas he was beaten. "Cousin Sally Dilliard," by Hamilton C. Jones, one of the earliest of the antebellum yarns, was the concluding tale in *The Big Bear*; his "McAlpin's Trip to Charleston" was included in *A Quarter Race*. Both stories develop suspense when the information a protagonist needs is not forthcoming; in the former a lawyer in rural North Carolina is never able to inform a jury about the fight that occurred at Colonel Rice's; in the latter an agent sent to Charleston causes his employer considerable discomfort with his lengthy account of failure. This formula appeared often in antebellum humor.

At Porter's urging, Carey and Hart brought out in 1845 one of the most celebrated books in the genre, Johnson Jones Hooper's *Some Adventures of Captain Simon Suggs, Late of the Tallapoosa Volunteers; Together with "Taking the Census," and Other Alabama Sketches.* Hooper (1815–1862), whom Porter had already spotted and befriended, spent a good part of his adult life in the Gulf South as a young man, emigrating from Wilmington, North Carolina, to Alabama, where he joined a brother in the eastern portion of the state. Moving from one to another Alabama town, for over twenty years he engaged in law, politics, newspaper editing, and writing, turning out the stories on which his twentieth-century reputation rests. The tales in the Suggs volume, which was dedicated to Porter, are particularly notable; going through eleven editions in eleven years after its initial publication, the book remains among the most widely read works by a Southern humorist.

Suggs is at once an early and important example of the backwoods picaresque novel and a burlesque campaign biography mocking the reverential treatment of Andrew Jackson in works by Amos Kendall and John Henry Eaton. This parodic element lets Hooper employ the familiar naïve narrator of satire, wildly exaggerating his stilted, pompous style and his worshipful manner in order to contrast his speech with Simon's pungent dialect. Suggs himself, the subject of much praise from humor scholars, is a rascally but engaging character—probably Southern humor's most artful trickster before Harris' Sut Lovingood, whom Hooper seems to have influenced. For his episodic treatment of Simon's adventures, Hooper appropriates some standard subjects of antebellum comedy—horse-stealing, gambling, the country militia, the camp meeting—along with such typical concerns of popular fiction as Indian customs, transforming both kinds of material through his satiric vision. His satire, like Mark Twain's and Harris', is many-faceted, directed at both the gullible frequenters of camp meeting or faro table and the clever rogue who fleeces them by pretending to be "General Thomas Witherspoon, the rich hog drover from Kentucky" or a recent Christian convert and a "poor worrum of the dust."

The deservedly high reputation of the Suggs volume has obscured Hooper's achievement in other books, notably *A Ride with Old Kit Kuncker* (1849). This work, which contains two further Suggs tales, is a varied collection of yarns based on Hooper's experiences in rural Alabama, particularly his stint as solicitor for the Ninth Judicial Circuit Court, revealing his talent for anecdote growing out of character in such pieces as the title story and "A Night at the Ugly Man's."

With the publication in the Library of Humorous American Works of *The Widow Rugby's Husband* (1851), a revised version of *Kit Kuncker*, Hooper's career as a humorist was virtually over, though he produced two further volumes that are part of a strong undercurrent in the humor field. In *Dog and Gun: A Few Loose Chapters on Shooting* (1856), drawing heavily on other authors, he treats such topics as choosing and charging a gun, training hunting dogs, and shooting game, setting forth his comments in a leisurely, genial manner. A pamphlet he had issued the previous year, *Read and Circulate: Proceedings of the Democratic and Anti-Know-Nothing Party in Caucus*, testifies to his growing involvement in politics. His death in 1862 in Richmond, where he was serving the Confederate government, deprived the country of an extremely talented minor author who had only begun to tap the comic resources of the South.

In late 1845 or early 1846, Carey and Hart published in the Library of Humorous American Works Solomon (Sol) Smith's *Theatrical Apprenticeship*, and their successors issued *Theatrical Journey Work* in 1854. Revised and enlarged, these two books became *Theatrical Management in the West and South* in 1868. Smith (1801–1869), a native of New York, managed theaters and acted in Mobile, New Orleans, and St. Louis. With his troupes he marched through Tennessee, Georgia, and South Carolina, and sailed often in Mississippi riverboats. Traveler, businessman, actor, manager, and correspondent of Porter, he collected experiences and tales that he recounted in the *Spirit of the Times* and then in his books. Spurning the dialect and misspellings of many of his fellow humorists, "Old Sol" nevertheless retailed incidents similar to theirs. Once in Tennessee he had to wait several days while most of the townspeople of Greenville attended a camp meeting. When the house was full for his final performance, he was shocked to discover that only seven people had paid admission. The reason became amply clear when the doorkeeper Sol had employed explained that he was not employed as a "window keeper" as well. On a trip up the Mississippi, Sol took passage on a boat whose captain loved poker. Too engrossed in his game to pay attention to the fact that they were making no progress up the river, the captain bought wood from the same wood yard three times. The events in Sol's tale are reminiscent of those in Thompson's "A Coon Hunt; or, A Fency Country," where inebriated hunters cross the same fence all night.

If Carey and Hart thrived by forging new paths for book selling in the aftermath of the panic, racing, a favorite pastime in the South and the star feature of Porter's *Spirit*, was badly crippled by the economic depression; and to its decline and the consequent gap left by the decline in racing news has been traced the spread of humorous yarns drawn from all over the South. Always a lively topic among gentlemen in wealthy circles, other sports, particularly hunting, came into their own during the 1820s, with developments in the North and South alike. The British author Henry William Herbert (1807–1858), who had emigrated to America in 1839, began his genteel sporting fiction like *The Warwick Woodlands* (1845) and the technical description of sport and game found in *Frank Forester's Field Sports* (1849) that forms a substantial substratum in the humor field. Porter in 1846 brought out an American edition of Briton Peter Hawker's *Instructions to Young Sportsmen*, expanded by valuable information about American game derived from Herbert and other authors. And in South Carolina, William Elliott (1788–1863), scion of a distinguished family of planters and politicians in the Beaufort area, during 1846 in Charleston issued *Carolina Sports*, a group of essays on fishing and hunting that he had published from the late 1820s onward in Charleston periodicals and in *Skinner's Sporting Magazine*, forerunner of the *American Turf Register*.

Elliott's book is particularly interesting because it distills and combines two elements important in the field: the so-called urbane or gentlemanly manner characteristic of tidewater writing with an almost exclusive emphasis on sports, while attempting (in Hubbell's term) the semiscientific description of game that Porter and Herbert were also attempting. His volume, a mixture of anecdotes, sketches, essays, and short stories, includes tales of the devilfish and the sea serpent (the latter added to the 1859 New York edition); four pieces on fishing and hunting; several narratives involving Chee-Ha, his plantation; "The Fire Hunter," a poignant story of race and class; and "Random Thoughts on Hunting," reflections on the value of sports, dance, and theater in siphoning off potentially destructive "animal passions."

Although not solely nor perhaps even chiefly comic, *Carolina Sports* contains elements familiar to Southern humor, raising them to the level of polite literature by its cultivated, frequently bantering tone, which constitutes for many readers the chief joy of the book. Elliott combines brisk dialogue, saucy colloquialisms, classical references, foreign phrases, baroque flourishes, and mock-heroic sallies, in playful manner swearing, for example, "By the Ghost of *Lignumvitae*," inquiring "*Que faut il faire?*" of a distressed boatsman, proclaiming that in narrative "I sin by design," and inveighing against his birthplace: "Oh, Beaufort! . . . Thou unmatchable town, that, devouring the oyster, still delightest in the shell!" He uses tall tales, the hoax yarn, lighthearted and sinister threads from folklore, and an Irvingesque story of the rationalized supernatural in his tale of the milk-white, indestructible Spectre Buck that presumably houses the spirit of an impious and drunken misanthrope.

Viewed one way, the devilfish story, the sea-serpent yarn, and the narrative of the spectre buck are literary versions of the magical-beast or the supernatural-animal-adversary strain in folklore; the last two pieces are also tall tales involving various degrees of spoofing. For readers unschooled in the art of devilfishing, the yarn by that title itself ostensibly contains some stretchers, as Elliott suggests when making "a fancy-sketch" out of a vague family tradition about a slave who had harpooned a devilfish after leaping upon its back. But elsewhere in the essay he soberly vouches for the truthfulness of his wild and breezy account of such escapades as being towed around Port Royal Sound all afternoon by the "novel, and *yet unpatented* impelling power" of another harpooned devilfish. Simms, who admired Elliott's writing, caught the flavor of the devilfish essay when he wrote its author, "I address you at hazard, at Beaufort, though with a lurking doubt whether, yoking a devil fish to your car, you are not cantering off to the antipodes." Ambling and loosely structured, *Carolina Sports*, as Hubbell and others have remarked, might have profited from some pruning; but the digressiveness of the book is one element in its charm, and it stands as a valuable record of the Carolina aristocracy at play.

Elliott's fellow South Carolinian Orlando Benedict Mayer (1816–1891), one of the "Dutch Fork" group of writers in inland Carolina, produced the lively dialect novel *John Punterick*, which remained unpublished until edited by James E. Kibler, Jr., in 1981. Its frame story, as Kibler notes, gives an interesting view of gentlemanly yarn spinners—planters, farmers, doctors—in action, and by doing so suggests some upper-class bases of humor from the Hotspur State.

In 1846, the year of *Carolina Sports*, Thomas Bangs Thorpe (1815–1875), who shared Elliott's interest in fishing and hunting, brought out his first volume, *The Mysteries of the Backwoods*. Digressive, sentimental, and almost devoid of comedy, *Mysteries* is nevertheless significant for humor studies because it shows a variety of sometimes conflicting influences at work upon an author whose most famous story, "The Big Bear of Arkansas," was virtually synonymous with the concept of Southern or Southwestern humor for scholars earlier in the twentieth century. The diversity of elements in Thorpe's work is in part explained by the circumstances of his early life and by his unfailing inclination to capitalize on trends in the popular literature of his time. Born in Massachusetts, he grew up in New York, where in the 1820s and 1830s he read Irving and Cooper, studied painting, and soaked up the Hudson River scenery that Irving had described compellingly. Moving to Louisiana in 1836, he alternated between painting and writing for a living, while also engaging in politics and newspaper editing. Never settling into a single mode of authorship, he typically wrote with an eye on the market, producing work that incorporates several strains from his literary predecessors. In *Mysteries*, for example, such nature essays as "Traits of the Prairies" and "Concordia Lake" with their painterly descriptions of landscape glance not only at Thorpe's profession as artist but also at an older mode in American letters found in Irving's and Cooper's work. Stories like "Place de la Croix" exploit the glamor of European explorations of America in the fashion of William Hickling Prescott, Robert Montgomery Bird, and Simms. Of the sixteen essays in *Mysteries*, in fact, only "A Piano in Arkansas" and "Tom Owen, the Bee-Hunter," an acclaimed and influential piece, contain significant humor. (Thorpe did not use "The Big Bear of Arkansas," which had appeared in the *Spirit* during 1841 and subsequently became the title story of Porter's first collection, as part of *Mysteries*.)

As both sportsman and nature lover, Thorpe in *Mysteries* is ambivalent about the killing of game for pleasure; in pieces like "Pictures of Buffalo Hunting," he echoes Cooper's distaste for squalid lower-class whites and his distress at wanton slaughter of game. Thorpe shows a lighter side in his "Letters From the Far West," published in the Concordia, Louisiana, *Intelligencer* and swiftly picked up by the *Spirit*. Here he parodies Matthew Field's sobersided epistolary treatment in the New Orleans *Picayune* and the St. Louis *Reveille* of Sir William Drummond Stewart's expedition into the Rocky Mountains, taking swipes at everything from western travel to the wonderful hunt. Thorpe contributed to the military-political strain that had long been present in Southern humor with two volumes on the Mexican War, *Our Army on the Rio Grande* (1846) and *Our Army at Monterey* (1847), and by *The Taylor Anecdote Book* (1848), an effort to ingratiate himself with Zachary Taylor.

In the middle of the next decade, Thorpe brought out *The Hive of the "Bee-Hunter"* (1854), essentially a reworking of material from *Mysteries* with several pieces added. The new material—particularly "Summer Retreat in Arkansas" (the *Hive* title of Thorpe's well-known tale "Bob Herring, the Arkansas Bear Hunter"), "The Big Bear of Arkansas," "Major Gasden's Story," and "The Way That Americans Go Down Hill"—substantially enriched Thorpe's humor, gave sports more prominence, and gave proportionately greater emphasis than *Mysteries* to characters who, so Thorpe claims in his somewhat glozing preface, are "truly *sui generis*—truly American." Also in 1854, Thorpe produced a novel, *The Master's House*, one of several Southern answers to *Uncle Tom's Cabin*.

Throughout the 1840s and the 1850s, regional newspapers continued, like the *Spirit*, to circulate sporting or comic tales. Particularly noteworthy papers were the *Intelligencer*, coedited by Thorpe and Robert Patterson; the *Picayune*, edited by George Wilkins Kendall, himself a humorist of some note; the New Orleans *Delta*; and the St. Louis *Reveille*, edited by Joseph Field, to which both Field's brother Mat and Sol Smith contributed. Kendall (1809–1867), who was keenly interested in military affairs, published in 1844 an account of his adventures in Texas, *Narrative of the Texan Sante Fe Expedition*, and in 1851 *The War Between the United States and Mexico*; his story "Bill Dean, the Texan Ranger" has been reprinted in anthologies of Southern humor. But Kendall's reporter Dennis Corcoran, who for a short time edited the *Delta*, made an even more substantial contribution to Southern humor in 1846 with his publication in the Library of Humorous American Works of *Pickings from the Portfolio of the Reporter of the New Orleans "Picayune."* The book consists of sketches of characters brought before police court in the Crescent City. As Noland's and Thompson's volumes show, the country yokel's visit to town had become a stock situation in American humor, one to which Corcoran helped add another dimension. New Orleans had grown to be a bustling, cosmopolitan port conducting its business with the developing Mississippi Valley, the West Indies, and beyond. Occasionally natives of New Orleans appear in Corcoran's court, but more often defendants are outsiders who, in addition to bumptious foolishness, display a wide variety of dialects—Irish, German, French, Mississippi black, Hoosier.

The existence and influence of the St. Louis *Reveille* raises the issue of the Midwest's relationship to the South and its humor, and also the fact that the type of comic writing we are considering was spread partly by means of the linked river systems. Important books emanating from the Middle West were Joseph M. Field's *The Drama in Pokerville* and John S. Robb's *Streaks of Squatter Life, and Far-West Scenes*. Both works were additions to the Carey and Hart Library in 1847, and both employ settings that usually lie outside the South. But both have ties to Southern humor, which obviously influenced the pranks, fights, and hunts that Field and Robb depict. Field (1810–1856) had been an actor and an associate of Sol Smith before becoming editor of the *Reveille* in 1844; he and his brother Mat were, like G. W. Kendall, humorists of some merit. Robb (*ca.* 1813–1856), a reporter for the *Reveille*, belongs in this account if only because he wrote one of the funniest and most widely circulated tales in the genre, "Swallowing an Oyster Alive."

If the 1840s had seen the establishment of Southern humor through book publication, the 1850s and 1860s saw it come of age, with new writers appearing and old ones consolidating gains. Prominent among the old ones was William Gilmore Simms (1806–1870), who, in border and Revolutionary War romances published earlier in the century, had created episodes and characters like those the humorists were using— bragging backwoodsmen, a windy preacher, a strolling actor, and wild adventures in the Alabama and Mississippi of the flush times. The enter- prising editor of a number of Southern periodicals, Simms with his sen- sitivity for popular writing knew that humor was a salable commodity, as his favorable notices of Elliott, Longstreet, Thorpe, Hooper, and similar writers suggest. Simms's move to humor, as indicated in the chapter on his writing, came with the short novel *As Good as a Comedy* (1852). More important than *As Good* for Southern humor is Simms's little-known *Paddy McGann*, serialized during 1863 but possibly be- gun earlier, an intriguing novelette whose frame story centers on the whiskey-loving Irish backwoodsman of the title and his gentlemanly drinking companions; the main narrative, told in Paddy's rich brogue, is an elaborate devil yarn embroidered with the kind of folk material that had always nourished Southern humor—a bewitched gun, a spirit deer, and a semicomic demon that inhabits a stump and goes "Hoo! Hoo! Hoo!" in the night. Simms's major work in humor would not appear until near the end of his life, but *As Good* and *Paddy* give an earnest representation of what he had learned from his fellow Southerners and the uses to which he was already putting his knowledge.

The major new humorists appearing in the 1850s were Henry Clay Lewis (1825–1850), Joseph Beckham Cobb (1819–1858), and Joseph Glover Baldwin (1815–1864). Lewis, born in Charleston, South Caro- lina, ran away from his brother's home in Cincinnati at the age of ten and found a home with another brother in Yazoo City, Mississippi. These difficult early years as well as his experiences as a doctor's apprentice in the backwoods of Mississippi contributed to some of the more grotesque events in his collection of tales, *Odd Leaves from the Life of a Louisiana Swamp Doctor* (1850). Lewis, writing as Madison Tensas, divided *Odd Leaves* into four sections: the first, "Runaway," details some of his experiences as a ten-year-old cabin boy on the river; the second, "Sawbones' Apprentice," occasionally introduces the grotesque and, one hopes, the surreal with accounts of the suffering wrought by the inexperienced physician; the third, "Grave Rat," is about the lives of students at the medical college in Louisville; the final section, "Swamp Doctors," includes stories about the doctor's experiences in his practice in Louisiana. Lewis is usually identified as the most grotesque of the humorists, but his book contains, in addition to medical lore, tales about horse racing and the wild animals of the Mississippi Delta that had become the usual fare in Southern humor. In fact, it is worth suggesting in Lewis' defense that the grotesque mode he used provided a barrier of artificial callousness between the suffering he witnessed and his sympathies with patients or victims.

A lesser figure in humor than Lewis, Joseph B. Cobb published three books, like Thorpe capitalizing on popular literary subjects. His first, the novel *The Creole, A Story of the Siege of New Orleans* (1850), treats the War of 1812 and Lafitte, the pirate; his third, *Leisure Labors; or, Miscellanies Historical, Literary, and Political* (1858), is a collection of essays. It is his second volume, *Mississippi Scenes; or, Sketches of Southern and Western Life* (1851) that earns him a place in the annals of humor. Cobb paid tribute to the primary influence on his collection of thirteen stories and sketches by dedicating his book to Longstreet. The urbane observations of Cobb's "Rambler" about events and characters in Columbus, Mississippi, are as reminiscent of Baldwin and Hall's observations as the name of Cobb's narrator is of Dr. Johnson. Another influence on Cobb was that of Washington Irving. The last two pieces of the collection, "The Legend of Black Creek" and "The Bride of Lick-the-Skillet," feature Southern incarnations of Brom Bones and Ichabod Crane.

With Elliott, Joseph Glover Baldwin was the best born of the humorists, and like Elliott's, his writing, in which the urbane manner attains a fine finish, reflects his genteel heritage together with his reading in Addison, Pope, Scott, Irving, Lamb, and Dickens. Exceedingly migratory, Baldwin moved from Virginia to Mississippi and then to Alabama in order to make a living from law; restlessly seeking new fields, in 1854 he settled in California, where he became an associate justice of the Supreme Court, an experience to which his uncompleted volume, *The Flush Times of California* (published 1966), is in part a literary memorial.

A Whig and an ardent supporter of the aristocratic South, in *The Flush Times of Alabama and Mississippi* (1853) Baldwin casts a nostalgic backward glance over the area commemorated in his title, giving vivid glimpses of the energy, zest, and chicanery in the Deep South of the 1830s and 1840s. Sketches he had published in the *Southern Literary Messenger* during 1852 through 1854, together with nine new ones, went into the volume, whose affectionate dedication to "The Old Folks" in the valley of the Shenandoah suggests Baldwin's continuing ties to his home. The book in fact shows a tidewater sensibility operating on standard aspects of Gulf South culture, rendered through Baldwin's carefully wrought style replete with literary allusions. His leisurely manner, his idealizing treatment of a vanished era, and his obvious alignment with patrician values connect him with the polite literature of his own and earlier times, as does his use of stock devices like the humorous character (Ovid Bolus, Cave Burton) and his frequent gentle mock-heroic manner, so finely fashioned that it obscures for all but his most sensitive readers the subtle humor of his treatment. Also connecting him to polite writing are his complimentary pieces such as "Hon. S. S. Prentiss" and "Hon. Francis Strother," which anticipate the strain he would explore in *Party Leaders* (1855), a knowing discussion of Jefferson, Jackson, Clay, and others. But his delight in puncturing pomposity (his own included), his relish for practical jokes, his use of tall talk, and his inclusion of rambling stories of the "Cousin Sally Dilliard" type indissolubly connect him with the humorists. Although some critics of *Flush Times* dislike its gentility and complain that it lacks the unity of such masterworks as *Simon Suggs*, the book nonetheless attains a considerable measure of coherence by its emphasis on politics and law and by the unfailingly urbane tenor of its narrative voice, whose refinement perhaps obscures the level of Baldwin's achievement in genteel comedy.

Appearing in the same year as *Flush Times* was Francis James Robinson's *Kups of Kauphy: A Georgia Book in Warp and Woof* (1853). Published in Athens, Georgia, Robinson's book did not enjoy the national circulation that books published by Carey and Hart obtained; nevertheless, *Kups of Kauphy* is a solid contribution to Southern humor. Of particular note is Robinson's use of a Negro narrator to defend slavery. Old Jack C———, "possessed of quick perceptive faculties, a lover of the ridiculous, cunning and smart," often gets the better of white travelers who visit the inn where he works as a waiter.

North Carolina, which had provided some of the earliest Southern humor in "Cousin Sally Dilliard," crops up again in the 1850s with Harden E. Taliaferro's *Fisher's River (North Carolina) Scenes and Characters* (1859). In 1857 Taliaferro (1818–1875), a Baptist minister preaching in Alabama, returned to Surry County, North Carolina, where he had grown up. During the trip he was reminded of tales he had heard and while there he began to collect new ones. *Fisher's River* has many of the stock incidents: the hunt, the revival, the fight, and the encounter with a mythical animal. This collection, however, lacks the rawness and narrative skill of Crockett or of Simon Suggs; the language is refined even though characters speak in dialect. These stories are quaint but have little reference to man's timeless conflict with himself or with nature. Crockett's famous "root hog or die" becomes "He rose early and worked late, obliged to do so or starve."

The outbreak of the Civil War in the 1860s obviously affected the writing and publishing of Southern humor. Porter, who for over twenty years had been the chief promoter of Southern humor, had left the *Spirit of the Times* in 1856, and two years later he was dead, leaving no comparable figure to replace him. Although there were no periodicals that circulated in the North and the South after the outbreak of war, and though Porter was gone, Southern humor, nevertheless, continued to be written during the 1860s, reaching perhaps its finest moment with the publication of the Sut Lovingood yarns by George Washington Harris after the war.

The tendency toward the genteel, always a possibility with gentleman narrators from Longstreet on, became more apparent in humorous writing in the years just before the Civil War, while after the war it became the foundation for Southern local-color writing. The movement from humor to genteel local color can be seen in comparing the stories of Richard Malcolm Johnston (1822–1898) and Kittrell Warren (1829–1889) with some of the earlier writing. In Johnston's first story, "Five Chapters of a History" which appeared in the *Spirit of the Times* in 1857, a little boy fights a bullying schoolmaster and defeats him. Even in the *Spirit* version, the fight is far milder than the eye-gouging, finger-biting fights of some of the earlier writers, but when Johnston revised the story in 1871 he felt compelled to replace a concluding apology for his long-winded tale with the boy's mother's sentimental epilogue about the justice of the outcome. Between 1883 and 1898 Johnston published four novels and eighty-two short stories. Johnston's first book, *Georgia Sketches*, obviously titled after Longstreet, appeared in 1864.

Kittrell Warren's *Ups and Downs of Wife Hunting* (1861) is also a relatively tame book in comparison with the humor that preceded it, but his *Life and Public Services of an Army Straggler* (1865) shows development in narrative skill that suggests that had Warren continued writing he might have achieved a great deal. *Ups and Downs* is about Jezebel Huggins, a pretentious, homely, and foolish admirer of women.

Jezebel looks down on the yokels among whom he was raised, but it is actually they who make a joke of him. Billy Fishback of *Life and Public Services* almost equals Simon Suggs as an accomplished prankster and confidence man. Selfish, greedy, and amoral, Fishback, a deserter from the Confederate army in Virginia, preys on the army and an unsuspecting populace.

Paralleling the development of more genteel local-color writing is the development of literary comedy in Southern humor during the late 1850s and the 1860s following national patterns set by Charles Farrar Browne (Artemus Ward), Henry Wheeler Shaw (Josh Billings), and others. An oral quality, a love of the sound of language and the fun of reproducing dialect on the printed page, had been characteristic of Southern humor, but the letters that Mozis Addums, a creation of Virginian George W. Bagby (1828–1883), began to publish in the *Southern Literary Messenger* in 1857 exhibit a somewhat different quality in that the language is crafted for the eye as well as the ear. Mozis Addums, an almost illiterate Virginia farmer, went to Washington seeking a patent on his perpetual motion machine and wrote his friend Billy Ivvins about what happened to him there. Mozis is an innocent of the backwoods, and everyone takes advantage of him. The strong anti-intellectual bias of the yeoman which dominated Southern humor, even that presented by some of the most sophisticated narrators, is replaced by an obvious appeal to learning in a language which develops humor from both the appearance and the sound of words. Hence Mozis writes about "4−farthers" and the "Deep-O," capitalizing on an orthographic tendency that had long been present in American humor and was even more carefully developed in the South after the Civil War by Bagby, Charles H. Smith (Bill Arp), the literary comedians who followed the piping of the Phunny Phellows. Bagby, in fact, was one of the more prolific and successful postwar Southern writers. His Mozis Addums letters appeared in several collections during and after the war.

Some of the energy of the realistic strain in Southern humor was sentimentalized into local color after the war, and some was diverted into the work of the literary comedians; but the original vein to its richest ore in the 1860s produced the final work of Gilmore Simms and the Sut Lovingood yarns of George Washington Harris. After *Paddy McGann*, Simms went on to excel in humor, and in so doing, he showed what he might have achieved had he chosen to abandon long fiction and work solely in the comic mode. The chief testaments of his talent, "Bald-Head Bill Bauldy" and "How Sharp Snaffles Got His Capital and Wife," are set in the Balsam Mountains of southwestern North Carolina that he had visited in 1847, when he spent about two weeks traveling with professional hunters, helping them bag game and sharing the drinks and yarns. Both stories use as framing device the hunters' Saturday night "lying camp," and both show creativity and authorial control beyond what is usually found in Simms. "Bill Bauldy," which remained in manuscript until it was published in the Simms centennial edition in 1974, is a combination tall tale and dream vision, in which Simms uses a parodic narrative of Indian captivity as scaffolding for Bill's fantastic underwater adventures. And "Sharp Snaffles," which appeared in *Harper's Magazine* shortly after Simms's death in 1870, interweaves the quietly comic details of the backwoods courtship yarn with the freewheeling fantasy of the wonderful hunt to create what Edd Winfield Parks called "one of the finest tall tales ever written by a Southern humorist."

And finally, as the mode matured, it bred a genius—G. W. Harris, in many ways the most original and gifted of the antebellum humorists. Harris (1814–1869) was born in Pennsylvania but spent much of his life in or near Knoxville, where he worked as a steamboat captain, a farmer, an owner of a metal-making and jewelry-working shop, and at other occupations. In the 1840s, encouraged by a Knoxville editor, he had written polemical political items for local papers and, using the pseudonyms Mr. Free and Sugartail, had published fairly conventional stories of mountain life in Porter's *Spirit*, where in 1845 appeared "The Knob Dance," forerunner of the Sut Lovingood yarns. The 1860s saw the capping of his literary career with the appearance of *Sut Lovingood: Yarns Spun by a "Nat'ral Born Durn'd Fool"* (1867), tales which had apparently been written in the middle 1850s and for which he may have sought a publisher as early as 1858. Of the twenty-four stories in the work, only eight had previously seen print, and these were heavily revised for the book version. The manuscript of another Sut work, "High Times and Hard Times," which Harris had with him at the time of his death, has never been recovered. To all but his most devoted fans, his sharp satires on political topics seem dated and dull today.

But the Sut Lovingood yarns remain a triumphant, astonishing achievement. In their emphasis on fear, pain, humiliation, and physical grotesquerie, they show a superficial similarity to Lewis' work. More fundamentally, however, they represent a highly original adaptation of standard elements of Southern humor. In the *Yarns*, Harris transforms the conventional features of framing narrative and tall tale, giving the dialect speaker dominance over the gentlemanly voices and thereby unleashing the violence, vitality, and crude exuberance of the primitive folk imagination. Through Sut's extravagant comic anecdotes, Harris allows us to witness, without being able to distinguish fact from fantasy, wildly comic practical jokes obviously partaking of the tall tale. By subordinating the tall tale to point of view, Harris has made it a function of the narrative method instead of the primary vehicle of meaning, as it tended to be in the hands of other humorists. With great ingenuity he similarly transforms such familiar topics of Southern humor as swindling Yankees, hypocritical parsons, funerals, jokes and superstitions, Negro-baiting, love, courtship, marriage, and adultery. In fact, almost the entire range of subjects developed and explored by earlier Southern comic writers comes under his wonder-wielding pen.

In public life an upright gentleman, a community leader, and a strict Presbyterian, Harris unrolled in Sut a demonic energy and apocalyptic fury perhaps inspired by the Calvinistic strain in his religious heritage. Although critics vigorously debate the fact, his book may have a moral purpose operating both through and beyond Sut's outrageous, revenge-ridden pranks. The *Yarns*, in fact, are perhaps best seen as myth with both classical and Christian dimensions functioning at the ironic level; they have many features of the myths associated with Western civilization—a rugged outdoor setting; close associations of people and animals; repeated transformations, through disguises, of human beings into animal forms; a pervading emphasis on sexuality or fertility and on uninhibited physical pleasure or pain. With all their moral fury, however, they are ironic, finally, in that they show no sense of cosmic or eternal justice operating behind Sut, who creates chaos to achieve not simply his fantastic forms of punishment but, in many cases, a rough approximation of what he considers earthly justice as well.

The Civil War, Reconstruction, and the self-consciousness of the New South may have modulated the voice of Southern comedy, but Porter's vein of ore was there. And from it the Southern genius has refined its Mark Twains and William Faulkners—and also its O'Connors, Weltys, Erskine Caldwells, and others, who, in one way or another, are indebted to the rich imagination of their antebellum forebears.

RICHARD J. CALHOUN

Literary Magazines in
the Old South

In two intentionally discouraging letters to Philip C. Pendleton, publisher of the *Magnolia*, William Gilmore Simms provided the authoritative statement on publishing and editing literary magazines in the antebellum South. Simms's letters are the most important contemporary source for a history of antebellum magazines, since they are based on the early experience of an important writer who already knew from two failed magazines, the *Album* and the *Southern Literary Gazette*, how quickly great expectations turned to personal disillusionment. Nevertheless, Simms continued to believe that literary magazines might eventually encourage what he and his fellow editors desired, a distinctively Southern literature that could make important contributions to American literature. For that reason Simms could not resist the call to try once more, and in July, 1842, he became editor of the magazine whose demise he had predicted, the *Magnolia*.

The first of the two letters, published in the *Magnolia* in January, 1841, not only described past failures but detailed a scenario for all future attempts at establishing a magazine, including Simms's own. The founding was always "the usual story of confident hope and bold assurance," the fair-weather encouragement of friends and the promise of contributions. Both promises were badly kept. "His contributors—men, generally, in our country, devoted to other professions,—can only write for him at moments of leisure. . . . He is necessarily compelled to wait upon them for their articles, which, good, bad or indifferent, he is compelled to publish. The constant drain upon himself, enfeebles his imagination and exhausts his intellect." When his subscribers fail to pay, the magazine fails. "The collections are to be made over an extensive tract of interior country. . . . the publication of the work becomes irregular. . . . the general dissatisfaction of all parties concerned—the editor being among the first—soon leads to the early abandonment of an attempt in which nothing has been realized but discredit, annoyance, and expense."

Simms has narrated succinctly the history of the expectations and the failure of nearly all literary magazines in the antebellum South from their true beginning, the *Southern Review* (1828–1832), to an impressive coda in *Russell's Magazine* (1857–1860). The *Southern Review* was scholarly and learned but too pompous and dull to attract a large audience. What inspired other editors to emulate it was the presence of Hugh Swinton Legaré, the exemplary professional man, distinguished enough as a lawyer to become attorney general under Tyler and secretary of state *ad interim*, who could display the kind of learning, especially of the classics, ideally expected of a Charleston editor.

The most interesting magazines that followed in the image of the *Southern Review* and failed in accordance with Simms's scenario were the *Southern Literary Journal* (1835–1838), edited by Daniel K. Whitaker, New Englander turned Charleston lawyer, with a desire to be a major force in the establishment of Southern letters; the *Orion* (1842–1844), coedited by William Carey Richards, a scholarly minister, and his artist brother, Thomas Addison Richards; the *Magnolia*, originally the *Southern Ladies' Book*, begun by Pendleton and continued by Simms, who tried admirably to prove his own predictions wrong; and *Russell's Magazine* (1857–1860), which followed Simms's script in spite of having the right ingredients for success—the firm support of Charleston professional men and editing by a talented young Charleston writer, Paul Hamilton Hayne, in close association with Henry Timrod.

All of these magazines were founded with the altruistic intention of promoting the cause of literature in the South. All were forced to try to find help outside the South, and all perished rather quickly. Even the survivors among Southern magazines existed constantly on the edge of disaster, some even moving from editor to editor and place to place. The exceptions to sudden death were the *Southern Quarterly Review* (1842–1857), begun by Whitaker then edited by Simms, this time with more stress on politics, which Simms knew to be "the bread of life" for the Southern reader; the *Southern Literary Messenger* (1834–1864), which lived on the fame of one of its editors, Edgar Allan Poe, and survived on the hard work of John Reuben Thompson, its editor for thirteen years, the longest tenure of a literary magazine under one editor. A third periodical, the *Commercial Review of the South and West* (1847–1861), known as *De Bow's Review*, had a longer survival under its sole editor, James D. B. De Bow; but it was, as the name indicates, a commercial review with an undistinguished literary department, mainly of interest because of the anti-positivistic and anti-industrial essays by George Fitzhugh.

Actually, none of these magazines was strictly a literary magazine in a *belles lettres* sense. A typical issue of even the most literary, the *Southern Literary Messenger,* or *Russell's Magazine,* featured essays (political, historical, travel, and literary) to fiction in a three-to-one proportion, scattering a handful of poems, often more sentimental and romantic than the editors would have preferred, variously throughout the magazine. Last were the reviews, by no means always of literature, intended to give what Southern books they could find the fair hearing the editors believed they were not given in Northern periodicals.

With an obvious shortage of professional writers in the South, contributions were needed from those Simms described as "devoted to other professions," the lawyers, physicians, professors, many well read in the classics, their critical ideas largely formed from their reading of the Scottish rhetoricians, Kames, Blair, Stewart, and Alison. A few (Legaré, Whitaker, Thompson, Richards) edited magazines. Others reviewed books and wrote scholarly essays and were much admired for their learning. Legaré had set the pattern with essays like "Classical Learning" for the *Southern Review.* He was succeeded by George Frederick Holmes in the *Southern Quarterly Review* and in the *Magnolia.* A few like Beverley Tucker contributed essays, reviews, and submitted poems and fiction to the *Southern Literary Messenger.*

Another possible source for contributors and subscribers, the planter class, proved a disappointment. A favorite theory of Southern editors had been that a leisure class was necessary for the support of literature and that the South with its "peculiar institution" would have a better opportunity for developing this class than the industrializing North. As part of a call to literary arms in the first issue of the *Southern Literary Messenger* (August, 1834), Thomas Willis White printed letters by James Fenimore Cooper and James K. Paulding espousing a theory of support by gentlemen who would be "above the necessity of laboring." In his letters to Philip C. Pendleton, Simms had made a point about the difficulties of even collecting on subscriptions "over an extensive tract of interior country."

By 1845 Simms had turned his attention to the possibility of support from the Southerners who were settling in the West. He even included them in the title of his new magazine, the *Southern and Western Monthly Magazine and Review* (known simply as "Simms's magazine"). When Simms's magazine foundered, and he merged it with the *Southern Literary Messenger,* its editor, Benjamin Minor, was briefly caught up in enthusiasm over the prospect of Western subscribers and included *West* in the new title of the *Messenger* (December, 1845).

In the 1830s and 1840s there had been hope of Northern support. Thomas Willis White, Daniel K. Whitaker, and William Gilmore Simms wanted to establish Southern magazines, but they also believed that a strong Southern literature would benefit American literature. They knew also that Southerners contributed to and subscribed to Northern magazines. For a while Southern editors were caught between their desire to promote Southern literature and yet not be so sectional as to drive away any potential Northern support. A desire to maintain that balance was a major reason for White's alarm over the attack by his editor, Edgar Allan Poe, on New York editor Theodore Fay's novel, *Norman Leslie*. William Richards of the *Orion* had always desired to fill his pages with "productions of Northern pens" and he had some success. And as late as 1858 Paul Hamilton Hayne was able to obtain a minor gem for *Russell's* from the pen of a young John W. De Forest (later famous for *Miss Ravenel's Conversion*) in a short story, "The Smartville Ram Speculation" (January, 1858).

However only the *Southern Literary Messenger* achieved any substantial success in attracting Northern contributors. The *Messenger* managed to enlist as regular essayists and reviewers Henry Tuckerman of Boston, Park Benjamin of New York City, and Henry C. Lea of Philadelphia. In 1905, when former editor Benjamin Minor listed the contributors in his book, *The Southern Literary Messenger,* he tabulated 294 contributors from the South and 134 writers from the North.

By the 1850s increasing sectional antagonisms gave Southern editors the last hope for financial solvency. Southern subscribers might be driven from Northern magazines by the radical abolitionist, utopian transcendental, democratic egalitarian literature that seemed to be increasingly featured there. By 1847 John R. Thompson had already characterized the Southern mind as "conservative in spirit" and in August, 1851, he mounted an appeal to Southern patriotism for the support of Southern magazines. He took the risk that he might lose his Northern contributors and did lose all his regulars except the faithful Henry Tuckerman. A decade later, Thompson's successor, George Bagby, was ready to admit failure too. Southerners had continued, even on the eve of conflict, to subscribe to the New York *Herald* for their news and to *Harper's* for their literature. Thompson had already resigned in 1860 for the less tiring and more rewarding job of editing the *Southern Field and Stream* at a salary of two thousand dollars.

Southern editors had faced what a reader today might recognize as a "catch-22" situation. They believed that Southern literary magazines were necessary to wake Southern writers from their lethargy, yet without an established literature they could not get enough contributors or subscribers to survive. William J. Grayson could see the illogic of the situation. It had been a reversal of the natural order of things to begin with quarterly reviews rather than with books to be reviewed.

In some respects the situation of Southern antebellum magazines was similar to that of little magazines in America a century later. The inability to pay contributors had made Southern editors dependent on submissions by writers not yet established enough to expect payment, on submissions by friends, and on a great deal of last-minute writing by the editors themselves. The most significant literature in antebellum magazines came from the editors. Poe alone contributed enough to make the *Southern Literary Messenger* important in the history of American magazines. Among his contributions in 1835, before he became the editor, were two examples of the new German horror tales, "Berenice" and "Morella," sent to a not-too-appreciative editor and publisher, Thomas Willis White. As editor Poe attracted more attention than White wanted with his attacks on Fay's *Norman Leslie* (December, 1835) and Simms's *The Partisan* (January, 1836). During the last year of his life, on good terms with John Reuben Thompson, Poe began contributing to the *Messenger* again with "The Rationale of Verse" (October, 1848), several of his *Marginalia* reviews, and his poem "Annabel Lee," intended for the *Messenger* but printed in New York before Thompson could be the first to publish it.

No writer helped Southern magazines more than Simms. He contributed major critical essays to Southern magazines, "Modern Prose Fiction," for example, in the *Southern Quarterly Review* (April, 1849), and he fought to keep the *Magnolia* alive with more than sixty contributions. Paul Hamilton Hayne showed the same kind of determination as editor of *Russell's Magazine,* with essays like "The Poets and Poetry of the South" (November, 1857), short stories, poems, and innumerable reviews.

Southern magazines made few important discoveries of Southern talent. Poe's career was advanced and Hayne could be regarded as a discovery by the *Southern Literary Messenger.* Timrod as a critic was the discovery of *Russell's Magazine,* to which he contributed some of his most important critical essays, including "Literature in the South" (August, 1859), and several of his better poems. The record of antebellum magazines in publishing local color and Southern humor was not distinguished, but they did publish A. B. Longstreet, Joseph Glover Baldwin, George Bagby, and William Elliott.

Perhaps most distinctively Southern of all the contributions to Southern magazines are the critical essays and the book reviews, often hurriedly done and impressionistic. There were few theoretical essays. The nearest approach to the genial criticism of the *Democratic Review* or the *Dial,* which was attuned to democratic content and to the reproductive appreciation of genius, was that in *Russell's Magazine,* where both Timrod and Hayne showed interest in some of the new romantic ideas about poetry and the imagination. Yet to Timrod the hold of eighteenth-century ideas on the Southern critical mind was still strong. "The opinions and theories of the last century are still held in reverence. Here Pope is regarded by many as the most *correct* of English poets, and here *Kaimes* [*sic*], after having been removed to the top-shelves of the libraries, is still thumbed by learned professors and declamatory sophomores" (August, 1859).

Timrod may have exaggerated the influence of a lingering neoclassicism on Southern criticism, but he is accurate about the long-lasting impact of the Scottish rhetoricians, especially Kames and Blair, on Southern critical practice. Their theories were discussed in essays in the *Southern Review* in the early 1830s, in the *Magnolia* in the 1840s, and in the 1850s in the *Southern Quarterly Review* and even in *Russell's,* where Paul Hamilton Hayne was trying to introduce the new critical ideas of Coleridge, H. N. Hudson, Edwin Percy Whipple, Margaret Fuller, and Matthew Arnold. The debate "What is Poetry?" between William J. Grayson and Timrod, featured in *Russell's* in 1857, represented the old—Grayson's preference for Pope and Dryden and the critical ideas of Kames and Blair—and the new—Timrod's excitement about the ideas of Wordsworth and Coleridge.

The stranglehold of a judicial approach to criticism is not surprising. The editors of Southern magazines saw their mission as judicial, "the proper development of talent and genius of a people." Critical standards were too low. To Simms, writing in the *Magnolia,* the critical obligation of the editor was "to elevate the standards of criticism to a proper level, and to strengthen the case of letters against the indiscriminate and dishonest trade in one of the besetting sins of our native criticism" (April, 1842). A new popular literature and the use of literature for practical effects were being encouraged by critics in the North. Evert Duyckinck in "The Prospects of 1845" predicted a miraculous era during which a great American literature would be produced. Southern critics often gave another, more pessimistic version. To both Hayne and Thompson, Walt Whitman's *Leaves of Grass* was an example of the new sensationalism in literature. To practically all Southern reviewers Harriet Beecher Stowe's *Uncle Tom's Cabin* was an example of propaganda, the misuse of literature for practical purposes. Transcendentalism was an example of the new obscurity in literature, based philosophically on the false doctrine of perfectionism.

From the perspective of a modern critic, the most grievous fault of Southern periodical criticism is that it missed the American Renaissance and pretty much failed to appreciate the great English romantics. Bryant was consistently the South's idea of a good American poet. Scott and Bulwer-Lytton were the favorite novelists because of their craftsmanship and the historical truth they portrayed. Lord Byron was the most admired romantic poet. There were, however, signs of change. Simms and Timrod praised Wordsworth; Tennyson's craftsmanship was beginning to find its admirers; Thackeray just might be a worthy successor to Fielding. It did not matter. The events of 1860 were to bring a long temporary close to all critical debates between the representatives of the old views and the new. No literary magazine would survive the war. The discussions of the 1850s would have to be taken up again in the 1870s and in the 1880s, and the "peculiar institution" would be gone.

LEWIS P. SIMPSON

The Mind of the Antebellum South

I n the *Education of Henry Adams* (1918), Adams states that the ante-bellum South expressed "no need or desire for intellectual culture in its own right." Personifying the Old South's intellectual condition in the figure of Robert E. Lee's son, Roony, whom he had known at Harvard between 1854 and 1858, Adams remarks that the Southerner was "handsome, genial," and born to command, yet could hardly conceive of an idea, let alone analyze one. He had "no mind; he had a temperament." While he renders a more involved judgment on the intellect of the antebellum South than Adams, Allen Tate in his well-known "A Southern Mode of the Imagination" (1959) suggests the author of the *Education* in portraying the "Old Southerner" as "wholly committed" to agrarian patriotism and the rhetoric of politics. He was, Tate says, a "composite image of Cincinnatus dropping the plough for the sword, and of Cicero leaving his rhetorical studies to apply them patriotically to the prosecution of Catiline." In *The Mind of the South* (1941), W. J. Cash assesses the intellect of the Old South more harshly than either Adams or Tate, declaring that the South was completely devoid of thought: "Satisfaction was the hallmark of Southern society; masters and masses alike were sunk in the deepest complacency; nowhere was there any tendency to question."

More recent inquiries into the culture of the antebellum South indicate that the images projected by Adams, Tate, and Cash are misleading, oversimplifying an intellectual life that was essentially continuous with the great secular critique of man and God, nature and society, and of mind itself, that in two centuries had "deconstructed" Christendom and instituted modernity, created the American Revolution, and embodied itself in a novel nation often referred to as the "Great Experiment." Save for Benjamin Franklin, no single American incarnated the great critique more graphically than the Virginia slave master and man of letters Thomas Jefferson. Celebrating Bacon, Newton, and Locke as the pre-eminent exemplars of the modern age, Jefferson recognized its central principle in the Baconian dictum: "Knowledge is power." Like the master of Monticello—and like George Mason, Richard Henry Lee, James Madison, and George Washington—postrevolutionary men of letters in Virginia and in the South generally assumed the power of mind to be the directing force of the new nation. They also understood it to be the guiding power of their increasingly self-conscious region. But even the most favorable evaluation of the intellect of the mid-nineteenth-century South cannot obviate the patent truth that it failed to fulfill the promise of thought and letters exemplified by the Jeffersonian generation. The failure resulted neither from intellectual complacency nor lack of mental activity. It was fundamentally owing to the complicated connection between the power of mind and the institution of chattel slavery. This relationship frustrated both scientific and literary achievement.

Researching the files of the *American Journal of Science* from 1850 to 1860, Clement Eaton discovered that the South had a "proper proportion" of theoretical scientists at work in such prominent fields as geology, geography, physics, chemistry, botany, and astronomy. Yet in *The Mind of the Old South* Eaton concludes that the region contributed comparatively little to science and that its cast of mind remained "on the whole, unscientific." Several antebellum professional scientists in America were Southerners. These included William Barton Rogers (1804–1882), who was born in Pennsylvania but brought up in the South. After he became professor of natural philosophy at the University of Virginia in 1835, Rogers undertook the studies (with his brother Henry, 1808–1866) that led to a classic paper, "On the Physical Structure of the Appalachian Chain as Exemplifying the Laws Which Have Regulated the Elevation of Great Mountain Chains Generally." Following the presentation of their work to the American Association of Geologists and Naturalists in 1842, Rogers was elected to membership in the Geological Society of London. A native Southerner who became a well-known scientist was Joseph LeConte of Georgia (1823–1901). Upon the completion of a period of study with Louis Agassiz at Harvard, LeConte was appointed to be his noted mentor's assistant in an investigation into the origin and structure of the Florida Keys and the adjacent coral reefs. Developing a twin interest in geology and zoology, in 1855 LeConte prepared a widely noted report for the American Association for the Advancement of Science, "On the Agency of the Gulf Stream in the Formation of the Peninsula Keys of Florida." In 1860 he was elected secretary of the association. A still more famous native-born Southern scientist was Matthew Maury (1806–1873). Maury, whose major work is *The Physical Geography of the Sea* (1855) and who drew the route for the first Atlantic cable, is most often remembered as the founder of the United States Weather Bureau. But though the ante-bellum South could claim prominent scientists like Rogers, LeConte, and Maury, it was heavily dependent on the North for scientists to teach in its colleges and completely dependent on the North for advanced scientific education. Southern natives who became scientists, moreover, were sooner or later attracted to positions beyond the South. LeConte, a slave owner and loyal secessionist who served the Confederacy as a chemist, stayed in the South until after the Civil War, when he left to become a professor at the University of California. Maury, like LeConte a supporter of slavery and of the Confederacy (he served as an officer in the Confederate navy) spent much of his career both before and after the Civil War outside the South. Rogers was less equivocal. Longing for "an atmosphere of more stimulating power," he left the South in 1854 to live in Boston. Establishing himself firmly in New England, in 1862 he be-came the founder and first president of the Massachusetts Institute of Technology. The only scientist of note who had an unequivocal devotion to the South was the gifted amateur in agricultural experimentation Edmund Ruffin (1794–1865). This Virginia planter, whose *Essay on Calcareous Manures* (1832) marks the beginning of scientific agricul-ture in America, is ironically commemorated as the intransigent seces-sionist who fired the first shot in the Civil War, and who upon its con-clusion, in a final act of defiance of the "perfidious, malignant, & vile Yankee race," killed himself.

Ruffin's irrational act terminated a period in the history of mind in the South that had begun definitively thirty years or so earlier. Moving from his interest in scientific agriculture to an absolute, obsessive com-mitment to the secessionist cause, Ruffin, the type of Southerner known as a "fire-eater," was the logical embodiment of a changed relationship between chattel slavery and the planting states. The origin of slavery in first one Southern colony and then another had been regarded in the light of historical circumstance. With the invention of the cotton gin and the steamboat and the rise of the cotton mills in the North and in England, slavery—expanding with the growth of the cotton kingdom—took on the aspect of a providential institution that must be considered as not only peculiar but indispensable to the Southern states; and the Southern region of the United States, in which the majority of white inhabitants did not own slaves but supported the institution of slavery, took on the aspect of a great slave society, stretching from the south Atlantic seaboard to east Texas. The central dedication of mind in the South—of its "men of mind," as William Gilmore Simms liked to call his literary and intellectual colleagues—became a struggle to define and interpret, to themselves, other Southerners, and the world, the nature and destiny of the evolving modern slave society in which they lived.

The meaning of this struggle may be better understood today than formerly. Introducing a recent collection of proslavery writings, *The Ideology of Slavery: Proslavery Thought in the Old South, 1830–1860* (1981), Drew Gilpin Faust points to the inclination among present-day historians of the South to see the advocacy of slavery not as "evidence of moral failure" on the part of the Southerners but as a key to "wider patterns of beliefs and values." As the slavery controversy increased in intensity during the thirty years before the Civil War, it became the means through which "Americans generally," Northerners as well as Southerners, reassessed the "profoundest assumptions on which their world was built." Seeking a conceptual basis for slavery as an institution, Southern intellectuals considered slavery, as the collection of essays *Cotton Is King and Pro-Slavery Arguments* (1860) asserts, to bear on "History, Political Economy, Moral Philosophy, Political Science, Theology, Social Life, Ethnology and International Law." One of the most learned of the proslavery writers, George Frederick Holmes (1820–1897), using the term *literature* in the broad signification it still had in his age, declared: "We shall be indebted to the continuance and asperity of the [slavery] controversy for the creation of a genuine southern literature. . . . For out of this slavery agitation has sprung not merely essays on slavery, valuable and suggestive as they have been, but also the literary activity, and the literary movement which have lately characterized the intellect of the South."

In 1822 the abolitionist Benjamin Lundy prophesied that slavery was doomed by the "modern march of mind." A relic of barbarism, it could not stand against the "mighty force of Public Opinion." The proslavery argument attempted to refute the abolitionist argument on its own terms. Southern writers, that is, formulated the argument for slavery not as a reaction against the Enlightenment quest for order but as a part of the modern movement of mind. Their motive, emerging clearly in the latter days of the Old South, was to establish the idea that the South was fulfilling the novel political and social order that had emerged out of the American Revolution.

This motive was implicit in the effort of John C. Calhoun (1782–1850) to resolve the slavery crisis by a "strict" interpretation of the constitutional structure of the United States. Expressing his views to a considerable extent through speeches and letters, Calhoun was the author of two classic treatises (both published posthumously in Calhoun's *Works* [1851–1855]): *A Disquisition on Government* and the unfinished *Discourse on the Constitution of the United States*. In striking opposition to the egalitarian premise of Jefferson, Calhoun argued that inequality is the basic condition of men and that liberty is not a natural but an earned right. In his reversal of Jeffersonian theory, he conceived that a rational consideration of human nature must conclude that it is inherently given to evil and requires strong social discipline. He did not, however, propose a case for slavery. His concern was the political necessity of maintaining the right to own slaves against the power of the opposing "numerical majority." Thus he interpreted the Constitution of the United States to define the source of freedom as being not in the submission to the rule of the majority of numbers but in respect for the will of the majority opinion, or "concurrent majority," which is made up of each interest or section. Defining the South to be a concurrent majority on the issue of slavery, Calhoun was primarily concerned not with overt acts of power against his region, but with the power exerted on its sense of identity through the depreciation of the Southern intellectual and moral character by a numerical majority. Equating slavery with "acknowledged inferiority," Calhoun saw the necessity of maintaining the power of mind in the South. "I ask whether we have not contributed our full share of talents and political wisdom in forming and sustaining this political fabric," he inquired in 1837 in a speech opposing the reception of abolition petitions by the United States Congress, "and whether we have not constantly inclined most strongly to the side of liberty, and been the first to see and first to resist the encroachment of power." The question was an anxious one, and Calhoun would seem to have addressed it as much to himself and his fellow Southerners as to the abolitionists. Fearing inferiority, in fact believing "acknowledged inferiority" to be equivalent to slavery, Calhoun implies everywhere in his writings that the South must maintain its status as a symbol of mind. This implication was still more plainly a motive in the tracts and treatises of the proslavery argument proper.

The full-fledged argument for slavery, like Calhoun's more indirect case for slavery, was a revision of the thought of the founders of the Republic, in particular Jefferson's. The proslavery writers agreed on the whole that, in establishing the "Great Experiment" through (as Alexander Hamilton said) the revolutionary process of "reflection and choice," the founders had tended to allow theory to obscure reality. In the aftermath of the Nat Turner rebellion and the famous debate about slavery in the Virginia House of Delegates in 1831–1832, Thomas Dew (1802–1846) wrote the prototypical document in a literature that was to flow unceasingly from Southern pens for the next thirty years. First published in the *American Quarterly Review* in 1832, Dew's essay was expanded and published later the same year as *Review of the Debate in the Virginia Legislature*. Observing that the Southerners lived in a long-established slave society, and urging them both to accept the actuality of their historical situation and to justify it to the South and to the world in the face of the abolitionist version of the Southern reality, Dew anticipated the voluminous proslavery argument that present-day students read in its two major consolidations: *The Pro-Slavery Argument as Maintained by the Most Distinguished Writers of the Southern States* (1852), and the volume already mentioned, *Cotton Is King* (1860).

Amplifying, and intensifying, Dew's presentation of the case for slavery, William Harper (1790–1847) of South Carolina declared in his *Memoir on Slavery, Read Before the Society for the Advancement of Learning of South Carolina at Its Annual Meeting at Columbia* (1838): "President Dew [Thomas Dew was president of the College of William and Mary] has shown that the institution of slavery is a principal cause of civilization. Perhaps nothing can be more evident than that it is the sole cause." Harper points out that the command of labor by means of the "coercion of Slavery alone is adequate to form man to habits of labour" and without it "there can be no accumulation of property, no providence for the future, no taste for comforts or elegancies, which are the characteristics and essentials of civilization." It is of the "order of nature and of God," Harper says, "that the being of superior faculties and knowledge, and therefore of superior power, should control and dispose of those that are inferior."

Tying the Baconian equation of knowledge and power to the notion of slavery as the redemption from barbarism of the enslaved (a redemption the white man must be the agent of no matter the "burden" it becomes), Harper incorporates slavery into the "march of mind" and enlists the Southern slaveholder in this movement. By implication he translates the Baconian dictum "Knowledge is power" into the sanction for slavery. Like Jefferson, who virtually divinized Bacon, Newton, and Locke as a secular trinity, proslavery men of letters, as Drew Gilpin Faust makes clear in *A Sacred Circle: The Dilemma of the Intellectual in the Old South, 1840–1860* (1977), considered Bacon to be an intellectual hero. James Henry Hammond (1807–1864), whose *Two Letters on Slavery in the United States Addressed to Thomas Clarkson, Esq.* (1845) is an important proslavery treatise, proclaimed in 1840 that a new "Baconian era in science & in morals" was in prospect. George Frederick Holmes looked forward to the South's participation in "an intellectual reformation analogous to the Instauratio Magna of Lord Bacon." Nathaniel Beverley Tucker, another leading proslavery figure, shared a similar enthusiasm for a Baconian renaissance in the South.

Claiming that Bacon's empiricism and experimentalism had been wrongly interpreted as materialistic in motive, the Southern proponents of slavery, as Faust shows, linked the discovery of physical truth with the discovery of moral truth, envisioned the South properly understood as the fulfillment of the American quest for a moral social order, and enlisted the Southern slaveholder as a leading figure in the progress of civilization. The purest champion of this idea of the South was probably Henry Hughes (1829–1862). A disciple of Auguste Comte, Hughes states in his *Treatise on Sociology: Theoretical and Practical* (1854) that the consummation of slavery's progress in history is imminent. It only awaits the world's realization that the slavery system in the American South embodies the scheme of "warranteeism" set forth by Comte. Identifying the Southern slave master as the warrantor and his chattel as the warrantee, Hughes describes the Southern order, governed by an absolute reciprocity of duties and obligations, to be potentially a near perfect society.

A religious skeptic, Hughes was probably unique among proslavery writers in attributing the role of social development entirely to man rather than assigning primacy to the directing hand of God. But he was not alone in ascribing historical singularity to the society of the South. Most proslavery writers tended to see slavery as a part of a special, divinely designed, organic social structure. Nonetheless they also recognized the slave society in which they lived as an integral part of the society of the Great Experiment—a society invented by man, announced by the Declaration of Independence, and put into effective operation by the Constitution adopted in 1789.

The tension generated in the proslavery depiction of the South—a portrayal which assumed that the South constituted on one hand an order rooted in tradition, and on the other an order modeled on the rational processes of the independent mind—is noticeably present in another proslavery exponent of the sociological mode, George Fitzhugh (1804–1881). Fitzhugh, who is best known for two books, *Sociology for the South: or the Failure of Free Society* (1854) and *Cannibals All! or Slaves Without Masters* (1857), rejected Locke and Jefferson, the Jefferson of the Declaration in particular. An absolute opponent of free labor and the capitalistic system, he argued that the modern politial economy, which defies the fundamental social principle that men are helpless when isolated from each other and sets every man up for himself, is destroying the social fabric, the basis of civilization. Since association by labor and division of expenses is the true secret of both national and individual wealth, and this combination of circumstances is fostered by slavery and prevented by free society, chattel slavery must become the universal labor system. Joining will and mind, men of letters in the American South, Fitzhugh said, can through will and mind create a convincing moral argument for the necessity of the worldwide adoption of its slavery system. But Southern thought must will to a "distinct thought—not a half thought." Vindicating slavery "in the abstract, and in the general, as a normal, natural, and, *in general*, necessitous element of civilized society, without regard to race or color," Fitzhugh asserted, the Southerners will "inaugurate a new philosophy of ethics or morals." Excluding all save Southerners from the American claim to novelty, Fitzhugh said, "We alone are a new people."

In spite of his energetic and prolific promotion of the Southern cause, Fitzhugh's contemporaries in the proslavery struggle regarded him with some trepidation. They sensed that the radical side of his argument implied the ultimate logic of the proslavery argument as a whole: namely, the total rejection of the South as a traditional order and the acceptance of its unique historical character as a modern historical mission to create a society in which the slavery system would be attached neither to capitalism nor race. Southerners drew back from a separation from the dynamics of capitalism; and they were unwilling to attempt to extend slavery, as Fitzhugh saw they must, to the lower orders of the white race. They were reluctant to follow the logical imperative of their history. This demanded, as Henry James envisioned retrospectively in his remarkable treatment of the antebellum South in *The American Scene* (1907), their "complete intellectual, moral and economic reconsecration of slavery, an enlarged and glorified, quite beatified, explication of its principle." Still, Southerners dreamed of the Southern singularity, and subscribed to the vision of the Confederate States of America proclaimed by Henry Timrod in "Ethnogenesis" (1861), which presents a great slave and cotton dominion as the salvation of the world.

> Could we climb
> Some mighty Alp, and view the coming time,
> The rapturous sight would fill
>   Our eyes with happy tears!
> Not only for the glories which the years
> Shall bring us; not for lands from sea to sea,
> And wealth, and power, and peace, though these shall be;
> But for the distant peoples we shall bless,
> And the hushed murmurs of a world's distress:
> For, to give labor to the poor,
>   The whole sad planet o'er,

> And save from want and crime the humblest door,
> Is one among the many ends for which
> God makes us great and rich!

The Southern appropriation of the messianic promise of the Great Experiment, the redemption of history through the agency of a novel slave society, was integrated with the religious or biblical argument for slavery. Voluminous in its expression from Protestant (chiefly Methodist, Baptist, and Presbyterian) pulpits and in printed sermons and tracts, this argument is well represented in *A Brief Examination of Scripture Testimony on the Institution of Slavery* (1850) by a Baptist preacher, the reverend Thornton Stringfellow (1788–1869). According to the evidence in the Bible, Stringfellow contends, the divine authorization of slavery is fully present in (1) the sanction of slavery by God in the patriarchal age and in the succeeding age from Abraham until the coming of Jesus Christ; (2) the recognition by Jesus of slavery as a "lawful relation"; (3) the merciful promise of slavery as the means of salvation for "millions of Ham's descendents" who save for their enslavement "would have sunk down to eternal ruin." The coalescence of the secular and religious visions of the institution of slavery in the proslavery argument is another instance of the phenomenon Hegel defined as "the secularization of the spiritual," by which he meant "the spiritualization of the secular." An economic institution or a labor system of fortuitous historical origins was identified with the operation of God's will in history. As the justification of chattel slavery became common in Southern pulpits the secular politics of slavery became a spiritual cause; and as politics in the Southern states became increasingly the politics of a slave society, religion and the state became unofficially yet closely identified in the South, and the Southern Protestant denominations severed themselves from their ties with their respective counterparts in the Northern states. In effect in the South the secular state, conceived on rational principles, and the institution of slavery, ordained by God, were joined. The church became the servant of the state, and the rational principle of the separation of church and state was abrogated.

If in a discernible sense the political republic and the "republic of Christ" (the *respublica* and the *respublica Christiana*) were reunited in the Old South, after their divorcement in the Jeffersonian age, so too were the republic of letters—the independent realm of secular letters and learning—and the political republic. Constituting an invisible order of mind, as Voltaire said at the height of the Enlightenment, everywhere independent in spite of religious and political oppression, the literary polity was essentially the source of the American Revolution and the new nation, a model state invented by the rational mind. But by the mid-nineteenth century in the South the politics of slavery had assimilated the modern realm of letters as well as the ancient realm of religion.

Alexis de Tocqueville illuminates the psychic state of the man of letters in the antebellum South when he observes (in the first volume of *Democracy in America* [1835]) that the Southern slave masters, unlike their ancient counterparts, do not rely on "fetters and death" to control their slaves, but, having discovered "more intellectual securities for their duration," employ "despotism . . . and violence against the human mind." Forbidding their slaves to learn to read and to write, the masters reduce them as nearly as possible to the level of "brutes" in order to guarantee racial segregation. But the prohibition against the dissemination of skill in letters among slaves was also dictated by another motive. While not as easily discernible as the racial motive (perhaps hardly separable from it), this was the unspoken fear of the potential mental capacity of the slaves. As has been remarked in the chapter "The Ideology of Revolution," Jefferson considered the Negro to be inferior in all human capacities yet was disturbed by the evident rational desire for freedom on the part of the slave. Query XVIII of the *Notes on Virginia* envisions a slave rebellion against the masters originating in the capacity of the slave to participate in the modern definition of history. In this definition, history has both its source and model in the human mind. The rational treatment of the slave demanded that his potential power to take part in the process of history be suppressed. To deny the slave the right to read and write by governmental decree was recognized as a strict necessity in the post-Jeffersonian South. Accepting this necessity, the Southern man of letters said that the slave had no mind at all and consequently did not participate in history. In its tacit denial of the liberal, cosmopolitan idealism of the republic of letters, this attitude implied the closure of the literary polity in the South in the realm of the state. When the editor of the *Southern Literary Messenger* was accused of "injudicious leniency towards Northern books and authors," Paul Hamilton Hayne, editor of *Russell's Magazine*, argued in his fellow editor's defense: "Now, it seems that when a work is purely *literary*, interfering in no way with the 'peculiar institution,' or our rights under it, common honesty requires that it should be reviewed without reference to the birth-place of its author, or the locale of the publication. A true literary spirit is essentially liberal, and the Editor who should arraign Irving's 'Washington' or Hawthorne's Tales, upon the charge that their authors were Northern men, would be guilty of the grossest absurdity."

Southern men of letters, in other words, subscribed to a literary ethos based on their "rights under slavery." Seemingly impervious to the irony of their ethical situation, they no doubt agreed with William Gilmore Simms's argument in his address "The Epoch and Events of American History, as Suited to the Purposes of Art in Fiction" (1842) that it is the artist who is the only "true historian"—the only one "who gives shape to the scattered fragments," who "unites the parts in coherent dependency, and endows with life and action, the otherwise motionless automata of history." But at the same time they effectually frustrated the concept of the mind of the writer as the true source of history by excluding from mind's authority the right to criticize slavery.* The situation of the man of letters in the antebellum South is reflected, indirectly but surely, in Simms's portrayal in *Woodcraft* (1854) of the relationship between the indolent planter and philosopher Porgy and Tom, his body slave. When Porgy offers to set Tom free, the slave replies: "Ef I doesn't b'long to *you*, you b'long to *me*! . . . You b'long to *me* Tom, jes' as much as me Tom b'long to *you*; and you nebber guine git *you* free paper from me long as you lib." Porgy argues, if futilely, against the utilitarian image of existence urged by his overseer Millhouse. But he cannot argue with Tom's image of reality. Porgy's consciousness is closed in the mind of his slave. Tom's refusal of his freedom is at once an idealization of the master-slave relationship by Simms, slave master and man of letters, and a profoundly ironic assertion that the mind of the slave is the source of Southern history.

* Not all men of letters in the antebellum South were assimilated by the official proslavery orthodoxy. In *The Other South: Southern Dissenters in the Nineteenth Century South* (New York, 1974), Carl Degler argues that there was never a general "blackout" on the expression of antislavery sentiments in the South. Degler points out in convincing detail the continuous existence of antislavery opinions by Southerners, who in a number of instances remained in the South in spite of their outspoken views. The minority opposition to slavery, he observes, stressed its harmful effects not on the enslaved but on the rest of the Southern population, slaveholders and nonslaveholders. Particular emphasis was often given to the bad influence of slavery on education, or, it may be said, on letters and learning, on the mind. But the Southern antislavery writers referred only to the education of the white South, not considering African slaves capable of intellectual development. In a curious way the antislavery Southern intellectuals (like Hinton R. Helper, author of the notorious *The Impending Crisis: How to Meet It* [1857]), were as assimilated to the Southern politics of slavery as proslavery men of letters.

THE WAR AND AFTER

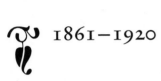 1861–1920

RAYBURN S. MOORE

Introduction to Part II

The coming of the war brought about some significant changes in the situation of the Southern writer. He now had to express his allegiance more openly in his work, whether he wished to or not, and even those authors like William Gilmore Simms and John R. Thompson, who had earlier defended the Southern way, were now expected to defend it even more consistently. The war led to other compromises, and the exigencies and difficulties of composition and publication were considerable. But the subsequent defeat of the Confederacy resulted in a serious though ultimately temporary discouragement of literature. Sources of publication disappeared and were not immediately replaced in the North, though gradually *Appleton's Journal, Lippincott's,* and *Scribner's* led the way in opening their pages to Southern writers, and all the great Northern literary magazines were printing Southern contributions and materials by the 1880s. Southern fiction in particular became popular; even Simms's novels were reprinted in the 1880s, and John Esten Cooke's new postwar stories sold well, but the main staple of the period was the local-color fiction published in magazines and thence in book form about plantation life in Virginia, mountaineers in Tennessee, crackers in Georgia, Creoles in Louisiana, and Negroes throughout the region. Poetry was less popular and paid less well, but even Hayne to some extent and Sidney Lanier to a greater extent were mindful of mundane matters like dialect, cotton, corn, and trade, and their verse expressed such realities in the context of the Anglo-American-Southern romantic tradition.

Interest in the community, the land and the people in it—the poor white and the black man as well as the planter—and the language of all levels not only characterizes the writing of the period but suggests ties with the past of Simms and Longstreet and also looks forward to the work of Faulkner, Wolfe, Warren, and Welty. Thus the writing of the period 1861–1920, even though separated from its immediate past by a war and from its future by another conflict of an even greater scope, is in important ways related both to its past and its future.

ELISABETH MUHLENFELD

The Civil War and Authorship

The literature of the Civil War era is the perennial poor relation of Southern literature; the product of a people drained by genuine crisis, it was impoverished and has been generally ignored. With the exception of Henry Timrod, no major Southern writer is linked inextricably with the war years, and in almost every comprehensive study of literature in the South, the nineteenth century divides neatly into the antebellum period, with emphasis on the 1830s, 1840s, and 1850s, and the postwar period beginning in the 1870s and flourishing in the 1880s with such writers as George Washington Cable, Joel Chandler Harris, Thomas Nelson Page, and, of course, Mark Twain. The nearly twenty years that were consumed in preparation for secession and in civil war, defeat, and reconstruction produced little first-rate traditional literature. Nevertheless, the Civil War era merits far more attention than it has received. Much work in the period develops antebellum ideas and structures, and it was in these years that many of the major themes and philosophical approaches of what we term the Southern Renascence began to form and receive expression by Southern writers.

The Civil War years were important to the development of Southern literature in several ways. First, the formation of the Confederacy and its national call to arms encouraged in Southerners an examination of their regional identity. Second, the war forced the South to rely more fully on its own literary resources rather than on those of New England or Europe. Southern writers found their readership altered almost overnight. No longer were they writing primarily for Northern readers, to whom they had perforce to defend an increasingly alien culture; instead, and suddenly, they addressed their work to men and women who shared their cultural background and concerns. These two related changes, coupled with the hardships of war itself, were accompanied by a slow abandonment of the self-consciously literary language, so widely employed by antebellum writers, in favor of simpler styles reflective of regional speech. At war's end, as the South began the difficult task of healing itself, its writers drew upon the two most distinctly Southern types of prewar writing: the historical romance and the coarse, realistic sketches of the Old Southwest humorists. Each type changed somewhat—the humor mellowing and taking on consciously literary structures, the historical romance shifting from colonial to antebellum settings—and blended with the other in the work of Cable, Clemens, and many popular local-color writers. Finally, though the war itself produced little meritorious literature in formal genres, it gave birth to a rich and relatively unstudied body of writing in the speeches, editorials, diaries, letters, and memoirs of a people seeking to explain, and ultimately to understand, themselves.

A discussion of these changes must begin with the 1850s, when the Southern writer's principal publishing outlets as well as his major readership continued to be in the North. The South had numerous publishers, to be sure. The 1852 *Bibliotheca Americana* listed nearly a hundred—fifteen in Charleston alone. But no Southern publishing house had the professional expertise to edit, advertise, and market serious literature effectively. Thus, a writer who wished to be read published in the North where he frequently found his work discredited as the product of a slave society.

In 1859, Timrod expressed the situation clearly in the essay "Literature in the South," published in *Russell's Magazine*. The fate of the "poor scribbler so unfortunate as to be born South of the Potomac" was grim indeed. "It is the settled conviction of the North that genius is indigenous there. . . . It is the equally firm conviction of the South that genius . . . is an exotic that will not flower on a Southern soil." If the Southern author published in the North, wrote Timrod, he was condemned by his countrymen; if he published in the South his book would not sell. If he wrote about his own culture, he would be abused by Northern readers and ignored at home. Ironically, Timrod's essay was itself a case in point, published in one of the best Southern literary magazines of its time but largely unread. *Russell's* boasted few subscribers outside South Carolina, could not pay even its best contributors adequately, could not pay its editor, Paul Hamilton Hayne, at all, and was forced to cease publication in March, 1860, three years after it had begun.

Southern men of letters such as Timrod and Hayne were anxious to avoid political rhetoric and sectional prejudices, but the times were against them. Hayne, writing in January, 1860, wanted to keep *Russell's Magazine* "as far removed as possible from tumult, passion, and deeds of violence and bloodshed!" Nevertheless, the intellectual climate in the South had already become thoroughly political, and as war became

179

likely, the South's most active pens poured out impassioned debate on political tactics, defense of regional custom, and, finally, a national call to arms. By April, 1861, even newspapers that had the preceding year come down firmly for the preservation of the Union now declared the South had no choice but to fight. Although scattered dissenters continued to speak out against the new Confederacy and a few writers and editors like Virginians Moncure Daniel Conway and David Hunter Strother (a successful journalist known as Porte Crayon) remained loyal to the Union, they represented a tiny minority. Southerners of every stamp invested themselves wholeheartedly in the "great revolution."

That the people of the Confederacy viewed their cause as nothing less than a revolution is immensely important for a study of the literature of the era. In revolutionary times, all thought, all energy of a people in revolt is necessarily devoted to the struggle at hand. Such was the case during the Confederacy. In the moving poem "Ethnogenesis," written early in 1861, Timrod gave joyful thanks for the birth of a noble nation, but the poem also offered a sober contemplation of impending war. For the time being, most writers found purely literary subjects irrelevant. Once the new nation was free, however, its leaders believed a genuinely Southern literature would flourish, producing a new classical age with the war itself inspiring great epics, poems, and romances. And from the beginning, the Confederate government demonstrated its determination to provide a healthy climate for such a literary flowering. It took a strong stand for freedom of the press and immediately enacted copyright provisions.

After war became reality, few writers had leisure for serious literary work. Instead, they entered the military or became involved in the new journals and newspapers that sprang up to support the war effort. Several publishing houses expanded operations, not only to fill the need created when Northern publishers were cut off, but also to accommodate the printing demands of the government and military. Among the most important publishers during the war years were West and Johnston and Ayers and Wade, both of Richmond; Burke, Boykin and Company of Macon; H. C. Clarke of Vicksburg; and S. H. Goetzel and Company of Mobile. Even for these major firms, publishing in the midst of war was an uncertain business that had to contend with military invasion, rampant inflation, and, perhaps most frustrating on a daily basis, the dearth of equipment and supplies. By 1863, S. H. Goetzel was routinely publishing books in wallpaper covers, and the poor quality of hastily manufactured paper became a source of annoyance to publishers and readers alike.

Almost all of the fiction and poetry published during the war was intensely martial. As the Richmond *Semi-Weekly Courier* put it in 1863, Confederate literature had "the ring of steel; its color is . . . blood-red and its perfume is that of sulphur and nitre." A few editions of British and European novels were pirated, among them works of Thackeray, Dickens, Wilkie Collins, George Eliot, and Bulwer-Lytton. Certainly the best-known foreign import was a translation in five parts of Victor Hugo's *Les Misérables*, published in 1863–1864, which soon had the Army of Northern Virginia calling itself Lee's Miserables. Burke, Boykin and Company brought out the first edition of Augustus Baldwin Longstreet's *Master William Mitten* (1864), which had appeared serially before the war, and West and Johnston issued a new edition of Nathaniel Beverley Tucker's *The Partisan Leader* (1836) in 1862. David Flavel Jamison's two-volume *The Life and Times of Bertrand Du Guesclin* appeared in 1864, and here and there appeared a poorly written tale of the American Revolution in the style made popular by Simms. But with these exceptions noted, virtually all original fiction, poetry, drama, biography, and history written during the war took war as its theme and polemics as its tone.

Prior to 1863, few nonmilitary books of any kind were published with the exception of songbooks and such peripheral items as Kittrell J. Warren's short jokebook for soldiers, *Ups & Downs of Wife Hunting* (1861). By 1862, instant histories of the war began to appear, and throughout the hostilities, eyewitness accounts continued to be published, precursors of the diaries and memoirs that were to appear well into the twentieth century. The death of General Thomas J. "Stonewall" Jackson in 1863 inaugurated a steady stream of biographies of war heroes.

By 1863, the war had become firmly established in the popular mind as, in John Esten Cooke's words, "the bludgeon against the rapier—the crop-eared Puritan against the Cavalier," and the romantic exploits of such colorful figures as John S. Mosby and J. E. B. Stuart cemented the image. As the war ground on, spreading death, pain, and privation into every echelon of Southern society, sentimental novels began to appear glamorizing battle and urging the honor of the cause. Titles such as James Dabney McCabe's *The Aide-de-Camp; a Romance of the War* (1863), Alexander St. Clair Abrams' *The Trials of the Soldier's Wife: A Tale of the Second American Revolution* (1864) and Reverend Ebenezer Warren's *Nellie Norton; or Southern Slavery & The Bible—A Scriptural Refutation of the Principal Arguments upon which the Abolitionists Rely . . .* (1864) reflected the spirit of the times.

Discerning contemporary readers dismissed most of this fiction as poor, but it served as escape literature for the soldier in the field. Printed in small runs because of the shortage of paper, such novels were usually read literally to pieces and hence have become rarities. They served a political purpose as well. The best of the Confederate novels, Augusta Jane Evans' *Macaria; or Altars of Sacrifice* (1864), for which General P. G. T. Beauregard had written out a full account of the first battle of Bull Run, was spirited through the blockade and pirated in New York. Union general George H. Thomas found the book dangerous and ordered all copies in his command burned. Similarly, copies of Cooke's 1863 biography of Stonewall Jackson found their way across enemy lines, and the United States Army subsequently banned the book because of its appealing presentation of the Confederate soldier.

Even more war-minded than the fiction of the period was the poetry, which poured forth in such astonishing quantities that some editors appealed to the public to send no more. As George W. Bagby commented in his *Southern Literary Messenger* in 1863, "We are receiving too much trash in rhyme." The work of Timrod, Hayne, John R. Thompson (editor of the *Southern Illustrated News*), James Ryder Randall (whose passionate and bloody "Maryland, My Maryland" quickly brought him acclaim), Margaret Junkin Preston, Francis O. Ticknor, and William Gilmore Simms represented war poetry at its best; most other work was amateurish. But professional and amateur alike reflected intense patriotism and religious conviction. The dirge for the fallen hero became a popular form.

Many interesting literary efforts of the war years were published only in journals and newspapers. When the war began, nearly a hundred journals existed in the Confederate states; the most prestigious was the long-established *Southern Literary Messenger*, which Poe had edited. Other journals that attempted to find and publish good fiction and poetry included *De Bow's Review, Southern Field and Fireside, Smith & Barrow's Monthly Magazine* and, most popular of all, the *Southern Illustrated News*, which brought out its first issue in September, 1862, and the following year published serially Simms's *Paddy McGann; or The Demon of the Stump*. Modeled on the English *Punch, Southern Punch* began publication in Richmond in 1863 as an outlet for war humor.

Few journals managed to stay afloat throughout the war. The plight of newspapers was even more difficult. Contending with everything from volunteer editors and the cutoff from Northern news services to the scarcity of paper and the encroachment of invading armies, papers were forced to cut back severely in size, and most folded. By the end of 1863, only nine of Mississippi's forty-five papers remained. To escape approaching enemy forces, the *Memphis Appeal* was forced to move so often that it became known as the "Moving Appeal."

By war's end, the Southern press was in disarray. The Vicksburg *Daily Citizen* was publishing on patterned wallpaper; newspapers in occupied territory had been taken over by Federal forces; Sherman had been careful to destroy printing equipment in his wake. And yet, in city after city, editors and writers set about to repair and replace presses and reestablish newspapers as a first order of priority. In Columbia, William Gilmore Simms joined with Julian Selby in March, 1865, to begin a paper they called the *Phoenix*. Its first lines were set up in a composing stick Simms found while rummaging through the ashes of the destroyed *South Carolinian* office, and the inaugural issue contained the first installment of his *Capture, Sack and Destruction of the City of Columbia*, a vivid account of the city's burning. Simms edited the *Phoenix* from late March to October 1, 1865, shaping the paper in the first months of the South's defeat into an organ for opinion and an outlet for fiction and poetry, including some of Simms's own best verses.

The work of Simms on the *Phoenix* was symbolic of the importance of letters in the defeated South. But Simms was also operating from sheer economic necessity. He, like his friends Timrod and Hayne, was living in real poverty. He mourned the deaths of his wife and several children and the destruction of his home and library of nearly eleven thousand volumes, one of the finest private libraries in the South. Writing to Evert Duyckinck, he described his destitution, inquired after his neglected copyrights, and noted quietly: "I could wish to have some books sent me. . . . I have had nothing to read for 4 years." By the end of the war, much of the South lay literally in ruins, and it had lost a generation of young men. In 1866, one fifth of the state revenues of Mississippi were spent on artificial limbs; Georgia was still spending $35,000 a year for the same purpose in 1881. In the face of such grim reality, the deferred dream of a truly Southern literature reemerged. An anonymous writer in *Scott's Monthly Magazine* expressed the hope in 1866 that "the next quarter of a century will be the Augustan age of Southern literature."

The problems of Southern writers in 1866, however, were far more serious than those of ten years before. Where they had once faced reluctance on the part of the Northern press to publish their work, now they encountered outright refusal. For the first several postwar years, Northern outlets were usually restricted to copperhead periodicals such as the *Old Guard*, which published works by Cooke, Simms, and Hayne, and the *Round Table*, but these had limited readership and paid poorly. Furthermore, when John R. Thompson succeeded in placing an article with *Harper's Monthly* in 1868, he was denounced as disloyal. (By the early 1870s the situation had improved. New journals such as *Appleton's Journal*, *Lippincott's Magazine* and *Scribner's Monthly* increasingly welcomed Southern writers.) War's end left the South with no major publishing firm equipped to produce and market books. Besides, Southerners were far too poor to buy them.

The South felt strongly the need to defend its action, to present its version of the war, to understand its defeat, and somehow to bridge the emotional chasm between itself and what Radical Reconstruction policies insured would be perceived as a conquering nation. Southern writers set about meeting these needs in a variety of ways. Several journals were founded to express Southern viewpoints. *Scott's Monthly Magazine* began in Atlanta in December, 1865; *De Bow's Review* was resurrected in Nashville in January, 1866, followed by such magazines as *Land We Love* (which published Francis O. Ticknor's "Little Giffen" in 1867), the *Eclectic* (which in 1868 became the *New Eclectic*, absorbed *Land We Love*, and finally published as *Southern Magazine*), the *Southern Review*, and *XIX Century*. The *Sunny South*, an Atlanta weekly begun in 1874, was edited briefly by Joel Chandler Harris. For the most part, these magazines published mediocre fare; all died before 1880.

The short-lived journals at least provided a forum for Southern opinion at a time when no other forum was available. One effective means of palatably packaging bitterness and unreconstructed views was in the humorous sketches popular in the 1840s and 1850s. Although the Old Southwest humor movement had begun to ebb several years before the outbreak of war, new sketches such as those by Harden E. Taliaferro in the *Southern Literary Messenger* and Richard Malcolm Johnston in *Southern Field and Fireside* were published in Confederate journals. Both George Washington Harris' Sut Lovingood and Charles H. Smith's Bill Arp pilloried Abraham Lincoln—Lovingood in travelogues published in February and March, 1861, in the Nashville *Union and American*, Arp in letters to "Mr. Linkhorn" which, with other wartime sketches, were collected in *Bill Arp, So Called* (1866). Kittrell J. Warren had written three humorous works during the war; the last, *Life and Public Services of an Army Straggler* (1865), contained a pair of rogues who anticipated Mark Twain's Duke and Dauphin in *The Adventures of Huckleberry Finn*.

The Reconstruction period saw dramatic changes in Southern humor that reflected changes in the attitudes of Southerners toward their past and future. Some of the finest sketches were published in the few years after the war, including Harris' *Sut Lovingood's Yarns* (1867) and

Simms's "How Sharp Snaffles Got His Capital and His Wife" in *Harper's* (1870); neither of these takes its strength from politics. But among humorists of a political bent, the cutting edge of immediate postwar humor modulated into far mellower nostalgic amusement that had more in common with the growing local-color movement than the vituperative satire of the war. Smith's Bill Arp, for example, changed from the feisty Yankee-hater who refused in 1865 to be "subjergated and humilyated" to a pipe-smoking bucolic philosopher who took comfort in sitting on his "piazzer" of an evening watching his farm. Such capitulation to the tastes of a largely Northern book-buying public was motivated by economic prudence, but it also suggested a growing desire for reconciliation.

Many writers moved north; others, like Simms and Hayne, reestablished contact with Northern colleagues. Hayne, who had moved with his family to a small, sparsely furnished cottage near Augusta after his Charleston house and library were damaged by Federal bombardment, carried on a remarkably prolific correspondence with leading writers, north and south, but barely managed to eke out a living by writing. Younger writers like Sidney Lanier also suffered. Lanier, whose allegorical apprentice novel *Tiger-Lilies* (1867) was one of the most interesting efforts in fiction written during the Civil War, pursued a career as poet in the face of ill health, poverty, and intellectual estrangement. In 1875 he wrote to Bayard Taylor, "with us of the younger generation in the South since the War, pretty much the whole of life has been merely not-dying."

By far the most successful means of avoiding starvation as a Southern writer in the late 1860s and 1870s was to publish sentimental, charming or humorous stories of life in the antebellum South for a Northern public curious to know more about the culture glimpsed during the war. So many women supplemented family incomes by writing subliterary romances that Hayne protested in an 1874 essay in the *Southern Magazine* entitled "Literature at the South: The Fungous School." More skilled writers entered the market as well. John Esten Cooke, author before the war of historical novels set in colonial Virginia, immediately put to use his military service with Stonewall Jackson and J. E. B. Stuart in a series of war novels: *Surry of Eagle's-Nest* (1866), *Mohun* (1868), and *Hilt to Hilt* (1869). Cooke's plots were contrived in what he called "the Reade-Collinsish style of mystery and sensation," and creaked mechanically, but his descriptions of famous military heroes, breathtaking night rides, and stirring battles, all based on people he had known well and events he had witnessed, rank high among the most vivid and skillful literature of the Civil War.

Cooke avoided any hint of bitterness in his war fiction. In the late 1860s, convinced that the only honorable course for the South was to abandon political rhetoric and turn instead to sheer hard work, he wrote *The Heir of Gaymount* (1870), one of the earliest novels to embrace New South articles of faith. The novel's message was the value of scientific farming. Interestingly, Sidney Lanier started a similar project, "John Lockwood's Mill," of which a forty-page fragment survives, that apparently intended to explore Southern potential for tapping into Northern industry and finance. Lanier also wrote a series of Georgia dialect poems between 1869 and 1871 focusing on the theme of personal integrity and solid work as the key to success. Cooke and Lanier—and many Southerners like them—struggled to integrate the chivalric ideal and the material benefits of what Lanier called "base 'Trade'." In the effort to face the economic and political realities of their region without abandoning a reverence for the past, they prefigured the local-color or New South writers of the 1880s.

While professional writers were straining to establish literary ties with the North, many Southerners were recording their memories of the conflict through which they had lived. Between 1865 and 1915, hundreds of memoirs and reminiscences were published, many written so far after the war that they are of little interest as Civil War literature. Of particular literary merit is General Richard Taylor's *Destruction and Reconstruction* (1879). Taylor, son of President Zachary Taylor, had an excellent vantage point, a discerning eye, a dry sense of humor (he asserted in 1867 that after all their dashing exploits, war heroes like Stuart "could scarcely have anticipated the fate of being exposed to Mr. [John Esten] Cooke's merciless admiration"), and a willingness to present the war as realistically as possible. Equally significant for its objectivity as for its account of the experience of a Confederate soldier is George Cary Eggleston's "A Rebel's Recollections," published first as a series in the *Atlanta Monthly* in 1874 and in book form the following year. The reality of day-to-day life in the Confederacy, the merging of personal and national destinies, may be more clearly seen, perhaps, in war diaries and such collections of letters as *The Children of Pride* (edited by Robert Manson Myers, 1972) or *Ham Chamberlayne: Virginian*, the letters of John Hampden Chamberlayne (edited by C. G. Chamberlayne, 1932). War diaries began to emerge long before Appomattox. Some, like that of Sarah Morgan Dawson (1913), seem intended solely as private documents; others, like *A Rebel War Clerk's Diary* (1866) by John B. Jones and *The Recollections of Alexander H. Stephens* published in 1910 but written during Stephens' imprisonment immediately after the war, clearly include material aimed at eventual publication.

Of all the books to come directly out of the Civil War, one of the most remarkable is that of Mary Boykin Chesnut, recently edited by C. Vann Woodward as *Mary Chesnut's Civil War* (1981). First published in a truncated version after the author's death as *A Diary From Dixie* (1905), Chesnut's book is not precisely a diary, but rather a conscious recreation and expansion of journals she kept during the war. Daughter of a South Carolina governor and wife of James Chesnut, Jr., a United States senator in the late 1850s who became a Confederate general, Mary Chesnut knew most of the major political and military figures of her day, and was a close friend of Jefferson Davis' wife, Varina. In the mid-1870s, Chesnut attempted to use her war material as fiction, writing two war romances, one of which survives in manuscript. Finally, in 1881, she began a full-scale revision of the diaries. Using the fictional techniques she had taught herself, she set scenes and rounded out characters, relying on her own instinct for metaphor and structure. The result is a massive and intelligent book which retains the diary form and remains faithful to her original journal, but which is also an important literary portrait of the Confederacy.

From our point of view, Mary Chesnut was fortunate to have no ties to the literary establishment, for thereby she avoided both the defensiveness and sentimentalizing of the writers of her generation. By the 1880s, the romances and formal "classical" poetry of the Civil War era had become outmoded. Realism was in full swing. As John Esten Cooke noted in the mid-1880s, the realists were right. "They see, as I do, that fiction should faithfully reflect life, and they obey the law while I can not. I was born too soon, and am now too old to learn my trade anew." Cooke died in 1886, the same year that marked the deaths of Hayne and Mary Chesnut. Timrod had died in 1867, Simms in 1870, Lanier in 1881. In an oration in 1872, Hayne had said of the war, "Many are the tongues that have essayed to narrate its history, but not for us, not in *our* generation, can the *Iliad* of the Southern war be 'said or sung'!" The dream of a classical age of Southern literature was itself history, but the legacy of the Civil War experience would be invested many times over in the years to come.

RAYBURN S. MOORE

Poetry of the Late Nineteenth Century

At the beginning of the Civil War, Southern poetry was in a stage of transition. Pinkney, Wilde, Poe, Cooke, Chivers, Lamar, and Legaré were dead. Simms, Grayson, Horton, Pike, O'Hara, and Meek had written their best poetry, though Simms lived to write a number of war poems and to collect the *War Poetry of The South* (1867) and Horton's work appeared once more in *Naked Genius* (1865). A few younger poets began to publish in periodicals in the 1840s and 1850s and to collect books of verse. John R. Thompson (1823–1873), editor of the *Southern Literary Messenger* (1847–1860), contributed verse to the magazines before the war, but his only collection was lost in the blockade during the war. John Williamson Palmer (1825–1906), a Maryland physician who subsequently gave up medicine for journalism, brought out *Folk Songs* in 1856. The free mulatto Baltimorean, Frances Ellen Watkins Harper (1825–1911), a popular antislavery and temperance lecturer, published the no longer extant *Forest Leaves and Poems of Miscellaneous Subjects* (1854). Margaret Junkin Preston, a native of Pennsylvania who moved to Virginia in 1848, contributed verse to newspapers and magazines but did not publish her first full collection until 1870. The most substantial work of the younger poets was contributed by two young Charlestonians, Henry Timrod (1828–1867) and Paul Hamilton Hayne (1830–1886), both of whose early work had appeared in Thompson's *Messenger*. Timrod subsequently collected his verse in 1860, whereas Hayne published three volumes before 1861.

The war, of course, changed everything. Poets who had seldom been restricted by politics, as writers of fiction had frequently been, were forced by circumstance to take part directly in the war or to deal with it substantially in their work. And even when occasion offered opportunity for study or meditation, the war interrupted and interfered; still it also provided material and theme and conditions for celebration of the new nation and its efforts to establish and defend itself. The response was full and immediate. Simms, Thompson, Palmer, Preston,

188

Hayne, and Timrod published frequently in behalf of the cause, and others—James Ryder Randall (1839–1908) of Maryland; Francis Orray Ticknor (1822–1874) of Georgia; and Abram J. Ryan, Father Ryan (1838–1886), of Virginia, Maryland, and states to the south— rose to the occasion and in lyrics such as "Maryland, My Maryland," "Little Giffen of Tennessee," and "The Conquered Banner" proudly sang of the glory of the states, the courage of the men in gray, and of the pathos of defeat. Timrod, with such poems as "Ethnogenesis," "The Cotton Boll," and "Carolina," became the laureate of the Confederacy.

After the war, the Southern poets turned to whatever economic means would keep bread in the pantry. Simms sought to reestablish his publishing outlets in the North, but few old-line firms were ready to accept his work, though Harper was an occasional exception. Poems need not be political or controversial in nature, but they paid little; and Simms, now over sixty, was forced to drudge for South Carolina and other Southern periodicals for little or nothing until he almost literally worked himself to death by 1870 at the age of sixty-four. Timrod fared even worse and died in 1867 before his artistic achievement during the war could be translated into the solid peacetime accomplishment his laureate performance surely presaged, though in 1866 he composed his beautiful "Ode" honoring the Confederate dead in Charleston's Magnolia Cemetery. Thompson, in the meantime, returned from England where he had promoted the Confederate cause and went to New York where he eventually became literary editor of the *Evening Post*, a position he held with distinction until his death in 1873. At the same time, Palmer also went to New York, worked in various editorial and journalistic capacities, and managed to write a few more poems, but never again reached the standard achieved in "Stonewall Jackson's Way" (1862). Preston, on the other hand, spent as much time on her poems as reduced circumstances, impaired eyesight and hearing, and the "mysteries of Sally-Lunn" would allow, and despite these handicaps, wrote her best poetry after the war. Hayne, too, overcame the obstacles of poor health and poverty and spent the last twenty years of his life in Georgia as man of letters and poet laureate of the South.

Of these poets, the work of Preston and Hayne merits full attention, and since much of Father Ryan's verse and some of Randall's best poetry were written after the war, their work may be noted. In addition, new poets such as Irwin Russell, John Banister Tabb, Sidney Lanier, Albery A. Whitman, Lizette Woodworth Reese, and Madison Cawein must be carefully considered.

If Henry Timrod was the laureate of the Confederacy, Abram Joseph Ryan was the voice of the Lost Cause. Priest, journalist, and poet, Ryan was born in Virginia and subsequently lived in Missouri, Maryland, Louisiana, Mississippi, Tennessee, Georgia, Alabama, and Kentucky. He edited the *Star*, a Catholic weekly in New Orleans, and the *Banner of the South*, another weekly, in Augusta. His best poems about the South—"The Conquered Banner" (composed in 1865), a requiem for the Confederacy; "The Sword of Robert Lee" (1868); and "A Land Without Ruins" (1879)—were all written after the war, and though Ryan maintained to the end that his lyrics were only verses and not poems, these and a few others have survived as sincere and patriotic responses to defeat and blasted hope.

Another well-known journalist and poet, James Ryder Randall, was celebrated in his own day as the author of "Maryland, My Maryland" (1861), one of the best poems to come out of the war, but "Pelham," "There's Life in the Old Land Yet," and "At Arlington" should also be remembered. After the war Randall devoted himself to journalism, editing both the *Constitutionalist* and *Chronicle* in Augusta, and failed to collect his poems until near the end of his life, dying before the book came out in 1908.

The antebellum poets who continued consistently to court the muse after the war and who eventually became devoted friends were Margaret Junkin Preston and Paul Hamilton Hayne. Preston (1820–1897), the daughter of a prominent Pennsylvania Presbyterian minister and founder of Lafayette College, came south with her father in 1848 when he became president of Washington College in Lexington, Virginia. There she met and married Major John T. L. Preston, a senior member of the Virginia Military Institute faculty, and began contributing poetry to periodicals, though her only book before the war was *Silverwood* (1856), a novel. During the war she continued to write poems when time was available, and in answer to a challenge from her husband, she composed *Beechenbrook: A Rhyme of the War* (1865), a long narrative in couplets broken occasionally by four- and eight-line stanzas. It was a very popular Confederate imprint, though many copies of the first edition were burned in the fire that followed the evacuation of Richmond. *Beechenbrook* was republished in 1866 in Baltimore, and a few other poems on the war were included with each printing. Subsequently, Preston brought together her poems in *Old Song and New* (1870), *Cartoons* (1875), *For Love's Sake* (1886), and *Colonial Ballads, Sonnets and Other Verse* (1887). She was almost as modest about her work as Father Ryan had been about his verses. She admitted once to Hayne that poetry had been for her only a pastime, and not "the occupation or mission" of her life. Nevertheless, she left a body of work that entitles her to more consideration than she has usually received. As Jay B.

Hubbell has pointed out, she was best at the sonnet, the ballad, and the dramatic monologue.

Her religious beliefs were strong and deep, as were her convictions about patriotism. No one can read *Beechenbrook* today without being impressed by the fervor of the religious and patriotic views expressed in behalf of the Confederacy by one whose father had returned to Pennsylvania at the outset and whose brother served in the Union army. She has an eye for character, even in sonnets such as "Equipoise," " 'Sit, Jessica,' " "Hawthorne," and "In Cripplegate Church," and more particularly in brief narratives (frequently monologues but not always) that deal with painters of the Renaissance—"Mona Lisa's Picture," "In the Sistine," and "Tintoretto's Last Painting." She also succeeds with poems in memory of friends, as in "The Shade of the Trees," a tribute to Stonewall Jackson, her sister Eleanor's husband, and "Through the Pass," an elegy based upon the last wish of Matthew Fontaine Maury to be borne through the Goshen Pass in May and buried where "my dead are lying." Altogether Preston's lyrics provide interesting psychological insights into human nature expressed in a graceful lyrical style; her numbers nevertheless strike the ear as less musical than the lush melodical lines inherent in Southern lyricism from Wilde and Poe to Hayne and Lanier. Her work is not cerebral in the Dickinsonian sense, but it demonstrates more interest in the mind and soul than is usual in the work of many of her Southern contemporaries.

On the other hand, her friend Paul Hamilton Hayne was a poet whose eye was on the English romantic tradition and whose ear was in tune with the Southern lyric back to Wilde and Poe. A Charlestonian and scion of a prominent family in Carolina politics, Hayne began contributing verses to newspapers in 1845 and later in the decade to the *Southern Literary Messenger* and *Graham's Magazine*. Subsequently, he edited the *Southern Literary Gazette* (1852–1854) and *Russell's Magazine* (1857–1860) and collected three books of verse before 1861— *Poems* (1855), *Sonnets, and Other Poems* (1857), and *Avolio* (1860). During the war he served briefly on the staff of Governor Francis Pickens, but his health failed and he spent the rest of the period writing poems and lecturing in behalf of Confederate causes. Having lost practically everything in the war, Hayne moved to a rural retreat near Augusta, Georgia, and committed himself again to a literary career, spending the last twenty years of his life contributing poems, essays, and criticism to periodicals throughout the nation and engaging in an extensive correspondence with American and British writers, including Longfellow, Whittier, Holmes, Bryant, R. D. Blackmore, Jean Ingelow, Swinburne, Philip Bourke Marston, and Wilkie Collins. He collected three additional volumes of verse—*Legends and Lyrics* (1872), *The Mountain of the Lovers* (1875), and *Poems* (Complete Edition, 1882)— and after the death of Simms in 1870 became the acknowledged literary spokesman of the South, the representative poet and the laureate of the South.

Hayne's accomplishment is clearly mirrored and demonstrated in sonnets, nature lyrics, and one or two narratives. Some of Hayne's best sonnets were published after his last collection appeared in 1882 and have seldom been reprinted. "The Renegade" (1885), for example, is an attack on George W. Cable and others who, in Hayne's view, turned on the South after the war was over. "Robert Lee" (1886), on the other hand, celebrates a leader whose "defeat but made him tower more grandly high." Tributes to Blackmore (1884) and Whittier (1886) also suggest a maturity of achievement, and "Death's Self" (1885) and "To Charles Gayarré" (1886), a sonnet of eighteen lines and presumably the last contribution he ever made to the genre, show him at top form.

Hayne's nature poems have been more frequently reprinted, though several good late ones—"In The Wheat Field," "Midsummer (On the Farm)," and "On a Jar of Honey"—have seldom reappeared. The so-called Copse-Hill poems—"Aspects of the Pines," "The Voice in the Pines," "The Wood Lake," "Golden Dell," "In the Pine Barrens," and "Midsummer in the South" among them—were written in the 1870s and published chiefly in the *Atlantic Monthly*, but Hayne's attainment along this line may also be observed in longer lyrics like "Muscadines" (1876) and "Unveiled" (1878) and in shorter pieces like "The First Mocking-Bird in Spring" (1876), "Hints of Spring" (1877), "The Mocking-Bird (At Night)" (1878), "The Pine's Mystery" (1879), and "To a Bee" (1880). Indeed Moses Coit Tyler always characterized "Muscadines" as immortal and Hayne himself thought that he had reached his "high-water mark" in "Unveiled," a Wordsworth-like irregular ode dedicated to Bryant.

In general, Hayne was less successful with long narratives, though two exceptions should be noted: "The Wife of Brittany" (composed in 1864 but not published until 1870), his most ambitious effort in the genre; and "Cambyses and the Macrobian Bow" (1873), a much shorter poem in blank verse. "The Wife of Brittany" is based upon Chaucer's "Franklin's Tale," but, as Hayne asserted, is an adaptation and no "mere modernization" of it. A nineteenth-century narrative in the romantic tradition of treating medieval problems, "The Wife" was praised by Longfellow, Whittier, and Lanier, but its characters and general standards of psychology seem hopelessly outmoded in the light of twentieth-century day. On the other hand, "Cambyses," stark and grim in a manner unlike many of his other poems, is Hayne's ultimate achievement in the form. Despite certain flaws, it creates in an unaffected style an unforgettable picture of power that begets perversity and a dramatic situation that by its terseness and laconic understatement highlights man's inhumanity to man.

As a whole, Hayne's canon is unabashedly in the Anglo-American tradition, and he is Southern to the core in his celebration of the land he loves, in his pride in his state and the virtues of the Old South, and in the natural melody of his lyrics, music that is heard in the forest and the sea, in upland and lowland, in pine, bee, and spirea, and in the voice of humanity everywhere. He was not a great poet, only an honorable minor one, but he committed himself to literature with a will and a conviction that neither Poe nor Simms before him exceeded or perhaps even equaled.

The new poets of the postwar period—Russell, Tabb, and Lanier, and later, Cawein, Albery Whitman, and Lizette Reese—frequently offered new wine in old bottles, though Russell and Lanier were among the first to publish dialect verse and Lanier experimented with line and meter, if not with theme and rhyme, throughout his brief career.

Irwin Russell (1853–1879), the author of "Christmas-Night in the Quarters" (1878), the best-known piece of verse in Negro dialect published in the 1870s, was a native of Mississippi who spent much of his youth in St. Louis, attended St. Louis University, studied law and practiced it while writing concurrently for newspapers and composing poems on the side. Many of his poems (usually in dialect) appeared in *Scribner's Monthly*, and though Lanier's dialect verse had preceded Russell's, the Mississippian was usually credited with discovering, as Joel Chandler Harris pointed out in 1888, "the literary possibilities of the negro character." Moreover, Harris praised Russell's "accurate conception" and "perfect representation of negro character," though he admitted that the dialect itself was "often carelessly written" and "not always the best." Whatever the verdict may be about Russell's interpretation of dialect (Harris obviously did not know much about the speech of Negroes in southern Mississippi), "Christmas-Night in the Quarters" is surely an achievement that transcends any inadequacies in the transcription of dialect. The poem is a nice contrast between speakers and points of view in terms of education, diction, and human nature; and the qualities of operetta—arias and spoken monologue, a sort of recitative on the action—are nicely realized in the Burnsian couplets of the educated narrator and the contrasting stanzas and rhyme schemes of the Negro speakers and singers. Altogether, it is an achievement that promises much to come, but Russell had only another year to live. Poor health, the yellow-fever epidemic of 1878 (in which he served his physician father as nurse and assistant), and other difficulties prevented him from fulfilling the promise of "Christmas-Night," and he died on December 23, 1879, at the age of twenty-six.

Tabb and Lanier, on the other hand, were born before Russell and both lived longer, Tabb (1845–1909) living well into his sixty-fifth year. The son of a Virginia planter, Tabb was born in Amelia County and was educated at home, where he acquired a knowledge of music and literature. Poor eyesight limited his activities both before and during the war, but by 1862 he managed to enter the Confederate service as a clerk to the captain of a blockade runner, a relative, and by June, 1864, when his ship was captured, he had run the blockade over twenty times. He was sent as a prisoner to Point Lookout, Maryland, where he met and formed a lifelong friendship with Lanier. After a prisoner exchange in February, 1865, he returned to Virginia and joined a regiment in defense of Richmond. Subsequently, he taught school, studied for the Episcopalian ministry, and was converted to Catholicism in 1872. In the same year, he matriculated at St. Charles College and completed his studies there in 1875. Continuing his studies for the priesthood, he entered St. Mary's Seminary in Baltimore in 1881 and was ordained in 1884. In the meantime, he taught English in schools in Richmond and Baltimore, contributed verse to *Harper's Monthly*, *Lippincott's*, and other magazines, and his first volume of poems was privately printed in 1882. After his *Poems* (1894) appeared, his work attracted more widespread critical attention in both the North and in England, and his reputation as the author of brief and finely finished lyrics on nature, religion, and literary topics was established and assured. Of such lyrics, "The Cloud" (1877) and "Mistletoe" (1883) may serve to illustrate Tabb's work on nature; "Interpreted" (1881) and "Easter" (1883), his verse on religion; and "Keats" (1880) and "Milton" (1885), his lines on literature.

Tabb's friend Sidney Lanier (1842–1881) composed verse and began his novel, *Tiger-Lilies* (1867), during the war, but his work primarily belongs to the postwar period. His health broken by a four-month stint in the Federal prison at Point Lookout, Maryland, where he met Tabb, he returned to Georgia in 1865 and spent the last sixteen years of his life writing poems, playing the flute in the Peabody Orchestra in Baltimore, contributing to magazines and doing such hack work as preparing editions of Malory and Froissart for boys, and generally trying to stay alive despite the ravages of tuberculosis. Nevertheless, despite poor health and poverty and divided loyalties to music and literature, Lanier managed in little more than a decade to write some impressive poems and to make his mark on the poetry of the period. Beginning in the aftermath of war, he contributed dialect verse, such as "Thar's More in the Man Than Thar Is in the Land" (1871, though written presumably in 1869), to newspapers, poems on Reconstruction, such as "The Raven Days" (1868) and "Night and Day" (1866), to magazines, and eventually poems embodying his ideas on nature and philosophy and the relationship between music and poetry to *Lippincott's, Scribner's Monthly,* and other publications. Those poems include "Corn" (1875), "The Symphony" (1875), "The Centennial Meditation of Columbia" (1876), "The Marshes of Glynn" (1878), and "A Ballad of Trees and the Master" (1881).

"Corn" brought Lanier to the attention of a national audience. *Lippincott's* did not have the circulation of *Scribner's Monthly* or *Harper's New Monthly,* but it served an Eastern audience and was generally well received in the South also. In "Corn" Lanier not only managed to express his ideas on nature, individualism, the single-crop system, and trade but also to experiment with line, rhythm, and meter. "Corn," in effect, is a prototype from which "The Symphony" and "The Marshes of Glynn," in particular, are developed. Similar themes in the three irregular odes and the relationships between music and poetry become more pronounced as Lanier's style evolves. Ironically, he seems less in control of his theme and material in "The Centennial Meditation," a poem commissioned for the celebration of the centennial in 1876. Criticized roundly in some quarters apparently because critics failed to take into account that it was a song meant to be sung and accompanied by music, the cantata, despite its controversial reception, brought Lanier's work to a more general audience in his own time than anything else he ever wrote. In 1877 appeared the only volume of his verse to be published during his lifetime, a collection of ten poems he had contributed to *Lippincott's Magazine,* and his reputation increased thereby, though the reviewers, as Charles R. Anderson has pointed out, were of two minds about the chief source of the strength of his theme and style— "the subtropical luxuriance of the deep South"—noting that occasional "overrichness and obscurity" were related to a corresponding lack of discipline. Such virtues and flaws—to say nothing of a penchant for poetic diction, a passion for rhyme, an ear for music, and an artistic involvement to the detriment of aesthetic distance—are to be found in Lanier's best poetry, including "The Marshes of Glynn." On occasion, as in "The Stirrup-Cup" and "A Ballad of Trees and the Master," when the demands of form provide boundaries, his lyrics approach perfection. What Lanier may have done had he lived is open to speculation and conjecture. In general, it seems clear that he (and Hayne, too, for both poets share certain strengths and weaknesses) owed much to Poe (de-

spite Lanier's well-known remark that Poe "did not *know* enough
. . . to be a great poet") and to earlier Southern poetry. His debt to the
Anglo-American tradition at large is another matter.

The last three new poets of the postwar period whose work merits
more than passing attention are Albery A. Whitman, Lizette Woodworth Reese, and Madison Cawein, though James Barron Hope (1829–
1887), a Virginia poet and journalist who had published a volume of
poems in 1856, the black poets T. Thomas Fortune (1856–1928) and
George Marion McClellan (1860–1934), both largely conventional lyricists, and Cale Young Rice (1872–1943), a Kentuckian who eventually
published twenty-one volumes of verse, may also be mentioned.

Albery Whitman (1851–1902), as a rather typical native of the cave
region of antebellum Kentucky, remembered slavery less in terms of big
plantations than of self-willed individuals. The years immediately after
emancipation he spent largely in southern Ohio, working, teaching, and
going to school. His formal education reached its highest level at Wilberforce University, where he welcomed his close exposure to the influence of Daniel Alexander Payne. For the rest of his life he served in the
ministry of the African Methodist Episcopal Church as an evangelist or
pastor (who sometimes established churches) in Ohio, Kansas, Texas,
and, finally, Georgia. An addiction to alcohol may have hastened his
death.

There were those who dubbed Whitman in his day the poet laureate
of the Negro race. For such an accolade he did have fairly impressive
credentials. He was, if nothing else, love of drink notwithstanding, a
poet who wrote. He published *Essays on the Ten Plagues and Miscellaneous Poems* (1871); *Leelah Misled* (1873); *Not a Man and Yet a Man*
(1877), over five thousand lines long and once assumed to be the longest
poem ever written by a Negro; *The Rape of Florida* (1884), reissued as
Twasinta's Seminoles (1885), both editions in Spenserian stanzas
throughout; a collection of lyric poems, *Drifted Leaves* (1890); the topical *World's Fair Poem* (1893); and a last attempt at a long narrative in
verse, *An Idyl of the South* (1901).

Whitman was a romantic with a love for seductive sound and for
imagery that pleases the senses. At various times he resembles first
Longfellow, then Byron, then Tennyson or Scott. His concepts of beauty
and, apparently, of the artist's true discharge of his vocation seem to
coincide with those of Poe. His heroes and heroines tend to be idealized
octoroons or Indians and his racial protest, therefore, somewhat escapist. Yet Whitman far from lacks either sincerity or skill. And even to
write as he did, with his measure of success, was to indicate his opposi-

tion to the racial stereotypes of an era when contempt for Negroes was as great as it ever has been in America.

Lizette Reese (1856–1935) was born and reared in Huntingdon (later in Waverly), Maryland, a suburb of Baltimore and the setting for much of her poetry. The child of a Welsh father who fought for the Confederacy and a mother of German descent, she taught school in the Baltimore area for over four decades. In 1874 her first published poem appeared in Baltimore's *Southern Magazine*, and in 1887 she published her first volume of poetry, *A Branch of May*, a collection that presaged the appearance of thirteen other books of verse and prose during her lifetime. Her work early and late is brief, direct, and spare, and the sonnet is a favorite form. Her themes and topics and subject matter are the country and people of her surroundings, and her language and ideas are based upon her experience and reading. There is little of the lushness of Hayne or Lanier in her work, but there is the same respect for traditional form and rhyme that one finds in Hayne but which is manifested in Reese's poetry in such a way as to suggest some of Preston's work and to anticipate the economy if not the angularity and wit of John Crowe Ransom. "Tears" (1899) is presumably still her best-known poem, but there are other sonnets and some short lyrics that are equally worthy of remembrance, including "A December Rose," "The Singer," and "Hallowmas" in *A Branch of May* and "April Weather," "Renunciation," "A Seller of Herbs," and "Compensation" in *A Handful of Lavender* (1891), to mention only those poems from her work before the turn of the century. Her poems are suffused with the locale of Huntingdon, and they abound with daffodils, lilacs, roses, hollyhocks, pinks, hawthorns, dogwoods, elders, white plum and apple and pear and cherry trees, blackberry blossoms, crickets, bees, thrushes, swallows, and wrens. She celebrates the seasons, particularly the months of April, May, and June, yet recognizes the values of September, November, and December. She knows meadow, grove, and town, but her characters are more frequently generalized than strongly local. Occasionally a personal note is sounded, as in "Renunciation" or "Compensation" or in tributes to Keats, Herrick, or Herbert. In general, however, her poetry is controlled by tone and form. Love is dealt with without sentimentality, and her preferences for sonnets, for traditional stanzas, meter, and rhyme contribute to the control she maintains over material and emotion. Subject to these self-imposed limitations, her work culminates in *Spicewood* (1920), *Wild Cherry* (1923), and *White April and Other Poems* (1930), and her canon in its concern for the local, for tradition, for poetry as song may serve as a transition between Hayne, Timrod, and Lanier (*A*

Handful of Lavender is dedicated to Lanier) and the work of Ransom and Donald Davidson in the 1920s.

Madison Cawein (1865–1914) also stresses locale in traditional forms, though his work encompasses a variety of forms not attempted by Lizette Reese. A native of Louisville, Kentucky, Cawein went to school there and, with the exception of three years in his youth, also spent the rest of his life there. His first collection of poems, *Blooms of the Berry*, appeared in 1887, the same year in which Reese's *Branch of May* came out. Subsequently his work was published in thirty-five other books, and William Dean Howells and Edmund Gosse praised his poems. In 1902 Gosse even selected poems for an English edition and wrote an introduction for *Kentucky Poems*. During his lifetime Cawein was best known as a nature poet in the nineteenth-century British tradition. The influence of Keats and Swinburne and even a note of Browning may be detected here and there in his poetry. In such brief narratives as "In Arcady" (1911), and in such sonnets as "Enchantment" (1911) and "After Long Grief" (1911), Cawein echoes Hayne's themes, diction, and form. There are, of course, poems that at least in subject matter and tone are hardly derivative—"Ku Klux" (1896) and "The Man Hunt" (1905), for example. But in his debt to acknowledged masters of British lyricism, in unquestioning acceptance of traditional forms, meters, and rhyme, in his sensitivity to verbal music and harmony and his awareness that verse is written for the ear, and in his concern for nature as it is manifested in his own locale, Cawein's canon is generally derivative and is clearly within the nineteenth-century Southern poetic tradition.

Altogether, Southern poetry of the nineteenth century developed very little from beginning to end. It is modeled on the standards set by British poets from Chaucer to Swinburne, and its exercises in experimentation by Poe and Lanier, for example, hardly challenge the tradition. It is also meant to be heard, as is clear from "The Lament of the Captive" to "Tears" or "In Arcady." It grows increasingly more concerned about natural surroundings from Wilde's "To the Mocking-Bird" to Cawein's "Dusk in the Woods." And it is characteristically chivalric in its consideration and treatment of love and of the relations between the sexes, though there are occasional notes or suggestions to the contrary in poems by Cawein and Reese. On the whole, however, Southern poetry of 1860 to 1900 is of a piece with antebellum poetry, and even if it seems old-fashioned and outmoded to present tastes, it clearly represented its culture, reverberated in the souls and memories of its audience, and served both historically and intrinsically to reflect and to respond to a way of life.

THOMAS RICHARDSON

Local Color in Louisiana

When the journalist Edward King visited New Orleans in early 1873 as representative of "The Great South" series for *Scribner's,* he discovered more for his Northern audience than he or his editors, J. G. Holland and R. W. Gilder, could have expected. "Louisiana to-day is Paradise Lost," he wrote. "In twenty years it may be Paradise Regained. . . . It is the battle of race with race, of the picturesque and unjust civilization of the past with the prosaic and leveling civilization of the present." King was perceptive, and the conflicts he described—past versus present, Creole versus American, black versus white, traditional versus progressive values—would help to stimulate a significant literary movement, what Warner Berthoff calls a "New Orleans renaissance in the '70s, '80s, and '90s."

To King's famous discovery of George Washington Cable, whom King assisted in placing "'Sieur George" with *Scribner's,* one may add Grace King, Kate Chopin, Ruth McEnery Stuart, the Creole historian Charles Gayarré, Alice Dunbar-Nelson, and Lafcadio Hearn, who lived and wrote in New Orleans from 1877 to 1887. These writers together produced a unique literature, considerably more complex than much other work of the local-color era. The books they wrote about Louisiana are not only numerous but impressive, including Cable's *Old Creole Days* (1879) and *The Grandissimes* (1880), Hearn's *Chita* (1889), and Chopin's *The Awakening* (discussed in a previous chapter).

The Louisiana writers owed much of their contemporary popularity to the quaint, quasi-foreign setting that Creole New Orleans and Acadian Louisiana offered a curious Northern public. Perhaps more than any other American locale, the bayou country with its rich French history and complicated social texture satisfied local-color impulses. The new national spirit after 1865, with its accompanying industrial and urban growth, stimulated a growing number of eager readers of emerging magazines both to celebrate sectional peculiarities and to escape from a world of growing complexity. As Americans looked back down the road not taken, the entire South was generally rediscovered as a field for fiction, for the vanished Old South had special appeal. Louisiana writers were especially successful, since the vanished community they portrayed was far removed from the reality of living in America. Louisiana, more than any other Southern state, and New Orleans, more than any other American city, worked to the writer's advantage. "After Louisiana," Robert Penn Warren would say years later, "nothing has been real."

Louisiana writers could immediately combine a tropical setting of magnolias, oleander, and ancient architecture with a social and economic cauldron. Because of its location at the mouth of the Mississippi, New Orleans was a city of all classes and customs, with a "polyglot variety" in its population—"Spanish, Creole, Acadian, Negro (with gradations of field hand and house servant, octoroon, quadroon, and mulatto), Italian, German, Yankee, Sicilian, mountain white and river tawny" (Warner Berthoff, *The Ferment of Realism: American Literature, 1884–1918* [1965]). The flatboatman from Kentucky milled in New Orleans streets, as did the Creole aristocrat, Caribbean sailor, American entrepreneur, and a sizable number of *gens de couleur libres.* Outside New Orleans there were French Acadian settlements, transplanted to Louisiana swamps and prairies, with colorful dialects among farmers, trappers, and fishermen. Finally, there was the Mississippi River itself, traveled by steamboats and river rats, and bordered by Negro shacks, antebellum homes, and fields of sugarcane. For the writer interested in sectional peculiarities, here were riches indeed. Louisiana local colorists were also in possession of historical material far more racy and challenging than the Old South alone could afford. By the 1880s, writers had nearly two centuries of Creole history, yellow-fever epidemics, quadroon balls, duels, the *Code Noir,* and characters like Jean Lafitte to use as source and background. Not only did writers draw directly on Louisiana history and legend for their stories, they found it so fascinating and so much a source of pride that considerable energy went into writing history itself.

The cankerous secrets revealed in Louisiana history, combined with the tensions in the contemporary postwar culture, help explain why this local-color literature has extraordinary strength and significance. As Shirley Ann Grau suggests, the Creole heritage in New Orleans reveals "the decline of an aristocracy under the pressure of circumstances"; it also mirrors the pressures that wracked the South after 1865. The classic conflict in New Orleans culture between the Creoles (the white descendants of the original French and Spanish settlers) and the invading Americans after the 1803 Louisiana Purchase, had been decided by the

1870s. By then, the Creole community was well past its zenith, though the city continued its polarization between the older, French-speaking Vieux Carré and the newer, more commercial American sections. The passing of the Creole community, its best values as well as its worst, afforded Louisiana local colorists appropriate themes of transience, defeat, and a tradition more authentic than history.

Cable's treatment of the Creoles has been variously criticized, but he, like Grace King and Gayarré, had roots in New Orleans. His stories, and theirs, develop a genuine attractiveness in the Creole culture— family, a sense of place, warm friendships, and personal dignity in the face of overwhelming odds. At the same time, the Louisiana literature generally avoids the shallow idealism so often found in local color. Cable saw the connections between the decline of the Creoles and their self-destructive racial pride, and his best work makes it clear that such racial arrogance has direct application to broader problems of Southern history, especially the black-white conflict after 1865. Although it is true that none of the other Louisiana local colorists matched Cable's awareness of the shadow in the Southern garden, the complexity of New Orleans' racial background is as important to the strength of the literature as is the Creole heritage.

Perhaps the most important Southern artist working in the late nineteenth century, George W. Cable (1844–1925) is now praised for his courageous essays on civil rights, such as *The Silent South* (1885) and *The Negro Question* (1890), as well as for his early fiction about New Orleans, especially *Old Creole Days* (1879) and *The Grandissimes* (1880). Not a Creole himself, Cable nevertheless knew his subject well. He was born in New Orleans, grew up there, served as a Confederate soldier, and returned to work there until 1884, when he moved north. As a clerk in the New Orleans Cotton Exchange, he began to study the colonial history of Louisiana while writing sketches for the *Picayune*; and his stories followed, he later told F. L. Pattee, because "it seemed a pity for the stuff to go so to waste." In his essay "My Politics," Cable tells how his reading of the *Code Noir* caused him such "sheer indignation" that he wrote the story of Bras-Coupé, first submitted through Edward King to *Scribner's* as "Bibi," but rejected because of its brutality. Later the story was incorporated as the foundation of *The Grandissimes*.

Cable's best stories from *Old Creole Days* illustrate his preoccupation with a doomed Creole community. Living in aged, ruined settings, his major characters often are isolated and self-destructive, yet their dignity in the face of defeat makes them attractive. In "'Sieur George," where the achievement is in the relation of setting and character, the reader glimpses the decay of two old men who slip along the "cobwebbed iron" of the Vieux Carré and up "rotten staircases that seem vainly trying to clamber out of the rubbish." "Belles Demoiselles Plantation" demonstrates the consequences of past sins on the De Charleu family, as an old Creole who "will not utterly go back on ties of blood" watches his mansion and seven beautiful daughters sink into the Mississippi. Old Jean-ah Poquelin, once an "opulent indigo planter," now lives isolated in a horrible swamp in an ancient house "half in ruins." He fails in his attempt to protect family secrets (his brother is a leper living on the grounds) from the callous Americans who are bent on developing his property, but his loyalty is more admirable than the materialism of his adversaries.

The Grandissimes, according to Louis D. Rubin, Jr., is "the first modern Southern novel," because it attempts "to deal honestly with the complexity of Southern racial experience." Like the best stories of Old Creole Days, The Grandissimes balances between sympathy for and judgment on New Orleans and the South, but it is stronger because it contains, as Cable says, "as plain a protest against the times in which it was written as against the earlier times in which its scenes were set." Here, Cable examines the connections between the decline of the best values in the Creole community, its self-destructive pride, and the far-reaching effects of its sins on the contemporary South. These themes achieve full significance in Cable's creation of Honoré Grandissime, a Creole who attempts to reconcile his sympathy for the Southern community, represented by his own family, with his judgment on its evils, especially slavery and racism. By setting his novel in New Orleans in 1803, Cable caught the conflict between Honoré's Creole family and the Americans. The arrogance of the Grandissimes is bearing dark fruit—especially "the length, the blackness" of the "shadow of the Ethiopian." Honoré must deal with his literal shadow, a half-brother, who is a free man of color also named Honoré Grandissime, and his family's brutal treatment of blacks, especially Bras-Coupé, whose curse continues to blight their fortunes. Honoré is also responsible to those traditional family values embodied in his uncle Agricola Fusilier, described in the novel as "the aged high priest of a doomed civilization."

Cable continued to write about New Orleans and Louisiana throughout his long career, in Madame Delphine (1881), Dr. Sevier (1884), The Creoles of Louisiana (1884), and the Acadian novel Bonaventure (1888). In all, he would publish fourteen more novels and collections, and his last book, Lovers of Louisiana (1918), written seven years before his death, returns to his original themes and subject matter. Curiously, The Grandissimes, his first novel, is also his best. Not enough has been said about the polarization in the world Cable and others knew after 1865. During Reconstruction, tensions between past and present were expressed dogmatically by what C. Vann Woodward calls "the doomed generation," those who remained loyal to the principles of the Old South, and another group who advocated the philosophy of the New South. Honoré Grandissime's dilemma mirrors Cable's own conflict as an artist working in the South after 1865. "As I watched the Great Reconstruction agony from its first day to its last," Cable says, "I found my emotions deeply torn—with my sympathies ranged upon the pro-Southern side of the issue and my convictions drifting irresistibly toward the other." In his career after *The Grandissimes,* Cable would be unable to reconcile his love for the South with his abhorrence of its evils. The result is a split in his life and art, social reform versus romantic escape. In his polemical essays, Cable the reformer and New South advocate assumes that the past can be redeemed in the present. In the pastoral *Bonaventure* and the romances beginning with *The Cavalier* (1901), he attempts escape through retrieval of an idyllic past, where the problems of racism are not present. Even in *The Grandissimes,* Honoré's dilemma shares importance with Cable's moral voice, represented by Joseph Frowenfeld, a character who exists outside the novel's major themes.

Grace Elizabeth King (1851—1932) has recently begun to receive the critical treatment she deserves, in part because of the appearance of Robert Bush's anthology, *Grace King: A Selection of Her Writings* (1973) and his *Grace King: A Southern Destiny* (1983). Rescued from her traditional role as a lesser figure who sought to correct Cable's views on New Orleans, King is seen by Bush as a writer whose work was influenced by her feeling about Cable's popularity, her French education, her allegiance to her family during Reconstruction, and the Cotton Centennial Exposition of 1884—1886, which brought outsiders like Richard Watson Gilder and Charles Dudley Warner to New Orleans. In her *Memories of a Southern Woman of Letters* (1932), King recalls her 1885 interview with Gilder about Cable. Cable, she said, had "stabbed the city in the back . . . to please the Northern press," proclaiming "his preference for colored people over white" and "quadroons over the Creoles." Gilder had replied, "if Cable is so false to you, why do not some of you write better?" King was so motivated to answer Gilder's challenge that she climbed the attic stairs the next morning and began "Monsieur Motte." King had deep personal feelings about the humiliation suffered by her family after the Civil War. She was not a Creole, but her aristocratic family had been intimate in circles that Cable knew mostly through observation and research. Like the Creoles, her education and background were exclusively French; like them, she had lost home and property to a new regime. Her "grand theme," Bush says, was "defending the character of New Orleans and upholding . . . its traditions." She naturally shared the anger of Creoles like Adrien Rouquette and Charles Gayarré toward Cable and his work.

However, "Monsieur Motte" and subsequent stories do not simply idealize the past; nor are they only important as "the defense of the Creoles." Anne Jones has recently made the point that King's portrayal of women (both black and white) is her real subject. In addition, King's reading of French realists stimulated her irony and her choice of contemporary subject matter. While the quadroon Marcélite of "Monsieur Motte" assumes a fictitious white identity to support the education of her former master's child—a devotion that readers might conclude "was the deserved reward of benign treatment"—her role as a black woman (and the role of other women in the work) is treated with surprising complexity. King draws back from uncomfortable conclusions about the traditional roles of blacks and women, but Jones finds a "cognitive dissonance" in her work, a "rebellious opposite" to orthodoxy. Likewise, in her later novel *The Pleasant Ways of St. Medard* (1916), King does not merely portray affectionate black-white relationships in the return of the former slaves Jerry and Matilda as servants to their old master; instead, "she is the sympathetic and . . . melancholy interpreter of the sorrows of Jerry's family as she sees it disintegrate."

King's cultivated friendship with Charles Dudley Warner led to the magazine publication of " Monsieur Motte" (1885) and to its expansion into a book (1888). As her stories continued to appear in magazines, she visited among friends in the Northern literary establishment and worked in Europe. Her collections of short stories, *Tales of a Time and Place* (1892) and *Balcony Stories* (1893), preceded a remarkable number of histories: a biography of Bienville (1892), for which she had done research in Paris; a textbook of Louisiana history (1893); *New Orleans, the Place and the People* (1895); *De Soto and His Men in the Land of Florida* (1898); *Stories from Louisiana History* (1905); and *Creole Families of New Orleans* (1921). King's final novel, *La Dame de Sainte Hermine* (1924), has received little attention. Until recently she has been remembered chiefly for *Memories of a Southern Woman of Letters* (1932), a disappointing book because, as Bush says, "it brought out the polite side of Grace King the lady rather than the perceptive . . . writer at her best."

One of Grace King's most significant friendships was with the Creole historian Charles Gayarré (1805–1895), an elder statesman in Louisiana society after 1865. Judge Gayarré is probably best known for his impressive *History of Louisiana*, but he is also remembered as an important representative of the culture which had to face tremendous social change in the years following the war. From a distinguished family, Gayarré was a well-traveled lawyer-planter whose political career before 1860 had included election to the United States Senate (a term cut short by illness in the 1830s) and service to Louisiana in a variety of important state offices. During the local-color era, he remained a well-known public figure, but one without power or privilege. He had lost his large personal fortune in the war, for he invested about $500,000 in the Confederate cause. Like other elderly aristocratic Southerners, he found the economic and spiritual climate after 1865 devastating.

With his friend Paul Hamilton Hayne, Gayarré has been described as the last of the literary cavaliers, but his historical work is professionally done. He wrote a history in French, *Histoire de la Louisiana* (1846–1847), and the *Romance of the History of Louisiana* (1848). His best work, however, is the multivolume *History of Louisiana. The French Domination* (2 vols., 1854) covered the years to 1769, *The Spanish Domination* (1854) to 1803, *The American Domination* (1866) to 1816, with a supplement sketching the history from 1816 to 1861. His political and historical novels, *The School for Politics* (1854), *Fernando de Lemos* (1872), and *Aubert Dubayet* (1882), are lightly regarded, but his articles written for magazines and newspapers after the war are rewarding. Hubbell especially praises "A Louisiana Sugar Plantation of the Old Régime," which describes Gayarré's childhood on the plantation of his grandfather Etienne de Boré. Gayarré reacted even more strongly than King to Cable's portrayal of the Creoles in *The Grandissimes*. Angry that Cable became respected as the formal authority on Louisiana culture while his own credentials were overlooked, Gayarré published a lecture, *The Creoles of History and the Creoles of Romance* (1885), which is perhaps the best definition of the adverse Creole reaction to Cable.

Even among specialists in Afro-American literature the memory of Alice Dunbar-Nelson (1875–1935) has grown dim. But in her day, Dunbar-Nelson was recognized as a worthy colleague of Charles W. Chesnutt. Born Alice Ruth Moore in New Orleans, a descendant of the proud colony of free Negroes in New Orleans which numbered no less than eighteen thousand at the beginning of the Civil War, she was educated through college in her hometown. In 1878 she married Paul Laurence Dunbar and never returned to the South. She and Dunbar separated by mutual consent in 1902, and after Dunbar's death she remarried. From 1902 until 1920 in Wilmington, Delaware, she headed a high school English department. From 1924 until 1928 she was a parole worker and teacher at a state industrial school for girls near Wilmington. She died in a Philadelphia hospital, still nationally prominent among Negroes, if only because of her connection with Dunbar and her associations with the Republican party.

Dunbar-Nelson wrote short stories, of which two collections appeared, *Violets and Other Tales* (1895) and *The Goodness of St. Rocque and Other Stories* (1899). Her fictive world is distinctly Creole. The characters she shapes speak French or, when they must, a broken English, and they live in or near New Orleans. Yet, rarely are they black. Racially typical of her protagonists are an aging violinist who loses his position in the orchestra of the New Orleans opera and a young girl who fortunately discovers before it is too late that nunneries are not for her. Dunbar-Nelson's nearest approach to the social protest that might be expected of her is a somewhat oblique indication of her approval of the conduct of some Negro stevedores who are involved as scabs in a strike. Romantic love, not always ending happily, and the Gallic culture in her native state are her two main themes. Of them she speaks sympathetically and gracefully, even though in muted tones and with a voice quickly permitted to cease once she no longer lived in the land of her childhood.

Lafcadio Hearn (1850–1904), the literary sojourner who lived in New Orleans from 1877 to 1887, estimated Cable more highly than Gayarré had. He was drawn to Louisiana, in part, by his impressions of "Jean-ah Poquelin," and he praised Cable's work in "The Scenes of Cable's Romances." As Lewis Simpson has suggested, the central problem in dealing with Hearn is his "literary and spiritual identity," for his ten years in New Orleans was only one stop in an international career that later carried him to the West Indies, New York, and, especially, Japan. Hearn had been born on a Greek island, and he had grown up in Ireland and France before being sent to America. In New Orleans Hearn found a culture more suitable to his interests than that of Cincinnati, where he had lived from 1869 to 1877.

Hearn's letters to his Cincinnati friends reveal a great deal of the sensuous appeal he found in the local color of New Orleans, as do his articles sent back to the Cincinnati *Commercial*. However, without money or employment, Hearn's first months in New Orleans were starving ones, and he was in desperate circumstances when he was hired by the *Item*. Yet his employment by the *Item*, and his later work for the *Times-Democrat*, were doubly fortunate, for the papers not only gave Hearn the means to live, they offered a flexible and creative outlet for his work. In a column called "The Foreign Press," in editorials, and in later collections, Hearn was able to offer his cultivated New Orleans readers translations from Gautier, Flaubert, and others, as well as a variety of exotic stories, collected as *Stray Leaves from Strange Literature* (1884) and *Some Chinese Ghosts* (1887). He also immersed himself in New Orleans culture; in his columns and in Northern magazines, he published a variety of local legends, street scenes, character sketches, and Creole songs. These are well represented in *Creole Sketches* (1924) and in *The Selected Writings of Lafcadio Hearn* (1949). Further documentation of the New Orleans culture he found so charming are the famous recipes he assembled in *La Cuisine Créole* (1885) and his "*Gombo Zhèbes*" (1885), a dictionary of Creole proverbs.

The most important work to spring from Hearn's Louisiana experience is *Chita: A Memory of Last Island* (1889), his first book of fiction. As Arlin Turner points out in the introduction to his recent edition, the book drew from Hearn's several vacation experiences at Grande Isle, from the variety of trips Hearn had made among the islands of the Gulf Coast, and from his reading of Herbert Spencer. Hearn had heard from Cable the story of a child saved from the complete destruction of L'Ile Dernière, a resort much like Grande Isle, in the hurricane of August 10, 1856, and he had read newspaper accounts of the event. *Chita* has three parts, "The Legend of L'Ile Dernière," a powerful description of the gathering storm, climaxed by the tide flooding the island and sweeping the hotel away; "Out of the Sea's Strength," which tells of the girl's rescue; and "The Shadow of the Tide," which brings the girl's real father, a wealthy Creole doctor, to the island ten years later. The first section, describing the awesome power of the sea, is so well done that Lewis Leary thinks it deserves a place beside "Old Times on the Mississippi." *Chita* has also been praised by Beongcheon Yu in *An Ape of Gods* (1964) as Hearn's "mastery of the . . . local color technique," especially regarding "primitive folkways" and "the exotic rhythm of outlandish dialects, especially Creole and Spanish."

Like Hearn, Cable used various dialects—Creole, German, Negro, Acadian—in his early fiction to capture accurate pictures of Louisiana; Grace King did not, since she sought realism in contemporary subject matter. Perhaps she was wise, for the dialect writing of the local-color era, more quaint than realistic, quickly became dated. Ruth McEnery Stuart (1852–1917), one of the most popular and prolific of the dialect writers of the 1890s, has, to some extent, been victimized by it. In twenty books and more than eighty magazine stories, Stuart used dialect to portray life as she remembered it in Louisiana and Arkansas. She grew up in a country home near New Orleans, married A. O. Stuart, a wealthy Arkansas planter, in 1879, and was widowed in 1883. Like

Grace King, she was friendly with Charles Dudley Warner; and it was through him that she launched a successful writing career, moving to New York in 1888.

From her first magazine stories of the late 1880s and her first novels, *The Story of Babette* (1894) and *Arlotta's Intended* (1894), Stuart moved quickly to the subject matter that made her popular—her portrayal of rural whites in Arkansas and her pictures of Southern blacks. Her books about the Arkansas farmers include *Sonny* (1896), one of the best representatives of dialect fiction during the local-color movement, and *In Simpkinsville* (1897), a collection focusing on the themes of courtship and marriage. Humorous treatments of marriage are also at the center of her fiction about blacks, as in *A Golden Wedding and Other Tales* (1893) and *Moriah's Mourning and Other Half-Hour Sketches* (1898). Although Joel Chandler Harris told Stuart, "You have got nearer the heart of the Negro than any of us," her treatment of blacks is generally idealized—faithful, smiling, sentimental. Her best book, *Napoleon Jackson: The Gentleman of the Plush Rocker* (1902), at least acknowledges the serious undercurrent in black-white relations after 1865.

Warner Berthoff says, correctly, that Louisiana local color has kept its "savor better than the work of any other regional school in late nineteenth-century American writing." In part, our continued reading of this surprising number of books reflects the reason for their popularity in their own era. The Louisiana culture the local colorists portray makes interesting reading. The French background, especially the decline of the Creole aristocracy, tells a story that "runs the gamut from sublime romance to smelly sordidness." More important, however, we continue to sense an unusual complexity in these works, a complexity not found in more idealized local color. Such strength springs directly from the tensions in Louisiana culture. Anne Jones finds in New Orleans after 1865 a commingling "of conflicts and resolutions that made [it] almost a perfect city for a writer." What Edward King really discovered in the Paradise Lost of 1873 Louisiana was the well-spring of a literary movement that would do considerably more than dominate the marketplace for over thirty years. The best books written in and about Louisiana during the local-color era—*Old Creole Days, The Grandissimes, Chita, The Pleasant Ways of St. Medard, The Awakening*—comprise a significant literature, well worth our attention a century later.

LUCINDA H. MACKETHAN

Plantation Fiction, 1865–1900

The literary phenomenon of the Old South, centered in the image of plantation culture, was the creation of writers pursuing careers in a very different South, dubbed "new" in economic, social, and political as well as literary structures. Thomas Nelson Page, the most durable of the post–Civil War plantation romancers, might assert that "the New South is . . . simply the Old South with its energies directed into new lines"; however, it was solely the newness of those lines that encouraged postbellum admirers of the plantation to turn a defeated way of life into a substantial legend. The design of images for a popular literature stocked with belles and cavaliers, courtships and duels, mansions and cotton blossoms, and, at the heart of the scene, wistfully reminiscing darkies, had to await the actual demise of the plantation world.

Beginning in the 1830s, with cotton as king and Northern industrial centers gaining economic victories in Congress, the creative minds in the Old South joined the region's general support of slavery as the only means of sustaining a plantation-styled agrarian society. Slavery, it seemed, had to be upheld though it could not easily be subjected to close scrutiny in the field of literature. In the North, Harriet Beecher Stowe's *Uncle Tom's Cabin* (1852) drew heavily on the minutely detailed, documented accounts of the plantation that poured from the pens of fugitive slaves supported by abolition societies in the late 1830s through the 1850s. While her very effective indictment of slavery incorporated tragic experiences recounted by escaped slaves such as Josiah Henson, Henry Bibb, William Wells Brown, and Frederick Douglass, she embellished her tale with some of the romantic qualities of plantation life that would be staples of postbellum Southern pictures designed to supplant her view: elegant mansions, handsome and delicate gentlemen and ladies, slaves who were childlike and loyal, cabins in the "quarters" that rang with songs and laughter. In the South, some, like William John Grayson in his didactic poem "The Hireling and the Slave" (1851), tried an uncritical defense of the region's peculiar institution. The South's leading antebellum novelist, William Gilmore Simms, included in much of his fiction a view that slavery was part of a proper ordering of men in society. Most explicitly in his Revolutionary War romance *Woodcraft* (1852, originally titled *The Sword and the Distaff*), Simms created a happy, familial master-slave relationship between the planter Porgy and his own "Tom" and a plantation symbolizing a threatened classical order. Other Southern fiction writers—George Tucker, William Alexander Caruthers, and John Esten Cooke—produced works combining romance and history, sometimes as a way to deal with their region without confronting increasingly controversial questions concerning the plantation. Southwestern humorists like Augustus Baldwin Longstreet, William Tappan Thompson, Johnson Jones Hooper, and Joseph Glover Baldwin were able to take the gentleman figure into new country bordering the Old South and thus avoid both the stereotyped pictures of chivalry that historical romance demanded and the problems connected with depicting a slave labor force that could scarcely be overlooked in treatments of the plantation.

In 1832, John Pendleton Kennedy wrote *Swallow Barn*, a work generally acknowledged as the fountainhead of plantation literature and popular enough with a Northern publisher to be reissued in 1851. Kennedy, self-consciously adapting and even parodying the social-historian stance of Washington Irving, conceived *Swallow Barn* as a series of letters from a gentleman visiting a tidewater Virginia plantation. Kennedy's first literary effort, it provided authoritative treatment of the plantation in three important areas: its image of the planter's house as social and moral center of order for the culture as a whole; its portrayal of the planter himself as a generous, unmaterialistic gentleman whose paternalistic relation to his slaves constituted an honorable, inescapable obligation; and its pastoral contrast of the simple grace of rural habits to the rude bustle of the expanding America Kennedy saw emerging in the 1830s. Yet Kennedy also saw and showed the humorous foibles of his plantation characters. He did not minimize their clannishness, provincial vanity, impractical self-indulgence, and intolerance of "foreign" views. In *Swallow Barn*, nostalgia finds its counterpart in parody. Kennedy aimed conscientiously at an authenticity that checked, for the most part, the urge to sentimentalize or exaggerate idyllic qualities that postbellum fiction writers would make into myth.

Thus while *Swallow Barn* might accurately merit the title "first plantation novel," in neither its form nor its tone did it sound the definitive note for the plantation fiction that would subsequently find wide acceptance in the 1870s and 1880s. A predilection for local color dominated literary tastes in the major popular magazines of the North immediately following the Civil War, but this new way of dealing fictionally with regional material, while it provided for minute attention to features of setting, speech, and quaint character, incorporated a sentimental rather than a critical vision of life in the Old South. Thus the plantation literature that arose from the ashes of the past had as its primary quality a tone of nostalgia evoking, without questioning, an aura of Camelot. What appeared was a vision of order and grace to communicate a new myth of a lost cause. For writers turning to the antebellum scene, the item second in importance to the nostalgic glow was the voice of the black slave, brought forward to authenticate a version of the plantation system as tragic Eden. Irwin Russell's banjo-picking darkie dancers, Thomas Nelson Page's uncles, and Joel Chandler Harris' Remus told their stories in convincing dialect to both a North and South ready to see slavery, once abolished, in a light that would facilitate reconciliation and make the Negro once again the Southerner's problem.

Joel Chandler Harris, in a biographical sketch of Irwin Russell (1853–1879) written for a posthumous edition of his poems (1888), names Russell as the first writer "to appreciate the literary possibilities of negro character." While the designation is far from accurate, Harris had good reason to see Russell's darkies as seminal portrayals of black plantation character. With Robert Burns his acknowledged master, Russell saw the slave as a folk figure whose poetic potential lay in his simplicity, his untrammeled and unrestrained response to life. Although he had been born in Mississippi, Russell had no close association with plantation life. Yet his "Christmas Night in the Quarters" (1878) gave to Southern writers who would follow the key to the problem of how to turn the character typifying the region's plight into a symbol of the simplicity and innocence lost to the nation as a whole with the destruction of the South's agrarian culture. A criticism of a diminished present could be accomplished through praise of "the simple race" that "'wuks the craps' on cotton places."

In Russell's poem are the seeds of the South's version of the pastoral. The black preacher's "blessin' on dis dance," the black fiddler "sound-[ing] his A" for the "fust kwatillion," the black mule driver exhorting his team, the black singer giving his rendition of Noah's flood—all these come forward to feed a nostalgia for the past, a need to contrast with the present, a desire to give a literary counterforce to modern realities. What Russell appreciated and was able to convey was not so much any true understanding of slave character but, following his beloved Burns, a feeling for a pastoral concept of peasantry rich in folkways, unashamedly natural, able to "dance bekase dey's happy—like de birds hops in de trees." Russell's contribution to plantation fiction was his use of a slave voice that was warmly natural, colorful in folk images, comic yet earnest, pastoral in its promptings. For post–Civil War plantation fiction writers, the figure of the slave provided an acceptable nostalgic perspective and even more; transforming the slave laborer of the Old South into the loyal sustainer and mourner of times gone by paradoxically both expedited the New South's entry into the industrial mainstream of a national future and salvaged a revitalizing sense of its glorious past.

What has long been known as a "plantation school" of white Southern local-color writers, coming into being to vindicate a lost cause, was actually a very diverse group whose experience within regional patterns differed widely and provoked responses that contrasted as often as they converged. One point seems to be settled; the most important contribution to the fictional shape given to plantation themes was made by Thomas Nelson Page (1853–1922). Sherwood Bonner published "Gran'mammy tales" told in Negro dialect in Northern periodicals in the 1870s, and Uncle Remus was firmly ensconced in his plantation cabin by 1880. Although Page's popularity began slightly later and he acknowledged many sources, especially Russell and his fellow Virginian George W. Bagby, his work was to surpass all others in forming the image of the plantation best suited to Southern aims, Northern expectations, and his own idealistic predilections. As Grace King, an admiring follower in the field, wrote, he "showed us with uneffable grace" that "we had now a chance in literature at last." Page's staples, "marsters," "mistises," and faithful retainers, provided the outlines for many disciples. When the Century published Page's first and most famous story, "Marse Chan," in 1884, the market had been tested and found eager for just what Page had prepared for it: a totally sincere, elegaic, uncritical rendering of the plantation scene as prose idyll, presented by black narrators who were the "chief 'pendence" of helpless owners and unable, in most cases, to survive their expulsion from Eden.

Page inherited an aristocratic past from prominent Virginia ancestors whose relics were enshrined at Oakwood, the tidewater plantation on which Page, born in 1853, lived out his boyhood during the Civil War, an experience recounted in his highly popular boys' romance, Two Little Confederates (1888). He made his way adeptly in the New South as a lawyer, diplomat, and husband in a second marriage to the sister-in-law of Marshall Field; however, he achieved renown as a persuasive yet conciliatory authority on the Old South. He captured and convinced Northern audiences through his pseudosociological studies, The Old South (1892), The Negro: The Southerner's Problem (1904), and The Old Dominion (1908); through his best-selling Reconstruction novels

Red Rock (1898) and *Gordon Keith* (1903); and, most significantly, through the stories of the antebellum plantation collected in his first book, *In Ole Virginia* (1887), after half of them had received appreciative notice through magazine publication. A special magic is worked in this collection through virginal damsels and sterling young gentlemen who meet threats to their garden world with tragic nobility of spirit.

The black narrators of Page's first book—Sam in "Marse Chan," Billy in "Meh Lady," and Edinburg in "Unc' Edinburg's Drowndin'"—bask in the reflected glories of white owners who give to them the only functions they will ever comprehend and the "bes' times" they will ever see. When Sam is made body servant to the infant Marse Chan, a stature is conferred that he wears proudly for life. Billy can engineer his lady's marriage to a former Union army colonel in the classic rendition of a plot device designed to signal happy sectional reconciliation, yet Billy is most content when "hit 'pear like de plantation 'live once mo'." And Edinburg is, like the other two slave characters, unappreciative of a freedom that only robs him of purpose. He mourns, "Dese heah free-issue niggers don' know what Christmas is." These characters were created to verify the simple beauty of the plantation and to reconstruct the image of the noble cavalier. Still, a modern audience perceives that their sad purposelessness in the postbellum present has been caused by a system that never granted them identity as human beings.

Page's black voices sometimes go beyond his conscious applications, exposing ironies within the system they exalt. Two stories of *In Ole Virginia* not told by former black servants reveal other facets of Page's restricted view of what slavery in the Old South actually meant. In "No Haid Pawn," Page attempted a Poe-like ghost story in which a cruel West Indian planter sets up housekeeping in Virginia and is finally hanged for decapitating one of his slaves. This operation of Southern justice comes too late for the slaves who have had to bear his viciousness. In "Ole 'Stracted" Page sympathizes with the plight of the freedman Ephraim who nurses a legitimate dream of owning his land. Ephraim's crazy old black neighbor turns out to be his father who, sold away from him and his mother by the creditors of a benevolent master, has come upon hard times. The old man has been driven "distracted" by the shock of this separation and by his frantic attempts to find his family and buy their freedom. Yet Page has the old man speak lovingly of his master and longingly of the good old days. He wants not to be free but to return home to the master, a phenomenon he explains by saying, "You know we growed up togerr?"

Page saw only the charm of master-slave relations that to him were secured by the honor and generosity of the Virginia cavalier tradition. Yet the grave deficiencies of the masters he created for "No Haid Pawn" and "Ole 'Stracted" have the inevitable effect of calling to judgment the system as a whole. Page's seeming blindness to such ironies was a disorder fostered by the atmosphere in which he lived and by the audience, both Northern and Southern, who actively encouraged his construction of a myth glorifying the Old South. A final irony is that, while Page did not acknowledge his black narrators as individuals apart from their masters' interests, he yet depended on the vitality of their individualized voices to convey his vision. They are his most memorable figures.

Joel Chandler Harris (1848–1908), the writer whose name is so often coupled with Page's as cofounder of a "plantation school," established a different order of consciousness for his characters, both black and white. Harris learned his plantation lore not on the veranda of the big house but in the slave cabin and, through it, in the briar patch. The humor tradition of middle Georgia, exposing Harris to writers such as Richard Malcolm Johnston and William Tappan Thompson, fostered in him a much less reverent perspective on the Old South than Page inherited in tidewater Virginia. Moreover, Harris learned a staunch democratic individualism from his Eatonton neighbors, and his own lowly origins kept him from denying human rights on grounds of artificial distinctions. He was the illegitimate son of an Irish laborer who deserted his mother shortly after his birth in 1848. At the age of thirteen he became a plantation employee of Joseph Addison Turner, a planter whose journal-printing ventures gave Harris a practical education in composition and literature. With his somewhat intermediary position at Turner's home, Turnwold, Harris had a vantage point far different from Page's to use in determining what to preserve for a plantation-life myth.

Calling himself "cornfield journalist" or "accidental author," Harris would have been famous if he had published only his first book, *Uncle Remus: His Songs and His Sayings* (1880), which in four months had created a tremendous demand for more tales and more descriptions of their black narrator. Harris wrote over thirty books of great diversity. In addition to the Remus series, he produced several popular works of fiction stressing slave themes. *Mingo and Other Sketches in Black and White* (1884) was the first; the next one, *Free Joe and Other Georgian Sketches* (1887), contains in the title story a sensitive but ambivalent portrait of a freed black man living in a slave world, and in "Aunt Fountain's Prisoner" presents yet another charmingly handled intersectional marriage story. *Balaam and His Master* (1891) gives in "Where's Duncan" a somber study of the effects of miscegenation on white master-father and black slave-son. Although Harris never gained control of the novel form, he penned some skilled character sketches within rambling plots in *Sister Jane: Her Friends and Acquaintances* (1896), a semi-autobiographical reworking of a tale serialized in a journal in 1878. His most ambitious novel, *Gabriel Tolliver* (1902), shows blacks trying to adapt to freedom and whites joining a Klan-like club to "protect" themselves. A far better treatment of Reconstruction occurs through the use of another black narrator, the aunt in *The Chronicles of Aunt Minervy Ann* (1899).

Harris was deeply interested in other Souths besides the old plantation South and was particularly sensitive to the "plain folk" of his home territory. A notable Georgia cracker, Billy Sanders, dispenses homespun rural folk wisdom in several works, most notably in "The Kidnapping of President Lincoln," which appeared in a collection of Civil War stories, *On the Wing of Occasions* (1900). In addition to fiction, Harris wrote an appreciative biographical sketch of Henry Grady (1890), his coeditor at the *Constitution* whose famous address, "The New South" (1886), contained not only the reconciliation theme that Harris always espoused but also a vision of an industrialized, trade-oriented South that Harris would find increasingly distasteful. And in editorials spanning his twenty-five-year career with the *Constitution* (1876–1900), he wrote important critical pieces on Southern literature as well as perceptive, meliorist studies of the race problem.

It was in the *Constitution* that Uncle Remus first appeared in 1876. No other figure in plantation literature would attain the depth of characterization that Harris achieved with his storyteller, who, unlike Page's blacks, is never dependent on the white adults of his world for identity. The early Remus of the newspaper sketches often shuffled along in his Atlanta setting. However, the Uncle Remus who moved to Miss Sally's plantation in the first collection (1880) tells his Brer Rabbit tales with a relish that indicates some consciousness on Harris' part of the black man's identification with the slave folklore subversions of white planter society. And in the three volumes that came after *His Songs and His Sayings*—*Nights With Uncle Remus* in 1883, *Uncle Remus and His Friends* in 1892, *Told By Uncle Remus* in 1905—Harris identified more with Uncle Remus, seeing himself, like his narrator, increasingly out of touch with a modern, moneygrubbing society. Partly because Remus' closest human relationship is not between a slave and his master but between a folktale teller and a white child, Remus retains greater independence. Remus' one other close relationship is to the hero of his stories, Brer Rabbit himself. While Harris never made up a rabbit story, but carefully compiled them and meticulously checked their authenticity as black folklore, he is artistically responsible for his black narrator's feeling for the rabbit's exploits, and that dimension adds complexity to Remus' character.

In the introduction to his first Remus collection, Harris indicated the tensions his narrator would always carry. A symbol of an Old South that Harris tended to idealize, Remus would have "nothing but pleasant memories of the discipline of slavery" and would thus provide a simplistic way back to a world of lost innocence. Yet as master of his folktale narratives, Remus would be a shrewd role player; Harris noted that it must be obvious why the Negro "selects as his hero the weakest and most harmless of all animals, and brings him out victorious in contests against the bear, the wolf, and the fox." Telling the tales was a kind of trickery whereby Remus could do what his rabbit did, using deception and slyness to win what, as a slave, he would never otherwise gain.

While Harris did not fully understand all the ramifications of Uncle Remus' role playing, still Charles Chesnutt (1858–1932), America's first important black fiction writer, understood it well enough to model his own narrator on Uncle Remus in order to achieve multiple levels of meaning. The Remus who says of his plantation days, "but dem wuz laughin' times," may be echoing the sentiment of editorial writer Harris that those days had "a romantic beauty all their own." Yet there is also the Remus who shrugs complacently while Brer Rabbit victimizes innocent opossums, the Remus who will simply explain, "In dis worl', lots er folks is gotter suffer fer udder folks sins." This Remus suggested a design to the young Charles Chesnutt who wrote in his journal that he wanted to write fiction that would "lead people out, imperceptibly, unconsciously, step by step" to a recognition of the black American's human rights.

Chesnutt, growing up after the war in Fayetteville, North Carolina, seems to have decided two courses early on; he would be a writer, if he could manage financially in such a career, and he would use his writing to better conditions for his race. About the same time that Harris was sending Uncle Remus back to the haven of Miss Sally's plantation, Chesnutt in 1881 moved to the North, settling finally in Cleveland (his actual birthplace) where he advanced in a career as a court reporter while writing stories and persistently sending them to magazines. The first story to appear in a major publication was also the first to use Uncle Julius in a postwar plantation setting where he tells a conjure story to a somewhat pompous Northern white businessman, John, and his more sympathetic wife, Annie. The *Atlantic Monthly* in 1887 published "The Goophered Grapevine," and Chesnutt's mission was effectively launched. Uncle Julius was designed not to adapt to conventional demands of plantation literature, as his fellow black storywriter Paul Laurence Dunbar was successful at doing, but to undercut the effect such fiction was having as proslavery, white supremacist propaganda. Julius' aims seem simple enough, and he reminisces about a quaintly rustic world, yet the stories he tells to divert his white patrons contain portraits of masters in whom greed is the sole motivation and slaves for whom plantation life means separation from loved ones, hard labor, and sudden reversals at the whim of the masters. The white world's dream is the slave's unrelieved nightmare, and Chesnutt uses dream motifs and fantasy to underline bitter realities.

In 1899, twelve years after the publication of the first conjure story with Uncle Julius, Houghton, Mifflin, through the energies of Walter Hines Page, finally published "The Goophered Grapevine" and six other similarly designed tales in *The Conjure Woman*. The book was highly praised, ironically from Chesnutt's standpoint for two reasons. First, readers including the influential William Dean Howells found "the spells thrown on the simple black lives" Julius depicted to constitute "enchanting tales." The public missed completely the ironic inversions by which Julius shows what the white lady listener in the stories can see quite clearly, "those horrid days before the war." Second, Chesnutt by 1899 had decided to move away from dialect folk tales in favor of realistic stories that he had been writing for several years about firsthand experiences of the color line. A collection of this new, more openly aggressive material entitled *The Wife of His Youth* was published later in the same year. Chesnutt never returned to the subtle forms of his first and only successful book. Three overtly judgmental, increasingly pessimistic, and excessively melodramatic novels followed: *The House Behind the Cedars* (1900), *The Marrow of Tradition* (1901), and *The Colonel's Dream* (1905). After these, which failed critically though they were no more overwrought than Thomas Dixon's successful white supremacist books, Chesnutt continued to write but never again found a publisher.

Chesnutt refused, as he wrote a friend, to depict old-time blacks "whose dog-like fidelity to their old masters" was one of their "chief virtues." This stand left him without the key element of popular plantation fiction design, as he well knew. Perhaps his best fictional twist of that design was a story in *The Wife of His Youth*, "The Passing of Grandison," in which the slave Grandison seems so full of dog-like fidelity that he makes his way back to his plantation after being kidnapped by abolitionists trying to free him. Grandison's return is hailed by the master happy to see all the proslavery platitudes vindicated by his devoted servant. Grandison, showered with gifts and treated as a hero, stays only long enough to get his whole family together to effect their escape to freedom. The story is the ultimate parody of plantation fiction's favorite ploys—the tested young lover, the generous master, the faithful retainer.

To bring together Page's *In Ole Virginia*, Harris' *Uncle Remus: His Songs and His Sayings*, and Charles Chesnutt's *The Conjure Woman* is to take the full measure of the potential for complexity that inheres in the exploitation of the plantation scene. The ground shared by these three works indicates common features that their authors saw as requirements for fiction treating the Old South. All placed the slave narrator at the center of the plantation scheme, not only because he fulfilled local-color standards but also because he provided an air of veracity and more subtly a persuasive doctrine of master-slave relations. These black narrators are the most valuable creations of the fictions for which they provided voice, for they embody the tensions that, with varying degrees of awareness, their authors brought to bear on the plantation they envisioned. Allen Tate, himself an agrarian drawn to the Old South as an image of order, would characterize nineteenth-century plantation literature as being in the "rhetorical mode," buttressed by the figure of the "old Southern *rhetor . . .* who was eloquent before the audience but silent himself." Tate names Mark Twain as the only writer of the period whose artistic scrutiny of his world included adequate self-questioning, an alert critical temper, and the genius to match these to a sincere attachment to a deeply felt Southern experience. Yet the best writers of the rhetorical mode made essential contributions. Page fashioned the staples that would demarcate the Old South's definitive myth; Harris created a black storyteller who demands attention as a multidimensional American character; with great agility, Chesnutt walked the color line, mining it (in a double sense) but also trapped in it, in his courageous and often highly skilled attempts to show the world the realities of being black in America. Plantation fiction of the last quarter of the nineteenth century, then, opened a necessary window on a world that, gone with the winds of war, became, particularly through the stories of Page, Harris, and Chesnutt, a viable landscape for exploring values at the heart of American experience.

MERRILL MAGUIRE SKAGGS

Varieties of Local Color

*L*ocal color is a general label for much of the writing produced in the American South between the end of the Civil War and the turn of the century. In the context of Southern literary history it covers the many different landscapes, tones, purposes, and forms of writing developed and used, along with a Southern setting, in the late nineteenth century.

It has been hard for the twentieth century to evaluate this late-nineteenth-century work properly, because local color does not conform to the norms of modernism. Simply put, local color is primarily story-telling, not prophecy; narrative, not symbolism; character sketch, not psychological analysis. Poe, Melville, Hawthorne, James—these are writers the twentieth century has valued much more than the story-tellers Cooper or Simms or Harriet Beecher Stowe. But in fact, one might better equate local color to eighteenth-century English fiction such as *Tom Jones* or *Pamela* than to the more moral and psychologically sophisticated romantic and Victorian novel. Or one might consider it an American form of pastoral.

Having been associated with nineteenth-century American modes and fashions, however, the local-color label has occasionally been used to denigrate the exceptional fiction of several twentieth-century women. But this association of local-color writing with women is not accidental. A startlingly high percentage of the Southern writers publishing in the late nineteenth century were female. And given our usual assumptions about the dire Southern economic plight during Reconstruction, an even more stunning fact is the percentage of those Southern women writers who not only published in America but also traveled in Europe during those end-of-century years—for example, Frances Courtenay Baylor, Sarah Barnwell Elliott, Sherwood Bonner, Constance Cary Harrison, and Molly Elliot Seawell. Sherwood Bonner, of course, traveled as another's companion in her European jaunts. And Ruth McEnery Stuart, who traveled almost as widely, though not in Europe, was featured as a lecturer throughout this country. Indeed, most of these women came from an affluent social background and could assume such travel. As a group, they represent a social and economic class much higher than that of the Southern men writers of the same period.

Examples tell the larger story. Sarah Barnwell Elliott was the daughter of a bishop in Georgia and sister of the first bishop in West Texas. Five kinsmen of Ruth McEnery Stuart were governors of Louisiana. Mary Murfree's ancestors left towns named Murfreesboro in both North Carolina and Tennessee. Molly Elliott Seawell's grandmother was the sister of John Tyler, the nation's tenth president. The high social status of these women before, and the relative affluence of these women even after, the Civil War may help to explain the conservative character of their works. Paving potential avenues to upward mobility with words— an impulse sometimes associated with such male writers as Joel Chandler Harris, George Washington Cable, or Harry Stillwell Edwards—is not an impulse appropriate to assume in these women. For them, writing furnished a different kind of self-assertion. One can even guess that they permitted themselves the unconventional aggressions of writing partially *because* their family status gave them a certain security. In any case, their class loyalties often appear stronger than their defense of the Confederacy as a political organization, and much stronger than their defense of the Confederacy's peculiar institution.

Initially, one must concede that the wide range of writing labeled local color does not easily render a great many sound generalizations. The work appears to have been written with diverse purposes in mind. Harry Stillwell Edwards, for example, appears to be trying to synthesize in his novels the best Southern literary models into a distinctively Southern kind of writing. Yet what one spots in his longer fiction often seems to be undigested chunks of Poe, Cable, and Simms. An independent agent by age fifteen who worked his way through Mercer University, Edwards (1855–1938) was the son of a minor poet who had moved to Macon, Georgia, from the North. Edwards tried both law and journalism as professions, and published nearly seventy stories as well as songs, poems, and two novels. His only moment of national glory came briefly in 1904 when he seconded the nomination of Theodore Roosevelt on behalf of the South.

Among other local-color works, Edwin Wiley Fuller's one novel, *Sea-Gift* (1873), written when he was eighteen, romanticizes his passage through a dull and happily normal childhood. Its connection to Southern uniqueness is strained. Francis Hopkinson Smith and James Maurice Thompson, literary opportunists of the clearest stripe, set out to write popular, formulaic potboilers capitalizing on the current interest in vaguely Southern settings; they apparently succeeded. Augusta Evans Wilson, conversely, tries to challenge the current debilitating views of women; but she does so with an astonishingly stilted version of how admirable Southern women really talk. Her heroine Beulah declares, "I tell you there is nothing a woman cannot do, provided she puts on the armor of duty and unsheathes the sword of a strong, unbending will." Cable seemingly wants to define two French types—the Creole and the Cajun—heretofore un- or underrepresented in American literature, and Grace King seeks to correct Cable's definitions. James Lane Allen wants to glorify his native state of Kentucky. Obviously, among such diverse fiction, setting is sometimes central and sometimes incidental to the writers' various purposes.

The local-color label puts a premium on the idiosyncrasies of habit and custom in a particular place. Yet sometimes the writer seems to have imagined the idiosyncrasies first, and the place in which they might appropriately occur only later. Rather, writers who do not know well the terrains they choose to use simply repeat the clever observations of earlier writers. Literary conventions are thus created. In this way, the mountaineers of Kentucky, Tennessee, Virginia, and Georgia became indistinguishable. What varies is the talent of their literary creators at writing good dialogue. Another undifferentiated group of plain folk are the crackers, whether of Georgia or Carolina or Arkansas. And the Creoles of Louisiana are all alike, whoever their creator. Further, all aristocrats, for practical purposes, derive from Virginia, wherever in fact their fields are planted.

What much local-color writing achieves, then, is not so much the delineation of distinctive locales as of several social types. Yet, particular social types reappear dependably in certain landscapes. Or to put it another way, a particular state location can dependably signal a predictable social type. Virginia signals gentry and gentry-imitating blacks; North Carolina signals somewhat melancholy but self-respecting tarheels, a word which by the end of the century means not shoeless intransigents but hardworking yeomen; Georgia and Arkansas both signal a cracker, which means an amusing provincial; Tennessee signals mountaineer as Louisiana signals Creole, at least until one is informed otherwise.

Kentucky, trying to have it both ways by mentioning both colonels and hillbillies, so obscures her state signals as to remain a literally borderline dark and bloody ground. As fictional ground, however, Kentucky was in a real sense outlined by James Lane Allen (1849–1925). Educator, scholar, and widely traveled bachelor, the gently retiring Allen remained by far the best-known Kentucky writer until Robert

Penn Warren appeared a half-century later. Allen's depiction of Kentucky life made it often seem as relaxing as a julep on the next-door colonel's front porch.

One way of calculating which locales were of greatest literary importance is to count the number of stories set in each place. Another way is to count the number of writers each setting produced. By either count, one notes in surprise that a high percentage of those who were writing in this period tried both plantations and mountains for their story settings. Among those using both settings are James Lane Allen, Sherwood Bonner, Frances Courtenay Baylor, Joel Chandler Harris, Thomas Nelson Page, John Fox, Jr., Harry Stillwell Edwards, and Mary Murfree. Each setting demands special character types; and the demand for those types, as well as those settings, extends well into the present century.

As a literary explorer who used mountains, plantations, country farms, and whatever else seemed fictionally viable for her settings, Sherwood Bonner (1849–1883) lived one of the most romantic lives of any woman writer in the nineteenth century. Born in 1849 to a planter family in north Mississippi, she spent the crucial years of her girlhood watching opposing armies raid her hometown of Holly Springs more than sixty times. After the Civil War ended, she married, soon bore a daughter, then left her husband and baby and journeyed alone to Boston to make her fortune as a writer. Naturally such an act outraged many, and Bonner became a conspicuous figure in the talk of both Mississippi and Massachusetts. Her satiric treatment of proper Bostonians contributed to the effect. She became the highly visible secretary and protégé of aging Henry Wadsworth Longfellow, who helped get several of her works published. Before she died of breast cancer at the age of thirty-four, she had experimented widely on behalf of American fiction and had helped to popularize "black mammy" tales, Negro dialect stories, hillbilly humor, backcountry tales of provincials, and reconciliation novels.

In this period the reading public stayed hungry for stories of the South. The market for mountain stories alone in the late nineteenth century is suggested by the almost annual publications of mountaineer volumes by both Mary Murfree and John Fox, Jr. Because the mountaineer stories published by Charles Egbert Craddock created a great fictional vogue, their author became the subject of much curiosity. Eventually she was revealed to be Mary Noailles Murfree (1850–1922), daughter of a prominent Tennessee family. Lame from her fourth year, Murfree wrote of the mountains around the health resort in which she vacationed. Her presentation remains that of an alert and eager tourist, full of sharp detail and shrewd observation but also external to the intimate life of the area. She eventually published twelve volumes, the most important of which remains *In the Tennessee Mountains* (1884), her first.

Not because he was first or best, but because he was among the last to mine the mountains for his literary materials, and because he therefore had all the generalizations of preceding writers available for his synthesis, John Fox, Jr. (1863?–1919), provides the most convenient source of mountaineer stereotypes. Fox was a Kentuckian and protégé of James Lane Allen, whose novels were popular enough later to be adapted to films. After completing his education at the University of Kentucky and Harvard, he served as war correspondent in Cuba and covered the Russo-Japanese war as well. But he aspired in his fiction to capture both the Kentucky mountains and the bluegrass country. He was perhaps most successful in *The Little Shepherd of Kingdom Come* (1903). Having mentioned at one point that "Charles Egbert Craddock put . . . [the mountaineer] in the outer world of fiction," Fox became adept at incorporating all Craddock's (or Murfree's) descriptive phrases into his own fiction. But Kentucky mountaineers replicate in speech and act all the residents of Appalachia from Georgia on to the North.

Repeatedly, Fox defined mountaineers as "people of another age." That is, though the mountaineers are of the same English or Scotch-Irish stock as the bluegrass folk, they have been cut off from contact with others for a hundred years; they therefore lack the "Cavalier element." Fox is at pains to distinguish mountaineers from "poor white trash," yet he associates them with "lazy Virginia blood that fought its way over the Cumberland." When Fox has described one mountaineer, he has described them all; "He neither drank nor gambled, and as he kept aloof from all social affairs, he wasted neither his energy nor his time"; he is "proud, hospitable, good-hearted and murderous"; and furthermore, he's "religious too: they talked chiefly of homicide and the Bible."

Despite this homogenized population, an occasional distinctive or interesting voice will capture our attention. Joel Chandler Harris can turn mountaineer violence, as other violence, into comic entertainment; and other, less well known, local colorists can use a mountain setting for enduring comic effects. Sarah Barnwell Elliott (1848–1928), in *The Durket Sperret*, reveals a considerable comic talent, especially for exploiting the impertinent comments that isolation apparently generates. Elliott was widely enough recognized as a writer to have her most popular novel, *Jerry* (1891), translated into German. But she was interested in the pathetic as well as the comic sides of mountain life. She also explored religious and philosophical themes, ventured into drama, and wrote a biography of Sam Houston.

Writing good one-liners is an important talent the local colorists developed extensively, illustrated by Elliott's *The Durket Sperret* (1898). Comparing two individuals, a speaker says, "nurther one o' you is stiffern hog slops." The folk wisdom of the mountaineers is an excellent source of delight, then as now. According to one mountain lesson, "'Fair-an-easy' is a good horse, Hannah, but 'Don't keer' is a galding nag." One rule of conduct teaches, "Work bars no grudges an' tells no lies." Rules of conduct are no less compelling for being taught obliquely: "Hit's better to git mud on you by prancin' [than] by crawlin'." Or, "Big-talkin' don't make big-doin'; hit's these still-tongue folks what's dangerous."

The Durket Sperret teaches us that those Southern local colorists who still arouse our interest are not necessarily the ones who write about any specific locale or social type. Rather, they are the ones who make us laugh with their dialogue. The only writers we remember from this hillbilly-sketching contest are those whose characters say something sensible in an arresting way. For mountaineers largely do the same things in the same ways all up and down the Appalachian chain. They fall in love and find their romances frustrated; they make good whiskey and find their income curtailed by the law; they feud with each other and ambush or kill off their neighbors, or are killed instead. They maintain their pride, and eye their neighbors warily. They are especially suspicious of lowland strangers—and with every good reason.

The local colorists perfect techniques for writing excellent dialogue. And the ones who are still in print—Joel Chandler Harris, George Washington Cable, Kate Chopin—are the ones who, like Sarah Barnwell Elliott or Ruth McEnery Stuart at their best, can fashion a shapely line that conveys pithy wisdom with comic flair. It also happens, however, that those lines are most convincing when placed in the mouths of characters who are allowed to speak improperly. These plain folk have been spared a repressive education as well as the social obligations of ancient family or ample wealth. They can provoke laughter because their absurdity is of no wide social consequence. Their isolated provinciality is their literary strength.

Beyond the need for an amusing line, Ruth McEnery Stuart also guessed another useful writer's secret: the mind's eye follows movement. So she begins her best stories—those in *Sonny* (1894), for example—in a setting that implies immediate action. Thus she captures attention and keeps it without the windy padding Maurice Thompson uses to state lazily, "The air had all the freshness and fragrance of the South." Stuart, on the other hand, having used her setting to initiate action, also masters the art of making drama out of the utterly banal. She convinces us that the everyday life of ordinary people can be interesting. That is, like all the best local colorists, she shows us the significant movement to be found in a seemingly static and familiar scene.

The humor to be found in a quiet and homely scene flavored the best fiction of Richard Malcolm Johnston (1822-1898), as well as that of Ruth McEnery Stuart. Johnston grew up as the son of a farmer and Baptist preacher around Powelton, Georgia. Offered several prestigious careers before the Civil War, he chose to be a professor. After the war, he fled Sherman's devastations, moved to Baltimore to run a school, and converted to Catholicism. He revealed no trace of such pattern-breaking potential in his fiction. In *Dukesborough Tales* (1871) and his many other Georgia stories, his tone remains genially comic, gently satiric, and fondly reminiscent.

Richard Malcolm Johnston's mid-Georgia crackers, Joel Chandler Harris' fashioners of animal fables, Thomas Nelson Page's plantation blacks, Ruth McEnery Stuart's Arkansas farmers, or George Washington Cable's half-French speakers of broken English all retain their power to entertain us after nearly a century. Such is rarely the case for the more respectable characters.

Respectable characters prove, with the hindsight of a century, to be the downfall of many an ambitious Southern writer. And with all the Kentucky-placed exceptions duly noted, no setting evokes the heart-sinking scent of unbearable magnolias more decidedly than Virginia. When F. Hopkinson Smith, for example, introduces a Virginia city setting in *The Fortunes of Oliver Horn* (1902) as a place of "birds and trees and flowers," the reader knows to expect the worst.

Francis Hopkinson Smith (1838-1915) was born in Baltimore to a family that once claimed friendship with Jefferson. His father's financial reverses forced his early independence, however, and he arrived in New York City only to work as a day laborer. Acquiring the leisure to write at the age of forty-seven, he soon turned out novel after novel, some set in the North and some in the South. The tales basically prove that life can be not only beautiful but also amusing. Their arch humor, however, appealed more to nineteenth- than twentieth-century readers.

But Smith is certainly not alone in screening from his narrative anything inconsistent with placidity. Molly Elliott Seawell (1860-1916) assures us that in the coastal country of Virginia "nature runs the whole gamut of beauty," though that gamut is especially defined by the "pale splendors of moonlight nights and exquisite dawns and fair noons." She quenches the last spark of literary hope by explaining, "It is impossible for anything in this tame, latterday age to be compared with the marvels of fifty, sixty, seventy years ago." With a staggering thirty-nine volumes of regional, historical, and children's fiction, plus journalistic pieces, Molly Elliott Seawell supported herself, her mother, and her sister after her father's death. Perhaps from assuming so patriarchal a role, she became a champion of conservative social values and argued, among other things, that women lacked the "Creative Faculty."

Constance Cary Harrison (1843–1920), too, asserted without irony that life on a Virginia plantation was "an earthly Eden." In Virginia and Maryland, Kentucky-born Constance Cary lived the life of a genuine Southern belle before she married Burton Harrison, Jefferson Davis' private secretary, and gained a participant's knowledge of upper-class Confederate social life. After the Lost Cause was buried, the Harrisons moved to New York, and Constance later moved to Washington. From these Yankee pinnacles she gazed back to the plantation South she depicted in a golden glow. Occasionally, however, her satiric attention lit on an absurd contemporary figure or scene and the resulting story possessed enough bite to require notice. Perhaps her best book is her autobiography, *Recollections Grave and Gay* (1911).

In Edenic Virginia plantation settings, the depiction of women is a matter of interest. For women may predictably serve as the last ingredients necessary to paradise and also as the disruptive conversants with the snake. With an impressive number of women writers in the local-color field, we wonder especially about their presentations of their own sex. Molly Elliott Seawell, for example, explains, "This status [that is, "a queer mixture of shabbiness and luxury"] is extremely common in Virginia, where, as a rule, the men have a magnificent but imaginary empire, and the women conduct the serious business of life." Constance Cary Harrison shows little respect for a mother who exists as "the belle of a passing generation, still rooted in the belief that men were born in the world to be footstools to womankind"; she shows more for a young girl who surmises that "one does not love a lady as one loves a gentleman." Yet Harrison assures us elsewhere, "In those days, a Southern beauty tripped through life on a path strewn with roses, hearts, and darts." Seawell summarizes the Southern lady: "She was of a type of woman which he had never seen until he came to Virginia—delicate, soft-voiced, pious, the chief and only hard worker on the estate, carrying easily the burden of thought and care for her family, her unbroken stream of guests, and an army of servants."

Given the ramrod righteousness of this stereotypic Southern lady, one especially appreciates the surprises generated by Georgia-born Augusta Evans Wilson (1835–1909). Wilson had the distinction of being banned by the American Library Association, while she was also dismissed as a lightweight by such peers as Constance Fenimore Woolson. She explored, albeit in unpruned prose, the ambitions and capabilities of women more honestly than most of the nineteenth-century writers could ever do. She also produced one extraordinarily popular and long-lived best seller—*St. Elmo* (1866).

In *Macaria, or Altars of Sacrifice* (1864), Evans Wilson introduced a heroine named Irene who refuses to let servants carry her burdens "as if I were a two year old child"; further, she refuses to be made either invalid or infantile, that is, made "a wax doll of." Her philosophy is as succinct as it is unorthodox. "If the Huntingdons stand high, it is because they won distinction by their own efforts; I don't want the stepping-stones of my dead ancestry; people must judge me for myself, not for what my grandmother was."

As a result of such independence, there is no end to the trouble a Wilson heroine can cause. When in *Macaria* a separating suitor says, "You belong to me," Irene replies, "No, I belong to God and myself." Such female self-reliance in a Wilson novel is always applauded, at least by the narrator. At the end of *St. Elmo*, Edna Earle, the heroine, has hit the international news as "the gifted and exceedingly popular young authoress." She tutors a pupil, keeps a salon, abhors *double entendre*, and insists on reverence for women and for "feminine delicacy, that God-built bulwark of feminine purity and of national morality."

But no Wilson heroine causes more trouble than Beulah, the ugly orphan. Beulah often expresses her extreme bitterness at society's habit of judging women strictly by the beauty of their faces. She herself is "so ugly that I hate myself." Under these circumstances, the most obscene word in the English language, to Beulah, is *dependence*. In order to escape it, she has established her emotional, intellectual, and economic independence by the age of eighteen. When queried, Beulah asks rhetorically, "Is it so extraordinary, then, that I should desire to maintain my self-respect?"

A respectable heroine created by Augusta Evans Wilson, however, is an astonishing cluster of exceptions to a mainly monotonous rule. Other interesting rule breakers appear in Southern local color whenever the hero or heroine escapes social respectability or lacks economic power. And regions from mountains to coastal swamps could convincingly boast such a resident, as long as he or she was not part of the gentry. For in a period that baked its fictional ladies and gentlemen in neat, cookie-cutter rows, all looking alike, our interest centers not on characters but on comic dialogue. And laughter, by definition, explodes conventions. Southern local colorists cultivated laughter-arousing dialogue and planted it in settings across the Southland. Nurtured carefully, it bloomed again later in many a twentieth-century comic masterpiece.

Kate Chopin

K ate Chopin's place in Southern literary history is a relatively small one, but it is replete with mystery, a hint of scandal, and some remarkably fine writing. A woman who made her reputation by publishing in a traditional mode, who shocked her audience by writing a bold novel, and whose work was eclipsed in the years after her death, Kate Chopin has begun to receive the critical and popular recognition she deserves only in the past two decades.

Kate Chopin's life began ordinarily enough, giving little hint of the controversy that would later surround her. Born in St. Louis on February 8, 1851, Kate O'Flaherty could claim a place in the local French Creole aristocracy. On her mother's side her ancestry could be traced to French settlers of the early eighteenth century, and perhaps her single most important childhood influence was her great-grandmother, Mme Charleville, who, according to Chopin's biographer Per Seyersted, mixed fact and fancy in her stories of the history of the Louisiana territory and the people who settled it. Mme Charleville's tales of the settling of the oldest settlement of French Louisiana, Natchitoches, would be especially important, for later Chopin would base much of her fiction there.

If Chopin inherited a strong sense of heritage and Creole breeding from her mother's side of the family, she also had the energy and self-reliance characteristic of her Irish father, Thomas O'Flaherty, a self-made man who had emigrated from Ireland as a boy and built a prosperous business in St. Louis. Unlike Ellen Glasgow, who was to write of her personal suffering caused by the mismatch of a genteel mother and a hard-driving businessman father, Kate Chopin remembered her early childhood as a happy time in a gracious home with loving parents.

This period in her life came to an end all too soon, however, when her father, who was one of the founders of the Pacific Railroad, was among twenty-nine people killed when a bridge collapsed during the run of the inaugural train. With the death of her father, before Kate O'Flaherty was five years old, the atmosphere of the household changed into one which was, as Seyersted describes it, "dominated by Kate's mother, grandmother, and great-grandmother, all of them highly religious widows."

The strong Catholic influence at home was reinforced in 1860 when Chopin entered the St. Louis Academy of the Sacred Heart. With the outbreak of the Civil War, her family supported the Southern side, and even though St. Louis was controlled by the Union army, her half-brother George joined the Confederate army, and Kate later remarked that she "tore down the Union flag from the front porch when the Yanks tied it up there." George's death from typhoid and the death a month earlier of Mme Charleville had a profound effect upon Kate, and she apparently underwent several years of withdrawal from most social activities during which she looked to escapist literature (Seyersted cites her reading of Scott) for relief.

By 1866 she had reentered active participation in school and social life, graduating from the academy in 1868 and becoming for several years "one of the acknowledged belles of St. Louis." In spite of her recognition as a belle, however, she actively pursued her interest in music and reading. She was now sampling widely among European as well as British writers—notably Cervantes, Molière, Mme de Staël, and others. Seyersted notes that at this period Kate O'Flaherty increasingly became an enigma to friends and family. She continued to play the role of the belle, but more and more she came to view herself as an independent woman. These latter feelings were heightened by a trip to New Orleans in May, 1869, where she thrilled to the cosmopolitan qualities of the city and even learned to smoke, at that time "still a rather daring indulgence for a lady."

If the young Kate was feeling the stirrings of independence, these feelings would be, if not eradicated, at least tempered by the events that would follow her meeting with Oscar Chopin, who had come to St. Louis from Louisiana. The two were married on June 9, 1870, and after a honeymoon in Europe, settled in New Orleans, where Oscar became a cotton factor and his wife began raising a family of six children. Although she was busy with the duties of wife and mother, Chopin was occasionally able to slip away and go on long walks about the city (something not considered entirely acceptable for a solitary lady), writing down notes about the jaunts. Her keen observations later would be translated into the rich description of New Orleans appearing in her final novel, *The Awakening*.

Chopin's life in New Orleans was apparently a happy one, but the era was brought to a close when Oscar Chopin suffered financial losses in 1878 and 1879, and by the end of the latter year, the family moved to

Cloutierville, near the Chopin family plantation. Here Kate observed the people and customs that she would later chronicle in local-color stories and sketches. Oscar's death from swamp fever in 1883 left Kate Chopin a widow with six children. Although she managed her husband's business affairs in the year following his death, she yielded at last to her mother's request that she return home with her children to St. Louis; in June, 1885, not long after her return to St. Louis, however, her mother died suddenly.

Characteristically, Chopin did not succumb entirely to her grief. A great help to her at this time was her personal physician, Dr. Kolbenheyer, who frequently visited her and encouraged her study of science and her reading of Darwin, Huxley, and Spencer. According to Seyersted, Kolbenheyer read to her the letters she had formerly sent to him while living in Louisiana, and he encouraged her to make use of her experiences there to write fiction. Writing was not new to Kate Chopin. She had kept a commonplace book as a young girl and later a diary, and had even written some short fictional pieces before her marriage, but now for the first time she turned seriously to her writing. If, as Seyersted suggests, Kolbenheyer's main reason for suggesting fiction to her was for therapy, the results would be much more far-reaching than merely a grief-stricken woman's attempt to recover some meaning for her life.

After a visit to Natchitoches in 1887, Chopin began to write in earnest. Her first published work was a poem, "If It Might Be," appearing in *America* on January 10, 1889. Before the end of the year she published two stories, "Wiser than a God" and "A Point at Issue," both of which explore the effect that marriage may have on a woman's ability to develop into an individual in her own right. *At Fault*, Chopin's first novel, was published at her own expense in 1890 after its rejection by a publisher, and follows the standard pattern of the reconciliation romance, popular in the decades following the Civil War. The novel is marred by a contrived plot in which the Southern heroine rebukes her Northern suitor because he had divorced his alcoholic wife instead of trying to rehabilitate her. He remarries, but Chopin conveniently kills off the wife, thus enabling the hero and heroine to marry with honor. Although the plot is mundane and the characters are largely stereotypes, two qualities are present in the novel that would characterize Chopin's later, better work: the vivid and realistic depiction of place, here the Southern plantation, and a perceptive treatment of such controversial topics as divorce and alcoholism.

After meeting with a publisher's rejection of a second novel, "Young Dr. Gosse," and subsequently destroying it, Chopin returned with renewed energy to writing short stories and sketches, twenty-three of which were collected in what was her most popular book during her lifetime, *Bayou Folk*, published in 1894. With this work, set largely in Natchitoches, Chopin achieved a national reputation, and her stories of Creole life were almost universally well-received. Chopin's attention to specific details of locale and to the importance of family, community, and honor in her stories was characteristic of Southern fiction of her time.

Three years later, in 1897, her second collection of stories, *A Night in Acadie*, was published. Like *Bayou Folk*, this collection contains stories set in Louisiana, frequently in Natchitoches, and with some of the same characters who appeared in the earlier collection. The critical reaction to this work, however, was less complimentary. Increasingly in her fiction, Chopin had taken to depicting independent, strong-willed women. She had met with resistance from editors of such magazines as *Century* and *Atlantic* because of the controversial nature of characters like the wives in "Athénaise" and "A Respectable Woman" who are chafing against the confines of marriage and are attracted by the worldliness of Gouvernail, who appears in both stories. Perhaps what most distressed Chopin's readers was not the suggestion that the women in these stories could be unsatisfied with husbands who met all the conventional requirements of what a husband should be (though this element is certainly present in the stories) but Chopin's refusal to condemn the women for their "transgressions."

Not dissuaded by criticism, however, Chopin went on to treat these topics at even greater length in her final novel, *The Awakening*. Published in 1899, *The Awakening* had the two-fold effect of bringing about during her lifetime a storm of scandal and controversy that silenced Chopin's literary output, and at the same time of securing her ultimate place in American literary history. The story of a young woman, Edna Pontellier, who is unsatisfied with her life as a wife of a successful businessman and mother of two small children, and who subsequently moves out of her husband's house and has an extramarital affair, evoked outrage both from literary critics and from some of Chopin's own circle. Although *The Awakening* contained some of Chopin's finest writing, marked by a clarity of style that reflected her reading of French authors and by richly evocative descriptions of New Orleans and the nearby resort of Grand Isle, the author's willingness to explore the dissatisfaction of the heroine and her refusal to provide a moral comment on Edna's activities seemed a violation of the code of this period of genteel literature. Although Chopin wrote several stories after *The Awakening*, she had difficulty in placing them.

The frankest of the stories written after *The Awakening*, "The

231

Storm," she did not even attempt to publish. In this brief tale Chopin describes an adulterous affair; the sort of passion alluded to in *The Awakening* is now pictured in more explicit terms. And at the end of the story, the wife, Calixta, after an interlude with her former lover, welcomes home her husband without a tinge of guilt. Although "The Storm" indicates that Chopin did not turn away from controversial topics, she did gradually retreat from public life. Her health weakened, and she died in August, 1904, from the effects of a brain hemorrhage.

Kate Chopin was, in many ways, a product of her time and place. Much of her fiction, especially the short stories, reflected the Louisiana setting that Chopin knew so well, couched in one of the most popular genres of the time, the local-color story. It was Chopin's expert use of her particular local-color material—the bayous and fields of Cloutierville, the cosmopolitan, exotic atmosphere of New Orleans—that led to her contemporary success. Additionally, her sketches of persons from all walks of life—landed Creoles, poorer whites, and blacks—provided a rich variety of characters in her works.

Had she only chronicled these settings, however, Chopin would probably be known today as a minor local colorist. But her exploration in short stories such as "The Storm" and her novel *The Awakening* of such controversial topics as a woman's right to question society's expectations of her, and Chopin's acknowledgment in her fiction of female passion, while silencing her during her lifetime, assured her place not only in Southern writing but in the history of American literature as well. Ahead of her time in subject matter and to a degree in her literary experimentation after the model of French writers, especially in *The Awakening*, Kate Chopin played an important role in the transition to modern American literature. Hers is a small but vital legacy for twentieth-century literature.

LOUIS D. RUBIN, JR.

Samuel Langhorne Clemens
(Mark Twain)

When Samuel Langhorne Clemens of Missouri first came upon the
post–Civil War American literary scene, it was in the guise of the
Wild Man of the Pacific Slopes, the truth-stretching Western humorist
who represented not the mannered gentility of the old Southern cultural
establishment but the outlandish humor and down-to-earth skepticism
of emergent frontier America. That was precisely what Mark Twain
wanted his audience to think. In the 1860s and 1870s it was not popular to be thought of as a Southerner; and for a humorist directly dependent upon public favor, popularity, one might say, was no laughing
matter.

As for those who wrote about Southern literature, Clemens not only
did not fit the model of what was generally held to be Southern, but his
writings were commonly thought of as something other and less than
genuine literature. Like the major figures of the twentieth-century
Renaissance, Clemens declined to serve as any kind of public spokesman
for his community's official attitudes and institutions. And it was his
failure to play this role that made possible the work in which his regional identity seems most clearly revealed. In Allen Tate's formulation,
Adventures of Huckleberry Finn (1884) may well be described as the
first modern Southern novel.

Clemens was born in Florida, Missouri, on November 30, 1835, and
grew up in the Mississippi River town of Hannibal. His father, John
Marshall Clemens, was one of many Virginians who as young men had
left the stagnant economic prospects of the Old Dominion to seek a
fortune in the West. In Kentucky he married a young woman of Virginia
ancestry, Jane Lampton. From there he moved to Tennessee and then to
Missouri, always in search of prospects that never materialized. Indeed,
the satirical portrait of the high-minded, impractical Virginians adrift in
the new territories sketched by Joseph Glover Baldwin in *The Flush
Times of Alabama and Mississippi* seems to fit the elder Clemens quite
accurately. Upon his death in 1847 his family was left all but destitute,

and first his oldest son, Orion, and then Sam were apprenticed as printers.

It was as a journeyman compositor that Sam Clemens left Hannibal in 1853 to work in Keokuk, St. Louis, Philadelphia, New York City, and Cincinnati; in 1857 he realized a childhood ambition by apprenticing himself as a cub pilot on the Mississippi River. Having mastered that trade he passed two years as an accredited pilot of steamboats between New Orleans and St. Louis. When the Civil War broke out and commerce on the river came abruptly to an end, Clemens enlisted in a Confederate volunteer troop, the Marion Rangers—an episode he later described in "The Private History of a Campaign That Failed" (1885), though significantly with the protagonist depicted as a thoughtless, callow youth instead of a twenty-five-year-old adult.

A brief period of soldiering was enough for Clemens. The troop disbanded, he returned home to Hannibal, and when his brother Orion, a Republican, was appointed secretary to the territorial governor of Nevada, he went along as Orion's secretary. As a journalist in the silver fields he acquired his pen name of Mark Twain and began winning a reputation as a humorist and platform raconteur. Subsequently he moved on to California. Meanwhile his writings, which were squarely within the tradition of Southwestern humor, were being read and admired in the East; in particular the sketch "The Celebrated Jumping Frog of Calaveras County" (1865) was widely reprinted.

In December, 1866, Clemens left the West Coast for New York City. The following summer he sailed aboard the S.S. *Quaker City* as part of a much-publicized cultural tour to France, Italy, and the Near East. Out of this grew Clemens' first major work, *The Innocents Abroad* (1869). Until then he was only one of a number of journalistic funnymen whose sketches and lectures toyed with the surface incongruities of changing American life. His main approach was still that of Southwestern humor. In rewriting his newspaper accounts of the voyage into a sustained narrative, however, he began developing a humorous inquiry into the contrasts between the ethical and moral attitudes of middle-class American society and those of the "Official Culture" of the day as exemplified in the historical, religious, and artistic heritage of Europe and the Holy Land.

In 1870 Clemens married Olivia Langdon, daughter of a wealthy Elmira, New York, coal merchant. After a brief spell as a newspaper proprietor in Buffalo, he took up residence in Hartford, Connecticut. In *Roughing It* (1872) he chronicled his years in the West; though like *The Innocents Abroad* it is ostensibly a nonfiction memoir, the new book constitutes the further development of a narrator who, in the guise of a tenderfoot being initiated into the rough-and-ready life of the territories, becomes increasingly a created characterization. *Roughing It* is not so much about the West itself as about the young Mark Twain *in* the West.

Meanwhile Clemens continued lecturing in America and England, writing on various projects including a collaborative novel with Charles Dudley Warner, *The Gilded Age* (1873), and involving himself in all manner of investments, inventions, and moneymaking ventures. To increase his already formidable literary earnings he set up his own subscription publishing house, which might have paid its way had he not constantly siphoned off its assets in hopeless subsidization of the Paige Typesetting Machine, which never could be made to function properly and ultimately consumed almost $200,000 of Clemens' capital. Throughout his adult lifetime he continued to become caught up in such activities, seeking like his character Tom Sawyer to discover hidden treasure in the everyday world about him.

It was in 1875 that Clemens' imagination moved a crucial step further back in time to discover his great subject: the experience of his boyhood and young manhood, as seen in the light of his adult knowledge of change, growth, and loss. For his friend William Dean Howells' *Atlantic Monthly* Clemens wrote a memoir in seven installments, "Old Times on the Mississippi" (1875), later incorporated into the early chapters of *Life on the Mississippi* (1883), in which he described his days as an apprentice pilot on the river. The ostensible genre is that of nonfiction, but Clemens shapes his cub pilot almost entirely in accordance with the demands of the narrative.

The development is from innocence to knowledge; the course of the apprenticeship is one of apprehending and mastering the responsibility that goes along with the river pilot's exalted status. Although told comically, the "Old Times" episodes explore what it means to acquire a vocation. Significantly, Clemens described piloting and the act of learning the river as analogous to a literary art: the river is a book whose language, though dead to the uneducated passenger, tells its mind to the pilot once its discourse has been mastered. Although the revelation serves to strip the river of its conventional scenic qualities, the trained reader now perceives, beneath the flowing surface, danger, direction, and change; and the vision is no longer static, but caught up in the flow of time. From the rhetorical set piece of abstract, "literary" language the writer moves into the vocabulary of a vernacular idiom closely attuned to real-life experience, and the pilot's apprenticeship is that of the writer learning to look beneath what is superficial and conventionally picturesque to identify what is important and vital. The Southern writer thus "gets out from under" the rhetorical mode and into a dialectic with his true experience.

The two novels that followed, *The Adventures of Tom Sawyer* (1876) and *Adventures of Huckleberry Finn* (1884), are universally conceded to be Clemens' greatest books. *Tom Sawyer,* which Clemens later described as "a hymn to boyhood," was in subject matter not unlike many other works of Southern local-color fiction of the day, describing village life and the good "bad" boy back when, in the narrator's words, "there was a song in every heart; and if the heart was young the music issued at the lips." The image of Tom and his comrade Huck, barefoot, bearing cane poles, going fishing on a sunny summer day, is instantly recognizable as symbol of the lost innocence of an earlier, simpler, preindustrial America. What distinguishes Clemens' novel from other such hymns to boyhood is the author's artistic vision, which was too truthful to delete from memory the darker aspects of the experience being remembered and recreated.

The truth is that *The Adventures of Tom Sawyer* is no idyll; at times it verges upon nightmare. The plot involves violence, terror, gore, and death; there are graveyard murders, corpses, drunkenness, dread superstitions, and ghost talk; sinister half-breeds talk of wreaking vengeance by slitting nostrils and notching ears; a man dies of starvation and thirst in a sealed-up cave; a small boy and girl are lost in the recesses of the cave and are mourned as dead; and so on. Reality breaks into the nostalgia for the Edenic village life of the prewar border South.

Yet what we remember finally is the sunlight, the two boys setting off for a day on the river; the evil and terror are gentled and made safe for the reader by the knowledge that the genteel narrator is not perturbed, and is recounting the boys' adventures from the vantage point of adult remembrance, as having happened *in* the past. The swift-paced, often melodramatic action is played against a backdrop of timeless nature, the white town drowsing (Clemens' favorite word) in the sun; and the adult Mark Twain is present to assure us that everything is bound to end happily. The hero has shown himself to be splendidly qualified for adult success in a future Gilded Age American society, too, having made his way to townwide fame and admiration and wealth through the discovery of buried treasure—and all this with a proper regard both for his own love of adventure and for a pure joy in the "theatrical gorgeousness" of the thing. It is just this tension between the pride in achievement that Tom Sawyer's successful entrepreneurial virtuosity affords the narrator, and his sense of loss, the end of the simple life of childhood, that makes the novel an enduring classic.

Adventures of Huckleberry Finn is not so much a sequel to its predecessor as a commentary on it. Late in the writing of *Tom Sawyer* Clemens discovered the storytelling possibilities in Huck Finn's viewpoint. Tom's own relationship to the community in which he functions is, though oblique, essentially affirmative; if sometimes for very different reasons, he operates within the framework of its beliefs, values, and assumptions. He represents something of what the young Sam Clemens might have been like, and the young Sam Clemens was no conscious dissenter from his community's values and institutions. Huck Finn, by contrast, is not emotionally, ethically, or socially a member of the community. Free of ties either of family or sentiment to the community that Clemens had been born into and grown up in, Huck Finn could bring to bear upon that time and place the perspective of the adult Sam Clemens.

Unlike its predecessor, *Adventures of Huckleberry Finn* has no genial adult narrator to mediate between protagonist and audience. The narrator is Huck Finn, whose vernacular vocabulary and syntax, inhibiting recourse to formal rationalizations and intellectual abstractions, enabled Mark Twain to get at his own deepest feelings about the nature of his experience. He could interpret the world of his childhood and young manhood—the border, slaveholding South, the institutions of church and state, class and caste, life on the river—in the light of everything he had come to think and feel about it.

The journey of Huckleberry Finn and the runaway slave Jim down the Mississippi on a raft deepens into a larger retreat from the human and institutional evasions and limitations of society itself. The further the raft drifts downstream, the more sordid, vicious, and morally enfeebled the community life along the shore becomes. The social ordering of human beings is progressively revealed as one in which the best truly lack all conviction and the worst are full of passionate intensity. Negro slavery, evangelical religion, family loyalty, popular culture, aristocracy, and democracy are alike shown as inimical to truth telling and incompatible with private integrity. At the Arkansas town of Bricksville the estimation of man and society sinks to its lowest ebb; the emotion-starved townsmen who loaf about the mud-mired main street of the wretched town can find amusement only in cruelty, excitement only in violence. The only response to a human society composed of their sort is the contempt of a Colonel Sherburn, who kills the drunk annoying him and then repels a mob. "Do I know you? I know you clear through. I was born and raised in the South, and I've lived in the North; so I know the average all around. The average man's a coward. . . . Now the thing for *you* to do is to droop your tails and go home and crawl in a hole. If any real lynching's going to be done, it will be done in the dark, Southern fashion."

It is the power and beauty of the raft voyage itself, however, that captured Clemens' imagination and still captures ours. At the outset the expedition upon which Huck Finn and Jim embark is mainly an escape from the institution of slavery, which threatens to sell Jim down the river away from his family. Once outside reach of these threats, Jim will make his way up the Ohio into free territory, and send for his family. But as the raft moves downstream, instead of a flight *from* slavery the voyage becomes a flight *into* a different kind of freedom: the freedom of the great river, the joy of life aboard the drifting raft, shed of the encumbrance and artifice of organized human society. "Other places do seem so cramped up and smothery, but a raft don't. You feel mighty free and easy and comfortable on a raft."

In the lyrical passages that describe existence aboard the raft, the author's memories of simpler times become infused and invigorated with the imaginative longing of an adult feeling himself trapped within the confusing and compromising morass of public and private life in post–Civil War urban America. The fusion produces a hymn not to boyhood, as in *Tom Sawyer,* but to an unfettered, unobligated, guilt-free life on the river, immediate and sensuous, with clock time suspended and the concerns of adult society put aside. To celebrate so enthralling a vista of human freedom Clemens marshals the full range of potentialities inherent in the vernacular discourse that Huck Finn's voice makes possible.

Yet it is, finally, only a fleeting glimpse of such freedom; the society of the shore cannot be evaded. It comes aboard the raft in the persons of the Duke and Dauphin, those two rogue-picaros. Without scruple or shame, at each successive venture ashore they bring out the worst in the inhabitants of the towns along the banks, until finally they sell Jim back into slavery. It is then that Huck, wrestling with the socially inspired "conscience" that tells him that to help free a slave is a mortal sin, decides that "all right, then, I'll *go* to hell," and sets out to steal Jim away from his confinement at Phelps Farm. And it is at that point, so many critics declare, that the novel undergoes a swift descent from its hard-won vision of human dignity and freedom and turns into comic farce, with Tom Sawyer reappearing improbably on the scene to stage a hilariously absurd rescue of Jim, who has regressed into the minstrel darky stereotype while Huck becomes a mere looker-on. Only then, as a last farcical note, do we learn that Jim has already been set free.

It was the only solution Clemens could find for his story. For the downstream journey could not go on forever; even the great Mississippi River must ultimately reach the open sea. The occupants of the raft can only return to life ashore. Huck says he will light out for the territory, but Sam Clemens knew all too well what he would find there; he had tried it himself in his day. The only way he knew to escape the social circumstance was through the private imagination, to pretend, like Tom Sawyer and Hank Morgan, that a Sunday school picnic was an affair of Arabs, elephants, and high adventure, that nineteenth-century industrial Connecticut was King Arthur's pastoral England, open for reform and conquest.

In *A Connecticut Yankee in King Arthur's Court* (1889)—the only other really major novel Mark Twain was to write—a master mechanic of the Colt Arms Factory receives a blow to the head that transports him back to feudal age England. What he finds there is a society that, in its attitude toward patrician privilege, human dignity, rank and caste, greatly resembles the slaveholding Old South of Clemens' boyhood. Setting out to reform and democratize it by virtue of his superior cleverness and freedom from outmoded, superstitious attitudes toward religious and secular society, he succeeds ultimately in achieving only a holocaust. Human beings, whether in Hannibal, Bridgeport, or Camelot, are, as Colonel Sherburn had concluded in *Huckleberry Finn*, beyond redemption. The gap between the ethical ideal and the actuality of human experience has become a chasm that even farce can no longer bridge.

In Clemens' own day, *A Connecticut Yankee* was generally treated as a spoof of the cult of medievalism and chivalry. It is that, but it is also a devastating denial of the possibility of any genuine improvement in human society through education, material progress, political or social reformation. Men will grovel or they will exploit; in the mass they are craven cowards, easily duped. All that "Progress" can do for them is exemplified in the senseless slaughter of the massed armies by the modern weapons of destruction introduced by the progressive Yankee, who issues a congratulatory order in the style of the Civil War generals.

The period that saw *Huckleberry Finn* concluded and *A Connecticut Yankee* begun and finished was one of steadily worsening prospects for Clemens. His business ventures were failing, the family spent much time living in Europe in order to keep down expenses, and increasingly the mood of his writings changed from sardonic burlesque to outright misanthropy and uncontrollable hopelessness and rage. His last full-scale work of consequence, *The Tragedy of Pudd'nhead Wilson and the Comedy of Those Extraordinary Twins* (1894) is a savage but formless indictment of racism, aristocratic pretense, and plebeian credulity; the would-be cub pilot's "white town drowsing in the sunshine of a summer's morning" has become the nightmarish social, political, and moral wasteland of Dawson's Landing.

In the same year it was published, Clemens was forced to declare bankruptcy. His friend the millionaire financier Henry H. Rogers helped him settle his debts; he embarked on a round-the-world lecture tour to earn money, and enjoyed financial security for the remaining years of his life. But the deaths of two of his daughters, Susy from meningitis and Jean from epilepsy, and the lingering illness and death of his wife left him lonely and bereft. He spent his final years as a traveling public figure, dictating a rambling autobiography and working on and failing to finish various projects, including a despairing, nihilistic account of two boys' friendship with a sad, transcendent figure named Little Satan, which in textually corrupt form was published after his death as *The Mysterious Stranger* (1916). He died on April 21, 1910, at the age of seventy-four.

He had traveled a long distance—from the little river town in the border South to a pilot's berth on the Mississippi, then westward to the silver fields and the Pacific Coast and Hawaii, then eastward to successful literary entrepreneurship and international renown. As a writer he had moved from the surface incongruities of Gilded Age journalistic humor to a fictional exploration of his Southern past that opened up into a lyrical exploration of individual freedom, only to darken speedily into despair at the recalcitrance of fallen human nature and the futility of all efforts to better the condition of what he came to know as the "damned human race." The border South of his boyhood, the industrial Northeast of his adult years are abandoned alike in hopelessness. In the course of that exploration he developed the idiom of Old Southwest humor into a vernacular literary discourse that could document and interpret everyday experience of time and change, so that in at least one very real sense, as Ernest Hemingway declared, "all modern American literature comes from one book by Mark Twain called *Huckleberry Finn*."

DEWEY W. GRANTHAM

Henry W. Grady and
the New South

Following the collapse of the Confederacy and the surrender of Lee's army at Appomattox, a movement gradually took shape to rebuild the South in the image of the victorious North. Against a backdrop of defeat, destruction, and poverty, the movement gave rise to the vision of an industrialized, prosperous, and economically independent South. Faith in the possibilities of such rehabilitation found expression in numerous quarters: in a developing community of interests between Northern and Southern businessmen, in the decline of agricultural prices during the generation following the war, in the optimistic reports of visitors from other sections, and in the support of public officials and political leaders. The movement was also encouraged by a cotton textile boom in the 1880s, by a series of industrial expositions, and by an extensive promotional literature. Most of the Redeemer governments that supplanted the Reconstruction regimes were friendly to industrial and developmental schemes. With the end of Reconstruction, a more sympathetic Northern attitude toward the South, and reviving prosperity in the late 1870s, many Southerners seemed ready to embrace a new design for economic progress.

Advocates of this New South elaborated a comprehensive creed to justify the doctrine of industrialization and progress. They cited the South's abundant resources, plentiful labor supply, favorable transportation facilities, and salubrious climate. They emphasized the potential benefits of industrial development, agricultural diversification, and urbanization; pointed to the progress being made in race relations; and called for an end to the politics of sectional confrontation. But they did not renounce the Southern past. While urging economic innovation, they accepted the prevailing racial attitudes among white Southerners. Their literature, as Paul M. Gaston has pointed out, was "permeated with a sense of the organic relationship between the old and the new."

Among the champions of the New South movement were Henry Watterson of the Louisville *Courier-Journal*, Francis W. Dawson of the

Charleston *News and Courier*, Richard H. Edmonds of the *Manufacturers' Record*, Daniel A. Tompkins, a Southern industrialist and publisher, Walter Hines Page, a North Carolina journalist who later founded and edited *World's Work* in New York City, and, though with his own tactfully expressed qualifications, Booker T. Washington, whose achievements at Tuskegee Institute and widely circulated autobiographical *Up From Slavery* (1901) helped to make him the chieftain of what has been called the Leadership of Accommodation among his race. But the most famous prophet of the New South was Henry Woodfin Grady of the Atlanta *Constitution*. None of the region's cities was more imbued with the New South spirit than Atlanta, which had risen like a phoenix from the ashes of destruction during the Civil War. The city's major newspaper, the *Constitution*, was probably the most widely read journal in the South. Grady himself embodied the New South creed almost perfectly.

Born in the north Georgia village of Athens in 1850, Henry W. Grady was the son of a local merchant who later lost his life in the military service of the Confederacy. Solid and respectable, families like the Gradys were the antecedents of the South's modern commercial and professional classes. Although Grady was too young to take an active part in the war and in its tumultuous aftermath, the events of that era made an indelible impression upon him. The young Georgian managed to attend the University of Georgia after the war, and in 1869 he began an apprenticeship in journalism that included several unsuccessful publishing ventures. In 1876 he was given an opportunity to write for the Atlanta *Constitution*. Thereafter, his reputation as an enterprising journalist grew, and in 1880 he was able to purchase one-fourth interest in the *Constitution* and to become its managing editor. Under his direction the Atlanta newspaper became a powerful factor in Georgia politics, an advocate of a revitalized Southern economy, and a symbol of the New South point of view. Still in his early thirties, Grady received mounting acclaim as a spokesman for the New South program—both in the columns of his newspaper and through his oratory. His boyish appearance, engaging personality, and irrepressible enthusiasm enhanced his effectiveness as a publicist and civic leader. The ideas that he championed, while not very original, were important in his emergence as a key figure in the New South movement.

By the mid-1880s, Grady was well known in his own section as a promoter of the economic and social rehabilitation of the South. In December, 1886, he addressed the New England Society of New York on "The New South." That address, the most celebrated in the literature of the New South movement, gave the Southern editor a national audience and a reputation throughout the country as a dedicated supporter of sectional reconciliation, Southern regeneration, and racial harmony. Until his unexpected death in 1889, Grady used his eloquent voice and pen to popularize the New South creed. The Atlantan envisaged a just and triumphant South, "the home of fifty millions of people, who rise up every day to call from blessed cities, vast hives of industry and of thrift; her country-sides the treasures from which their resources are drawn; her streams vocal with whirring spindles; her valleys tranquil in the white and gold of the harvest; . . . her wealth diffused and poorhouses empty, her churches earnest and all creeds lost in the gospel."

Instead of depending on staple agriculture and a cotton economy, the New South should be diversified and industrialized. The region needed Northern capital and technology in order to process its own raw materials, make full use of its own labor supply, and end its industrial and financial bondage to the North. "The old South," Grady explained, "rested everything on slavery and agriculture, unconscious that these could neither give nor maintain healthy growth." The New South, on the other hand, was developing "a social system compact and closely knitted, less splendid on the surface, but stronger at the core—a hundred farms for every plantation, fifty homes for every palace—and a diversified industry that meets the complex need of this complex age." Coupled with the theme of economic change and renewal was a composite of related ideas emphasizing hard work and thrift, the dignity of labor, the image of the self-made man, and the ideal of success and material achievement. Labor in this context was clearly viewed as a redemptive force, both to the individual and to the community.

Another component of the New South creed was the depiction of race relations. It was a vital consideration, not only for the development of a dependable source of labor in the postwar South, but also for the reassurance and support of Northerners in the economic and political spheres. Grady and like-minded spokesmen assured the North that the South's racial problems were being solved in a way that would be acceptable to all concerned. As the Georgian asserted in 1886, "No section shows a more prosperous laboring population than the negroes of the South, none in fuller sympathy with the employing and land-owning class. He [the black man] shares our school fund, has the fullest protection of our laws and the friendship of our people." At the same time, the New South publicists defended racial separatism and the Solid South. Racial peace and fair play were necessary, but as Grady declared, "the supremacy of the white race of the South must be maintained forever."

A third element in the ideology of the New South was the theme of sectional reconciliation. Southerners, the apostles of the New South affirmed, accepted the outcome of the war and were loyal to the Union. "The South found her jewel in the toad's head of defeat," Grady said. "The shackles that had held her in narrow limitations fell forever when the shackles of the negro slave were broken." Notwithstanding such avowals of nationalism, champions of the New Order appealed to Southern tradition and stressed the continuity between the Old South and the New South. Finding much to praise in the grace and heroism of their ancestors, and discovering a heritage of nationalism and industrialism in the Old South, they fashioned a history of the South that was compatible with their needs. The myth of the Old South, the valor of the Lost Cause, and the imagery surrounding the New South elicited an increasingly sympathetic response from other sections. The North, it appeared, had discovered a new and more acceptable South: a region that was loyal, peaceful, and forward-looking as well as exotic.

In literature, no less than in business and politics, the New South seemed to be entering more fully into the life of the nation. Southern writers such as Thomas Nelson Page, F. Hopkinson Smith, and George Washington Cable, exploiting local and regional materials, demonstrated a new vitality in the 1880s, and their work attracted readers in all parts of the country. Several of these writers and others like Thomas Dixon, Jr., and Will N. Harben became proponents of the New South movement, and that fact no doubt helps explain their popularity in the North. But the creative writers of the late nineteenth-century South, led by Page and Smith, also made use of the plantation legend and other images of the Old South and the Civil War, and in that respect they contributed to the growth of a lush mythology about the section.

Despite its widespread support, the New South creed was not approved by all contemporary Southerners. Southern writers responded ambivalently to the ideology of the New South, and a number of them, including Sidney Lanier, Joel Chandler Harris, Charles W. Chesnutt, and Ellen Glasgow, turned against the movement. They disliked its extreme materialism, recalled with nostalgia a more pastoral South, and yearned for an "arcadian alternative" to the dominant direction of American life. There were also political leaders and professional men who found fault with the New South creed, and in the early 1890s the Populists rudely challenged the basic assumptions of the movement. In later years the agrarian manifesto *I'll Take My Stand* (1930) subjected the New South ideas to critical scrutiny, and other talented writers of the Southern Renascence, including Thomas Wolfe and William Faulkner, among others, were indebted to the literary opponents of the New South movement.

Still, the New South creed had a profound effect on the course of modern Southern history. It provided an agenda for politics in the twentieth-century South. The search for economic development through industrialization, agricultural diversification, and modernization never ceased to preoccupy Southern leaders. The idea of an enduring racial settlement and a *modus vivendi* based on the "separate but equal" treatment of blacks became a fundamental part of the moderate white outlook in the region. Support of intersectional accommodation remained an important aspect of the New South orientation. The commitment to Southern values and the effort to blend the old and the new long characterized the ideological descendants of Henry Grady. These salient themes were expressed in the efforts of Southern progressives to reconcile progress and tradition, in the urban boosterism of the 1920s, in the South's industrial expansion following World War II, and even in a New South school of historians early in the century.

Eventually new circumstances and pressures weakened some elements of the New South ideology. The passage of time revealed that the New South approach had relatively little to offer poor farmers and unskilled workers. Indiscriminate industry hunting on the basis of cheap labor and generous community subsidies proved costly in social terms. The benefits of industrial growth and rampant urbanization seemed to become less certain in light of adverse environmental and social consequences. Even more significant was the collapse of the New South racial program in the face of the modern civil rights movement and the Second Reconstruction.

Perhaps the most lasting manifestation of the New South was the mythology that quickly enveloped it and the role that the concept played as a catalyst for Southern writers. Men like Henry W. Grady were themselves partly responsible for the mythic view of the New South. They persuaded many Southerners to believe that the section was not only capable of economic development and progress but that it was already becoming the scene of great industrial growth, harmonious race relations, and success in the national arena. While the myth of regional progress and triumph may have given the Southern people much needed hope and confidence, it also bred in them a false sense of success and an unrealistic view of their true situation. Nevertheless, Grady and his collaborators are significant in the literary history of the region, for the image of the South they created became a strong and somewhat paradoxical factor in the production of a distinguished body of Southern writing. It also contributed to the mystique of the South that seized the American imagination.

Humor, Romance, and Realism at the Turn of the Century

Surveying the arts in the South in 1917, H. L. Mencken described the region as the "Sahara of the Bozart," finding few writers there that merited serious consideration. Scholars since have referred to the years 1890 to 1920 as the forgotten decades and the dark night of Southern literature. In the main, the writing of the period failed adequately to reflect the region's experience. The strength of the legend of the Lost Cause that idealized the Old South and the Confederacy and of the New South creed that optimistically and mistakenly proclaimed the triumph of a new industrial order—romantic myths that curiously reinforced each other—made it difficult for Southern writers at the turn of the century to portray their region with critical realism. Moreover, if their works were to sell, these writers felt bound to heed readers' demands for a genteel literature that encouraged escape either into a romantic past or an idealized present. As participants in an intellectual awakening that especially affected historical scholarship and in social and literary criticism that often found an outlet in such journals as the *Sewanee Review* (begun in 1892) and the *South Atlantic Quarterly* (begun in 1902), some imaginative writers, despite tight constraints, tried to free their work from sentimentality.

So strong was the influence of sentimental romance, however, that it affected even Southern humor. Vestiges of the Southwestern humor that had been the Old South's original contribution to national letters lingered in the writing of the mid-South humorist Opie Read (1852–1939) with his use of the box narrative, colloquial speech, and frontier hyperbole. In Read's work, though, and to a greater degree in the work of Southern humorists who came after him, there was a weakening of the Southwestern tradition. Writing for an audience composed increasingly of Northerners and including many more women than before, Southern local-color humorists often reduced the vernacular humor of the Old Southwest to mere dialect tales replete with malapropisms and stereotyped characters and imbued with melodrama and sentimentality. As

Read's humor weekly, the *Arkansas Traveler*, put it in 1885: "The days of vulgar humor are over in this country. . . . The humorist of the future must be chaste."

With the ascendancy early in the twentieth century of the newspaper humorists, Southern materials were used with diminishing frequency. Before William Sydney Porter (1862–1910), a native North Carolinian, left his adopted Texas, he could write the hilarious farce "Vereton Villa" (1896) burlesquing Northern misconceptions of the South. Once settled in New York as O. Henry, only occasionally did he write Southern stories, which usually perpetuate stereotypes. Significantly, his best Southern story, "A Municipal Report" (1910), contains relatively little humor. A similar shift in the use of material characterized the humor of Irvin S. Cobb (1876–1944) after he left Kentucky for New York in 1904.

Following the dictates of their readers, the newspaper humorists often forced sentimental endings upon their stories and sketches, in O. Henry's case pleasantly surprising the reader but sometimes altering the tone of the piece itself. In the work of the Kentucky novelist Alice Hegan Rice (1870–1942), sentimentality abounds from first page to last. Her novels *Mrs. Wiggs of the Cabbage Patch* (1901) and its sequel *Lovey Mary* (1903) exemplify the "crying humor" popular at the time. Blending humor and pathos, these novels elicit what the *Arkansas Traveler* described earlier as "a tear of joy, a tear of sadness." In Rice's work the joy far outweighs the sadness. Never is there a hint of bitterness in the incredibly optimistic Mrs. Wiggs, a widow with five children forced from the country to a city slum where the family lives at the edge of starvation and where she watches her older son die from worry and overwork. The humorous treatment of such a situation tortured credibility but failed to daunt readers who, uplifted by a tale extolling the virtues of adversity, purchased *Mrs. Wiggs* by the hundreds of thousands.

Considerably more faithful to life than the crying humor of Rice is the work of the Tennessean Frances Boyd Calhoun (1867–1909) whose only novel, *Miss Minerva and William Green Hill* (1909), delighted thousands of readers young and old. Describing the antics of young Billy Hill and his friend Jimmy Garner, Calhoun fashions an ambience somewhat similar to that in Mark Twain's tales of Tom Sawyer and Huck Finn. Contrasting the masculine, natural world of Billy to the feminine, artificial world of his aunt and guardian Miss Minerva, Calhoun opts for the vitality of the masculine. True to formula, however, she diminishes an often realistic story with a romantic conclusion that transforms Miss Minerva from a character of independent mind to one simperingly submissive to her suitor, who has championed Billy all along. But the characters and scene contain sufficient vitality for Emma Speed Sampson

(1868–1947) to have used them in eleven books, including *Billy and the Major* (1918).

Like other Southern writers of the time, Calhoun uses "darky humor" to a large degree. But if blacks could sometimes be treated as clowns and as foils for whites, to one Southern writer they were beasts. There is little that is funny in the novels of the North Carolinian Thomas Dixon (1864–1946). The author of nearly thirty books, Dixon is best known for *The Leopard's Spots: A Romance of the White Man's Burden 1865–1900* (1902), *The Clansman: An Historical Romance of the Ku Klux Klan* (1905), and *The Traitor: A Story of the Fall of the Invisible Empire* (1907), which purport to reflect postbellum Southern history in the form of fiction. As Dixon had little grasp of the novelist's craft, the fiction is amateurish, suffused with the stuff of popular romance: clumsily contrived plots, characters typed by features, daring rescues, obtrusive moralizing through authorial intrusions, and jejune treatments of sex. The history, notwithstanding Dixon's claims that it was authentic, is often fictitious. Unrestrained sentimentality and racism characterize the novels, each of which, appearing as Jim Crow became supreme, was immensely popular, selling around a million copies.

If Dixon was certain that the South had been right in its militant resistance to Radical Reconstruction, he believed that it had been mistaken in breaking from the Union. While defending the motives of the Confederates and praising their valor, he rejoiced that the burden of slavery had been lifted from white Southerners, freeing them to join in the quest for material success, which they would attain without becoming materialistic.

All that Dixon stood for was anathema to the Negro novelist Sutton Elbert Griggs (1872–1930). Griggs, a Texas-born Baptist clergyman, published *Imperium in Imperio* (1899), *Overshadowed* (1901), *Unfettered* (1902), *The Hindered Hand* (1902), and *Pointing the Way* (1908). *Imperium in Imperio* somewhat anticipates the black nationalism of a later day. One of its protagonists is a leader in a secret order that plans to seize Texas from the United States as a step toward the establishment of a separate Negro state. In *The Hindered Hand* Griggs explicitly condemns Dixon, particularly for Dixon's insistence that the Negro is a beast. Griggs's last novel, however, is conciliatory and apparently is a call for aristocratic Southerners, out of their social superiority and sense of *noblesse oblige*, to play a leading role in the building of a South palatable both to blacks and whites. Griggs, as a literary artist, performs no better than Dixon. Moreover, most of Dixon's faults are Griggs's also.

Portraying the rise of the New South in an optimistic manner was Will N. Harben (1858–1919), most of whose thirty novels and nearly sixty stories are set in his native Georgia. Praised by contemporary critics for his lifelike rendering of the speech, customs, and character of northern Georgia hillmen, Harben could compose a strongly realistic work such as "The Heresy of Abner Calihan" (1894), a moving story of the power of religious orthodoxy. In many of his novels, however, the tone and the effect are essentially romantic, in large part the result of seldom resisting the lure of the labored happy ending, treating the theme of sex with startling sentimentality, and typing characters by social class. To varying degrees in *Abner Daniel* (1902), *The Georgians* (1904), *Ann Boyd* (1906), *Gilbert Neal* (1908), and *Dixie Hart* (1910), he records the ascendancy of sturdy, hardworking, longheaded yeomen, usually contrasting them with the old gentry whom he often portrays as effete or dissolute. Busily discarding outworn tradition and building a prosperous, progressive New South, Harben's protagonists, sanguine over the South's prospects, are happily unaware of the reality of the region's colonial dependence upon the North. As local color, Harben's work contains much realism; as social history, it falls victim to the romanticism both of the genteel tradition and of the New South movement.

More critical of the results of postbellum industrialization is *The Bishop of Cottontown: A Story of the Southern Cotton Mills* (1906) by the Tennessean John Trotwood Moore (1858–1929). Setting his novel in his native Alabama in the mid-1870s, Moore condemns the practice of using child labor in textile factories, which he attributes to the greed of absentee directors and parents alike and to the lack of state regulation. His descriptions of how labor in the mills affects the workers are grimly realistic. Yet the story is attenuated by undue length, a multiplicity of plots, and maudlin love scenes.

Like Harben, whose creativity declined markedly after 1910, and Moore, who never again achieved the success reached in *The Bishop of Cottontown*, Opie Read traveled the road toward realism and often stumbled over the obstacles of literary convention. Remembered primarily as a humorist because of his early career on the *Arkansas Traveler* and his later years as a chautauqua lecturer, Read wrote more than twenty novels between 1888, the year after he moved to Chicago, and 1906, when the chautauqua began to consume his time, that are more pertinent to the study of the South's literary development than his humor is. His work enormously popular, Read often conformed to the strictures of sentimental romance through the use of happy coincidence, stereotyped characters, and language ornate enough to satisfy the most genteel of readers. On occasion, however, he moved beyond such banality. Without resort to sentimentality his work sometimes conveys a sense of loss as the myth of the Southern arcady falls victim to progress. His complex portrayal of the aristocratic General Lundsford in *The Jucklins* (1896) partially redeems an otherwise inferior work. In *My Young Master* (1896) he tells a sensitive story of a Kentucky family before and during the Civil War through the narrator Dan, a mulatto slave whose delineation approaches the fullness of some of George W. Cable's black characters. *The Wives of the Prophet* (1894) treats sexual passion in a manner suggestive of Kate Chopin. Moreover, in that novel, a somber story of carnality and duplicity set in Tennessee, Read had the artistic integrity to write an unhappy ending, a practice contrary to the dictates of popular fiction and one that other incipient realists might well have emulated more often.

Likewise remembered as a humorist, Irvin Cobb is nevertheless more significant to Southern writing because of short stories in which humor is less direct, less important to outcome than it is in most of his other work. Usually set in his native Paducah, Kentucky, these stories—more than twenty-five of which were published before 1920—center upon the character of Judge William Pitman Priest, a kindly old Confederate veteran who spends most of his time righting wrongs and otherwise making decent people happy. To be sure, Judge Priest is a stock character, but with a difference. Rather than the conventionally tall, slim, sonorous Confederate colonel with iron-gray hair who had served with the Army of Northern Virginia, Judge Priest is a short, plump, bald, unlikely hero with a wheezy voice who had fought as a private in the Army of Tennessee. The Confederate veterans who gather at the reunions pictured in Cobb's stories are old men in nondescript uniforms, their muscles gone loose, their feet aching—a little comical, a little pathetic, but more human for all that. Writing after the plantation romance had exerted much of its influence, Cobb intended to modify stereotypes, for as he wrote in the preface to *Back Home* (1912), the first volume of Judge Priest stories, he wished to show the North what life was really like in "an average southern community." In part he succeeds, but his stories are usually too formulaic to achieve the verisimilitude he professed to seek.

Few Southern authors at the turn of the century set out more consciously to portray the South with critical realism than Corra Harris (1869–1935) of Georgia. In numerous essays on Southern literature that were published in national magazines, she laid the blame for the pervasiveness of sentimental romance upon the cultural captivity of the region's writers. Reactionary, defensive, and greedy, Southern writers, she argued, were too enamored of the past, romantic accounts of which sold well, to criticize the present, whose culture had been manufactured largely by clubwomen intent upon creating a gilded image of the region.

In her fiction, too, Harris hammered away at that image. *The Recording Angel* (1912) ridicules the polite culture of small-town matriarchs, satirizes the cult of the Lost Cause, and welcomes the changes brought by the return of a native who cares little for convention. As she criticized what she considered to be specious in Southern tradition, however, Harris cherished what she believed to be worthy, notably the vitality of fundamental Christianity. In *A Circuit Rider's Wife* (1910) and *A Circuit Rider's Widow* (1916) she attacks the hierarchy of the Methodist church, which her husband served as a minister until his death in 1910, for neglecting pastors and flocks, for placing form above substance, and for fostering a religion of joyless sterility. Yet because she could not resist preaching in her fiction, the arguments overwhelm the art. Moreover, her vision and talent were too limited to enable her to treat adequately the social issues she raised, and her novels often sink to domestic bathos.

The inability of most Southern writers at the turn of the century to use what talent they had to produce work that treated the region with thoroughgoing realism resulted from their acquiescence to the demands of an audience that desired a literature of escape, romance, and ideality and from the writers' own immersion in the lingering Victorian culture of the time. Thus a phenomenon like the Populist revolt went untreated—except for an occasional mention to condemn it as demagogic—because many of the agrarian rebels were marginal men, beyond the bounds of the dominant culture that owed them no consideration. Thus the themes of sex and romantic love could only be treated, except in a rare instance, with a mawkishness that would have amused someone like George Washington Harris. Thus almost always a happy ending had to be forced upon a story even if it vitiated the story's effect.

Nevertheless, some aspects of the work by many of the ten Southerners treated here anticipated characteristics of later regional literature: grisly depictions of violence that were hardly sentimental; admiring portrayals of the black man's savvy and fortitude; an uneasiness over the impact of material progress upon the region's folk culture; a love of the South that was made more authentic by a willingness to acknowledge certain of its shortcomings. Ironically, many of these writers, whose work has been severely diminished by time, believed that their writing was much superior to the work of the poetasters and literary chauvinists that they satirized. And it was.

FRED HOBSON

The Rise of the Critical Temper

In the quarter-century following the American Civil War, William P. Trent contended, there existed no native criticism of Southern life and letters worthy of the name. Professor Trent of Sewanee, however, was not altogether correct. George W. Cable of Louisiana, Atticus Haygood of Georgia, Thomas U. Dudley of Kentucky, and Lewis Harvie Blair of Virginia were among Southerners who had challenged Southern racial attitudes or social and economic assumptions during that period. They followed in the tradition of Southerners of the mid-nineteenth century—including Daniel R. Goodloe, Benjamin S. Hedrick, and Hinton Rowan Helper of North Carolina, Moncure Daniel Conway of Virginia, and Cassius Marcellus Clay of Kentucky—who had proved that the critical spirit in the South had not disappeared completely with the passing of the Jeffersonian age.

But Trent, generally speaking, was correct. For half a century or more the South had lain under the sway of what Wilbur J. Cash would later call the "savage ideal"—that ideal "whereunder dissent and variety are completely suppressed and men become, in all their attitudes, professions, and actions, virtual replicas of one another." For that reason in particular, the mission that Trent, Walter Hines Page, John Spencer Bassett, and their Southern compatriots undertook in the waning years of the nineteenth century and the first decade of the twentieth was a courageous one. They would reintroduce the spirit of free inquiry and bold examination that they associated with Jefferson. They would be critics of the South, not apologists or press agents for it.

The rise of the critical temper in the Southern states just before the turn of the century resulted largely from a new point of view held by various young Southerners, particularly academics. Although most of the new social and cultural critics had received their undergraduate education in the South, they had gone elsewhere for further education and had seen the South with new eyes. Page, a North Carolinian, had been one of the first students in the new Johns Hopkins University; later Trent of Virginia and Bassett of North Carolina, along with Woodrow Wilson, had studied with the noted historian Herbert Baxter Adams at Johns Hopkins; William Garrott Brown of Alabama studied history at Harvard University; Edwin Mims, originally of Arkansas, studied literature at Cornell; William Malone Baskervill of Tennessee, John Bell Hennemann of South Carolina, and William Dodd of North Carolina all studied in Germany. The geographical detachment brought a new objectivity that these Southerners employed when they cast their eye on Dixie.

Walter Hines Page (1855–1918) was the acknowledged leader of the new native critics—though, unlike most of the others, he launched much of his criticism from a vantage point outside the South. He had left North Carolina in 1885 after a year as a rebellious but frustrated newspaper editor in Raleigh, and had established himself in New York and Boston where, by the 1890s, he had become a highly successful writer and editor. But Page continued to look south. Not only did he comment on Southern affairs in the pages of the *Forum*, the *Atlantic Monthly*, and *World's Work*, all of which he edited at one time or another, but he also corresponded with, encouraged, and provided a forum for numerous other progressive Southern spokesmen—Trent, Bassett, Brown, Dodd, Mims, Edgar Gardner Murphy, Edwin Alderman, and C. Alphonso Smith. Although he supported the New South movement of Henry Grady, Page was at the same time far more critical of the New South—and Old South—than any other prominent New South spokesman.

Page contended that public education and social reform were the keys to Southern progress. From the beginning of his career he had blasted traditional Southerners, the "Confederates" and "Mummies" who lived in a bygone age. His native state, he charged in 1886, was a prime example of intellectual vacuity: it was characterized by an "insufferable narrowness and mediocrity," was governed by "provincial and ignorant men," and contained not a single being "who is recognized by the world as an authority on anything." It boasted "no man or no woman who . . . has ever written a book that has taken a place in the permanent literature of the country. . . . It is the laughing stock among the States." Page continued his criticism, though modified it, in articles for *Forum* and the *Atlantic*, a book of essays entitled *The Rebuilding of Old Commonwealths* (1902), and an autobiographical novel, *The Southerner* (1909), in which he condemned three ghosts that haunted the South after Appomattox: the Negro, religious orthodoxy, and the Confederate dead. He also began his own publishing house, Doubleday,

Page and Company, which became at the turn of the century a leading publisher of notable Southern books—including those of Sidney Lanier, Ellen Glasgow, and Booker T. Washington.

But Page as cultural force and social critic, at least after 1890, was first and foremost a diplomat—as befits one who in 1913 would become ambassador to the Court of St. James. So committed was he to his particular form of Southern uplift that he was often hesitant to risk antagonizing moderate Southerners with whom he needed to work; thus he included most of his harshest criticism in letters to like-minded Southerners, usually avoided the subject of race altogether in his public utterances, and published his highly critical novel *The Southerner* under a pseudonym.

Somewhat less diplomatic than Page, at least for a time, were William P. Trent (1862–1939) and, particularly, John Spencer Bassett (1867–1928). Their criticism was perhaps the more significant because they were living and working in the South when they voiced it. In 1888 Trent had left his graduate study at Johns Hopkins for a post at Sewanee, carrying the influence of Thomas Jefferson and Matthew Arnold with him, and four years later published a life of William Gilmore Simms that was as much social criticism as biography. He condemned the Charleston of the early and mid-nineteenth century in which Simms had come of age, portraying its leading class as a "blind, exclusive, and thoughtless aristocracy"—and, Trent added, he spoke not only of Charleston but of the entire antebellum South. In the Southern states existed "a life that choked all thought and investigation that did not tend to conserve existing institutions and opinions." Southerners led "a primitive life," and "evils . . . flowed from an unsound social and political system." It was obviously no environment for the independent thinker or the aspiring creative artist. Of Simms, Trent concluded, "Perhaps there has never been a man whose development was so sadly hampered by his environment."

What Trent had written was something virtually new in the postbellum South—a biography highly critical of the culture that had shaped his subject—and he accepted the condemnation he received as proof of his charges. But he had only begun his assault on Southern complacency and mediocrity. As he later wrote, "my work on the 'Life of Simms' brought me in contact with the *Southern Quarterly*, and other old Southern Reviews, and the criticism my book received emphasized the fact that the South not only needed a literary organ but was less fortunate in that respect than it had been before the war." Thus in 1892 he founded a journal, the *Sewanee Review*, which pledged itself to a free and open inquiry of life and literature and opened its pages to Southerners, mainly academics, who were equally devoted to the critical spirit. "The REVIEW did not become quite as much a Southern organ as I had hoped," Trent later wrote, by which he meant most of the articles were not specifically about the South, but it distinguished itself by its free spirit and its role as model to subsequent Southern reviews. When Trent left Sewanee for Columbia University in 1900, he left his mark. As he wrote in his preface to another book, *Southern Statesmen of the Old Régime* (1897), he "disdained to pander to a provincial sentimentalism that shivers at honest and fair criticism of any man or cause that may have become a shibboleth."

Trent was not the only Southerner at the turn of the century who believed the literary scholar had to adopt a critical approach to Southern life and letters. William Malone Baskervill (1850–1899), chairman of the English Department at Vanderbilt University, was not so outspoken as Trent, but in his pioneering volume of *Southern Writers* (1897) he set out to discuss postbellum Southern writers from a national, not provincial, perspective. In chapters on George W. Cable, Joel Chandler Harris, Sidney Lanier, Maurice Thompson, Irwin Russell, and Mary Noailles Murfree (Charles Egbert Craddock) he treated the writers as products of Southern society, though his view of that society was kinder than Trent's. Baskervill died in 1899, before he completed a planned second volume of *Southern Writers*, but a group of his former students produced in 1903 the second volume with essays on Thomas Nelson Page, James Lane Allen, Grace King, Sherwood Bonner, and other writers.

Other, younger literary scholars joined the new critical movement that Trent and Baskervill had begun. John Bell Hennemann (1864–1908), a native South Carolinian who had come to the University of Tennessee in 1893, then Sewanee in 1900, was a staunch supporter of Trent who served briefly as editor of the *Sewanee Review*. In his essay "The National Element in Southern Literature" (1903) he became one of the first Southerners to identify and defend the new critical movement in Southern literary studies and to proclaim Trent and Baskervill its founders. Edwin Mims (1872–1959), professor of English at Trinity College in North Carolina (and, after 1912, Vanderbilt), produced in 1905 a biography of Sidney Lanier in which he maintained a critical distance from his subject and acknowledged Lanier's glaring artistic deficiencies, all the while admiring his heroic life. In a chapter entitled "The New South" Mims allied himself strongly with the Southern progressives. Another literary scholar, C. Alphonso Smith (1864–1924) of

Louisiana State University and the University of Virginia, wrote several essays pointing to the poor quality of most antebellum Southern literature, though Smith's criticism of Southern life was mild.

But none of the literary scholars was as outspoken as Bassett, the Trinity College historian, and no Southern journal bolder than that Bassett founded in 1902, the *South Atlantic Quarterly*. Inspired by the *Sewanee Review* but more self-consciously Southern, the *Quarterly* devoted more than half its articles during its first ten years of publication to Southern history and the contemporary South. Bassett had as his aim not only critical inquiry into the Southern past but actual reform of the contemporary South, and he dared to venture into the only area largely avoided by both Trent and Page—Southern race relations. One of his editorials, "Stirring Up the Fires of Race Antipathy" (October, 1903), gave rise to a controversy much greater than any Trent or Page had ever incited. In perhaps the strongest indictment of white supremacy since George W. Cable's *The Silent South* (1885), Bassett attacked Jim Crow laws, restrictions on the Negro vote, and the white assumption that the Negro had his place: "The 'place' of every man in our American life is such a one as his virtues and his capacities may enable him to take."

But it was not Bassett's attack on white supremacy that roused white outrage, nor his prediction that the Negro would "in spite of our race feeling . . . win equality at some time," but rather his reference to Booker T. Washington as "the greatest man, save General Lee, born in the South in a hundred years." Although Bassett added in the next line, "but he is not a typical negro," the damage had been done. Southern editors, led by Josephus Daniels of the Raleigh *News and Observer*, demanded Bassett's resignation, and the young professor's job was saved only by a courageous stand by the Trinity College faculty and administration.

Bassett was even more outspoken in other *South Atlantic Quarterly* editorials. He denounced the South's "spirit of ignorance," its "poverty of scholarship," and its "intolerance of criticism." Southern politics was characterized by fraud, provincialism, appeals to racial hatred, "a tyranny of ideas"; the intellects of its politicians were "pauperized." The South exhibited deep feeling but crude thought. "We write as a people who are not yet out of the stage of uncultured animalism." He asked, "Shall we of all people be those among whom self-examination and self-criticism shall have no place?"

Bassett, like Cable twenty years before, could not last in a South dominated by a savage ideal; and also like Cable, he moved in 1906 to Northampton, Massachusetts, where he hoped to find, he later wrote, "a peaceful atmosphere." But his criticism in the *South Atlantic Quar-*

terly was the most notable example of the Southern critical temper at work in the realm of social issues just after the turn of the century. The year before Bassett drew the ire of tarheel editors, Andrew Sledd, a Virginian who had become a Methodist minister and professor of Latin at Emory College, wrote an article, "The Negro: Another View," for the *Atlantic Monthly* in which he bitterly condemned lynching and the white attitudes that contributed to it. Less fortunate than Bassett, he was fired from his position. Sledd left for graduate study at Yale, though later he returned to the South and finished his career at Emory. Other Southerners cast a critical eye upon the South and escaped with livelihood and reputation: William C. Dodd, the historian at Randolph-Macon College (and, after 1908, the University of Chicago) whose *South Atlantic* essay "Some Difficulties of the History Teacher in the South" earned him criticism in some quarters as a traitor to the South, but gained him respect in others; William Garrott Brown, the Jeffersonian from Alabama whose essays in the *South Atlantic Quarterly*, the *Atlantic Monthly*, and other journals attacked a politically solid South; Quincy Ewing, an Episcopalian minister from Louisiana and author of an outspoken *Atlantic* essay, "The Heart of the Race Problem" (1909); and finally, Edwin Mims, who was not only the biographer of Lanier but also an apostle of Walter Hines Page and Bassett's successor as editor of the *South Atlantic Quarterly*. A social as well as a literary critic, Mims contributed essays to the *Atlantic* and *World's Work* on Southern progress and poverty, but always exercised such caution—some charged timidity—that he rode out the Southern storm and emerged as a bona fide Southern booster in his book *The Advancing South* (1926).

Mims, in most respects, was different only in degree from his fellow Southern spokesmen. Except for brief outbursts by Page in his 1886 "Mummy" letters, Trent in his Simms biography, and Bassett and Sledd in their isolated attacks on white supremacy, the social and cultural critics at the turn of the century still wrote with a certain caution, an awareness of consequence. They knew the necessity of an honest investigation of Southern life and letters, and they possessed a critical temper alien to the generation before them; but they also knew the price that criticism exacted. They wrote with conviction but not often with abandon or iconoclastic glee. That task and pleasure would await H. L. Mencken, Gerald W. Johnson, Wilbur J. Cash, and other Southern critics of the next generation.

THE SOUTHERN RENASCENCE

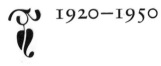 1920–1950

THOMAS DANIEL YOUNG

Introduction to Part III

For some reason that no one seems to understand completely, at specific periods in the nation's history many of the most significant literary figures seem to have resided in the same geographic region. From about 1790 to 1830, with Washington Irving, James Fenimore Cooper, James Kirke Paulding, and William Cullen Bryant furnishing the nucleus, New York was the literary capital of the United States. About 1830 it moved to Boston where it remained until the beginning of the Civil War. Between 1830 and 1860 almost every literary figure of any importance lived within a few miles of that New England city—James Russell Lowell, Oliver Wendell Holmes, and William Wadsworth Longfellow at Cambridge; Ralph Waldo Emerson, Henry David Thoreau, and Nathaniel Hawthorne at Concord; and Herman Melville at the height of his career in nearby Pittsfield, Massachusetts. Certainly that area had no serious challenger to being the literary center of the country. From 1860 to 1900, because of the Civil War and its aftermath, the United States had no literary capital. There were distinguished writers—Walt Whitman, Emily Dickinson, and Mark Twain—but they lived miles apart and had little communication with each other. There is no evidence that any one of them read seriously the writing of either of the other two. About 1912 important writers began again to congregate in the same vicinity. This time, with Hamlin Garland, Theodore Dreiser, Carl Sandburg, and Edgar Lee Masters leading the way, and assisted by *Poetry* magazine, many persons with literary aspirations migrated toward Chicago. When the young Ernest Hemingway wanted to find a sympathetic audience for his plans for a career in literature, he had merely to ride a streetcar from his home in suburban Oak Park to the downtown Loop.

Although there is broad disagreement on the reason why, the compass needle moved again in about 1920—and pointed South. For thirty years or more that region dominated literary activity in America. During this period, three of the most significant literary groups in twentieth-century America were centered in the South—the Fugitives, the Agrarians, and the New Critics—and some of the nation's most enduring writers lived and wrote there—William Faulkner, Eudora Welty, Robert Penn Warren, John Crowe Ransom, Allen Tate, Thomas Wolfe, Caroline Gordon, Cleanth Brooks, and Andrew Lytle. Ellen Glasgow and James Branch Cabell, because their literary careers were launched before World War I, are not included in the Southern Renascence, though some of their most important work was done in the twenties, thirties, and even later.

Most literary historians and critics would agree that there is no clear sociological explanation for the Southern Renascence. The South in the 1920s was the last place one would expect significant literary activity to occur. According to Howard W. Odum and Harry Estelle Moore's influential study, *Regionalism: A Cultural-Historical Approach to National Integration* (1938), during the 1920s the cultural index or plane of living of the South was the lowest in the nation. It was at the bottom of the list in almost everything: ownership of automobiles, radios, residence telephones; income per capita; bank deposits; homes with electricity, running water, and indoor plumbing. Its residents subscribed to the fewest magazines and newspapers, read the fewest books; they also provided the least support for education, public libraries, and art museums. It would not appear to have produced an economic and intellectual climate conducive to the creation of significant literature. As Donald Davidson once remarked, one wonders how "Faulkner managed to survive, much less write." Apparently there was little change even in the thirties; in one of his fireside chats President Roosevelt proclaimed the South the nation's number one economic problem.

Despite these adverse circumstances, however, the Renascence did occur. The South, as Randall Stewart once observed, suddenly became a "nest of singing birds." Many explanations for this unexpected phenomenon have been offered. One of the most interesting and illuminating is Allen Tate's: "With the war of 1914–1918, the South reentered the world—but gave a backward glance as it slipped over the border: that backward glance gave us the Southern renascence, a literature conscious of the past in the present" ("The New Provincialism" [1945]). He and his friends, he wrote in "The Profession of Letters in the South" (1935), came to realize that the Southern attitude was different from the dominant American one, which he defined as "a social point of view," one that did not require a literature of "conviction and experience" but one supported by "statistical survey." The total purpose of Donald Davidson and his fellow Agrarians, Davidson wrote in *Still Rebels, Still Yankees* (1957), was "to seek the image of the South which we could charge with high conviction and to give it, wherever we could, the finality of art." The Southern writers whose best work began to appear in the period between the two wars attempted to find, as Lewis Simpson writes in *The Dispossessed Garden* (1975), "the meaning of the past," to discover or reconstruct some viable relationship to the Southern tradition as it differed from that of other sections of America. The specific characteristics of this tradition, as it was presented in the poems, essays, novels, and stories of the third, fourth, and fifth decades of this century, are summarized by Cleanth Brooks in "The Southern Renascence: A Traditionalist View": a feeling for the concrete and the specific, an awareness of conflict, a sense of community and of religious wholeness, a belief in human imperfection, and a genuine and never wavering disbelief in perfection ever developing as a result of human effort and planning; a deep-seated sense of the tragic, and a conviction that nature is mysterious and contingent. Any attempt to harness nature and make it a servant of man will always be doomed to failure. "This is the ground," Richard King writes in *The Southern Renaissance* (1980), "in which the South's artistic promptings took root and flourished."

EDGAR E. MACDONALD

The Ambivalent Heart: Literary Revival in Richmond

The Southern Renascence of the twentieth century is generally adjudged to have gotten under way in the years immediately following the First World War. It was in these years that a new generation of Southern authors emerged who were able to look at and within themselves and their region with critical discernment as well as passionate involvement. A restrictive sectional identification was no longer present to interfere with a thoroughgoing artistic exploration of human experience in Southern guise.

Yet, what the bold modernists of the 1920s and 1930s were able to achieve was already well under way almost a generation earlier, in and about the one-time capital of the Confederate States of America—Richmond, Virginia. It is the Richmond writers, Ellen Glasgow and James Branch Cabell and to a certain extent Mary Johnston and Amélie Rives, who exhibit the first really important break with the aesthetics, social attitudes, and community assumptions of the older, late-Victorian South, and who speak with voices that are recognizably of the emerging twentieth century rather than the nineteenth.

Richmond as an industrial center in an agrarian state early attracted a polyethnic citizenry that gave it a diversity uncommon in most of the South. A plebeian mixture of Virginians and Southerners resulted from Richmond's being the capital of the Commonwealth in 1779 and the capital of the Confederacy in 1861. Its numerous nineteenth-century newspapers attest that it was diverse and literate, and the book firms flourishing there indicate that it aspired to be literary.

In 1906 the national publication *Book News* featured Richmond in its series "Lesser Literary Centres of America." Alice M. Tyler traced its literary history from its founding father, the man of letters William Byrd II, through the nineteenth century. About the twentieth century she wrote, "The list of literary workers today in Richmond is large." She included editors, historians, journalists, including Henry Sydnor Harrison before he became famous for *Queed* (1911) and *V. V.'s Eyes*

264

(1913). The stars of her article, aside from the inevitable references to Poe, were Amélie Rives (Princess Troubetzkoy), born in Richmond and whose *The Quick or the Dead?* (1888) was still considered mildly shocking in 1906; Mary Johnston (latest novel *Sir Mortimer* [1904]); Ellen Glasgow (*Wheel of Life* [1906]); and James Branch Cabell (*The Line of Love* [1905]). "Miss Johnston and Miss Glasgow are very warm friends," Tyler observed. These two friends, along with Glasgow's sister Cary McCormack, Lila Meade Valentine, Mary Branch Munford, and other forward-looking ladies, formed the Equal Suffrage League of Virginia in 1909. The Southern male was to be enlightened that his chivalrous pose was a sham long overdue for public exposure. The year 1913 saw three feminist novels flower from these activities: Glasgow's *Virginia*, Johnston's *Hagar*, and Harrison's *V. V.'s Eyes*. All three scrutinized the Southern belle; was she victim or victimizer? Ironically both, the three writers postulated.

Symbolically, Amélie Rives's *The Quick or the Dead?* (1888) foreshadowed the direction Southern fiction would take with Faulkner's "A Rose for Emily." Rives was born in Civil War Richmond on August 23, 1863, next door to St. Paul's on Grace Street; her father, Colonel Alfred Landon Rives, was a member of Lee's staff, and the general himself was her godfather. Her grandfather was twice minister to France. The war was little more than a background drama for her education and travels. Such works as *World's End, Shadows of Flames,* and *Hidden House* treat international themes reminiscent of Edith Wharton and Henry James. But the heroine of *The Quick or the Dead?* embodies a theme that becomes pervasive in Southern letters; she is torn between the past, the memory of her dead husband, and the present, his cousin who hauntingly resembles the dead man. Her irrational responses to her morbid sentimentality, especially those scenes set in a Gothic church, are redolent of Poe, but Rives prefigures Faulkner in the final scene when the heroine retrieves her wedding ring from the hearth, blows ashes from it, and replaces it on her finger. She has clearly chosen the dead over the quick. But in a sequel, *Barbara Dering* (1892), the handsome cousin returns; the past has not permanently repressed her rational will.

Mary Johnston too had made her literary reputation earlier. *To Have and to Hold* (1900), a historical romance of the bartered brides at Jamestown, is a work of enduring popularity (evidenced by two film versions). Johnston was born on November 21, 1870, at Buchanan in Botetourt County, Virginia. Her family, like Amélie Rives's, moved to Alabama, and like Rives, Johnston traveled in Europe and lived in New York. On the death of her father, Major John William Johnston (CSA), cousin of Confederate general Joseph Eggleston Johnston, Mary and her sisters moved to Richmond in 1905 and lived there until 1912. *Lewis Rand* (1908) and *The Long Roll* (1911) include scenes laid in Richmond.

As Ronald Cella observes, "At the same time Johnston was discharging her duty to the Lost Cause by writing *The Long Roll* and *Cease Firing* (1912), she developed a serious commitment to some contemporary causes" (*Mary Johnston* [Boston, 1981], 25). In 1912 she spoke for women's suffrage before the Virginia House of Delegates, a group dedicated to Confederate ideals. Her first "cause" novel was *Hagar* (1913), little more than a suffrage tract, but her interests broadened to criticisms of ignorance and intolerance in *Witch* (1914), to evolution and progress in *Wanderers* (1917), to mystical philosophy in *Foes* (1918), *Michael Forth* (1919), and *Sweet Rocket* (1920). Her later works, *Silver Cross* (1922) to *Drury Randall* (1934), are marked by experiments, renewal, and nostalgia. Mary Johnston's recreations of the struggles of the past to guide an interior search for meaning in the present are the prototype of a Southern tradition that flowered into a legacy.

Ellen Glasgow both accepted Richmond and rejected it, refusing to take any of its inherited notions as gospel. One of the younger children in a large family, her self-confessed morbid sensitivity made her side with a delicate mother, the ideal of Southern womanhood, against a father who enjoyed remarkable bodily vigor, one who could reconcile his Calvinistic stoicism with his physical pleasures. Her gentle, Episcopalian mother died when Ellen was twenty; her father remained an enduring enigma until she was forty-three. In the disparity of parental temperaments, the resulting stress for Ellen Glasgow would give her the double vision of life that results in protest, in art. The code of male chivalry as practiced in Virginia, more immediately in Richmond, would become the focus of her attack. The church, which upheld the code, would be the first institution openly rejected. Earlier, a very young Ellen had rebelled against formal education, especially that decreed as proper instruction for the female. She read omnivorously and eclectically, forming a mind delicately perceptive and toughly resilient.

When Ellen Glasgow put aside the holy books of her father's church, she picked up the writings of Darwin. The result was a short story entitled "A Woman of Tomorrow," published in 1895 when Ellen was twenty-two. Significantly the story is concerned with a woman's conflict between marriage and career. The young author published her first novel two years later: *The Descendant* was accorded serious attention by the critics, and the novel went into three editions. Its hero, an illegitimate poor white from Virginia, goes to New York and becomes editor of a radical newspaper. Its heroine is a Southern girl who studies painting in New York, art symbolizing liberation in a male-dominated society. *Phases of an Inferior Planet* followed in 1898, with another Southern heroine in New York, this one seeking fulfillment as a singer. She meets a young biologist, a rebellious nonconformist. They marry, but poverty wrecks their happiness, and he becomes a priest celebrated for his rebuttals to a series of anonymous antireligious articles of which he too is the author. Young Miss Glasgow's irony may appear heavy-handed, but no perceptive reader could doubt that she had experienced large doses of male double-talk in her native Richmond.

With her third novel, Ellen Glasgow came home. *The Voice of the People* (1900) is an analysis of Virginia and Virginians that marks the beginning of a multivolume social history spanning the transitional period from the Civil War to World War II. In *Voice* she contrasted aristocratic-democratic Williamsburg, the eighteenth-century capital of Virginia, and plebeian-dissembling Richmond, the latter-day capital. In like manner Ellen Glasgow's heart was divided, loving the nobility of the past but scorning the evasions of those who worshipped it blindly. Her fourth novel, *The Battle-Ground* (1902), is a novel about the Civil War but is by no means an apology for the Confederacy, and its depiction of wartime Richmond is not presented sentimentally. The hero returns to the valley to find his ancestral hall in ashes, but there are no lamentations in the elegiac tradition of Thomas Nelson Page or John Esten Cooke. His wife says firmly, "We will begin again, and this time, my dear, we will begin together." No war was totally lost if it liberated the female from a passive role.

The Deliverance (1904) marked a new stage in Glasgow's development. A reversed social order sets up a delicious if grim irony of situations. Old Mrs. Blake, blind and crippled, has never been told by her children that the South lost the war and that she is living in the overseer's house, her son Christopher grubbing a bare subsistence from the soil and her daughter Cynthia slaving in the house. Mrs. Blake is the post–Civil War South, happily recounting the glorious days of her youth. "Lies, lies—there had been nothing but lies spoken within her hearing for twenty years."

With *The Miller of Old Church* (1911), Glasgow served up a new combination of red and blue blood. In this work the heroine has both, and when she marries the miller, the implication is clear that the character with the best possibility for happiness is one with the blood of both classes, combining sensitivity and fortitude. We see Miss Glasgow moving toward her prescription for the ills of the South: "Blood and Irony."

The significantly entitled *Virginia* (1913) is the first classic study of the evasive idealism that stifled thought in the South. An illuminating portrait of a Southern girl raised according to the precepts of her father, a tradition that expostulated that the less a girl knew about life the better prepared she was to cope with it, the title character Virginia is sent to Miss Priscilla Batte's school where girls are taught what Southern males expect of their wives. In this work Glasgow resolutely faced the ultimate in Southern misalliance, the blood union of white with black; Cyrus Treadwell's instincts "permitted him to sin against his race's integrity, yet forbade him to acknowledge, even to himself, that he bore any part in the consequences of that sin."

In *Life and Gabriella* (1916), the well-born heroine rejects the enslaving code of the Southern lady and makes her way in New York as a fashion designer. At the age of thirty-nine (then Glasgow's), she marries a virile Irishman. Glasgow wrote this novel in New York, but upon its completion she returned to Richmond, where she met the embodiment of the "new man" in the South. Dynamic Henry Anderson, rising from post–Civil War poverty, gave Richmond much to talk about with his success as a lawyer in Washington and New York, his championing of the Republican party, his British style and servants. His political aspirations interested Glasgow, for they opposed another entrenched institution in the South, the Democratic party. Her success and strength of mind appealed to him, but the novel they wrote together, *The Builders* (1919), was neither a good political study nor an interesting romance. Then Anderson, as a colonel in the American Red Cross, was sent abroad and was irradiated by the charming Queen Marie of Romania. At home, disillusioned by the war and the disaffection of the "new man," Glasgow turned out another therapy novel, *One Man in His Time* (1922).

Recovered from romance, the curse of the South, a mature woman and artist produced *Barren Ground* (1922). Philosophy and art coalesced into a classic: theme, characterization, and style evidence a new mastery. Glasgow's heroine, Dorinda Oakley, with a saving Presbyterian vein of iron, succumbs briefly to romance but rises from the inevitable disillusion, conquers the broom sedge, the symbol of nature triumphant over will, and emerges as a new image of independent woman. Like Glasgow herself, she stood above any male, father or lover or any paternal diety, who would rob her of her self-realization. Cheered by the critical and public success of this work, Glasgow turned her matured talents to three delightful comedies of Richmond society. *The Romantic Comedians* (1926), the story of a May–December marriage, satirizes the unhappy alliance of the Old South with the New South. Wit sparkles on every page. "The worst of all possible worlds would be one invented by good women," Glasgow wickedly has Judge Honeywell, a model of conventional thinking, say. Honeywell ironically is the natal twin of Edmonia Bredalbane, a Wife-of-Bath character. She observes of her brother, "You look as if you had lived on duty and it hadn't agreed with you." The judge muses on her popularity with younger Richmonders: "They treated her scarlet letter less as a badge of shame than as some foreign decoration for distinguished service." In *They Stooped to Folly* (1929) Glasgow analyzes three generations of the fallen woman, a male invention. Aunt Agatha, assigned a third-floor back bedroom and resigned to spinsterhood, "had fallen like a perfect lady." Mrs. Dalrymple is not received by Richmond ladies, but she holds an allure for their husbands who continue to call. Milly Burden is unaware of any such classification as fallen woman. Virginius Littlepage, witness of the changing mcres, has a daughter militantly dedicated to social reform. He is reconciled to a war "that diverted Mary Victoria's mission from the Congo, where faces were incurably black, to the Balkan kingdoms, where, he charitably assumed, they were merely sallow."

In *The Sheltered Life* (1932) Ellen Glasgow achieved a masterpiece that can stand with the best works in this century. Her superbly handled irony is blended with compassion to give us a perfectly realized portrait of Eva Birdsong, inevitably destroyed in attempting to embody the concept of the Southern ideal. Like her younger contemporary Faulkner, Glasgow acknowledged the beauty of an agrarian South—the pastoral garden—but exposed its evasive idealism. Neurasthenic Aunt Etta is the unloved old maid, handsome Aunt Isabel another "compromised" female. The latter, however, with the saving grace of beauty and spirit, crosses the invisible social boundary and marries handsome Joseph Crocker, a carpenter. Mrs. Archbald with a Cabellian wand metamorphoses Joseph, her new brother-in-law, from plain people to quiet people, and finally with the aid of a genealogist into old family. The novel's ultimate irony is poetically evocative. Surrounded by the dead birds her husband intended to present to his friends, the beautiful Eva Birdsong sits gazing silently into the twilight of the past, having shot her profligate husband. In Richmond no romance could end with divorce, only with death.

Ellen Glasgow published two more novels before her death in 1945. *Vein of Iron* (1935), a nostalgic return to the fortitude of her Calvinist ancestry, records the dark days of the depression in Richmond, but the hero returns to the Great Valley of his ancestors to die. *In This Our Life* (1941), the effort of an ill and disillusioned woman, has as its hero Asa Timberlake, attempting to hold his disintegrating family together in a disintegrating Richmond. It received the Pulitzer Prize in 1942, primarily in recognition of Glasgow's long literary career, and it was made into a film with the leading Hollywood stars. Her unfinished sequel was published posthumously in 1966. In *Beyond Defeat* Asa is liberated from his old-line family and joins a new family based on love and respect, out of Richmond, down on James River near where Pocahontas had welcomed the Old World to the New World.

But Richmond permeates the Glasgow opus. Its houses, parks, gardens, and streets serve exclusively as background for seven of her novels: *The Romance of a Plain Man, The Builders, One Man in His Time, The Romantic Comedians, They Stooped to Folly, The Sheltered Life,* and *In This Our Life.* Richmond also provided settings for *The Voice of the People, The Battle-Ground, The Deliverance, Life and Gabriella,* and *Vein of Iron.* Characters in other novels make trips to Richmond. Its Jeffersonian capitol and her own house at One West Main are described in *Voice of the People.* In *The Sheltered Life,* thirty years later, a mature Glasgow sat in her garden at One West Main and poured her hard-won stoic philosophy into the mind of General Archbald. Today, fifty years later, the garden is much as she described it, with its wall, its stone birdbath, its old sycamore. Ellen Glasgow died in the big gray house that Richmond had swept past, leaving it a lonely relic among the antique shops, the parking lots, the human derelicts abandoned by every city.

While Ellen Glasgow, in her preface to *The Sheltered Life* (1938), classified her fellow Richmonders as "a shallow and aimless society of happiness-hunters, who lived in a perpetual flight from reality, and grasped at any effort-saving illusion or pleasure," she could look on them with an amused, even affectionate tolerance. James Branch Cabell, on the other hand, was early subjected to subtle social pressures that further inhibited an already shy youth. The Cabells were old family, physicians, dedicated to public service; the Branches, his mother's family, were new and had used their coal mines in West Virginia as collateral to obtain Yankee money to open the Merchant's Bank in war-devastated Richmond. James Branch Cabell was born April 14, 1879, in what he liked to refer to as an upstairs room of the Richmond Public Library. The latter was built on the site of his maternal grandmother's house; his parents, Dr. Robert Gamble Cabell and Anne Harris Branch, followed the local custom of newlyweds living on the third floor of a parent's home until the children started arriving. Cabell grew up in a Richmond that was industriously mythologizing the war. King Arthur had returned from Avalon in the form of General Lee with the Knights of the Round Table becomingly dressed as Confederate generals. Mordred's great evil host was the Yankee. Cabell observed, however, that the public affirmation of his elders' faith in their gods did not conform to their private talk at home. There one learned that the heroes had human failings which were not part of the official history.

At the age of fifteen, Cabell was sent to the College of William and Mary, safer than the sophisticated university. The Williamsburg college was then small, private, a normal school dedicated to preparing male students for public teaching careers. Cabell's attire, with yellow gloves and cane, marked him in the eyes of the other students as someone outside their rurally oriented experience. His nickname was Sister. He was relatively happy there for three and a half years. A young lady, four years his senior, listened to his verses, but aside from two or three literary students, he turned to the faculty for intellectual companionship. In the middle of Cabell's senior year, the idyll in "Fairhaven" (Williamsburg) came to an end. Rumors associated Cabell and several other students with homosexuality. Charles Washington Coleman, the college librarian, likewise figured in the talk. The faculty minutes reveal that none of the evidence supported a finding against the students or Coleman, but Cabell's verse diaries of this period prove that he suffered a profound sense of shame from the gossip.

When Cabell returned to Richmond in 1898, he found a disturbing alteration in his parents' relationship: his father had moved out. Annie Branch, twelve years younger than her husband, was pleasure-loving and disregarded the strictures of society. Presbyterian Calvinism was still a meaningful part of Richmond's social fabric, but freed from Branch Methodism by her mother's Patteson Episcopal heritage, young Mrs. Cabell smoked and drank cocktails before other ladies freely confessed to these pleasures. While his mother entertained the Richmond gossips, Cabell worked for three different newspapers: the Richmond *Times* (1898), the New York *Herald* (1899–1901), and the Richmond *News* (1901). In 1901, he submitted five short stories to magazines and had three of them accepted by leading periodicals. His output in the short story form was prodigious, and always an economical writer he later reworked many of these stories into longer works. Between 1902 and 1911 he traveled in France, Ireland, and England doing genealogical research for a wealthy Branch uncle. His writing reflects his ancestral delving just as it reflects the vagaries of Richmond gossip. Generally Cabell favored the episodic tale; shorter works take the form of the philosophical *conte* and his longer journeys that of the eighteenth-century picaresque novel.

Just when Cabell began to rejoice in having his first works accepted in 1901, he became the subject of more painful gossip in Richmond. Rumor established him as the murderer of his mother's lover, a cousin.

While Cabell's name did not appear in print in the four Richmond papers that speculated on the murder, they hinted at his identity; gossip supplied his name. Like the college rumors, these could not be openly denied without giving them wider currency. The reclusive Cabell turned to work for solace while his mother braved the world. She took the manuscript of his first novel to Walter Hines Page in New York and succeeded in getting it published. *The Eagle's Shadow* (1904) was also serialized in the *Saturday Evening Post*.

The year 1907 brought another stage of the events that kept alive the gossip surrounding Cabell's name. His mother determined upon a divorce, a step not lightly taken at that time. That same year, Cabell decided he would take his revenge on Richmond society by satirizing it in a work that would expose its multiple hypocrisies. *The Cords of Vanity* (1909) followed his penchant for reworking his short stories, and thus the highly romantic stuff of magazine fiction is cemented together by a protagonist who is Cabell's age and who speaks in the first person. Much of the cement is thinly disguised autobiography. But Cabell's sentimentalism interfered with his irony: "For the rest, Lichfield, and Fairhaven also [Richmond and Williamsburg], got at and into me when I was too young to defend myself. Therefore Lichfield and Fairhaven cannot ever, really, seem to me grotesque." He would indulge in more thinly disguised biography in *The Rivet in Grandfather's Neck* (completed 1911, published 1915) and *Something About Eve* (1927). Like Glasgow, Cabell saw evasion as a way of life in his native environment, and his one great character, Jurgen, embodies the traits of those Cabell saw as most representative of the Southerner: a middle-class pawnbroker who assumes any role—duke, pope, God—but who sees through all the pretenses associated with role playing.

By 1919, at the age of forty, Cabell had published eleven books and numerous stories. While his work had aroused a limited critical acceptance, he was by no means a popular author nor one who had received attention from the ruling critics. The publication of *Jurgen* in September and its suppression by the courts in New York as a lewd and lascivious book made its author known overnight. Although two years later the charges against his book were overthrown, Cabell remained in the popular mind an "indecent writer." While *Jurgen* was still banned, *Figures of Earth* appeared in 1921. The perceptive saw it as a vindication of Cabell's artistic powers, its hero more representative of questing man than the philandering Jurgen, but it confused others who expected another "pornographic" work. *The High Place*, considered by many scholars as Cabell's best work, followed in 1923, and finally with *Straws and Prayerbooks* in 1924 Cabell revealed that all his work up to that time fitted into an overall epic scheme, as yet incomplete. *The Silver Stallion* appeared in 1926, *Something About Eve* in 1927.

Over the years critics had observed that Cabell essentially wrote the same story over and over, that of a questing Faust–Don Juan forced to compromise with a dubious reality in the end. Cabell admitted that the criticism was in part true, that he had intentionally depicted the universal male in what he would term a Biography of Man. In 1923, pushed along by the critics, he conceived the idea that all his work from its genesis could be arranged in epic form. Thus in the mid–1920s, at the height of his creative powers and popular acceptance, he turned back to resurrect his early and immature work to be a part of "The Biography of the Life of Manuel," embodied in the Storisende (story's end) Edition. This ambitious and inflated rewrite (1927–1930) appeared in "twenty volumes," in reality eighteen. Cabell misjudged the temper of the times. Not even enthusiasts longed to read a twenty-volume work, and the booming American economy was hurrying to its bust. In the end, even Cabell grew weary of the attempt to make his early romances an organic part of his more sophisticated work. He made a public farewell to the "Biography" in 1930 and dropped the James from his name, leading reviewers to surmise that he was retiring from writing. Confusions resulted, some believing that James Branch Cabell and Branch Cabell were two different people. In the epilogue of *Let Me Lie* (1947), an affectionate acceptance of his native state, he bid farewell to Branch Cabell and resumed the James. In the exile phase some ten titles had appeared— essays, fiction, and more allegorized biography.

Cabell never attained a large following in Richmond despite his excellent newspaper coverage, but two relatively late works almost won the locals over. In *Let Me Lie* (a pun) he paid his respects in a collection of essays to "the remarkable Commonwealth of Virginia" as well as to General Lee. In *As I Remember It* (1955) he humanized himself in recounting his deep affection for his first wife, Priscilla Bradley Cabell, a charming widow with five children whom he had married at the age of thirty-four. Ballard Hartwell Cabell arrived as her sixth child, and very clearly her writer-husband became her seventh. Ballard was born with Down's syndrome and remained an endearing child; when his mother died in 1949, he requested his seventy-year-old father to marry the following year. Ballard's choice was Margaret Freeman with whom Cabell had been associated as an editor of the *Reviewer* in the early 1920s. Cabell died in May, 1958.

Cabell is generally classified as a comic poet. In *The Cords of Vanity* and *The Rivet in Grandfather's Neck*, he set out to write the social comedies that Ellen Glasgow produced in her best three novels of Richmond life, but sentiment intruded on his irony. Allegory and his fictional Poictesme were later to give him a remove from his subject matter that allowed him to maintain his ironic pose. While Ellen Glasgow's tragic despair occasionally intruded on her irony, she could look on Richmond with amused detachment. Cabell, haunted by old loves, could not write of Richmond objectively until after his major work was accomplished. In his cosmic comedies, Cabell appears to stand outside time and place, but it would be difficult to find an American writer whose environment played a larger role in creating those stresses that result in literature.

Apart from the national recognition that Glasgow and Cabell brought to Richmond in the early decades of this century, a group of local writers helped to focus attention on literary activity there by founding the Virginia Writers Club in 1918. Cabell was president of the club until 1921 when he was succeeded by Margaret Prescott Montague, then internationally known for her short story "England to America," winner of the 1920 O. Henry Award.

Several members of the Writers Club combined journalism with publishing. Sally Nelson Robins, long a writer for the *Times-Dispatch*, published *Romances of Illustrious Virginians* in 1920 and *Love Stories of Famous Virginians* in 1923. Another member capable of a prodigious amount of work was Emma Speed Sampson. Emma Keats Speed, descended from John Keats's brother George, grew up in Kentucky and studied art in Paris and New York before marrying Henry Aylett Sampson of Virginia (whose *Sonnets and Other Poems* was published after his death in 1920). Emma Speed Sampson's sister Nell Speed was a successful New York newspaperwoman and author of pulps for teenage girls. On her deathbed, she prevailed on her sister Emma, then forty-five, to continue the *Molly Brown* series (three more), *The Tucker Twins* (six), and *The Carter Girls* (four). The publishers of the popular *Miss Minerva and William Green Hill* by the deceased Frances Boyd Calhoun suggested that Sampson write a sequel. *Billy and the Major* (1918) was the result, and the book went into seven editions selling 100,000 copies. A new sequel appeared about every two years until 1939.

Margaret Prescott Montague, the club's first vice-president and Cabell's successor as president, was also a versatile writer—novels, short stories, poems, and essays flowing from her pen. Her first novel, *The Poet, Miss Kate and I*, was published in 1905. Between 1910 and 1935, the *Atlantic Monthly* alone published thirty-eight of her articles. Another member of the Writers Club was Kate Langley Bosher, a pioneer suffragist, child welfare activist, and popular writer. Her first novelette, *Bobbie*, set in Civil War Virginia, appeared in 1899. Her best seller, *Mary Cary* (1910), was made into a film entitled *Nobody's Kid* in 1921.

Several members of the Writers Club played assisting roles in the birth of the *Reviewer*, the publication that gave a focus to the cultural ferment at work in Richmond and which attracted the attention of literary circles outside Richmond. By 1920 the *Evening Journal*, under the guidance of the widely traveled editor and publisher Samuel Travers Clover, had attracted to its Saturday book page and its Sunday magazine section several prolific reviewers and feature writers, among them Very Palmer, Emily Clark, and Hunter Stagg. Clark developed "Browsings in an Old Book Shop," and Stagg had begun producing extended critiques such as "The Art of James Branch Cabell" based on Hugh Walpole's article in the *Yale Review*. Unexpectedly, the *Evening Journal* announced its demise on September 25, 1920, its assets passing to the Richmond *Times-Dispatch*. The last issue of the *Evening Journal* appeared on a Saturday, its book page a reminder of passing glory for its contributors. "Hunter Stagg and I had assisted at its death-bed," Emily Clark would write in *Innocence Abroad* (1931), her account of the birth and death of the *Reviewer*. A few days later, at a Sunday afternoon gathering at the West Avenue home of Helena Lefroy Caperton, compiler of *The Richmond Social Register* and other minor fictions, the idea of continuing their literary careers in a publication of their own occurred to Emily Clark and Hunter Stagg. Margaret Freeman, a close friend, agreed to find a printer and credit; two weeks later another school acquaintance, Mary Dallas Street, joined the enterprise and contributed two hundred dollars for printing and postage.

Of the book reviewers metamorphosed into editors, Hunter Stagg was the most far-reaching in his literary associations. Emily Clark enjoyed literary contacts for their social aspects, and they led to her marriage to the elderly but wealthy Edwin Swift Balch of Philadelphia. They also gave birth to two books: *Stuffed Peacocks* (1927), her satires of thinly veiled contemporary personalities, and *Innocence Abroad* (1931), a history of the *Reviewer* and her literary conquests. Margaret Freeman enjoyed meeting literary people to debate with, but her drive was toward the business of telling "new" people how to appear otherwise. These interests led to her marriage late in life to James Branch Cabell. Mary Dallas Street produced her poems and two novels, *At Summer's End* (1936) and *Christopher Holt* (1946), but she sought the special friendship rather than wide associations. Hunter Stagg, however, was a dedicated lionizer, the one who sought out writers for the thrill of associating with creative genius. Carl Van Vechten, leader of avant-garde cultural circles in New York, responded to Hunter's appeal and opened literary doors for him. Their correspondence constitutes a history of the 1920s.

The history of the *Reviewer* is something of an anomaly, a combination of its Richmond origins, its Northern influences, and its Southern impact. Cabell introduced its editors to Joseph Hergesheimer who brought in established writers and recruited the crusading talents of Henry Mencken, whose "The Sahara of the Bozart" had been reviewed in the first issue. Mencken would determine the *Reviewer*'s direction, an attack on the old Southern school of writers and the discovery of new voices in the South. Hergesheimer, a frequent visitor in Richmond, also led Emily Clark to Carl Van Vechten who would insist on sophistication and an international seasoning. The first volume of the *Reviewer*, twelve issues as a fortnightly, was primarily a local product, its editors calling on friends for material. Volume II, a monthly, with Cabell setting its tone as guest editor for its first three issues, marked a move into its major phase, a rich mixture of established writers (its four godfathers along with Glasgow, Johnston, Robert Nathan, John Galsworthy), new Southern voices (Frances Newman, Julia Peterkin, Allen Tate, Gerald Johnson, Josephine Pinckney, DuBose Heyward, Paul Green), wealthy dilettantes (Beverley Randolph Tucker, Amanda Bryan, David Bruce, who later became ambassador to London, Paris, and Berlin). Beset with financial woes throughout its four years of existence in Richmond, the *Reviewer* became a pawn between its improvident and iconoclastic editors and the Richmond establishment. When Emily Clark and Hunter Stagg relinquished their editorial management in October, 1924, they were free to present the periodical, untinged with any shadow of Confederate gray, to Paul Green in Chapel Hill. The *Reviewer* died there a year later, but J. B. Hubbell, editor of the *Southwest Review*, agreed to fulfill Green's commitment to his subscribers by sending them copies of his journal.

Without the *Reviewer*, the literary scene was less exciting in Richmond, but the springs did not run dry. The Richmond Woman's Club, formed in 1894, continued to pay handsome fees for guest speakers, including leading writers and critics. The Book and Author Dinners continued under the sponsorship of the Junior League. Ellen Glasgow continued to receive a steady stream of literary guests, including Gertrude Stein (1934). Hunter Stagg was appointed successively as the editor of the book page for the *Times-Dispatch* and the *News Leader*. When Douglas Southall Freeman announced the latter appointment, he editorialized (February 8, 1927), "As far as the News Leader knows, he is the only literary editor of a Southern newspaper, charged with no other duties and responsible for an entire page." Hunter Stagg was peculiarly gifted to lead his Richmond readers to accept new writers; he had met those people; to be liberal in one's acceptance of diversity was Jeffersonian. His review of Jean Toomer's *Cane* (*Times-Dispatch*, October 21, 1923) was wholly admiring. He had even met Negro writers, entertained them in his home (Langston Hughes, 1926, Walter White, 1928). The editors of the *Reviewer* had always called their business meetings parties, and "poor Hunter" may have attended too many parties; he died an alcoholic.

When prizes were given to Richmond writers, they were nicely divided between "Confederates" and "new voices." Douglas Southall Freeman received a Pulitzer in 1935 for his four-volume *R. E. Lee*. Ellen Glasgow received her Pulitzer in 1942. Virginius Dabney, a Jeffersonian, received his for editorial writing (*Times-Dispatch*) in 1948. David Mays, biographer of Edmund Pendleton, was awarded one in 1953, and again Dr. Freeman was a recipient, posthumously in 1958, for his biography of Washington (shared by Mary Wells Ashworth, his assistant and coauthor of Volume VII). Clifford Dowdey's *Bugles Blow No More* (1937) won for him a Guggenheim Fellowship, and he received the Fletcher Pratt Award in 1965 for *The Seven Days: the Emergence of Lee*. John Latouche was granted a Guggenheim in 1949, and in 1954 *The Golden Apple* received the New York Critics Circle Award as the best musical.

The careers of Ellen Glasgow and James Branch Cabell reaffirm the observation that art is preeminently provincial, that it springs from a certain age and a specific locality. Richmond's post–Civil War class structure allowed Glasgow to write "English" novels, and when World War I accelerated the evolutionary into revolutionary changes, the results were her novels of manners, wherein her gift for irony came to fruition. Cabell's pre–World War I work was flawed by its reflection of Richmond's ambivalent attitude toward itself, a mixture of public sentiment and private derision. World War I liberated Cabell, allowing him to be openly satirical in his philosophical comedies of disenchantment, and it provided a mundane society ready for sophisticated innuendo. The duality of Richmond's penchant for Queen Anne facades and Mary Ann behinds had become the national allegory of the American dream versus the Gopher Prairie reality. Ellen Glasgow saw clearly in *In This Our Life* that World War II would mark a final dissolution of values an older Richmond had cherished. As it would other cities throughout the

South, the war would homogenize it, making it nearly indistinguishable from other American cities, culturally as well as architecturally. But if Richmond is in truth a state of mind, a social attitude, a mythic symbol, a moment in Glasgow's novels, it remains recognizable, a geographical nexus, still Janus-like. All moves forward, Jurgen observed in his encounter with Pan, to the sound of laughter.

JOSEPH M. FLORA

Fiction in the 1920s: Some New Voices

In the aftermath of World War I when iconoclasm was fashionable among American intellectuals, the South joined and sometimes led in questioning old messages and old ways. An impressive number of writers from the South gained national prominence for fiction reflecting this cultural shift. Although most of them are not often read now, they were immensely important in their own time and prepared the way for the great writers of the Renascence. Familiarity with the work of writers like Frances Newman (1883–1928), Julia Peterkin (1880–1961), DuBose Heyward (1885–1940), T. S. Stribling (1881–1965), Evelyn Scott (1893–1963), and Elizabeth Madox Roberts (1881–1941) increases understanding and appreciation of the Renascence.

H. L. Mencken (1880–1956)—Baltimore newspaperman, critic, and essayist—personified the national spirit of iconoclasm. He excoriated the entire American culture for being second rate, and in the 1920s younger intellectuals considered him a hero. As literary editor of the *Smart Set* (1908–1924) and as editor of the *American Mercury* (1924–1933), Mencken encouraged a host of new writers while mocking genteel traditions virtually out of existence. His prejudices—published in six volumes from 1919 through 1926—delighted, shocked, and sometimes repulsed readers, but they decidedly helped direct the national literature. Reviewing Mencken's work in 1930 and seeing it as likely to lose its influence in the years after 1930, James Branch Cabell honored him as "King Mencken" of the decade just passed.

Although Mencken took the literary and cultural life of the entire nation as his subject, his special interest was the literature and culture of the South—or the literature and culture that in 1920 he lamented was not there. No prejudice of his six volumes of *Prejudices* produced more definable results than his essay "The Sahara of the Bozart." At the start of the 1920s, Mencken threw down the gauntlet, declaring that the "south has not only lost its old capacity for producing ideas; it has also taken on the worst intolerance of ignorance and stupidity." Mencken cited Cabell as the exception to the rule, and he was one of Cabell's most able defenders—before, but especially after, the suppression of *Jurgen*. The attack of the Philistines on Cabell's romance (the book had grown out of the story "Some Ladies and Jurgen" published in the *Smart Set*) was grist for Mencken's mill. He celebrated Cabell for being a writer of style and poise, a writer who transcended the local and deserved respect and admiration from cultured readers everywhere. Cabell was, Mencken declared, the remnant of the greatness of vision and achievement that had marked an earlier Virginia. If Virginia had something going in its favor, Georgia, the least cultured of the Southern states, had virtually nothing.

If many Southerners rankled under Mencken's attack, others—particularly younger Southerners like W. J. Cash, Gerald W. Johnson, and Paul Green—welcomed Mencken's criticism and seized it as an opportunity for an extended symposium. Mencken could not be ignored. Southern intellectuals might sometimes disagree with Mencken, but most of them appreciated his advice. When in 1926 Emily Clark and friends founded the *Reviewer* in Richmond, she sought Mencken's guidance and contributions. Mencken was similarly a confidant to the editors of the *Double Dealer*, the little magazine born in New Orleans in 1920. Scarcely had Mencken unleashed his attack on the South before he could assert that "the South begins to mutter." Many of the new generation of Southern writers kept contact with Mencken; increasingly he felt himself one of them. He wielded a large influence, directly and indirectly, on Southern culture, especially in fiction.

When Cabell surveyed the achievement of the 1920s in American literature, he foresaw that the literature of the 1930s would be very different and singled out ten writers for epitaphs—writers who had played a major part in the 1920s, but who would not in the 1930s. In addition to himself and Ellen Glasgow, he chose one other Southerner, Frances Newman. Since Newman had died unexpectedly at age forty-four, the promise of her abilities had not been realized. But Cabell had found a great deal to praise in the work she completed; earlier Mencken had named her one of the violets of the Southern Sahara.

Newman's career, however brief, was impressive. A librarian, first at Carnegie Library in her native Atlanta and then at the Georgia Institute of Technology, she earned a reputation as caustic judge of contemporary literature because of various reviews and pieces she wrote for the *Carnegie Library Notes*, the Atlanta *Constitution*, Emily Clark's little magazine the *Reviewer*, and various New York papers. These caught the attention of both Cabell and Mencken. Responding to her request that he autograph her *Jurgen*, Cabell wrote Newman on November 16, 1920:

"Are you not 'doing' a book of some sort? If not, you ought to be ashamed of yourself. . . . You will see, I know, Mencken's Second Prejudices, and surely his Sahara of the Bozarts [sic] should incite you to rehabilitate the fame of Georgia." Mencken himself began encouraging Newman to set her hand to the task.

Newman's first book, *The Short Story's Mutations: From Petronius to Paul Morand*, appeared in 1924; in her commentary to her anthology, she sided with the modern preoccupation with form. In 1924 she also became a published writer of fiction. Her short story "Rachel and Her Children" appeared in Mencken's *American Mercury* and won an O. Henry Memorial Award.

Newman's claims as a writer rest, however, on two novels. The first of these, *The Hard-Boiled Virgin*, was published in 1926; Cabell pronounced it a "minor masterpiece, flawless in all save in its most abominable title." The novel was unmistakably avant-garde. Like Cabell's, Newman's manner would not appeal to every reader; as the title suggests, the subject matter was, also like Cabell's, not what genteel readers were looking for. Just as Cabell benefited from the suppression of *Jurgen*, Newman's sales were bolstered when the novel was banned in Boston. Although Katherine Faraday, Newman's heroine, is indeed much concerned with the issue of her virginity, the novel is scarcely salacious. It requires a patient reader. Preferring "a cynical and suave prose," Newman likened her style to that of George Meredith. Her syntax is often involved and weighted with allusions. There is no dialogue in this novel of many minute chapters. Newman always calls her heroine by her full name, emphasizing in part her focus on a new kind of Southern woman. Newman was avowedly showing a woman thinking the thoughts a woman was not supposed to think. In every way, Newman questioned the approach to the Southern woman by earlier writers.

Her second and last novel, *Dead Lovers Are Faithful Lovers* (1928), also challenged earlier presentations of Southern women. In her portraits of two women (one bent on holding her handsome husband by means of physical beauty and sexuality, the other finding favor with the same husband because of her intelligence), Newman again used sophisticated literary methods. Virginia Woolf, as much as anyone, was the major influence on her, especially Woolf's emphasis on small moments and her attention to form. Newman also liked Woolf's ability to reach beneath surfaces. Withal, her instincts were to agree with Mencken about the fiction of the past. She was a rebel who supported Mencken's cause through pronouncement and by example; her career illustrates the support the gifted writer often received from Mencken.

Just as Mencken prized Cabell and encouraged Newman, he found other Southern writers whose work he could praise and encourage, writers whose appeal was very different from the modern sophistication of Cabell and Newman. An important writer in this group was Julia Peterkin, who wrote of the life of the Gullah blacks from the plantations of coastal South Carolina, a life that Peterkin knew as mistress of a plantation after her marriage to William Peterkin in 1903. Henry Bellaman, her piano teacher, encouraged her to write about the life she vividly reported, and in the early 1920s her sketches and stories appeared first in Mencken's *Smart Set* and then frequently in the *Reviewer*. Although Glasgow, Cabell, and Newman were by no means blind to the condition of blacks in the South, the theme was minor in their writing. Peterkin, like other white writers of the decade, made clear that the new fiction of the South would differ greatly from that of the popular fiction preceding it in its presentation of the black experience.

Peterkin's scope was purposefully small, select. She focused on the lives of the blacks who lived near and on her own plantation, insisting on the authenticity of character and incident. She seldom allowed a white into her pages. Black-white relations were not her subject, in part because the characters she observed accepted their place in the scheme of things; most of her characters seldom saw whites and thought of the white world as largely unrelated to their own. Peterkin wanted to preserve a record of the folk beliefs of the people she had come to know. She did so with understanding and sympathy, as many readers—black and white—judged.

Her first book, *Green Thursday* (1924), collected those *Reviewer* sketches, emphasizing in its cumulative force the price the blacks paid for some of their folk beliefs. The title emphasizes one such belief: he who plows on Green Thursday, Ascension Thursday, will not fare well. Against the protest of his wife, Killdee plows and his misfortunes mount. Throughout the book Killdee and his wife debate their beliefs in a world where the struggle for survival demands most of their energy. Typically, Peterkin does not show religious faith as working toward the happiness of her characters. What is most important about *Green Thursday* is its pioneering role in asserting the validity of portraying the lives and beliefs of the Gullahs. Peterkin proved that there was a market for a more penetrating view of the black experience than had been obtained in the earlier fiction of the South.

Peterkin followed *Green Thursday* with three novels, and her greatest fame rests on the first two of them. *Black April* (1927) celebrates the elemental force of April, the foreman of Blue Brook plantation. April spreads his image throughout the land, though the proud man is finally brought down. In *Scarlet Sister Mary* (1928), Peterkin's heroine has a vibrant sexuality and strength; like Defoe's Moll Flanders, she continually triumphs. The novel won the Pulitzer Prize. In a third novel, *Bright Skin* (1932), Peterkin complicates the dynamics of her world, for her heroine is a mulatto in a black society. The response to this novel, however, was discouraging. Peterkin continued to write sketches and essays on her Gullahs, but she ceased writing novels.

Although Peterkin's fame was considerable in the 1920s, few were reading her when she died in 1961. Her presentation of the black, important as it was for its time, has not met the needs of later generations; her interest in the primitive aspects of Gullah life has seemed too exclusive. But Peterkin unquestionably pioneered in portraying the black as human being; she broadened the scope of modern fiction. It was needful that the white South try to get inside the black psyche.

Peterkin was not the only Southern white to make that attempt in the 1920s. DuBose Heyward, also a South Carolinian, was to achieve his greatest fame for his portrayal of blacks. His novel *Porgy* (1925) achieved a reputation more lasting than that of any book by Peterkin. It was the source of the successful play *Porgy* (1927), written with his wife Dorothy Heyward, and also of George and Ira Gershwin's opera *Porgy and Bess* (1935), one of the great works in American music. There were also practical results from Heyward's study of the black experience. He became identified with the Harlem Renaissance, and his work provided greater opportunities for serious black artists in New York.

Mencken assisted Heyward's meteoric career, but not in the same way that he had assisted Newman and Peterkin. Heyward was defensive about Mencken's indictment in the "Sahara." In direct response to it, he and a group of poets in Charleston had formed the Poetry Society of South Carolina. Heyward became a writer in several genres and was important to their history, but he achieved his greatest artistic success with the novel. Literary General Sherman (as Heyward accused) or not, Mencken praised Heyward's fiction portraying the black, finding it important just as he found Peterkin's work important.

Although Heyward also aimed at authentic portrayal of blacks, his characters convey a larger sense of both the exotic and heroic than do Peterkin's. Ultimately, Heyward was more concerned with social change than Peterkin was, though his novels are not novels of social protest. Usually he was concerned with revealing his characters in the realities of their own intense living.

Porgy, Heyward's first novel and his best, is a folk novel in that it presents the homogeneous culture of Catfish Row, revealing a group of people whose lives are mainly untouched by the realities of the world beyond the Charleston wharf. Their lives are essentially duplications of those of their parents and grandparents; they do not expect their children's lives to be different. They are not defeatists; rather their subculture is vibrant and intense. Sometimes the white world intervenes, but the blacks always close ranks, viewing the white world as remote, largely unrelated to theirs. Heyward knew this subculture was passing and wished to capture it in a novel.

The folk novel always deals with basic emotions, and *Porgy* is about the rhythms of love and death, but more about love. The novel is one of the moving love stories of the period, as play and opera would stress by giving stronger emphasis to the affirmation of Catfish Row than the ending of the novel provides. In the novel the crippled beggar Porgy returns from a brief stay in prison to find that Bess has run off. In play and opera, Porgy returns to find Bess gone, but he is soon on his way to find her.

Heyward's other important novel about black life, *Mamba's Daughters* (1929), is more ambitious in structure and theme. Its action proceeding from Charleston to New York City, it presents the white world as well as the black world and shows them coming into greater understanding. Although the black story line and the white story line are not mutually successful (the memorable characters of the novel are black), *Mamba's Daughters* was also recognized as an important novel; with his wife, Heyward later wrote a play based on it.

Heyward wrote three other novels, the most successful of which was probably *Peter Ashley* (1932), a portrayal of Charleston aristocracy just before the Civil War. He turned to the black experience again for his last novel, *Star Spangled Virgin* (1939), a study of the effects of the New Deal on the blacks of St. Croix. The novel, published the year before Heyward's death, received only lukewarm praise from critics.

Another pioneer among white writers of the decade who looked at the black experience in their fiction is T. S. Stribling, whose second novel, *Birthright* (1922), made clear that the "ole massa" school had passed. In his novel Stribling recounts the efforts of Peter Steiner, a black educated at Harvard, to improve the condition of the blacks in his small Tennessee town. But not even Steiner's mother grasps what he is about, and when the novel ends Steiner is moving to the North, his project abandoned. Stribling's blacks are less compelling as characters than are Peterkin's or Heyward's, his purpose seemingly more didactic than theirs, but his novel received wide critical attention, being viewed as a triumph for Mencken's camp, and gave Stribling a solid base from which to pursue his career as novelist.

Stribling, a native of Clifton, Tennessee, had prepared to teach school and to practice law, but writing attracted him more. He started his writing career doing assignments for Sunday school magazines and then turned to the writing of adventure stories. He became a prolific writer, and much of what he wrote, like his first novel, *The Cruise of the Dry Dock* (1917), was merely entertainment. But he was also a serious writer who deserves to be remembered for his social novels, like *Birthright*, that examine various aspects of Southern life. He achieved his best results when he studied the poor white. Mencken was immensely pleased by *Teeftallow* (1926), a novel satirizing the narrowness of middle Tennessee small-town culture for its bigotry, materialism, and violence. The novel became, along with Ellen Glasgow's *The Romantic Comedians* and Elizabeth Madox Roberts' *The Time of Man*, a main selection of the Book-of-the-Month Club; thus three of the nine novels so designated in 1926 were by Southerners. Stribling followed *Teeftallow* with a sequel, *Bright Metal* (1928), exploring further the same culture, even some of the same characters of the earlier novel. His 1930 *Backwater* satirizes life in the Arkansas lowlands.

Stribling's most ambitious work belongs to the 1930s, for he had a panoramic vision of the South that anticipates the Faulkner of *Absalom, Absalom!* and the Snopes trilogy. In *The Forge* (1931), *The Store* (1932), and *The Unfinished Cathedral* (1934), Stribling chronicles the fortunes of the Vaiden family from the years before the Civil War to the 1930s. He won the Pulitzer Prize for *The Store*, the tale of the rise of Miltiades Vaiden from poor white to rich landowner through methods that would find their personification in Faulkner's Flem Snopes. The third volume of the trilogy studies the Protestant clergy in this milieu and recalls characters of Lewis' *Babbitt* and *Elmer Gantry*. Critical realism was the mode in favor with most critics in the 1930s though Donald Davidson and others of the best Southern critics criticized Stribling's results. Stribling enjoyed great acclaim for his trilogy, but he is now scarcely read except by a small group of readers in the South. Faulkner's mythical histories, slow to win the day, have by now all but obliterated Stribling's work.

Stribling followed his popular trilogy with two other novels, both set in the North, one debunking lawyers and businessmen, the other the American college education. The last of these, *These Bars of Flesh*, was published in 1938 when Stribling was fifty-seven years old. Although he did not die until 1965, he wrote mainly detective fiction after 1938, and his reputation declined rapidly.

Another Tennessee writer to whom Mencken gave encouragement was Evelyn Scott, a writer who in many ways seemed made to Mencken's order. By the age of thirteen, Scott had virtually thundered "no" to the expectations of her culture and class: Dixie has seldom had a more rebellious daughter. As such, she naturally prized the work of Mencken. When *Ideals*, a collection of her short stories was published in 1927, she sent him an inscribed copy: "To H. L. Mencken. Though no critic's approval has given me more courage than his, this book is sent with no implied stipulations. If he doesn't like it, I expect him to ignore it or 'roast' it. And I will continue to wish there were more in America with his implacable directness."

Scott, born Elsie Dunn, spent her girlhood in her native Tennessee and later attended Sophie Newcomb College and Newcomb School of Art in New Orleans. At age twenty she left New Orleans to live in Brazil with Tulane's already married dean of the School of Tropical and Preventative Medicine. Both changed their names to mark the bold step. Scott never again lived in the South, though it was the locale for a good part of her fiction. She did not perceive the land in any mystical sense and so was not interested in describing it in her fiction. Rather she sought to portray the destructive effects of its mentality on its people, particularly its women. She told parts of her story in two autobiographical volumes. *Escapade* (1923) is essentially a journal of her six years in Brazil. She states, "I want to poison the whole world with my own suffering." She described her childhood and youth and made her brief against the South in *Background in Tennessee* (1937). Her rebellion was also useful to her in her fiction, especially in *Eva Gay* (1933). The need for individual freedom and development was her abiding subject.

Although Scott was a prolific writer throughout the 1920s and 1930s, perhaps her best work belongs to the 1920s; certainly she achieved her greatest fame during that period. Her first published book was a collection of poems, *Precipitations* (1920), but she made her first real mark as a novelist. Sinclair Lewis greeted her first novel, *The Narrow House* (1921), as a major literary achievement: "Salute to Evelyn Scott! It would be an insult to speak with smug judiciousness of her 'promise.' She has done it!" *The Narrow House* is the first volume of a trilogy that portrayed a Southern family, the Farleys, through three generations, but indicated that the binding ties were destructive. As the title reveals, death rather than life triumphs. In 1929 the Farleys could be compared with Faulkner's Compsons. There are important similarities and differences. Scott appears more intent on finding solutions than does Faulkner; his virtue of endurance is hardly a virtue in her work. Scott admires rather those who might break away.

Scott recognized Faulkner's genius as soon as she read *The Sound and the Fury* and wrote a memorable appreciation; however, readers coming to Scott would more likely be reminded of D. H. Lawrence than of Faulkner. Her characters are bothered by their sexuality, in part because of social mores. But the problem is deeper, and in the Farley trilogy the division between mind and body is everywhere apparent. *Narcissus*, the title of the second volume of the trilogy, underscores the difficulty the characters have in finding a meaningful transcendence of self in marriage. There is an intimation of the Laurentian rainbow in *The Golden Door*, the final volume of the trilogy. The first two volumes focus on the two unsatisfactory marriages of Laurence Farley; in the *Golden Door* his daughter comes much farther toward finding marriage a workable solution for men and women who have begun to face themselves. In the later *Eva Gay*, there is an abundance of talk about marriage. The reader will sometimes feel impatient at the characters' preachments about the problems facing men and women.

Scott followed her trilogy of contemporary life with a historical trilogy, proving herself more Southern than her first work suggested. Like many other Southern writers, she also took a long backward look—and she was as much interested in her family's history as in her nation's. In *Migrations* (1927) Scott studies westward expansion in nineteenth-century America. Because her characters as they move and strive for new frontiers take their old notions with them, they do not find freedom, but new bondage. War is sometimes a means for people to attempt to escape from their bondage, but it often results in overpowering realization of individual failure and insignificance. Thus it happens in *The Wave* (1929), Scott's panorama of the Civil War. The characters from *Migrations* take their place with scores of other characters, some from history, from both North and South, and from every condition. Using various techniques, including some stream of consciousness (she was also an admirer of Joyce), Scott tells interesting stories of people caught up in a huge, destructive movement. The families portrayed in *Migrations* come to the fore again in the two-volume *A Calendar of Sin* (1931), structured as a calendar of events from 1867 to 1914. Subtitled *American Melodramas*, the novel exposes false ideas about marriage and sexuality—false notions of sin—that would make understandable the deceptions that were the subject of her first trilogy.

In the 1930s Scott turned more to the problems of the writer in an unsatisfactory world. The autobiographical Eva Gay seeks to find part of her meaning through writing. In *Breathe Upon These Slain* (1934), a writer on vacation in England invents stories about the lives of the people whose pictures are on the wall. Rejecting the demand of Marxist critics that art serves political ideology, she maintains that the writer must continue to value the individual. In *Bread and a Sword* (1937) her protagonist is a writer who compromises by writing to exemplify Marxist doctrine. In *The Shadow of the Hawk* (1941) her protagonist is an inventor who refuses to compromise his ideals.

Although Scott lived some twenty years more after writing *The Shadow of the Hawk*, the two novels she wrote in those years remain unpublished. When she died in 1963, she was virtually forgotten. In her time she had been highly praised by leading spokesmen like Mencken and Sinclair Lewis, but her brand of realism was not what influential critics of the 1930s were seeking. Despite the many difficulties that plagued her as a writer in the last two decades of her life, especially in connection with the writing of the unpublished "Before Cock Crow" (an almost completed draft was stolen), Scott remained dedicated to her vision to be an artist and continued to seek meaning through her art.

Mencken did not have a hand in all of the literary careers beginning in the 1920s. Generally he paid less attention to the trans-Appalachian writers of the South. One he missed was Elizabeth Madox Roberts, whose work is now more widely read than that of either Stribling or Scott. But Mencken surely heard of Roberts' work, for two of her novels, *The Time of Man* (1926) and *The Great Meadow* (1930), were popular and critical successes.

Born in Kentucky, Roberts was a lifelong student of its past and spent most of her life there. Her first published book was a book of poetry, *In The Great Steep's Garden* (1915). Although she is known primarily as a poet for children, poetic sensibility also marks her fiction. Louis Untermeyer observed of *The Time of Man* that "every chapter has the effect of a poem." Roberts' technical accomplishment transcends that of Stribling and of most of her contemporaries. Although her fame declined rapidly after her death in 1935, reprints in the 1960s of her two most famous novels with introductions by Robert Penn Warren and Willard Thorp stress her larger claims. Roberts' modest but steady reputation as a poet has also reminded readers of her achievement in fiction.

When placed next to work like that of Cabell and Glasgow, the work of Elizabeth Madox Roberts makes clear the expansiveness of the South. She relates a vastly different kind of experience from that portrayed by writers of the coastal plain and piedmont. Her work is significantly Western as well as Southern. Indeed, the contemporary writers with whom she associated and learned were Western and Midwestern. One of her great subjects was the Kentucky pioneer; he was not far removed from Roberts' time or experience.

Roberts viewed the pioneer in mythic patterns. There is a strong core of realism to her work, but her lyrical prose and use of literary allusion make her work anything but parochial. *The Time of Man* is modeled on the *Odyssey*. Like her protagonists in later works, her Odysseus is a woman, and that angle of vision colors all. Despite emphasis on the physical struggle for subsistence, Roberts is primarily interested in the introspective. Ellen Chesser, the Odysseus of *The Time of Man*, is the wife of a tenant farmer who unjustly becomes known as a "barn burner." But Ellen does not surrender to the adversities that result from that charge, nor to other adversities from nature and human nature; and the reader admires her inner strength as she continues to endure, paradoxically even to triumph "in the time of man."

My *Heart and My Flesh* (1927) is the story of aristocratic Theodosia Bell, who, Roberts said, "went to hell and returned to walk among you." Like Job rather than Odysseus, Theodosia loses all that she values and aspires toward, especially her desire to be a violinist, but finally rejects suicide, and moves toward affirmation. Because Theodosia discovers that she has mulatto half-sisters, her story is an important forerunner of *Absalom, Absalom!* Roberts' third novel, *Jingling in the Wind* (1928), is in yet another mode—light farce. Her satire on industrial civilization is not now well known, but it suggests something of her persistent concern with new modes.

The Great Meadow, Roberts' fourth novel, has a spirit similar to that of *The Time of Man*. Although Diony Hall, the heroine of *The Great Meadow*, has a broader frame of reference and a greater sense of herself than Ellen Chesser has, both novels celebrate pioneer endurance. Set in the time of the western migration from tidewater Virginia to Kentucky at the time of the American Revolutionary War, *The Great Meadow* must count as one of the major novels exploring the American past. Coming at the beginning of the decade of the Great Depression, the novel benefited from the nation's need to review its past and to fortify itself.

Roberts' reputation declined after *The Great Meadow*, but several critics have found much to admire in *He Sent Forth a Raven*, perhaps her most ambitious novel. Published in 1935, Roberts' story of a Southern misanthrope had been written by 1927; tonally it is similar to *My Heart and My Flesh*, but its method—evoking the allegory of *Moby-Dick* and the story of Noah—is more complex. Her last novel, *Black Is My Truelove's Hair*, was published in 1938. It was followed by *Songs in the Meadow* (1940), a collection of poetry mostly about Kentucky, and by a gathering of her stories, *Not By Strange Gods*, in 1941 (the year of her death). By then Roberts was narrowly identified as a regionalist and since then as a poet. Willard Thorp wrote in 1960 that *The Time of Man* and *The Great Meadow* "are among the classics of our literature," but interest in her work has been modest.

The reputations of Newman, Peterkin, Heyward, Stribling, Scott, and Roberts have paled considerably since the time when "King Mencken" reigned. Nevertheless their works had a profound influence and prepared the way for the great writers of the Renascence who began to emerge around 1929, the year of the publication of *Look Homeward, Angel* and *The Sound and the Fury*. Southern writers of fiction broke new ground in the 1920s and helped the South view its heritage with greater vision and to look for new modes of literary expression.

THADIOUS M. DAVIS

Southern Standard-Bearers in the New Negro Renaissance

New York City's Harlem of the 1920s seems a long way from the South. The psychological distance between the two localities is explicit in a saying popular during the decade when Harlem was an emergent "Culture Capital" for blacks: "I'd rather be a lamp post in Harlem, than the mayor of Atlanta." Harlem, not Georgia or any other location in the South, was *the* place to be for blacks in general and for black writers in particular. In the years after World War I, Harlem became a Mecca for black authors, because it offered what the South at the time could not: an intellectual and artistic community replete with opportunities for publishing and acquiring an audience. Yet, it was precisely because of the South that Harlem could become the center of black America and of a major literary and cultural movement, the New Negro Renaissance.

The influx to Harlem began during the war years, when critical labor shortages in the Northern industrial areas brought blacks out of the economically depressed South. Prompted both by the federal government and labor agents for industries, blacks migrated from the rural South in record numbers. During this "Great Migration," Alain Locke observed, "a railroad ticket and a suitcase, like a Baghdad carpet, transport the Negro peasant from the cotton-field and farm to the heart of the most complex urban civilization." Although blacks left the agrarian South in search of economic and social opportunities, they did not leave behind their Southern heritage, practices, and beliefs, but instead transposed them to Harlem. By 1925, one result, according to Locke, was that the black "poet, student, artist, thinker, by the very move that normally would take him off . . . from the masses, finds himself in their midst, in a situation concentrating the racial side of his experience and heightening his racial consciousness." Not only did Southern blacks contribute a critical mass to Harlem, but they also made a viable folk culture evident to those blacks of "the Talented Tenth," who could give voice to that culture in art. Harlem provided a place for black life to seize, Locke concluded, "its first chances for group expression and self-determination" because the "moving, self-awkward new comers provide an exceptional seed-bed for the germinating contacts of the enlightened minority" (Alain Locke, "Our Little Renaissance," in Charles S. Johnson [ed.], *Ebony and Topaz* [New York, 1927]).

By November, 1919, W. E. B. Du Bois, editor of the NAACP's *Crisis* magazine, had named Jessie Redmon Fauset as literary editor. The *Crisis* began to provide a forum with a national audience for black writers, and Fauset, a consistent supporter of young writers, announced in its pages, "The portrayal of black people calls increasingly for black writers." The literary works in the *Crisis* confirmed a New Negro movement; for example, in June, 1921, it published Langston Hughes's "The Negro Speaks of Rivers," a poem celebrating the proud heritage and fusion of black American and African identity.

> My soul has grown deep like the rivers.
> I bathed in the Euphrates when dawns were young.
> I built my hut near the Congo and it lulled me to sleep.
> . . . I heard the singing of the Mississippi when Abe Lincoln
>   went down to New Orleans, and I've seen its muddy
>   bosom turn all golden in the sunset.

Hughes's poem inspired other young writers, such as Arna Bontemps, Countee Cullen, Rudolph Fisher, Sterling Brown, Gwendolyn Bennett, and Jean Toomer, all of whom published in the *Crisis*.

In January, 1923, the National Urban League joined the NAACP's efforts to bring the works of promising New Negro authors into print by founding *Opportunity: A Journal of Negro Life* and naming sociologist Charles S. Johnson as editor. From the outset, Johnson, a Virginian, was committed to including poetry and fiction; two poems, Leslie Pinckney Hill's "Voyaging" and Countee Cullen's "The Dance of Love," appeared in April, 1923, and from that issue to the end of the decade, *Opportunity* published a number of the new black writers, including Georgia Douglas Johnson, John Matheus, Zora Neale Hurston, Langston Hughes, and Willis Richardson. Particularly between 1925 and 1927, the years of the *Opportunity* literary contests and awards dinners, Johnson did much to nurture the New Negro Renaissance.

Along with *Opportunity* and the *Crisis,* the *Messenger,* the official publication of the Brotherhood of Sleeping Car Porters headed by the Florida-born A. Philip Randolph, was crucial to the cultural activities of the 1920s, both in New York and throughout the nation. Politically radical at its founding in 1917 by Randolph and Chandler Owen, the *Messenger* was a socialist organ for union activities; however, between

1923 and 1928, the journal became more involved with literature. Its functional editors, George Schuyler and Theophilus Lewis, published Langston Hughes, Georgia Douglas Johnson, Countee Cullen, Zora Hurston, Arna Bontemps, Bruce Nugent, and others, particularly after 1926 when the *Messenger* paid for literary contributions. The *Messenger, Opportunity*, and the *Crisis* not only carried messages of the New Negro awakening to their own national readership, but they also inspired the founding of other black little magazines, such as *Black Opals* in Philadelphia, and the designating of special "New Negro" issues of white periodicals, such as the *Carolina Magazine* at Chapel Hill.

The same collective spirit that produced *Crisis, Opportunity*, and *Messenger* as vehicles for literary expression also marked the work of two Southerners in sustaining the movement. Georgia Douglas Johnson (1886–1966) and Walter White (1893–1955), both Atlanta natives educated at Atlanta University, were to emerge as minor authors, but they were essential to the period and its cultural impact because of their social consciousness and commitment to black artists.

Georgia Douglas Johnson's first book of poems, *The Heart of a Woman* (1918), appeared just on the eve of the awakening. She had spent much of her life in the South, growing up in Georgia and teaching in Alabama, but her career as a poet coincided with her years in Washington, D.C., where she worked for the government. Throughout the twenties, she published widely in the leading journals. Two of her books coincided with two phases of the renaissance; *Bronze* (1922) ushered in a period of concerted effort to change the image of blacks in American life, as her author's note points out. "This book is a child of a bitter earth-wound. I sit on the earth and sing—sing out, and of, my sorrow." *An Autumn Love Cycle* (1928) came when the concentrated period of renaissance writing was nearing an end; it was reviewed in *Opportunity*, April, 1929, the last year that the journal published a substantial amount of creative writing.

Johnson's poems are competent in technique and traditional in form, but they are mainly ordinary and slight, as Du Bois concluded in his foreword to *Bronze*. "Her work is simple, sometimes trite, but it is singularly sincere and true." The poems collected in *Bronze* are Johnson's most sustained explorations of a black historical consciousness. Some of the poems are distinctly connected with racial uplift, while others, such as "Prejudice" and "The Old Men," record the effects of oppression: "They have learned to live it down / As though they did not care." Johnson's favorite form is the brief lyric, which does not sustain anger or outrage, but which adequately conveys her sensibilities.

Despite Johnson's life in genteel poverty, her "Saturday Nights" were overt expressions of dedication to literary pursuits among the New Negroes, and perhaps her greatest contribution to the renaissance. During Saturday evenings of talk and readings, she opened her S Street home to artists such as Jean Toomer, Langston Hughes, Waring Cuney, May Miller, Sterling Brown, Angelina Grimké, Alice Dunbar-Nelson, and Bruce Nugent; in the process, she nurtured their art and sustained her own.

Significantly, Johnson, who was the first black woman since the nineteenth-century Frances Watkins Harper to gain recognition as a poet, participated in the Harlem Renaissance primarily from her Washington home. Her position as a practicing poet outside the New York circle is similar to that of several other Southerners among the New Negro writers, particularly Joshua Henry Jones, Jr. (1876–?), from Orangeburg, South Carolina, who contributed his poems and novel from Boston where he worked as a journalist and, for a time, in city government, and Leslie Pinckney Hill (1880–1960), a Lynchburg, Virginia, native who taught at Tuskegee Institute and at the Manassas Industrial School in Virginia, but contributed his poetry and fiction from Cheyney, Pennsylvania, where he was principal of a training school for teachers.

Jones's two collections of poetry, *The Heart of the World and Other Poems* (1919) and *Poems of the Four Seas* (1921), contain formal poems that do not reflect racial themes, which is perhaps why they were frequently anthologized in the twenties but rarely since. Although he does not use his Southern background or idiom in his poems, Jones relies upon both in his one novel, *By Sanction of Law* (1924). Leslie Pinckney Hill, on the other hand, appeared more frequently in anthologies of New Negro writers, even though he published only one book of poetry, *The Wings of Oppression* (1921), and a dramatic history of Toussaint L'Ouverture in 1928. His poems encompass several of the main concerns of the renaissance. Hill does not use the idiom of blacks, but he makes effective use of traditional forms for modern messages. More sensitive to topical issues than Joshua Jones, he is nonetheless linked to Jones and to Georgia Johnson as representative of the well-educated blacks from the South who believed in the power of art to alter negative images and racial stereotypes either by its instructive themes and messages or by the fact of its creation by black writers.

While Georgia Johnson was a major presence during the renaissance, another Southern woman, Anne Spencer, was a major poet even though she neither joined the migration to New York nor conducted a salon in her home. Born in Branwell, West Virginia, but a resident of Lynchburg, Virginia, for most of her adult life, Spencer (1882–1975) is typical of a group of Southerners, in particular Jonathan Brooks and George Leonard Allen, who contributed to the renaissance from their homes in the South. Anne Spencer's poems were published in all of the major anthologies of the time, including James Weldon Johnson's *The Book of American Negro Poetry*, Alain Locke's *The New Negro*, Countee Cullen's *Caroling Dusk*, and Charles S. Johnson's *Ebony and Topaz*, but she rarely left her home in Virginia.

Spencer was one of the most lyrical poets of the renaissance, as well as one of the most gifted. Her poems show a meticulous concern with the craft of writing and a noticeable command of verse forms. Her talent for creating a textually rich poetry especially reveals itself in her use of imagery and symbolism. Perhaps the most painstaking craftsperson among the New Negro poets, she produced a small body of works during the period and her lifetime, but it is marked by a finely wrought merging of form and idea. Spencer wrote in response to things that moved her personally, but her poems are not primarily topical and are rarely controversial. In her self-introduction in *Caroling Dusk*, she revealed: "I write about some of the things I love. But I have no civilized articulation for the things I hate. I proudly love being a Negro woman— its [*sic*] so involved and interesting. *We* are the PROBLEM—the great national game of taboo."

Whereas she could write about the roles or treatment of women, in her poetry she could seldom treat the conditions of blacks. During the 1920s, however, she wrote a few poems of racial protest, but they were not accepted for publication. One exception, "White Things" (*Crisis*, 1923), is a clearly articulated protest against the treatment of blacks.

> They pyred a race of black, black men,
> And burned them to ashes white; then
> Laughing, a young one claimed a skull,
> For the skull of a black is white, not dull,
> But a glistening awful thing.

"White Things" is direct and suggestive, but one of her lesser efforts.

The presence of Spencer's poetry among the major poems of the period reiterates that the flowering of New Negro literature was neither confined to New York nor to urban areas in the North. Other Southerners were, like Spencer, engaged in creative writing in remote sections of the South, and like her, they submitted their works to the leading journals. Jonathan Henderson Brooks (1904–1945) and George Leonard Allen (1905–1935) were two such poets.

Brooks was born on a farm twelve miles from Lexington, Mississippi, where he farmed on shares until he was fourteen. His first published poem, "Garnered the Yields," appeared in *Opportunity*, January, 1924. His works were primarily religious in theme and written in conventional forms and language. His best-known poem, "The Resurrection," won a third prize in the 1927 *Opportunity* poetry contests; it was published, along with "The Last Quarter Moon of the Dying Year" and "Paean," in *Caroling Dusk*. Although his formal education in the high school divisions of Jackson College and Lincoln University and in the college course at Tougaloo College was interrupted repeatedly by periods of farming and teaching, Brooks did not incorporate images of Mississippi rural life into his poetry. He continued writing competent, but unoriginal, verse while serving as pastor of a Baptist church in Kosciusko, Mississippi, and later as a postal worker in Corinth. His book, *The Resurrection and Other Poems*, was published posthumously.

Like Brooks, George Leonard Allen was also from a farming community in the South, but his father's position as a school principal in Lumberton, North Carolina, enabled Allen to complete his education without interruptions. He began writing while a student at Johnson C. Smith University in Charlotte, North Carolina, where he published works in both school and local periodicals. After his graduation in 1926, Allen taught at the Kendall Institute in Sumter, South Carolina, and published his poetry in journals with a national circulation, *Opportunity, Lyric West,* and *American Life*. Although Allen's poetry eschews racial issues and lacks complexity, it shows potential in its minimal effort to use the local imagery of his familiar Southern world in lyric expressions.

For the most part, however, Allen, Brooks, and Spencer, much like Johnson, Hill, and Jones, made little use of the raw materials of Southern life and language in their poetry, even though they were among the New Negro poets most familiar with the South. These Southerners notwithstanding, the writers who achieved stature in the renaissance or its wake were attracted to New York and moved there to participate in the cultural activities. One such Southerner was Walter White, who became a major figure, but not a major writer.

White, the blond, blue-eyed assistant to James Weldon Johnson at the NAACP, is similar to Georgia Douglas Johnson in the social function he served in bringing writers together and in helping them form contacts with publishers. White's arrival in New York in 1918 coincided with the first stirrings of the New Negro's political consciousness. His investigations of lynchings during the Red Summer of 1919 gave him a unique perspective about the treatment of blacks and attitudes toward them. Visibly white, he collected information about violence against blacks by moving undetected among whites. Because of his formative experience in defending his family's home against attacking whites in the Atlanta riot of 1906, Walter White was proud of his racial identity, as he pointed out about his revelatory experience in *A Man Called White* (1948). "I was gripped by the knowledge of my identity, and in the depths of my soul I was vaguely aware that I was glad of it. . . . I was glad my mind and spirit were part of the race that had not fully awakened, and who therefore had still before them the opportunity to write a record of virtue as a memorandum to Armageddon."

Much of White's racial consciousness converged in his first novel. Written during a twelve-day retreat, *The Fire in the Flint* (1924) relates the tragedy of Kenneth Harper, a Northern-trained physician who returns to his Georgia hometown to practice among his people. The novel has been called melodramatic and propagandistic, but it is also dramatically moving. Told without great technical skill, *The Fire in the Flint* captures the idealism of a black man loyal to the South. At the same time, it makes clear the reasons why an educated black person cannot live impervious to racism.

White's second novel, *Flight* (1926), also treats the dilemma of a middle-class black, Mimi Daquin, who is a New Orleans Creole of color. She passes for white for a time, but eventually returns to her race. Although episodic like *The Fire in the Flint, Flight* is a better structured work. The portraits of Atlanta's black bourgeoisie and of Harlem's social life are authentic.

In attempting to depict the lives of blacks who had proven themselves in the white world, Walter White was also attempting to write not merely about Southerners but primarily about the newly emerging black middle class. The missing key was a language and voice to depict black life, whether of the middle or lower class. In focusing closely on the subject matter of a black life in its outward approximation of white life, writers such as White did not adequately consider that even the black bourgeoisie needed a language that could contain the distinctiveness of blacks, and they failed to find an appropriate narrative voice to express their visions.

Two major conceptions permeated the literature of the New Negro; both were related to black cultural identity. One conception celebrated and explored for meaning the Southern folk roots of black life, which included attention to the African heritage and survival of Africanisms in the practices and beliefs of Southern black folk. That conception offered a way of defining the uniqueness that Langston Hughes called "our individual dark-skinned selves." The second conception understood American blacks in terms of the dualism that W. E. B. Du Bois had identified in

The Souls of Black Folk (1903) as "twoness," the black and the American existing within the same individual. According to Du Bois, to deny either of the two was to deny the essence of one's very being.

These two conceptions led to conflicting visions of art and literature produced during the renaissance. On one hand, attention to folk roots and to an African past individualized blacks, but also separated them from the dominant white culture, perhaps to a greater extent than the intellectual proponents of culture wished. On the other hand, the dualism Du Bois identified suggested that the American part of black life and spirit was as vital and as valid as the other. Although Du Bois understood that the American identity of blacks was inextricably tied to the South, he frequently stressed a transcendency of lower-class associations of blacks in the South, and so appeared disinterested in a rich folk culture. What this meant to some writers was that blacks were no different from their white counterparts living in America, and that they should be portrayed as white only in a "darker hue," as Jessie Fauset explained in the introduction to her novel *The Chinaberry Tree* (1931). There were other writers, for instance James Weldon Johnson and Jean Toomer, who early in the 1920s recognized the significance for black artists of exploring inherently black materials.

A distinct line can be drawn from Jean Toomer (1894–1967) and James Weldon Johnson (1871–1938) to the younger generation of New Negro writers because Toomer and Johnson announced and reiterated the importance of the South in all of its beauty, complexity, and pain, but especially in its models in language and form for black writers. The two writers understood that the South, whether treated directly or not, was essential to the formal or folk art that would emerge among black artists. For them the language of blacks was of primary significance; in its richness of tone and color, language distinguished Southern blacks, and their descendants or relatives in the North, from most Americans, just as it was one of their links to white Southerners, who were at the same cultural moment uncovering the resources of their oral heritage.

Jean Toomer, a Washington, D.C., native, was cut from the same racially mixed mold as Walter White, but had no formative experience that made him black for life. Yet, for a concentrated period in the early twenties, Toomer was the quintessential voice of the black Southern artist heralding a new consciousness of black life and a reinterpretation of the South for that life. Toomer came from a family of Southerners, the most notable of whom was his grandfather, P. B. S. Pinchback, who was born in Macon, Georgia, and served as acting governor of Louisiana during Reconstruction. Nevertheless, Toomer's discovery of the South as material for his writing originated during a three-month stay in rural

Sparta, Georgia, where he was temporarily principal of a school for blacks.

Toomer wrote into the stories, poems, and vignettes in *Cane* (1923) his passion in the discovery of a place and a people. His collage of the conflicting realities in a Southern black heritage served as an "emotional release and freedom," according to Saunders Redding, both for himself and for other black writers. He uncovered a beauty and a strength worthy of black pride, and he exposed an identity and a spirit existing despite repression and victimization. In a unique lyrical voice, he captured the folk spirit, which he believed "was walking in to die on the modern desert."

Cane celebrates racial self-discovery in three sections that thematically trace a modern black's search for meaning. The cyclical form begins in rural Georgia with six stories linked by ten separate poems. As one of the poems, "Georgia Dusk," reveals, the setting becomes

> An orgy for some genius of the South
> With blood-hot eyes and cane-lipped mouth,
> Surprised in making folk-songs from soul sounds.

Poetic devices—rhythm, repetition, symbols—unify the impressionistic treatment of ordinary people, mainly women, rooted in the soil and in the social, racial, and psychological limitations of Southern life. At the same time, Toomer presents the spiritual essence of black life through experimental explorations of consciousness. Four of the stories, "Karintha," "Becky," "Carma," and "Blood-Burning Moon," reverberate with songs echoing the thought and mood of the entire section: women ripened too soon, men destroyed by bigotry, a world rife with contradictions, but compelling in its "muted folk who feel their way upward to a life that crushes or absorbs them." Throughout there is the sentiment of "Cotton Song," a work song in the dialect of men in the fields who express their strength and determination to change their own lives.

> We aint agwine to wait until th Judgment Day!
> . . . .
> Cant blame God if we dont roll,
> Come, brother, roll, roll!

Toomer's main statement occurs in the first part, which also contains his most vivid symbols (pine needles, cane fields, and cotton flowers) and shows best his mastery of form and technique. Lush images and lyrical patterns recur throughout the thematic emphasis on the soil as the soul of black life. The second section, however, focuses attention on the harsh existence of blacks in an urban environment where they are alienated from the soil and from their roots. Each character, as a result, has a "body [that] is separate from the thoughts that pack his mind." The city causes a different set of problems: in "Rhobert" materialism crushes the individual's spirit; in "Box Seat" bourgeoisie values obscure the individual's worth; in "Avey," "Theater," and "Bona and Paul" unspecified aspects of the Northern socialization process cause the failure of human interaction and communication.

The final section, "Kabnis," is a return to the South, where the ritualized search for identity and meaning has the potential for completion. Unlike the other two sections, it is a novelette in the form of a play, and relies less upon lyric expressionism and more upon the ordinary speech of black folk. While the allusions are more difficult, they reiterate the theme that identity is possible in the soil and in the South despite its painful heritage. All of the characters seem representative of types who, though having complex emotions about the region, have found ways of surviving in it. Religion and, to a lesser extent, education (suggested both by schools and by unions), while problematical, symbolize hope for the future.

In *Cane*, Toomer announced the major themes of the New Negro Renaissance: the search for and discovery of a black-centered identity; the unearthing of roots in the soil, the South, and Africa; the realistic conception of the North in the lives of blacks; the reassessment of religion; the exploration of class distinctions among blacks; the realization of beauty and the consciousness of pain caused by racial, social, and economic conditions; the consideration of how the past ought to be viewed and how modern blacks can come to terms with their history and still maintain personal dignity and self-worth; the value of folk traditions and practices. Although Toomer wrote other works in the 1920s, especially the plays *Balo* (1927), *The Sacred Factory* (1927), and *The Gallonwerps* (1928), he did not return to the material of *Cane*, and thereafter wrote little that was directly associated with black life.

James Weldon Johnson, though a contemporary of Paul Laurence Dunbar and not seemingly a groundbreaking stylist, recognized, much like Toomer, that one of the most important areas for the art of the New Negro would be the folk expressions from the oral tradition of Southern blacks. Born in Jacksonville, Florida, Johnson was the primary man of letters in the renaissance. Educated at Atlanta University, Johnson began his multifaceted career as a newspaper publisher and lawyer in Florida, continued as a songwriter and lyricist in New York, a diplomat in the foreign service, an executive with the NAACP, a writer of fiction, poetry, autobiography, and history, and ended as an educator at Fisk University in Nashville.

Johnson's novel, *The Autobiography of an Ex-Coloured Man*, written while he was a United States consul at Corinta, Nicaragua, was published anonymously in 1912, but was reissued under his own name during the height of renaissance activity in 1927. It did not make a major impact on the renaissance, but it treated one of the primary themes—passing—and created a new type of black protagonist, an unheroic vulnerable human being. In portraying a black man who rejects his race in spite of his love for it, Johnson did not preach about racial conditions; rather he simply presented them objectively, if loosely, in the episodic work.

Early in his career, Johnson had written "coon songs" and dialect poems, largely influenced by Paul Laurence Dunbar and collected in *Fifty Years and Other Poems* (1917) as "Jingles and Croons," in which "The Rivals" and "July in Georgy" are skillful, but undistinguished. The folk blues in dialect, "Sence You Went Away," however, is a more memorable effort. Johnson also wrote the lyrics for the popular songs "Oh, Didn't He Ramble," "The Congo Love Song," and "Under the Bamboo Tree," but his finest early work is "O Black and Unknown Bards," a highly imaginative formal poem that celebrates the nameless slave composers of spirituals.

> O black and unknown bards of long ago,
> How came your lips to touch the sacred fire?
> How, in your darkness, did you come to know
> The power and beauty of the minstrel's lyre?

From the beginning of his writing, Johnson's inspiration came from black music and oratory, yet his work did not satisfy his own desire to capture black life, especially its speech, in artistic forms.

He expressed his concerns in the preface to *The Book of American Negro Poetry* (1922).

> What the colored poet . . . needs to do is . . . to find a form that will express the racial spirit by symbols from within rather than by symbols from without, such as the mere mutilation of English spelling and pronunciation. He needs a form that is freer and larger than dialect, but will hold the racial flavor; a form expressing the imagery, the idioms, the peculiar turns of thought, and the distinctive humor and pathos, too, of the Negro, but will also be capable of voicing the deepest emotions and aspirations, and allowing the widest range of subjects and the widest scope of treatment.

He was actually searching for a means of encompassing the richness of the black oral tradition and Southern folk heritage more fully into a written literature than literary dialect had been able to do. Although some critics now dismiss his discussion of dialect because, like Stephen

Bronz, they believe that "language was not a crucial problem in the Negro Renaissance," they overlook the connection between the writers' overt search for appropriate forms to embrace black life and their underlying problem with an appropriate language. Only Johnson addressed the problem in critical discussions that raise the question of how the essence of black life and thought might be expressed without falling into the linguistic clichés and racial stereotypes of conventional dialect or avoiding the inherent richness and special resources of black speech. He believed in the "power of the Negro to suck up the national spirit from the soil and create something artistic and original."

Johnson discovered that the folk life and oral tradition contained the idiom and language for which he had searched. In December, 1920, he published "The Creation" in the *Freeman*. As the first stanza indicates, its poetic patterns stemmed from black speech.

> And God stepped out on space,
> And he looked around and said:
> *I'm lonely—*
> *I'll make me a world.*

Following the model of sermons, the poem freed the voice of the speaker from formal poetic or rhetorical conventions, but replaced them with expressive patterns and imagery from black traditions. For example:

> Darkness covered everything,
> Blacker than a hundred midnights
> Down in a cypress swamp

or

> This Great God,
> Like a mammy bending over her baby,
> Kneeled down in the dust
> Toiling over a lump of clay.

"The Creation" was reprinted throughout the decade, and in 1927, it and six additional sermons appeared together as *God's Trombones: Seven Negro Sermons in Verse*. The sermons resulted from Johnson's research for *American Negro Spirituals* (1925), a collection of sixty-one spirituals for which his brother Rosamond made piano arrangements. Importantly, in *God's Trombones* Johnson experimented with form; he used free verse, intonation, cadence, pauses, stresses, repetition, and rhythm in translating the verbal inventiveness of black speech. The work confirmed the creative possibilities of black Southern materials. In 1935, Johnson published his last collection of poems, *St. Peter Relates an Incident of the Resurrection Day and Other Poems*. The thirty-nine poems, mainly from his first volume, included "Lift Every Voice and Sing," which had long been considered the black national anthem, but none of the poems matched the achievement of God's Trombones.

Johnson's achievement is, as Arthur P. Davis concluded in From the Dark Tower (1974), that he "inspired changes in the development of Negro literature both by precept and example." Johnson's work made clear that an educated black could respect and value black folk and oral materials as primary matter for serious art, and it gave a major impetus to their use as essential to renaissance art by showing what could be achieved if a black writer wished "to give a distinctly racial tone and color" to his or her work.

Johnson's God's Trombones and Toomer's Cane prepared the way for a younger generation of writers, particularly Langston Hughes (1902–1967), Zora Neale Hurston (1901–1960), and Sterling Brown (1901–   ), whose works revalued a South that gave them the most vital materials for their art. Hughes, Hurston, and Brown, the major young writers to emerge from the renaissance, were all Southerners either by actual place of birth or by their own identifications with the South as the signal inspiration for their writing. They understood, as had Johnson and Toomer, that the South, whether treated directly or not, was crucial to a lasting formal or folk art that had or would come from New Negro writers. They not only shared a belief that the speech of blacks was richly poetic, but they also used a metaphorical language in imagining and creating black speakers. They believed that the black masses must be portrayed by means of their own language and experience. None of the three authors attempted to follow a dictum of false sophistication in their portrayals of black life, and none was given to emphasizing the achievements of a black middle class, though none of them denied the validity of that experience as well in the history of black Americans.

Importantly too, the three were among the writers most concerned with the shape of the telling, whether in poetry or prose. Their interest in formal concerns made them more attuned to the multitude of possibilities inherent in folk art and forms: oral tales, folklore, popular music, blues, jazz, gospel, and spirituals. While Blyden Jackson's observation that the New Negro writers "promised much more than they actually performed" is accurate, it is also true that the performances rendered by Hurston, Brown, and Hughes were unmatched by prior generations of black artists and would remain the primary artistic inspiration for the generations to follow.

Langston Hughes, born in Joplin, Missouri, and raised in Lawrence, Kansas, and other Midwestern towns, had limited direct contact with the Deep South during his boyhood, but his early experiences were shaped by his maternal grandmother, Mary Sampson Patterson Leary Langston, who had been a free black in North Carolina and the wife of Lewis Sheridan Leary, a freedman and one of five blacks with John Brown at Harper's Ferry. Hughes's own maternal grandfather, Charles Langston, had been active in the Underground Railroad at Oberlin, Ohio. In a sense, Hughes was a Southerner twice removed from the South, but one whose formative world remained intimately connected to the South by the Southern black migrants to Missouri, Kansas, Ohio, and Illinois.

He was the writer-in-residence who perhaps best understood that the folk of the South were crucial to the imaginative impulse of black writers attempting to define themselves and to declare their independence from restrictive literary traditions and expectations. For his art, two things were seminal: the experience of the South and his love of black people. His first published poem, "The Negro Speaks of Rivers," which succeeded Claude McKay's "If We Must Die" in giving literary articulation to the new racial awareness, had been inspired by the sight of a sunset on the Mississippi River. In 1923 Hughes had been profoundly moved by *Cane*, which he believed "contained the finest prose written by a Negro in America. And like the singing of [Paul] Robeson, it is truly racial." When his first book of poems, *The Weary Blues*, appeared three years after Toomer's work, it was also in his opinion "racial in theme and treatment." His subjects and his techniques stemmed from what he termed the "colorful, distinctive material" of black individuality, particularly the music of the blues and jazz, which became his primary means of identifying with the black folk of the South and their lore and customs.

From the beginning of his career, Hughes showed himself to be a master in manipulating the masks in folk culture and in exposing a speaker in his or her own voice to an audience. His poems in *The Weary Blues* are marked by an efficiency and economy of style and by a clear colloquial idiom. Hughes produced another of the major works of the renaissance, *Fine Clothes to the Jew* (1927), that identified the poetic concerns that he and others would have for the duration of the cultural awakening and throughout their careers. In a letter to Dewey Jones, who reviewed *Fine Clothes* for the Chicago *Defender*, Hughes maintained about his second book: "It is harder and more cynical . . . and it's limited to an interpretation of the so-called 'lower-classes,' the ones to whom life is the least kind. I try to catch the hurt of their lives, the monotony of their jobs, and the veiled weariness of their song. They are the people I know best." Only one of the sections, "Railroad Avenue," is set in a Northern, urban environment; the others, particularly "Beale Street Love," "From the Georgia Roads," and the two sections of blues, treat Southern blacks and folk materials. The poems are in the idiom of blacks and make use of the oral tradition of both their secular and religious lives.

Hughes may have been a topical poet who took up the immediate issues that affected the lives of blacks and who worked within the times that he lived, but as he himself revealed, he also built his "temples for tomorrow" and wrote a wide range of excellent poetry, including the "Madam to You" poems (*The Life and Times of Alberta K. Johnson*), *The Dream Keeper* (1932), *Ask Your Mama* (an elegantly sustained long poem), *Shakespeare in Harlem* (1942), and *Montage of a Dream Deferred* (jazz poems with his greatest variation in mood and tone).

Throughout his long career as a poet, novelist, playwright, editor, newspaper columnist, and translator, Hughes remained in touch with the folk spirit. Although he was not so optimistic as to believe that the folk spirit would overcome oppression, he did not abandon his belief that it would survive and survive intact. One of his major achievements as a writer, the creation of the folk hero Jesse B. Semple is an affirmation of the endurance, wisdom, and truth of the black life.

By the end of the twenties, Hughes had come to recognize the changing attitudes and moods of the renaissance. He wrote both the play *Mulatto: A Tragedy of the Deep South*, which was not produced until 1935, and the novel *Not Without Laughter*, which was published in 1930, as the most active period of the New Negro movement came to an end. Written during the summer of 1928, *Not Without Laughter* tells the story of a boy, Sandy, growing up in a small Kansas town, but it incorporates the spirit of the renaissance by presenting blacks in a new modern age.

During the thirties, much of Hughes's attention was devoted to drama. He founded the Harlem Suitcase Theater in 1937, mainly as an outlet for *Don't You Want to be Free?*, one of his more popular plays. In 1930, Hughes had begun collaborating with Zora Neale Hurston on the folk comedy *Mule Bone*, which was never produced. Their association in the aborted project, however, reiterates their similar concerns with Southern folk and folk expressions.

Hurston was a Southerner from Eatonville, Florida, who retained her ties with the South and its people. She alone of the writers who gathered in Harlem was irrepressibly Southern in her mannerism and speech. Perhaps better than anyone except Hughes, she understood that the renaissance might not last forever, but that the work of the artist could last, if the artist paid attention to the abiding folk spirit and to the enduring roots of folk life. Hurston's spirit and wit, her assurance with words, and her sense of herself enabled her to become one of the more active figures of the period. Yet, she was also different in her audacious, down-home antics and her storytelling, or "lying" as she called it, both of which made the uncultured blacks of the South all too vivid for her cultured associates who preferred to idealize Southern folk life.

Hurston arrived in Harlem in 1925. She had been a student of Alain Locke's at Howard University, where in 1921 she had published her first story, "John Redding Goes to Sea," in the student literary magazine *Stylus*. Charles S. Johnson had printed her story "Drenched in Light" in the December, 1924, issue of *Opportunity*, and encouraged her to join the literary activities in New York. The fiction and drama that she contributed during the twenties all made use of her Southern background. Hurston's most important works of the 1920s, the play *Color Struck*, a second-prize winner in the 1926 *Opportunity* contests, and "Sweat," a story published in *Fire!*, have received more attention; both are set in Florida and show a genuine understanding of the complexities of ordinary black life. With these stories and their awards, Hurston became one of the more visible writers in Harlem.

"I was glad," Hurston wrote in *Mules and Men* (1935), "when somebody told me, 'You may go and collect Negro folklore.'" That somebody was Franz Boas, who taught anthropology at Barnard College and Columbia University and who was Hurston's mentor in a field that perfectly matched her talents. But as she went on to explain, collecting folklore was not a new experience for her; she had listened to and absorbed the stories and customs of her family and neighbors in her all-black hometown.

The people of Eatonville, first sketched in "The Eatonville Anthology" (1926), were the origins of Hurston's fictional characters in her two major literary works, *Jonah's Gourd Vine* (1934) and *Their Eyes Were Watching God* (1937). A diverse gallery of Southerners from real life endowed the fiction with the substance of black folk culture. Both novels are especially successful in rendering the language and voice of the folk in literary narratives that retain the oral quality of storytelling. As Lucy Pearson approaches death in *Jonah's Gourd Vine*, a work based on Hurston's parents, she speaks with assurance: "Don't worry 'bout me, Sister Clark. Ah done been in sorrow's kitchen and Ah done licked out all de pots. Ah done died in grief and been buried in de bitter waters, and Ah done rose agin from de dead lak Lazarus. Nothin' kin touch mah soul no mo'. It wuz hard tuh loose de string-holt on mah li'l chillun." *Jonah's Gourd Vine*, Hurston's biographer Robert Hemenway maintains, is "less a narrative than a series of linguistic moments representing folk-life of the black South."

Hurston's second novel, *Their Eyes Were Watching God*, is both a stronger narrative and a broader representation of folklore. In depicting the maturation and development of Janie Crawford, Hurston carries her heroine through multiple aspects of life in rural Florida and captures the importance of language in giving shape and meaning to her private and communal experiences. Her story is rich with metaphors, "speeches with rhymes," story swapping, "front porch" tales, boasts, and other verbal exchanges that characterize the strength and the promise of a particular black culture. By the end of her experiences, Janie has become one of the "big picture talkers . . . using a side of the world as a canvas."

Hurston's achievement is primarily in her use of language and voice, her authentic descriptions of black folkways and oral traditions. With naturalness, yet precision, she tapped the richness of community and created fictional folk whose spirit, humor, style, and speech expressed the vitality of a Southern black heritage for literary works.

Hurston virtually dismissed the negative impact of racism in her portrayals of Southern blacks and ignored the reality of racial oppression in creating self-contained black worlds. But Sterling A. Brown, who had as wide a knowledge of black folk life and lore as Hurston, believed that the racial climate restricting blacks could not be overlooked in truthful creative writing. A Washington native whose early poems were infused with the same folk spirit that inspired Hurston and Hughes, Brown was not a physical part of Harlem during the New Negro Renaissance, but he had a keener vision of emotional and psychological realities at the core of black existence.

Brown was one of the young writers who benefited from Georgia Douglas Johnson's "Saturday Nights," because they provided him with an access to the cultural activities of the renaissance. The son of a former slave from Tennessee who became a distinguished minister, he was a student at Williams College (A.B., 1922) and Harvard University (M.A., 1923) during the first years of the reawakening in Harlem, but by the middle of the decade, he had begun to publish poetry in *Crisis, Opportunity, Carolina Magazine, Caroling Dusk*, and *Ebony and Topaz*. At the same time, he pursued a career as a critic and teacher at Virginia Theological Seminary in Lynchburg, Lincoln University in Missouri, Fisk University in Nashville, and Howard University, where he taught from 1929 until his retirement in 1969.

Although urban born, Brown, from his earliest works, showed an affinity for people of the soil. His poem "Foreclosure" (*Ebony and Topaz* [1927]) treats the flooding river, Father Missouri, which reclaims land from the poor farmer Uncle Dan, who

> Curses, and shouts in his hoarse old voice,
> 'Aint got no right to act dat way at all'
> And the old river rolls on, slowly to the gulf.

His people are primarily poor black folk whose lives are a struggle for survival and whose voices reflect their folk roots.

Some critics have questioned placing Sterling Brown in the chronology of the New Negro Renaissance, yet he clearly belongs there because he functioned as a distinct presence and voice during the twenties. His poem "When De Saints Go Ma'chin' Home" won first prize in the 1927 *Opportunity* poetry contests; that same year, "After the Storm" appeared in the *Crisis*, while seven of his other poems, including one of his major works, "Odyssey of Big Boy," were presented in *Caroling Dusk*. Although his first book, *Southern Road*, was not published until 1932, much of the work had been written during the twenties and had already appeared in print. Known as a careful craftsman who stressed the importance of folk materials in his poetry and critical works, Brown did not appear to be a prolific creative writer; however, his poetry was severely underestimated until the appearance of his *Collected Poems* in 1980.

The epigraph to *Southern Road* suggests the message and vision in most of his poems: "O de ole sheep dey knos de road, / Young lambs gotta find dy way." The lines come from a spiritual, and the selection shows his concern with forms indigenous to black culture and with themes addressing black history. In the introduction to *Southern Road*, James Weldon Johnson linked Brown to McKay, Toomer, Cullen, and Hughes as the most outstanding "younger" poets.

> Sterling Brown is one of this group and therefore has been instrumental in bringing about the more propitious era in which the Negro artist now finds himself. . . . Mr. Brown's work is not only fine, it is also unique. . . . He infuses his poetry with genuine characteristic flavor by adopting as his medium the common, racy, living speech of the Negro in certain phases of *real* life. For his raw material he dug down into the deep mine of Negro folk poetry. . . . He has actually absorbed the spirit of his materials, made it his own; . . . he has taken this raw material and worked it into original and authentic poetry.

Popular tales, epics and ballads, such as "John Henry," "Casey Jones," or "Stagolee," provide the models for his forms and for his heroes.

Brown's second book of poetry, *No Hiding Place*, submitted a few years after the first, was not accepted by a publisher until it appeared as part of *The Collected Poems*, which included *Southern Road* and *The Last Ride of Wild Bill* (1975). Although two sections treat Harlem and Washington, the six main sections of *No Hiding Place* are set in the South: the cotton South, rural Louisiana, Atlanta, Georgia, Tennessee, and Virginia. Many of the poems focus attention on the pilgrimage of contemporary blacks to the places of their past, such as "Remembering Nat Turner" in which the lone signpost marking Turner's rebellion has "rotted in the hole" and "tenants split the marker for kindling." These poems reveal Brown's intimacy with Southern life not only as he understood it from his former-slave father, but also as he himself experienced it teaching and traveling throughout the region.

While his poetry follows that of Johnson, Toomer, and Hughes, it differs from theirs in that it explores with greater authority, sensitivity, and detachment the folklore, humor, and strength of Southern blacks, whose stories, tales, ballads, and legends are fundamental to his art. Brown's achievement is that he encompasses the broadest vision of black experience in his poetry. Lives circumscribed by racism, poverty, ignorance, or injustice are not reduced to one level; they are multilayered, multidimensional, and rich with experience and meaning. His best-known poems, "Slim Greer," "Strong Men," "Sporting Beasley," "When De Saints Go Ma'chin' Home," "Crispus Attacks McKoy," and "Old Lem," all depict the survival and endurance of blacks and their ability to laugh, both at themselves and at the ways of the white world, and their capacity to "keep comming," as his symphonic poem "Strong Men" portrays through its litany of abuses suffered by blacks who nonetheless "keep a inchin' along" and "gettin' stronger."

Although the achievement of the renaissance is most evident in its premiere artists, its broad-based literary significance manifests itself in the accomplishments of writers who, at best, earned modest reputations during the concentrated years of renaissance activity, but who later attained the status of major authors. The primary example among those with Southern roots or backgrounds is Arna Bontemps (1902–1973), who was recognized as one of the New Negro poets in the 1920s but whose main literary works, though shaped by his participation in the renaissance and his associations formed in Harlem, appeared in the 1930s and afterward.

Born in Alexandria, Louisiana, Bontemps is typical of the youths who arrived in Harlem when the excitement of the New Negro Renaissance was just under way. His reasons for going to New York were obviously inspired by the cultural awakening, as his memoir of the South, "Why I Returned," indicates. "So what did one do after concluding that for him a break with the past and the shedding of his Negro-ness were not only impossible but unthinkable? First . . . he went to New York in the twenties, met young Negro writers and intellectuals who were similarly searching, learned poems like Claude McKay's 'Harlem Dancer' and Jean Toomer's 'Song of the Son,' started writing and publishing in this vein himself, and applauded Langston Hughes when he wrote . . . 'We younger Negro artists . . . intend to express our individual dark-skinned selves without fear or shame.'" Raised in Los Angeles, California, Bontemps graduated from Union Pacific College in 1923; within the year, he had decided against teaching in California and planned his move to Harlem because, as he said, he wanted to view the remarkable happenings in New York "from a grandstand seat."

In the foreword to his only book of poems, *Personals* (1963), he recalled: "It did not take long to discover that I was just one of many young Negroes arriving in Harlem for the first time and with many of the same thoughts and intentions. Within a year or two we began to recognize ourselves as a 'group' and to become a little self-conscious about our 'significance.' When we were not too busy having fun, we were shown off and exhibited . . . in scores of places and to all kinds of people. And we heard the sighs of wonder, amazement and sometimes admiration . . . that here was one of the 'New Negroes.'"

His first published poem, "Spring Music," appeared in the *Crisis* in June, 1925; the next year was one of his most productive as a publishing poet. When Bontemps, who was described by Hughes as "quiet and scholarly, looking like a young edition of Dr. Du Bois," won the Alexander Pushkin Prize a second time in 1927 for "The Return," he was considered the most promising New Negro writer of serious formal poetry. "The Return," a long poem in four parts, is typical of Bontemps' use of somber landscapes to create tone poems.

> Let us go back to the dusk again,
> Slow and sad-like following the track
> Of blown leaves and cool white rain
> Into the old grey dreams; let us go back.

Nature, ever-present in his poetry, evokes memory and longing, which are both racial and individual. Bontemps' combination of melancholy landscapes with memories of loss makes much of his poetry elegiac in tone. While his language is sonorous, it is never in an inventive black musical form or colloquial idiom.

His poems, particularly the longer ones, incorporate images of Africa that rival those of Hughes or Cullen, but sadness rather than joy pervades Bontemps' vision. Africa is part of the memory and the dream in

Bontemps' finest poems, but it symbolizes the accumulated sorrow in the lives of blacks. Bontemps' poetry is not so distinctly individualized as that of other poets of the period. His three novels of the thirties, *God Sends Sunday* (1931), *Black Thunder* (1936), and *Drums at Dusk* (1939), reveal more of his individual talent, especially his interest in the historical roots of black life. His first novel is set in the South at the turn of the century. Dedicated to his father Paul, it derives from Bontemps' roots in the Red River area of Louisiana. The frail hero, Little Augie, grows up in the quarters of a Louisiana plantation where his mother was born a slave, but by becoming a famous jockey, he escapes a life of work in rice and cotton fields. Augie wins money and women, and moves in the fast world of racetracks and gambling in New Orleans and St. Louis. Despite setbacks, Augie is a resourceful hero who can make his own way in the world. The novel is uneven and at times superficial; nevertheless, its narrative is engaging and the subject matter is distinct.

God Sends Sunday, written in the late twenties, was influenced by the general reconsideration of the past that characterized the renaissance, but *Black Thunder* and *Drums at Dusk* are the only historical novels by a New Negro writer. The two works reflect Bontemps' serious concern with black heritage, roots, and identity. *Black Thunder* presents the story of Gabriel Prosser's slave rebellion in 1800. It has a fascinating plot, well-rounded characters, particularly the heroic but human Prosser, and its innovative technique and suggestive symbols make it Bontemps' finest piece of fiction. More than any of his other novels, *Black Thunder* displays his gift for rendering folk speech and manners, yet it has not received its due acclaim.

Drums at Dusk is a weaker novel of the Haitian revolution. Although it treats a complex subject, the work is melodramatic and its characters unconvincing. As in *Black Thunder*, the main theme is freedom, but the dramatic power of the earlier novel is missing, perhaps because Bontemps' strong imaginative identification with historical black figures did not encompass Haitians as fully as it did Southern blacks. Nonetheless, his achievement in both novels is that he constructed visions of the past that made the Harlem modernists' abstract concerns with earlier periods of black life both concrete and accessible.

During his career as a teacher in the South and as a librarian at Fisk University, Bontemps continued to write. Much of his work was done in collaboration with Langston Hughes, his lifelong friend. During the 1960s, he was rediscovered as a major author from the New Negro Renaissance.

In addition to writers such as Bontemps who achieved recognition after arriving in Harlem in the 1920s, other youths looked out "over the rooftops of Negrodom" in New York and tried to convey what they saw in creative writing. Melvin B. Tolson (1900–1966), born in Moberly, Missouri, arrived to study for a master's degree at Columbia, but was attracted by the creative energy in black New York. He began *Harlem Gallery* (1965) as a sonnet on Harlem at the end of the twenties, and expanded it into a long free-verse poem in 1930. Unable to find a publisher, he put it aside for the next twenty years before he finally rewrote the poem as the first of an epic treatment of Harlem. Tolson's primary verse form was the Pindaric ode, which he used successfully in his long erudite poem, *Libretto for the Republic of Liberia* (1953), which, along with the prizewinning "Dark Symphony" (1941), was his major poetic achievement. In large measure, Tolson's work was influenced by the literary activity of the New Negro Renaissance that allowed young writers to see the possibilities for blacks as artists and to define what their subject matter could be.

Like Tolson, other young black writers were also inspired by the renaissance and were able to achieve more of the kinds of literary work it had called for, precisely because of the groundbreaking activity and cultural climate created by the New Negroes. Many of them did not travel to New York and did not begin their careers until well into the 1930s. One of the most important of these writers is Frank Marshall Davis (1905–   ), who was born in Arkansas City, Kansas, and who was just completing his education in the twenties. In 1931, Davis moved to Atlanta and helped to found the *Daily World*, which became the major black daily newspaper in the South. His first book of poems, *Black Man's Verse* (1935), reflects his interest in jazz and cabarets as matter and mode for black poetry and shows the influence of Langston Hughes. His second book, *I Am the American Negro* (1937), reveals the major impact of social realism on the black writers of the thirties. Both volumes also continue the concern with racial identity that marked the literary ferment of the twenties. Davis' long poem "Snapshots of the Cotton South," one of his most effective poems of the thirties, shows the fullness of his understanding of the Southern condition for underclass blacks and whites alike in a segregated world.

The commitment to exposing racism and to exploring the dilemma of a new generation of blacks felt by Davis and other writers of the thirties was a legacy of the ideological concerns of the twenties and the major renaissance writers. The second wave of New Negro writers followed the example of the first by making a distinctive art from racial materials. The use of a black idiom, the refinement of voice, the stress of rhythm, and the style of imagery that had been part of the experiments of the renaissance became the major resources for black writers in the later periods. The end of the twenties, then, did not mark the end of the flowering of black writers.

In his portrait, "Black Renaissance," Langston Hughes, who associated the beginning of the movement with the advent of *Shuffle Along* on Broadway rather than with political events, remarked that when A'Lelia Walker, the heiress and renaissance party giver, died in 1931, "that was really the end of the gay times of the New Negro era in Harlem," and that "spring for me was the end of the Harlem Renaissance. . . . The cycle that had charlestoned into being on the dancing heels of *Shuffle Along* now ended in *Green Pastures* with De Lawd." Hughes, as well as Bontemps, ended the New Negro Renaissance in 1931, the year he left Harlem. But though the center could not hold in Harlem, the renaissance continued, dispersed even more than before to the far places that had kept up with the activity in New York, imitated it, and spawned other New Negro artists, who like Hughes, Bontemps, Hurston, and Brown, continued creating, producing, and publishing throughout the bleakest years of the depression. Although no mass exodus took place from Harlem, the out-migration of artists in the early years of the 1930s, ironically often to the South and the harbor of its black colleges, reflected both the precarious financial position of black writers and the devastating economic conditions for blacks in urban areas. By 1935, the year of the sobering Harlem riot, the New Negro Renaissance with a strong nucleus in New York was over.

Alain Locke, who had some of the first words heralding the renaissance, addressed the end of the period as well. "Negro artists are just the by-products of the Negro Renaissance; its main accomplishment will be to infuse a new essence into the general stream of culture." Locke also observed, "If conditions in the South were more conducive to the development of Negro culture without transplanting, the self-expression of the 'New Negro' would spring up just as one branch of the new literature of the South, and as one additional phase of its cultural reawakening. The common bond of soil and that natural provincialism would be a sounder basis for development than the somewhat expatriated position of the younger school of Negro writers" (Locke, "Our Little Renaissance"). Locke was as perceptive in the end as he had been at the beginning. Unfortunately, because the New Negro Renaissance was not treated as an added part of the South's Renascence, the history of Southern literature can only claim those Southern standard bearers in the New Negro Renaissance from afar; nonetheless, the reclamation acknowledges the vision and the achievement of the New Negro writers, especially those who helped to shape the art of modern black literature out of the resources of the South.

MARK ROYDEN WINCHELL

The New Poetry

The Fugitives so dominated Southern poetry during the period between the two world wars that one is likely to think that outside of
that group the South was indeed what Mencken declared it to be—the
"Sahara of the Bozart." The truth, however, is that the twenties and
thirties saw a considerable amount of interesting minor verse being
written by non-Fugitive Southerners. An examination of these efforts
should provide greater appreciation of the heterogeneity of modern
Southern poetry and additional perspective on the concerns and achievements of the Fugitives themselves.

For some idea of the state of poetry in the South during the 1920s,
one can turn to Addison Hibbard's anthology *The Lyric South* (1928).
Of the thirty poets featured in Hibbard's volume, all but two or three
are local-color artists who never gained a national reputation. Although
Hibbard argues that the new generation of Southern poets represented a
break with the tradition of Lanier, Timrod, and Hayne, those whom he
anthologizes seem very much continuous with that tradition. Despite
eleven selections from the Fugitive leader John Crowe Ransom, *The
Lyric South* gives little indication that Southern letters had been affected
by the modernist revolution in poetry. As Hibbard himself concedes: "In
comparison with the poetry of the country as a whole, the product of
the Southern poets strikes one as strangely satisfied with things as they
are. It is, in a very real sense, a lyric South concerned with beauty and
emotional ecstasy almost to the exclusion of anything like actuality."

The poet with the most selections in *The Lyric South* was William
Alexander Percy (1885–1942) of Greenville, Mississippi. By all accounts a remarkably kind and humane individual, Percy was essentially
a lonely man who seemed to feel out of place in the modern world.
While readily admitting that he wrote his poetry primarily for himself,
he was intent on keeping himself out of that poetry. One must therefore
ignore his four books of verse—*Sappho in Levkas* (1915), *In April
Once* (1920), *Enzio's Kingdom* (1924), and *Selected Poems* (1930)—

314

and look instead to Percy's engaging autobiography *Lanterns on the Levee* (1941) to glean any sense of his personality.

Part of the impersonality of Will Percy's verse may have been due to its author's basic shyness and reticence. As a classical stoic in the tradition of Marcus Aurelius, he would have considered an overt display of personal emotion to be in bad poetic taste. Ironically, however, his prosodic models came not from neoclassical but from romantic and Victorian verse. Reviewing *In April Once* for the University of Mississippi student newspaper, an aspiring poet named William Faulkner noted that the best qualities of Percy's verse belonged to the previous century, that the sensuousness of his imagery rivaled that of Swinburne. As Louis Dollarhide concludes, Percy was "Swinburne in a Wordsworthian form."

Like other Southern poets of his time, Percy found some of his best materials in his own region. Touring Mississippi with his father LeRoy during the latter's 1911 Senate campaign against James K. Vardaman, Will Percy discovered that he need not set his poems in faraway places and long-ago times. As Phinizy Spalding observes, the verse that Percy wrote after 1912—particularly the "Delta Sketches" section of *Enzio's Kingdom*—owes much to the landscape of his native state.

Six years prior to the publication of Hibbard's anthology, Harriet Monroe devoted an entire issue of *Poetry* (April, 1922) to Southern verse. The guest editors of that volume were DuBose Heyward (1885–1940) and Hervey Allen (1889–1949), two prominent members of the Poetry Society of South Carolina. In addition to publishing copious selections from their own work, Heyward and Allen featured poems by Henry Bellaman, Josephine Pinckney, Beatrice Ravenel, and several lesser lights. Although the Fugitives had been around for several years at this time and John Crowe Ransom had published one book of verse, the work of the Nashville group apparently was not deemed worthy of inclusion in a volume representing the current state of poetry in the South.

In the commentary that concludes their special issue of *Poetry*, Heyward and Allen stress the distinctively regional aspects of the verse produced in their part of the country. They regard the Negro and the poor white as rich sources for local color. Moreover, they see the predominantly rural topography of the South as ideally suited to a landscape poetry fundamentally different from the verse being produced in the great American cities. Such a poetry must necessarily keep its distance from the main currents of modernism. According to Heyward and Allen, the South "will accept with modern spirit the new forms in verse, but accept them as being valuable for their loosening effect upon the old rather than as being all satisfactory in themselves."

Although the Poetry Society of South Carolina did not have nearly as much impact on American (or even Southern) verse as the Fugitives later would prove to have, the Charleston group sought to make poetry a civic asset. Heyward, Allen, and company recruited prominent members of the Charleston aristocracy for their organization, sponsored readings and lectures, and awarded prizes. They saw poetry more as a celebration than as a critique of culture. For this reason, they sparked a genuine enthusiasm for literature within the Charleston community. Some critics, however, feel that the group suffered from the defects of its virtues. Cleanth Brooks argues that by excluding from their verse elements that might be inimical to the moods they were seeking, the South Carolina poets, like their Victorian counterparts, achieved those moods too easily and were thus guilty of sentimentality.

It is arguable that in the person of Beatrice Witte Ravenel (1870–1956) the South Carolina group came closest to transcending the limitations of local color and participating in the main currents of literary modernism. Although she published only one book, *Arrow of Lightning* (1925), and is now largely forgotten outside of Charleston, Ravenel exhibited a greater originality of diction and imagery than any other non-Fugitive Southerner of the 1920s.

Born and raised in Charleston, Beatrice Witte was very much a lady of her time and region. Nevertheless, she spent five crucial years in the 1890s as a student at the Society for the Collegiate Instruction of Women (now Radcliffe College) in Cambridge, Massachusetts. While studying under such luminaries as William James, George Lyman Kittredge, George Santayana, and George Pierce Baker, Miss Witte associated with the young poets William Vaughn Moody and Trumbull Stickney and began publishing her own work in both local and national magazines. Despite the promise of her early career, Beatrice Witte returned to Charleston and in 1900 married Frank Ravenel. From then until 1917, she wrote virtually no poetry.

When Beatrice Ravenel did begin to write again, apparently inspired with patriotic fervor by America's entry into the First World War, her verse remained technically similar to that which she had written at Cambridge. It was, according to Louis D. Rubin, Jr., "highly abstract and very sentimental." In the early 1920s, however, her work developed a new power and maturity. In his introduction to *The Yemassee Lands: Poems of Beatrice Ravenel* (1969), Rubin maintains that "it is as if she had come upon the poetry of Amy Lowell, the Imagists, and other moderns, and suddenly realized what it was possible to do with language in a poem, whereupon she began doing it. Almost overnight she put aside the sentimental ideality of the poetry of the waning genteel tradition, with its poetic abstractions, ornate and artificial literary language, and its strained diction, and began writing in free verse, with notable economy of diction, a sharp precision of language, and vivid, evocative imagery."

Like her colleagues in the Poetry Society of South Carolina, Beatrice Ravenel was a regional writer who drew upon the materials of her particular locale. What makes her superior to her fellow Charlestonians is what she did with that material. For example, in her most famous work of the 1920s, a three-poem cycle dealing with the Yemassee tribe of the Carolina low country, she resists the temptation to exploit the quaint and picturesque qualities of Indian life. In addition to being an original and imaginative craftsman, she possessed the sort of artistic integrity that sacrifices cheap and immediate effects for a more subtle and lasting impact. Like Whitman, whose influence on her verse is unmistakable, Beatrice Ravenel was able to respond to nature on both a sensuous and a spiritual level.

If Ravenel was an inchoate modernist trying to break out of a local-color tradition, several Southern poets of the 1920s and 1930s were even more insistent on shunning their provincial roots. To varying degrees, these individuals reflected the cosmopolitan influences that would shape the main course of twentieth-century poetry and make the verse of the lyric South seem antiquated by comparison. In this regard, one thinks of West Virginia's John Peale Bishop and Georgia's Conrad Aiken (whose lifelong expatriation from the South puts him beyond the scope of this study). Because of his association with the imagist movement, however, no poet is more deserving of the label *Southern modernist* than Arkansas' John Gould Fletcher (1886-1950).

Although an early disciple of Ezra Pound, Fletcher was more intimately involved with the Imagists during the movement's final phase, after Amy Lowell had supplanted Pound as its dominant presence. (Pound, who was as tactless as he was brilliant, offended the thin-skinned Fletcher, whereas Miss Lowell provided him with the sisterly encouragement that he needed.) When Pound had moved on to vorticism with its emphasis on the integrity and uniqueness of each art form, Fletcher, who had no interest in any modern art other than poetry, was still seeking to incorporate the virtues of painting and music in his verse.

Fletcher's philosophical relationship to imagism consisted largely of a shared renunciation of the inflated rhetoric, archaic diction, and sentimental feeling that dominated much nineteenth-century verse. For him, imagism meant an honest, nondidactic approach to poetry. That Richard Aldington, Hilda Doolittle, and Pound himself understood the term also to imply a specific doctrine of the image (a hard visual impression rendered in an instantaneous moment) seemed not to affect Fletcher. He believed that by manipulating the various musical devices of poetry (assonance, consonance, alliteration, and the like) within a free-verse structure he could evoke a poetic excitement in the reader. As a result, his verse was more suggestive and less literal than that of the more conventional imagists. If an Aldington or an H. D. poem seems like an austere pencil sketch, a Fletcher poem more closely resembles a lush Oriental painting with musical accompaniment.

Despite his deviations from the imagist party line, there can be little doubt that Fletcher wrote his best poetry while associated with Pound and Lowell (1913–1916). His major works during this period include *Irradiations* (1915), a group of poems based on American themes and settings (written in 1915), *Goblins and Pagodas* (1916), *Japanese Prints* (1918), and *The Tree of Life* (1918). His *Selected Poems* was awarded the Pulitzer Prize in 1938.

After his association with the imagist movement, Fletcher became involved with the Nashville group. He was both an outside contributor to the *Fugitive* (a select company that included Hart Crane and Robert Graves) and one of the twelve participants in the Agrarian symposium *I'll Take My Stand*. By 1927, he had concluded that the imagist revolution had reached a dead end and that the only salvation for modern poetry lay in the classicism of the Fugitives. Dionysus in the city had given way to Apollo on the farm.

In the last analysis, there are perhaps three senses in which a poet can be regarded as Southern: if he is from the South; if he writes about the South; and if his work is informed by some sense of the region's internal contradictions. According to these criteria, the poets we have considered here are at best two-thirds Southern. Although they are from the South and have, in different ways, relied on their native locale for poetic material, neither the local colorists nor the deracinated modernists have confronted the meaning of contemporary Southern experience as resolutely as have the major Fugitives. Had the Nashville group never existed, there would have been no Southern poetry—only poetry in the South.

THOMAS DANIEL YOUNG

The Fugitives: Ransom, Davidson, Tate

In the summer of 1920 a group of young men—Vanderbilt University faculty members and students plus a few townspeople—began meeting at the home of James M. Frank on Whitland Avenue in Nashville, Tennessee, about two miles from the university, so that each member of the group could read his poems and have them criticized by the other members. These young men, including John Crowe Ransom and Donald Davidson (later Allen Tate and Robert Penn Warren would join the group), knew each other because they had belonged to an informal circle of townspeople and university affiliates who met from 1914 to the outbreak of World War I, first at informal social gatherings and later at discussion sessions covering a wide range of topics—literature, art, religion, and philosophy. These prewar meetings were presided over by Sidney Mttron Hirsch, a Jewish mystic, etymologist, and world traveler, but in the days immediately following the war the mantle of leadership passed to Ransom, who had just published his first book of poetry. The character of the meetings soon changed, for Ransom was interested in the *craft* of poetry.

The nature of the meetings was again altered after Allen Tate joined the group in November, 1921. Tate possessed "a knowledge of literary matters," Ransom remarked in "In amicitia," an essay published in the *Sewanee Review* (Autumn, 1959) to honor Tate on his sixtieth birthday, "which were not the property of our own region at that time." What Tate brought to the group was literary modernism.

In April, 1922, the group published the first issue of a little magazine entitled the *Fugitive*. Between then and December, 1925, nineteen issues of the now internationally known journal of poetry and brief critical commentary were published.

Born in Pulaski, Tennessee, on April 30, 1888, John Crowe Ransom grew up in the small middle Tennessee towns in which his father served as Methodist minister. He attended Bowen Academy in Nashville, from which he was graduated in 1903. The following fall he entered Vanderbilt and graduated first in the class of 1909, after dropping out for two years following his sophomore year to teach in secondary schools. In 1910 he entered Christ Church College of Oxford University, from which three years later he was awarded a Bachelor of Arts degree in *Litterae Humaniores*. He taught for one year in the Hotchkiss School before joining the faculty of the department of English of Vanderbilt University. He remained in that position until August, 1937, when he accepted a post at Kenyon College of Gambier, Ohio. Two years later he founded *Kenyon Review*, one of the most distinguished literary quarterlies ever published in America. He edited the *Review* for twenty years, retired and lived the remainder of his life, except for occasional visiting professorships, in Gambier. He died on July 3, 1974.

Ransom's first poem was published in the *Independent* for February 22, 1919. It expresses the irritation a young man feels because a young lady, with whom he is watching the sunset, seems little moved by the beauties of the natural surroundings. As Ransom would express the attitude later, she was not aware of "the world's body." Encouraged, no doubt, by the fact that his poems were being accepted by that journal and the Philadelphia *Public Ledger*, for which his Oxford friend Christopher Morley was a columnist, Ransom continued to write verse. Much of it, he commented later, "made considerable use of the word God . . . that ultimate mystery to which all our great experiences reduce." By the time he and Davidson, who were both in officer training school, met at Fort Oglethorpe, Georgia, in late summer of 1917, he had a "whole sheaf of poems," a copy of which he gave Davidson, who pondered over them while he was serving in France. These were the poems published as *Poems About God* (1919) while Ransom was still serving as an artillery officer in Europe.

They were not the kind of poems one would expect from the dutiful son of a Methodist minister, for they clearly reveal Ransom's skepticism, the schism that had developed in his thinking between orthodox religion and secular philosophy. The reader is constantly aware that the poet is troubled by the way God makes himself manifest in the world. God hears the pious old lady's prayer, but his only response is a frown. The God the poet presents in "Geometry" seems to be a crazy man. The man in "Worship" finds God in a crockery stein at the local pub. "God's oldest joke," the poet writes, is the "fact that in the finest flesh / There isn't any soul." "For all his mercies," the poet concludes, "God be thanked / But for his tyrannies be blamed."

The reader of Ransom's mature poetry would probably doubt that these early efforts were written by the same man who wrote "The Equilibrists" and "Bells for John Whiteside's Daughter." The irony is too obvious, direct and heavy-handed. These poems reflect, as Thornton Parsons has noted, "a simple amateurism, a complete freedom from aesthetic self-consciousness" (*John Crowe Ransom* [New York, 1969], 17). This less-than-perfect verse does have some characteristics, however, of the later poetry. These early efforts are fables, anecdotes, or simple little narratives concerned with mutability, death, and the passing of youthful energy and beauty, or with man's dual nature. Many characters in these early poems, as in the later ones, come to grief because they cannot accept the nature of the world in which they live.

> Dick's a sturdy little lad,
> Yonder throwing stones;
> Agues and rheumatic pains
> Will fiddle on his bones.

Perhaps the basic difference between these poems and the later ones is that the identity of the persona who appears in them is transparent. The speaker is obviously Ransom himself. He is voicing some queries that have shaken the faith of an orthodox middle Tennessee lad who has gone to Oxford for three years. Never again would Ransom write poems with such an apparent autobiographical bias.

Before the *Fugitive* was begun, Tate recalls in *Memoirs and Opinions* (1975), Ransom "had written a poem which foreshadowed the style for which he has become famous; it was 'Necrological,' still one of his better poems; I marvelled at it because it seemed to me that overnight he had left behind him the style of his first book and, without confusion, had mastered a new style." The poem, which appeared in the *Fugitive* for June, 1922, was suggested by Ransom's reading of the death of Charles the Bold of Burgundy, who after being slain in battle was left to be eaten by the wolves. Ransom imagines a young friar coming into the field soon after the battle, attempting to devise some means of justifying the suffering and human slaughter that have occured there. He thinks of its obvious inconsequence for those who won today but go to be slain elsewhere. By what means can one justify human love and sacrifice, devotion to a cause however sacred, if the winner of today's engagement goes to find death in tomorrow's? He ponders these and related questions until his faith is seriously challenged. He learns as he looks at the body of the lady, who has sacrificed both her reputation and her life for her lover, that the body is more than a mere enclosure for the soul, that there is a kind of love far different from the adoration he feels for his Lord. It would seem that Ransom believes an important lesson can be learned here—the monistic system of the friar and his church will not explain the many paradoxes of the world around him. As he stands in "a deep surmise," his head bowed "as under a riddle"; he is "So still that he likened himself unto those dead / Whom the kites of Heaven solicited with sweet cries." The experience has rendered him impotent, unable to act or reason.

Most of the poetry by which Ransom will be remembered was written between April, 1922, and December, 1925, the years in which the *Fugitive* was published, and most of it first appeared in that journal. The combined characteristics of that poetry, which Tate described as in the "mature manner," are most distinctive: the subtle irony, the nuanced ambiguities, the metaphysical conceits, the wit, the cool detached tone. Most of the poetry was collected in *Chills and Fever* (1925) and *Two Gentlemen in Bonds* (1927). Ransom also published three selections of his poems, all of which contain new and revised verses but few new poems: *Selected Poems* (1945) includes only five poems written after 1925; *Selected Poems* (1963), *Selected Poems, Revised and Enlarged* (1969) includes twelve sonnets from *Two Gentlemen in Bonds* and markedly revised versions of several earlier poems. Finally, however, Ransom chose to preserve only 80 of the 153 poems he published.

Ransom's conviction that aimless, purposeless modern man cannot know the redemptive qualities of human love is best expressed in "Spectral Lovers" (1923) and "The Equilibrists" (1925), the latter considered by many Ransom's best poem. In the first poem the man and woman know they are in love so why, they wonder, are "they frozen apart in fear?" They remain spectral lovers because of their own weaknesses and because they cannot bring themselves to the point of decision. They will remain spectral lovers, potential lovers; they can never consummate their love, but they will never be without the desire to love. "The Equilibrists," a more suggestive and evocative poem, explores a similar situation. The lovers are in "a torture of equilibrium" because they burn "with fierce love always to come near," but honor keeps them apart. The lovers yearn for an ideal world in which the conflicting forces of honor and desire can be reunited, but this is not such a world. The one to come also offers little hope to them. The state of painful equilibrium in which they find themselves will be continued throughout eternity. Knowing their plight, one in which their "flames were not more radiant than their ice," the poet can only offer an epitaph, "lines to memorize their doom."

> Equilibrists lie here; stranger, tread light;
> Close, but untouching in each other's sight;
> Mouldered the lips and ashy the tall skull.
> Let them lie perilous and beautiful.

"Bells for John Whiteside's Daughter" (1924), Ransom's best-known poem, is also one of his best, one that Randall Jarrell has called "perfectly realized . . . and almost perfect." Like many of Ransom's other poems, this one is on the precariousness of human life, the fleetingness of feminine beauty. It demonstrates a quality of Ransom's artistry that Graham Hough has noted: the poet's ability to present important problems through delicate subject matter. Since it concerns the death of a little girl, the poem could easily deteriorate into trite and shabby pathos, but Ransom handles his material admirably. He achieves aesthetic distance by presenting the essentials of the poem from the "high-window" of an interested but uninvolved bystander. Then, as Robert Penn Warren has pointed out, the burden of the poem lies in the poet's development of his attitude to the girl's death. First he is astonished because the news is so unexpected ("There was such speed in her little body, / And such lightness in her footfall"); after a moment's reflection, however, the astonishment turns to vexation. The speaker has confronted another of the inexplicable mysteries of the world he must live in. There is no piteous cry to heaven for justification or solace; the poet uses a usually lamentable occasion for some of his most effective irony, achieved by contrasting the stock response to death to the one addressed in the poem.

In his use of wit and irony, in the tension of paradox and ambiguity of his best verse, Ransom is distinctively a modern poet. His basic attitudes, however, as well as the poetic forms he employs, reflect his continuing interest in tradition. In "Old Mansion" (1924), Ransom suggests that only through participation in the culture out of which one comes can he develop a sensitive awareness of the past and create a feeling of stability and permanence in the flux of an ever-changing world. One can tolerate the harsh unpleasantness of the present world if he will glance backward to the felicities of a previous age. Ransom expresses the same attitude in "Antique Harvesters," which he calls his Southern poem. Here the persona calls upon the young men to get to know their famous lady, to realize the myth that in its full bronze maturity retains all the vigor and vitality of its green youth. They must experience it now for soon it will pass into the grayness of death and oblivion.

Any final estimate of Ransom's literary achievement must take into account his poetry. In a small handful of poems his achievement is remarkable. He has provided, as Isabel Gamble MacCaffrey has pointed out, an "accurate mirror of the modern sensibility." Few poets of his generation have been able to represent with greater accuracy and precision the inexhaustible ambiguities, the paradoxes and tensions, the dichotomies and ironies that make up modern life.

At Allen Tate's first meeting of the Fugitives he reports that Donald Davidson (1893–1968) was writing poems about "lovers and dragons, and . . . one about a tiger-woman that I thought remarkable." Among Davidson's first poems were some whose titles suggest the qualities Tate mentions: "A Demon Brother," "Tiger-Woman," and "Following the Tiger." The poet's choice of subject may reveal an inclination to escape some of the unpleasantness of the materialistic present by creating an imaginative realm where lovers, singers, and others of sensibility and taste can be shielded from the harsh realities of an unsympathetic society.

Soon after he joined the Fugitives, Tate translated Baudelaire's sonnet "Correspondences," which suggests that the poet is often required to transpose an image from one order of experience to another. This idea interested Davidson, and he shifted the emphasis in his poetry. No longer was he interested in trying to create a kind of natural lyricism like that of the early Yeats; instead he turned to writing what he and Tate called the "Pan" series—poems that sought "to take a thoroughly contemporary, even commonplace, subject and sublimate it by giving it a mythologizing or quasi-mythological treatment." On July 24, 1922, he wrote Tate, "I am trying to capture the elusive thing you are always getting into your poems." His chief fault, he felt, "is largely due to restraint" and in "saying the pat obvious thing." In a deliberate attempt to attain the effect achieved by "dressing up one experience by using the language of another," he wrote in the summer and fall of 1922 a series of poems: "Corymba," "Dryad," "Naiad," "Avalon" and "The Wolf." In these poems, which Allen Tate thought were among the best Davidson ever wrote, Davidson tries to control their form in order to exclude the excesses of imagery and diction characteristic of his earliest verse. He strives for simplicity of execution. His approach is indirect; his intentions more deliberately poetic; his tone more consciously ironic. He attempts, as he wrote Tate, "to combine a certain satiric touch, a hardness of texture with lyrical beauty."

By 1925, however, Davidson had discovered that the kind of poetry he wanted to write was not the brief lyrics that could be published in the limited space of a small journal like the *Fugitive*. He had concluded, as Louise Cowan has noted, that he no longer wished to be a "detached observer of society, isolated from it." He felt that he must be with society, not against it. "The South," he wrote his publisher, Houghton, Mifflin, in 1927, "has arrived at a crisis. It has always possessed great individuality which under modern influences it runs a great risk of losing. To retain its spiritual entity the South . . . must become conscious of its past and not repudiate whatever is worth saving in its tradition." Davidson's artistic problem, as he saw it, was twofold. First, he had to identify those elements that are traditionally his as Southerner; then, he had to suggest a way to preserve them.

Since mid-1925 he had been working on a ten-part poem (later reduced to nine) in which, as he expressed it, he wished "to name, to set apart from time / One sudden face, built from clay and spittle." This persona bears a close resemblance to Davidson, who had grown up in several small towns of middle Tennessee. The unifying metaphor of the poem is that of the protagonist's march down a long street searching for his past. He finds the dust of battles, bones "rotting with antique lace," tales of old men, silk gowns "crumbling in attics," hunting shirts, Bibles, ruffled shirts "of gentlemen in forgotten graves." Wherever he goes the protagonist is haunted by reflections of his past. He moves from "the tall men," the pioneers who settled Tennessee, through the tragic days of the Civil War and Reconstruction, to World War I (when former enemies fought a common foe), and, finally, returns to the post–World War I world. Immediately he finds everything drastically changed. As he seeks a means of earning a living, he is struck by the fact that his world is controlled by acquisitive materialism. Only in the company of his new bride does he find aim and purpose in modern living.

The book-length poem ends with "Epilogue: Fire on Belmont Street," in which, as he wrote John Hall Wheelock on February 4, 1949, he wished to emphasize "that modern science . . . [is] willing to go to any lengths of destructiveness which modern business . . . [will] subsidize or for which modern liberals . . . [can] get up slick excuses." He was committed to a poetry and to social and political attitudes completely foreign to the "closed circle of the Fugitives." The direction of his artistic future—including *I'll Take My Stand* (1930), *Lee in the Mountains and Other Poems* (1938), and *The Attack on Leviathan* (1938)—was irretrievably fixed with the creation and publication of *The Tall Men*. Poem after poem in *Lee in the Mountains and Other Poems* expresses Davidson's Agrarian views. In "Aunt Maria and the Gourds," "The Last Charge," and "Randall, My Son," he utters a prophecy of doom for the modern industrial society. The title poem in this volume, surely Davidson's best-known poem, demonstrates how Lee in the period from 1865 to 1870 illustrates a "living tradition," a heritage of "heroism and humanism." The poem is Davidson's best because it is his least didactic. He does not plead Lee's case; he allows it to rest on its merits. During the period covered by the poem Lee is constantly piqued by an insoluble problem. Did he surrender too quickly? Should he have taken his army to the mountains and continued to fight until the enemy wanted peace badly enough to offer reasonable terms of surrender? Although the physical surrender at Appomattox was honorable, the conditions he must now submit to are not. He is "alone / Trapped, consenting, taken at last in the mountains"; now he must "surrender all." Although he now has neither arms nor men, he has knowledge, and he knows he must struggle continuously to keep from surrendering his dignity as a human being. He is fighting the most demanding battle of his career. Davidson's last two books of poetry were *The Long Street* (1961) and *Poems: 1922–1961* (1966).

The background that Allen Tate (1899–1978) brought to the Fugitive group was different from that of Ransom and Davidson. He did not grow up in the small towns and villages of middle Tennessee as they did. Born in Winchester, Kentucky, Tate was descended on his mother's side from Virginia gentry. His father, an unsuccessful businessman, moved his family from place to place until finally he relinquished his position as family provider to his oldest son, Benjamin. Allen accompanied his mother to Washington; Fairfax County, Virginia; and the many famous watering places in the area. His childhood was one of loneliness, of recognizing his vast difference in interests and inclinations from his contemporaries. As a consequence of his sporadic attendance at many different schools and his attitude toward the ones he attended, his early education was uneven. A voracious reader with an inquisitive and far-reaching mind, by the time he entered Vanderbilt in 1919 he was aware of the modern movements in English, French, and American literature and philosophy. His training in mathematics, however, was so meager that he had to employ a tutor to prepare him for the exacting examination required for admission to Vanderbilt.

His performance in his English classes and his contributions to the campus literary magazine brought him in the fall of 1921 an invitation to the fortnightly meetings of the Fugitives. There is little evidence to indicate that Tate seriously thought of any career other than literature after "To Intellectual Detachment" and "Sinbad" appeared in the *Fugitive* for April, 1922. Although he was not in Nashville during the entire period in which the *Fugitive* was published, an issue of the magazine seldom appeared without including at least one of his poems. Little of his mature poetry, however, appeared in the magazine. He was a young man still learning his art and searching for his subject. Nevertheless, with the exception of Ransom's, the most interesting poems published in the *Fugitive* were Allen Tate's. He was an inveterate experimenter, both in subject and technique.

Vanderbilt offered him exactly the kind of intellectual environment he needed for the development of his literary talent, and he gave to a small circle of poets just beginning their careers fully as much as he received. He confirmed the dignity of the profession of letters and the potentialities of literature as a legitimate mode of dealing with human experience. The poetry he wrote at Vanderbilt was for the most part, if not amateurish, at least experimental. Much of his verse did have verbal audacity and genuine poetic excitement, but the language is usually more brilliant and daring than the situation merits.

What Ransom objected to most in Tate's early verse was that its structure was never clearly developed and even its rich texture seldom contained a coherent pattern of imagery. The poetry he contributed to the *Fugitive* was so displeasing to Tate that he included only one piece in a book until he brought out the *Collected Poems* (1978). That poem, "Horatian Epode to the Duchess of Malfi," appeared in the *Fugitive* for October, 1922, and shows the influence of both Ransom and Eliot. It treats a favorite theme of Ransom's, the fleetingness of youthful beauty and energy. Like Ransom, too, Tate attempts to achieve a specific effect through the use of obscure Latinate language. The duchess, stricken in the prime of life, has no more chance of personal immortality than an "infusorian / Lodged in the hollow molar of an eohippus." This obviously naturalistic attitude toward death is explored through the remainder of the poem. Tate's treatment of his theme lacks Ransom's ambiguity. The use of a learned, erudite vocabulary is not playfully overstated, as Ransom's often is, for wit and irony. Tate uses *infusorian, eohippus,* and *megalith* not as circumlocutions. Instead they represent the level at which his poetic intentions can be best accomplished: he is attempting to create "emotional violence" through intellectual abstraction. He is emphasizing human mutability and the fleetingness of feminine beauty, and he wants his reader to know the change is permanent and absolute. Unlike Eliot, his emphasis is not on the theological and philosophical significance of this development but on the pain one experiences because of the spiritual disorder of the age. Treatment of this theme in later poems, such as "Seasons of the Soul" (1944), will be closer to Eliot's.

Tate's first collection of poems was *Mr. Pope and Other Poems* (1928), and the title poem, which appeared in the *Nation* for September 2, 1925, shows Tate much nearer his mature form. The poem has been variously interpreted. Radcliffe Squires believes it states a basic doctrine of Tate's poetic creed: "The nature of Pope's poetry cannot be found in the discoverable man, yet the world would have it so." M. E. Bradford suggests that the reader of poetry should not be interested in the character or personality of the author but in "the thing made," the poem. Louis D. Rubin, Jr., argues strongly that Tate was not preaching a sermon; he was writing a poem. Around a crooked tree, alive and growing, a "moral climbs"; this climbing vine, Rubin believes, is Pope's poetry, which still exists and its meaning continues to grow. "What we now see when we look for the poet" is the poetry. It will forever conceal the "grotesque shape and adorn the personality of the long-since-hidden man" who wrote the poems. In short, it would seem, Tate is insisting that it matters little why the poet wrote the poem, or the state of his health or disposition, or even how good or bad his reputation was in his day. The important thing is that which lives, the poem. It will last.

In 1925 to 1926 Tate was deeply involved in writing "Ode to the Confederate Dead," which he revised for the next ten years. (During this period he wrote two biographies: *Stonewall Jackson: The Good Soldier* [1928] and *Jefferson Davis: His Rise and Fall* [1929], as well as many of the poems that appeared in his first collection, *Mr. Pope and Other Poems.*) Although it was far from his favorite, it remains his best-known poem. While the poem carries "Ode" in its title, Tate insisted that he wrote it to demonstrate that the form is no longer accessible to the modern poet. "Fragmentary chaos" has succeeded the "active faith" of the traditional society, the poem reiterates, and try as he may, the protagonist of the poem, standing at the gate of the Confederate ceme-tery, cannot imagine that the falling leaves are the "charging soldiers" of the Confederacy who lie buried in the graves before him. He is aware of the changing seasons—he can see the falling leaves of autumn—but he has lost the faculty of explaining mystery through myth. Modern man is like a blind crab who has "energy but no purposeful world in which to use it." Like the "hound bitch / Toothless and dying" in the cellar, mod-ern man can hear the wind only. He has lost his creative imagination, the means by which he could transcend the knowledge circumscribed by reason and sensory perception.

Tate wrote several other of his best poems between 1925 and 1927 while he was in New York trying to establish himself as a man of letters. One of them was "Subway," in which he attempts to give his reaction to his metropolitan experience. Like Hart Crane, he sees the spiritless life surging under him as a terrestrial inferno, the symbol of which is the subway. The people hurrying from place to place, without aim or pur-pose, are like the residents of hell for whom there is no rest. They are forever involved in useless activity. The speaker in the poem is a mod-ern, whose life is as aimless and purposeless as the riders of the subway. He is involved in a fruitless experience, one that he does not understand and can do nothing about. He comes back into the daylight, into the common actuals of everydayness, after his brief visit "into the iron for-estries of hell," but he is no longer able to perceive of the universe in any terms except those abstractions created by the subway.

Another poem of this period is "Causerie," which Tate wrote in re-sponse to a newspaper account of a party on the stage of the Earl Car-roll Theatre during which Joyce Hawley, a chorus girl, is reported to have bathed nude in champagne. The persona of the poem is an insomniac who muses on the possibility of doing a heroic act in modern times. How unlike his Elizabethan ancestors is modern man! The heroic men of the Renaissance could not rest until "they had scanned the earth." But again, though Tate laments the lack of direction in modern life, he is both prosecutor and accused. He is one of those moderns who knows not who he is nor where he is going, except to death. Like all moderns, he sorely needs the direction that religion would give his life. What modern man misses most is the ability to sin and the hope of Resurrection. Like Joyce Hawley, modern man can be guilty only of social indiscretion.

During his two years in Europe (1928–1929 and 1930–1931) Tate's poetry gradually became more affirmative. Although he sees no easy solutions to the problems he has raised in the earlier poems, the tone of his verse seems a little less somber, and there is an occasional faint glimmer of hope as he moves toward the affirmation of the later poems. From Paris in 1929 he sent to Andrew Lytle a poem dedicated to him and entitled "Home Thoughts from Abroad." The persona of the poem is musing about his ancestors and about the fact that as an American he, unlike the European, is confronted with a lack of history. He feels he is an exile, separated from the past and cut off from a meaningful tradition. Some cultures, he speculates, "Provence, / The Renascence, the age of Pericles" move clearly into the future. Others are lost, he thinks, because they lack "poetry and statues," art and myth. The next year he published "The Cross" in the *Saturday Review of Literature*. The Christian myth, to which he is powerfully drawn, the speaker says, is available to him only as an intellectual position. He cannot accept it through faith. He realizes he is blind to the world that no longer nourishes him, but he is powerless to effect a transformation that cannot be accomplished through the reason; it must be performed by an act of the will. He needs to *see*, to *know*, but he cannot because he is spiritually blind. He cannot accept the myth through which he can know ultimate reality.

At about the same time, Tate began to think of himself in relation not only to the Southern tradition but to that of Western Europe, a particular concern central to "The Mediterranean" (1932) and "Aeneas at Washington" (1933). If modern man is to discover his sense of mission, which once anchored his life, he must repudiate the material acquisitiveness with which America is obsessed and retrace his steps with the hope of rediscovering the natural rights theory, the respect for the natural world, and the love of God that once dominated his thoughts and actions. From this point Tate moved certainly, if somewhat hesitantly, toward the affirmation of Christian principles that render to man a level of dignity toward which, from the beginning of his career, Tate had constantly aspired.

"Seasons of the Soul" (1944), which some consider Tate's best poem, is a definite step toward the affirmation Tate had sought for twenty years or more. The poem is divided into four sections of sixty lines, each section having six stanzas. Each section bears the title of a season of the year and each carries connotations of one of the four elements of ancient natural philosophy. Summer corresponds to air, autumn to earth, winter to water, and spring to fire. Together the four sections may be considered a spiritual autobiography of modern man.

At his death in 1978 Tate had completed only three parts of a proposed nine-part poem. All of the completed poems—"The Maimed Man" (1952), "The Buried Lake" (1953), and "The Swimmers" (1952)—are in terza rima, and Tate stated publicly his intention of writing the entire poem in this form. He ended his career where he began it, with a desire to see, but to see beyond the bounds of pure perception so that he might know metaphysical reality.

Few modern poets have written poems that are as difficult to penetrate as Tate's. The opaqueness of the poetry is in part due to the difficulty of the ideas. Evil permeates the poems, and it is of a kind that cannot be removed by social reformation. Those living in the present must suffer for the evil committed by those who preceded them. One must forever confront the consequence of impaired human faculties. Not only are these ideas difficult for the modern reader to accept, but they are always presented in a highly intellectualized frame of reference, usually embedded in obscure, esoteric, and apparently unrelated images clustered in the rich texture of the poem. The style is elliptical but powerful, allusive and witty, tantalizingly flavored with a maze of metaphysical metaphors and religious imagery. Although Tate published a dozen or more books of poems over a period of fifty-odd years, all the poems he wished to preserve are included in Collected Poems (1978).

Two other poets should be included in a consideration of the Fugitive group: Merrill Moore (1903–1957) who for a time was closely associated with the Fugitives, and John Peale Bishop (1892–1944) whose career was obviously influenced by his friendship with Allen Tate. Merrill Moore was born in Columbia, Tennessee, the son of John Trotwood Moore, writer, editor, and state librarian. After attending Montgomery Bell Academy, Moore entered Vanderbilt University in 1920 and joined the Fugitive group two years later. He contributed prolifically to the Fugitive during the years of its publication. Many years later Donald Davidson observed that Moore, unlike the other Fugitives, never revised a poem in the light of the criticism he received after he had read it at a Fugitive meeting. He merely went home and wrote four or five new ones. He wrote so facilely and with so little apparent expenditure of energy that Ransom once remarked that he came as near writing "automatic poetry" as anyone he had ever seen. Davidson attributed Moore's fertility in the composition of verse to the fact that his "poems tended to be mere observations of the phenomenal aspects of life, unaccompanied by judgments." Although he was graduated from the Vanderbilt Medical School and studied psychiatry with Dr. William Herman and Dr. Hanns Sachs, and later taught psychiatry at the Harvard Medical School—at the same time carrying on a demanding private practice—he continued to write poetry. In his lifetime he is reputed to have written fifty thousand sonnets, though many of them have few characteristics of a conventional sonnet except the usual fourteen lines. His best poems, according to Tate, "have a flavor, an ease and a subtlety of statement which give them a definite place in contemporary verse."

John Peale Bishop was born in Charles Town, West Virginia. His father, for whom he was named, was a physician from the Connecticut Valley who died when Bishop was nine years old. His mother's family roots were Southern. Throughout his life Bishop's attachments to the South manifested themselves in many ways. In subject matter and setting, almost all his fiction and much of his poetry focus on the South. Yet he lived much of his adult life on Cape Cod. Although the best of Bishop's work does not constitute a large body of material, two dozen of the poems from *Now With His Love* (1933) and *Minute Particulars* (1935), the novel *Act of Darkness* (1935), and a dozen of the essays from *Collected Essays* (1948) deserve a wider audience than they have received.

Few modern readers would agree with Edmund Wilson's assessment of Bishop's poetry. "The verse of John Peale Bishop is probably the *finest* poetic instrument that we have had in the United States since Pound and Eliot left. Trained in the great tradition of European poetry, his ear has a delicacy and a precision which elsewhere have hardly survived." This estimate, enhanced by Wilson's friendship for Bishop, is clearly inflated. On the other hand, most readers of modern poetry would disagree with R. W. Stallman's observation that "Bishop's poetry is the collective catch-all of the chief fashions which his age made current." Too often Bishop's verse has been dismissed as being derivative, his manner and his matter being mere pale imitations of the French Symbolists, Eliot, Pound, and Yeats.

His verse is always sensual and often sensuous in its affirmation of physical passion. More than a dozen lyrics (his entire canon comprises less than 125 finished poems) deal frankly with sex, such as in "Les Balcons Qui Rêvent," which contains these lines:

> The lovers sleep, their dreams increased
> By shudders from the night before.
> His breath upon his parted lips,
> Sleeping he flows into her sleep.
> Her belly slumbers, but the tips
> Of both dusk breasts are bright awake.

Structurally, his poems are superior works of art. Typically he uses a two-part structure employing either contrasting symbols or a scene followed by elaboration on its meaning. The latter is the method of "The Ancestors," which he wrote as a companion piece to Tate's poem by the same title. The first two stanzas portray a scene and suggest a mood that is extended and explained by the last two. The opening lines

> The house leaks and leans. Night's roof-timbers glut
> To rain on those wide planks the dead have thinned
> With their loud feet

lead into a controlled symbolic meditation on the collapse of tradition, concluding with the ironic exclamation: "What calm to send the mind on the stone ease / Of passions ruining in the sculptured tomb!"

Bishop's finest and most sustained poem is his elegy on the death of F. Scott Fitzgerald, "The Hours." Along with two dozen or so other poems, it deserves more attention than it has received to date. In addition to their own merit, these poems are important indications of the range of poetic styles in vogue during the twenties and thirties.

William Faulkner

Although the hill country of north Mississippi in the waning years of the nineteenth century would seem to promise a prospective novelist meager cultural and literary nourishment, Faulkner was actually most fortunate in the place of his birth. That countryside was to prove rich in the very materials his genius required. The specific place of his birth was the little county-seat town of New Albany, but before he was five, his parents had settled in another county-seat town not too far away, Oxford, in which Faulkner grew up with his three brothers, had his schooling, and which he came to regard as home for the rest of his life.

He was born on September 25, 1897, and baptized William Cuthbert Falkner—the *u* in his surname appeared only years later. He represented the fourth generation of his family in the state. His great-grandfather, William Clark Falkner, had arrived in north Mississippi as a penniless boy in about 1840 and grew up with the new country that was just opening up. Faulkner was clearly fascinated with his ancestor's character and career. In a letter to Malcolm Cowley he described his great-grandfather.

> My great-grandfather, whose name I bear, was a considerable figure in his time and provincial milieu. He was prototype of John Sartoris [an important character in *Sartoris* (1929) and *The Unvanquished* (1938)]: commanded the 2nd Mississippi infantry, etc. Was a part of Stonewall Jackson's left at Manassas that afternoon [July 21, 1861]; we have a citation in James Longstreet's longhand as his corps commander after 2nd Manassas [August 29–31, 1862]. He built the first railroad in our county, wrote a few books, made grand European tour of his time, died in a duel and the county raised a marble effigy which still stands in Tippah County.

Faulkner and his brothers played boys' games, fished, hunted, and William played football for the Oxford high school, but he did not graduate. He was, however, a voracious reader. All distinguished writers are essentially self-educated, but Faulkner's education was more self-accomplished than most. Except for French, his high school courses bored him. He did poorly even in English, and he eventually dropped out of school. Oxford was the seat of the University of Mississippi, and later on he was allowed to take some courses there, but again soon ceased attending.

He read, as one would expect, the usual things: Sir Walter Scott, *Ben Hur, Robinson Crusoe*, Dumas. But he read poetry too, and from an early age. At sixteen he was enamored of the poetry of Swinburne, and wrote fair imitations of Swinburnian verse. He read the early Yeats and the English poets of the nineties. He wrote a play echoing Oscar Wilde's *Salome* and further enhanced the *fin de siècle* atmosphere by providing illustrations reminiscent of Aubrey Beardsley's. He read the French Symbolist poets and attempted translations of Verlaine and Mallarmé.

Faulkner's romantic interests and impulses did not, however, express themselves only in literary pursuits. As World War I went on, his imagination was fired by the notion of being a fighter pilot, one of those glamorous knights of the air. Disappointed when his boyhood sweetheart, Estelle Oldham, became engaged to another man, he tried to enlist in the United States air arm, but was rejected because he was not of the required height and weight. In July, 1918, however, he was accepted by the Royal Air Force, Canada, and went to Toronto for training, though the war ended before he could be sent overseas and even before he had received flight training. Yet that circumstance did not prevent his buying a British officer's uniform, complete with swagger stick, and letting it be known that he had been wounded in combat.

Back home in Oxford, he wrote a great deal of verse and some romantic prose. Yet other elements began to make their appearance in his work; as early as 1920 he had discovered T. S. Eliot, and lifted a line from one of Eliot's less well-known poems and inserted it in one of his own. He probably owed such acquaintance with the new modernists to Phil Stone, a local attorney and friend who bought the books of the newer authors, subscribed to avant-garde magazines, and encouraged his younger friend in his effort to become a poet. It was Stone who, when Estelle Oldham was about to marry, persuaded Faulkner to leave Oxford and join him in New Haven, where Stone was studying law at Yale. It was Stone also who helped him get into the RAF. He also paid part of the publication costs of Faulkner's first book, *The Marble Faun* (1922), a long pastoral poem. The landscapes described in this poem are clearly English; there are downs and leas; the cottages are roofed with thatch; and the birds are British songsters. The young Mississippi poet had not yet learned to call his muse home.

Faulkner was not only fortunate in his place of birth. He was also fortunate in his time of birth, for a man growing up during the first two decades of the twentieth century was well aware of the older culture, which had not yet passed away, and yet alive to the new forces that were already altering that culture. Memories of the devastating war that had put an end to the Old South were still vivid. One could get firsthand accounts from Confederate veterans and elderly matriarchs who had been brought up in the older ways. But the South was at last beginning to enter the world of American industrialism and finance-capitalism. Thus, the older world helped one judge the new and vice versa. Furthermore, the so-called Southern Renascence, itself an aspect of the new modernist literary movement in Britain and America, was just gathering impetus.

The year 1925 was a most important one in the process of Faulkner's maturation. At about this time he discovered Housman's *A Shropshire Lad* and was much moved by the stoic endurance it expresses and by its celebration of a particular region—significant qualities in terms of Faulkner's own subsequent career. Housman's ironic realism was a useful ingredient in the young poet's literary diet. By this time, he had also discovered Cabell's *Jurgen*, as his own ironic retelling of a "chivalric" tale in *Mayday* amply attests. *Mayday* was a hand-lettered, illustrated, and bound booklet that he presented to Helen Baird, a young woman whom he met early in 1925 and with whom he fell deeply in love. (It was not published until 1977.) He also prepared for her a short sequence of sonnets in hand-lettered format like *Mayday* (published in 1981 as part of *Helen: A Courtship and Mississippi Poems*).

The love affair was a hopeless one, but the poetry (perhaps as a consequence) is the best that Faulkner ever wrote. It may also be the last that he ever wrote, for though in 1933 he published a collection of verse entitled *A Green Bough*, the poems it contains were written much earlier. Henceforth Faulkner committed himself to prose. Later he would call himself a failed poet, but the phrase is too deprecatory. His true poetry is to be found in some of the more rhapsodic passages of his novels.

Faulkner spent the first half of 1925 in New Orleans. To a young man reared in a Protestant, even Puritanic culture, New Orleans, with its French-Spanish atmosphere and its charming relaxed ways, was a revelation and an intense stimulation. In New Orleans he met and was befriended by Sherwood Anderson and other writers and artists of the French Quarter. In July, in company with the young architect Bill Spratling, he embarked on a freighter for Genoa. Thence he walked through Switzerland and France to Paris, where he remained except for a brief trip to England. By December he was back home in Oxford.

During the first half of 1925 Faulkner was occupied with his first novel, *Soldiers' Pay*, published in 1926. It is a novel of postwar disillusionment and reflects the themes and mood of *The Waste Land*, though the young author never lapses into abstract philosophizing but sets the story firmly in a cultural environment that he knew firsthand. By this time Faulkner had evidently read Joyce and was well acquainted with *Ulysses*, stylistic devices from which turn up in Faulkner's second novel, *Mosquitoes* (1927).

In 1929 he published *Sartoris*, a condensed version of a novel to be published in 1972 in its full dimension as *Flags in the Dust*. With *Sartoris*, Faulkner first enters into his Yoknapatawpha County and initiates his great creative period—1929 through 1942—in which he published eleven novels, seven of them reckoned to be his masterpieces. Although Yoknapatawpha, with Jefferson as its county seat, exists on no map of Mississippi, it is clearly modeled upon the geographical and cultural area in which Faulkner had grown up. It provided its creator with literary material beautifully apt to his developing purposes. The population was richly diverse: old plantation families, some of them still living on their lands, others having moved into town; the poorer whites, many of them sturdy yeoman farmers, but others landless who worked farms on shares with the owners; still others the "white trash," looked down upon by the blacks as well as the other whites.

The land was still important, the number of shopkeepers and mechanics still small, though growing. Jefferson had the usual complement of physicians and lawyers, many of them coming from the old gentry. The number of clergy, all Protestant, was large and diverse, representing a half-dozen or more religious denominations. Last, there were the many blacks, most of them still on the land, but some with various kinds of jobs in town, many of them working as household servants.

The action of *Sartoris* occurs in 1918 to 1920. As in *Soldier's Pay*, the young men have just returned from World War I. Horace Benbow is romantic, dreamy, arty, introspective, and a failed poet who writes a mannered prose in the style of the nineties. Young Bayard Sartoris is also a romantic, but of another order. He is the man of action, high-spirited, daring, even foolhardy; he had been (what Faulkner himself had endeavored to become) a fighter pilot in the RAF. Bayard can find no activity in which he can fulfill himself in the slow-moving, traditional community to which he has now returned. Neither can Horace find any fulfilling life. Both men have been disastrously uprooted. In this novel it is plain that Faulkner has not given up his interest in the romantic, though he is now able to hold the problem at arm's length and view it with detachment.

If *Sartoris* sprawls a bit, a second novel published in 1929, *The Sound and the Fury*, is beautifully, though intricately, structured. The story of the Compsons comes to us through three stream-of-consciousness sequences taken from the minds of the three Compson brothers: Benjy, retarded to the threshold of idiocy; Quentin, another vulnerable, idealistic romantic; and Jason, the crass, would-be rationalist. Only in the last section, related by the author speaking in the third person, does the reader come upon an objective world.

Faulkner's interest in the young male as romantic continues in *As I Lay Dying* (1930), a brilliant novel, again presented through interior monologues of each of the several characters. Darl Bundren, who breaks down into madness as the novel ends, is the poetic dreamer, ineffectual as a man of action, but with a poet's insights. Darl's brother Jewel, like Bayard Sartoris, is unreflective and impulsive. He can and does achieve heroic feats of action. Another brother, Cash, is patient, methodical, uncomplaining. Dewey Dell, their sister, is instinctive womanhood. The youngest brother, Vardaman, is the typical young child. He will presumably grow up, whereas Benjy Compson has been locked into permanent childhood.

With these two novels Faulkner had made a brilliant beginning in his literary career, but his novels did not have a wide commercial appeal. As a bachelor, he could make do, but in 1930 his financial problems became pressing; on June 21 he and Estelle Oldham Franklin were married. She had returned to Oxford, divorced and with two young children. To Faulkner she was to bear two children, a little girl who died in early infancy, and Jill (now Jill Faulkner Summers), who became her father's literary executor. Faulkner's marriage did not prove to be a particularly happy one for either partner, though no divorce occurred. Yeats would have described Faulkner's literary triumphs as emerging from a sense of deprivation and loss. But then he might have added that such were the springs of his own creativity—and that of Dante! There were worse fates. It was at this time also that Faulkner purchased an antebellum house on the edge of Oxford. He made repairs, restored it, and renamed it Rowan Oak. The old house gave him great satisfaction, but it obviously added to his financial burdens.

Sanctuary (1931) had a kind of *succès de scandale* and as such enjoyed rather good sales. But Faulkner's financial anxieties were chronic, right on through the period in which he was producing his masterpieces. Those financial pressures drove him to Hollywood, where over a period of years he worked as a scriptwriter for months at a time.

The reputation of *Sanctuary* has suffered from Faulkner's having stated frankly that he wrote a horrifying tale in order to make money.

Regardless of the reasons for its creation, *Sanctuary* contains some of his most powerful writing. As for its moral import, it is neither frivolous nor cynical, for it has to do finally with the need to confront and admit the fact of evil. Nor did Faulkner depart from the concerns that characterized his earlier work. In this novel he has Horace Benbow, the dreamy idealist, suffer his final comeuppance in his shattering discovery of the depth and power of evil.

Thus, the romantic-idealist, whether the contemplative or the rebel against society, continued to fascinate Faulkner. We see versions of him in the defrocked clergyman Gail Hightower (*Light in August* [1932]); a more sympathetic example in Isaac McCaslin (*Go Down, Moses* [1942]); even in the powerful and ruthless Thomas Sutpen (*Absalom, Absalom!* [1936]), who never loses what General Compson terms his innocence, refuses to accept the limits that are imposed on humankind, and finally destroys his children and himself in his effort to achieve his great dream of founding a dynasty.

In a more purely romantic aspect, Harry Wilbourne (*The Wild Palms* [1939]) and his paramour, Charlotte Rittenmeyer, achieve the most desperate commitment of all: making no concessions to the demands of society or even of their own flesh, they vow to keep their relationship at the intensity of one long honeymoon. In its idealistic aspect, the simple Christ-like corporal of *A Fable* (1954) represents a commitment of the same absolute sort.

Faulkner remained enough of a romanticist himself to accord his romantic characters full dramatic sympathy. A few of them learn to accept reality and their own limitations without turning into cynics or, like Quentin Compson, taking their own lives. Nor do all his idealists suffer defeat. Old Bayard Sartoris (in *The Unvanquished*) at the age of twenty-four wins a victory over himself and a moral victory over the prejudices of the community of which he feels himself a part. Yet in spite of his sympathy for the romantic rebel struggling to achieve his proper individuality, Faulkner is careful to provide his rebels with something solid to strive against—no faceless abstraction, no gray *anomie*, no mere impersonal system. The opposition is composed of believable human beings, and human beings who are not necessarily stupid or vicious.

Such provision for a real clash of wills obviously makes for more intense drama; but Faulkner evidently had in mind more than increased dramatic tension. He accepted the necessity of life in a community if human beings were to lead full lives. As a citizen of Oxford, Faulkner at various times quarreled with his own community—over its attempt to prohibit the sale of beer and over far more serious issues such as civil rights and the desegregation of the public schools. But his story "Golden

Land" depicts the horrifying emptiness of a society, which may be defined as a collection of people bound together merely by ties of economic convenience and utility (a *gesellschaft*). A true community (a *gemeinschaft*) is held together by manners and morals deriving from a commonly held view of reality. The common values that bind a given community may be defective, even wrongheaded. In such case, all praise to the individual who tries to amend them. Faulkner provides such an instance at the conclusion of *The Unvanquished*. But a sense of community is in itself good, and the absence of all sense of community is a serious loss.

In that view, Faulkner joins himself with other serious representatives of Western culture. The growing feeling of alienation, of isolation, of being homeless even among one's own people, has become a prominent theme in contemporary literature. Faulkner's Horace Benbow, young Bayard, Quentin Compson, the barnstorming stunt flyers of *Pylon*, and, most clearly of all, Joe Christmas of *Light in August* are alienated men.

Joe Christmas is cut off from any community, black or white; he has tried and rejected both. He is cut off from womankind and from nature itself. In his lonely defiance of the world at large and his insistence on his own independence, he exhibits qualities of nobility; but his is a desperate quest. One cannot kick the very earth out from under one's feet. By contrast, in the same novel Lena Grove, a young woman with absolutely no resources, makes her way into Jefferson in the course of an equally ridiculous quest—to find the father of her soon-to-be-born child. But Lena is not alienated; she seems to feel completely at home in the strange town. Almost effortlessly she finds her protector and, though with a certain rolling of eyes and pursing of lips among the respectable women, the community accepts her.

Lena is not exceptional among Faulkner's female characters. Faulkner had his special notions about women. They were instinctively wiser than men. They viewed with almost amused contempt the codes of honor and the facades of rationality behind which men lived. They were closer than men to nature and the instinctual life. As a consequence, they were the great sustaining forces in a family or a civilization, displayed by the black women Dilsey and Molly Beauchamp and, among the whites, by such matriarchs as Miss Rosa Millard and Aunt Jenny DuPre. Rarely does Faulkner depict one of his women characters agonizing over a decision. They usually know at once what is to be done. What Faulkner stresses in his novels is their power to nurture, to sustain, and to hold steadfast. If this view of women is old-fashioned, so be it. Faulkner was in many ways an old-fashioned man and wrote about an old-fashioned society.

339

In any case, his women characters are memorable: Eula Varner, the earth goddess; Lena Grove, instinctive wisdom masked as simplicity; Candance Compson (with whom Faulkner confessed he was in love), who for all her misfortunes remained a whole person as none of her brothers could be; Joanna Burden, warped by her upbringing as sadly as was her paramour, Joe Christmas, but resolute to the end. And if one is to find the most admirable character in Faulkner's great novel *Absalom, Absalom!*, it is surely Judith Sutpen, who inherits her father's iron will but, unlike him, is not ruthless but compassionate.

Thus, it is Faulkner's men who tend to be the romantics, rarely the women. And since women seem to know from the first what they are, they do not have to go through the rites of passage demanded of every young man. The specific subject matter of at least three of Faulkner's novels is precisely this process of growing up. Each of the following may be regarded as a typical bildungsroman: *The Unvanquished, Go Down, Moses*, and *The Reivers* (1962). Without too much exaggeration, one might claim that most of Faulkner's failed and defeated characters are men who somehow failed to grow up.

The case of Gavin Stevens, the resident intellectual of Yoknapatawpha County, calls for special comment. He is a romantic-idealist, and Faulkner subjects him to a number of comic pratfalls, but no tragic defeat. Faulkner is amused by some of his romantic delusions (see *The Town* [1957]) and his rather quixotic idealism. But then Don Quixote, Faulkner has told us, was one of his favorite characters.

The horizontal ties that knit together the community of a particular time find a counterpart in vertical ties that bind a community back to its past. Yoknapatawpha has a history of its own, one handed down through oral tradition from generation to generation. Experiences, memories, attitudes, values, are part of its heritage. To Faulkner, the past was also important. He has more than one of his characters declare that the past was not really *past*. The past was alive in the present. Indeed, the present had to be understood as an extension of the past. For the individual human being the past may be a powerful resource or a crippling burden, as it proves to be for Gail Hightower or Quentin Compson, but it cannot be simply dismissed.

Several of Faulkner's novels deal specifically with a period in the past. *The Unvanquished* and *Absalom, Absalom!* are examples. Yet even those novels are not mere costume extravaganzas with stock characters decked out in antebellum dress. In *Absalom, Absalom!*, for example, Quentin Compson, a young man of the twentieth century, is trying to make sense of what happened fifty and more years earlier, and clearly he applies the issues involved to himself. In 1865 Henry Sutpen had taken the desperate expedient of killing his best friend, a murder which was also a fratricide, in order to defend his sister's honor. Quentin is conscious of having utterly failed in trying to defend his own sister's honor.

Shreve, Quentin's Harvard roommate, may regard their discussion of this terrible episode in the faraway past of a faraway region as no more than an evening's diversion—melodramatic deeds enacted by rather grotesque people. Now that the curtain has rung down, the exciting story read through, one can leave the theater or put the book aside. But the story of the Sutpens touches Quentin to the quick. He cannot shake off the experience. Lest we put down Faulkner's preoccupation with past history to a nostalgic yearning for the Old South, we should reflect that international figures of the caliber of Pound, Eliot, and Yeats have also been much concerned with the past as a necessary means for understanding and coming to terms with our disordered present and our perilous future.

Faulkner was a master of the short story. "Red Leaves," "That Evening Sun," "Mountain Victory," and even the early "A Rose for Emily" are among the most accomplished short stories in modern fiction. If we add to these some easily detachable sequences from Faulkner's two most episodic novels (*The Unvanquished* and *Go Down, Moses*) such as "The Old People," "An Odor of Verbena," and "Pantaloon in Black," Faulkner's ability to handle short fiction becomes plain. Yet he also produced a great many stories to sell to popular magazines in order to make a living during the long period in which his masterpieces did not sell. Some of these stories are mediocre; a few, clearly mere potboilers.

Faulkner wrote five novels that have their setting outside Yoknapatawpha County—actually only four, for *Soldier's Pay*, though its formal setting is a little Georgia town, makes use of small-town Southern material. Of the four, only *The Wild Palms* has any claim to greatness. Much of Faulkner's effort, and some magnificent writing, went into *A Fable* (1954), but most qualified judges regard it as at best a splendid failure.

Although a few critics in this country and in France had, from the beginning, regarded Faulkner as a great literary artist, he had little general public appeal. The appearance of Malcolm Cowley's *The Portable Faulkner* in 1946 and Robert Penn Warren's intelligent and enthusiastic review of Cowley's introduction to it did much to call attention to Faulkner's true stature. The award of the Nobel Prize in 1950 set the seal of international approval on his work. So the last decade of his life saw him loaded with honors from every quarter. He died on July 6, 1962.

Faulkner profited enormously from using his local material. It provided him with an excellent means for presenting the characteristic problems of modern man living in a world of drastic change; yet at the same time it gave him an opportunity to insist upon what he regarded as the eternal truths about the age-old and essentially unchanging human predicament. Employing his native materials, he found that he could stay home and yet touch upon universal issues.

Although Faulkner's world view was essentially traditional, and though he usually referred to himself as just a storyteller, his formal and technical strategies are exciting. He experimented boldly and tirelessly, and, far more often than not, successfully. His special quality is variety and plenitude. For instance, he is one of America's great comic writers, but again and again he attains the dignity and intensity of tragedy. He has provided us with many fine and subtle psychological studies, but he also poured out a profusion of characters, vividly portrayed yet often struck off in the brief compass of two or three hundred words. He had fully absorbed the oral tradition from tales told around a hunter's campfire or yarns heard on the front porch of a country store. Yet he also dared to venture high-flown rhetoric—flamboyant language, rich cadences, and elaborate imagery. He is an original. There is no one else quite like him in American literature. His place in the canon is secure.

LOUIS D. RUBIN, JR.

Thomas Wolfe

Whatever the year 1929 brought to the South and the nation in the way of economic debacle, for Southern literature it was nothing less than an *annus mirabilis*. William Faulkner published *Sartoris* and *The Sound and the Fury*. There were new books by Ellen Glasgow, James Branch Cabell, DuBose Heyward, T. S. Stribling, Allen Tate, and Stark Young. Among authors publishing their first books were Robert Penn Warren, Erskine Caldwell, Hamilton Basso, Merrill Moore, and Thomas Wolfe.

Of all these writers, none seemed more promising than Wolfe. His first novel, *Look Homeward, Angel*, not only received extremely good reviews, but it appeared to constitute an unusually favorable augury for the future of Southern writing. Stringfellow Barr wrote in the *Virginia Quarterly Review* that "it is the South's first contribution to world literature." In London the *Times Literary Supplement* asked, "What is going to be done with this great talent, so hard, so sensual, so easily comprehending and describing every sordidness of the flesh and spirit, so proudly riding to the heights?" And when Sinclair Lewis received the Nobel Prize in literature he informed his audience in Stockholm that *Look Homeward, Angel* was "worthy to be compared with the best in our literary production, a Gargantuan creature with great gusto of life."

While literary historians might agree nowadays that it was the publication of the first two Yoknapatawpha County novels of Faulkner, far more than the appearance of *Look Homeward, Angel*, that makes 1929 so momentous a date in Southern literature, there can be little doubt that Thomas Wolfe's advent onto the literary scene, at the age of twenty-nine, was an event of magnitude. If Wolfe's critical reputation, always rather ambiguous even when his fiction was at the height of its popularity during the late 1930s and the 1940s, is somewhat clouded, his novels do not lack readers. And if his relationship to the literary Renascence that his generation of Southern writers created seems in certain significant respects to be different from that of almost all his contemporaries, nonetheless it is impossible to comprehend his life and work without keeping in mind his strong ties to the twentieth-century Southern community.

Wolfe was born in Asheville, North Carolina, October 3, 1900, the youngest child of Julia Elizabeth Westall and William Oliver Wolfe. The Westalls were a North Carolina mountain family of many generations' standing, while W. O. Wolfe was a Pennsylvania-born stonemason who came to Asheville in the 1880s. The Wolfes were not among the town's elite; in his fiction Wolfe makes much of their lower-middle-class status and the ambivalence of their social position. As readers of the highly autobiographical fiction know, the family life was often turbulent. W. O. Wolfe went on periodic alcoholic binges. In 1906 Mrs. Wolfe purchased a boardinghouse, the Old Kentucky Home, with her youngest son thereafter dividing his time between it and the family home on Woodson Street.

In 1912 Wolfe was enrolled in a private school, the North State Fitting School, where the woman he called the "mother of my spirit," Margaret Roberts, encouraged his literary interests. Four years later, in 1916, while still fifteen years old, he entered the University of North Carolina at Chapel Hill. There he played a prominent role in campus affairs, debating, contributing to the campus newspaper and the literary magazine, and writing plays for Frederick H. Koch's Carolina Playmakers workshop. Upon his graduation in 1920 his mother sent him to Harvard University to study playwriting in George Pierce Baker's famous 47 Workshop. He stayed for three years, writing two full-length plays, Welcome to Our City (published for the first time in 1983) and Mannerhouse (published in 1948). He also earned a master's degree in English; one of his teachers was John Livingston Lowes, whose lectures on the English romantic poets thereafter constituted a strong influence on Wolfe's thought and art.

Bent upon becoming a playwright, Wolfe secured an instructorship at Washington Square College of New York University and submitted his plays to various Broadway producers, but without success. After his first year of teaching he went to England and France. Meanwhile he had begun to try his hand at prose fiction. It was on the return voyage, in September of 1925, that he met Aline Bernstein, a wealthy stage designer. In the several years that followed, she encouraged and helped him as he began the novel that was to be Look Homeward, Angel. The Esther Jack of the later Wolfe fiction, she was fifteen years older than Wolfe, was married and with grown children, and was Jewish. It was a tumultuous affair, with repeated quarreling and reconciliations. Wolfe

soon grew to envy and resent the fashionable and sophisticated metropolitan theatrical and literary set of which Mrs. Bernstein was a part,
and his provincial xenophobia came to the fore. His novel, provisionally
titled "O! Lost!," was going the rounds of the publishing houses, and
Wolfe took each rejection hard. He was away in Europe when Maxwell
Perkins, the senior editor at Charles Scribner's Sons, read and was impressed with the manuscript, and upon Wolfe's return home in January,
1929, Scribner's offered him a contract. *Look Homeward, Angel* was
released on October 18 of that year.

The novel received generally favorable reviews and sold steadily,
though not sensationally. The reaction in Wolfe's home city of Asheville
was violent; the autobiographical nature of the work, its evocation of
the everyday and familiar, only intensified its realistic depiction of much
that was unsavory and unflattering in community life. Asheville was not
accustomed to being made into the locale of twentieth-century-style realistic fiction. Wolfe's college friend Jonathan Daniels, writing in the
Raleigh *News and Observer*, remarked that "North Carolina, and the
South are spat upon." Wolfe received threatening letters, and close
friends such as Margaret Roberts were bewildered and hurt by his depiction of them and their families. His own family, however, stuck
by him.

That Wolfe was paying off some old scores in *Look Homeward, Angel* is beyond doubt. Yet the matter is not so easily disposed of as that.
The depiction of the town of Altamont and the mountain country of
North Carolina, seen through the eyes of the child and youth Eugene
Gant from an aesthetic perspective of autobiographical recall, is rich in
remembered life and detail, with much that is admiring. For good and
for ill Wolfe was striving to recreate a time and a place as he remembered it; that the picture thus rendered might often be unflattering did
not matter nearly as much to him as that it convey the emotional intensity of his attitude toward it. To describe, to delineate in detail, was an
act of repossession.

Look Homeward, Angel is a novel of growth; the protagonist is born
into a Southern family and community, experiences childhood and
youth, goes away to college, and at the end is preparing to leave for the
North. Along with the developing personality of Eugene Gant there are
characterizations of his mother, his father, his brothers Ben, Steve, and
Luke, and his sister Helen. The process chronicled is that of estrangement and loss in time. The death of Ben severs the last tie that fastens
Eugene to Altamont and the family. Yet at the same time the story is
being told by a remembering narrator whose recreation of his earlier

experience invests family and setting, people and place with dignity and vitality, so that if at the close Eugene Gant is ready to put Altamont behind him forever, clearly the autobiographical author has taken the community right along with him.

In 1930, following publication of the novel and its growing success, Wolfe gave up his teaching job at Washington Square College, broke off with Aline Bernstein, and went to Europe again. He returned the next year, settled in Brooklyn, and sought to begin a second novel. The process was arduous and often painful, with many false starts. It was Maxwell Perkins' belief that *Look Homeward, Angel* must be followed by another novel equally as large and imposing, and Wolfe, whose emotional dependence on Perkins was very strong, agreed with the view, even though the literary form that seemed to come naturally to him was the novella, or short novel of from fifteen thousand to thirty thousand words. During 1933 and 1934 Wolfe and his editor worked to put together a novel, with Wolfe writing transitional scenes and passages to knit together the various episodes. Most of the manuscript was originally written as first-person narrative, about an autobiographical protagonist named David Hawke. Perkins convinced Wolfe that what he had written was the continuation of Eugene Gant's story, and should be published with that name and in the same third-person narrative form as *Look Homeward, Angel.* He also persuaded Wolfe that a great deal of the material describing Wolfe's life in the late 1920s and the early 1930s should be kept for another novel.

In the summer of 1934 Wolfe went out to Chicago to see the world's fair, and when he returned was told that the manuscript had been sent to the printer. Although irate because he wanted to work his book over and give it greater unity and cohesion, eventually he acquiesced in Perkins' belief that the process of revision had to be brought to a halt or it would never be concluded. *Of Time and the River,* subtitled *A Legend of Man's Hunger in His Youth,* was published on March 8, 1935. It was prefaced by a fervent dedication to Perkins. The novel received many glowing reviews, and also some that were highly critical. It made the best-seller lists, and its author was now a famous man. In the autumn of 1935 Scribner's published a collection of some of Wolfe's shorter pieces, *From Death to Morning.*

In a little book, *The Story of a Novel* (1936), based on lectures that he gave at the University of Colorado Writer's Conference in the summer of 1935, Wolfe has described the process of writing *Of Time and the River.* He saw the book as an account of "man's search to find a father, not merely the lost father of his youth, but the image of a strength and wisdom external to his need and superior to his hunger, to which the belief and power of his own life could be united." Apparently Wolfe himself never fully understood what the novel was about; its development is much more specific than that, and involves not so much a search for a father figure (if anything, it is a mother figure who was being sought) as for a perspective from which he could view his experience artistically.

Eugene Gant at the outset of the novel is in full flight from his mother's world and his middle-class Southern community and social situation. He goes to Harvard and the dramatic workshop, but is repelled by the mannered artificiality, the fashionable avoidance of everyday American experience as being not sufficiently artistic. In New York City, as a teacher and would-be playwright, he finds real life enough and to spare, but he feels lost in the massive impersonality of the metropolis and is unable to write. (The provincial antisemitism of this section in particular often shows Wolfe at his least attractive; as he remarked later, he had to learn everything the hard way.) At an estate he visits along the Hudson River he encounters the very wealthy, and perceives that rank and position mean everything there, while the talents of an artist, however successful, would count for little. He journeys to England, the fabled home of the poetry he loves, but feels himself very much an outsider. The literary life of Paris, the legendary *vie Bohème*, does not seem real at all; he is too middle-class, too American. At an estate near Orleans he encounters the authentic aristocracy of Europe, of which the country-club set back in Altamont and the money-crafted estates along the Hudson are only imitations, and finds there the same materialism, social injustice, snobbery, and insensitivity to literature that had sent him northward from Altamont.

Only after all this has taken place, and he ends up alone in the South of France, thinking of home, does he begin to discover the true lineaments of his art, the memory of "the life of twenty years ago in the quiet, leafy streets and little towns of lost America." It is then that he begins to write. In the search for lost time, the exploration of his own past, and his identity within time and change, is located the kind of artistic reality that he seeks. It will be an art grounded in history, textured by the remembrance of the past and the recreation of ordinary experience as it had been for him in his time. That, in however uneven form, is what happens in *Of Time and the River*, and it gives to a lengthy, sprawling, lyrical (sometimes to excess) novel most of its progression and meaning.

The several years that followed publication of *Of Time and the River* were a time of confusion for Wolfe. He was embroiled in several lawsuits, including one for libel, and his relations with Charles Scribner's Sons and Maxwell Perkins went into a sharp decline. Wolfe's excessive reliance upon Perkins carried with it a suppressed but implicit resentment of such dependency. When Bernard DeVoto, in a savage attack in the *Saturday Review of Literature* for April 25, 1936, entitled "Genius Is Not Enough," proclaimed *Of Time and the River* formless and adolescent, and declared that no good novelist would ever depend upon "Mr. Perkins and the assembly line at Scribner's" to shape his prose into novels for him, a break became inevitable. Various other factors were involved in the eventual termination of the tie with Scribner's, but it seems clear that it was the dependence upon Perkins that rankled most. *Of Time and the River* as published was not the book he intended; there was no escaping that.

Wolfe continued to work at a new novel, which bore various working titles. He traveled to Germany for the 1936 Olympics, and on the train trip out an incident occurred, in which a Jew attempting to flee the Nazi regime was seized by police, that made Wolfe recognize the true evil of Nazism. The novella he wrote about it, "I Have a Thing To Tell You," was published in the *New Republic*. Wolfe also, for the first time since before publication of *Look Homeward, Angel*, went home to Asheville, where he was lionized. He also began looking around for another publisher. Impressed with a young editor at Harper and Brothers, Edward C. Aswell, and an offer of a ten thousand dollar advance on royalties, in December of 1937 he signed a contract with that firm.

Wolfe was bent upon putting Eugene Gant behind him and creating a less directly autobiographical protagonist. As he worked and reworked his material the new protagonist assumed various names, but it was not long before Wolfe was back in the customary autobiographical mode. George "Monk" Webber was heavyset and simian rather than tall, and the details of his family relationships differed slightly from Eugene Gant's, but the sensibility was the same, though given to less lyrical evocation and more of a satirical thrust.

In the spring of 1938 Wolfe grouped and reshuffled the hundreds of episodes and many hundreds of thousands of words he had written into a very rough chronological order, worked out an overall outline of contents, and began revising and filling in episodes. In May he left New York to speak at Purdue University and take a vacation in the Far West. In July he was hospitalized in Seattle, Washington, brought back by train to the Johns Hopkins Hospital in Baltimore, Maryland, operated upon for tubercular infection of the brain, and he died on September 15, 1938. He was thirty-seven years old.

His literary career, however, was far from concluded. Faced with a ten thousand dollar advance royalty payment made to Wolfe by Harper and Brothers and a huge cache of manuscript that dated from the days of *Look Homeward, Angel* up to the previous spring, Edward Aswell, with the help of Perkins and Elizabeth Nowell, Wolfe's literary agent, went to work. He combined, spliced, selected, deleted, and rearranged; he changed names, scenes, descriptions; he used material from letters; he even wrote some transitional sequences himself. Under the titles of *The Web and the Rock* (1939) and *You Can't Go Home Again* (1940), Harper and Brothers published two novels supposedly left behind by Thomas Wolfe when he died. In a subsequent collection of fragments, *The Hills Beyond* (1941), Aswell included a brief account of the editorial process, which concealed far more than it revealed.

Not until after Aswell's death was Richard S. Kennedy permitted to publish a close study of the actual Wolfe manuscripts, *The Window of Memory: The Literary Career of Thomas Wolfe* (1962), and scholars could grasp the full implications of Edward Aswell's editorial work. What Wolfe had turned over to Aswell to look over and familiarize himself with when he departed for the West was a mass of material from which he intended to shape a novel, but so far had done little more than arrange it chronologically, produce a rough outline, and begin to provide introductory sequences. Thus, if *Of Time and the River* had been put into print before Wolfe thought it was ready, *The Web and the Rock* and *You Can't Go Home Again* were, in the sense of being shaped, unitary works of the imagination, not his doing at all.

The Web and the Rock begins with Monk Webber's childhood in Libya Hill, takes him briefly to college and then to New York City; and then suddenly we find him aboard the same boat from Europe that Eugene Gant had boarded at the close of *Of Time and the River*, ready to begin the romance announced in that book. The subsequent love affair is a very uneven narrative, and it seems obvious that had he lived, Wolfe would have scrapped much of it and rewritten more, or perhaps begun all over again with the sequence. *You Can't Go Home Again* deals with Monk Webber as he publishes his first novel and enjoys and endures fame and fortune thereafter. It contains some sequences of biting satire and some of overinflation, while of narrative development it has almost none at all. Most of its episodes were written as independent entities, and they cohere only in a very loose fashion.

In the clumsy, uneven shape they were published in, the two posthumous "novels" did abiding harm to Wolfe's critical reputation. They seemed to confirm everything that hostile critics had said about Wolfe's formlessness and addiction to empty rhetorical assertion; no one realized that Aswell, not Wolfe, had put them together out of a mass of separate stories, novellas, and first-draft manuscripts. Perkins at least had secured Wolfe's reluctant acquiescence in what was done to *Of*

Time and the River. Aswell's editorial job can scarcely be defended on grounds other than of economic expediency.

So the fiction of Thomas Wolfe, more than a half-century after the first novel appeared and forty-five years after the author's death, occupies a secure but controversial position in the literature of that region he once referred to as "the dark, ruined Helen of his blood." He was the single full-fledged romantic of the Southern Renascence, and his novels and stories provide, in their poignancy, their intense lyricism, their rhetorical excess, and their depiction of change and loss, a special and unique view of a Southern time and place.

JAMES MELLARD

The Fiction of Social Commitment

Although the South and its writers escaped almost none of the so-cial, economic, and political changes affecting the nation in the 1930s, authors such as Faulkner, Wolfe, Glasgow, Cabell, and Tate were never to make their dominant themes ones of political protest. Still, there was a socially committed fiction between the crash and America's entry into World War II, and it continued interests already announced in the 1920s: agrarian reform, industrial change, social deracination, and racial relationships. The best or the best known of these socially com-mitted fiction writers—Erskine Caldwell, T. S. Stribling, Harry Harrison Kroll, and Lillian Smith—were not protesting social conditions arising from the Great Depression so much as aiming for reform of historical conditions. Others, such as the trio of "proletarian" women novelists—including Olive Tilford Dargan (aka Fielding Burke), Grace Lumpkin, and Myra Page—wrote under the influence of the American Commu-nist party and inevitably protested social conditions directly connected with the depression. But the almost invariable result of the efforts of all Southern liberal or radical novelists was to demonstrate the resilient power of Southern culture and history. For whatever the accomplish-ment of any of these, the issues of place, race, and history are more important, finally, than the temporary bursting of the economic bubble.

The fiction of social commitment, however much it might have been intended to overthrow tradition, retained its roots in traditional images, themes, and values. In Southern protest fiction, the tradition of the landed gentry and the "good farmer" continued to play a major role. These two social images, threading through the history of Southern lit-erature and culture, together represent the positive element in the sign system Southern history provides. The negative element in the system is provided by their antitypes—the evil plantation owner and the degener-ate poor white (or "white trash"). Inevitably, writers who focused atten-tion on the negative features of the older agrarian or the newer indus-trial socioeconomic structures also located major characters in the

351

underside of the sign system. Thus, the basic structure of signification found in reform-minded writers depends upon the positive traditional images, for without them their inversions and transformations of types could not work.

The aristocratic images within the agrarian tradition are generally better known today than the demotic ones, since best sellers and popular films such as *Gone With the Wind* have carried the plantation theme. But in the 1920s the yeoman farmer, or the poor white, saw various manifestations and even occurred significantly within a feminist context. Apart from those in Faulkner (*Sartoris* [1929]), the important poor white farmers were women, appearing in Glasgow's Dorinda Oakley, of *Barren Ground* (1925), and Roberts' Ellen Chesser, of *The Time of Man* (1926). Her earlier works having depleted the theme of the aristocratic agrarian ideal, Glasgow came to the conclusion that the old order was beyond restoration and that the future must reside in the plain farmer once again rooted in the land. *Barren Ground* makes quite plain that the land is a transcendent agency, capable of restoring one's spirit and with it one's "permanent self," as Glasgow calls it. Something of this same spirit infuses Roberts' *The Time of Man*, but Roberts seems more inclined to locate the transcendent ideal, the restorative or creative power, in human consciousness. Ellen Chesser seems a soul out of Virginia Woolf transplanted into a simple tenant farm girl. Although Roberts subjects Ellen to all the physical and material hardships of the Southern tenant farmer, she also endows Ellen with a consciousness that seems almost to transform reality, yet never seeming merely to escape reality into naïve fantasy.

The writers of the 1930s who take up the agrarian theme focusing on the woman are more novelists like Glasgow than lyric modernists like Roberts. Olive Tilford Dargan, Grace Lumpkin, and Myra Page are, in addition, more committed to a specific revolutionary social vision than either Glasgow or Roberts. The proletarian novels of these women seek to transform the values of agrarian life into a set of parallel values suitable to a more urban, industrial future. As Walter Rideout says of them in *The Radical Novel in the United States, 1900–1954*, their first novels, Dargan's *Call Home the Heart*, Lumpkin's *To Make My Bread*, and Page's *Gathering Storm*, "are in effect local-color fiction performed with a radical purpose." Among more than half a dozen novels dealing with the 1928 strike of textile workers at Gastonia, North Carolina, these three novels depict the transformation of the good farmers from the mountains into the good workers of the mills, the landowners (good and evil) from the agrarian tradition into the mill owners (good and evil) of an emergent industrial economy.

The best of the proletarian novels depicting the transition from rural to urban life, agrarian to urban industrial values, is Dargan's *Call Home the Heart* (1932), published under the *nom de plume* Fielding Burke. Like some of her earlier work, *Call Home the Heart* combines general social criticism with a feminist theme. The novel, as Sylvia Jenkins Cook says, "is about the predicament of a woman morally and intellectually committed to communism but drawn by a powerful urge to an idyllic and independent agrarian life that embodies the best of Jeffersonian and native American traditions." Dargan's central character, Ishma Hensley, is a young woman of the North Carolina mountains who becomes so dissatisfied with her plight as wife, mother, and maidservant that she throws over the lot, descends into the mills of Winbury, and undergoes the ideological transformation that carries the burden of the novel's contradictory themes. Her transformation involves a growing awareness of the value of the social mass, the rewards of "transmuting daily life into an ideal." But the proletarian symbol of the masses always stands in contrast to the other major symbol of Ishma's life—that is, the land, or idyllic nature and its restorative beauty, peace, and tranquility. Significantly, the agrarian tradition finally seems to triumph over the emerging proletarian commitment. Repelled by an unideological personal distaste for the wife of a black union leader whom Ishma had heroically saved from a lynch mob, Dargan's protagonist flees back to the land, where she can regain a semblance of purity from the far valleys, sunlit peaks, long, dreamy ridges, and pale rivers. Returning to her life with her husband and daughter, Ishma at the end dreams of bringing children of the mill towns to the mountains so they too might experience the beneficence of the natural world.

But this dream seems, finally, a pale copy of the bolder dream of the social revolutionary with which Ishma had been tempted. Largely because of the Marxists' negative reaction to this novel's apparent sellout, Dargan soon followed it with a sequel, *A Stone Came Rolling* (1935), that shows Ishma as a clearer-eyed social revolutionary. The sequel is better Marxist propaganda, but it is inferior as a novel whose characters can really move readers. Much the same might be said of Grace Lumpkin's *To Make My Bread* (1932) and *A Sign for Cain* (1935); it certainly can be said of Myra Page's *Gathering Storm* (1932). The best of the novels (as opposed to social tracts) written by these three proletarians is probably Lumpkin's *The Wedding* (1939), which has retreated from the acerbity of social propaganda to social comedy—the comedy of manners associated with Ellen Glasgow. All of these women saw the demise of Marxist revolutionary ideals toward the end of the 1930s, and Lumpkin, for one, shifted all the way across the political spectrum, becoming quite conservative in the 1940s, as well as returning to earlier religious convictions. Thus, it appears that for these proletarian novelists the traditional values—the agrarian ideals of independence, hard work, and the land—ultimately triumphed over the more transient political ones.

Although the proletarian women novelists are interesting historically, they were not the only writers to address socioeconomic issues. Male authors of the 1930s such as Harry Harrison Kroll, T. S. Stribling, and Erskine Caldwell were more typical of Southern fiction in their sociological critiques. The traditional themes associated with the virtues of the land and the good farmer or mountain dweller are represented in novels by Kroll. Kroll's *Mountainy Singer* (1928) extols the values of the mountain existence, which he finds conducive to arts associated with the uplands—folk music and oral tales—and the pastoral virtues of character that mountain isolation can protect, particularly innocence that formal education has not yet spoiled. Kroll clearly foresaw that literacy would destroy any true oral culture. In *Cabin in the Cotton* (1931) and *I Was a Sharecropper* (1936), Kroll trades nostalgia for social polemicism in his treatment of traditional values. Having grown up as a sharecropper's son, Kroll could translate lived experience into his exposés of the cropper system, with its owners' corrupt accounting, the farmers' debt-enslavement, and the system's endorsement of cheating as a way of life for owners and tenants. These two novels continue a line of fiction begun in the early 1920s by Edith Summers Kelley's *Weeds* (1922) and represented in Texan Dorothy Scarborough's *In the Land of Cotton* (1924) and *Can't Get a Redbird* (1929), as well as Glasgow's *Barren Ground* (1925). Kroll brings to his social critique the commitment not of a proletarian idealogue, but of one who has endured the evils of the system and risen above them. His own life thus forms the positive aim of the typical cropper novel's plot, for he saw the injustices, recognized a need for changes, and escaped to a better life when he saw reform was impossible.

Erskine Caldwell is perhaps the only writer of the 1930s classified as a liberal on social issues who turned to the antitype of the poor white or the good farmer for his subjects. Caldwell's subjects are the Southern grotesques who to the poor white stand as the aristocratic planter stands to Simon Legree. Descended from the comic white degenerates of Southwestern humorists such as Augustus Baldwin Longstreet and George Washington Harris, Caldwell's subhuman figures seem designed primarily to show people turned into mechanical objects as a result of all-consuming material or sexual manias. Caldwell creates his best-known comic grotesques in *Tobacco Road* (1932) and *God's Little Acre* (1933), in such characters as Jeeter Lester and Ty Ty Walden. Although

Caldwell usually remains dispassionately objective in recording the unmitigated greed, untrammeled sexuality, and animal cunning of his one-dimensional characters, occasionally he drops the mask and provides overt social commentary, as in the critiques in *God's Little Acre* of the mill towns or the love-hate relationship of the small farmer to the land. Since Caldwell's readership was more interested in the novels' depictions of overt sex than in social commentary, his most effective work for the cause of economic reform probably came in the documentary photography and essay books, such as *You Have Seen Their Faces* (1937), that he did with Margaret Bourke-White. When Caldwell is read today, moreover, he is read for the incredible humor of his grotesques, not for the social reform the early novels might have engendered.

More than any other social issue, the problem of racial relationship was one subject any Southern writer could treat, regardless of political persuasion. From the beginning of the Southern Renascence in the early 1920s, race was a major subject of socially committed writers of fiction. For the liberal, reform-minded novelist, the plight of blacks in the South—as in the nation generally—was especially interesting, for it offered ample opportunity to include issues shared with the poor whites. The world of the tenant farmer and sharecropper, the factory worker and the culturally uprooted, was not relegated to blacks. Thus white writers like T. S. Stribling in *Birthright* (1922), DuBose Heyward in *Mamba's Daughters* (1929), and the proletarian novelists—Dargan, Lumpkin, and Page—could also involve blacks in novels concerning poor white workers or mountain folk. A major project of social revolutionaries in the proletarian novels is to effect a union of black and white workers in the mill towns of the Carolinas. Dargan's *Call Home the Heart* and Lumpkin's *A Sign for Cain* both attempt to show that white and black workers alike were much exploited by mill owners, though these novels also show they were equally exploited by the promises of fundamentalist religion. Erskine Caldwell's *Trouble in July* (1940) also turns to black characters and a theme of racial injustice. Finally, Lillian Smith's *Strange Fruit* (1944) is perhaps the best known of the many militantly antiracist novels written by whites during the first two decades of the Renascence. Although Smith's black woman and white man are presented as too naïvely innocent of the world's meanness, *Strange Fruit* is nonetheless effective in presenting, if not dramatizing, the social, ethical, and economic impact of white upon black, black upon white. The issue of race relations would not go away, of course, and the socially committed novelists could not resolve it. But they would not let American readers forget it either.

JOHN PILKINGTON

The Memory of the War

During the decades of the 1920s and 1930s readers by the millions turned to the image of the Civil War as depicted by Southern novelists, some good and others bad. The astonishing popularity of Stark Young's *So Red the Rose* (1934), which numbered its readers by the hundreds of thousands, and Margaret Mitchell's *Gone With the Wind* (1936), which sold a million copies within a year and went on to become the most popular book of the century, testifies to the intense zeal with which the public of the depression years devoured Southern Civil War fiction.

Scores of Southern Civil War novels appeared first in hardback covers only to be later dispensed in paperback from drugstores and grocery markets. Most of these novels should be classed as popular literature, written without a serious purpose beyond the immediate entertainment of the reader; nevertheless, in large measure they seem to have satisfied that generation's desire to know how people lived during the war and to learn about Southern history in a more palatable form than that of the classroom textbook. Despite the ephemeral existence of such fiction, many of the writers conformed to a respectable standard of authenticity and literary skill. What they lack is the shaping hand and intellectual insight of the literary artist.

For the permanent memory of the war, as revealed in works of lasting value, the literary historian must deal with a selection of historical novels written by first-rank authors who wrote to interpret the Southern past for the discriminating reader. The line between these authors and the professional historians, biographers, editors, sociologists, and essayists who during the 1920s and 1930s sought to reinterpret the Southern experience is not always easy to draw. Those who explored the South and its history, however, shared a common belief that the Civil War was the single most significant and symbolic event in the Southern past. Understanding the meaning of the South, its strength and weakness, its glory and defeat, and its present problems, must begin with the

356

war. The novelist had, perhaps, a single advantage over his nonfiction colleagues; as a literary artist, he could deal with his material in an emotional, imaginative manner, not always fettered by the reality perceived by the academic mind.

Although not every literary historian or critic would make exactly the same selections, the first-rate Southern Civil War fiction includes, in addition to Stark Young's *So Red the Rose* (1934) and Margaret Mitchell's *Gone With the Wind* (1936), James Boyd's *Marching On* (1927), Clifford Dowdey's *Bugles Blow No More* (1937), William Faulkner's *The Unvanquished* (1938), Caroline Gordon's *None Shall Look Back* (1937), Andrew Lytle's *The Long Night* (1936), Thomas Sigismund Stribling's *The Forge* (1931), and Allen Tate's *The Fathers* (1938). Included also should be the treatment of the war in John Peale Bishop's *Many Thousands Gone* (1931) and Faulkner's *Absalom, Absalom!* (1936).

So divergent in focus, theme, and treatment are these works and the prodigious outpourings of their second- and third-rate siblings that not many generalizations about them can be safely made. One may observe that, with perhaps the exception of Boyd in *Marching On*, none of these novelists seeks to analyze the emotional psychology of the common soldier in battle after the manner of Stephen Crane in *The Red Badge of Courage*. Crane's influence seems to have been greater in the direction of realistic treatment of fighting scenes, notable in Caroline Gordon's *None Shall Look Back* and in T. S. Stribling's depiction of the battle of Shiloh in *The Forge*. Virtually all of the Southern writers, however, are faithful to the facts of recorded history. Many, like Stark Young, Margaret Mitchell, and William Faulkner, make good use of family stories, letters, and diaries. Faulkner's use of his great-grandfather, Colonel William Clark Falkner, as the basis of the fictional Colonel John Sartoris is well established. Young builds the plot of *So Red the Rose* around his McGehee ancestors and in the novel mentions by name his father, Alfred Alexander Young, who enlisted in the Confederate army at the age of sixteen and fought in the battles around Memphis, Vicksburg, Jackson, and Atlanta. Several novelists, including Boyd, Dowdey, Lytle, and Tate, were themselves authors of formal histories.

The war itself, however, is often present only in the background, its progress being noted through letters, the talk of returned soldiers, and newspaper accounts. Novelists generally preferred to concentrate upon the effect of the war on those who remained at home, but they were not averse to evaluating Confederate leadership. They have high praise for Robert E. Lee, Nathan Bedford Forrest, Stonewall Jackson, and Jeb Stuart and often bitter denunciation of John C. Pemberton for the defeat at Vicksburg, Braxton Bragg for ineptness in the Chattanooga campaign, and Jefferson Davis for indecision, favoritism, and stubbornness. In *So Red the Rose*, Malcolm Bedford says "it was Jefferson Davis who had ruined the South."

Although slaves appear in virtually every Southern Civil War novel, slavery itself remains unchallenged, though an occasional individual expresses disapproval of the institution. The McGehees, for example, owners of large numbers of slaves, did not believe in slavery, yet they knew no way of stopping it. Edward McGehee had been an officer in the Colonization Society until the movement collapsed. Slaveowners, slave traders, and overseers who mistreat slaves are seen as villains. Slaves tend to remain in the background, except in *So Red the Rose* where they receive remarkable prominence. As might be expected, the novelists of the 1930s make little or no effort to view the war of slavery from the Negro's point of view. Faulkner's account in *The Unvanquished* of the disaffected Loosh and the bands of slaves moving along the roads at night toward their "homemade Jordan" represents the exception rather than the rule.

No single Southern Civil War novel towers above all others as a masterpiece of fiction uniting the causes, events, waste, and public significance of the war with the private, emotional, and moral life of the individual. No character of the stature of Tolstoy's Bezukhov in *War and Peace* emerges from the accounts of what these novelists consider the central event in the American experience. Perhaps one reason for the lack of development of a single figure embodying all elements of the struggle lies in the pervasive emphasis of these authors upon the Southern family as the unifying image of the novel. If the Southern Civil War novel can be said to have one central theme, it is the decay or collapse of the Southern family from forces both without and within, public and private. Southern novelists have viewed the fate of the family as emblematic of the decline of the South since the war. Its military defeat has been understood as the immediate cause, the precipitating event, the dramatic climax of a much longer historical development. More fundamental has been the triumph of Northern industrialism, the deterioration of agrarianism as a way of life and the concomitant decline in the humanistic values of classical civilization. In one form or another, these themes appear in scores of Southern Civil War novels of the 1930s and even into the 1940s, but they are best handled by such writers as Tate, Gordon, Lytle, Faulkner, and Young, who, except for Faulkner, had direct association with the Southern Agrarians, and all of whom, including Faulkner, were not only sympathetic to the Agrarians' criticism of modern industrialism, but also felt themselves to a degree alienated from the urban culture of the twentieth century. One cannot say, however, that they held the South entirely blameless.

In *The Fathers*, Allen Tate explores the effect of the war upon the Buchan family. Major Buchan, owner of Pleasant Hill plantation in Virginia and representative of the old, traditional order, makes a moral decision to side with the Union. His son-in-law George Posey declares that he is "not choosing sides, I am chosen by circumstances," though he prefers the Union. Major Buchan finds himself wholly unfitted to participate in the methods of living demanded by the new order brought by the war. To succeed he must violate his own code and approve the compromises made by his son-in-law. Refusing to compromise, the major commits suicide. Posey, however, who profits by selling supplies during the war, succeeds because of his moral pliability. In many respects, he seems a male analogue to Margaret Mitchell's Scarlett O'Hara, who by abandoning the traditional code exemplified by Ashley and Melanie Wilkes—who appear helpless in the new order—saves the Tara plantation but debases herself morally in the process. For Tate in *The Fathers*, the public crisis and the personal trials have been united in the Buchan family, and the traditional order has proved inadequate to function in the new antitraditional society.

The inadequacy of the traditional order to meet the conditions of modern life as accentuated by the war finds expression in Andrew Lytle's *The Long Night*. Responding to the obligation of his family to revenge his father's murder, Pleasant McIvor discovers too late the fallacy of his moral position. Deserting his army post, he lives out his life in isolation, alienated from the postwar life. Like Lytle, Caroline Gordon writes from the Agrarian position. In *None Shall Look Back*, she depicts the dissolution of the family through the breakup of a traditional, agrarian society and its replacement by a commercial order. Of the major characters in the two branches of the Allard family—one at Brackets plantation in the Cumberland Valley and the other in northern Georgia—Ned and Rives Allard fight with the Confederates. As the ultimate defeat of the South approaches, Rives and George Rowan, Love Allard's fiancé, choose to fight on until they are slain. Jim Allard, however, the oldest brother who could not go to war, marries Belle Bradley, daughter of a merchant who prudently put his money into United States bonds in Cincinnati, and clerks in his father-in-law's store. The Bradleys, despised by the older Allards for their commercialism, represent the new order. They survive and flourish. When Ned returns broken in health from deprivations in a Federal prison, he finds Brackets destroyed, Jim and

Love compromising with the Bradleys, and only Cally and Lucy Allard, Rives's widow, loyal to the cause. Like the women in *The Unvanquished* and *So Red the Rose*, they will "never know when they are licked." The hope for the future seems to lie with General Forrest, who also has never surrendered.

Although Faulkner's fiction receives major treatment elsewhere, his contributions to Southern Civil War fiction in *Sartoris*, *Absalom, Absalom!*, *The Unvanquished*, and *Go Down, Moses* have special pertinence here. He shared with Stark Young the belief that the war had been a powerful catalyst in the decline of Southern aristocratic families, particularly Faulkner's Sartorises, Compsons, and McCaslins. Faulkner embodied courage, resourcefulness, energy, and honor in such figures as Colonel John Sartoris and Granny Millard; but he also saw the violence, recklessness, and greed that flawed their class. The war never ceased to anchor Faulkner's thinking about the South. What he saw most clearly was that the war had hastened the decline of the great families and destroyed slavery as an institution, but that in its aftermath had come the sharecropping, tenant farmer system that enslaved both Negroes and whites and the creeping eruption of Snopesism that corroded the human spirit.

Stark Young was well prepared to defend the Southern position in the Civil War. Having spent his early years in north Mississippi, Young, the son of a Civil War veteran and a member of the huge McGehee family with its branches in Como and in Woodville, Mississippi, had also lived for almost twenty years in Amherst and New York. In his earlier novels—*Heaven Trees* (1926), *The Torches Flare* (1928), and *River House* (1929)—he had effectively written of his love of the land, the warmth of family affection, the personal integrity, and the devotion to the art of living well that had been his Southern heritage. But Young had also expressed forcibly his criticism of the South, its absence of cultural resources, lack of energy, and decline into formalism. As an artist in the South, he had personally felt alienated from the sources of his creativity; he could not live in the South and participate in the life of the theater or in the other arts. But Young was also alienated from the urban society he saw around him in New York. Responding to Herbert Croly's liberalism, he deplored the money values, the deadening effects of industrialism on the individual spirit, and the passion for the acquisition of material goods that he saw in New York. He felt keenly the caustic attacks of Northern critics on the South, the embarrassment of the Scopes case and the Scottsboro trial, and the efforts of Northern liberals to reconstruct the South a second time. He welcomed the opportunity to participate in *I'll Take My Stand* (1930), for he saw in the Agrarian symposium a chance to deplore the sterility of the machine age and to defend what he thought valuable in the Southern tradition. *So Red the Rose*, written several years later, derives much of its vitality from Young's restatement of these principles in fictional form.

Young begins *So Red the Rose* by establishing the values of the large Bedford and McGehee families. Family life emphasizes personal integrity, standards of conduct external to the individual, respect for the feelings of others, and the desire to live life as an art. Children are taught to subordinate their desires to the well-being of others, to know instinctively what should or should not be done, and to enjoy the continuity of life through the generations that came before them and will come after them. What happens in the novel is the impact of the war upon these two families.

In its larger terms, the conflict is, as one character says, the industrial North against the landed South; and it has been going on for a decade, perhaps since the beginning of the Industrial Revolution. Implicitly, Young recognized the war as marking the great shift in American society from a nation of small towns, small farms—agrarianism—to a developing urban, industrial country, a process still continuing even as Young was writing *So Red the Rose*. The war hastened the movement. For the Bedfords and the McGehees and their kind, the war brought physical suffering, the destruction of property, and the death of loved ones. Symbolic of the war is General Sherman, the divided man, mourning the death of his young Willy while unable to respond to Edward's death and callously planning the replacement of Hugh McGehee and his kind. As harbingers of the future, Young offers the Snopes-like industrialist Sam Mack, who sees society as a state of war, and the poor white Sam Shaw, whose crowd will soon have political control. Sallie Bedford says the bottom rail is now on top.

The double wedding at the conclusion of the novel illustrates Young's affirmation of the continuity of life. Afterwards, Hugh McGehee thinks that there is "still goodness that comes of harmony." That goodness rests upon both a physical harmony and a manner of life and arises from "the natural springs of feeling, where interest, pressure, and competition have not got in the way." It is this goodness that Young wished to retain from the past. As for the old way of life, Young knew that "we can never go back" and that no intelligent person would wish to return to the old Southern life.

Young, Faulkner, Gordon, Tate, Lytle, and other serious novelists of the Civil War share a desire to create an image of the past that would harmonize with the conditions of the 1920s and 1930s. Like the nonfiction historian, they fashioned the past from the recorded facts of history but presented it emotionally in terms of character and incident to convince their readers of the rightness of the novelist's own understanding of the meaning of the war in Southern history. The best of this fiction has enriched Southern literature and retains a permanent value.

ANNE GOODWYN JONES

Gone With the Wind and Others: Popular Fiction, 1920–1950

Like many other Southerners of her generation, Margaret Mitchell spoke of William Faulkner and Erskine Caldwell in the same breath: both betrayed the South for Yankee bucks, feeding the Northern appetite for Southern decadence. But Faulkner has his own chapter in this history, and even *Tobacco Road* has landed in a more exclusive neighborhood. Mitchell (1900–1949) alone remains in "popular fiction," with her book that did not contain, in her words, a "single sadist or degenerate." And with reason. For rarely did popular fiction writers share with Faulkner the least desire for formal experimentation; only in the case of Faulkner's own brother did they exploit with Caldwell the distancing possibilities of the tradition of Southwest humor. Most of them tell plain stories—more than half of them historical novels—with old-fashioned plots of love and adventure. And they found a public that heard in their stories a voice it could understand and trust. Yet almost to a person, these writers use those conventions not to avoid but to express the motive energy of deeply felt concerns, concerns that in fact formed the great theme of the greater writers of the Southern Renascence: the meaning of the past for the present.

Between the First World War and midcentury, and despite important differences between the jazzy 1920s, the depressed 1930s, and the wartime 1940s, Southerners of every stripe stepped into "an unfamiliar terrain of diversity and change." In that material and psychological frontier lay "a thousand threats to the older orthodoxies," and, historian George Tindall continues (*The Emergence of the New South* [1967]), the response of this "comparatively static society" was "a mixture of hope and fear, of anticipation and nostalgia." The scars and structures on that new terrain—industry, cities, mill villages, sharecropping farms; the labor movement, the women's movement, the depression, jazz-age ungentility; lynchings, nativism, fundamentalism, the Scopes trial, the Klan—take no explicit shape in these popular novels. They are concerned less with material than with mental change, with orthodoxies and heresies; to borrow a phrase from Daniel Joseph Singal, their war is within. Displacing it onto the past, even onto another country, each tells of the conflicts of feeling and idea that divided the mind of the white middle-class South. A substantial minority lament the loss of a sense of wholeness and greatness imagined to have existed in the past; some, in their fictions, reinstate that past, often by force; others simply mourn. They are, in Richard King's terms, monumentalists. But even fewer are the full-fledged proponents of the divorce from the past implied by King's term *modernizers*. (See *A Southern Renaissance: The Cultural Awakening of the American South 1930–1955* [1980].) The majority aim for both continuity and change. Because their characters and plots embody the conflict of past and present, in revising them these writers revise tradition, stitching together past and present. And if some of them have suffered neglect and obscurity, it may have been, as Tindall said of T. S. Stribling, "at the hands of critics who derogated liberalism."

Jay Hubbell has pointed out that the postwar literary revolt took the form in the South of challenges to "the traditional ideals of the southern gentleman and lady" and the glorification of "Negroes and poor whites." Indeed, in these novels, gender, race, and class often accompany or embody a thematic concern with history. In general, the men take history, and the women gender, as the means for their meditations on past and present. That should be no surprise. Among these writers, the central point of distinction is not race or class but gender. Men assumed a role in the public world, hence in history; women assumed a private role, profoundly shaped by gender, and (until recently) outside history. Thus for the men, gender is a function of history; for the women, history is a function of gender. (There are exceptions, of course.) The writers are grouped here in terms of their focus on history or on gender; though such a strategy necessarily obfuscates certain individual differences and certain other similarities, it should help us to see how so various a group as this shared the deepest concerns of now better known (but then less popular) writers of this time and place.

Margaret Mitchell did like the works of Virginia novelist Clifford Dowdey (1904–   ). And Dowdey is a good writer with whom to begin, for *Tidewater* (1943) takes as its subject history itself, the protagonist's stance on his aristocratic past and his role in shaping the democratic future. Most of Dowdey's work, including his better known *Bugles Blow No More* (1937), is set during the Civil War. *Tidewater* takes place roughly a quarter-century before it. When young Virginia planter Caffey Wade ("Tidewater") arrives in Chemauga City on the Mississippi, he seems, with his carriage and his slaves, to be a "cotton-eyed, indolent dandy of a dying line." Wade's mental baggage is Jeffersonian:

the enlightened few should govern the many in the interest of all; slaves and women and lower-class whites should be treated well and kept in their place. But by virtue of his role in a political scheme, Wade comes to respect the small planters and the river people of the "Pitch," and to despise the aristocratic scheme, fueled by amorality. Even his own revered ancestors had, he learns, in their time been mean. For a time, Tidewater is "not sure what [his] kind is." By the end, however, he chooses another class, not of society or money or even blood, but of the heart. But it is a fugitive community, with a fate as uncertain as Huck Finn's; freed slaves, outlaws, "new" women, and Caffey Wade are going to Texas.

Such a frontal assault on the traditionalist vision, though set before the Civil War, clearly speaks to conflicts contemporary with Dowdey. The more conventional historical novels of James Boyd (1888—1944) exploit formulaic narratives of adventure and romance to make similar statements about the present. *Drums* (1925), for instance, Boyd's first and very successful novel, tells the story of Johnny Fraser's coming of age during the American Revolution. The North Carolina son of a Scot and a Wilmington aristocrat, Johnny fulfills his fantasy of being a gentleman when he goes to England. But, as courtly life palls, the values of the backwoods emerge. John Paul Jones, Daniel Boone, and the ragged revolutionaries are the normative figures for Johnny at the end, just as his socially smart English flame Eve is supplanted in his affections by his strong country neighbor Sally. It is a mental journey his mother has made before him; thus does the novel celebrate the democratic ideal and the plain folk by working through a version of the Old South fantasy so that the protagonist rejoins his own family.

In *Breakfast at the Hermitage* (1945), one of a series of domestically titled novels set in Nashville, Alfred Leland Crabb (1884—) embodied the old aristocratic dream in houses—old landmarks and new Greek revivals that one "can die in with a sense of completeness." With them, an exact replica of the Parthenon built during the novel's action (the 1890s) reflects a yearning toward a lost past of order and clarity. The antitheses to these structures are Victorian gingerbreads shoddily built for quick profit. Yet the plot celebrates certain changes. It is the story of Hunt Justice, a bright country boy with an eye for beauty who works hard, makes a name for himself, goes north to school, and marries the daughter of a prominent plantation family, herself a strong-minded woman who plans to work in the world. Even the building of the Parthenon uses modern energies and techniques to reinstate ancient values. Like Kingsley plantation, which stands "not too near the highway to be defiled by it; not too far away to lose its common touch," the novel aims despite implicit contradictions for a didactic balancing act between the best of the old and the best of the new by the ingenious method of literally creating the past in the present.

Still more conservative in its implications for the place of the Southern past in the present is James Street's *Mingo Dabney* (1950). Street (1903–1954) wrote this novel and *Tomorrow We Reap* (1949) about the Dabneys of Lebanon, Mississippi, though he became famous for historical nonfiction and fiction, like *The Velvet Doublet* (1953). Although most of the action in *Mingo Dabney* takes place in Cuba during the revolution of 1895 to 1898, young Mingo's search for love and land in Cuba is in fact a displaced search for the Old South. Mingo organizes a group of outlaws, becomes a revolutionary hero with his daring feints and ploys, and despite the failure of the revolution, stakes out a claim at the end to a piece of land where he will self-consciously replicate his Mississippi home. In this novel, though the untouchable woman (Southern lady) discovers her capacity for sensuality and love, she discovers it at the cost of all her enormous political power, becoming "only obedient" to Mingo. He will now rule, imperial, over land and woman, a successful Sutpen.

Unlike these historical novelists, John Faulkner (1901–1963), Frances Gray Patton (1906–   ), William March (1893–1954), and Joseph Mitchell (1908–   ), set their works primarily in the present; this does not mean they fall into the modernizers', or even the liberals', camp. John Wesley Thompson Faulkner III suffers the fate of literary identification as the brother of William, though apparently they never discussed their writings with one another; born four years after William, John wrote mainly of the people of the hill country he came to know when he ran his brother's Beat Two farm in Lafayette County, Mississippi. *Cabin Road* (1951) was the first of a five-novel series published by Gold Medal/Fawcett and never widely reviewed; recently reissued by Louisiana State University Press, it was apparently designed mostly as comic entertainment, roughly in the tradition of Southwestern humor. The jokes are at the expense of those outside the implied audience of white middle-class men: the cuckolded redneck, the prolific black man, the slow-witted hillman, the cagey prostitute, the insatiable wife, hanging, incest, theft, a "Negro hunt," all are meant to make readers laugh. John Faulkner does thread throughout a theme that is consistent with his implied social conservatism. The hill folk do not understand or care about money, a point made repeatedly by their inability to change a five-dollar bill. Nor is work valued over "setting around" to "ketch up on" oneself. The government man—the straight man, linear, goal-oriented— with his car stuck in the mud and his money worth about nothing, seems a parody of the modern world. But no: at the end (and in vivid contrast to the rescue of the car in Eudora Welty's *Losing Battles*) a tractor comes and simply pulls out the car. The novel does not take traditional hill values seriously for long, but neither does it celebrate the new.

Like John Faulkner's novel, North Carolinian Frances Gray Patton's most famous work, *Good Morning, Miss Dove* (1954), though set in contemporary times, monumentalizes the values of white middle-class Southern tradition. When Miss Dove learns as a young woman of her father's shady financial dealings, she determines to control reality from then on by making it over into a set of rules and laws which, if obeyed (as her father did not), give one control over one's destiny. The town where she teaches for decades loves and respects her for this; students like her classes because there they are permitted a "complete suspension of the will." Miss Dove not only teaches continuity but she embodies it; thus her illness, as change, threatens the psychic fabric of the town. Although there are suggestions that her choices have been made at great personal cost, to take such an interpretation seriously is to indict the town for a sentimental and hypocritical exploitation of their Miss Dove, a conclusion the novel does not sustain. The plot finally endorses Miss Dove's hierarchical and authoritarian stance. Not only does she survive her operation, but her teachings have enabled a former student to survive without water on a raft in the ocean during World War II. Personal survival and history itself are shaped by those determined enough to impose their views on others.

William March, too, used a contemporary setting in his best-known works, *Company K* (1933) and *The Bad Seed* (1954). Although it is hard to find in his work peculiarly Southern characteristics, March's vision is consistent with that of other American male modernists. Through the voice of the entire company, including the dead, *Company K* recreates the horrors of trench warfare; the ironies March exhibits, though familiar, are moving. And if March's themes are familiar to readers of Hemingway, so is his treatment of women; male camaraderie, as in John Faulkner's very different setting, seems the only source of human sustenance left.

North Carolinian Joseph Mitchell spent his adult life in New York City, never wrote fiction, and had practically nothing to say about the South in the feature stories about Manhattan that gained him fame. Yet the stance and subjects of those stories place him squarely with the liberals of his period back home. In language, Mitchell preferred the exact vulgar word to the "nasty genteelism"; he fumed at his role with the news media, which he called "pimp[ing] for the status quo." He chose as his subject outsiders and eccentrics. In his first collection, *My*

Ears Are Bent (1938), one finds Harlem blacks who show "what the depression and the prurience of white men could do"; prostitutes and fan dancers; Father Divine; a female boxer; a racing-cockroach salesman; a marijuana party; and a women's hostel. Unlike John Faulkner, Mitchell eschewed parody. He likes his subjects, and dislikes the artful—society women, authors, preachers, and officeholders. But times have changed. Mitchell has to explain to his readers what a piazza is; and today his assumption of the artlessness of anthropologists and prostitutes seems a bit naïve, his choice of subject determined perhaps more by its variance from the genteel than for its own complexity. Mitchell's work nevertheless suggests some of the strengths—he brings into history those traditionally outside it—and some of the limits of the mind of a liberal white Southern man at the time.

Very few of these writers deal directly with race as an issue or black folk as a subject. Roark Bradford (1896–1948) and Lyle Saxon (1891–1946) are exceptions. Bradford retells the story of John Henry in an artfully ritualistic and repetitive style that echoes the ballad form of the song. Despite occasionally compelling dialect—"Yo' wif' might be de four-day febers, but I'm de wastin' disease"—the novel suffers from obvious white stereotyping. All the blacks are obedient, willing workers; the only tensions in the novel are sexual, never racial or economic. Bradford—most famous for *Ol' Man Adam an' His Chillun* (1928), which Marc Connelly adapted for the stage as *Green Pastures*—implies a monumentalist vision of history in his evocative but traditional and sentimental treatment of blacks.

Lyle Saxon does a better job of imagining black life with some sensitivity to the fullness of black experience. Saxon, a native Louisianian, like Bradford worked with the New Orleans *Picayune*. Most of his work is not fiction. His only novel, *Children of Strangers* (1937), is the story of mulatto Euphémie Vidal. The crossfire of race and caste and sex controls Famie's history. At fifteen, in 1905, she yearns for whiteness and money and status. By the end, her child by a white lover has deserted her and is "passing," her mulatto husband is dead from tuberculosis and overwork, she has suffered from disease and poverty, has sold her birthright, has been ostracized by the mulatto caste, and has married a black man. On the fringe of the novel are the rich white folks, one of whom closes the novel with an unconscious but doubly ironic comment on Famie: "Niggers are the *happiest* people." If Bradford seems to want to monumentalize the old view of blacks, Saxon seems to want to deconstruct it.

Whereas most of the men discussed in this chapter revise or repeat the images of the traditional lady and gentleman as a function of their meditations on history, most of the women make the meditation on gender their main project, thereby revising or repeating the past. And while those women who concentrate on revising manhood explore directions similar to those of the revising men, creating a "new man" who sheds the habit of command and gains some sensitivity to feeling, those who concentrate on revising womanhood move into more complexity than do their revisionary brothers, who may limit themselves to awakening sexuality in the Southern lady and who do not avail themselves of the literary tradition of woman's fiction. Inglis Fletcher (1879–1969), Frances Gaither (1889–1955), and Marjorie Kinnan Rawlings (1896–1953) turn their eyes to traditional manhood; the lone man in this group, Edwin Granberry (1897–   ), locates his text in the anxiety of masculinity.

Fletcher wrote some dozen historical novels about her adopted state in her Carolina series, beginning with *Raleigh's Eden* (1940), set in 1765 to 1782, and ending with *Rogue's Harbor* (1964), set in 1677 to 1689. *Roanoke Hundred* (1948) starts the series with the story of Sir Richard Grenville's shortlived island colony, 1585 to 1586. She begins the novel in England; we meet Sidney, Hooker, Ralegh, and an early Scarlett O'Hara with a raunchier view of sex, a larger capacity for love, and a much better education. But Philippa disappears as the exigencies of the plot (all the hundred are men) and possibly of conventional attitudes about gender make the novel into a celebration of the romantic Civil War masculine ideal: swashbuckling Grenville, perfect knight, whose authority rules in war, in peace, and in love, dies courageously leading his ship against impossible odds. Only the shepherd boy Colin—with his Grenville blood and his devotion to his lord—survives to carry on the traditionalist Southern dream.

If the design of Fletcher's plot made her drop the new woman she had recaptured from the Renascence, Edwin Granberry, looking at modern man, finds loss embedded in what he sees as permanent if primitive human needs. Although he wrote plays, stories, and novels, the story "A Trip to Czardis" (1932), Granberry said, "so overshadowed my other writings that one might suppose it to be the only thing I have written." Thirty-four years after the story, the novel appeared. The only work in this chapter that veers significantly from realism, *A Trip to Czardis* is neoromantic in almost every sense. Jim Cameron, a man in harmony with his wife, his sons, and nature, is tempted to lose it all for a harp-playing, night-swimming *belle dame sans merci* who is married to his boss. Added to the pressures is his boss's revelation that his wife will go mad if she cannot bear a child, and that he, Ponce Logan, is sterile. The tragedy is inevitable. And the implications, including the setting (a "big white house set like a Greek temple in the cypress glooms") place this book with others that accept the past as the immutable shape of the future. The novel assumes that a woman is happy only if she has borne a child (better, a son); that a man is happy only if he has fathered a son; that women prefer violent sex; and that the siren song of female sexuality will turn sane men into maniacs and moral men into animals.

Where Fletcher and Granberry assume its persistence, Frances Gaither systematically deconstructs the traditional image of Southern man. Like Granberry, Gaither grew up in Mississippi; she began writing adult fiction in 1940 at age fifty-one; *Follow the Drinking Gourd* (1940), *The Red Cock Crows* (1944), and *Double Muscadine* (1949) are all set before the Civil War. The frame story of *Double Muscadine* is a historical event, the (re)trial of a mulatto slave in Mississippi in the 1850s for the murder of her master's son; the title is the name of a traditional "coverlid" pattern woven by a strong white spinster; and the deconstructed gentleman is a well-loved, generous master. Kirk McLean's easy assumption of his slaves' sexual availability may be the motive for the murder; layers of violence, arrogance, and emotional dishonesty gradually appear from beneath the courteous surface of this gentleman. In fact, no traditional idea escapes scrutiny in this complex novel; both plot and point of view contribute to the reader's experience of unpredictability and change.

If Gaither deconstructs traditional manhood, Marjorie Kinnan Rawlings reconstructs it in *The Yearling* (1938) when she invents Penny Baxter as a struggling backwoods farmer whose story may have been obscured by the well-known story of his son Jody and his fawn. Penny gets his name from his small size. Unlike Grenville's, Penny's courage is private and understated; he reads feelings and responds to them with intelligent care; and he lives in the grip of the daily exigencies of post–Civil War frontier life. All are historically female experiences. But Rawlings' depiction of Jody's mother is static; she remains bossy, insensitive, and boring, and Rawlings' achievement remains the reinvention of manhood.

One reason for Mrs. Baxter's callous detachment cited by the narrator but never imaginatively explored is that before Jody she bore baby after baby after baby, all of whom died. Caroline Miller (1903–), who won the Pulitzer Prize for *Lamb in His Bosom* (1933)—and one of the four novelists in this chapter mentioned in James D. Hart's *The Popular Book*—tells the story missing from *The Yearling*. Set in the pre–Civil War south Georgia woods, the central experience of the novel is mothering: pregnancy, childbearing, childrearing, and the sickness and death of children. The protagonist, Cean Carver (then Smith, then O'Connor), is pregnant almost every year, and lives with the guilt of secretly practicing birth control for two years. Many of the memorable scenes—giving birth, killing a panther, escaping from the burning house—take place while she is alone with the children because all the men have gone to the coast, a journey too "dangerous" for women. Thus Miller revises gender by turning to the past to claim a character that challenges Victorian stereotypes of fragility and dependence. Implicitly she revises history as well by turning in a historical novel to a class and sex traditionally outside history. (By 1933 Ellen Glasgow had created Dorinda Oakley in *Barren Ground* [1925]; Elizabeth Madox Roberts had created Ellen Chesser in *The Time of Man* [1926]; and Edith Kelley had created Judy Pippinger in *Weeds* [1923]—all strong backwoods women. Eudora Welty in *Losing Battles* [1970] would continue the characterization.)

In her seven novels set in rural eastern North Carolina, Bernice Kelly Harris (1892—1973) likewise says something new about gender in history, specifically in literary history. *Sage Quarter* (1945), an excellent example, seems to fit the formula of nineteenth-century women's fiction: we have orphaned twins, one dark and assertive (Ruby) and the other pale and sacrificing (Pearl); we have the handsome outsider who disappears while the protagonist Pearl (this might have been Melanie Wilkes in *Gone With the Wind*) lives and supports herself alone, learns anger, and finds a voice that "fills the room"; and we have the final romantic return and marriage. Indeed, as had its prototypes, *Sage Quarter* permits unconventional female growth within a conventional frame. But to express a fuller range of female experience, Harris subtly revises the literary convention itself. She incorporates the real into the genteel: the fear of girls whose uncle molests them when their parents send them to spend the night; the quiet slow madness of the childless aunt who tries to nurse others' babies. Or she turns the tables on Mark Twain, making a girl's graveyard fascination plausible and unsentimental. Most of this Harris achieves with her point of view; though there are lapses, she for the most part succeeds in stretching Southern women's fictions still further.

A less experimental writer, Frances Parkinson Keyes (1885—1970) in *Came a Cavalier* (1947), one of her over fifty still popular novels, repeats rather than revises the women's fiction plot. But because even that plot revised womanhood, if covertly, she accomplishes ends similar to Harris'. Thus on the surface, traditional gender survives: Constance Galt earns her French cavalier (Southern gentleman), Tristan de Fremond, by her almost unbearably good behavior as a nurse in France during World War I and is a protected child in a playhouse chateau (plantation), which has "for centuries epitomized culture and hospitality and gracious living," through much of the marriage. Yet Constance's real story—that is, the story of her growth—takes place, predictably, when the men are away at World War II (Civil War). Constance resists the Germans, endures their enforced encampment in her chateau, labors in the fields, heroically spies, and ultimately earns such respect that "no one questions her judgment or authority." The novel ends just at the point where the resumption of the conventional marital relationship might conflict with her growth; interestingly, Constance undergoes an odd, brainwashing illness and a therapy of the S. Weir Mitchell type before she returns to her prewar role.

But the biggest blockbuster of all these popular novels was *Gone With the Wind* (1936). It sold a million copies in the first six months, and now endures in popular American mythology. Well it might, for *Gone With the Wind* merges its readers' interests in history and gender by means of a further revision of the female domestic literary traditions. Thus Mitchell self-consciously uses her experiment in gender to investigate the contemporary South's capacity for continuity with the past. She never clearly answers the questions she raises; yet leaving uncertain the relation of past to present—popularly expressed in the question, "Will Rhett ever come back?"—makes the novel interesting to almost everyone.

Mitchell uses the conventions of women's fiction. She pairs protagonists; Scarlett and Melanie present the varying difficulties of female self-assertion and self-sacrifice. She sends the men off to war to permit female autonomy and growth. And she gives Scarlett the final love recognition scene that conventionally offers the chance for a woman to have love as well as a voice. Mitchell's focus on the dark twin is not unusual; it follows the pattern set by Augusta Evans Wilson in the previous century. But unlike Miller and Keyes and even Harris, the field for her Scarlett's autonomous growth is, rather than the home, the plantation, or border worlds like teaching and writing, clearly the male, public, economic, competitive world. Scarlett, of course, runs a sawmill, hires and fires, and rides alone on business, taking the risks traditional to men; the "Gerald" in her heart emerges from the facade of ladyhood. Further, what conventionally would be a joyful love scene at the end becomes only Scarlett's recognition and articulation of her love for Rhett; he no longer gives a damn. The implications are considerable: Mitchell has given us a woman who has entered (traditional) history, and for whom love is not the reward.

This emergence of a "new woman" is related to questions of change and continuity, of history as subject, in two further ways. Mitchell fully intended Scarlett to symbolize Atlanta; in her strengths and weaknesses, in her continuities and breaks with the past, we are to see those of the New South. But unlike Ashley and Rhett, Scarlett never gains the analytic capacity to envision herself as a meaningful part of history. Thus as she challenges gender, as she enters history, and as she represents the South, she embodies Mitchell's meditation on history; but she herself will, at best, think about it all tomorrow.

With Ashley and Rhett, Mitchell explores a "new man" as well. In certain respects each is a Southern gender stereotype, like Melanie and Scarlett; Ashley is the Southern gentleman of culture and sensitivity, and Rhett the swashbuckling reincarnation of Sir Richard Grenville. Yet Rhett's choice of personal gain over regional piety, his directness, his challenges to codes of female behavior, all make him potentially new, a Grenville without his Virgin Queen. Because he stands for the Old South of his Charleston birth, Rhett embodies the possibility of continuity, of the South's incorporating new values into its tradition. But the thoroughness with which he rejects his new values at the end of the novel, in his unequivocal decision to return to the old ways, suggests the depth to which Mitchell despaired of that continuity, as expressed in a revision of Southern manhood. (Similarly, the ultimate weakness of both Ashley and Melanie suggests her abandonment of what had been a sustained effort to revitalize the idea of the Old South.) Only with Scarlett, daughter of an aristocrat and an immigrant, raised in the red clay up-country, does the novel leave some ambiguity. On one hand, Scarlett's return to Tara means a return to the (now metaphoric) "gentle cool hand" of her mother Ellen and the "broad bosom" of Mammy, possibly then to a past of preautonomous childhood. Yet on the other hand, we as readers—knowing her history and presumably capable of analyzing it—might well anticipate that now, freed from the self defined in loving Ashley and then Rhett, back at private, agricultural, feminine, antebellum Tara with her skills and self learned in the public, business, masculine, postbellum world, she may manage to solve simultaneously the riddles of Southern womanhood and of Southern history by incorporating the new into the old. The question we should ask then is not "Will Rhett ever come back?" but "If he comes back, who will *he* be?"

Perhaps the failure of *Gone With the Wind*, like other novels in this chapter, to use the possibilities of language more fully than it does made it popular; perhaps that failure of language also keeps it from greatness. For under these bushels we find no brilliance like Faulkner's or Porter's. Nevertheless, the light these writers made helps us to see that the yearning for a stable past and the sense of its inadequacy, the excitement of liberation into the new and the anxiety of the shapes it was taking—in short, the conflict between monumentalist and modernizer—informed the works of popular as well as high culture writers, women as well as men, of the period 1920 to 1950. And a good number of these writers, even if it was at the cost of sentimentality or irresolution, imagine that neither tradition nor innovation must be forsaken.

M. E. BRADFORD

The Passion of Craft

K atherine Anne Porter (1890–1980), Caroline Gordon (1895–1981), and Andrew Lytle (1902–) all published their first important work in the 1930s. But from the beginnings of their careers, these writers had in common connections far more important than those of mere chronology. They were acquainted, wrote sometimes for the same audience, spoke often out of personal memories of an earlier, agrarian South, and emphasized the relations of the sexes in their finest productions. They looked out upon the world from a place within the corporate life of Southern civilization, even when their immediate subject was something unrelated to the patrimony. But it is in the similarities of their aesthetic theories, their attitudes concerning the formal properties of their art, that we find a ground for treating their fiction in the confines of one brief discussion. For Porter, Gordon, and Lytle are all makers in the same tradition, disciples of Flaubert, James, and Joyce—and of the other modern masters of their craft—who invite their readers into the invented universe of imaginative experience by way of a dramatic representation of consciousness. They render rather than simply tell a story, are careful of texture and detail, point of view, and the archetypal resonance of frequently repeated patterns of human action. Perceived as part of literary history, these authors appear in the character of conscious artists. Therefore, what they have written is more likely to survive the test of prolonged critical scrutiny than the more fashionable lyric or topical novels and stories popular with their contemporaries.

Much of Katherine Anne Porter's earliest writing, as we can see from her *Collected Essays and Occasional Writings* (1970), is more properly described as journalism than as fiction. Indeed, her career began with work for newspapers. But she made the transition from reportage to art by natural stages, using Mexico as the subject of one kind of work and as the setting for another. In the essays, she made distinctions concerning Mexican art and interesting observations on various Mexican revolutions. She was sympathetic with Latin aspirations for social and

375

economic improvement. Later, irony and experience tempered these melioristic expectations. But there is nothing doctrinaire or partisan in the six short stories set in Mexico that were originally intended for *Flowering Judas* (1930), her first collection, or in the Mexican sections of her only novel, *Ship of Fools* (1962). What we find instead is evidence of the submissive imagination at work, evocations of an organic life rooted in the earth like trees, and of the confusion generated in deracinated moderns out of touch with immemorial ways.

"Maria Conception" (1922), the earliest of these stories, concerns an Indian woman who recovers her ne'er-do-well husband by murdering a rival for his affections and then adopting the child produced by the illicit union—a replacement for the baby she had lost. Maria is a kind of goddess, a natural force treated with sympathy by the narrative voice in the story. Even when she has stabbed Maria Rosa, her conduct has about it an inevitability acknowledged by her husband and others around them. Here the action has the primitive severity of myth. Porter concedes nothing to the sensibilities of her North American or European reader. And the same is true of "Flowering Judas," in which a young woman from the United States has come to Mexico to teach children and promote rebellion. Yet she is not comfortable with Mexicans, is disconcerted by their attentions; and in overreaction she imagines herself guilty of complicity in the death of the young revolutionary Eugenio. Laura is like the gross and cynical Braggioni, her mentor in radicalism: a "professional lover of humanity" who does not wish to be troubled over people. Or, rather, she is worse, for Braggioni is capable of redemption. But Laura, in the purity of her ideology (and the fastidiousness that is its source), works hard for the revolution without ever loving "some man who is in it." The story concludes with Laura's nightmare of the dead Eugenio. In what Ray B. West has described as a "sacrament of betrayal," she eats the flowers of the redbud, called the Judas tree because in legend Judas Iscariot hanged himself from its branches, and Eugenio's ghost cries out in accusation, "Murderer! Cannibal!" In its economy and symbolic suggestiveness, "Flowering Judas" is one of the best-made American short stories.

"Hacienda" is a longer and less successful fiction, but it does extend Porter's artistic reflection on the distance between gringo expectations and Latin reality. A group of leftist film makers descend on a pulque estate, where the beneficiaries of the latest Mexican revolution brew the ancient national drink. These, of course, are not the Indians who actually ferment the pulque. Peons are to be the heroes of the Russian director's interminable project, but they are despised by the Europeans and North Americans who intend to glorify "the revolution of blessed memory." The categories of class struggle and *ressentiment* will not, however, apply to the changeless, elemental rhythm of the hacienda. The entire enterprise of socialist realism is an absurdity fueled by ideology and money from the United States. Hanging over the delusions of the intellectuals and the progressive rhetoric of the Mexican regime is the sour smell of pulque, the stench of decay. The American woman who serves as our post of observation on the fiasco leaves in disgust.

Katherine Anne Porter's most memorable stories, however, concern the South of her girlhood and the experiences of her fictional surrogate, Miranda, not Latin America. These are "Old Mortality" (1937), "Pale Horse, Pale Rider" (1938), and the stories gathered under "The Old Order" in *The Collected Stories* (1965). In these works irony is balanced by affection and the certainties of blood. Yet they are not merely nostalgic evocations of ancestral piety. For Miranda is a rebel, one who understands the special mythology of her family as a self-protective idealization; but in "Old Mortality" she prefers these legends to the antimyth of Cousin Eva, a disillusioned feminist. In "The Grave," "The Fig Tree," "The Circus," "The Witness," and "The Last Leaf," Miranda seeks self-definition through a juxtaposition of her past and present, knowing throughout the effort that "of the three dimensions of time, only the past is real" and that love provides us a better access to truth than hatred. "The Source," which concerns Miranda's grandmother, is full of love, as is "The Journey," a rich account of the character and strength of the matriarch Sophia Jane. Miranda takes that example with her as she moves beyond her Southern milieu—in an "exhilaration of having faced one's destiny," resting on the memory of a life where "everything . . . had meaning." In "Pale Horse, Pale Rider," Porter's finest work, this strength is tested and proves to be sufficient.

In this short novel Miranda is a reporter for a Western paper published in a town near the mountains. The time is 1918, the year of the great influenza epidemic. Far from home, she meets a fellow Texan, a young army officer. When Miranda is stricken with the flu, her young man helps her fend off the pale horseman of death and, in consequence, falls ill himself. Sustained by a "stubborn will to live" by that "particle of being" deep down in her consciousness, Miranda emerges from her long delirium. But Adam Barclay dies. Porter captures beautifully the relations of these two young lovers caught by one of the endemic human tragedies. Her control of the material is as impressive as the treatment of the dying matriarch in "The Jilting of Granny Weatherall." Miranda in her final grief is the "one singer left to mourn," the stoic figure in the old Negro song that is the source of the story's title. The rendering of her sorrow and courage in the moment of complete bereavement is both poignant and convincing. The same cannot be said of the most important episodes in *Ship of Fools*.

Porter's novel is structurally a replication of *Das Narrenschiff* (1494) by the medieval moralist Sebastian Brant. Its action follows the voyage of a German ship from Mexico to Bremerhaven, and its burden is both topical and dark, reminiscent of Melville's *Confidence-Man*. But in its analysis of venality, malice, and bigotry, *Ship of Fools* is overwrought and repetitious, almost an invective upon the human race. As in "The Leaning Tower" (1941), in her nautical allegory Porter surveys a human cross section in order to comment on her times. The results are depressing. John W. Aldridge is quite correct in observing that the Southwest and South were Porter's "most potent imaginative material." When writing of people with whom she could identify, she produced a small body of fine work that continues to command respect.

Caroline Gordon also began her career as a journalist. Like Porter, she drew inspiration from a rich treasury of regional and familial memories: of the Black Patch of Kentucky, the Southern frontier, the Civil War, and the South's Old Regime, both in its health and in its decline. Like her Texas contemporary, she grew up a Protestant but converted to Roman Catholicism; and both authors honored the same fictional examples in their artistic maturity. However, there are useful distinctions with reference to their respective achievements. For one, with nine novels and three volumes of short fiction (not to mention her distinguished criticism), Caroline Gordon was a much more productive writer. In addition, Gordon did not (as was the habit of Porter, according to Robert Penn Warren) "balance rival considerations" in handling her chosen material. For she spoke out of a settled point of view derivative of the most traditional species of Southern conservatism and of a substantial Christian orthodoxy, and was thus a direct challenge to the intellectual context within which her work first appeared. Therefore, she has not enjoyed the general audience which her talents should command. Her critical reputation among men and women of letters has, however, survived the neglect. Her place in the history of Southern literature is that of an anomaly, a major artist whose books were difficult to find or purchase during much of her career.

With encouragement from her husband, Allen Tate, and their good friend the English novelist Ford Madox Ford, in 1929 Caroline Gordon started to work on her first serious fiction. *Penhally* appeared in 1931. Before the publication of this novel she had published only two short stories. Yet it is a mature work. *Penhally* is, like Faulkner's *The Unvanquished* and Welty's *Delta Wedding*, the story of a family, the Llewellyns, and their stewardship of the Kentucky plantation that gives the book its title. It is thus a dynastic novel, though unlike its distinguished counterparts, concerned with the destruction of a corporate life, a patriarchal order where the master spirits are expected to embody the common good of their ancestors, heirs, and descendants but are finally overwhelmed by irresponsible individualism. Some of the disintegration has its source in Yankee penetration of a defeated South. The rest follows from a failure of character among the Llewellyns themselves. *Penhally* begins in the 1830s with a quarrel between brothers over the entail of their father's holdings and ends a century later with a fratricide brought on by a selling of the land that the entail would have prevented. In the intervening sections there are tensions between Llewellyns and their wives that result finally in a corruption of the blood and loss of place. In the course of the action, various Llewellyns preside at Penhally and represent the composite protagonist of the family whose tragedy they accomplish. A Southern novel more illustrative of the special qualities of the region's literature is difficult to imagine.

After *Penhally*, Gordon published *Aleck Maury, Sportsman* (1934) and *None Shall Look Back* (1937). The former is an exceptional book, a pastoral: the story of a retired professor and his passion for hunting and fishing—arts through which he resists the efforts of the women of his house to tame him. Aleck Maury preserves in himself some sense of the terms on which the value of life survives, though most of the masculine role as understood within his heritage has been abolished. By way of contrast, in *None Shall Look Back* the masculine role is displayed in its most uncompromised version, mounted with sword in hand. In her criticism Gordon has maintained that the characteristic action in serious fiction is masculine in gender, a gesture toward the observing world "which from time immemorial has been personified in the feminine consciousness." In *None Shall Look Back* the manly figures are under the command of that Tennessee Achilles who "bought a one-way ticket to the war," General Nathan Bedford Forrest. His campaigns are the enveloping action within which Rives Allard chooses death over the possibility of domestic felicity. His wife and mother are witnesses of Rives's transformation into a summary figure, representative of an entire society in its decision to leave to their children the memory of commitment and sacrifice offered on principle, against terrible odds. No Southern novel captures better the experience of the region during its effort to achieve a national independence.

Gordon's *The Garden of Adonis* (1937) continues with the Allard family, this time under contemporary, depression-era circumstances. Ben Allard is destroyed while attempting to care for his land and retainers—killed in his own field by the best of his tenants, Ote Mortimer.

These adversaries are surrounded by lesser men and by women who subvert them. In *Green Centuries* (1941), Gordon's novel of frontier settlement, the betrayal is the other way around. Orion Outlaw persuades the gentle Jocasta Dawson to become his wife and to join him in pioneering. They journey through Cumberland Gap to the new life of the frontier.

Unlike his brother, who becomes a Cherokee, Orion is the male principle untrammeled by the restraints of civilization, and thus fails Cassie. In the end, after a short agrarian interval, he is what his name suggests, the hunter and companion of Daniel Boone, not the farmer and husband. In his life, at the level of myth, Indian attitudes toward nature and ritual are played off against the white man's will to dominate the creation, the frontiersman's joy in the struggle to achieve that dominion. *Green Centuries* is a profound exploration of the dangers of a state of nature, and it is perhaps Caroline Gordon's finest novel.

These first five books, with the excellent short fiction finally gathered in *The Collected Stories of Caroline Gordon* (1981), provide the basis for Gordon's future reputation. Apart from *The Glory of Hera* (1972), a late retelling of the legend of Hercules, the novels written out of her growing concern with religious questions and with the diseases of the spirit that plague modern life are not so impressive as their predecessors. These books, *The Women on the Porch* (1944), *The Strange Children* (1951), and *The Malefactors* (1956), despite their interesting use of symbolic naturalism, the roving narrator, and stream of consciousness, have too many qualities of the *roman à clef*. Gordon's most accomplished fiction reflects the values and concerns of her Agrarian phase. In that work she gave a more powerful expression to the principles announced by her husband and his friends in *I'll Take My Stand* than was possible for them to achieve in the discursive mode, principles that were hers by birthright and inheritance, not by association.

Andrew Lytle was one of the original Nashville Agrarians before he began to write fiction. Moreover, his first book was not a novel but a biography, *Bedford Forrest and His Critter Company* (1931). And he continues to write essays of opinion and social comment that demonstrate that he has not retreated from the positions that he assumed by contributing to the 1930 manifesto. We would therefore anticipate finding in his art reflections of a traditionally Southern view of the world such as is apparent in his statements as a public man. In this expectation we are not disappointed. But the connection between argument and art is often subtle and oblique. Moreover, the issues raised by Lytle's fiction go deeper than the topical surface of regional analysis. They probe the significance of human pride and presumption in the history of Western man since the Renaissance. Speed and mass, the Faustian dream of god-like power over the creation, are the occasions of action in Lytle's narratives—and to a lesser extent, exaggerated versions of attitudes that would be virtues if constrained by a corollary commitment to the network of families well situated on the land that had been Christendom before the modern deification of will and intellect had occurred.

The Long Night (1936) is a powerful evocation of the role of family in antebellum Southern life, but is not a historical novel or "about" the Civil War—except when the enveloping action converges upon Lytle's central character, Pleasant McIvor (a figure borrowed from a family story of his friend Frank Owsley), and checks him in his role as the avenger of blood. Pleasant's father, Cameron McIvor, is murdered in Alabama by neighbors whose complicity in a slave-stealing ring he has discovered. The culprits first label McIvor an abolitionist, then determine they can attack him with impunity and make a travesty of the McIvors' effort to punish them at law. At that point Cameron's relations assemble and determine to judge the killers of their kinsman according to an older law well-known to Scots. Once most of the principal murderers are dead, the clan is satisfied. Only Pleasant persists, in isolation from his own blood and all human society. But the war interrupts his vendetta and brings into focus the impropriety of concentrating on his private affairs when the very survival of honor and dignity is at stake in a larger conflict. A young kinsman who in later years is told the story by an aging Pleasant repudiates his extravagance by refusing to extend it. Robert Penn Warren has described the book as "more a ballad than a novel." Whatever its form, *The Long Night* is a window on an older world of feeling within which family loyalty was the basis of all social reality.

Both *At the Moon's Inn* (1940) and the related novella "Alchemy" (1942) treat the conquistadors de Soto and Pizarro from the viewpoint of an engaged spectator who, after being for a time overcome by the presence of a great captain, sees in his commander the Promethean pride that finally dissolved Christendom. The two narratives are beautifully constructed. In *At the Moon's Inn* Tovar draws back from the dream of a worldly beatitude at the behest of de Soto's ghost. And the nameless narrator in "Alchemy" rejects Pizarro after years of reflection on the conquest of Peru. The two heroes are finally like their prototype, Christopher Columbus, in their search for Eldorado: alchemists who make their own miracles. Lytle discovered a shape in their history, an image that helped him to interpret the character of modernity, long a motif in the calculus of the Agrarians.

At the Moon's Inn and "Alchemy" are profound studies in the history of European man in this hemisphere "reducing a union composite of spiritual and temporal parts to the predominance of material ends." The scope of these works gives them a special authority, a resonance possible only when the enveloping action links its central characters to the great times of test and transition. But as in Lytle's first novel, family, its problems, and its importance are the themes in most of his mature work—his excellent short stories; the extraordinary memoir/chronicle *A Wake for the Living* (1975); his fine short novel *A Name for Evil* (1947); and his masterpiece, *The Velvet Horn* (1957). *A Name for Evil*, which calls to mind Henry James's *Turn of the Screw*, renders the pride of Henry Brent, who destroys his wife and his life by repeating (in the name of the patriarchal tradition) the self-centered severity of his ancestor, Major Brent. The major, he imagines, is present and intent upon his ruin. The Eden of Henry Brent is too private even for an Eve. In *The Velvet Horn* the Fall is reenacted in the context of another excessive isolation. During Reconstruction, the members of the Cropleigh family retreat from the world and through incest are corrupted by that vanity. Lucius Cree, the child of this violation, is compelled by his relations (mother, stepfather, ostensible father and uncle) to learn the truth about his origins. Soon thereafter he marries a mountain girl who carries his child. Living in a ruined world, he will seek the "paradise within, happier by far" than any Eden left in Tennessee. Finally, his uncle, the "hovering bard" of the family who understands the pattern of these events, sacrifices his own life for that of his nephew, and the Cropleighs are humbled and reunited with the world. In "The Working Novelist and the Mythmaking Process" Lytle has given us an insight into the genesis of the novel and the levels of action that intersect within its structure. *The Velvet Horn* is one of the major achievements of the Southern Renascence.

The works of the three masters examined here repay the closest critical scrutiny. Katherine Anne Porter, Caroline Gordon, and Andrew Lytle have, out of the passion of their craft, honored the imperatives of their art and deserve a high seat in the house of fiction.

Black Novelists and Novels, 1930–1950

The depression in the 1930s and World War II in the 1940s are central events in American social history. Yet Southern black novels during these two decades rarely do more than hint at the effects either event had on the lives of Southern blacks. Otherwise, the variety of thematic concerns in Southern black novels between 1930 and 1950 is as wide and as rich as during perhaps any other period in Southern black literature. Richard Wright clearly is the leading Southern black novelist of this two-decade period. Novelists Zora Neale Hurston and Arna Bontemps are second only to Wright. Although three of Hurston's four novels and all of Bontemps' three were published during the 1930s, as writers they more properly belong to the latter stage of the literary movement of the 1920s. George Wylie Henderson (1904–), George Washington Lee (1894–1976), Waters Turpin (1910–1968), William Attaway (1911–), Frank Yerby (1916–), and Saunders Redding (1906–) are Southern black novelists of the period 1930 to 1950 who still remain in the shadows of Wright, Hurston, and Bontemps, even though some of their novels rank with the best of the period and are clearly surpassed in literary and historical significance only by Wright's *Native Son*.

Much more than chronology provides the continuity between the Southern black novel of the 1920s and that of the 1930s. The earliest of the best novels of the decade—Henderson's *Ollie Miss* (1935), Bontemps' *Black Thunder* (1936), and Hurston's *Their Eyes Were Watching God* (1937)—are closely aligned with the evolution of form and technique and a primary emphasis on the affirmation of black culture and character that stem from the Harlem Renaissance of the 1920s; these novels do not adhere to the emphasis on social and racial polemics that characterize much of the literature of the late 1930s and of the protest era of the 1940s. For Bontemps and Hurston, affinity with the literary movement of the previous decade is quite logical. Both belonged to the literary circles of the Harlem Renaissance, and in the 1930s both were reaching an apex in a literary career molded to a large extent by literary trends and writers of that set. Henderson, however, had limited contact with the intellecual and literary coteries of the Harlem Renaissance.

Born in 1904, Henderson was a native of Alabama. The son of a Methodist minister and educated at Tuskegee Institute, Henderson himself was essentially of the black middle class, through his two novels portray black Alabama peasants. Arriving in New York during the early years of the depression, after the Harlem Renaissance formally had ended, he worked as a printer for the *Daily News*. He also wrote short stories during his early years in the city, some of which were published in the *News* and others in various magazines. Henderson is at his imaginative best in his first novel, *Ollie Miss*, whose expert depiction of the lives of folk characters against the background of a rustic Alabama landscape is rather far removed from his own personal experiences. With *Ollie Miss* he launched his career as a novelist in the middle of the Depression decade and produced one of the period's literary gems.

The narrative style of *Ollie Miss*, *Black Thunder*, and *Their Eyes Were Watching God* reflects stylistic innovations associated with the Harlem Renaissance, innovations represented most fully by the prose sections and the dramatic dialogues of Jean Toomer's *Cane* (1923). The overall poetic qualities of these three novels—especially their economy of language and precision in the use of image (rather than narrative exposition) to convey idea and action—signal continuity with developing techniques in style and form that extend from *Cane*.

The earliest novels of the 1930s emphasize the inner strength and moral visions of the Southern black character. The moral strength, self-assuredness, independence, and spiritual beauty of Henderson's Ollie Miss, Bontemps' Gabriel, and Hurston's Janie Crawford are qualities of black character consistent with the concept of the New Negro that intellectuals and artists of the 1920s embraced in their writings. The content and much of the form of Bontemps' *Black Thunder* is controlled by the novel's historical setting. Nevertheless, Bontemps' style of narrative presentation allows him to create a protagonist whose personal identity derives more from innate strengths and ethnic visions than from the interracial strife consequent to the setting. The white world is barely visible in Henderson's or Hurston's novel. Black characters, therefore, are not defined in terms of their juxtaposition to or conflict with whites, as is the case in many novels about Southern black life published before the 1920s or after the 1930s. The early novels in this decade focus on the ethnicity rather than the sociology of Southern black life.

Writing in the middle of a decade noted for its economic austerity and racial tension, both Hurston and Henderson use the Southern black woman as a symbol of the spiritual essence of a Southern black life still untainted by materialistic values and undefeated by racial hostility. Ollie Miss could easily belong to the gallery of Southern black women portraits that fill the first section of Toomer's *Cane*. To be sure, *Ollie Miss* is a celebration and affirmation of Southern black womanhood and in turn Southern black folk life. The title character embodies the best of the race and the region and is a symbol of the spiritual force of femininity that gives life and creates harmony. She possesses the masculine strength and fortitude of *Cane*'s Carma, the hauntingly feminine beauty of *Cane*'s Karintha; like many of the women in *Cane*, Ollie Miss is spiritually estranged from her human environment. Her closest affinity is with the earth; her demise comes only when during a love affair she allows the material world, represented by her spiritually unbalanced lover, Jule, to supersede her sense of self.

Ollie Miss precedes by two years Hurston's portrait of Janie Crawford. In both novels folk realism rather than social realism is the dominant context. *Their Eyes Were Watching God* has enjoyed a much wider readership and greater critical acclaim than has the little-known *Ollie Miss*. However, in *Ollie Miss* Henderson is a master of those techniques of the black folk novel that have given *Their Eyes Were Watching God* its continued readership and critical acclaim. As a black folk novel, *Ollie Miss* is superior to *Their Eyes Were Watching God*, for Henderson is more firmly in control of the techniques of the folk novel than is Hurston. His use of language, aphorism, and image derived from the folk culture is tightly and intricately woven into the novel's thematic fabric in such a manner that the folk elements do not call attention to themselves. These elements blend harmoniously with techniques of narrative voice, dramatic dialogue, and character delineation.

Among the best novels of the 1930s and one of the purest examples of the black folk novel, *Ollie Miss* is second to none in its sophistication and innovation of fictional technique during the decade. In terms of literary history, George Wylie Henderson is a less important novelist than Richard Wright, and *Ollie Miss* is a less important novel than *Native Son*. Yet in terms of how well the author sustains control over his materials and is a master of his fictional craft, it is *Ollie Miss*, not *Native Son*, that bridges the span in the evolution of fictional technique in black fiction between Toomer's *Cane* in 1923 and Ralph Ellison's *Invisible Man* in 1952.

Published in 1937, two years after *Ollie Miss*, Turpin's *These Low Grounds* and Lee's *River George* can be considered transitional novels in that both exhibit characteristics of folk realism and social realism. Turpin emphasizes the perspective of the folk realist; Lee, the social realist. The setting in each novel is confined primarily to the first quarter of this century, and in neither novel does the action progress chronologically into the 1930s. The greatest weaknesses in the artistry of each novel result from the author's attempts to be inclusive in dealing with a variety of traditional issues relevant to black life (social, economic, educational, artistic, religious) as well as the attempts to incorporate topical references to people, events, and conditions consequent to the time and place in which each is set (World War I, Harlem's cultural life, historical and political figures, baseball). Like several black novels from the late nineteenth and the early twentieth century that attempt a panoramic survey of black life, these two novels are marred by thematic didacticism, romantic and wooden character portrayal, and disjointedness in plot structure. They lack the artistic control that James Weldon Johnson, for instance, maintains in surveying black life in America in *The Autobiography of an Ex-Coloured Man* (1912).

Indeed, Turpin is a far less successful purveyor of the range and complexity of black American life than Johnson. Turpin's knowledge of the eastern shore of his native Maryland, and of Baltimore, was meticulous, as is evident in his first and last novels, *These Low Grounds* and *The Rootless* (1957). Only in *The Rootless* does he integrate his intimate knowledge of historical Maryland with the ability to tell a tale well. Like Yerby and Redding, Turpin was for many years a college teacher of English; he also was a college football coach for a short time. He spent most of his academic life in Baltimore and at Morgan State College, from which he received a bachelor's degree and at which he taught for seventeen years until his death in 1968. Although he wrote and produced plays, his significance in literary history is as a novelist. The first of his three novels is his least accomplished.

Set on Maryland's eastern shore, *These Low Grounds* traces chronologically the struggles of three generations of a family (from the eve of the Civil War to the 1920s) to improve the conditions of their lives. While several of the novel's concerns are economic and social and to some extent parallel issues associated with the depression, the novel's focus is on various kinds of problems that affect the harmony of an intrafamily structure. Its chief character, Jim Prince, the family patriarch, is a strong-willed and independent person. Yet he lacks the basic qualities of the New Negro that Henderson, Bontemps, and Hurston use to delineate their protagonists in *Ollie Miss, Black Thunder,* and *Their Eyes Were Watching God*. Neither does he typify the protagonists of the proletarian fiction of the period. Overall, there is a close similarity of themes and characters (as well as of glaring shortcomings in fictional technique) between this novel and novels from earlier periods in Southern black literature.

During the depression many Southern black novelists reached a pinnacle in their literary careers; others published their first novel; still others began the preliminary stages to a publishing career that was to blossom years later. Many of these writers are intricately involved in social, literary, and political activities which conditions of the depression engender. Bontemps, Attaway, Wright, Yerby, Ellison, Margaret Walker, and other black novelists who published during that or later periods were connected with the Federal Writers Project of the Works Progress Administration. Yet seldom is the depression a focus in their novels. Southern black novels of the 1930s are not topical discussions of the economic realities of the depression. They do not exhibit that intense focus on the decade's socioeconomic issues which is an earmark in the writings of black social and political theorists and in the literature of several whites during the period. What the Southern black literary artist during the 1930s had to say directly about the issues of the depression period was confined primarily to the short story. In general, the short story, rather than the novel, has been the fictional form the Southern black writer has found most serviceable for a literary discussion of issues contemporary with his time.

Southern black novelists of the latter half of the nineteenth century usually set their novels (either in part or in whole) in the antebellum period; those between the turn of the century and World War I often chose the post–Civil War years as the setting; those between World War I and the depression most often used a contemporary setting; and those of the 1930s and the 1940s in general confined the settings of their works to the two decades surrounding World War I. Even Southern black novelists of the 1960s and the 1970s generally looked not to the contemporary scene but to the World War I period and the antebellum South for theme, setting, and artistic inspiration. Thus, in a comparison to novels by blacks from other parts of the country or to those by whites, it is apparent that setting in the Southern black novel basically is in the recent or remote past, rather than in a time corresponding to the period in which the work was published. This in part explains why novelists of the 1930s did not focus on contemporary issues of the depression era.

When looking to the past for theme and setting, novelists even of the 1950s, 1960s, or 1970s rarely chose to highlight the depression years. That fact suggests an additional explanation for the lack of a direct relationship during the 1930s between the Southern black novel and the most prominent social issues of the time. Southern black novelists have always maintained a close fidelity to the actuality of Southern black life, and have tended to highlight the most important social issues that affect the lives of Southern blacks. Despite any artistic shortcomings, Southern black novels of the 1930s are basically truthful in their portrayal of black life in the South. To be sure, the economic realities of the depression era affected the lives of blacks in the South, yet not as traumatically as they did the lives of blacks in the urban and industrial North or those of whites throughout the country.

Blacks in the North during the decade or so prior to the depression were enjoying relatively prosperous lives economically, especially when compared to blacks in the South. The improvement in their economic status over the previous years had resulted primarily from opportunities opened to them in the labor force because of the decline in European immigration, the continued industrial growth of the region, and other factors associated with the economics of World War I and its aftermath. The depression changed their lifestyles markedly. They were victims not only of displacement and other deprivations brought on by the depression, but also of the racism that tarnished the implementation of various government programs designed to ease the plight of Americans during the crisis period. For the white masses, the change was even more traumatic. Their lives and lifestyles were dramatically and drastically altered by the austerity of an economic crisis the likes of which they had neither known nor envisioned.

The change in lifestyles among blacks in the South, especially in the rural areas, was not nearly as drastic. Certainly, the depression brought a measurable change to their lives, but since they always had lived at the bottom of the economic stratum, the change for them was not as austere as it was for other Americans. Southern blacks had survived lesser but similar periods of economic crisis that had affected the region and them in particular, such as those brought on by the boll weevil. Thus, in presenting black life during this period, Southern black writers were not as concerned with dramatic or drastic alterations in lifestyles as were, for instance, white writers who depicted the effects of the depression on whites.

The economic crisis of the 1930s sharply delineated America's privileged and underprivileged classes. The plight of the underprivileged class becomes a subject for numerous American works that, espousing a prominent political ideology of the period, attribute the ills of the society primarily to the capitalists' economic exploitation of the proletariat. The relatively large body of imaginative writing in this vein has come to be known as proletarian literature. For Southern black fiction writers, life among the poor class of blacks in the South was also a predominant subject. The body of fiction they produced is in marked contrast to the general body of literature of the 1920s that focused on the lives of middle-class blacks or on Northern black urbanites. Yet one cannot readily classify black fiction of the 1930s as proletarian literature. While William Attaway's *Let Me Breathe Thunder* is set against the background of the depression, it is not a novel about blacks. Only a few black short stories during the period directly espouse the contemporary political, social, and economic ideologies that shape much of the white literature. Southern black fiction of the 1930s is rather uniform in suggesting that the social and economic problems of black sharecroppers did not emerge during the depression, but that these problems had become entrenched in Southern black life by the time the depression occurred.

While selected stories in Wright's *Uncle Tom's Children* (1938) are directly in line with the political and economic ideology of the 1930s, Wright's retreat from this stance in *Native Son* (despite the long section that tacitly supports Communist ideology) is indicative of Southern black novelists' ambivalence toward viewing the problems of black Americans as problems primarily of class rather than of race. Few Southern black novelists of the 1930s or the 1940s suggest in their works that interracial cooperation in the fight against the capitalistic overlords will gain equality for and sharply reduce the economic hardships of blacks. Instead, their works assert that racism is the overriding problem of the black masses—that social, political, and economic problems the race faces stem from the racism ingrained in society. Indeed, the economic austerity of the time actually intensified racism against blacks in the South and elsewhere in the country.

That perspective on the political economy affects black life in Turpin's *These Low Grounds* and Lee's *River George*. These and other novels from the period are less a reflection of the political ideologies of the time than they are a continuation of traditional treatments the Southern black novelist has given to Southern black life. For instance, in *River George* the protagonist, Aaron George, attempts to organize a committee among local sharecroppers to help defend themselves against the landowners' economic exploitation. Yet the perspective through which Lee presents this and similar socioeconomic issues in the novel is not one of Marxism, but one that is aligned with traditional literary stances Southern black writers have used to protest white racism. Aaron tries to organize the committee to fight racists; from the authorial perspective, it is little more than coincidental that most of the racists are also capitalists. In the rural landscape that provides the thematic context for the novel, the economic problems of poor blacks are viewed almost totally in terms of a conflict of races rather than of classes.

At places in the novel, Lee seems even to repudiate Marxist perspectives on the novel's contents. At one point the author-narrator, speaking of Aaron's situation and by implication that of other sharecroppers, states that the root of Aaron's problem is that he "was a Negro in a world made and ruled by white men." From the perspective of the sharecroppers (and that of the narrator), it is essentially a situation of white versus black, not capitalist versus proletarian. In addition, Lee handles religious themes in the novel in a manner that basically contradicts a Marxist view of religion. Many political ideologues of the period supported the contention that religion was an opiate that kept the poor, downtrodden masses oppressed. At one point Aaron questions the efficacy of his mother's and other sharecroppers' religious faith as a panacea for their social and economic ills. Yet he does not reject their faith in religion as an opiate to keep them oppressed; rather, he asserts that social activism should supplement their religious faith. The narrator goes on to affirm the value religion traditionally has held as a force that spiritually unites the black community.

Aaron's attempts to organize a collective resistance to the whites' economic exploitation of black sharecroppers, his verbal challenges to other forms of racial discrimination, and his active support of black migration to the industrial and urban centers of the North infuriate local whites. His social activism, educational training, and display of self-worth brand him a "bad nigger." Yet his death by lynching at the novel's end is not precipitated by his threat to the economy of the oppressive white power structure, but by his supposed commission of one of the most deadly sins a black could commit against white society at the time. Defending himself against Fred Smith, a white man who is his rival in a love affair with a black woman, Aaron beats Smith brutally. Shortly thereafter Smith and other whites plot Aaron's destruction by circulating a rumor that he murdered Smith. Given the time and the place, the fight alone would be sufficient justification for whites to brutalize Aaron with impunity. They accuse him of murder in order to garner widespread support, incite mob violence, and hasten his death.

Lee places the fight between Aaron and Smith in the center of the novel. Aaron flees in order to escape impending mob violence, and Lee uses his flight as a device to shape the narrative structure of the second half. Yet he severely weakens the novel by using Aaron's flight as a means to survey black life in America. The flight-from-violence theme, however, is a standard structuring device in novels of this and earlier periods. A similar act of interracial violence motivates narrative action in

Attaway's *Blood on the Forge*, a novel that thematically concerns the economic deprivations of a black family in rural Kentucky who, fearing mob violence, seek a better life in the steel mills near Pittsburgh. What is clear in both novels, then, is that racism, which often manifests itself as white-on-black violence, is at the core of black-white relations in the South. With an emphasis on sexual racism this theme is to run through most of the Southern black novels of the 1940s.

Born in 1894 in Indianola, Mississippi, George Washington Lee graduated from Mississippi's Alcorn College and spent most of his professional life as an agent and as an executive for insurance companies. His knowledge of the Mississippi Delta area is borne out in scenes and characters in *River George* (1937), one of the very few black novels whose setting focuses on a Southern city that, like Harlem, was a major center of black life and culture during this century. The low life of Memphis and its Beale Street is included in *River George* and is the subject of Lee's book *Beale Street: Where the Blues Began* (1934).

In Southern black novels of the late 1930s and in most of those of the 1940s the experiences of the Southern black migrant in the industrial and urban North are the central focus. The title of Waters Turpin's second novel, *O Canaan!* (1939), alludes to the religious mythology associated with the black migration from the South to the promised land of the North, a migration dating back to the early years of the slavocracy. The novel's thematic structure is consistent with that of most other novels on the subject. In fact, thematically and structurally those novels about the Southern black migrant published during the first half of this century are rather formulaic. Violence, or the threat of violence, is the primary factor to precipitate the migration, a migration that is reinforced by promises and visions of vast improvements in the social and economic quality of the migrant's life once he is in the North. The migrant brings with him a set of values molded by his life in the black South, values that clash with those of the urban environment. If the values he brings are strong and deeply rooted in Southern black culture, he comes eventually to recognize and to reject the deceptive and superficial Northern environment, and to affirm the authenticity of his personal and ethnic identity. Thus, he avoids becoming either a spiritual or a physical victim of the urban environment. If the system of values he brings with him is weak or flawed, the urban North claims him as one of its own and he spiritually degenerates, often to the point of physical destruction. It is, to some extent, the Southern black literary perspective on the traditional country-versus-city theme in American literature. Wright's *Native Son*, Ellison's *Invisible Man*, and several other major and minor novels about Southern black migrants are variations on this basic formula.

Like most Southern black novelists of this period, William Attaway was a migrant in the North. Attaway lived only a short time in Mississippi, where he was born in 1911. His father's medical practice afforded the family a middle-class existence for the time and place. But with visions of a better life, the family joined the host of Southern black migrants and moved to Chicago when Attaway was still a boy. By the time he was in high school, Attaway already was displaying his artistic interests by attempting to write scripts. After he entered the University of Illinois, his writing interests turned to one-act plays and short stories. Leaving the university, he worked as a seaman, a salesman, a labor organizer, and at other odd jobs before returning to complete his degree program. No doubt his vagabond experiences as a young man during the depression years provided him with materials for content and character in *Let Me Breathe Thunder*. But in *Blood on the Forge* Attaway incorporates very few of his personal experiences.

For this or any other period, *Blood on the Forge* is a superior example of the novel of black migration. Conditions of the depression had slowed the black exodus to the North during the 1930s, but in the 1940s the war industry gave the migration renewed impetus. Life for the Southern black peasant during the World War I and World War II periods was basically the same. Thus, Southern black life during the period in which the novel is set and the one in which it was published are basically the same. For setting, Attaway chose a time when the great black migration was in full swing, the period surrounding World War I. He chose his chief characters, the three Moss brothers, from the Southern black peasantry. Focusing on the lives of Big Mat, Melody, and Chinatown, the novel follows the basic formula of the black migration novel.

The Moss brothers are victims of racism and economic deprivation in rural Kentucky. As victimized sharecroppers, their lives are a short step from total economic destitution. They are bound to the soil—overused soil that barely affords them an existence, yet soil from which they derive spiritual sustenance. After Big Mat kills a white man, the three escape to the industrial North, one step ahead of the inevitable lynch mob and, they think, one step closer to realizing their visions of economic prosperity among the steel mills near Pittsburgh. Their Southern black values are not strong enough to sustain them in their new environment. Gradually, each is demoralized and Big Mat is physically destroyed. Although Attaway uses the basic migration formula, he handles his material with an expertise that makes this novel one of the best black migration novels of any period.

Published in 1941, *Blood on the Forge* was released at a time when Wright's *Native Son* (1940) was still gaining popularity among contemporary readers and critics, a popularity that reduced the attention *Blood on the Forge* probably would have received otherwise. Despite the novel's achievement and the author's promise, *Native Son* held the day and Attaway concluded his literary career with the publication of this second novel, though since then he has written television and film scripts. The artistry of *Native Son* and *Blood on the Forge* is the best to be found in the Southern black novel of the 1940s. Neither attempts to be inclusive in depicting scenes from black life, and thus both avoid the artistic pitfalls that marred several previous novels about black Americans. Nevertheless, both novels are representative portrayals of black American life, and both exhibit the continuing growth of sophisticated fictional techniques in the Southern black novel.

Like *Native Son*, *Blood on the Forge* weaves the theme of violence into the totality of the novel's artistic fabric. In the 1940s, violence was a predominant theme, even though the lynching of a black, a symbol of the pervasiveness and intensity of white-on-black violence in the South, had been sharply curtailed. Since the turn of the century the lynching scene had been a stock device in novels about the black South; yet before the 1930s novelists were little more than descriptive in their inclusion of this scene as part of the reality of the South. Beginning in the late 1930s, however, violence becomes pervasive in the technique of the Southern black novel, often functioning as a central structuring device. With Wright and Attaway, the violence associated with black life— interracial and intraracial, physical and psychological—pervades form and meaning in the novels of Southern blacks. It is used to define thematic structure, to delineate character and setting, to undergird patterns of imagery, and to shape narrative voice. The group of black writers during the 1940s who emphasized violence as the index to black life in the South and in America came to be known as the protest school of. writers, or, in the example of Richard Wright, the Richard Wright school. Those writers dominate the period, and violence is the thematic and structural core of novels of folk realism, novels of social realism, problem novels, and propaganda novels. Even those writers whose works are considered a reaction to the protest school or the Wright school use interracial violence as a preeminent theme.

George Wylie Henderson used the violence of Southern black life as a central (though too obviously forced) structuring device in his second (and last) novel, *Jule*. Published in 1946, *Jule* is a sequel to *Ollie Miss*, and in the first third of the novel, Henderson works with the same setting and characters from his earlier work. While this is the novel's best section, Henderson's characterization, setting, style, and theme in *Jule* are noticeably weakened since *Ollie Miss*. In the remainder of the novel, he abandons the folk realism of *Ollie Miss* for the social realism that dominates most Southern black fiction of the 1940s. He rather abruptly brings the first third of the novel to a close by inserting an obviously contrived scene of interracial violence. The stock scene precipitates Jule's (the protagonist's) flight from rural Alabama to the urban North, Harlem, and thus motivates narrative structure for the rest of the novel.

The familiar plot Henderson used in *Jule* is forced and hackneyed. Young Jule, son of Ollie Miss, grows into manhood, defiantly confronts his human environment, and becomes the third member of a love triangle that includes a young black girl (Berta Mae) and a white landowner (Boykin Keye). He physically attacks Keye, consequently gets into trouble with the white folks, and thus is forced to flee to the North to avoid mob violence. In Harlem he succumbs to the city's vices, eventually reverses his degenerate plight, returns South (too late) to visit his dying mother, reaffirms his love for Berta Mae while there, and, fortified with the values of his Southern black past, returns to Harlem at the novel's end to live happily ever after.

With only a few variations, *Jule* is constructed on the familiar and well-worn formula of the Southern black migration novel. Henderson brings little to the novel that is fresh, innovative, or aesthetically pleasing. The richness of character creation and setting that distinguishes *Ollie Miss* gives way in *Jule* to wooden and static character portrayal; the expert handling of familiar folk types and themes in *Ollie Miss* becomes a faulty portrayal of outworn stereotypes; the economy of style and vividness of imagery becomes trite prose, empty dialogue, and scattered purple passages. Artistically, *Jule* certainly is one of the glaring failures among novels about black life published during the decade.

Although violence is a preeminent concern in Southern black fiction of the 1940s, few Southern black writers, however, write of the violence of black life within the context of World War II. The best treatment of the subject comes from Ralph Ellison and from Frank Yerby, a prizewinning writer of short fiction who by the middle of the decade had essentially abandoned the short story form for the novel. Once again, the Southern black fiction writer chose the short story as the forum for a fictional discussion of contemporary issues. In "Health Card" (1944), "Roads Going Down" (1945), and "The Homecoming" (1946), Yerby showed considerable talent and promise as a writer. He launched his career as a novelist in 1946 with the publication of *The Foxes of Harrow*, the first in a series of three novels (including *The Vixens* in 1947 and *Pride's Castle* in 1948) about the South and Southerners that together span the last three quarters of the nineteenth century. Yerby's chief characters are white, and as historical works the novels are rather formulaic. Nevertheless, their public appeal was widespread, spawning Yerby's sustained career as a prolific and commercially successful novelist.

Yerby was born in Augusta, Georgia, in 1916. He received a bachelor's degree from Paine College and a master's from Fisk University; he later did additional graduate study at the University of Chicago. During the depression he worked with the Federal Writers Project in Chicago. Between 1939 and 1941 he taught English at Florida A & M and Southern universities. Whatever motivated him in the mid-1940s to turn from a promising literary artist to a commercially successful writer, his decision has brought him success. In addition to the series of three novels listed above, both of his other novels published by 1950 were commercial successes—*The Golden Hawk* in 1948 and *Floodtide* in 1950. In the early 1950s he moved to Europe and has spent most of his life since then in France and Spain. Almost yearly since 1946 Yerby has published a best-selling novel in the typical Yerby fictional vein.

Since the publication of his first novels, Yerby has remained an anomaly among Southern black novelists. Few (including Yerby) would claim that he is a great literary artist, and even Yerby has expressed surprise at the immense popularity of his particular brand of novel. Nevertheless, he is a writer of considerable talent. He seldom has focused his novels on black American themes and characters. (*Speak Now*, set in Paris and published in 1969, is the primary exception.) Yerby is not, however, singular among black American novelists whose novels are primarily about whites rather than about blacks. Like those writers, Yerby has been both praised and condemned. To a large extent, critical evaluations of his works have been predicated less on his talents as a writer than on the fact that as a black writer he has not chosen to write about black themes and characters. His works have been labeled costume and historical novels. Although his most severe critics have accused him of writing only potboilers, Yerby's historical novels, despite other shortcomings, reveal his acute attention to the accuracy of historical details. On the whole, his novels are equal or superior to the typical American potboiler; those published by 1950 are in general written much better than the so-called raceless novels published by blacks during the period.

The approach Saunders Redding takes to black life in *Stranger and Alone* (1950) more closely resembles Southern black novels of the 1930s than those of the 1940s. Rather than concentrating on interracial violence and social protest themes, Redding uses racial conflict and social protest in *Stranger and Alone* primarily as backdrops to a story about a familiar and important character type in the Southern black community. It is the story of Shelton Howden, a story about the genesis and organic development of an accommodationist who uses the power and influence he acquires from and has with whites and other black accommodationists to betray the aspirations of his race.

As an accommodationist black educator, Howden is a character type well known in the life and the literature of the black South in the twentieth century. The frequency with which this character type appears in black American literature is second only to that of the black preacher. Portraits of the type in the black American novel are quite varied, ranging from Chesnutt's Jeff Wain (*The House Behind the Cedars* [1900]), to Toomer's Professor Hanby (*Cane* [1923]), to Larsen's Dr. Anderson (*Quicksand* [1928]), to Shaw's Principal Johns (*Greater Need Below* [1936]), to the quintessential example of the type, Ellison's Dr. Bledsoe (*Invisible Man* [1952]), whose literary twin by the same name also appears in *Stranger and Alone*. As a literary type, the black educator almost always is intended for ridicule; quite often he is presented as a character who deserves the narrator's and readers' scathing condemnation. Unlike his literary compatriots, however, Howden (though he is to be ridiculed) is presented in a rather sympathetic manner.

Howden belongs to an impressive list of character portraits in the twentieth-century Southern black novel, a list which, since the 1930s, includes Bontemps' Gabriel, Henderson's Ollie Miss, Hurston's Janie Crawford, Wright's Bigger Thomas, Ellison's Invisible Man, and Ernest Gaines's Jane Pittman. Howden certainly is not a stranger to black American literature and life. Yet he does stand alone among major protagonists in the Southern black novel as one who is to be denied rather than affirmed, as one who elicits the reader's sympathy but not his empathy. It is for the superb creation of the novel's protagonist that Redding's novel deserves praise; unfortunately, most other aspects of the novel's fictional technique are flawed.

The best parts of the novel no doubt are shaped by Redding's personal experiences and observations. The Delaware-born author is, among other things, a noted educator. After his freshman year at Lincoln University in Pennsylvania, Redding transferred to Brown University, from which he received a bachelor's and a master's degree. Although he never attended a Southern black college, Redding knew his subject well. Before going on to teach at several white universities after 1950, including Brown and Cornell, Redding taught at black colleges in Georgia, Louisiana, North Carolina, and Virginia. He has had an illustrious career as an astute educator, social critic, historian, literary critic, and creative writer.

His technique in *Stranger and Alone*, his only novel, is neither spontaneous nor inspired. He approaches his subject with the eye of a clinician, with a style that is conscious rather than natural. His cerebral language and images characterize him as a prose technocrat rather than a prose stylist. Nevertheless, his fictional treatment of the Southern black college, despite the novel's shortcomings, and of the accommodationist black educator is the most thorough and aesthetically satisfying to be found among Southern black novels. From early childhood to young adulthood, Howden is victimized by an intricate system of racial oppression; yet as an adult, he consciously works to perpetuate that very system. Using a detached and sophisticated authorial and narrative stance, Redding allows the reader to witness the maturation of a character type who is an inevitable product of a complexity of social and psychological forces over which he has no control. Prominent traces of twentieth-century naturalism help give shape to this study of a character who, molded by a racist and accommodationist environment, becomes the thing itself.

Artistically, *Stranger and Alone* is a much less polished novel than *Native Son* or *Invisible Man*. But Redding's handling of the environment's impact on the psychological development of black character in many ways recalls Bigger Thomas and foreshadows the Invisible Man. In terms of the evolution of fictional technique in Southern black novels, particularly theme and character, *Stranger and Alone* is a natural bridge between *Native Son* and *Invisible Man*. Beginning with *Native Son*, Southern black novels become more concerned with emphasizing the psychological complexity of their protagonists than with creating protagonists who are representative victims of racism or who are intended essentially as familiar or social types. Racism remains a preeminent force in shaping the black protagonists' psyche, but after *Native Son* the best of the novels that deal with racial oppression and conflict give these themes a prominent position in the novels' background rather than in the foreground. *Stranger and Alone* is exemplary of the trend, a trend that has been sustained since the 1950s. Given the emphasis on the affirmation of black character stemming from the Harlem Renaissance, the tendency since the 1930s to create black protagonists who are much more than one-dimensional victims of racial strife, and the continuity in the evolution of sophisticated fictional technique in the Southern black novel since the turn of the century, Ralph Ellison's *Invisible Man* in 1952 was inevitable.

The years 1930 to 1950 represent an even more sustained period of growth for the Southern black novel than does the Harlem Renaissance, a period dominated more by poets than by novelists. Four of the six novelists highlighted in this section published all of their novels during this period. Waters Turpin's historical novel, *The Rootless*—his last and best novel—was published in 1957. After 1950 Frank Yerby published several other best sellers in a career that is still in healthy progress. Other Southern black novelists, such as Margaret Walker and Ralph Ellison, as well as black novelists not of the South, have their literary roots in this period. And, of course, the period produced Richard Wright, a Southern black writer whose works probably have had the greatest influence on the shaping of black American fiction since he published *Native Son* in 1940.

HERSCHEL GOWER

Regions and Rebels

Late nineteenth-century local-color writing flourished in the American South because, in part at least, the various subregions and localities in which Southerners lived were markedly distinctive and identifiable. In their own time the local colorists of the nineteenth century developed a brand of realism that was an answer to American romanticism. They emphasized the importance of ordinary folk, commonplace events in a community, the indigenous strains of a culture. But their realism was sometimes severely undermined by bathos and by characters too predictable and stereotyped to come alive as individuals. Too often place and a span of time were presented for their own sake, the result being that vivid characterizations and strong themes were often overshadowed or neglected. Southern local colorists presented to Northern readers a South that was quaint, docile, and no longer a national threat.

In a sense, the local-color tradition has continued into modern times. There were during the 1920s, 1930s, and thereafter, and there still are, Southern authors whose work places a strong emphasis upon the peculiarities and uniqueness of specific locales. But in the fiction of authors such as E. P. O'Donnell, Marjorie Kinnan Rawlings, Brainard Cheney, James Still, Jesse Stuart, Harriette Simpson Arnow, and Bowen Ingram, such emphasis does not come at the expense of wholeness and depth of characterization, the willingness to look long and hard at human nature at its least attractive as well as its best, or a subordination of life to landscape. These writers did indeed make conscious choices in writing about a particular place, and though they were undoubtedly familiar with the work of such local colorists as George Washington Cable, Kate Chopin, Joel Chandler Harris, and Charles Egbert Craddock, they learned to avoid many of the excesses of their predecessors. In general they do not go as tediously far as Craddock, Harris, or John Fox into phonetic spelling of speech, for example, or depend as often on coincidence in the plot of a short story or novel, or violate tone by authorial

399

comment and "educated" exposition. When most of the seven began their serious writing in the 1930s and 1940s, they were already sufficiently versed in the basic techniques of the craft to avoid the blunders made by the generation before them; they consciously labored to overcome both the preciousness and the pitfalls of their predecessors. As students they had the advantage of exposure to literature that was critically sound; they also had teachers who read what they wrote, criticized it, and encouraged them to find their individual voices. For example, Cheney, Still, and Stuart were indebted to the influence of John Crowe Ransom, Donald Davidson, and other writer-teachers at Vanderbilt. The exception is E. P. O'Donnell, who left school in the seventh grade and, like Faulkner, taught himself to write.

E. P. O'Donnell (1895–1943) was born in New Orleans of second-generation Irish parentage and was a lad of many parts who read voraciously but apparently had little regard for formal education. Biographical data is at best sketchy, but the young O'Donnell is reputed to have tried his hand at a number of jobs—from shining shoes on the Algiers ferry to serving as an altar boy. He said he knew he wanted to be a writer but recalled, toward the end of a brief life, thirty-three different jobs on land and sea.

Like his literary godson John Kennedy Toole, whose Confederacy of Dunces was published posthumously in 1979, O'Donnell had an uncommonly keen ear for Louisiana speech. His people live in the flat lowlands of the Mississippi River delta one hundred miles below New Orleans and speak a patois part Cajun and part broken English. The sounds rise from the printed page to the reader's ear; diction, intonation, and emotion commingle in a point-counterpoint of voices. O'Donnell is equally successful in transcribing the speech of the Slovenian family of Kalaviches, Catholic peasants on the lower Mississippi in Green Margins (1936).

Natural sounds that accompany the flow of the mighty, noisy river strike the ear with the same freshness that we find in the opening paragraph of Green Margins. "The Delta blackness was deep and hollow. The girl shivering on the deserted levee heard the wind's strange noises, the troubled squeaking of floating hyacinth bulbs rubbing together in the void, the thudding of driftwood logs, the swishing of unseen grasses. And farther out, the river's laughter, a ceaseless bitter din." His gift for dramatizing the sounds of the delta takes O'Donnell into the techniques of synesthesia and a wealth of images that convey more than one sense impression simultaneously. "There would be no rain: the wind-polished moon was high and lonely, having driven back all but the fiercest stars. . . . The dull gray earth sent up its bristling cold through the woman's soles. But she knew it was warm under the ground where the baby roots were. The wind was very dry. She could feel endless areas of vegetation curling. She was aware of sap everywhere creeping downward." To read passages with such striking images is almost to believe, for the moment, that John Keats had moved to the bayou and recorded his sensual responses in the prose of Louisiana. After placing stories in *Harper's, Collier's,* and the *Yale Review,* E. P. O'Donnell was given a writing fellowship by Houghton Mifflin, who published the five-hundred-page *Green Margins* in 1936. It is a structured, detailed, remarkably rich first novel that in recent years has been reissued in paperback.

A second, even finer, more impressive example of O'Donnell's gifts—this one exhibiting a humorous and ironic stance—is *The Great Big Doorstep: A Delta Comedy* (1941). Published when the author was forty-six and selected for the Book-of-the-Month Club, this major novel shows an artist who has found his voice and can command the attention of both a popular and a scholarly audience. The story of the Crochet family is the struggle of every family to outwit outrageous fortune.

Unfortunately E. P. O'Donnell died of a heart ailment in 1943 at age forty-eight in Charity Hospital, New Orleans. He and his work were virtually forgotten for a generation of readers and critics. Then in 1979 the Southern Illinois University Press in the Lost American Fiction series reissued *The Great Big Doorstep* with a brief but perceptive afterword by Eudora Welty. Appreciative of the speech and characterizations, Welty sums up the thematic achievement of this novel when she says, "We learn that the life of complete poverty is very rich." Published simultaneously in paperback by the Popular Library in 1979, this last novel by one of the most gifted of the regionalists is not entirely forgotten.

Born in Washington in 1896, Marjorie Kinnan Rawlings was educated in Wisconsin, lived and worked as a journalist at various places in the North before settling down to a writing career in 1933 at Cross Creek, Florida. In the next twenty years she published four novels: *South Moon Under* (1933), *Golden Apples* (1935), *The Yearling* (1938), and *The Sojourner* (1953). The best known of these is *The Yearling,* which won the Pulitzer Prize, was selected by the Book-of-the-Month Club, and was an overwhelming popular success. The movie version, which appeared in 1946, has remained a perennial box-office attraction.

The Yearling is set in 1870—1871 and is the story of young Jody Baxter, his parents, and their daily struggles in clearing pines in the scrub country east of Ocala and southeast of Gainesville. Around the Baxters there is the dense wilderness where game abounds and where man lives close to nature but in a precarious, uncertain relationship. There are trips on the creeks and rivers, the rituals of hunting and fishing, and the planting of crops for subsistence. Because his pet fawn eats the tender shoots in the garden, the boy Jody must kill the deer in the symbolic act of growing up and becoming a man. He must sacrifice the fawn for the sake of his own initiation and knowledge of the real world. Except through the paradox of destruction, he would never awaken to the tragedy of the human predicament.

Brainard Cheney (1900–) was born in Fitzgerald, Georgia, grew up in Lumber City, was graduated from Vanderbilt, became a newspaper man and political analyst and literary critic. His novels are set in the pine barren country of South Georgia where his family first settled on the Oconee River in 1813. The four published novels—*Lightwood* (1939), *River Rogue* (1942), *This Is Adam* (1958), and *Devil's Elbow* (1969)—are sequential in that they encompass a fifty-year span from about 1875 to 1925.

James Still (1906–), Jesse Stuart (1907–) and Harriette Simpson Arnow (1908–) are regionalists from Kentucky. Stuart was born in Greenup County, an area where his many volumes have been written and where he continues to live. Although born in Fairfax, Alabama, Still has spent most of his adult life near Troublesome Creek, Knott County, and has written a novel, stories, and poetry set in this remote area of Kentucky. Harriet Simpson was born in Wayne County and first pursued a career as a teacher in various rural and urban areas of Kentucky. She married Harold Arnow, a newspaper reporter, in 1939 and moved to Michigan in 1945, where with the exception of *Mountain Path* (1936) all her books have been written and where she still resides.

James Still and Jesse Stuart are contemporaries who attended, at the same time, Lincoln Memorial University, Harrogate, Tennessee, and were at Vanderbilt for graduate work in the 1930s. Still received the master's degree in 1930, the year Stuart was principal of Greenup High School. Stuart spent the school year 1931–1932 at Vanderbilt; his unfinished thesis on John Fox, Jr., was destroyed in a dormitory fire, and he did not take a degree. Still and Stuart have shared the same teachers, academic backgrounds, and abiding love for Kentucky. But there are major differences that have persisted during the courses of their two careers.

Still has maintained the stance of the "splendid isolationist," the private man from Troublesome Creek, the librarian, the gardener, and the figurative mountain climber who happens to write stories now and again. If we consider volume alone, Still (along with Ingram) has been the least productive of the writers here under consideration, having thus far published *Hounds on the Mountain* (poems [1979]), *River of Earth* (novel [1940]), *On Troublesome Creek* (stories [1941]), *Pattern of a Man and Other Stories* (stories[1980]), and four children's books. In an afterword to the stories, Still said: "My writings drew on everyday experiences and observations. I only wrote when an idea overwhelmed me. . . . I wrote in an isolation that was virtually total. Whether that was good or bad I cannot say. More than one rescue party came to try to persuade me back to 'civilization.'"

Still is concerned with such basic themes as honor, loyalty, self-reliance, and independence. He dramatizes these human qualities vividly. His people learn endurance, self-preservation, and ways to respond to the world with a wry humor. Like the dramatist, he gains powerful effects as the effaced narrator who never stands between the characters and the reader. Words carry their own force in Still's narratives. "Fiction is drama," he remarked. "I include only actions I can visualize, and I have to hear the characters talking. When they quit talking to me I know something is wrong. In one story I left a character tilted back in a chair for two years because he quit talking to me." Thus, Still as author has been willing to wait, even for a long time, to get a story or a poem set down the way it seems right to him. A strong individualist, he writes first to please himself; others can be pleased if they choose. James Still generalized on the difference between his outlook and Stuart's when he stated that no writer needs to exhibit himself and promote his own work. "We can't know how good a writer is unless we can forget how great he keeps telling us he is." Small though the output at hand, Still's readers usually are impressed by its quality.

In contrast to Still, Stuart is essentially a teller of tales, a writer one step away from the oral tradition in which he grew up in the dark hollows of Kentucky. Stuart assumed the role of bard, minstrel, and entertainer. He read his stories and poems aloud at public gatherings, writers' conferences, at colleges and universities. He took his tales and poetry off to the marketplace and lost few opportunities to promote a homespun Jesse Stuart for the public. He learned how to hold an audience with his balladlike prose. Thus he settled on being a performer as well as a writer.

By 1967, the year Jesse Stuart was sixty, he had published twenty-six books and three hundred short stories. He suffered a severe heart attack in 1954, at age forty-seven, but in 1960 lectured for a year at the University of Cairo, Egypt, and made a goodwill tour overseas for the State Department in 1962. The most prolific writer Kentucky has produced, Stuart may be unequalled in America, for since 1967 he has published another ten books—autobiographies, many poems, articles, and commentaries. He out-talked and out-wrote everybody until a few years ago when he became permanently bedridden with paralysis.

Clearly outstanding in the Stuart canon are *Man with a Bull-tongue Plow* (1934), a collection of 703 sonnets varying in number of lines, all written in the course of a year, a kind of hill farmer's autobiography in poetry with death as central unifying theme. *Beyond Dark Hills* (1938), the prose autobiography that Stuart began for a class at Vanderbilt, establishes the major and recurring themes in his work: endurance, fortitude, the inevitability of laughter, love, and survival. These are the qualities from which life springs in Stuart's isolated W-Hollow. *The Thread That Runs So True* (1949) recounts Stuart's experiences as a teacher and the hard, often bitter physical battle—as well as the intellectual battles—before discipline and book learning can win the respect of a hill-country community. An intrepid believer in education as a moral force to fight the powers of darkness, Stuart combined teaching, lecturing, and writing throughout a lifetime. Among the novels, *Taps for Private Tussie* (1943), a raggedly humorous presentation of a Kentucky family and the effects of World War II on their lives, is certainly Stuart at his best—wry, witty, idiomatic, vigorous, and conscious of life's bittersweet ironies. It was a popular success and sold over two million copies in two years.

Ruel E. Foster's study (*Jesse Stuart*, in the Twayne United States Authors series [1968]), concludes that Stuart "embodies better than any other American writer the dual lives of a man of action and an artist." A practicing and philosophical agrarian, Stuart in his prime successfully ran a farm of one thousand acres. Foster comments that "he holds everlastingly for the efficacy of tiny, invisible, molecular moral forces that work from individual to individual and in time destroy the hardest monument of man's pride. From boyhood he has believed that one can do anything if he wants to badly enough." However repetitive his later works may seem, Stuart has made no compromises with his earliest affirmations and convictions.

Before her marriage to Harold Arnow, Harriette Simpson had published one novel, *Mountain Path* (1936), and three short stories. Cleanth Brooks, John Thibaut Purser, and Robert Penn Warren selected "Washerwoman's Day," a story that was first published in the *Southern Review*, for their influential anthology, *Approaches to Literature* (1936). Since the 1940s, however, Arnow has felt more at ease with the novel and local history. She has published *Hunter's Horn* (1949), *The Dollmaker* (1954), *Seedtime on the Cumberland* (1960), *Flowering of the Cumberland* (1963), and *The Weedkiller's Daughter* (1970). The most popular of her four novels, *The Dollmaker*, the story of Gertie Nevels, who with her family moves from Kentucky to Detroit, is the saga of all displaced, uprooted individuals suddenly shoved into a cold, seemingly ruthless environment. Living in a housing project in a large city is almost disastrous for the Nevelses. Gertie loses her bearings until she resumes wood carving (a mountain craft) as a means of creating and finding order and a chance to understand the paradoxical nature of the world.

In spite of personal tragedy and the deaths for which Gertie Nevels cannot pretend to assign a meaning, the heroine's attitude ultimately affirms that there is courage, forbearance, and a will to survive in most human beings. Gertie comes to know something of the magnitude and universality of the human experience: "the alley [in which she lived] and the people in it were bigger than Detroit."

Bowen Ingram was the name under which Mildred Prewett Ingram (1925—1981) published stories and novels set in Nashville and the small towns of Middle Tennessee. She was born in Gordonsville and educated in Lebanon, where, after an early marriage to Daniel Ingram, she spent most of her life. Bowen Ingram was a sensitive reporter of the currents that ebbed and flowed through a country village, a rural county seat, or Nashville itself. Her people are neither folkish in speech nor local in their outlook. They are educated (but not intellectuals); they are aware of the world beyond; and they observe manners and decorum naturally without having to think. Like Jane Austen and the author's fellow Tennessean Peter Taylor, Bowen Ingram presents characters with breeding and a sense of values. All the stories are set in the twentieth century, though the dominating patterns of behavior have been carried over from the nineteenth. Her novels are If Passion Flies (1945) and Light in the Morning (1954).

Neither conformists nor nonconformists in any strict philosophical or literary sense, the regionalists of the South in the twentieth century surpassed their predecessors in the school of local colorists. If they rebelled against the older generation it was a matter of art. They disdained one-sided, stereotyped characters; they avoided easy, predictable solutions; they explored modern themes that were not "easy" or shopworn. Growing up with the sledgehammer irony of Poe and Maupassant, they elected to make irony more subtle and ambiguous. They obviously rebelled against excesses in the phonetic spelling of speech, shifts in tone within a story, and most of the literary extravagances of the nineteenth century. At their best, these writers were competent craftsmen and natural storytellers who were keenly aware of the poetry in good prose.

They were not rebels, however, in matters of fictional or poetic techniques. For example, among them there are no major innovators like Henry James or William Faulkner in the presentation of point of view, or stream of consciousness, or juggled chronology. For the most part, they practiced with competence the traditional techniques of the trade without the daring of a James Joyce or a Thomas Wolfe. Like Ernest Hemingway, they did what they did well, but as Faulkner said about Hemingway, "he did not try for the impossible." These seven regionalists, memorable for the settings and texture of their work, do not exhibit the genius of the great writers in Southern literature. Taken altogether, however, they reaffirm the *pietàs* of the Southern community, the unique elements of life in the South, and the severity of the human condition in whatever region they represent.

THOMAS DANIEL YOUNG

Editors and Critics

B y the early 1920s John Crowe Ransom was teaching in his classes
at Vanderbilt the approach to literature that later became known
as the New Criticism. When he first began to offer the introduction to
literature course required of all freshmen, one quarter of which was devoted to Shakespeare, he included six or seven of the plays. He gradually
decreased the number, however, until he was doing only one play. He
had concluded that to teach Shakespeare as poet he must concentrate
not only upon the structure of the play (its narrative and meter) but also
upon what he was later to call its *texture* (its diction, imagery, sound,
figurative language—the irrational elements of art that furnish many of
the insights that literature offers). If he was to teach the plays as poetry,
he was convinced, he must concentrate on passages from one play, with
only complementary references to the others that the students were required to read. It was not until the fall of 1937, however, that Ransom
published "Criticism, Inc.," the essay that has often been cited as "the
clarion call for the New Criticism, a new approach to literary study, for
criticism concerned with formal analyses and literary judgments." In
"Poetry: A Note in Ontology," published three years earlier, he had attempted to identify the unique nature and function of poetry—a task
that consumed much of his creative energy for the remainder of his
life—by dividing verse into three types: physical, Platonic, and metaphysical. The first of these he calls genuine poetry because it attempts to
present "things in their thingness," but despite concentration on the
basic ingredient of all poetry—images—it is only "half poetry" because
it carefully excludes all concepts and, therefore, it possesses little intellectual and emotional content. It is all texture and no structure. The
second classification he labels "bogus poetry." The writers of this kind
of verse have no faith in images. They use them merely to illustrate ideas.
His illustration of this bogus poetry (from Robert Browning's *Para-
celsus*) is illuminating.

The year's at the spring
And day's at the morn;
Morning's at seven;
The hill-side's dew-pearled;
The lark's on the wing;
The snail's on the thorn:
God's in his heaven—
All's right with the world!

This, he concludes, "is a piece of transparent homiletics; for in it six pretty, coordinate images are marched, like six little lambs to the slaughter, to a colon and a powerful text." The third kind of poetry he called metaphysical—though he later was convinced that this designation was too restrictive. This is "true poetry," because it has both idea and image, structure and texture. It is constructed upon a "metaphor that is meant," one that is "developed so literally that it must be meant, or predicated so baldly that nothing else can be meant." The fully developed metaphor presents a likeness between two objects that in its initial statement is "partial though it should be considerable," but after its full development its "identification is complete."

These essays Ransom included in The World's Body (1938)—along with "Poets without Laurels," "A Poem Nearly Anonymous," "Forms and Citizens," and "The Tense of Poetry"—and the New Criticism was formally launched; for in this collection he indicates the function of poetry is to help us recover "the body and solid substance of the world" from the "fulness of memory" into which "it seems to have retired." Because we "cannot know constitutionally as scientists" the world "which is made of whole and indefeasible objects," we must depend upon poetry to recover this world for us. Poetry, then, "is the kind of knowledge by which we must know what we have arranged that we shall not know otherwise."

In late winter, 1940, Ransom submitted an untitled book-length essay on contemporary critics to the New Directions press. The manuscript was accepted by James Laughlin, president of the press, but he suggested the addition of another chapter, as Ransom wrote Tate, "to include my own doctrine and save myself from having to write another book." When Tate, after he had read the manuscript, agreed with Laughlin, Ransom continued his search, now more than twenty years old, to find appropriate terms to describe the specific *nature* of poetic discourse as he had presented its precise *function* in The World's Body. The result was "Wanted: An Ontological Critic," the final essay in The New Criticism (1941), the book that gave the new approach to literature its name.

Ransom begins the essay by asserting that a critic must be able to distinguish between poetic and scientific discourses. A poem differs from prose not in moralism, emotionalism, or sensibility, Ransom asserts, but in the kind of structure it has, a structure that "is not so tight and precise on its logical side as a scientific or technical prose generally is" but one that "imports and carries along a great deal of irrelevant or foreign matter which is . . . obstructive." To complete the poetic discourse an irrelevant local texture is added to the loose logical structure. "The structure proper is the prose of the poem, being a local discourse of almost any kind, and dealing with almost any content suited to a logical discourse. The texture, likewise, seems to be of any real content that may be come upon, provided it is so free, unrestricted and large that it cannot properly get into the structure. One guesses it is an *order* of content, rather than a *kind* of content, that distinguishes texture from structure, and prose from poetry."

Structure contains, then, the logical argument of a poem, its fable, the part that may be reduced to prose, along with its meter and the denotation of the words it employs. Although this structure is not as tightly organized as a scientific essay, it bears some resemblance to a prose discourse. Poetry also contains "an irrelevant local texture," which a scientific discourse would rigorously exclude; that is, its patterns of imagery, the connotation of its language, and its tropes.

As Ransom was attempting to work out his theories of the nature and function of poetry, so was his gifted student, Allen Tate. In "Whose Ox" (*Fugitive*, December, 1922), Tate clearly allied himself with modernism by arguing against the traditional concept that poetry "must *represent* some phase of life ordinarily perceived" and that the poet must "look for his effects in a new combination of images representing only the constituted material world." Instead, he insisted, poets must be allowed to attempt to achieve the effect they pursue by "rearranging, remaking, remoulding in a subjective order . . . the material world." It is obvious that Tate, like Ransom, is considering the unique nature of poetic composition as he searches for a means of retaining the traditional elements of verse while permitting it to incorporate the most effective of the modernistic techniques.

In a later essay, "Literature as Knowledge," included in *Reason in Madness: Critical Essays* (1941), Tate comes even closer to Ransom's insistence that poetry is about the only source of a specific quality of knowledge when he states: "In the poem we get knowledge of a whole object, . . . complete knowledge, the full body of the experience. . . . However we may see the completeness of poetry, . . . it is a problem less to be solved than . . . to be preserved." In "Tension in Poetry" (*On the*

Limits of Poetry: Selected Essays, 1928–1948 [1948]) Tate suggests that the poet is less interested in making the reader's response to his work logical than he is in creating a definite response. Every poem, he continues, has both extensive and intensive meaning. The traditional poet interested primarily in constructing a logical argument "begins at or near the denotative end of the line"; that is, he is emphasizing the accepted definition of the words he is using. The less traditional poet—the modernist or symbolist, for example—begins at the other end, the intensive one. Tate argues that "by a straining feat of the imagination," each poet "tries to push his meaning as far as he can toward the opposite end, so as to occupy the whole scale." One kind of poet wants the meaning that the word suggests; the other, that which it explicitly names or describes. The tension created by the reaction between these two opposing forces—the intensive and the extensive—gives the poem its unique meaning. Above all else, Tate reiterated, a poem intends to move its readers to a significant action or reveal a fundamental truth.

Tate agreed with Ransom that writing and reading poetry in the twentieth century is not considered a significant activity; therefore, it is ill-taught in school and college. In fact, poetry teachers, because they do not understand the unique function of poetry—that is, to reveal a quality of knowledge available almost nowhere else—do not know how to deal with their subject. They are learned men (they know the data of literature), but they are not critical men (they are unable to render a literary judgment). They do not have the skill to read literature as literature; therefore, they read and teach it as philosophy, history, theology, linguistics, or something else.

Two important media made the New Criticism the most important force in critical thinking for three generations, and the effect it has had on the way literature is experienced today is far from dead. First of all, three influential journals—the *Southern Review*, the *Sewanee Review*, and the *Kenyon Review*—opened their pages to critics who for the most part agreed with Tate and Ransom on the nature and function of poetry. For many years these magazines have been filled with the most significant criticism written in Europe and America. Each quarter they carried the illuminating and convincing remarks of Ransom, Tate, T. S. Eliot, William Empson, R. P. Blackmur, Robert Penn Warren, Cleanth Brooks, Robert B. Heilman, F. O. Matthiessen, Lionel Trilling, John Peale Bishop, L. C. Knights, Phillip Rahv, Arthur Mizener, Randall Jarrell, Yvor Winters, Austin Warren, Kenneth Burke, Ray B. West, and many, many others. It was indeed, as Ransom pointed out, an age of criticism.

As these critics were busily establishing the principles and demonstrating the means by which literature should be read, some of them—notably Brooks, Warren, and Heilman—were preparing textbooks from which literature (especially poetry) could be taught. Their work, however, was not confined to school texts. The year following Ransom's publication, Brooks brought out *Modern Poetry and the Tradition* (1939), the primary purpose of which, he wrote in the introduction, was "to assist those readers whose conception of poetry . . . is primarily defined . . . by the achievements of the Romantic poets." Although some of the poetry by modern poets is admittedly obscure, he continues, it is both significant and understandable. Furthermore, it is very definitely anchored in the tradition, though one must often go back beyond the nineteenth and eighteenth centuries to the seventeenth to find the poetry it most resembles. Like their seventeenth-century forerunners, many modern poets consider their proper role that of maker; they are attempting to reconstitute human experience through appropriately blending emotion and intellect. They feel that if they truthfully render this experience, they must include the whole of it, even its discordant elements, and, above all, they must not oversimplify it.

Even as he wrote this book, Brooks and Robert Penn Warren were preparing *Understanding Poetry* (1938), a widely used textbook designed to convert college teachers of poetry and their students into those critical men and women whom Ransom had called for in "Criticism, Inc.," a group prepared to deal adequately with the "poetic or individual object which tends to be universalized, but is not permitted to suffer this fate." This book, and the several different editions of it that have been published in succeeding years, has revolutionized the way literature is taught in the classroom. Direct in purpose, it simply aims to demonstrate that if poetry is to reveal the unique knowledge it contains, it must be read as poetry and not as something else. At the outset the editors point out the three most commonly used substitutes for the poem in many classrooms: "1. Paraphrase of logical and narrative content; 2. Study of biographical and historical materials; 3. Inspirational and didactic interpretation." In many instances, the editors continue, a paraphrase of the poem may be useful, or a discussion of the author's life and when he lived may aid in understanding and experiencing the poem; this kind of reading and this supplementary information, however, should be used as means and literary constructs, not as historical or ethical doctrines. They should be employed to assist the reader in his approach to the poem and not as a substitute for the poem itself.

Most college textbooks place obstacles between the reader and the poem and encourage him to be satisfied with a vague, impressionistic interpretation of the poem. The editors of *Understanding Poetry* demonstrate the kind of impediments they have in mind. After reprinting Keats's "Ode to a Nightingale," one anthology of English poetry adds the following note: "The song of the nightingale brings sadness and exhilaration to the poet and makes him want to be lifted up and away from the limitations of life. The seventh stanza is particularly beautiful." If this poem is read in an attempt to allow it to reveal the unique knowledge it contains, however, the reader must be concerned with such matters as the following: "1. How is the paradox of 'exhilaration' and 'sadness' related to the theme of the poem? . . . 2. The seventh stanza is referred to as 'beautiful,' but on what grounds is the student to take any piece of literature as 'beautiful'? 3. Even if the exercise quoted is relevant, there is a real danger that the suggestion to the student to look for beautiful objects in the poem will tend to make him confuse with poetic excellence the mention of beautiful or agreeable objects."

The editors of *Understanding Poetry* explain in clear, concrete, and unambiguous language the manner in which they believe poetry should be experienced: "1. Emphasis should be kept on the poem as a poem. 2. The treatment should be concrete and inductive. 3. A poem must be treated as an organic system of relationships, and the poetic quality should never be understood as inhering in one or more factors taken in isolation."

Such a tightly structured selection of verse—complemented by a series of closely focused, inductively argued explications of many of the poems—had never before been placed in the hands of students. Beginning with the simplest kind of verse and following each poem with appropriate commentary and questions revealing its aim and purpose, highlighting its basic structure and causing the reader to study closely its significant elements of texture, provide an entirely novel manner of experiencing a poem. This book along with *Understanding Fiction* (1943), and *Understanding Drama* (1945), edited by Brooks and Robert B. Heilman, have surely had more effect on the way literature is taught in American colleges than any others ever published.

After *Modern Poetry and the Tradition* appeared, some commentators protested that Brooks believed the English literary tradition did not include the writers of the eighteenth and nineteenth centuries, that it leaped from the metaphysicals to the moderns. Almost as if to prove this claim fallacious, Brooks published *The Well-Wrought Urn: Studies in the Structure of Poetry* (1947) in which he demonstrated that poetry from almost every literary period can be explicated in the manner suggested by the New Critics. These readings prompted Ransom to label Brooks "the best living 'reader' or interpreter of difficult verse." These readings and such essays as "The Heresy of the Paraphrase" also reveal that in a few particulars there is, to use Ransom's phrase, a little divergence between his theories and Ransom's. Brooks feared that Ransom's insistence on separating a poem into its logical structure and its irrelevant texture might result in the age-old error of dividing a poem into form and content. Ransom retaliated with the comment that by refusing to recognize the poem's logical structure Brooks "goes straight from one detail [or image] to another in the manner of the bee who gathers honey from the several blossoms as he comes to them, without noticing the bush" that supports them. Too, they each placed different demands upon the metaphor. Ransom insisted upon a single and consistent development of the metaphor, from a similarity though slight to an identification that is complete. Brooks argued that the coherence of a poem depends not on its ideational core but upon the development of its dominant metaphor through a series of resolved stresses. These differences, though significant, obviously were not irreconcilable. Both men always insisted that the reading and writing of poetry are essential activities in any civilized society. Although Brooks has never altered his opinion of the importance of poetry, in his later years he has established a reputation as being one of the most illuminating and perceptive commentators on the works of William Faulkner. His two books on Faulkner, *William Faulkner: The Yoknapatawpha Country* (1963) and *William Faulkner: Toward Yoknapatawpha and Beyond* (1978), are masterpieces of rational and persuasive argument presented in lucid and supple prose.

As any reader of modern literature well knows, Robert Penn Warren did not spend his entire career editing textbooks demonstrating the manner in which literature should be read. The most versatile writer in modern Southern letters, he wrote books of poetry, fiction, and criticism that have won for him every important literary prize except the Nobel. With the possible exception of Allen Tate and Edmund Wilson, he is the leading candidate for American man of letters of the twentieth century. His literary career is ably covered in James H. Justus' essay appearing elsewhere in this volume and surely does not need to be rehearsed here. A few words about his criticism, however, would seem appropriate. In addition to such theoretical and speculative essays as "Literature as Symptom" (1936), "Pure and Impure Poetry" (1943)—in which he argues that poetry wishes to be pure but poems do not— "Knowledge and the Image of Man" (1955), "A Poem of Pure Imagination: An Experiment in Reading" (1946), and "Democracy and Poetry" (1975), no other Southern critic has written as well on so many important Southern writers at very crucial times in their careers. In many instances these essays set the perimeters of the deluge of criticism that

413

was to follow. Among the most helpful of these are "John Crowe Ransom: A Study in Irony" (1935), "A Note on the Hamlet of Thomas Wolfe" (1935), "Irony with a Center: Katherine Anne Porter" (1941–52), "Love and Separateness in Eudora Welty" (1944), "William Faulkner" (1946–50), Introduction to *A Long Fourth and Other Stories* by Peter Taylor (1948), "Elizabeth Madox Roberts: Life is from Within" (1963).

WILLIAM C. HAVARD

The Search for Identity

One of the ironies of Southern literary history is the closeness with which the Southern Renascence followed H. L. Mencken's scathing portrayal of the South as a cultural wasteland in "The Sahara of the Bozart." And if that coincidence in timing is precise enough to suggest a cause and effect relation, other ironies, some clearly intended by the author and some apparent only in retrospect, run throughout Mencken's best-known short piece of social criticism. In their pleasure with Mencken's flamboyant imagery, or in their Puritanical assurance of cultural superiority, those who quote from "Sahara" often tend to overlook two things in the essay that may be more pertinent to the whole question of the personal and social identity of the South and the Southerner than what either Mencken or those defensive Southerners who tried to answer him directly had to say about the state of Southern culture *circa* 1920. The first is that, after the hyperbolic statement that "it would be impossible in all history to match so complete a drying-up of a civilization," Mencken went on to say (in an oddly balanced additional bit of hyperbole) that the pre-Confederate South "was a civilization of manifold excellences—perhaps the best that the Western Hemisphere has ever seen—undoubtedly the best that These States have ever seen." Second, he compared the qualities of this early Southern civilization with its New England counterpart, much to the disadvantage of the latter.

> The New England shopkeepers and theologians never really developed a civilization. . . . They were, at their best, tawdry and tacky fellows, oafish in manner and devoid of imagination; one searches in vain for mention of a salient Yankee gentleman. . . . But in the South there were men of delicate fancy, urbane instinct and aristocratic manner—in brief, superior men. . . . To politics, their chief diversion, they brought active and original minds. . . . A certain noble spaciousness was in the ancient southern scheme of things. The Ur-Confederate had leisure. He liked to toy with ideas. He was hospitable and tolerant. He had the vague thing that we call culture.

415

What makes this multiple comparative perspective interesting in retrospect is that it conveys to the reader, either directly or by implication, virtually every historical issue leading to the renewed search for Southern identity that played so important a part in the Southern Renascence from the 1920s onward. The totally negative opening of the essay mirrors the dominant view of Southern culture set forth in William P. Trent's 1892 biography of William Gilmore Simms. Trent's critical judgment that intellectual life in the Old South was virtually nonexistent, having been perpetually stifled by the presence of slavery, was elaborated by others into the conception that the potential Southern man of letters became so heavily engaged from the 1820s into the 1860s in legal and political defense of the South as a plantation culture rooted in a slave-based economy that there was no time or opportunity to cultivate the creative mind and produce a literature (and a high culture generally) worthy of the name. In the aftermath of the Civil War (the ultimate defense by arms), the Southern writers withdrew into the never-never land of the Lost Cause, out of which they created a romantic vision of a grand, tragically doomed civilization that they were determined to make live in historic memory. Sentimentality rather than the effort to confront reality thus replaced the political ideology of separatism (or Southern nationalism) as the moving force behind Southern literature during the last third of the nineteenth century. Thomas Nelson Page is the writer usually identified as the main exemplar of this dominant trend.

As Mencken moves into the comparisons of the older Old South with the South of his day and with the North, his personal affinity with the social and cultural characteristics of that earlier Southern civilization show through most clearly. The Virginia planter-cavalier image mirrors Mencken's views on society, politics, and the general culture: pro-aristocratic, deeply skeptical about the excesses of egalitarian democracy, and strongly adherent to the idea of cultivated leisure as the foundation for the practice of the arts and gracious living. The contrast between this essentially romantic vision of a properly constituted society (once nearly completely realized) and the desiccated South that succeeded it is paralleled by the comparison of both with the Puritanical dogmatism and commercialism of New England in combination with the "bumpkinry of the Middle West—Bryanism, Prohibition, vice crusading" which have found their way into the post-Reconstruction South that had fallen into the hands of the former poor whites who were now part of the boosterism associated with "all the progress . . . [the South] babbles of." Although Mencken did not mention the New South as such, nor relate its doctrines to the attempts by Henry Grady and other of its proponents to conflate the later Southern romantic myths with the progressive dogmas of the Northern industrial age in an effort to promote sectional reconciliation and industrial development in the South, his understanding of the recent South in those terms is unmistakable.

Despite its philippic cast, "The Sahara of the Bozart" is more than a fortuitously timed onslaught on the South and all things Southern. In its exaggerated and unqualified way it set forth the essential questions about the South and Southerners that would occupy the minds of those Southern men and women of letters—the creative writers of the Renascence and after, as well as a host of historians, social scientists, and journalists—for the indefinite future as they sought to understand and portray men and women as Southerners, and the South as a social, political, and cultural historical entity. Because most of those who engaged in this quest for Southern identity during the early days of the Renascence were creative writers and as much aware as Mencken of the moribund state of Southern letters, one of the first questions to engage them was the place of the literary artist in the South and the kind of culture or cultures most conducive to the cultivation of the literary vocation generally, and in the South in particular. The nature of the Southern historical experience also loomed large in this search. Included in this consideration were such questions as the distinctiveness of the South and the consequences of that distinctiveness (if more than superficial) for both the South and the nation in the light of rebellion, secession, and the return to the Union of a conquered territory and people. In the anthropological sense, the cultural ethos of the South was also a part of any special social identity one might perceive both in subjective terms and in the moral, aesthetic, and religious values Southerners held in common. Those values were revealed symbolically through their arts, rituals, and myths, as well as in their economic, political, and sociological manifestations in institutions, social structures, and the habits and customs displayed in the day-to-day activities of life.

These complex issues and more were treated in all their diversity and interrelatedness in the creative literature that constitutes the Southern Renascence. Like all recognized major works of the imagination, much of that literature has been judged to have lasting value because of its ability to convey universal truths about man, nature, and society through the portrayal of the concrete and particular. The characters, as well as the natural and social settings that provided the materials on which these writers set their imaginations to work, were distinctly and uniquely Southern.

The chapters on the individual authors or groups of authors in this section of this volume show the ways in which this era of Southern literary achievement developed and how it altered the self-identifying

417

images of the South between the first and second world wars. What is not included, however, is a related development that was in its own way as much a part of the reawakening of the active life of the mind in the South as the literary Renascence. The student of Southern culture is aware of the appearance on the post–World War I Southern scene of a number of outstanding historians, social scientists, and journalists whose intellectual interests were focused on the South and who sought through methods of analysis appropriate to their respective academic disciplines or vocations to grasp the meaning (or identity) of the South in its larger moral, social, political, and especially historical dimensions. As in the case of the creative writers, the variety of perceptions and theoretical differences among these essentially scholarly and critical men and women created tensions that stimulated their efforts and broadened the scope of the inquiry in ways that have kept the quest very much alive. And despite the range of interpretations that have resulted, one can discern commonalities among the protagonists in the debates and other exchanges that seem to divide those involved in these intellectual and artistic pursuits, a sense of a common purpose that is paradoxically both the product of the Southern experience and the essential component in the shaping of that particular experience. The present essay proposes to supplement the several discussions of the Southern literary artists with some illustrations drawn from those "other" members of the Southern republic of letters who were engaged in the Southerner's search for identity.

That the pursuit of the identity theme has not been carried out separately by the creative writers and the historians *et al.*, but has been a common enterprise, is amply supported in the case of the Nashville Agrarians. The Agrarians may be considered either an outgrowth or a continuation of the earlier Fugitives who had been informally organized before World War I. At least four of the Fugitives had been influenced by the modernist literary movement in Europe, a phenomenon growing out of the alienation of many members of the Western literary culture from the modern rational progressive industrialized society that had been launched by the Enlightenment and had culminated in the disillusioning events leading to the physical and cultural destructiveness of the First World War and the economic and political disintegration of its aftermath. Following the dissolution in the mid-twenties of the Fugitives, whose members had developed what might be called a Southern literary consciousness, another informal gathering took place on the Vanderbilt campus to discuss the social and political problems confronting the South and the nation. Participants included two of the leading Fugitives who were still on the Vanderbilt faculty, John Crowe Ransom and Don-

ald Davidson of the English department, who were joined by other colleagues, notably historian Frank Lawrence Owsley, psychologist Lyle
Lanier, political scientist H. C. Nixon, novelist-to-be Andrew Lytle, and
John Donald Wade, biographer, essayist, and a fellow teacher of English.
Allen Tate and Robert Penn Warren, though away from Nashville, remained in touch and were, along with Ransom and Davidson, the former Fugitives who carried over to the Agrarian movement.

Along with two internationally prominent literary figures and a former Vanderbilt student who was a sometime journalist and federal ad-
ministrator, this group was invited to participate in writing the book
that evolved out of these "agrarian" discussions. The book was *I'll Take
My Stand* (1930), the "Southern Manifesto" that was to all purposes a
translation of the aforementioned Southern literary consciousness of the
Fugitives into a public statement about the social, economic, and political conditions for a coherent Southern culture that could express symbolically the meaning of its existence in history. As Davidson never tired
of explaining, the immediate stimulus for entering into a discussion of
these questions of social and political philosophy was the Scopes trial in
Dayton, Tennessee, in 1925 over a Tennessee statute prohibiting the
teaching of evolution in the public schools. Conducted in a circus atmosphere fomented by publicity featuring Mencken's uncompromisingly
savage satire, Davidson, especially, perceived the whole thing as a contrived occasion on which the dominant national culture—that urban-
industrial, centralized, modern materialistic one that had prevailed in
1865—could ridicule and humiliate the traditional agrarian, fundamentalist, plain-folk culture of Tennessee even as the Northern industrial order continued to exploit the area economically.

I'll Take My Stand was a controversial book from the outset, and
remains so to this day. We cannot rehearse all the arguments it provoked. But as Ransom indicated in his introductory "Statement of Principles," it was an expression of a certain way of looking at man and
society that the contributors to the book held in common. In order to
render those abstract convictions in concrete terms, it was stipulated
that all the articles in the book tended "to support a Southern way of
life against what might be called the American or prevailing way." And
in what Louis D. Rubin, Jr., has identified as a metaphoric expression of
the appropriate social and economic arrangements for a good life in the
classical sense, Ransom noted that all the contributors "as much as
agree[d] that the best terms in which to represent the distinction are
contained in the phrase, Agrarian *versus* Industrial."

Taken at its immediate face value (and it was misconstrued even at
this level) the book was a scathing criticism of the dehumanizing conse-

quences produced in a society organized around an industrial mode of production. Under a fully developed industrial system, the individual's identity is reduced to that of a producer and consumer of material goods; or as it was stated in Emerson's earlier formulation, "things are in the saddle and ride mankind." Man is isolated from nature in his very exploitation of it to satisfy the unending cycle of production and consumption. As Ransom said, "the latterday societies have been seized—none quite so violently as our American one—with the strange idea that the human destiny is not to secure an honorable peace with nature, but to wage an unrelenting war on nature." Man's proper relations with nature, including respect and piety towards its grandeur and mysteries, are the ground of religion and of art, and these expressions of the life of the mind and spirit cannot find room for cultivation in an industrial system whose goods are entirely material, and whose idea of progress is "incessant extension of industrialization." Modern man is similarly beset by the compulsions of the industrial society in his effort to establish the right relation of man-to-man, which includes the individual's cultivation of the social sensibilities that affect this internal harmony, as well as family and community affairs. The industrial order imposes its conditions in abstract ways that fragment society, create personal insecurity, and turn even the leisure that its productive capacity increases into occasions for the exercise of the consumer function on which the infinite series "characteristic of industrial progress" depends.

For a short time the Agrarians acted as spokesmen for the principles they perceived as the basis for a good life in an ordered society, and they never ceased to associate literature and politics as they returned to the pursuit of their literary arts. Tate's essays are full of references to the political philosophies (sometimes "shadowy") in the works of the modern man of letters, and how they have failed in those philosophies to face up to the problems of modernity. He also refers to the way the man of letters has connived, perhaps disdainfully, in society's ignoring him by withdrawing into the self. Davidson was never reconciled to the abandonment of an activist role in politics for the literary expression of the truth about man and society in the effort to understand and to act. Warren later entered the lists of public debate, especially on the problems of racial reconciliation, but also in other ways. In whatever any of them did later, creative writers, historians, and social scientists alike, they accepted the fact that all issues involving man start with the nature of man, not just his physical and psychological nature, but social and spiritual natures as well. And they all continued to write about the infinite permutations of these positive qualities and defects of man within the frameworks of a Southern setting, especially as that setting continued to be a society that never totally abandoned its historical roots in a civilization that was older and wiser than modernity. Even when, as with Warren, they remarked about the South having no place for them, they were never alienated from it. Although not recognized for doing so until much later, the Agrarians also faced up to the South's great moral deficiencies because, like its virtues, the flaws were inherent in the possibilities and limits of a human nature that is not perfectible in the world but is such that man is compelled to keep trying to find some form of redemption from the evil that results.

The critical reception of *I'll Take My Stand* was more negative than positive. In many circles, North and South alike, the Agrarians were regarded as being a rather simple extension of the romantic mythmaking of the old moonlight and magnolia genre, and the fact that many of its defenders also received it in that spirit lent credence to that perception. The validity of parts of its critique of historical modernity and the idea of infinite progress, especially as manifested in the triumph of the modern urban-industrial society over a traditional one that had developed through experience rather than by way of instrumental (essentially technological) reason, was not widely recognized until it was confirmed by further experience over the next two generations.

In the meantime an intellectual (and practical) movement was taking shape that provided a defense of the assumptions and purposes informing the concept of modernity in terms of their applicability to the economic, social, and political conditions of the traditional South. That intellectual movement closely paralleled the Fugitive-Agrarian one in time, though its program for practical action extended far beyond the limited attempts on the part of the Agrarians to implement their ideas. As in the case of the Agrarians, too, what might with some retrospective justification be called the movement for Southern modernization (or Southern development) began in a university. In this case it was a public institution—the University of North Carolina—in a state that already had the reputation of being among the most progressive of the Southern states. The leadership in this case was clearly vested in, or assumed by, one man, Howard W. Odum, a sociologist out of rural Georgia who went to Chapel Hill in 1920 to head the Department of Sociology and School of Public Welfare (both newly established) at the university. His accomplishments at North Carolina were so remarkable that he is given credit by many social scientists and intellectual historians for having made a real place for the social sciences generally in institutions of higher learning in the South, and for having been responsible for turning the University of North Carolina not only into a nationally recognized center for study and research in the social sciences, but also into a center for public service directed toward improving the conditions of life in the South by application of social technologies to problems revealed by the scientific study of Southern society and culture. As part of these efforts he founded the Institute for Research in Social Science and the *Journal of Social Forces*, both of which are still flourishing and continue to be concerned with both pure and applied social science research.

On the surface Odum gave every impression of representing the modern mind in its purest form. He exhibited great confidence, amounting to a secular faith, in man's capacity to use the methods of natural science to gain knowledge of man and society that would enable him, through application to the problems of Southern society, to change that society for the better. The largest of the goals he set was displacing ideological sectionalism, which not only kept the South separate from the nation but erected other barriers against improving economic and social conditions in the South, with a concept of regions based on natural geographic, economic, and social coherence. In that respect he appeared to be a rationalist in the sense attached to that term in the age of the Enlightenment. Comprehensive physical and social planning also played a great instrumental role in his conception of a proper social order. To those ends he was a prodigious laborer in the area of scientific sociology and on practical means of effecting changes in institutions as the basis for modernizing the South. Parts of Odum's voluminous works (an excellent sample of which can be found in *Folk, Region, and Society: Selected Papers of Howard W. Odum* [1964]) could be folded into contemporary social science literature on third world development, and readers would have difficulty distinguishing between the basic concepts and methods of the respective works.

In other respects, however, Odum was an interesting example of one who sought to combine a socially organic traditionalism with the products of rational change in social structures to create a social order that reflected a complete harmony between the self (or inner being) and the objectively (or outwardly) structured society. His analysis of Southern society was comprehensive, demographically and anthropologically, but as a science that deals largely with external phenomena, sociology could not always penetrate to the moral ethos that is basic to a civic culture born of the wisdom of experience. In their special studies, the professional associates and students of Odum discerned and analyzed many social, economic, and political problems in the South, including those of the tenant farmers, black Southerners, and laborers in the textile mills, as well as the limitations imposed on personal and social development by poor education, health, and income levels generally. Even so, there remained in Odum's mind and heart many attachments to the traditional culture he wanted to change radically but not completely, thus indicating that while *Agrarian* became almost as bad a word in the lexicon of the North Carolinians as *sociology* did for the Nashvillians, the two groups had more in common than they cared to admit.

These commonalities may be best illustrated by reference to a collection of essays entitled *Culture in the South* (1934), edited by W. T. Couch, a prime figure in the development of the University of North Carolina Press and an associate of Odum's in several academic enterprises. *Culture in the South* was regarded by some as a response from North Carolina to Vanderbilt, and in some respects it was. But in its contents, which included contributions by three Agrarians—Wade, Davidson, and Nixon—it proves to be more of a corrective supplement to *I'll Take My Stand* than an adversarial treatise. (One should note, however, that Andrew Lytle's essay, which he was invited to contribute, was refused.) General agreement seemed to be reached on opposition to a culture entirely based on material acquisitiveness. Although differing over the means of handling commonly recognized problems within the traditional culture, the Agrarians conceded here and elsewhere that change was inevitable and some deliberately induced reforms were a necessary part of that change. And the critical and the constructive tended to unite in the devotion to a shared culture in which at least as many distinguishable parts of it deserved preservation as required alteration.

Historiography in the South underwent a massive change during this period. The older epideictic style gave way to a realistic look at the region's political and social history; major revisionist works were produced on such topics as Reconstruction; and intellectual history and biography came into their own. Although some of these changes have been traced back to the last quarter of the nineteenth century (see Wendell Holmes Stephenson, *Southern History in the Making* [1964]) a reasonable starting point in the present context might well be the work of Ulrich B. Phillips, the first historian who studied plantation life and its extended ramifications, using previously unexamined sources to bring a new realism to the economic and social history of the South. Although *Life and Labor in the Old South* (1931) is Phillips' best-known and most influential work in relation to the development of Southern historiography over the quarter-century following its appearance, his statement of the central theme of Southern history in a 1928 article in the *American Historical Review* proved to be a stimulus, possibly unmatched in any other source, to the continuing search for a unifying theme in Southern history that might explain the South's distinctive identity as a cohesive society. Although Phillips resisted broad generalizations about history, the central theme he advanced was the determination by the white Southerner that the South should remain "a white man's country." Many central themes have been proposed subsequently, but no matter how diverse these have been, rarely have any of them failed to include the relations between blacks and whites as a heavy thread running through Southern history, and thus a major shaping influence on the perception of the South and the Southerner.

Going beyond Phillips in both time and importance to the quest for identity on the part of Southern historians is the distinguished multivolume *History of the South*, published by the Louisiana State University Press in cooperation with the Littlefield Fund. The book in that series that has drawn most attention is *The Origins of the New South, 1877–1913* (1951) by C. Vann Woodward. Of all the Southern historians since World War I, Woodward has been the most widely recognized for giving new dimensions to Southern historiography, mainly by providing a place in Southern history for the so-called common man in his struggles to enlarge his political role by populist means.

Woodward's first book was a biography of Tom Watson, the enigmatic Georgian who articulated the economic and political goals of Southern populism perhaps better than any of the other leaders of the movement. Frustrated with his inability to break the hold of the large farmer–New South business alliance, Watson turned bitterly to racial demagoguery, which made him into a scapegoat prototype of the anti-intellectual, amoral, and irresponsible, if often egomaniacally clever, Southern mass leader. Woodward pointed out how the Populist era (*circa* the 1890s) and the Great Depression of the 1930s had had much in common— depression and economic dislocation, the development of strong antipathies on the part of farmers and laborers toward the increasingly dominant business interests, and an urgency born of desperation on the part of these large segments of the population about finding solutions to agricultural problems through agrarian reform.

In the same year in which *Origins of the New South* appeared, Woodward published a book entitled *Reunion and Reaction* that set the scene for the treatment of the New South by providing evidence that the "reaction" was not a return to Old South planter paternalism, but a takeover of economic and political power by prewar Whigs, thus setting New South politics at odds with, rather than complementary to, the South's dominant agrarianism. This change helps to explain why the Southern Populist party (or parties) tended to be so deeply opposed to the New South's programs for the advancement of the region and so intent on remaining mainly a farmers' movement. In the New South the Populists perceived nothing by way of a revitalized agricultural economic base, but perceived a continued exploitation of the South by way of national economic policies that limited the role of the region to that of a producer of raw materials and a tributary of the rising industrial powers, with all the problems of absentee ownership, low wages, lack of opportunities, and continuing poverty. In many respects the farmer's rebellion mounted an attack on New South politics that combined the later strictures of the Vanderbilt Agrarians and something of the rural reformist proclivities of the Chapel Hill sociologists.

In some of his essays in *The Burden of Southern History* (revised edition, 1968), Woodward talks about the ironies of Southern history that result from a mind divided between perceptions of an Old South and a New South, with all of the implications that division has for preserving some of the region's distinctions in face of the temptation to merge without residue into the dominant national pattern by having all the Southern cultural norms conform to those of the North. He also points out that the South's distinctiveness is rooted in its having had a different historical experience from the nation at large: where America has known only success and affluence, the South has known failure, defeat, and poverty; where the nation has thrived on its myth of innocence, the South has experienced, in the awful burden of slavery, the reality of evil and a sense of guilt; where the country as a whole has been optimistic and secure in its progressivist creed, the South's historical experience has generated pessimism in Southerners, an awareness of the limitations of the human condition, and a realization that everything one wants to do cannot be accomplished. The Southern historical experience has been closer to the experience of humanity at large than has the national experience, and out of that different experience and the identity the South has achieved through it, the South has much in its tradition that it should take care to preserve and much of value to offer the nation.

Woodward also notes that "the most reassuring prospect for the survival of the South's distinctive heritage is the magnificent body of literature produced by its writers in the last three decades. . . . After Faulkner, Wolfe, Warren and Welty no literate Southerner could remain unaware of his heritage or doubt its enduring value. After this outpouring it would seem more difficult than ever to deny a Southern identity, to be 'merely American.' To deny it would be to deny our heritage." At the 1956 reunion of the Fugitives in Nashville, during the course of a discussion of the relation between the poet and the politician and the poet and the philosopher, one of the participants noted that the poet and the philosopher had a much closer relation than the poet and the politician. It was the function of the poet (artist) to express experience in the images that came as close as possible to recreating for his audience the experience as it came to him, and it was then the philosopher's task to analyze that experience as expressed by the poet in a way that made it rationally apprehensible and coherent in relation to the general realm of experience. It might well be said that as philosopher-historian, Woodward has come as close as anyone to standing in that relation to the literary artists of the Southern Renaissence, and has performed the function arising from that connection about as well as the poets carried out their task of originating the symbols of experience.

A summary overview of any subject necessarily concentrates on a small number of illustrative examples to support its main points. A few other writers and their works are so striking in their uniqueness or in the completeness with which they exemplify a special aspect of the search for a Southern identity that failure to mention them would suggest serious oversight. A brief comment on three such cases is indicated.

The first of these is Wilbur J. Cash's *The Mind of the South* (1941). Cash was a North Carolina journalist who worked on his one important book for more than a decade, despite considerable prodding from Alfred Knopf. This book, described by one commentator as a modern miracle, is still regarded by some historians and other students of the South as having said all there was to say about the collective consciousness of the white Southerner. *The Mind of the South* is in its essence a demythologizing treatise in the Mencken vein, and indeed parts of it were published in the *American Mercury* as early as the 1920s, while Mencken was editor of that magazine. Although both slightly more restrained in its language and somewhat more sustained in the coherence of its analysis than Mencken's work, it is still colorfully and aphoristically written, featuring clever turns of phrase and sweeping generalizations. In holding that the South did not have time to develop a planter aristocracy, Cash paints a satirical portrait of an acquisitive family's rapid rise from illiterate dirt farmer status to slave-owning, pseudo-aristocratic planter and political leader, and in striking phrases he characterizes the Southerner by ascribing to him traits that reflect habits born of temperament rather than of intellection, of an exaggerated romanticism rather than rational calculation, of emotion more than mind. A sense of community derived more from the raw and restless frontier than from a settled sense of tradition, and it possessed a social cohesion established by a "proto-Dorian" bond of white supremacy that bound Southern whites of all classes and conditions into a unity against the blacks. In some of the traits thus assigned to the South and Southerners, Cash found merits that the South might use in putting its house in order. Indeed, his was a love-hate relation with his region rather than total alienation from it. In the practical sense *The Mind of the South* could be viewed as offering the possibility of a catharsis that would open the way to the restoration of mental and social health through the prescriptive changes held out by the North Carolina sociologists.

The Southern identity as seen by William Alexander Percy and Richard M. Weaver involves the possibilities of a defensive preservation of a traditional Southern culture as opposed to displacement by a totally rationalized one. Although Percy and Weaver come from different parts of the South, and differ considerably in background and in the conduct of their lives, they are essentially defenders of the same faith; that is, they both espoused a traditional way of life as opposed to what they perceived as a threat to the destruction of that way of life by the forces of modernity. Their intellectual ties are thus obviously with the Agrarians, as indeed were their ties of friendship.

Percy was from and of the Mississippi Delta, son of a Greenville planter-lawyer who was also a political leader of the antebellum South. One of the traumatic experiences of his life was observing his father being replaced by the demagogue James K. Vardaman. The younger Percy was a graduate of Sewanee and Harvard Law School, a Rhodes scholar, heroic young army officer in World War I, and a minor poet. He returned home after the war and settled quietly into the sequestered life of Greenville, Mississippi, and its plantation environs. His single prose work, *Lanterns on the Levee* (1941), is a lyrical valedictory to Southern aristocratic paternalism, based entirely on his personal experience and reflecting the characteristic Southern traits of personalism, sense of time and place, and classical stoicism. Here is the personification of the cavalier ideal, self-revealed as an anachronism who belonged in another century, but was also a living saint, as his Greenville writer friends David L. Cohn and Hodding Carter, Jr., have described him.

Weaver was by birth a North Carolinian who spent his early years in Lexington, Kentucky, and was graduated from the University of Kentucky in 1932. He was a socialist in his younger days, but abandoned that persuasion in favor of the traditional agrarian outlook. He did graduate work at Vanderbilt and Louisiana State University, from which he received his doctoral degree in 1943. Weaver spent most of his professional career (foreshortened by his death in 1963) at the University of Chicago where he taught classical rhetoric and wrote extensively on that subject and on philosophical issues that linked both rhetoric and other concerns of the humanities with the moral and social values of Western civilization. His principal work on the South was his unorthodox doctoral dissertation originally entitled "The Confederate South 1865–1910: A Study in the Survival of a Mind and a Culture," which was published posthumously (but practically unchanged) in 1968 under the title *The Southern Tradition at Bay*. In that book Weaver in a sense completes the statement of a part of the Agrarian position that was suggested on numerous occasions by Tate and others, but never developed fully by them, on the connections (unique with the South as distinct from the nation at large) of the Southern traditional culture with the European or Western traditional culture, thus broadening the historical basis out of which the South emerged.

This brief survey of contributors from a variety of perspectives to the search for Southern identity in the age of the South's intellectual Renascence is far from complete, but is amply supplemented by other parts of this literary history. It can only be reiterated in conclusion that a general revival in the life of the mind occurred in the South during this period in response to prior and incipient changes within and outside the South that produced a literature which not only established a fuller identity for the region but in varying ways prepared for a Southern reentry into the nation that may be more than a mere final absorption by the dominant culture—a reentry that brought with it some preserved, if still threatened, values that the dominant culture had mistakenly rejected during the long separation.

The Agrarians

When the *Fugitive* ceased publication in December, 1925, Ransom promised in the brief statement announcing the demise of the influential little magazine that the group that had produced it would continue its meetings and would possibly contribute to other communal projects. The meetings did continue sporadically, and in 1928 the group brought out a collection of verse under the title *Fugitives: An Anthology of Verse*. It was evident, however, that the force that had held the young poets together—that is, the writing of verse and the frank and detailed discussions of it—was losing its cohesiveness. Everyone was pursuing other interests or had left Nashville. Allen Tate was in New York trying to make his way as a free-lance journalist while he wrote *Stonewall Jackson, The Good Soldier: A Narrative* (1928). Robert Penn Warren was in graduate school at Berkeley and later at Yale and Oxford, where he was writing *John Brown: The Making of a Martyr* (1929) and composing a draft of his first story "Prime Leaf," later expanded into his first novel, *Night Rider* (1939). Davidson was writing his first book-length poem, *The Tall Men* (1927), and Ransom was engrossed in the contemplation of the nature and function of poetry, which would be the subject of a book of criticism he would soon begin.

The differing literary creeds and professional expectations seemed inevitably to be drawing the four men farther and farther apart when suddenly an event occurred that reunited them. It was the Dayton, Tennessee, trial of John T. Scopes for teaching evolution to his high school students. In *Southern Writers in the Modern World* (1958), Davidson writes his reaction to the treatment of this trial by the liberal Eastern newspapers. "I can hardly speak for others, but for John Ransom and myself, surely, the Dayton episode dramatized, more ominously than any other event easily could, how difficult it was to be a Southerner . . . also a writer. It was horrifying to see the cause of liberal education argued in a Tennessee court by a famous agnostic from Illinois named Clarence Darrow. It was still more horrifying—and frightening—to realize that the South was being exposed to large-scale public detraction and did not know or much care how to answer."

Davidson mounted his defense of the South immediately by publishing "The Artist as Southerner" in the *Saturday Review of Literature* for May 15, 1926, and "First Fruits of Dayton: The Intellectual Evolution in Dixie" in *Forum*, June, 1928. At the same time Ransom and Tate were exchanging letters in which they discussed means of retaliating against these absurd attacks and finally decided they should attempt to collect a "Southern symposium of prose" that would include contributions from the "ablest men in the region." Davidson enthusiastically agreed to this proposal, and the three began months of correspondence and discussion trying to attract the "best minds in the South" as contributors to the symposium. When the book was finally published as *I'll Take My Stand: The South and the Agrarian Tradition* by Twelve Southerners (1930), it contained "Introduction: A Statement of Principles" by Ransom and essays by Ransom, Tate, Davidson, Warren, Frank Lawrence Owsley (history, Vanderbilt), John Gould Fletcher (poet), Lyle H. Lanier (psychology, Vanderbilt), H. C. Nixon (political science, Tulane), Andrew Lytle (novelist and biographer), John Donald Wade (American literature, Vanderbilt), Henry Blue Kline (graduate student, Vanderbilt), and Stark Young (novelist and drama critic). Even allowing for the fact that 1930—with the country deeply mired in the worst depression in its history—was not the best time to argue that quality of life is a more valuable social possession than material goods, surely none of the Agrarians was prepared for the reception the book received. Most reviewers, both North and South, were apparently appalled that supposedly sane men could not see that the only solution to the nation's economic plight was more, not less, industrial progress. A columnist in the *Macon Telegraph* called the book "a high in the year's hilarity." Henry Hazlitt accused the Agrarians of trying to stem "the tide of progress" and H. L. Mencken attacked the book in two separate reviews, declaring that farmers are "doomed to becoming proletarians and the sooner the better."

Although the book was far more often ridiculed than championed, it was certainly not ignored. Davidson declared later that it probably ranked very high among "the most often misunderstood books in America—both read and unread." Immediately after its publication the book aroused so much controversy that the Agrarians were given an opportunity to present their case directly to the people. Several public debates were scheduled, and Ransom, as spokesman for the group, appeared against Stringfellow Barr before thirty-five hundred people in Richmond and against William S. Knickerbocker before one thousand in New Orleans (Davidson also faced Knickerbocker in Columbia, Tennessee); Barr and Ransom met again in Chattanooga, and Ransom debated William D. Anderson, a Georgia industrialist, before an Atlanta audience estimated to be in excess of fifteen hundred.

Unlike the Fugitives, the Agrarians were not a closely knit group bonded together by a series of regularly scheduled meetings. In fact, the Agrarians never met as a group, and it is doubtful that some of the members ever met. When *I'll Take My Stand* was published, its contributors were broadly scattered across two continents, and some of them had never read "Introduction: A Statement of Principles," which was supposed to unify the book by providing several basic issues around which each contributor could build his argument. Even the four contributors who had formerly been Fugitives apparently joined the movement for vastly different reasons. Donald Davidson was reacting against what he thought was a basic insult to his intelligence. He was convinced, he wrote years later, that all Southerners were being forced to accept in the name of progress ideas and attitudes vastly inferior to those they were giving up. He never surrendered, he wrote, "to the servile notion that the existence of a powerful 'trend is a mark of its inevitability.' All the works of men result from human choice, human decisions." He did not believe industrialism could provide a cure for human ills; therefore, he was compelled to argue against the possibility of help coming from that source. Tate hoped to convince his readers of the compelling need for a return to religious humanism. At the Fugitive reunion at Vanderbilt in 1956, Robert Penn Warren said he was attracted to the Agrarian movement because of his concern for the "disintegration of the notion of the individual in the society we are living in." In modern society, he continued, there is "no awareness that the individual has a past and a place." John Crowe Ransom was pleading for a mature society, one that nurtures both its economic forms (the means by which we gather the material necessities) and its aesthetic forms (the means of civilized living). No civilized society, he warned, has existed without a poetry, and we should not expect ours to be an exception. He was, in short, calling for a society in which poetry is written and read.

I'll Take My Stand remains today, as Richard M. Weaver referred to it thirty years ago, "one of the few effective challenges to a monolithic culture of unredeemed materialism." The place of the black man in the social order provided the Agrarians with a dilemma they could not solve. (Warren tried to argue that society must provide equal if separate facilities, and was so dissatisfied with his proposed solution that he attempted to retract it in *Segregation* [1956] and *Who Speaks for the Negro?* [1965].) It is hardly fair, however, to say with F. Garvin Davenport in *The Myth of Southern History* (1970) that the Agrarians were therefore impotent to deal with a much larger problem: the evils inherent in "the decision of society to invest its resources in the applied sciences." Few scholars would admit today that the symposium attempted either to develop utopian conservatism or to destroy the realities of a mechanistic materialism. Instead, one is inclined to agree with Louis D. Rubin, Jr.'s conclusion in *The Wary Fugitives* (1978) that *I'll Take My Stand* "makes no real economic proposals for dispensing with what the machine age can offer; it hardly even defines what agrarianism is, other than something generally involving a society in which farming is of importance; it says a great deal about what is wrong with industrialism, but almost nothing about how to get rid of it."

The importance of *I'll Take My Stand* is that it is a frightening description of what can happen to a society that deifies the machine, that attempts at all costs to establish an all-out technocratic society, even at the risk of stripping from man his basic humanity. Above all, it is a passionate protest against the creation of an intellectual climate that stultifies and destroys what Ransom called the aesthetic values. The Agrarians reiterated the belief—and many of them repeated this conviction many times after the symposium was published—that no amount of social legislation or social planning will effect a perfect society inhabited by perfect men and women. They presented modern man as one who has lost his sense of vocation, his attachment to a specific place, and his conviction that he is performing a valuable function. One of the book's basic values, as William Pratt points out, is that a "satisfying way of life cannot be produced by economic forces, with their shifting cycles of poverty and wealth, but can come only from an adherence to stable human values and ideals" (*Mississippi Quarterly*, Fall, 1980).

Nearly a hundred years before the publication of *I'll Take My Stand*, Henry David Thoreau undertook an experiment, the purpose of which, in part at least, was to test the validity of a statement made by his mentor, Ralph Waldo Emerson: "Things are in the saddle and ride mankind." He went to Walden, where he spent two years, two months, and two days, "to drive life into a corner and reduce it to its lowest terms." He wanted to see how much of one's life had to be exchanged in order to obtain the essentials of the good life. He found what he suspected: the meaningless clutter of urban centers tends to corrupt man and place needless obstacles in his way. The intentions of Thoreau's masterpiece were misunderstood and for nearly a century he was virtually unknown. He was called a "skulker," one unable or unwilling to meet the challenges of modern living. His early readers—and few indeed they were—tended to miss his point. He was not recommending the abandonment of the materials available in a fairly advanced and complicated society, but he was insisting that one should limit his dependence on these products to those that were essential and use *them* and not let them use *him*.

Of course one must point out that the differences between the Transcendentalists and Agrarians are far more obvious than their similarities. Unlike Emerson and Thoreau, the Agrarians were distrustful of transcendental voices, as they were of man's possible divinity while he lived. The Agrarians devotedly believed that any attempt to march to the beat of a different drummer was a threat to the social order that stands between man and the abyss. Despite these differences, however, both groups abhorred the "slavish, unexamined bondage to material possessions." For seventy-five years or more the principal thrust of Thoreau's writings was misunderstood, and he was accused of being a social hermit, trying to reverse the tide of progress. The failure of Americans to heed his warnings resulted in a virtual breakdown in the great American experiment in democracy and cleared the way for the robber barons. This development convinced Henry James that America was destined to become a cultural desert; he escaped to the more hospitable intellectual and tradition-conscious climate of Europe.

Now, fifty years after the publication of the symposium we have finally discovered that we are doomed, in the words of Andrew Lytle, "to hop about like sodium on water" and burn up in our own energy. Now when the quality of life has deteriorated to the point that it is difficult to find clear air to breathe and pure water to drink, when we realize that almost every nation in the world and even a few individuals who have closely read articles in the popular technical journals have the means of destroying all of human life—only now have we come to regard seriously the basic intent of *Walden* and *I'll Take My Stand*: we must simplify our lives or perish.

Although Agrarian activity did not cease with the publication of *I'll Take My Stand*, that symposium contained almost all the significant contributions the Agrarians were to make to American cultural criticism. Nevertheless, they attended many meetings—in Chicago, Atlanta, and elsewhere—and joined discussions, served on committees, and wrote papers intended to meet the economic crises of the Great Depression. Since the twenties many members of the group had attempted to secure means of disseminating their attitudes and convictions, including the acquisition of a county paper, a magazine, and a press. In the spring of 1933 Seward Collins promised to open the pages of the newly established *American Review* to the Agrarians, and during the next four and a half years various members of the group published more than fifty essays in the journal: Davidson (20), Ransom (11), Fletcher (8), Lytle (3), Owsley (6), Tate (6), Wade (1), and Warren (7). Every Agrarian except four—Young, Kline, Lanier, and Nixon—published at least one essay. The newly formed *Southern Review* at Louisiana State University, with Cleanth Brooks and Robert Penn Warren as managing editors, also welcomed and printed many contributions from the Agrarians.

In the spring of 1933 the group at North Carolina, headed by W. T. Couch, approved plans to publish a book related to Southern economic problems, and four Agrarians—Davidson, Wade, Lytle, and Nixon— were to contribute. Davidson wrote on literature, Wade on American humor, and Nixon on higher education (Lytle's essay was rejected). When the book appeared, Ransom read it, disliked most of it, but he thought it "publicizes our cause" because "some of us are mentioned in almost every essay." He wanted Tate to review it and advised him to make his remarks "wise, fixed and not repelling." Tate's commentary appeared in the *American Review* for February, 1934. Although markedly restrained for him, his reactions clearly reveal his conviction that this book is not a sequel to *I'll Take My Stand*. "Although labor problems in the South," Tate wrote, "have been grievous, they have not been grievous enough. We must catch up with the world; we must completely industrialize the South so that we shall have a problem that must be solved in socialistic terms. . . . This point of view . . . is realistic; that of the Agrarians backward looking and sentimental." After the review was written, he cautioned Ransom that he might not like it, but he would have to admit that none of the "Nashville group had been allowed to discuss economic issues."

Tate began almost immediately, with the assistance of Herbert Agar, a well-known journalist from Louisville, Kentucky, to prepare a second Agrarian book. Although the volume that appeared, *Who Owns America? A New Declaration of Independence* (1936), contains essays from eight contributors to *I'll Take My Stand* (Tate, Lytle, Davidson, Wade, Ransom, Nixon, Owsley, and Warren) and three from new converts to the cause (Cleanth Brooks, George Marion O'Donnell, and James Waller), it is a far different book from its predecessor. It contains points of view other than those of the Agrarians, particularly those of the Anglo-Catholics and the distributists, and the appearance of complete dedication to a single cause is conspicuously absent. With the exception of Warren's contribution (one of his best essays as well as one of the most impressive in the collection), the selections written by the Agrarians are noticeably weaker than those they contributed to *I'll Take My Stand*. The essays written by the Agrarians for *Who Owns America?*, like many of those published since *I'll Take My Stand*, tend to be more practical and less theoretical than the earlier ones. Ransom's contribution "What Does The South Want?" demonstrates that his cast of mind and idiosyncratic prose style will not permit him to write simple, straightforward solutions to economic problems with the same facility and effectiveness that he could deal with theoretical concepts. Tate's "Notes on Liberty," though hardly more clearly argued than his "Remarks on Southern Religion," seems to lack the ring of sincerity and the urgent call for action that characterized the earlier essay. Warren's "Literature as a Symptom," though among his most distinguished critical writings, clearly demonstrates how peripheral his interest in agrarianism really is. Only Davidson's "That This Nation May Endure" is a significant contribution to the fundamental theory on which the movement was based.

On September 17, 1936, Ransom wrote a letter to Tate in which he insisted that Tate's "*patriotism* is eating at *lyricism*," that not only was he writing fewer poems but that those he was producing were inferior to the earlier ones because they came dangerously close to propaganda. A little later he wrote Tate that "I am signing off" from agrarianism "a little by degrees." In response to a query from Edwin Mims, who wanted to know how Ransom could write "so far removed from his material," Ransom, who was contemplating a move to Kenyon College, indicated that he could do the kind of writing he wanted to do in Ohio as well as he could in Tennessee. "It is true," he wrote, "that if . . . [the writing he proposed to do] were on regionalism or agrarianism, I would be going into foreign parts. But I have about contributed all I have to those movements, and I have of late gone almost entirely into pure literary work." In the fall of 1937 he moved to Kenyon and continued writing the essays that would make up *The World's Body* (1938). Agrarianism, as a significant influence on his thinking, thus moved far into the background. Tate quickly followed Ransom back into literary criticism, and again took up seriously the writing of fiction and poetry. Only Davidson's interest in the movement remained as completely absorbing as ever, and the only other important Agrarian document produced by any member of the group was his *The Attack on Leviathan* (1938).

JACOB H. ADLER

Modern Southern Drama

With isolated minor exceptions, American drama, as opposed to hack writing for the stage, did not exist until the advent of Eugene O'Neill in the second decade of this century. At its best, from the twenties to the sixties, it became almost a flood, with such playwrights as O'Neill, Maxwell Anderson, Elmer Rice, George Kaufman and his various coauthors, Thornton Wilder, Clifford Odets, William Saroyan, Arthur Miller, William Inge, Edward Albee, Lorraine Hansberry, Leroi Jones, and the many important writers and composers of the American musical, such as Jerome Kern, Oscar Hammerstein II, Richard Rodgers, and Lorenz Hart.

In the South, some novelists, such as Carson McCullers, Thomas Wolfe, DuBose Heyward, and even William Faulkner, wrote a play or two, or adapted some of their own novels for the stage—most notably, in the latter category, McCullers' *Member of the Wedding* and Heyward's *Porgy* (first turned into a play by Heyward and his wife, then into the famous opera with text by Heyward and Ira Gershwin and music by George Gershwin). Also, novels by Southerners were turned into plays by other writers, including Wolfe's *Look Homeward, Angel,* and Caldwell's *Tobacco Road.* Actual dramatists from the South include Laurence Stallings, whose play *What Price Glory?* (coauthored with Maxwell Anderson) was the most important American play about World War I, and Randolph Edmonds, a black playwright, college teacher, and director of drama whose many short plays have been published in three collections. But among the dramatists who gave American drama a special eminence, three Southerners are of major importance: Paul Green, Lillian Hellman, and Tennessee Williams.

Of the three, Paul Green (1894–1981) was the earliest. A student and later a professor at the University of North Carolina, his one-act plays were produced by the Carolina Players. He then wrote full-length plays for the New York stage, most importantly *In Abraham's Bosom*

(Pulitzer Prize, 1926), *The Field God* (1927), and *The House of Connelly* (1928), which in their day gave him a high rank among American dramatists. All three are laid in the South. Later, Green turned to writing historical pageants, such as *The Lost Colony* (1937) and *Wilderness Road* (1956), for the open-air, summer-long productions that became, and remain, popular in various parts of the South and are a peculiar American phenomenon. With the collaboration of the author, Green also adapted Richard Wright's *Native Son* for the stage (1941). As this collaboration might indicate, Green's plays show deep compassion for the problems of the lower classes, white or black; but they are likely to be remembered more as significant social history than as plays to be revived on the stage.

The plays of Lillian Hellman (1905–1984), however, are revived, and her reputation has, if anything, grown with the publication, after she stopped writing plays, of her four books of memoirs, especially *An Unfinished Woman* (1969) and *Pentimento* (1973). Hellman was born in New Orleans, as was her father, and her mother was from a family long settled in a small town in Alabama. The families were Jewish, though like Arthur Miller and unlike Clifford Odets, there is little or nothing in her plays directly reflecting that background, in spite of the fact that some of her plays draw on her father's and mother's families for characterization and plot elements. On the other hand, some of her plays include blacks as more or less important characters, especially *The Little Foxes* and *Another Part of the Forest*. Like Green, Hellman displays great sympathy for, and understanding of, blacks; and her memoirs make clear that a black servant who was her close friend in childhood and another who worked for her later in life were strong influences upon her.

After attending both New York University and Columbia, but never earning a degree, Hellman presently settled into a job of playreading for producer and director Herman Shumlin; during those early years she met many young people who were later to be literary figures; her longtime friend Dorothy Parker; the budding playwright Arthur Kober, with whom she had a brief marriage; the novelist Dashiell Hammett, with whom she maintained a lengthy relationship. With Hammett's encouragement she wrote *The Children's Hour*, which Shumlin read, liked, produced, and directed, as he also produced and directed her next four plays. *The Children's Hour* (1934) had the longest run of any of her plays in spite of the fact that one of its basic subjects, lesbianism, was then very nearly taboo. Her choice of forbidden subject matter is one of the many evidences in her work and in her life of Hellman's courage, and also one of the many reminders of Ibsen in her work. An impressive first play, *The Children's Hour* has no noticeable Southern connections.

After one more play in a Northern setting, Hellman's next success, *The Little Foxes* (1939,) is wholly and unmistakably Southern. Like Williams' *Summer and Smoke*, and like some of Faulkner's novels, it concerns the South in the early years of the century—in this case, 1900. We see three small-town Alabama siblings, Ben and Oscar Hubbard and Regina Giddens, as beginners in the establishment of Southern industrialization. The family's rapacity and cruelty, leading to theft, blackmail, murder, oppression of the poor (black and white), are the center of the play. They are contrasted with the helpless gentility of Oscar's wife, Birdie, the last member of an aristocratic family ruined by the Civil War; with Regina's husband, Horace, a moral and sensitive well-to-do banker who is aware, but insufficiently aware, of the evil of the family into which he has married; and with the Giddenses' daughter, Alexandra, who rebels against her mother's evil but who will never, Hellman apparently believes, be strong enough to fight meaningfully against the forces it represents. This successful Hellman play is the one most frequently revived.

To a Southerner it seems clear that *The Little Foxes* could have been written only by a Southerner. Its dialogue sounds Southern, though not obviously so. The family's lower-class origins are easy to recognize, and the North is viewed as a faraway world, so different as to be incomprehensible. The place of blacks is illustrated in a variety of ways: their not daring to hunt game, in spite of genuine hunger, because Oscar (and presumably other Oscars) orders them not to, and their being unable to inherit money in a white man's will; and on the other hand, by the loyalty that Ben feels toward an old black servant, and the protectiveness and even domination that the black woman servant displays in Regina's household. Unlike Williams' plays about the South, however, Hellman's have not been particularly successful abroad. Apparently the Southern world that she presents is less comprehensible to foreigners, less universal, than that of Williams.

Hellman's Washington plays (*Watch on the Rhine* [1941] and *The Searching Wind* [1944]) have perhaps some of the atmosphere of the aristocratic culture of the upper South, but the center of interest is the war in Europe. Indeed, *Rhine* is almost certainly the most impressive American play concerned with World War II; and Hellman displays in it, as she does less centrally elsewhere, a belief in the power of goodness and a compassion for the oppressed, and also a skill at humor and even comedy, that is likely to be insufficiently recognized in her work. The play is also a demonstration of her lifelong interest in politics, an interest that was to bring her serious difficulties in the McCarthy era, though it seems probable that she has never espoused any specific ideology or political movement. As she herself recognizes, Hellman is not easy to pin down. The wealthy family in *Watch on the Rhine* is viewed, on the whole, favorably. They have something to learn, and they learn it. Like the penniless German anti-Nazi who is the husband of the daughter of the family, they represent culture at its best.

Another Part of the Forest (1946) shows the Hubbard family twenty years earlier, in 1880—again a reminder of Faulkner, who also deals with families in more than one generation and in more than one work. The Hubbard siblings' father, Marcus, has established himself in the town financially, though he is of poor-white origin. Oppressive and unscrupulous like his offspring, he is unlike them in his interest in something besides money—culture. And he is a more complex character than his children. The play provides further Southern insights: Marcus, in spite of his money and cultural interests, is unaccepted in the town; Oscar is a member of the "new" Klan, very different from what it was immediately after the war; and Marcus' wife, Lavinia (modeled after Hellman's mother), feels a closeness to the blacks, an eagerness to help them, and an affinity to their sort of Christianity. Although over melodramatic, the play is good, and Marcus one of Hellman's most impressively drawn characters; but it is unlikely ever to have the popularity of *The Little Foxes*.

These four plays all show strong affinities to Ibsen: in their well-made qualities, taut dialogue, unresolved endings, use of the end-play technique, interest in social issues, symbolic titles, use of blackmail, and depiction of clearcut characters, including, in two of the plays, children. Hellman's last two original plays (*The Autumn Garden* [1951], set on the Gulf Coast, and *Toys in the Attic* [1960], set in New Orleans) may move toward Chekhov: in technique in the first, in story in the second. Both are fine plays. Hellman is the most important American Ibsenian with the exception of Arthur Miller and the most important Southern playwright other than Tennessee Williams. Since *Toys in the Attic*, aside from one adaptation from a novel in 1962, she has left drama and has written her memoirs. A New York dweller in most of her adult life and part of her childhood, she has homes there and in Martha's Vineyard.

Tennessee Williams (1911–1983) has done perhaps more than any other single writer to make the world aware of the South. After an early failure (*Battle of Angels* [1940]), his major plays run from *The Glass Menagerie* (1944) to *The Night of the Iguana* (1961). He continued to write plays until his death, but while some certainly have quality, such as

439

Small Craft Warnings (1972), none achieved the success or quality of the earlier plays. Except for the St. Louis of *Menagerie*, the expressionistic Central America of *Camino Real* (1953), and the Mexico of *Iguana*, all of his plays in the major period are laid in the South: New Orleans, the Gulf Coast, or small-town Mississippi, where Williams was born in 1911. Williams' maternal grandfather was a minister, and he and his mother and his sister lived with the grandparents. Somewhere around 1919 or 1920, Williams' father, a traveling salesman, was transferred to the home office in St. Louis; and the trauma that the move from small-town Southern gentility involved for Williams and his sister Rose is reflected in much of his work, especially *The Glass Menagerie*. That play is certainly autobiographical, but it cannot be taken as literal presentation of the family's circumstances: Williams' father never deserted his family, as the play shows him to have done; the family's circumstances were almost surely never as bad as the play indicates, and were sometimes excellent, as Williams' *Memoirs* (1975) make plain; and Williams' brother is omitted from the play. The play does present Williams, his mother, and his sister (in the persons of Tom, Amanda, and Laura Wingfield) as closely true-to-life in both personality and Mississippi background. One aspect that is understandably omitted is Williams' homosexuality, though homosexuality occurs as an element in several later plays, including *A Streetcar Named Desire* (Pulitzer Prize, 1947), *Cat on a Hot Tin Roof* (Pulitzer Prize, 1955), and *Suddenly Last Summer* (1958), and Williams deals with it in his *Memoirs*. *Menagerie* depicts Laura as a young woman near to emotional breakdown, a breakdown that actually occurred to Rose, resulting in a prefrontal lobotomy and the need for lifelong institutionalization. In the play, Tom leaves home, giving the impression that he will never return or take care of his family. In actuality, Williams too became (and remained) a wanderer, but he took care of his sister for many years.

Menagerie seemed to critics and audiences alike to break new ground, though its use of a character as narrator and presenter seems to derive from Wilder, and its use of symbols and sound effects from Chekhov. In any case, Williams uses them, as well as lighting effects, brilliantly. *Menagerie* was unusual in that it played in Chicago for six months before moving to New York, where it had a long run.

Williams had worked in a factory and attended Missouri and Washington universities before completing a degree at Iowa and beginning his wanderings. From early on his major interest had been writing, and he began to break into drama with a collection of one-act plays that won him a group theater prize, the resultant backing of the prominent literary agent Audrey Wood, and a Rockefeller grant. *Menagerie* initiated his fame and standing as a playwright that were confirmed with his next and still most powerful play, *A Streetcar Named Desire*. The triangle of Blanche Dubois, fallen representative of a faded aristocracy and culture, her sister Stella, and Stella's husband Stanley Kowalski from the New Orleans slums is one of the most fascinating and effective in modern drama anywhere. From its opening, with Blanche timidly entering the slum—ironically, Elysian Fields—in clothes suitable for a garden party, to its end, with Blanche led willingly to a mental institution and Stanley and Stella in each other's arms after Stella has taken Blanche's true story of Stanley's having raped her as an insane illusion, the play holds audiences spellbound. As in *Menagerie*, but even more effectively, it uses symbols and sound effects. And it deals with Williams' almost constant subject of the contrast between the culture of the Old South and its lack in the New South, and the need, somehow, to find a new integration.

Although almost all the Southern plays have memorable qualities, notably *Summer and Smoke* (1948), the most successful and effective of Williams' plays after *Menagerie* and *Streetcar* were *Cat on a Hot Tin Roof* and *The Night of the Iguana*, the first totally Southern, the second not Southern at all. *Cat*, like Hellman's Hubbard plays, concerns a wealthy family of poor-white origin, the Pollitts; but the set is at least partly symbolic rather than realistic and the story very different. Taking place on the family's huge estate in the Mississippi Delta, it concerns, centrally, a father, Big Daddy, doomed by cancer; a son, Brick, emotionally handicapped by an apparently unfounded fear of homosexuality, who has a lengthy and fascinating dialogue with his father revelatory of them both and central to the play; and Brick's wife, Maggie (the "cat"), agonized by her husband's lack of communication on any level, including sexual, and fiercely determined to win him back. As is not true of *Menagerie* or in any significant sense *Streetcar*, there is the possibility of a happy ending. (Another play, *The Rose Tattoo* [1951], is a comedy and hence does have a happy ending, and two others, *Camino Real* and *Night of the Iguana*, end at least affirmatively.) *Cat* is perhaps the most notable example of a frequent problem with Williams. The play exists in two versions, the second being one in which, at the director's insistence, Williams significantly revised the third act, providing, among other things, a greater likelihood of a happy ending. Williams has, of his own volition, heavily revised other plays before and after production, most notably *Battle of Angels*, turned into the relatively successful *Orpheus Descending* (1957), and *Summer and Smoke*, becoming the much later and very different *Eccentricities of a Nightingale*.

The Night of the Iguana (which was printed in two versions and originally produced somewhat differently from either) concerns a group of "lost" persons at an isolated hotel in a Mexican jungle. Its central character, Hannah Jelkes, is a new creation for Williams, a virginal woman who will always remain so, a woman who can handle almost any hardship, any catastrophe, who has conquered her own emotional fragility and fears. She apparently succeeds in the play in enabling the other central character, a defrocked minister named Shannon, to overcome similar and deep emotional problems and to begin to accept her healthy, realistic view of life.

Throughout the plays, from *Menagerie* to *Iguana*, Williams is noted for his repeated use of certain character types: the insensitive and outspoken, probably older, woman; the fragile young woman; the "gentleman caller," frequently a blatantly sexual, but not necessarily unsympathetic, young man. On the other hand, his plays range over a wide variety of Southern life: fallen aristocracy, established rich, the middle class, *nouveau-riche* poor whites, politicians (especially in *Sweet Bird of Youth* [1959]), slum dwellers, and a variety of foreigners who range, as they do in Hellman, from the sympathetic to the despicable. Oddly, however, and unlike Hellman, his major plays do not portray blacks. Sex and violence are frequently important in his works, but in the best plays they are credible and essential; and the violence is likely to have an extremity and Gothicism reminiscent of Faulkner and Poe.

Williams also published one-act plays, short stories, poems, and two novels. He is recognized worldwide as one of the outstanding dramatists of the modern era, in spite of the fact, again like Chekhov, that most of his plays center on a very special world unfamiliar to most foreigners. Like Chekhov, Williams at his best succeeds in turning the eccentric particular into the universal.

Richard Wright

A native of the area most typical of the cotton-growing South, Richard Nathaniel Wright was born September 4, 1908, near Natchez, Mississippi, of a mother who had been a rural schoolmistress and a sharecropping father unable, it has been said (his relatives challenge this), either to read or write. In 1910 Wright acquired a brother. The four Wrights moved to Memphis in 1912 where the father, infatuated with a loose woman of that city, abandoned the family. On the mother's meager earnings the three remaining Wrights survived under constant duress until their retreat into the home in Elaine, Arkansas, of one of the mother's younger sisters, Wright's Aunt Maggie, wife of the owner of a prosperous saloon. This sister's husband, however, was killed in cold blood by whites, apparently because he was, for a black, overly affluent. Aunt Maggie later fled North from an adjoining Arkansas town, leaving Wright's mother and the two Wright boys alone again. Then, in a climactic catastrophe, Wright's mother became paralyzed in a house where she was the only adult. She would remain an invalid until her death in Chicago in 1959. Wright's brother was sent North to rejoin Aunt Maggie. Wright himself sojourned briefly, and unhappily, with a brother of his mother in Greenwood, Mississippi. But by 1920 both he and his mother were domiciled with his mother's parents in Jackson, Mississippi.

Wright now found himself in a household fanatically Seventh Day Adventist, and was forced to attend a Seventh Day Adventist school. An almost armed rebellion won for him his grandmother's permission to transfer to a public school. In 1925 he finished, as valedictorian, the ninth, and highest, grade of the black public schools in Jackson. He worked menially in Jackson and in Memphis for two long years, near the end of which he was able to reunite himself with his mother, his brother, and his Aunt Maggie. On a bitterly cold morning in December of 1927, he arrived, with his Aunt Maggie, in Chicago.

As soon as he could, Wright brought his mother and his brother to

Chicago, where he eked out a living for himself and them by means of various jobs, including a substitute clerkship in the post office. For a while during the depression, he was both unemployed and on relief. Then he benefited from the Rooseveltian policies of governmental aid that sought to give work as well as money to victims of the nation's economic crisis. In consequence, he held, successively, positions as a staff member at the South Side Boys' Club, a publicity agent for the Federal Experimental Theater, and a writer on the Federal Writers Project. Meanwhile, through a John Reed Club he had encountered Marxism.

From 1932 until 1944, according to his own testimony, he belonged to the Communist party. He moved to New York City in 1937. His first book, *Uncle Tom's Children*, a collection of novellas, appeared in 1938. The novel he wrote before it, *Lawd Today*, was not printed or circulated until after his death. But his first published novel, *Native Son*, almost overnight in 1940 catapulted him into fame and a fair amount of instant financial gain. The marriage he had contracted in 1939 not even a sup-posedly idyllic residence in Mexico could preserve. He dissolved it through divorce in 1940, and in 1941 he married Ellen Poplar. Also in 1941 he published *Twelve Million Black Voices*, a so-called (by him) folk history of the American Negro featuring the mass exodus of hun-dreds of thousands of an ill-treated black peasantry from the South into the big cities of the North. His autobiographical *Black Boy* appeared in 1945. After spending much of 1946 in Paris to see how life could be there for him, his wife, and their daughter, Julia, who had been born in 1942, Wright settled permanently in the city of boulevardiers and artists in 1947.

Wright never renounced his American citizenship, but he also never lived again in America. His second daughter, Rachel, was born in 1949 in Paris. Wright traveled widely, Australia the only continent he did not visit, and he spent six months in Argentina for a filming of *Native Son*. From trips to what is now Ghana, to Spain, and to a summit conference of Third World nations at Bandung in Indonesia, he obtained material for the books *Black Power*, *Pagan Spain*, and *The Color Curtain*. Some of the lectures he delivered in countries of Western Europe were pub-lished as *White Man, Listen!* Three of his novels, *The Outsider*, *Savage Holiday*, and *The Long Dream* were written in France. So were four of the eight stories in his posthumously published *Eight Men*. He died unexpectedly in Paris on November 21, 1960.

Of Wright's fifty-two years of life, thirty-three were spent outside the South. The novel by which he is best known, *Native Son*, is set com-pletely in the North. Not even his remains lie in the South. His ashes rest in an urn in the famous Parisian cemetery Père Lachaise, more than an ocean away from the Southern earth and sky near which he first saw the light of day. Even so, he was, in every way that really counts, no less a Southern writer than his fellow Mississippian, William Faulkner. Not only did he retain, and never cease to value, vivid recollections of the South as an appealing form of a physical world—an appreciation of the grip of the beauty of the Southern land upon his senses, for example, can be easily derived from his pastoral prelude to the tragic events that set the prevailing tone of "Big Boy Leaves Home"—but also, to an arresting degree, the South was, in his literary work, almost always his subject, if not everywhere as forthrightly as in his earliest short stories, then at least, in many places, by readily perceived broad implications, as in *Native Son* and *The Outsider*, both of which have Southern protagonists brought North by their parents. Moreover, nothing may seem to have affected his creative powers so beneficently as the South. He, in effect, began his writing career in Chicago, where transplanted Southern Negroes were all around him, and the fiction he was writing tended, at first, to be placed within a Southern landscape. As he advanced into middle age he moved east and, socially, up. At his death he was consorting with Sartre and Sartre's friends, among others. It has been argued that his last fiction was his worst, and that a negative correlation may be detected between his distance from his roots in actual, or migration-extended, Mississippi and his ability to write. Certainly, it does appear that the farther he got in space and time from his Southern home, the poorer became the harvest in themes and subject matter from his creative imagination.

One charge has been made against him, however, that may be far too unjust. There have been critics who have said that he wrote badly. Those critics, moreover, once were prone virtually to weep (if crocodile tears) because, sympathetic as they said they were with Wright's attacks on racism, they were simultaneously deeply pained that he should sabotage his own effectiveness as an agent for the elimination of color caste through the regrettable execrableness of his art. He was, some of them specified, another Dreiser with an elevated mission and a hopelessly flatulent prose style. But genuine familiarity with Wright's work hardly supports these critics. Wright was anything but indifferent to aesthetic discipline. He could not deny his relative lack of formal education. In *Black Boy*, however, he speaks persuasively of his passion, even before he reached Chicago, to write good sentences and convincingly of the time and care he devoted to trying to do just that. In the years of his youth he published poetry as well as prose. At the end of his life he not only studied existentialism and negritude, but also experimented quite admirably with haiku, the Japanese verse no sloppy artificer can employ. In any case, it is the whole corpus of his work—poetry and prose, fiction and otherwise—that refutes the allegation that he could not, or did not, handle respectably the mechanics of composition. He wrote a lot. Michel Fabre's bibliography in *The Unfinished Quest of Richard Wright* credits him with, in addition to his books and poems, 161 other publications. These other publications include articles, essays, lectures, prefaces, newspaper stories, reviews, and two dramatizations of *Native Son*. Any writer so prolific and, in genres, so catholic as he could hardly be expected not, occasionally, to nod. Nevertheless, given our human capacity to err, he rarely does. The much more significant discovery about him in connection with his attention to writing as writing is the high ratio of success he achieves, when all the appropriate evidence is collected and appraised, in his felicitous wedding of form to the elements that may be considered content in his practice of the writer's art. The brilliant authenticity of the vernacular of his proletarian Negro characters throughout *Uncle Tom's Children*; his memorable descriptions of bullfighting in *Pagan Spain*, which compare admirably with similar descriptions by Hemingway; the ingenious orchestration of inspired nuances of verbal, rhythmic, and syntactic effects consistently in the big scenes in *Native Son*, except the scene of Max's much too protracted plea to Bigger's jury—all show how remarkably often Wright handled his form superbly, and at those exact moments in his writer's odyssey when the very desire to perform at his absolute best could have pressured him into performing poorly. Without being altogether perfect, he did tend to be one of the elect in his use of craft. He wrote the long preface to the classic study by St. Clair Drake and Horace Crayton of Negro urbanization, *Black Metropolis*. There he says that in America it is "right to treat black men wrong, and wrong to treat them right." Such an aphorism hardly fits the picture of a writer unable to control his writing.

At the level beyond form in its simpler senses, Wright joins the very small circle of major writers who have been able to create at least one character endowed with epic stature. Two American writers who easily belong to this circle are James Fenimore Cooper and Mark Twain—Cooper for Natty Bumppo, the deerslayer, and Mark Twain, if for no one else, for Huckleberry Finn. Bigger Thomas is Wright's character who lifts him into the company of such writers as this exemplary pair. It is ironic that during Wright's lifetime a host of scholars labored for some five years or so on a project that generated fifteen thousand pages of typewritten manuscript, four published monographs, and thirty unpublished papers, all as preliminaries to a monumental two-volume study of the American Negro, entitled *An American Dilemma*, written by the project's director, Gunnar Myrdal, and published in 1942. It is no reflection upon those scholars to suggest that most people will learn much more about the American Negro, especially as he was between World War I and World War II, from Bigger Thomas of *Native Son* than from *An American Dilemma*. A reader is drawn into *Native Son* at its beginning by an episode in which Bigger, impoverished sharer of a small one-room apartment with the three other members of his family, two of them his mother and his sister, kills a rat, his family's uninvited guest. Before all is over in *Native Son*, the American social order, through its legal execution of Bigger, in effect kills another rat. The whole point of *Native Son* is Bigger's condition, actual and perceived, in the environment that Wright obviously believes is responsible for virtually everything that Bigger is. That, in terms of all America's Biggers, is really the point of *An American Dilemma*. But this point has not been made nearly so effectively at the end of *An American Dilemma*, either in application to one Bigger or to all American blacks, as it has at the end of *Native Son*. For Bigger Thomas is no creature of abstractions. He is tremendously, though vicariously, an experience of life itself. His crowning glory is the immediacy of contact with reality that he provides. Moreover, through the thaumaturgy of great art he is, as we have already intimated, both one person and a common denominator in personality for a whole community of individuals caught in the same environmental web. He is also the richest, truest possible answer, with one exception, to the question of what it meant in Wright's day to be a Negro in America. The only answer more valid and more satisfactory is actually to have been one of those Negroes.

To Wright, being a Negro meant being something of a monstrosity, even if a monstrosity fabricated, not by nature, but by the machinations of men. The depiction Wright presents of blacks as victims of a social order greatly affected the depiction of blacks by other Negro writers. It is at least arguable that no other Negro writer has ever rivaled him in his influence upon his racial colleagues. In John A. Williams' novel, *The Man Who Cried I Am*, a fictive writer obviously molded upon Wright is told by another fictive writer, a black novelist, "You are the father of us all." And, after *Native Son*, Wright did become, more or less, the father of every black writer who succeeded him. In this regard he predisposed both the higher cerebrations and the predilections in craft of his disciples. It was he, as well as generational changes, that accounted for the ways in which black writers of the 1940s and the 1950s did not sound like black writers of the Harlem Renaissance or like either Chesnutt or Paul Laurence Dunbar. Wright cut his writer's teeth on naturalism, and

447

much of the reason that most black writers for more than twenty years seemed decidedly more akin to Frank Norris than to Henry James may be discovered in the simple circumstance that Wright was similarly so akin, just as most of these same writers were hard-boiled largely because Wright had been hard-boiled before them. Additionally, in the 1930s, Wright fed his mind, not only upon Marxism, but also upon the data banks and the deductions in general theory therefrom by social scientists who were employed or trained or esteemed at the University of Chicago. Apparently, in his inner core he was not nearly so much a European radical as an American populist infected with intellectual ardors as well as with the indestructible optimism of the typical American democratic liberal. He was, therefore, resolutely an integrationist. The beckoning future of *The Long Dream*, his last novel, is an integrationist's future. Wright respected blackness. There are no octoroon protagonists in his fiction. He went to Africa and wrote *Black Power*, about Ghana just as it was escaping its colonial status, at least partly out of his conviction that black Americans were right to cherish Africa. Moreover, he felt and professed a genuine affinity with all colored peoples everywhere, whether they were yellow, brown, red, or black. But black nationalism in the United States was not part of his ideal for black Americans. He left America because America was not integrated. What he did, he never repudiated in any of his fancies. He never thought of the America he wanted as one in which whites were to be kept eternally separate from blacks.

In France, Wright owned both an apartment in Paris and a farm in Normandy. On the farm he grew vegetables that an American Negro might well have cultivated for his own favorite diet in the American South. Wright's friend, the noted black cartoonist Ollie Harrington, tells of Wright's occasional proud distribution of these vegetables among his Parisian friends. At the base of any cosmopolitanism Wright had acquired were his Southern roots that he did not forget. Yet Wright, the black writer, had conquered a true lion in the path of all black writers. He was not the parochial. He was universal. He did speak to, and for, all men and women everywhere, especially on the great issues of equity and human brotherhood. And he spoke with power, which was his long suit. In comedy he may be suspect, but at his best, as he often was, he could inflame the viscera of his readers. He did not want, he explicitly averred, to write weakly, so that bankers' daughters could enjoy the slight shivers they might get from him—he was too serious about his aims for that. Against the old, hackneyed, viciously dishonest stereotypes about Negroes that were circulated throughout America to justify the mistreatment of Negroes, he had launched his own holy war. That war he prosecuted with fervor. He had the right also to feel that he was prosecuting it with some success. For when he died, his Negro was a part of the American consciousness which no earlier travesty from the plantation school or from the lore of those who claimed that blacks were as low as beasts could easily erase. Largely with one book he had greatly altered the terms of the dialogue about color endemic to America. He had challenged a status quo. And he had won.

JAMES H. JUSTUS

Robert Penn Warren

By the time Robert Penn Warren graduated from Vanderbilt in 1925, his actual literary output would not have suggested that he was the most promising of that remarkable association of poets and intellectuals known as the Fugitives. The youngest of the group, he was remembered by his friend and roommate Allen Tate as one of the most remarkable persons he had ever met, his mentor John Crowe Ransom had quickly spotted him for an advanced class for creative writers, and his contributions had appeared in the *Fugitive*; but his poetry was stiffer and more mannered than that of his more experienced friends, much of his artistic energy went into sketching murals inspired by *The Waste Land*, and his talent for discursive prose or fiction was yet to be tested.

Neither Warren nor any of the other Fugitives was self-consciously Southern; the group was simply a gathering of like-minded men, mostly from Kentucky and Tennessee, committed to the high calling of the poet and the practical exercise of his craft. But by 1928, when the appearance of *Fugitives: An Anthology of Verse* signaled the formal end of the Nashville group, the concerns of many of its members had already begun to shift to regional matters, especially as they illuminated the crucial issue: the survival of what they perceived as a traditional Southern identity. Even the explicit urgencies that stirred Tate, Ransom, and Donald Davidson to action in the late 1920s, however, when their correspondence and informal conferences led to the planning and writing of *I'll Take My Stand* (1930), affected Warren in markedly different ways. From his perspective outside the South, the economic and cultural problems resulting from industrialism, political demagoguery, technological farming, religious fundamentalism, and the growing popularity of the radio, the phonograph, and the automobile touched him mostly as abstract issues—partly because he had left the South more definitively than some of his friends and partly because those issues were beginning to be transmuted by memory into the stuff of art.

Warren once commented that he "became a Southerner by going to California and to Connecticut and New England." At Berkeley, where he went for his master's degree, and at Oxford, where he went as a Rhodes scholar, the contrasts between the South and elsewhere emphasized his Southernness for the first time. In England he dutifully wrote "The Briar Patch," a well-written but evasive defense of segregation, for the Agrarian symposium; more vitally, he began his first fiction, a long story based on the tobacco wars of Kentucky and Tennessee that had raged about the time of his birth. "Prime Leaf" (1931), which would later be rewritten as his first published novel, *Night Rider* (1939), was an imaginative reconstruction of local history focusing on the clash of opposed moral principles. If the narrative of both the novella and the novel suggests the oral transmission of history and legend, the more immediate texture of the story is threaded by personal memory of steamy tobacco fields, the hacking of grackles, and the idioms and rhythms of ordinary folk with whom Warren had grown up.

That process of becoming a Southerner by not being in the South is reflected in Warren's first book, *John Brown: The Making of a Martyr* (1929), a revisionist account by an amateur historian openly scornful of moral idealism. Not only John Brown but also those Yankee philosophers, professors, entrepreneurs, and canny businessmen who tendered him moral and financial backing are viewed from a perspective often characterized as Southern: one that shows a wariness of abstractions and appeals to categorical principles of ethics and morals because they so often fail to account for the grimy facts of experience and the human weakness for masking self-interest and egoism with high-sounding declarations. Both his first fiction and his first essay in historical writing also established certain tendencies that would recur in Warren's work in various modes for the rest of his career: the fondness for choosing characters with a disposition toward romanticizing the self—an innocence that can turn murderous when the delusion is violently exposed; a flair for a style that simultaneously projects the complexity of situations and the clarity of understanding their significance; the aesthetic uses of the South and the past, especially the Civil War and its aftermath, as times and places susceptible of moral reinterpretation; and a philosophical bent for dramatizing human experience through large dialectical patterns—good and evil, aspiration and consummation, dream and fact, word and flesh, idealism and pragmatism. Such characteristics, most of them evident in all the literary forms Warren chose, became especially marked in his fiction, his favorite mode from 1939 to 1955. In these years that saw the steady accrual of his technical mastery in his most popular novel, *All the King's Men* (1946), and his most complex, *World Enough and Time* (1950), Warren also wrote and published the only short stories of his long career, the finest of which, "Blackberry Winter" (1946), quickly became a classic in the literature of initiation.

If self-division generates the dramatic interest of many of his fictional characters, it also dramatizes itself on a grander scale in the Civil War itself, which Warren has called the most searing, most meaningful event in our national lives. That large-scaled conflict is the symbolic backdrop for the personal dilemmas of the protagonists of *Band of Angels* (1955), *Wilderness* (1961), and the inset narrative of *All the King's Men*; its tangled causes Warren explores in *John Brown* and its mingled consequences in *The Legacy of the Civil War* (1961); its magnetic influence on two American writers who experienced it preoccupies Warren in his lengthy introductions to his anthologies, *Selected Poems of Herman Melville* (1970) and *John Greenleaf Whittier's Poetry* (1971); and the doughty survivors, inheritors, and victims of that war recur, sometimes obsessively, in the poetry from *Promises* (1957) onward.

Throughout his writings that make significant use of the Civil War, Warren exercises freely his powers to humanize the participants in history, to free them from the confining categories invariably designed for them not merely by the needs of historians but by certain impulses in us all to reduce and compartmentalize in order to make sense of the complex affairs of complex men. Yet, despite his insistence upon acknowledging the ranges of complexity in that pivotal historical event, the Civil War looms for Warren as the concrete manifestation of an abstract dichotomy: history is both the blind force sweeping guilty and innocent alike in its wake, and the salvation of those persistent seekers of self-identity. Self-understanding, the goal of so many of his morally frail and ambiguously motivated protagonists, is frequently attained only when they acquire a historical sense, the application of lessons learned in the past to unchanging human problems.

That achievement, like similar moments in Faulkner and many of his Southern contemporaries, is invariably accompanied by what might be called functional violence, physical and psychic wrenchings as a necessary stage in the ongoing drama of the self. The constitutive melodrama of the individual self is inherent in the historical reality that forms the base of almost every fiction Warren has written, from the tragic excesses of the Civil War (*Band of Angels*) to the political and financial chicanery of the New South (*At Heaven's Gate* [1943], *All the King's Men*), from the clash of seaboard and frontier values (*World Enough and Time, Brother to Dragons* [1953]) to a contemporary South of TVA dams, media manipulators, and racial and class confrontations (*Flood*

[1964], *The Cave* [1959], *Meet Me in the Green Glen* [1971], *A Place to Come To* [1977]). Adultery and betrayal, murder and suicide, slaughter, passion, and ruth dominate so many narratives because they conform not only to the visceral reality of daily headlines but also, as symbolic extensions, to that of all lives struggling toward self-definition. Even in the poetry with residual narrative lines, Warren turns again and again to those lives in which obscure hurts intersect with fate or in which private motives mesh with public causes: "The Day Dr. Knox Did It" (1966), *Audubon* (1969), "School Lesson Based on Word of Tragic Death of Entire Gillum Family" (1957), "The Ballad of Billie Potts" (1944), "Internal Injuries" (1968), "Two Studies in Idealism" (1960), "Recollection in Upper Ontario, From Long Before" (1980).

But if melodrama is one constituent of Warren's art, it is balanced by another equally prominent one—meditation—as if the unbearable ironies and visceral excesses require the mediation of time and the moral exercise of mind to justify their ineradicable presence. His most accomplished meditations, *The Legacy of the Civil War* and *Jefferson Davis Gets His Citizenship Back* (1980), are impressive not for the reportorial facts that lend them documentary credibility, but for the visible play of a mature intellect sorting through the data for their personal, regional, national, even universal meaning. Through his historical writing, characteristically a creative amalgam of acquired knowledge, philosophical speculation, personal memory, and the skillful application of analogy and metaphor to undifferentiated fact, Warren assembles patterns of action worthy of contemplation. The results are meditations in which the disparate and the distant are transformed into human continuity, a theme repeated in his fiction and poetry. Except for his first two novels, his protagonists and personae are meditators as well as actors. Some, like Jack Burden of *All the King's Men* and R. P. W. of *Brother to Dragons* (1953), come across as garrulous moralizers whose deliberations outstrip their deeds; others, like Amantha Starr of *Band of Angels* and Jed Tewksbury of *A Place to Come To*, whine, wheedle, and rationalize their lacerating way to wholeness. Still others, like Angelo Passetto of *Meet Me in the Green Glen*, Adam Rosenzweig of *Wilderness*, and Monty Herrick of *The Cave*, become such adept glossers of their own existential acts that they confute the credible limitations of their characters. The less dramatized, more overtly personal voice of the poet broods over the terrors and griefs of the separated soul from "Original Sin" (1942) and "The Ballad of Billie Potts" to the truncated elegies of "Tale of Time" (1966) and "Mortmain" (1960) and in the exquisitely remembered moments of joy, pain, and ambiguous discovery meditates on the relation of the self that he was to the self that he now is.

In its sometimes violent yoking of dramatized incident and iterated moral significance, Warren's fiction struggles toward an aesthetic state in which the necessary question—"What happened?"—is never fully and definitively balanced by the other question, "What does that happening mean?" Warren's is a moral fiction in which the moral slides uneasily into paradox and contradiction; the fiction is the formal enactment of a restless mind that explores potentialities and alternatives in the most basic human acts. His most conventional novel is his first, but even in *Night Rider* the most notable effect is a deliberate disjunction between subject and style. The narrative is filled with violence—indeed, it suggests the human need for violence when a man, staggering through life with unfulfilled needs and ambitions, seizes the chance to force himself into a clarifying identity supplied by others. The scaffolding of the action is a series of eruptive acts—bombings, burnings, group punishments, and organized vandalism—nocturnal violence glimpsed through the light of torches—but the telling has no matching verbal incendiarism. The style is restrained and austere, suggesting the futility of using human violence to effect human wholeness in the very process by which the protagonist, coolly distanced throughout as "Mr. Munn," is attempting to do just that.

If *Night Rider* is Warren's most austere novel, *World Enough and Time* is his most rococo. It too concerns violence as a weapon not to be unsheathed only in emotional emergencies but brandished as conscious policy, to satisfy a projected sense of personal completeness; his fourth novel also explores alternative courses for making the self whole—the consolations of philosophy and the immersion in community. The various means by which Jeremiah Beaumont undergoes his difficult search constitute a case study in the pathology of romanticism, and Warren formally presents his case study through the patient's own account, a florid outpouring of a deluded egoist, and a detached, bemused commentator on that confession. Although Warren counters his nineteenth-century patient with a twentieth-century analyst, the attempt of a narrator-historian, who has learned his lessons from William James, to understand the quaintness of an earlier troubled spirit is itself subject to errors, miscalculations, oversimplifications. *World Enough and Time* is a rhetorical masterpiece. It begins as dialectic—text and commentary, confession and injunction, apologia and debunking—and ends with both the protagonist and his historian rising in chorus to sing of the inevitable disillusions involved in the human struggle for perfection.

The most crucial issues in Warren's work center on the dynamics of extravagant hopefulness in conflict with corrosive despairs that would deny any possibilities of hope; and his most resonant characters are those who, though they begin by trying to reshape a recalcitrant reality according to their preconceived versions, end by coming to terms with the imperfections they share with the world and their fellows. Beaumont is perhaps Warren's purest example of the innocent and idealist, the character type established in *John Brown* and continued with Percy Munn of *Night Rider* and Jerry Calhoun of *At Heaven's Gate*. In the mode of the suffering innocent, whose prototype is Beaumont, are also Amantha Starr and Adam Rosenzweig. In the mode of the bruised cynic, whose prototype is Jack Burden, the twentieth-century wise guy, are Brad Tolliver of *Flood* and Jed Tewksbury of *A Place to Come To*. Behind both modes is a Warrenesque assumption that all brands of idealism carry threat as well as promise. Finally rejecting grand gestures and single solutions, they earn their humanity by dramatizing their creator's own belief in the only kind of achieved continuity, moral and social, that is possible: "You have to nag along inch by inch."

Although Warren characterizes himself a yearner rather than a believer, his vision, implicit in his earliest work and explicit in his later, derives from orthodox Christian doctrine yoked to a tough secular existentialism. That man is fallen, that to be whole he must commit himself to rigorous self-evaluation and, ultimately, to both the consoling responsibilities to society and the bracing realities of history, is a conviction that energizes the narratives and the poetry as well as the nonfiction prose. And because they represent doctrines that run counter to the vision that emerges so consistently in his work, Thomas Jefferson and Ralph Waldo Emerson are those historical figures who preside ambivalently over much of it.

In his reading of American history, Warren seems to attribute to Jefferson's rational optimism the inspiriting of a society in which democratic man adopts anarchic individualism as a national habit; he emphasizes the dark consequences of egalitarian ideology in *Brother to Dragons*, in which the father of the American Enlightenment is forced to acknowledge the beastliness of man that even he shares. Equally beguiling is Emerson's romantic optimism, which culminates in a transcendental proclamation of human divinity. For Warren such beneficence turns out to be a mischievous heritage that he finally confronts directly in the ambiguously titled poetic suite, "Homage to Emerson," even though he had done it fictively in secondary characters in *All the King's Men*, *Band of Angels*, and *Wilderness*. If the malevolent side of rational optimism is Lilburn Lewis, Jefferson's unmazed Minotaur, the malevolent consequences of romantic optimism produce John Brown, in whom the seventeenth-century fervor of the true believer flowers in the secular creed of abolitionism, Emerson's instrumental bloody hand. At once too partial and too capacious, with an exaggerated respect for man's possibilities and too little recognition of his boundaries, these forms of human liberation recur in Warren's work as attractive but false abstractions. Diversity and multiplicity are the conditions to which Warren's characters must learn to accommodate themselves. If the rage for one's confirming and confirmable identity often constitutes the drama of his characters, the very frequency of the pattern suggests the difficulty by which the full self can be known; because so many characters are reluctant or unable to acknowledge their composite natures, their rigid insistence on identity is often a longing for illusory comfort. That Warren does not send his characters on their anguished search with the kind of adversarial brio we see in *Candide* attests to his unresolved attraction to the kinds of idealists so powerfully represented by Jefferson and Emerson.

In some instances—notably the idealistic protagonists of *World Enough and Time*, *Band of Angels*, and *A Place to Come To* and the personae of the retrospective poems—even their disabling flaws are shown sympathetically, as if their stories are one story and one common enough to be our own. It is not just Jack Burden who struggles against his inclination to "brass-bound Idealism"; Willie Stark the boss was once Cousin Willie from the country with inchoate urges for the betterment of his own class as well as himself. To be innocent and idealistic is to be fated for pain, disillusionment, and despair without any real assurance of ultimate psychic recovery; but to be incapable of innocence and idealism is to be worthless from the outset. If his intellectual affinities are for the darker nay-sayers in America's literary tradition, Warren's unresolved attraction to the hopeful visionaries has never been dispelled; the interaction of both provides the energy for his most compelling work, the warp of Jefferson, Emerson, and Whitman patterning itself with the woof of Hawthorne, Melville, and Faulkner.

Warren began his career as poet, achieved academic recognition as pedagogical innovator, gained his greatest public reputation as novelist, and in recent decades has emerged again as poet, the role to which this distinguished man of letters is most committed and in which he feels most comfortable. Impeccably schooled in the formal shapes and studied intricacies of English metaphysical verse, Warren gained his own poetic voice when he learned to mingle the compressed, striking images of Donne and Marvell with the vernacular syntax and brittle tonalities of the great modernists, especially evident in "Original Sin" and others of *Eleven Poems on the Same Theme* (1942). The self-conscious juxtaposition of the learned and the colloquial in such a poem as "The Ballad of Billie Potts" gradually developed into a more unified idiom, first seen in a sustained way in *Promises*, a volume that also signaled a more personal involvement with his subjects. The most successful poems of Warren's later maturity are his lyric meditations in *Incarnations* (1968), *Now and Then* (1978), and *Being Here* (1980), especially those in which the poet of the present seeks to make sense of events compulsively recalled from the past. What keeps such poems from being merely nostalgic is Warren's need to formulate, test, and redefine not only his impressions and his memory but also larger problems of the philosophic mind: self-knowledge, ambivalent love, and the continuity of identity through time.

Like his fellow Fugitives Tate and Davidson and many other American poets of the twentieth century—Eliot, Pound, William Carlos Williams, Hart Crane, Archibald MacLeish—Warren also reasserted an earlier century's penchant for the long poem, the importance of which lay in its possibilities for philosophical extension, complex meditation, and quasi-narrative development of historical or legendary materials. His most notable, *Brother to Dragons*, is the most sustained in imagery, characterization, and narrative thrust; the later *Audubon: A Vision* and *Chief Joseph* (1982), with their greater range and variety of techniques, reflect Warren's increased shaping of loosely grouped lyrics into poetic suites ("Mortmain," "Ballad of a Sweet Dream of Peace" [1957], "The Day Dr. Knox Did It") and his experimentation with what he has called snapshots—frozen moments of revelation from a variety of perspectives.

From the beginning Warren has written a poetry freighted with both hard imagery and philosophical speculation. The strong auditory and visual metaphors characteristically summon up people, places, and things from the past; the speculation of the speaker articulates the considered response to them in queries demanding the meaning of what he has done and his relationship to the large abstract orders of time and space. The claims of memory in the later poetry continue to generate in Warren both the image and the speculation; but the landscapes of his Kentucky boyhood, of Italy, of Vermont, of the American West also generate an intensity, a compelling confrontation with the mysteries of meaning, rarely seen in the earlier verse. Like pedagogues without faith in their pedagogy, Warren's later speakers leave behind the more obtrusive wise-guy assertiveness, the laconic observation, the superior perspective, and candidly enter into their investigations of meaning with little confidence that definitive answers are possible. Although the emotional impact of experiences dredged up from the past can often be recounted with an astonished clarity, the considered gloss on those experiences is always hedged by ambiguity and puzzled awe.

Reflecting the substantial emphasis on the search for meaning, the poems after *Selected Poems: New and Old, 1923–1966* (1966) show the complex ways that ontological and existential issues converge from many directions. From earlier fiction and poetry comes the motif of the burdens of creatureliness in *Incarnations*, in which the transfiguring possibilities of brute flesh are ominously balanced by the brutalizing human qualities attributed to mammals, fish, fowl, vegetation, stones, and the energies of nature. Many of the poems in *Or Else* (1974) are structured as internalized debate, and the text is dominated by the rationalist's vocabulary (*evidence, logic, proof, fact, principle*). *Now and Then* is structurally balanced by "Nostalgic" poems and "Speculative" poems, as if the tentative, subliminal knowledge derived from dream states and near-mystical moments of recall must be tested against a rationalist's daylight sensibility. In the poems of *Being Here*, where the byplay of time and timelessness, of identity and extinction, is both intellectual and emotional, Warren's characteristic rhetorical mode is interrogative: central points are not so much asserted as speculated on, the titles of two poems are questions, and the mood of many is set by repetitive questions. In *Rumor Verified* (1981) satisfactory answers to looming questions seem even more remote. A theme from the poems of the 1960s, the "frail integument of flesh," is resurrected, now provided with a context no longer merely domestic. Here the closely observed and heard present dominates the experience of recall. Metaphors of helplessness (nestlings' beaks agape for sustenance) and human insignificance (the particle, dislodged from mountain crag, evolving over eons into a single grain of sand on a beach "where no foot may come") are linked imaginatively to images of life held in a fragile balance between obliteration and continuity. Threatened by avalanche, volcanic eruption, geologic catastrophes, the human identity becomes a nearly irrelevant concern, and the persona in poem after poem dramatizes its sense of fragility in images of galactic distances and earthly depths, of mountains and plains forming and unforming out of seas. Coming to terms with one's mortality begins in the thump of heartbeat and rhythm of pulse, in a sleeplessness beyond insomnia, but it ends in a grand but chilly vision in which the self "flows away into the unbruised / Guiltlessness of no-Self." Death becomes "Nature's Repackaging System," and as slow ages "shift and crumble / Into the noble indifference of Eternity," so do individuals: "We let ourselves flow from ourselves into / The vast programming of the firmament."

The naturalistic vision projected so vividly in Warren's early verse is not transformed in the later volumes into an old poet's peaceful affirmation of faith. Situations change, but the same questions haunt and nag the questing speakers. Bereft of sureties once provided by religion, philosophy, and history, they are forced to rely on minimal assurances—to assert the virtures of the *merely* human in a natural world that is *only* natural. As its title suggests, *Being Here* quietly affirms a tenuous victory of simple existence; but as in *Now and Then*, in which the ineradicable erosions of time qualify the poems of celebration, the fact of survival triggers speculations about truth as well as perspectives on past experiences distorted and occasionally ennobled by memory. If some poems celebrate the persistence of being here, others record with awe and wonder the place of human nature in great nature, and still others extend the search for continuities between the self that was and the self that yet remains.

After the mid-1950s, each successive volume of verse confirmed Warren's primary commitment, made initially in Nashville in the early 1920s, to poetry as his preeminent mode. The continued vitality of his work in the 1970s and early 1980s derives in part from a creative openness both to personal risk taking and to formal experimenting. His most successful later poems celebrate the discoveries yet possible to old age in which the poet meditates on and speculates about the distribution and use of his powers to love, to question, and to evaluate what is left.

THE RECENT SOUTH

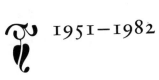 1951–1982

LOUIS D. RUBIN, JR.

Introduction to Part IV

If the impact of the First World War on the South had been profound, decisively altering its relationship to the Union and setting into motion crucial changes in the fabric of its social and economic life, the coming of the Second World War and its aftermath not only confirmed those changes but created a modern-day South that in numerous respects seemed to bear little relationship to the community in which the leading writers of the Southern Renascence had been born a half-century or so earlier. The Solid South, the Land of Cotton became today's Sun Belt.

When World War II was done, the manufacturing plants, the military installations, the influx of wartime workers from the Midwest and the Northeast, did not shut down or move away, as happened after 1918. Instead, industrialization moved into high gear; towns became cities and cities became huge metropolitan areas; cotton lost its dominance and sharecropping became a thing of the past; the trend of outward migration that had drained the region of many of its best young people was reversed; and by the 1970s what had once been described as "America's Economic Problem No. 1" was the fastest-growing, most rapidly prospering section of the United States.

Most dramatically of all, the South finally got out from under its centuries-old burden of racial segregation. Well before the promulgation of the *Brown* vs. *Board of Education* decision of the Supreme Court of the United States in 1954 that decreed an end to segregation by race in public education, forces were at work that were altering the racial status quo; but *Brown*, and subsequent landmark decisions decreeing an end to all forms of legal segregation and securing the right to vote for black Southerners, permanently and thoroughly revamped almost every facet of Southern life having to do with race. The political impact of all this was momentous. Southern politics largely ceased to revolve around segregation and questions of race; the one-party system that had functioned for a hundred years in order to safeguard segregation was de-

463

cisively ended. From being the most segregated, the South changed into the most racially integrated region of the United States, and the single factor that had separated the South politically from the rest of the country was eliminated. The election in 1976 of a white Southerner, campaigning *as a Southerner*, to the presidency of the United States, an election that was importantly secured by the votes of black Southerners, confirmed the end of an era. To be sure, the South of the 1980s is no racial paradise; vexing racial problems, particularly those having to do with economics, remain to be solved. But in ways that would have been virtually inconceivable even a few decades earlier, the states of the one-time Confederacy constitute an integrated community and are no longer either set apart from the remainder of the nation or united among themselves by the racial equation.

It was only to be expected that such momentous social, political and economic change would have its impact on the literature of the South. Much of the strength of the literature of the 1920s, 1930s, and 1940s lay in the richness and profundity with which it mirrored and interpreted the life of the Southern community, white and black. Now, as a new, second generation of modern Southern writers began publishing their books, the close literary engagement with the Southern community continued. Authors such as Eudora Welty, Walker Percy, William Styron, Flannery O'Connor, Ralph Ellison, Ernest Gaines, James Dickey, Randall Jarrell, Elizabeth Spencer, George Garrett, and numerous others continued to draw on the life of their native region in ways that, however informed by the individual imagination, involved pervasive elements of continuity in form, theme, and language. Applied as modifier to the noun *literature*, the adjective *Southern* continued to signify a distinction that was more than geographical.

Yet there were differences, not only in individual talent but in shared attitudes and concerns, differences that grew out of a changed and changing situation, a developing experience of community, society, and belief. For if it was the human transaction in change and resistance to change, in the pervasive workings of the historical imagination upon individual and community circumstance, that has provided so much of the distinctive quality of modern Southern writing, then the effect of such change was bound to have an impact upon the successive generations of writers.

Nor has it ended. Still another generation of Southern authors began publishing their stories, poems, and plays in the 1960s and 1970s, a generation that was born and grew to maturity in a greatly different South than their predecessors had known. What does the adjective *Southern* mean when applied to a generation of writers now in their thirties and forties? If life in the South has changed so drastically over the past half-century, then at what point does the community experience become more dissimilar than similar to that of an earlier time?

When presented in those terms, the problem becomes the concern of scholars, not of novelists, poets, and playwrights. The latter write their stories, poems, and dramas not about ideas and theories but about people and places. In what is written, the scholars of literature perceive and seek to identify relationships to time and place. What they have found constitutes in part the final section of this history of Southern literature.

THOMAS DANIEL YOUNG

A Second Generation of Novelists

M ost of the important Southern writers whose best work began to appear following World War II, as Lewis P. Simpson has noted, were not concerned primarily with the "meaning of memory and history," nor were they principally engaged in a struggle to demonstrate the redemptive "meaning of the classical-Christian past in its bearing on the present." Instead, many of them were trying to find their place in an apparently meaningless and absurd universe. To make their separate existence plausible and significant in a universe from which the gods seemed to have disappeared, these writers felt compelled to resort to techniques that would make their world appear, as Lewis A. Lawson has written, extra-real. The techniques most often employed were the grotesque—as in Flannery O'Connor's *Wise Blood* (1952) and Eudora Welty's "Keela, the Outcast Indian Maiden" (1940)—and the existential/phenomenological. One can detect influences of the latter attitudes in the early novels of John Barth and in any of those of Walker Percy.

If the concerns just mentioned encouraged some of the contemporary writers of the South to create stories and novels that were more like those written elsewhere in the Western world, the changes that have occurred in a society that is rapidly shifting from agrarian to urban have been a primary concern of Peter Taylor's for thirty years or more. His fictional domain, as well as that of Anne Tyler for the most part, embraces a society with a disintegrating tradition, one in which family structure is deteriorating, and love is no longer a dominating force (see *The Collected Stories of Peter Taylor* [1969] and Tyler's *Dinner at the Homesick Restaurant* [1982]). A related theme that threads its way through much contemporary fiction is that of loneliness, of separateness from family, society, and the natural world—the feeling of aloneness, in Ralph Ellison's phrase, that follows the realization that a materialistic, bureaucratic society has reduced the individual "to an abstraction, has made him invisible."

What one misses in the fiction of this period, however, is the all-pervasive, dominating presence of William Faulkner. Although most of her life has been spent in Mississippi and her writing based on her experiences there, Eudora Welty does not claim, as Faulkner did, to be "sole owner and proprietor" of the fictional world she has created. Her fiction is rooted in a specific time and at a particular place, but she has not created an apocryphal county and a dozen or more stories and novels in which the same characters reappear and facets of the same theme recur, novels so closely interrelated that one has to read all of them before he can fully understand any of them. However, her stories comprehend more than one time and one place. She is not a regionalist or local colorist; anyone who has read any of her nearly flawless fiction knows that the range and depth of her view of reality are not restricted to any one section of the country. In story after story, Welty probes the depth of the human sensibility attempting to identify the motives that initiate specific actions. Above all, as Albert J. Devlin has written, her stories and novels emphasize that "changeless human values" exist within a definite time and in a single place. Although Welty has written convincingly of the effect of place on fiction and has examined the need of communally shared values and traditions, in some of her best fiction— *The Golden Apples* (1949) and *The Optimist's Daughter* (1972)—she has explored the possibility of one's becoming so stifled by a closed community that individual development is impossible. Her reflections on the past and its influence on the present cannot be expressed, nevertheless, in a manner so concrete as the stereotypical statement that the underlying design in the Yoknapatawpha novels can be detected by following the development of the conflict between the flawed and deteriorating Sartoris family and the amoral clan of Snopses. Although she used much of the same raw material as her gifted neighbor, each of her stories or novels, like his, bears the unmistakable stamp of its creator.

One theme that runs through much of the fiction written in the South since World War II is that of the complex and ambiguous relationships between blacks and whites. From Elizabeth Spencer's *Voice at the Back Door*, through Madison Jones's *A Cry of Absence*, Jesse Hill Ford's *The Liberation of Lord Byron Jones*, and Ernest Gaines's "The Sky is Grey," one can note the unique characteristics of a biracial society. Just as Rider in Faulkner's "Pantaloon in Black" is dehumanized by the white men who think that because he is black he is unable to feel grief, so in *Voice at the Back Door*, *A Cry of Absence*, and *Lord Byron Jones*, the confrontation of black and white sends destructive tremors through entire communities. Anne Tyler's "The Geologist's Maid" reveals the unbreachable gap between a white man and his black maid, as thirty-five years before Peter Taylor in "The Long Fourth" had treated the same kind of misunderstanding between a Nashville woman and her black servant of many years. No one in contemporary America has presented more vividly the myriad kinds of relationships that may exist between white mistress and black servant than Peter Taylor has. Perhaps no contemporary writer has succeeded as well as Doris Betts in showing how much the relationships between the races have changed in two decades. In "The Ugliest Pilgrim" Betts presents an intimate sexual affair between a white girl and a white man and indicates that the girl would have been willing, had the opportunity developed, to have had the same kind of relationship with a black man. The reader finds the girl a sympathetic character because Betts treats Flick's blackness as if it were no different from Violet's scarred ugliness. Flick is presented as if he, like the white Monty, is merely another imperfect human being, no stronger and no weaker than anyone else. Such a story would not have been written by a Southern author for a Southern audience thirty years ago.

All contemporary stories do not concentrate on the ways the region has changed, but some suggest that though the surface may seem different the fundamentals are much the same. The grotesquerie and the violence are everywhere evident. In the 1930s and 1940s there developed a disturbing picture of a society whose citizens had lost all their respect for traditions, rituals, rites, and ceremonies. Peter Taylor and Anne Tyler write of a people moving from a closely knit, ordered community to a society without traditional values. Organized religion has no effect upon the process by which their characters reach a decision. Tyler's stories do not have Taylor's thin veneer of a social order composed of polite, well-mannered, civilized, compassionate people, but in the work of both writers there are too many loveless marriages, too much sham and hypocrisy, too many empty and meaningless gestures. Cormac McCarthy's fiction is filled with episodes of animalistic fornication, incest, murder, and necrophilia. After reading his work, however, the certainty of man's depravity, in the South and elsewhere, no longer seems anything less than fundamental truth.

Despite these continuities, however, there are significant changes. Mildred Haun's stories suggest that the lines separating folk fantasies and supernatural truths are often indistinctly drawn. But Haun's granny woman, who assists the inhabitants of her isolated region in understanding the signs of a metaphysical world, becomes in David Madden's hilariously funny story, "The Singer," a young girl, a Christ-like figure, who has received a "call to sing for God." The age-old theme of leaving home and innocence and the inevitable acquisition of knowledge and experience, along with the awareness of the omnipresence of evil, an archetypal action in the writings of Truman Capote and Robert Penn

Warren, is used by Andre Dubus to present a pathetic story of loneliness, infidelity, and hopelessness.

From the carefully crafted and ironic prose of Peter Taylor through the skillfully structured fiction of Eudora Welty to the lyrical realism of Ralph Ellison's great novel, one can move to the well-paced (though sometimes seemingly chaotic) narration of David Madden and the deceptively simple (and often quasi-surrealistic) stories of Barry Hannah and not exhaust the possibilities of contemporary Southern prose. There remain Reynolds Price, Elizabeth Spencer, William Styron, James Agee, Madison Jones, Shelby Foote, Anne Tyler, Walker Percy, Doris Betts, Ernest Gaines, and many more. At no other time in our history, not even in the period between 1920 and 1950, has the Southern prose writer provided more divergent themes treated more evocatively and convincingly than at the present.

PEGGY WHITMAN PRENSHAW

Eudora Welty

With the 1936 publication of "Death of a Traveling Salesman,"
Eudora Welty began a career marked by literary distinction.
From the outset she enjoyed the support of other writers and sympathetic
editors and literary friends, particularly fellow Southerners Cleanth
Brooks and Robert Penn Warren, who were editing the *Southern Review* in the late 1930s. They published seven of the seventeen stories
that later composed her first collection, *A Curtain of Green and Other
Stories* (1941). Katherine Anne Porter, who was living in Baton Rouge
at the time, wrote the introduction to the collection. For all the early
encouragement, however, it has been Welty's extraordinary talent and
insight that have sustained the steady rise in reputation and readership
throughout her long literary career. When *The Collected Stories of
Eudora Welty* was published in 1980, the author's literary achievement
was celebrated in countless retrospective reviews in the United States
and abroad.

Welty was born in Jackson, Mississippi, in 1909, where she has maintained her residence throughout her life. Her parents were not native
Mississippians, her father having come from Ohio, her mother from
West Virginia. Both schoolteachers before their marriage, the Weltys as
a young couple moved to Jackson to establish a life and a family. In the
years of Welty's youth, the family's means were comfortable but always
moderate. At his death in 1931, Christian Welty was president of the
Lamar Life Insurance Company. In various recollections of her childhood, Welty has spoken of the love and stability provided by her parents, two brothers, and a close community of friends and neighbors. In
some respects, her experience was atypical of her time and place. For
example, she regularly traveled to West Virginia to visit her mother's
family, and she made other trips outside Mississippi. At home there were
spirited political discussions between her mother, who was a "Southerner and a Democrat," and her father, who was a "Yankee and a Republican." In a 1981 interview included in *Mississippi Writers Talking*

(1982), she spoke lightly of her concern as a child over her father's differentness. "At that time there weren't very many Republicans in Mississippi. I think there were maybe two in Jackson that I knew of." Undoubtedly her parents' opposite outlooks cultivated in Welty an early habit of seeing life in a dialectical pattern. "It was interesting to grow up learning there were two sides to everything," she said. "It made you think."

Welty's experiences of her college years, like those of her childhood, incorporated the distant and new as well as the local and familiar. For two years she attended Mississippi State College for Women and then completed her bachelor's degree in English at the University of Wisconsin in Madison. Doubting that the profession of letters could be counted upon for a living, her father urged her to prepare herself to earn an income. Following his advice, she attended the Columbia University School of Business and had, as she has said, her "year in New York."

In 1931, she returned to Mississippi and worked for a local radio station, as a part-time correspondent for the Memphis *Commercial Appeal*, and as "junior publicity agent" for the Works Progress Administration. In her introduction to *One Time, One Place* (1971), the collection of photographs she took during the 1930s, she writes that the WPA job gave her "the chance to travel, to see widely and at close hand and really for the first time the nature of the place [she had] been born into." The sights and sounds of the Mississippi countryside deeply impressed her, furnishing a storehouse of images for many later works of fiction.

Beginning with the earliest stories, the world view embodied by Welty's fiction is that of an almost classically balanced temper. She understands and writes about the conflicting and complementary claims of the separate self and the group, represented by the family and the larger society. Like the generation of Southern writers just preceding her, she views the South from within and outside the tradition. In fact, she has portrayed the clash between the old and new South most notably in *Losing Battles* (1970), where she creates a 1930s hill-country family who might have served to illustrate the agrarian culture defended by the essayists of *I'll Take My Stand*. The Beechams and Renfros are farmers, or are not far removed from farming. They have a strong sense of place; they are self-sufficient and close knit, even clannish, and they take pride in the family's history, which is an oral history maintained in the form of favorite family stories. Communal and ritualistic values are more important to the family than any individual's aspirations for freedom and self-fulfillment. The Faustian force that for a lifetime threatened their satisfied complacency is represented by the schoolteacher

471

Julia Mortimer, who alternately cajoled and scolded her charges in an attempt to move them toward enlightenment and pragmatic rationalism. She called for industry, if not industrialization, and argued for cultural improvement or progress, which she was confident would come with education.

In this novel, as in most of her fiction, Welty is not ideological; she does not take sides. But contrary to Richard H. King's thesis in *A Southern Renaissance* (1980), she has assuredly placed the region at the center of her imaginative vision. Welty grounds her cultural critique in such vivid local detail that one may miss the larger outline. For Welty, the validity of fiction's truth and the power of fiction to persuade the reader to believe its truth lie in "the achieved world of appearance," as she says in her famous essay "Place in Fiction." She sees the life around her in its time and place, with a sharp eye and ear for the details of the region. Like John Crowe Ransom, she holds that art's way of getting at truth is through the local and particular. She understands that strains between historical forces and cultural traditions have their counterpart at the personal and local level, and it is here that she focuses her fictional lens.

The balance found in Welty's view of the South and the world beyond is also manifest in her style and technique. *A Curtain of Green*, which foreshadows the later fiction in its range and diversity, shows Welty's skill with both the dramatic story that is built upon dialogue and the lyrical story that is marked by figurative, almost poetic language. In the stories developed through action, dialogue and humor, the characters are as vigorous and varied as Canterbury pilgrims. For example, the retarded Lily Daw, contrary to the expectations of the respectable ladies of Victory, Mississippi, marries a red-headed xylophone player. The women of Leota's beauty parlor expose their mean-spiritedness in "The Petrified Man." And in a comic monologue of the kind Welty used later in *The Ponder Heart* (1954), Sister explains to a passerby in China Grove why she has taken residence in the post office. Welty's approach in such stories anticipates her creation of a chorus of voices in *Losing Battles*, in which the family members, like the narrator Edna Earle Ponder in *The Ponder Heart*, explain, defend, recall, and finally celebrate themselves in their spirited tale-telling.

By contrast, in such early stories as "The Whistle," "A Curtain of Green," "Death of a Traveling Salesman," and "A Worn Path," Welty employs an essentially lyrical style to explore themes of human loneliness, courage, and endurance. She portrays through significant details and suggestive metaphors the arduous journey of the aged Phoenix Jackson along a worn path of the Natchez Trace. The technique Welty uses to evoke an image of love and sacrifice owes much to the modernist technique of subtlety and indirection. This lyrical style is particularly suited to certain Weltian themes: the mysteries of the inner life, the subtle but palpable life of the imagination, the tenuous and tenacious forces that hold people together and push them apart. This was the kind of story much admired by the editors of the *Southern Review*. Among American writers Welty is one of the most gifted creators of lyrical prose. In her second collection, *The Wide Net and Other Stories* (1943), which includes some of her most memorable stories—"Livvie," "A Still Moment," "The Wide Net"—the lyrical technique predominates. Some contemporaneous reviewers found the prose style excessively indirect and complained of the author's obscurantism, a charge Robert Penn Warren answered in "Love and Separateness in Eudora Welty," an influential essay that set the direction of much subsequent Welty criticism.

The 1940s were extremely active years for Welty. Following the 1941 collection, the novella *The Robber Bridegroom* appeared in 1942. Here she moved beyond the twentieth-century settings and characters of her first stories to the Mississippi wilderness of the early nineteenth century. She also blended fantasy and realism, fairy tale and history in ways she had not before explored. A tale of Indians and Natchez Trace outlaws, it links a settler's family, including the princesslike daughter Rosamond and an evil stepmother, with the robber bridegroom, Jamie Lockhart, and such characters as Mike Fink and the infamous bandit Little Harp. In a letter to Welty, William Faulkner praised the novella's blend of history, myth, humor, and cultural critique.

Delta Wedding (1946), Welty's first full-length novel, elicited mainly positive reviews, though some reviewers objected to the indirectness of the style and what they saw as Welty's unwillingness to subject the Mississippi Delta to social criticism and political scrutiny. It was a short-sighted view of the novel's complex portrayal of the region. Welty depicts a plantation family in 1923, caught up in the preparations for daughter Dabney Fairchild's wedding. It is chiefly through the perception of the nine-year-old cousin Laura, the onlooker and outsider, that the story unfolds. Here, as earlier, Welty explores the relation between love and separateness, the individual's need for loving connections and a private selfhood. In the novel she portrays not only the reflective inner life of Laura but the bustling activity of the Fairchild family, in which the women are steady managers of people and the men are the life-force bringing spontaneity and vitality. The agents of memory and tradition, the women codify and pass on the values of the family to succeeding generations. Male characters like George Fairchild and the groom, Troy

Flavin, may delight and rejuvenate the family, appearing like field gods in the spring, but ultimately it is the Fairchild women who inherit the land and decree the rituals that sustain the family.

Welty's fifth book of fiction, *The Golden Apples* (1949), is one of her most distinguished and experimental works. Although many critics have regarded the book as a novel, Welty's inclusion of the cycle of related stories in *Collected Stories* indicates her preference. The book represents perhaps Welty's finest achievement in fusing material drawn from classical and folk myths with realistic characters and settings of the twentieth-century South. She also employs imagery and forms derived from painting and music—elaborate fictional forms suggesting musical motives, counterpoint, recapitulation. The result is a brilliant book that has not yet found its proper place in the American literary canon. Welty writes of the inhabitants of the fictional town of Morgana, Mississippi, King and Snowdie MacLain and the twins Ran and Eugene, and the Raineys. With subtlety, and yet with a kind of playful exuberance, Welty weaves the stories of these characters into patterns that hint of the exploits of Perseus, Odysseus, Zeus, Leda, Atlanta, Irish heroes, and American tale spinners, to name a few. At the conclusion, Virgie Rainey emerges as a heroic wanderer who has made her journey into the world and her return home. Remembering a painting that hung years earlier in her piano teacher's studio, one depicting Perseus slaying the Medusa, Virgie in middle age understands the human drama reflected in the painting and in the music her teacher had offered her. Through Virgie's perception, Welty develops a striking metaphor that expresses her own generous, comprehensive vision of life, one that celebrates both the vaunting hero and the tenacious adversary.

During the writing of *The Golden Apples*, Welty spent three months in San Francisco, where she set the story "Music from Spain." In the next few years she made several trips to Europe and the British Isles, drawing upon her experiences for two major stories in *The Bride of the Innisfallen and Other Stories* (1955). The fifteen years intervening between that collection and *Losing Battles*, Welty's next major publication, saw the illness and death of her mother and two brothers, a period of considerable family responsibility.

In 1972, Welty published *The Optimist's Daughter*, which had appeared originally in 1969 in a shorter, different form in the *New Yorker*. The novel won the Pulitzer Prize, and like *Losing Battles* enjoyed wide sales and popular attention. Welty dedicated the book to the memory of her mother (C. A. W.) and drew upon her mother's childhood in West Virginia for some parts of it. In theme and form it has the balance of a formal elegy. The protagonist, Laurel Hand, like Laura McRaven of

Delta Wedding, is both outsider and family member. She epitomizes the kind of Weltian character who seeks both to belong to the world and understand it. She is like Psyche, whose myth Welty has employed in earlier fiction, who is impelled to see the face of love. Here, as elsewhere, Welty shows that one of life's most demanding and heroic ventures is the act of seeing. To see and then to accept the consequence of one's vision requires a high order of courage. As some critics have pointed out, this pattern of heroism, recalling Psyche, is of a persistent if not distinctly female order.

In addition to writing fiction, Welty has engaged in many other forms of literary activity throughout her career, as reviewer, essayist, and lecturer. In 1978 she published *The Eye of the Story*, which includes essays and reviews spanning nearly forty years. She writes of aesthetic theory and practical, everyday matters of writing, of favorite authors, including Jane Austen, Henry Green, and Katherine Anne Porter, as well as of her childhood and the Mississippi settings that have so often informed her imagination. The collection mirrors the remarkable breadth of her reading and thought.

In the early years of her career, Welty was frequently linked with Carson McCullers, Truman Capote, Flannery O'Connor, and others, particularly by critics who focused on the Gothic and grotesque branch of the Southern house of fiction. Because of the proximity of their time and place, Welty has also often been compared to Faulkner. By the fifth decade of her career, however, Welty is generally recognized by the literary world as an extraordinarily singular writer. She resembles Faulkner not in style, subjects, or settings so much as in her broad, generous vision and acceptance of life, a Keatsian negative capability, marked perhaps by a bit more of Jane Austen's joy and geniality than typically found among twentieth-century writers. Welty is not dispirited by human foibles, nor overawed by human tragedies and epics. She sees the human comedy with piercing vision, and she writes of it with empathy and deep affection.

475

James Agee

O f modern American writers, perhaps only Charles Olsen has left us with as much sense of promise unfulfilled as James Agee. Poet, fiction writer, journalist, screenwriter, literary and film critic, James Agee saw only three of his books published within his lifetime—his early collection of poems, *Permit Me Voyage* (1934), his documentary masterpiece, *Let Us Now Praise Famous Men* (1941), and a novella, *The Morning Watch* (1951). Two years after his death on May 16, 1955, the popular reception of his posthumously published novel, *A Death in the Family* (1957), awakened critical interest in Agee's work. In the decade and a half following his death, Agee's short fiction, poetry, film scripts, film reviews, and correspondence have been published in collections. Several books and numerous articles attest to the critical interest in Agee's work.

James Agee was born in Knoxville, November 27, 1909, and grew up there and in a mountain community near Sewanee, Tennessee. After leaving Knoxville in 1925 to attend Phillips Exeter Academy and later Harvard University, Agee never lived in the South again for any lengthy period. As a reporter for *Fortune* and later as reviewer and critic for the *Nation*, Agee spent most of his adult life in New York and Hollywood. Yet, if he never publicly took his stand as a Southerner, much of his poetry and most of his fiction result from the experiences of his childhood in Tennessee. Agee's literary affinities with other Southern writers are marked. His recasting of Elizabethan and classical forms in his poetry often closely resembles the work of the Fugitive poets, especially that of Allen Tate, whom Agee knew well. The Shakespearean rhythms and diction of his prose are similar to Faulkner's. The moving elegiac passages of *Let Us Now Praise Famous Men* and *A Death in the Family* and Agee's insistence upon personal experience as the subject for fiction have direct parallels with the work of Thomas Wolfe. Most importantly, Agee's concern with history and with the role of religious faith and his belief in the wholeness and the integrity of the individual in the face of the multiplicity of modern life place him into the mainstream of twentieth-century Southern literary tradition.

Let Us Now Praise Famous Men, which includes photographs by Agee's friend Walker Evans, grew out of an assignment by *Fortune* magazine to investigate tenant farming in the South. This documentary of the lives of three Alabama tenant farmer families is generally regarded as Agee's most important work. It is in this remarkable book that Agee's versatile talents find their fullest realization. His concern with the symphonic possibilities of language and his interest in the visual expressiveness of the camera are combined in his prose style. Much of the "Clothing" and "Shelter" sections is cinematographic—the focus of the narratives moves like a camera panning the poor families' houses and presenting the objects found there as synecdoche for the whole fabric of their lives. Other sections of the book, especially "On the Porch" and "A Country Letter," are richly meditative and elegiac. Still in other sections of *Let Us Now Praise Famous Men,* such as "Education" and "Conversation in the Lobby," Agee as author directly interprets, lecturing the reader. Interspersed throughout is the narrative of Agee's relationship with the tenant families and his retelling of their own stories. As disjointed as each section may appear at first to be, taken together they constitute a prose symphony of separate movements with themes that run throughout the story and are brought together again on the porch at the end of the book.

Early in the book, Agee discusses the work as a problem of fusion of four planes of communication. The first plane is that of his personal experience; the second is that of facts, "as it happened"; the third plane is the situation of the past recalled by the imagination of the author in the present; and the fourth is the actual "problems of recording," or the writing of the text. Roughly the first three planes correspond to the narrative, cinematic, and interpretive modes of the work while the fourth is the work as a whole. The elaborateness of the design of *Let Us Now Praise Famous Men* not only is a testimony to Agee's meticulous working out of theories of technique and function in literature, but also in its complexity suggests perhaps the reason for the comparatively small number of works produced in Agee's career.

Let Us Now Praise Famous Men is the imaginative documentary of reality. *A Death in the Family,* set in Knoxville in 1915, is the fictionalization of Agee's actual experience of the death of his own father. Although the novel is, in part, the product of the editors who compiled it after Agee's death, *A Death in the Family* is also technically complex. The basic narrative itself is tripartite—Jay and Mary before Jay's death, the period of waiting, and the funeral. It is the interspersed chapters, the nonsequential lyrical fragments, however, that give the novel much of its power. Although written earlier and included by the editors, "Knoxville, 1915" creates the world of the novel and helps to explain how that world changes for Rufus with the death of his father. The "dream sequence" section of the novel and the interspersed italicized sections of the book, though not sequentially part of the main plot, further adumbrate the loss the boy experiences with his father's death. Like *The Sound and the Fury, A Death in the Family* finally moves more by resonances than by narrative events.

Agee's works often appear to predict the directions American letters has taken today. *Let Us Now Praise Famous Men* is the forerunner of the "new journalism" of Mailer and Capote. Agee's strange beast fable, "A Mother's Tale," would be labeled today as "metafiction." Agee's movie reviews are well respected as important works of film criticism. His film *The African Queen* is now considered a classic. But important also is Agee's portrayal of Southern tenant farmers in the thirties, his re-creation of domestic life in Tennessee, his reinvigoration of folk tradition into finely honed poetic forms. Perhaps of most importance is Agee's determination that the life of the individual in the South in the twentieth century is mysterious and complex and a fitting subject for literature.

LEWIS A. LAWSON

William Styron

Although William Styron has not lived there since he was a young man, he is still a son of the South. Indeed, much of his time in Roxbury, Connecticut, or at Martha's Vineyard, or in Europe over the past forty years has been devoted to an uncovering of his Southern past. Born in Newport News, Virginia, June 11, 1925, he lived out his childhood there with his widower father, an engineer at the shipyard. The Newport News area, both Southern/agricultural and American/industrial, presented him with shifting perspectives and competing appeals. From the very beginning, he must have had that double vision so useful to the artist, the ability not merely to see a thing, but to question it. Thus he never simply accepted "place" unconsciously, but sensed that its impact, either for good or ill, upon an individual could never be escaped.

Styron's schooling was decidedly traditional. He went to a nearby Episcopal boarding school, Christchurch. Then he entered Davidson, a North Carolina college with a strong Presbyterian tradition. After a year, in order to participate in a wartime officer training program, he transferred to Duke University. After serving as a Marine Corps officer toward the end of the war, he returned to Duke, graduating in 1947.

At Duke, Styron had enrolled in William Blackburn's creative writing course, but his stories give little evidence that he was soon to be regarded as Faulkner's heir. Nor, apparently, did he dream of such a future, for after graduation he went to New York to take a job in publishing. But the job was not congenial, and after a few months he was unemployed. In the period that followed, he enrolled in Hiram Hadyn's fiction course at the New School for Social Research, while living among the bohemians in Greenwich Village. In time he decided that if he was to write, it would be novels, and so he began to explore the imaginative possibilities in a story that he had heard of a girl from Newport News.

In his first novel, *Lie Down in Darkness* (1951), Styron seems strikingly derivative. He had read his Fitzgerald, his Warren, his Wolfe.

479

Above all, he had read Faulkner, and so strong was that influence that on first reading it very nearly swamps the novel. *Lie Down in Darkness* seems to be a grafting of the family situation in *The Sound and the Fury* upon the narrative structure of *As I Lay Dying*. A Southern girl just into her twenties, Peyton Loftis has committed suicide in New York City, and now her body must be transported from Port Warwick (Newport News) to its Virginia burial place, companied by her estranged parents and three other people who are caught in the battlefield that separates Milton and Helen Peyton Loftis.

Closer attention reveals, though, that the novel possesses its own profound vision, which is based upon a wisdom extremely rare in a first novel. Peyton Loftis is caught in what Gregory Bateson would later identify as the "double bind." Milton Loftis possesses that outlook traditionally identified as the cavalier manner; Helen Peyton has those Southern Calvinist values that provided so much of the durability—and obsessiveness—of the Southern tradition. Styron has, in other words, captured the paradox of Southern character that is too often missed by commentators on its history. A dutiful child, Peyton tries to please her parents, only to displease one every time she pleases the other; her only escape, as R. D. Laing would see it, is to split her self, that is to say, go insane. On the personal level, it is certainly a Southern novel, but like any good Southern novel it is universal. "What's the matter with this world?" is a hillbilly refrain heard in the novel, and the implied answer is that more and more the individual is subjected to mutually antagonistic value systems, to which he can respond only by adopting bad faith or sinking into mental illness.

The reviews of *Lie Down in Darkness* were almost all very enthusiastic, but Styron could not completely enjoy them, for he had been recalled to service during the Korean War. Although he was discharged rather soon, the experience provided him with the materials for a short novel, *The Long March* (1953), that is increasingly being regarded as a classic. The setting is a Carolina marine base, and Styron describes the "boondocks" with sweltering immediacy. But the setting eventually fades away, for the theme is the conflict between Colonel Templeton, the representative of authority, and Captain Mannix, a marine reserve who rebels against it. Styron seems well aware that he is creating an answer to the fable of *Billy Budd*, for his position clearly favors "Man-nix," the naysayer who refuses to accept the absurd, which claims respect simply because it is the authority. For his refusal, Mannix suffers agony—but he maintains his basic humanity, the ability to say no.

There followed a period in which Styron seems to have suffered a severe alienation from his native land. He spent considerable time in

Europe, becoming acquainted with the existentialist literature that was influential there. His novel *Set This House on Fire* (1960) reflects some of his main concerns of those days. Cass Kinsolving, the Southern-born painter, has exiled himself in Europe, only to fall prey to Mason Flagg, the rich American who seems to have the right connections into the military industrial complex. When Cass kills Mason, he receives no punishment, but neither does he experience any sort of purgation; it is only when he realizes that his guilt originated with his Southern past that he can return to the South and begin to work again.

Such a resolution prefigured Styron's decision to develop an idea that had intrigued him since boyhood. He knew of Nat Turner, a slave who had led a rebellion in Southside Virginia, and he must have thought that it was time for him to meditate upon the complexity of the institution of slavery. *The Confessions of Nat Turner* (1967) caused a great outcry among black readers, for various reasons; there was, for some time, a great deal of debate about the novel. Now, though, it is increasingly accepted as a novel and, moreover, as a study of slavery in general. Styron never claimed that it was any more than that, and he will yet be generally acknowledged for the depths of his insight.

After *Confessions*, Styron returned to his experience as a marine during the Korean War in a novel tentatively called "The Way of a Warrior." But he put it aside to publish *Sophie's Choice* (1979), a novel about a young man like himself, Stingo, who goes to New York to work after World War II. There he finds his life recast by Nathan, a Jew, and his mistress, Sophie, a Polish Gentile, who become, in a way, parent figures who preside over his growing up. Chiefly, what they teach him is the great, fearsome strength of chaos and death: Nathan, for all his brilliance, is incurably insane, while Sophie, for all her beauty, is sick to death in her soul, unable to live with the memory of having had to decide which of her children would be spared in a German concentration camp.

After *Sophie*, Styron offered a precise identification of his life theme: "I would think my concerns are by now pretty obvious. They involve . . . human institutions: humanly contrived situations which cause people to live in wretched unhappiness." His statement places his canon in sharp focus. In *Lie Down in Darkness* he was concerned with the way in which the historical institutions affecting Milton and Helen Loftis could pervert their role as parents; in *The Long March* he studied, in high allegory, the conflict between the institutional man and the individual; in *Set This House on Fire* he pitted an individual against the rich but hollow power of an institutional representative; in *Confessions* and *Sophie* individuals are so twisted by an institution that they destroy themselves. But in *Sophie*, there is a survivor, Stingo, and perhaps he holds the key to Styron's message: while it is true that institutions grow ever stronger (the capacity for world destruction provided by the bomb is never far from Styron's imagination), still they can only vanquish an individual if they can destroy his spirit. Styron commemorates the victims, but his primary purpose is to inspire the individual with the will to endure.

Truman Capote

B orn in New Orleans, September 30, 1923, Truman Capote (Truman Streckfus Persons) lived in Monroeville, Alabama, until the age of ten when he left for schools in New York and Connecticut. His early interest in Poe, especially "The Tell-Tale Heart"; his friendship with neighbor Harper Lee (Lee and Capote each has appeared as a character in the other's work); his interest in people observed through his youthful roman à clef, "Old Mr. Busybody"; and a homelife broken by a parental separation suggest the dimensions of the literary works that would come from Capote, who at seventeen began to work for the *New Yorker*.

As a Southern writer seeing the wake of William Faulkner's writing, Capote set his course early to avoid being caught in its wash. Although he spent time periodically through the years in New Orleans, he resided in New York and traveled widely. The settings for his fiction have moved from Alabama to New York to Kansas. And in several interviews, he disclaims being a Southern writer. However, the weight of his Southern childhood, its influence on his writing, and his literary response to Southern authors indicate otherwise. Capote, indeed, belongs to the post–World War II generation of writers, which includes Harper Lee, Carson McCullers, Flannery O'Connor, and William Styron.

His prose, both fiction and nonfiction, possesses a descriptive style with a crispness and precision enhanced by his tendency to rewrite and by his lifetime of journalism. The travel reports on New Orleans and Ischia, written during the 1940s, reveal Capote's ability to capture tone and mood of setting through selective use of specific detail. His skill in character portrayal is suggested by Mrs. Morris Otto Kunz and Gioconda from these early efforts. In 1957, when Capote wrote "The Duke in His Domain," a sustained sketch of Marlon Brando, he reached a high level of personality and character development through vivid description and dialogue, a power that appears in *In Cold Blood*. Unlike writers who work and live in relative isolation, Capote thrust himself into the public sphere, especially large gatherings. Although his becoming a part of the social scene at times eclipsed his literary reputation, his reporting and experiences in the frequently eccentric world brought some rewards—*The Muses Are Heard* (1956) and *Breakfast at Tiffany's* (1958).

Despite his journalistic endeavors, Capote's early stories show that his literary focus was introspective and autobiographical. As he gained more experience through his varied reporting assignments, his fiction evolved into a near-complement of his journalism. His youthful fiction has a strong Gothic influence and bears resemblance to Nathaniel Hawthorne's concept of romance, in which there is little if no transition from physical reality into the mindscape of dreams. "A Tree of Night" (1943) is the story of a college girl nearly forced into the close company of rural grotesques on a railroad journey. In "The Headless Hawk" (1946), terror and nightmare dominate in the person of Mr. Destronelli and in the visions of Vincent's "old and horrid" self. Mr. Revercomb from "Master Misery" (1948), acting in the manner of Chillingworth, steals Sylvia's dreams. The most comprehensive treatment of these themes and moods comes in *Other Voices, Other Rooms* (1948), an autobiographical novel set in the Deep South, one which clearly places his work in the same context as Harper Lee's *To Kill a Mockingbird*. Joel Knox seeks identity and love amid a house and setting surrounded by people leading meaningless lives. Fear has both a physical and a psychological presence in this short novel.

In contrast to much of the earlier work, "A Christmas Memory" (1946) and "House of Flowers" (1951) explore an environment of love and comfortable dreams. The characters often possess a vitality, a kind of active peace, that affects not only themselves but those around them. These stories depend more on the interplay of characters than on the interior struggles, but it is *The Grass Harp* (1951) that shows Capote truly emerging from the world of personal vicissitudes. Here the eccentric dreamers of the tree find conflict with the realists of the community who do not accept them. Although the narrative contains devices of dream sequences like memory and the recurring images of Indian grass, it expands Capote's previous social range of characters; Judge Cool, often speaking with the voice of the author, does not foresee the reconciliation of both worlds.

In *Breakfast at Tiffany's*, Capote uses the New York setting and his adult experiences to create comedy congruent with its extroverted surroundings while retaining an understated tie to his own past and the South he knew. He concerns himself with Holly Golightly's illusions and presents them as part of reality: "she's a *real* phony." An innocent abroad to an extent, Holly moves as easily among the members of the underworld as among the wealthy public figures at her party. The narrator, who seems much like Capote, stays at the edge of the stage. For the first time Capote seems to be able to discriminate among his own experiences and approach them nearly objectively.

In 1959, Capote's years of journalism had their most profound effect. After seeing a news item about the murder of a family in Kansas, he went to that state to begin research on *In Cold Blood* (1966), an innovation that he termed a "nonfiction novel." The narrative begins on the day of the murders with focus on the victims and concludes with the executions of the murderers, Perry Smith and Dick Hickok, whose decisions and actions threaten and violate the morality inherent in the idea of the American dream. Capote continues to maintain the objectivity achieved in his previous novel; he appears as the journalist in a few instances, however. As a form of fiction, the nonfiction novel has some precedent in the documentary novel, but Capote saw it as a completely different form. A second effort in this genre is "Handcarved Coffins: A Nonfiction Account of an American Crime," published in *Music for Chameleons* (1980).

When the narrator of *Breakfast at Tiffany's* comments on the fact of change and the naturalness of it, he could as well have been observing the literary career of Truman Capote. For the only constant in his professional life, from its beginnings in the 1940s until Capote's death in 1984, was that of journalistic writing.

Carson McCullers

Carson McCullers' literary career presents a complicated, curious history. Although she was hailed as a wunderkind in 1940 for her first novel, *The Heart Is a Lonely Hunter*, which she published at the age of twenty-three, her subsequent books, *Reflections in a Golden Eye* in 1941 and *The Member of the Wedding* in 1946, were generally less well received. The stage version of *The Member of the Wedding* in 1950 solidified her popular, if not her critical, success. The 1951 omnibus edition of *The Ballad of the Sad Café* gathered into one volume her work of the previous decade, including her three novels, the title novella (written in 1941), and six of her best stories. For the first time, serious critics joined reviewers and fellow writers in admiration of McCullers' unique talents. Her ensuing silence, caused by her serious illness, once again weakened her critical reputation, which was not enhanced by her play *The Square Root of Wonderful* in 1958, nor her novel *Clock Without Hands* in 1961. Since her death in 1967 and the publication of the posthumous collection *The Mortgaged Heart* in 1971, renewed critical attention has again been paid to McCullers, with her work being compared favorably with that of the other leading women writers of the Southern Renascence.

Born in Columbus, Georgia, in 1917, Carson McCullers grew up in that small mill city, passing a childhood remarkable only for her weak health and strong attachments to artistic mentors. Her passions were music and literature, and she worked with incredible zeal toward accomplishment in both. She finally settled on literature as a vocation after her move to New York in 1934 at the depths of the economic depression, when a new documentary impulse was felt throughout the culture, in the various artistic mediums as well as in the social sciences. Fiction, poetry, and drama, as well as painting, photography, and film, all recorded the harsh reality of the American dream gone sour. McCullers' earliest work reflects many of the same interests, particularly the pieces that directly prefigure her first novel, *The Heart Is a Lonely Hunter*.

Carson McCullers is not a realistic writer, yet in her best works she matches the documentary detail of social surface to a complex understructure of grotesque allegory drawn from the modernist tradition. She explains her method in the essay "The Russian Realists and Southern Literature" (1941) where she rejects the "Gothic School" as a "tag" for Southern writing and posits instead "a peculiar and intense realism . . . a bold and outwardly callous juxtaposition of . . . the whole soul of man with materialistic detail." In *The Heart Is a Lonely Hunter*, the allegorical structure, the complex solar system of grotesque "lonelyhearts" in complementary orbits, is perfectly balanced by an intensely realistic documentation of the social surface found in a Southern mill city during the depression. It is a prodigious fiction, and remains her finest effort.

Her second novel, *Reflections in a Golden Eye*, was more directly influenced by modernist fiction, in particular, Isak Dinesen's *Seven Gothic Tales*. When viewed as an example of the modern Gothic, McCullers' tale of bizarre sexuality on a peacetime army base demonstrates versatility and artistic daring. This critically neglected second book seizes many of the grotesque aspects of the modern South and develops them as symbols of a more universal alienation.

The Ballad of the Sad Café is a more traditional work in the Gothic mode. Written quickly during 1941 when McCullers was stalled during the writing of *The Member of the Wedding*, the novella remains McCullers' literary ballad. The distancing effect of the balladeer-narrator allows the larger-than-life characters and strange events to be unified in one of the most intriguing short works in modern Southern fiction.

McCullers recreated some of the literary and popular success of her first novel in *The Member of the Wedding*. This smaller portrait of the mill city probes social relationships and individual feelings through the symbolic use of the alienated adolescent. Yet her concentration on what was only one aspect of *The Heart Is a Lonely Hunter* limits the achievement of *The Member of the Wedding*; the novel evidences a loss of intellectual vigor and emotional intensity. It is a narrower achievement, though more accessible for a popular audience in the stage and screen versions that made the author financially secure.

McCullers worked for over a decade on *Clock Without Hands*, her last novel, in which she attempted a major social fiction, a realistic assessment of the postwar South. She intended it and *The Heart Is a Lonely Hunter* to stand as a pair of major Southern novels. Unfortunately, her declining creative power made successful completion impossible. The novel's weak characterization and stereotyped action, undoubtedly influenced by the author's long and debilitating illness, cannot create a structure strong enough to order the complicated changes that transformed the region in the days of integration. Carson McCullers died on September 29, 1967.

Born and raised in the Deep South, Carson McCullers came of literary age at the end of the most important decade in the history of Southern letters, and she extended the tradition by employing the modern South as setting in all of her major fictions. More importantly, she used the harsh symbolism of Southern life to recreate the universal failures and anxieties of the modern world. However, like many Southern writers, she developed an ambivalent attitude toward her native land; she cut herself off from the roots of her vision in the South, yet she never developed a replacement. Her achievement, however, still proves unique in the fiction of the Southern Renascence.

LOUISE Y. GOSSETT

Flannery O'Connor

Ellen Glasgow's prescription of blood and irony for Southern literature was filled by Flannery O'Connor (1925–1964) in ways that were more complex than Glasgow or any other proponent of realism or social criticism in Southern fiction had foreseen. O'Connor made rural central Georgia her place as forcefully as Faulkner and Welty made Mississippi theirs. She once acknowledged the intensity of her locale by saying that even if she were to write about characters as exotic to her as the Japanese, they would all sound like Herman Talmadge. Few in her generation of Southern writers remained both literally and fictionally anchored in place as she.

Her decision to stay in her own region was, in part, made for her when she developed lupus. After 1950, illness kept her permanently at Andalusia, the family farm near Milledgeville. The farm and town, the cities of Macon and Atlanta, and their surrounding country furnished the geography of her fiction. A dark row of pines, for example, like that which bounds scenes in "A Circle in the Fire" and "A View of the Woods" edged the pasture below the Andalusia farmhouse. A red clay road ran from the highway to the house, and peafowl tacked and strutted across the lawn. The more intricate merging of actual and fictional milieu is suggested by Barbara McKenzie's photographs in *Flannery O'Connor's Georgia*. There are the ramshackle stores, the kudzu-bordered roads, the religious and commercial billboards, the collapsing barns, the thin crops guarded by scarecrows, and the river baptisms that speak of the struggle by which O'Connor's characters live and die. Subsistence land and towns or cities indifferent to people challenge and baffle the characters. Sometimes beauty transfigures the scene: trees sparkle in hoarfrost or a peacock's tail shimmers like the Transfiguration.

Only once did O'Connor use a setting outside the South. In "The Geranium" (1946), her first published story which was later rewritten as "Judgement Day," the old Southern father, transplanted to New York, lives in memories of his South, where blacks and whites, he says, know

489

their proper stations. It is not a land in which devoted agrarians preserve humane values. It meagerly supports small farm owners, who, in turn, pay small wages to their tenants and smaller to blacks.

The South as landscape figures most vividly in O'Connor's short stories, which were brought together in two collections: *A Good Man Is Hard To Find* (1955) and *Everything That Rises Must Converge* (1965). The posthumous volume *Flannery O'Connor: The Complete Stories* (1971) contains all her short stories, including those written for her master's thesis at the State University of Iowa (1947). O'Connor located her two novels largely in the urban South, but the central characters have the mind-set and speech of their rural or small-town origins. Hazel Motes and young Francis Marion Tarwater bring to the cities in *Wise Blood* (1952) and *The Violent Bear It Away* (1960) an obsessive singlemindedness that appears elementary and primitivistic but deals with complex matters.

Urgent themes and their swift, vivid enactment charged O'Connor's fiction with unusual power from the first publication to the last. O'Connor did not so much expand and build themes from one work to another as she learned to select and deploy details with increasing exactness. The concision and the rapid tempo generate an intensity more suited to the short story than the novel. The resistance to psychological or spiritual illumination that is characteristic of all the main characters is more difficult to sustain in novels than short stories, though the process by which illumination arrives can be more fully traced in the novels. In both forms, denouements occur quickly. The crux of the fiction is the human being's need to recognize the peril of damnation in which he lives. The religious implications of this need do not eventuate in reassurances that the characters who come to recognition will live cheerful, successful lives. For O'Connor, the nonnegotiable, incontrovertible terms of the demand that man change constituted the drama. The human being hears, refuses to listen, persists in his own ways, attempts to escape, and is finally struck down by his conceit, which proves to have been working in the cause it has resisted.

The hound-of-heaven paradigm describes the fundamental course of action in O'Connor's fiction. The doom that envelops Faulkner's or Glasgow's characters in the tragic dignity of recognition and final loss prepares O'Connor's characters for the divine comedy of redemption. The most obsessively active resisters are the prophet figures like Hazel Motes and young Tarwater. In resisting their vocation, Haze and Tarwater overturn the proprieties of ordinary business, religion, education, psychology, social service, and journalism, thereby exposing the limitations and hypocrisies of respectable citizens and their institutions.

Haze, who worships by denial, preaches the Church Without Christ. Through his encounters he exposes the false religions of the evangelist Hawkes, the radio personality Onnie Jay Holy, and the primitivist Enoch Emery. His reading the letters of a "Dear Mary" column mocks the superficialities of a psychology of adjustment.

In a similar vein, the encounters of young Tarwater with his school-teacher uncle Rayber expose the false faiths of education, psychology, and rationalism. He defeats the reasonable efforts of Rayber to free him from his compulsion to baptize his idiot cousin Bishop. Both Motes and Tarwater are possessed men, driven by cataclysmic power. The violence of their resistance and capitulation, like the magnitude of Lucifer's rebellion, measures the omnipotence and omniscience that overwhelms them. Motes grinds quicklime into his eyes and puts rocks in his shoes to mortify his body into a bottomless vessel that will hold more of the light into which he contracts at death. After being drugged and raped by a homosexual, Tarwater, who had simultaneously baptized and drowned Bishop, burns the woods around his old home and sets off to the city to fulfill the command that he prophesy the "terrible speed of mercy." These apocalyptic versions of human experience are usually narrated by an omniscient voice and are as clear and inexorable as those of an Old Testament prophet. In *The Violent Bear It Away* there is an additional voice within Tarwater that keeps up a descant of temptations. Action occurs in linear time sequences that may be broken by flashbacks. Usually narration moves from episode to episode of violent, unexpected, disruptive, extreme behavior, the bold lines of which O'Connor felt were necessary to make graphic the perversion that human beings no longer recognized.

The narrator is neither prurient, sordid, nor sentimental. The certainty of O'Connor's moral vision controls the perspective. The errors, or the sins, of characters, subject as they are to the great reversal of redemption, are treated ironically. At short range the errors are put in their place verbally. For example, the author says of Mrs. McIntyre, impatiently listening to Father Flynn in "The Displaced Person," that "Christ in the conversation embarrassed her the way sex had her mother." At long range the errors are turned around by the ironies of the plot. Events in "The Displaced Person" reveal that Mrs. McIntyre tacitly wills the death of the displaced person who has disrupted her farm by his efficiency and true charity. The shock of this kind of violence is fundamental to O'Connor's fiction. By destroying human pride and ordinary expectations, it forces an encounter with the hidden self that frees the character to change. O'Connor may leave this change open as a possibility, as she does for Mrs. McIntyre, whose deterioration at the end of the story reduces her to hearing doctrines from the priest. Or O'Connor may declare the change accomplished, as it is for Mr. Head in "The Artificial Nigger" when he feels his pride consumed by mercy. Or she may let another character assess the likelihood of change as does The Misfit by pointing out that the grandmother had a potential goodness that frequent shocks could have activated ("A Good Man Is Hard To Find").

In her last posthumously published collection, *Everything That Rises Must Converge* (1965), O'Connor more surely controls the telling of the stories by using a central intelligence. Figures like Mrs. May ("Greenleaf"), Mrs. Turpin ("Revelation"), Parker ("Parker's Back"), and Tanner ("Judgement Day") develop more psychological consistency and complexity than do the parable figures in the stories of *A Good Man Is Hard To Find*. They enact the same moral drama, however, in which spiritual and intellectual pride perversely struggles against grace and mercy, or divided selves struggle to integrate hostility and love, fear and confidence. The thrust of O'Connor's folk idiom, realistic details, and ironic tone into the level of anagogical meaning raises issues, difficult to settle, about the credibility, consistency, and coherence of the fiction, issues peculiar to O'Connor's work. The arguments, which are aesthetic and theological, reflect divisions within her audience that O'Connor expected. She took part in the discussions through her essays, lectures, and letters, published both before and after her death on August 3, 1964. The major prose pieces, chosen and edited by Robert and Sally Fitzgerald, appear in *Mystery and Manners* (1969) and the letters in *The Habit of Being*, edited by Sally Fitzgerald (1979).

In *Mystery and Manners*, three essays, which were originally lectures, make an apologia distinguished in its intelligence, wit, common sense, self-knowledge, and humility. O'Connor spells out the premises of her literary realism and orthodoxy that set her treatment of themes and characters apart from the secularized culture in which she lived and in which she knew most of her audience believed. In "The Fiction Writer and His Country," O'Connor discusses the importance of manners and mystery for her art. From the manners of her fellow Southerners she drew the substance of human relationships that she considered essential to storytelling. The mystery of Christian faith gave her the moral vision essential to an artist's seeing with meaning. In "The Grotesque in Southern Fiction" she defines her realism as that which moves toward religious mystery, and she acknowledges the violence and outlandish comedy that result from yoking the recognizable external reality of manners with religious reality. The consequent grotesque distinction she identifies as prophecy, that is, seeing the eternal in the everyday, however defective and distorted the latter may be. The disjunction of Southern writers, she asserts in "The Regional Writer," is that their region with its Civil War and Fundamentalism gives them the great drama of the Fall and the means of interpreting it.

No other Southern writer, except perhaps Walker Percy, so boldly connects art and religion in fiction. She takes the risk also of being misread and dismissed, because though her fiction originates in the social, political, psychological, and historical reality of her region, no interpretation of it on these grounds alone is complete. These essays, and those referring specifically to her role as a Catholic writer, reveal how clearly O'Connor understood the problem of literature and belief and how fully she was an artist who dealt with the issue through the literary resources of point of view, symbol, iconography, character, dialogue, place, tone, and humor.

The astute, often acerbic judgments and the ironic humor of O'Connor's essays also characterize her letters. Written as conversations with friends, the letters are important accounts of O'Connor as artist: her struggle to write with the exactitude an art requires, her willingness to work without recognition, her humility before her talent.

Although she was not an experimentalist to the extent that Faulkner, Cabell, and McCullers were, O'Connor often claimed for herself the freedom of writing in "the modern romance tradition." Clearly, she had Hawthorne's distinctions in mind, for however tangibly her stories begin in local facts, they continue into situations and revelations that are parabolic or anagogical, levels seldom approached by her contemporary American writers. In the power with which she dramatizes her orthodox Catholic vision of redemption, she is unique in American fiction.

Peter Taylor

Peter Taylor was born January 8, 1917, in Trenton, Tennessee, and spent his youth in Nashville, St. Louis, and Memphis. He attended Southwestern University, Vanderbilt University, Kenyon College, and Louisiana State University. He had as mentors Allen Tate, John Crowe Ransom, and Robert Penn Warren. Although never an Agrarian himself, Taylor examines in his fiction many themes common to the work of his famous teachers—the breaking down of old loyalties, manners, faiths, and relationships by the pluralisms of modern life. As a teacher at Kenyon, the University of North Carolina at Greensboro, the University of Virginia at Charlottesville, and elsewhere, Taylor has guided and inspired a new generation of Southern writers.

Although he has published one short novel, *A Woman of Means* (1950), and has shown an increasing interest in drama throughout his career, Taylor's literary reputation justifiably rests upon his short fiction, which has appeared in journals and magazines for over four decades. A majority of these stories have appeared in Taylor's collections, *A Long Fourth and Other Stories* (1948), *The Widows of Thornton* (1954), *Happy Families Are All Alike* (1959), *Miss Leonora When Last Seen* (1963), *The Collected Stories of Peter Taylor* (1969), and, most recently, *In the Miro District and Other Stories* (1977). Most of these stories, though set in urban environments, often Nashville, Memphis, or St. Louis, are stories of persons and families whose roots are in small Southern towns, most often in Taylor's fictional Thornton, Tennessee. Although these small-town Southerners move to the city, their values, often parochial, are not left behind, and the central conflicts of the stories are often the result of the intersection of the older values with the demands of modern life. Taylor's allegiances, however, are neither exclusively on the side of the small town nor of the modern world.

Taylor's stories generally fall into two groups, though many overlap. The first group of stories might be termed modern tales of manners; the second consists of psychological tales in the tradition of the Southern grotesque. In the first group, which encompasses the majority of Taylor's fictional production, are remarkable stories of unremarkable people. These are tales in the genteel tradition, if such a term may be used without pejorative associations. Basically such stories depict small crises that reveal greater underlying dilemmas. In "Guests," for example, the visit of country relatives to Nashville occasions domestic quarrels that subtly illuminate not only the essential differences in the values of the country couple, but also the gap in communication and understanding between the urban wife and her husband. In "At the Drugstore," a neo–New Yorker's morning expedition to the drugstore during his visit to his Southern hometown allows the man to put his past and his present into a meaningful perspective. In the best of these stories, Taylor's ability to present the ineffable and fragile moments of recognition in his characters' lives exhibits as subtle a fictional touch as Katherine Anne Porter's Miranda stories and Ernest Hemingway's "A Clean Well-Lighted Place." Like these two authors, Taylor, in his finest work, becomes a poet of the extraordinary ordinary.

The second group of stories, which include Taylor's most famous pieces, are tales of Southern grotesques. These stories, such as "A Spinster's Tale" and "Venus, Cupid, Folly and Time," are in the same tradition as Faulkner's "A Rose for Emily" and many stories by Flannery O'Connor and Carson McCullers. In "A Spinster's Tale," a young woman's fear of male sexuality, personified to her by the neighborhood drunk, becomes generalized to include all of the male members of her family and by extension all males. When the drunk falls off her porch and injures himself, she cannot bring herself to help him and leaves him lying in the rain while she calls the police. "Venus, Cupid, Folly and Time" is the story of a dance party for adolescents given by a sexually bizarre elderly brother and sister. In such stories, Taylor explores the subrational mysteries behind the facade of public character.

Sexuality is often a theme in Taylor's work. Although presented in its perverse manifestations in "Venus, Cupid, Folly and Time," in its psychological intricacies in "A Spinster's Tale," "Sky Line," and "A Fancy Woman," or at its most comic in "Reservations," Taylor's approach to his subject is always urbane, never lurid or sensational. Often prevalent in Southern fiction, violence, when present in Taylor's works, is usually psychological and is often coupled with sexuality, particularly in his more recent stories. But Taylor's grotesques are not always sexual cripples; some, like Miss Leonora of "Miss Leonora When Last Seen" and Aunt Munsie of "What Do You Hear from 'Em'," are the victims of a debilitating alienation. In fact, in Taylor's fiction, alienation is most often the cause for many psychological deviations.

Taylor has assiduously avoided the commentaries on art so common to writers who have found a home in the academy. Only in one story, "1939," does he directly deal with the artist as a central theme, and the message of the tale is that the artist must finally exist as an equal in the community.

In recent years, literary scholars have focused an increasing amount of attention on Taylor's work. The publication of *The Collected Stories* in 1969 was greeted with enthusiastic praise by reviewers. The *New York Times Book Review* proclaimed Taylor "one of the best writers America has ever produced"; another reviewer has asserted that "no one writing in English can do more with a short story than this man." But because he has chosen to work predominantly in short fiction, because the magazine market for fiction is steadily diminishing, and because today's reading public has eschewed the short story in favor of the novel, Peter Taylor's reputation in Southern letters has not achieved the levels that his work merits.

Elizabeth Spencer

Elizabeth Spencer, a native of Carrollton, Mississippi, is a writer of unusual versatility and subtlety. To date, she has published eight novels and several collections of short stories, works that exemplify an extraordinary range in style and subjects. In some respects, her fiction has reflected a course of change similar to the events in her life, depicting in the early novels rural settings and characters drawn from her youth in Mississippi, and later, foreign places and cosmopolitan figures suggestive of international cities like Rome and Montreal. In 1956 Spencer married John Rusher of Cornwall, England, and since 1958 they have lived in Montreal.

Spencer was born in Carrollton, July 19, 1921, grew up in Mississippi, graduated in 1942 from Belhaven College in Jackson, and took a master's degree in English at Vanderbilt in 1943. In several interviews she has acknowledged the considerable influence Donald Davidson, one of her professors at Vanderbilt, had on her early career. In 1945–1946, Spencer worked as a reporter for the Nashville *Tennessean*, but finally quit her job to devote herself full time to her writing. She published *Fire in the Morning* in 1948. The book received unusually wide attention, particularly for a first novel, and Spencer was praised for her skillful handling of a complicated plot involving four generations of hill-country Mississippians. The novel's protagonist, Kinloch Armstrong, is a young man who contends with the many-layered, intricate relationships of life in a small Southern town. The focus of his emotional and moral journey is the unraveling of a secret from the past having to do with the rightful ownership of one of the largest tracts of land in the county. Eventually his determination to uncover the past, largely motivated by his desire to expose his hated enemies, the Gerrards, leads to painful and ambiguous discoveries. Spencer's themes and subjects are often somewhat reminiscent of those of Faulkner and Warren, but her handling of these is fresh and original. In style, Spencer employs several modernist techniques—irregular chronology, flashbacks, multiple points of view—but the

497

strength of the novel lies in its vital, credible characters and its vigorous, engaging narrative, attributes chiefly of the traditional novel.

Spencer continued to draw the attention of national reviewers with her next two novels, both set in Mississippi. In *This Crooked Way* (1952) she creates one of her most memorable characters in Amos Dudley, son of an impoverished hill family, a man obsessed with a vision of God and a dream of wealth and power. Although Amos' daughter Elinor figures in the earlier *Fire in the Morning*, Spencer clearly is not concerned to create a Mississippi saga. Instead, she concentrates on the intersecting forces of psychology and theology in the life of a man who exemplifies the prototypical American Adam, one whose arena for action is the rich, untamed land of the Mississippi Delta in the early twentieth century. When Amos leaves the hills to make his short westward journey, he is confident that his desire for success, as well as his destined achievement, is the will of God. Spencer opens the novel with an omniscient narrative portraying Amos' youthful entanglement with God and his rise as a plantation owner. Using multiple narrators very effectively in the remaining sections, she explores the emotional costs of Amos' grand plan in the lives of those closest to him.

In *The Voice at the Back Door* (1956), written largely while in Italy on a Guggenheim grant in 1953, Spencer turns to the complex, often tense relationships arising from racial conflicts and divisions in a small town. The plot is intricate, the cast of characters large, and the depiction of a mid-twentieth-century Southern town richly detailed. The novel's action is centered upon Duncan Harper, formerly an admired football hero, who in his role as acting sheriff threatens the established racial caste system by protecting a black man over the protests of the white citizenry. Here Spencer demonstrates her skill in writing social criticism that is ultimately a compelling portrait, not a commentary.

With the publication in 1960 of *The Light in the Piazza*, which won the McGraw-Hill Fiction Award, Spencer shifted the scene of her fiction from the American to the European South. The novella continued Spencer's preoccupation, however, with the ambiguities of moral action. The protagonist Margaret Johnson, vacationing in Italy with her daughter Clara, faces a decision that appeals to desire and tests the conscience. Margaret has long hoped for a normal life for Clara, the twenty-six-year-old victim of a childhood injury that has left her with the mind and *joie de vivre* of a ten-year-old. When Clara meets a young Italian who proposes marriage, Margaret at first demurs, then she acquiesces to and finally promotes the marriage, convinced that she has done "the right thing." Many reviewers noted the Jamesian matter of the book, and indeed the delicate sensibility of Margaret is reminiscent of James's heroines, but Spencer's treatment of the international theme comes of her own vision. The book's moral stance is finally ambivalent, infused with the slightly ironic acknowledgment that Clara's diminished mentality offers no serious diminution of her ability to succeed as a traditional wife and mother in Italy. In contrast to the moral convolutions, the prose style is lucidly straightforward. Its transparency is beguiling, however, for beneath the surface lie murky and irresolvable human dilemmas.

A second novella set in Italy, *Knights and Dragons* (1965), represents a further development in Spencer's career, that of her growing fascination with the mysterious, hidden forces in life. The central character, Martha Ingram, is entrapped in a web of relationships with three men, her former husband, her superior at the United States cultural office, and an American economist traveling in Italy who becomes her lover. Martha is haunted by a sense that, by some strange necessity, she is compelled to be either destroyer or victim in these relationships. Furthermore, she is convinced that somehow life in Italy blurs her judgment and makes discriminating between the roles impossible. She is frightened by the fanciful and demonic impulses she feels within herself, and yet she attends them, knowing that her vitality depends upon the tension between her fear of and attraction to mysterious people and inexplicable motives.

In her next two novels, *No Place for an Angel* (1967) and *The Snare* (1972), Spencer returns to her exploration of psyches that are stimulated and damaged by mysterious malevolence. Catherine Sasser and the group of world-weary Americans who surround her in *No Place for an Angel* contend with a fragmented and hapless, bomb-threatened existence. The setting is Europe and the United States of the late 1950s and 1960s. In one way or another they all suffer the pain of trying to reconcile a religious instinct—at least, a longing for purpose—with the frenzied secular world. Spencer effectively employs narrative devices in the novel, particularly the fluctuating sequences of time, and unstable, almost hallucinatory memories to suggest the dissolving interior world of the characters.

Like Catherine Sasser, Julia Garrett of *The Snare* is impelled by fate, or curiosity, or some attraction to evil, to risk life's danger zones in her determination to get beyond the bland and conventional. But Julia is better conditioned to traverse the "human swamp," having been early introduced to it by the sensual father of the guardian she lived with in New Orleans. Unlike Catherine, she does not retreat as she uncovers life's depravities; she is "life infected," and the infection safeguards her from morbid ennui. Julia's odyssey takes her from the affluent Garden District in New Orleans to the exotic, if dangerous, underworld of drug

499

trafficking, and finally to a modest, self-controlled life with her infant child. *The Snare* is a powerful, ambitious novel that has largely been neglected by critics of contemporary Southern fiction.

In 1981 Spencer published with Doubleday *The Collected Stories of Elizabeth Spencer*, which included the ten stories of the 1968 *Ship Island and Other Stories* (that she had dedicated to Eudora Welty), the novella *Knights and Dragons*, and twenty-two other stories previously uncollected. Also in 1981, the University Press of Mississippi brought out *Marilee*, a collection of three stories all narrated in the first person by the character Marilee Summerall, a young woman of fictional Port Claiborne, Mississippi. The Marilee stories, which also appear in *Collected Stories*, illustrate especially well Spencer's excellent ear for the vernacular and her unerring artistic control of fictional forms. Overall, Spencer's short stories evince the range in style and subject that distinguish her novels; such stories as "Ship Island," "Judith Kane," and "I, Maureen" represent some of her most artful and engaging fiction. Her vision of the human experience in whatever setting it is enacted is generous and penetrating.

Shelby Foote

Although most readers know Shelby Foote as the author of a distinguished three-volume history of the Civil War, he has consistently thought of himself as a novelist. His career includes to date six novels about characters who either live in Jordan County, Mississippi, or who come from there. By creating his mythical county Foote appears to be imitating William Faulkner, but the Mississippi Delta in Foote's novels differs radically from Faulkner's Yoknapatawpha. Although there was some settlement before the Civil War, the Delta is largely new country, cleared and planted in the last third of the nineteenth century. It is land that Foote knows well. He was born in Greenville, November 17, 1916, and though the family soon moved away, he returned there in 1927 with his mother, his father having died in 1921. As a boy, Foote was as often in the home of William Alexander Percy as he was in his own home; Walker Percy was his closest friend. It was perhaps because of Walker's presence there that Shelby spent two years, 1935 through 1937, at the University of North Carolina at Chapel Hill.

When Foote left Greenville for service in World War II in 1941, he left behind a manuscript of what was to become his first novel, *Tournament* (1949). After serving with the army and the marines he returned to Greenville and to writing. In 1946 the *Saturday Evening Post* accepted "Flood Burial," an excerpt from *Tournament*, and the following year the *Post* took another story, "Tell Them Good-by." The year 1947 also saw the local publication of "Merchant of Bristol," another excerpt from *Tournament*. In 1949 the Dial Press published the novel that Foote had been revising. The press had expressed interest in a novel about the Battle of Shiloh (Foote had written a short story about the battle, which *Blue Book Magazine* had accepted), but the editors at Dial felt that he should first publish some other novel. The success of *Tournament* postponed the publication of *Shiloh* (1952) until two other novels, *Follow Me Down* (1950) and *Love in a Dry Season* (1951), had been written and published.

501

In some respects, Hugh Bart in *Tournament* resembles Foote's grandfather, Huger Foote. Bart came to Jordan County in 1878 and soon established himself as one of the most successful planters on the shores of Lake Jordan. Other men admired Bart, but his three children failed him, and in his growing realization of their failures he recognized his own. Bart's life was a game, a tournament, but the rules of the game were too narrow and artificial to allow Bart a richly conceived existence. He was a victim of an encompassing wasteland.

Luther Dade Eustis, the central figure in *Follow Me Down*, was a tenant on Solitaire Plantation, the farm Hugh Bart sold in *Tournament*. Luther's fanatical devotion to evangelical religion warped his understanding of sexuality and led him to drown the woman with whom he had spent several days on an island in the Mississippi River. It was she, his furies said, who was his temptation, the cause of his sin. Luther's story is told from multiple points of view—those of the circuit clerk, a reporter, a deaf-and-dumb boy who lived on the island, Eustis himself, and Parker Norwell, the lawyer who saved Luther from the electric chair.

Most of the action in Foote's third published novel, *Love in a Dry Season* (1951), takes place in Bristol, the county seat of Jordan County. The four principal characters, however, occupy an emotional and spiritual vacuum; they strive without much understanding of themselves to bring about their undoing. Harley Drew, an outsider, comes to Bristol, and conceives that his way to success lies in marrying Amanda Barcroft, the daughter of one of Bristol's prominent citizens, the major, who opposes the marriage for his daughter's sake. Amanda's emotional needs prevent her understanding Drew's motives, and she agrees first to elope and, when that fails, to wait until the major dies. Drew in the meantime has found a sexual partner in Amy Caruthers, wife of Jeff Caruthers, who has inherited a plantation on Lake Jordan. Jeff, who before he was blinded had been a voyeur, nearly kills Amy and Drew. The Carutherses and Drew leave Bristol abandoning Amanda to lifelong spinsterhood.

Shiloh: A Novel is a narrative of the Civil War battle seen from multiple points of view, Union and Confederate. The narrative technique enables Foote to present the battle from the view of foot soldiers—including Luther Dade from Jordan County—who experience the gore of battle on the blossom-littered field, and from the view of officers who see the battle in larger perspective. The narrative of Lieutenant Palmer Metcalfe, an aide to General Johnston, opens and closes the novel. Metcalfe helped write the battle order, and at the close he speculates on the difference between the design and its execution. For Metcalfe the failure is symptomatic of the fatally flawed South, which had given too much to the love of the ideal and too little to actuality.

Jordan County: A Landscape in Narrative (1954), a collection of stories, might also be defined as a novel told from multiple perspectives. The collection opens with a tale about a soldier who returns to Bristol after World War II; subsequent stories trace the history of the county back through its development and settlement. These stories depict the failed attempts of men—black, white, and red—to tame the fertile land and live in harmony with themselves and each other.

The Civil War: A Narrative, one of the great achievements of American letters, must be ranked with and perhaps above the nineteenth-century "literary" histories written by Henry Adams, Francis Parkman, George Bancroft, and others. Just as Foote had approached fiction with an eye clearly focused on history, so he approached the writing of military history with the mature novelist's interest in dramatic action, form, characterization, narrative method, and style. Random House originally contracted for a single volume, but the plan soon expanded to three volumes, which took almost twenty years to complete: *Fort Sumter to Perryville* (1958), *Fredericksburg to Meridian* (1963), and *Red River to Appomattox* (1974). Foote's acknowledged models were historical—Gibbon, Tacitus, Thucydides—and they were literary—Proust, Faulkner, Homer. To the four years of war Foote has given epic form. Sweeping judgments do not occur; rather from the accumulation of facts and concrete details judgments grow. The carefully crafted style is plain and forceful, but it also has a typically Southern quality of the oral tale that allows the high seriousness with which mass slaughter must be treated to be punctuated by humor in description and detail. Mules are mules, and Leonidas Polk, the Episcopal bishop, becomes a "transfer from the Army of the Lord." The men who fought the war may have seen themselves as knights or saints, but fundamentally, Foote keeps reminding us, they were ordinary human beings.

After the completion of *The Civil War*, Foote resumed his career as a novelist, a career he had actually never abandoned, as both the form of the history and the action of *September, September* (1977) make clear. With a historian's interest in the accuracy of events, he set *September, September* during that month of 1957, the month the integration of Central High School in Little Rock swept Orval Faubus onto the front pages of newspapers nationwide. With a novelist's eye he sought in the events those human elements that strike more deeply: just thirty days after the introduction of the Edsel on September 4, a commercial disaster for the Ford Motor Company, "the Russians put the Sputnik up from

Kazakhstan, a polished steel basketball . . . beeping in A-flat around and around a world that would never be the same." But change for Foote has more to do with human action than with technology. Through the course of events in a novel in which three whites from Bristol, Mississippi, come to Memphis and kidnap the grandson of one of the city's wealthiest black businessmen, the father of the little boy awakens to the responsibilities his own manhood demands of him. No more will Eben Kinship be dominated by his father-in-law, Theodore G. Wiggins, or by the white world Theo has managed to manipulate.

Running through Foote's fiction, and in *The Civil War* as well, is a contrast between the conception of an action and its execution. However good the plans are, whether they are the general ideals Bristol chooses or the plans for a specific act, they will likely fail if human beings are not mature enough or wise enough to execute them properly. After the writing of *The Civil War*, Foote finds in *September, September* a black protagonist who survives his initiation to establish a sound basis for future success.

Walker Percy

To judge from his age when his first novel, *The Moviegoer* (1961), was published, Walker Percy at forty-five came late to his literary career. But to judge from the evidence provided by that novel and those following, his need to write began when he was thirteen. For at that time he discovered loss, which would become the constant subject of his fiction. On July 9, 1929, his father, LeRoy, killed himself with a shotgun blast, thus following his own father, Walker, who twelve years before had used a shotgun to end his life. LeRoy's action so staggered his son that it was nearly twenty years before he could recover his health and his world. Then he began to reconstruct himself, necessarily using the old materials to build a new life. It seems inevitable that his fiction would have the search for a father as its primary theme and that the search would take place in a fallen world of lost values.

Walker Percy was born May 28, 1916, and spent his childhood in New-South Birmingham, living in a contemporary home just off the number six fairway of the New Country Club. He was to spend adolescence in Old-South Greenville, Mississippi, in the old Percy house on Percy Street. For Mrs. Percy and her three sons had been invited to live with William Alexander Percy, LeRoy's first cousin. When the young widow died in an automobile wreck a short time later, Walker and his younger brothers were adopted by Uncle Will.

Life for Will Percy was duty. He was constantly engaged in a variety of community activities out of a sense of historical responsibility: both his father and grandfather had "done" for the community, and he would never dishonor their memory, regardless of his personal inclinations. His view of life is summed up in *Lanterns on the Levee: Recollections of a Planter's Son* (1941), written as a devoir to his fathers and a manual for his sons. The theme is stated in the primary title, an image immediately meaningful to the locality: every man of goodwill must carry a lantern on the levee to watch for breaks. Will Percy saw culture as the levee between chaos and humanity, and so he sponsored "levee-raising" activities for both his sons and the community. Ultimately, though, he felt that man could not ward off the chaos that inhabited both nature and human nature. He thus was tempted to yearn for the apocalypse, out of which a new order would emerge. Until that time, deterioration would continue, against which he was obliged to contend.

When it was time, Walker Percy went to Chapel Hill to major in chemistry. After that he went to Columbia's College of Physicians and Surgeons, gaining a degree in medicine in 1941. Life was not so tranquil as these accomplishments might suggest. During medical school he had felt so distressed that he underwent three years of analysis. When treatment was discontinued, both patient and physician agreed that the ailment had not been identified. Then shortly after beginning his residency at Bellevue, he contracted tuberculosis and had to enter a sanitarium for what was to be a three-year period of withdrawal from the active world, which seemed to be engaged in the apocalypse that had so fascinated Uncle Will before his death in 1942. As Walker Percy had dutifully followed the role that he felt his uncle desired, he suffered a threat from first one quarter and then another. It could never be established that there was any connection between those illnesses and a dissatisfaction, perhaps unconscious, with the life that he was leading, but such a speculation would help to explain the radical turn that his life took.

Having lost his function, Walker Percy seized upon reading as the only available way to express his being. He had always read widely and had even tried a little writing in high school and college. Now he began to read, not for diversion, but to find a reason for a condition that tuberculosis had made him realize. While he had found science aesthetically and intellectually satisfying, he had never read any book employing the scientific method to speak to his own experience of living. He began to read those writers who are loosely identified as the existentialists—Kierkegaard, Dostoevsky, Heidegger, Marcel, Jaspers, Bergson, Sartre, Camus, Buber. Dutifully following the view of the world provided by a culture of consensual rationalism, Walker Percy had learned to look at everything as an object under a microscope; tuberculosis both turned the instrument on him to make him aware of his objectivity and also revealed himself as a suffering existant who must die; thus he experienced the "coming-to-oneself" that figures in each of his novels.

A relapse, after he had tried to return to medicine, convinced Percy that even more withdrawal was necessary. Finding that he was out of place in Greenville, he went to Santa Fe. The desert was sure to be good for his body—but it turned out to be vital to his mind and soul. Novel by novel he was to sketch in the realizations that he came to in New Mexico. Just as he was becoming aware of the limits of science, he discovered in the summer of 1945 that it was unlimited; it could assuredly create the apocalypse that most people seem secretly to desire. He could see his vocation: to describe the alienation caused by the cultural frame created by empiricism. For if the enemy could be known it could be fought. At the same time, his soul responded to the desert as so many have; his fiction argues that he found faith in Santa Fe.

Thus Percy withdrew and returned, not in obedience to some Toynbeean law of history, but in exercise of will. Then he married, moved to Louisiana, and became a Catholic. Although he kept his name on the physicians' register, he did not practice. Instead, living on an inheritance, he continued to read, now adding Thomas Aquinas, such contemporary Catholic thinkers as Maritain, Guardini, and Dawson, and writers in various fields who were developing a deeper understanding of language—Langer, Barfield, Mead, and, later, Chomsky. After a while, he began to publish essays and book reviews in the journals of several specialties, from the Catholic *Thought, Modern Schoolman,* and *New Scholasticism* to the cultural reviews *Sewanee* and *Partisan* to the academic *Journal of Philosophy, Personalist, Philosophy and Phenomenological Research,* and *Psychiatry.* Some of these essays were later collected in *The Message in the Bottle* (1975), a study of human utterance as the ground of intersubjectivity, the answer to alienation. Following John, he was beginning with the Word.

In the 1950s Percy began to feel a need to write a novel. It was time to see if out of the wreckage of his past, existential phenomenology, and Catholic orthodoxy he could construct a world view for himself. He wrote "The Charterhouse" and then another fiction—neither of which was published. Then, like Faulkner with *The Sound and the Fury,* freed by failure, he wrote a novel for himself, "Confessions of a Moviegoer." Stanley Kauffmann, an editor at Knopf, recognized at once that it was publishable. With his encouragement, Percy revised it four times before it was printed.

The protagonist of *The Moviegoer* is Binx Bolling, who records the week of his life prior to his thirtieth birthday. As a stockbroker, he tiptoes through life in bad faith, secretly sickened by the Cartesian world that he seems to support, unable to accept either the Stoic/Gnostic course cherished by his Aunt Emily or the Christian way lived by his half-brother, Lonnie. For the most part he self-consciously views the world as a moviegoer, a Platonic spectator, though there are times when he risks pain by searching for an explanation of his father's need to escape "everydayness," a need so acute that he gambled his life in World War II and lost. But then, inspired by acts of faith by others, he grasps for faith himself. Thus the novel brilliantly leaps from Plato's *Republic* to Augustine's *Confessions*, from *The Waste Land* to *Ash-Wednesday*, as a new father is found.

In his second novel, *The Last Gentleman* (1966), Percy, this time in the third person, once again addresses the subject of loss. Will Barrett staggers through adolescence completely unable to integrate his experiences. The South of his birth offers him opposed and equally unsatisfactory alternatives. The unreflective Southerner (his Uncle Fannin) is so tranquil in his Shut Off home that he exists in a child's world, while the reflective (his father, Lawyer Barrett) can only pace under the water oaks, proclaiming the tag end of an embittered Southern Stoicism, until he is ready to go to the attic and the shotgun. Having been through analysis without recovery, Will tries a cheap version of the engineer's world view, which subtly becomes the romantic world. This leads him back to the South—and all too quickly to the horror of the past. Thus he flees to the Southwest. The genial and comic tone and the apparently happy ending only stress the irony of Will's successful quest.

Love in the Ruins (1971) continues Percy's exploration of both the South and the Southwest. Tom More has lived in Edenic Paradise Estates with Doris, his Shenandoah Valley Apple Queen, very much at home in his Southern world. Then, unable to deal with his daughter's death, which mockingly proclaims the malfunction of the cells, he creates an instrument, the "lapsometer," which starts out as a measurement of object, the brain, but with the Devil's help winds up as a control of subject, the mind. Thus Tom plans to separate the two, to silently deny incarnation. He woos both his Southern girl Lola—all body—and his Southwestern girl Moira—all (air)head. Just as he two-times womankind, so he will lobotomize mankind during the apocalypse. If he can do this, he can surpass his father-figure, Sir Thomas More, accomplishing a technological Utopia. He succeeds only in getting stumbling-down drunk and exaggerating the mess the world is in. He is saved only at the last moment by confessing his need for both godly father and goodly nurse. It is impossible to conceive of a more hilarious religious novel.

Lancelot (1977) is Percy's most "Southern" novel in that he situates it in the Southern literary tradition and he uses it to launch a savage attack upon a certain aspect of the Southern way of writing history. The protagonist is in effect a Southern fictionist in the tradition of Poe, creating from selected bits of the past a legend that satisfies both his obsession with his "family romance" and his need for a cosmic philosophy that validates his own behavior. As such he is much like the Quentin Compson of *Absalom, Absalom!*. Inspired by Voegelin and other students of Gnosticism, Percy dreamed a nightmare of the world to come if consciousness continues to separate itself from its ground in being, and yearns only for the apocalypse.

The Second Coming (1980) is literally just that, for it reintroduces Will Barrett. It is also Percy's answer to the apocalyptic dream that his earlier fictions had warned against. Here is the heaven on earth that man can have, not omniscience, but love. Returning from the Southwest with a false faith, Will had thrived in the concrete world of consumerism before retiring to Southern Eden, a Carolina golf course. But then he develops the staggers and falls prey, after all these years, to such alienation that he continually plays with toys of desperation as he is Hamlet-haunted by recollections of his father. At the same time he meets Allie Huger, a graceful figure, who, having been labeled a distressed creature and confined for such altering as Dr. More would prescribe, escapes to reconstruct her life in a greenhouse. When the two converge, will and grace, they respond to each other's communication problems so as to comprise an intersubjectivity, a communion that must be the closest human approximation of the bliss that the faithful await. Love can indeed be found in the ruins, if love seeks not the rotation but the repetition.

What has Walker Percy accomplished? It is clear why he has not removed his name from the physicians' register: he continues to diagnose and prescribe. Most fundamentally he has used fiction to articulate the competing forces that have beset his existence and thus, with help, reclaimed his life. Beyond that, he has succeeded in crafting a technique for storytelling that gives pleasure to readers. Still he has steadily and purposefully used his individual talent to create a literature that responds to all literature before it, has thus walked the levee as forcefully as anyone else in twentieth-century American literature.

Ralph W. Ellison

Ralph Waldo Ellison was born in Oklahoma City, March 1, 1914, of Deep South parents who had migrated to Oklahoma from Tennessee. His nurture and his formal and informal education there were not limited by accidents of race and geography. For example, young Ralph's reading, as had been true for his father (who died when Ralph was three years old), was avid and catholic, considering that Oklahoma was at that time a frontier state; and he absorbed as well the oral lore and traditions of the region. "I knew the trickster Ulysses just as early as I knew the wily rabbit of American lore," he wrote in *Shadow and Act*. And his boyhood appreciation of music encompassed blues, jazz, religious, and classical music. Indeed, as a boy he aspired to develop into a Renaissance man. The early exposure to and interest in broad, inclusive culture might reasonably be considered fundamental to Ellison's lifelong aestheticism, both theoretical and applied.

Ellison left Oklahoma City at the age of nineteen to enter Tuskegee Institute in Alabama, where he majored in music. His cultural pluralism is illustrated by his ambition at the time to compose a symphony that would exhibit his varied interests and experiences and that would incorporate both jazz and European music. He was also, by this time, highly appreciative of creativity and artistic craftsmanship, integrity, and virtuosity, whether in the music of Walter Page and the Blue Devils Band or in the poetry of T. S. Eliot.

Ellison's atypically broad humanistic vision and absence of any feelings of racial inferiority did not permit acceptance on his part of the relatively open, dehumanizing racism he encountered in Alabama. Nor had he been conditioned to be sympathetic with the subservience of some Negroes of the Deep South. He did not immediately understand their sense of helplessness and their belief that their lives were restrictively predetermined and anonymous. The formal, liberal education of Ralph W. Ellison at Tuskegee, therefore, was augmented by his vicarious and experiential education in the ways of the Deep South, including significantly Negroes' Darwinian mechanisms for dealing with the realities of a white-dominated, frequently hostile world. When after three years at Tuskegee he left for New York in 1936, ostensibly for summer work, Ellison had had experiences, made observations, and developed interests and ideas about Southern life that would find expression in his writing. For instance, in the Golden Day scene in *Invisible Man*, Supercargo (superego) controls the Negro mental institution inmates, who are "crazy" in that they had dared to aspire to professional occupations. Their incarceration is contrasted to the freedom of Trueblood, who has committed incest and is rewarded by whites because he fulfills their projections of immorality/amorality among Afro-Americans. Another example may be found in an early short story, "Flying Home," in which Ellison's central character, a cadet in a novel program to train Negroes to be airplane pilots, flies (aspires) high and fast, hits a buzzard (Jim Crow), crashes, and awakens in the presence of a folk-wise Negro sharecropper who knows the craziness and danger—as well as the personal exhilaration—inherent in a Negro's aspiration to rise above society-imposed restrictions. (At the same time that its immediate perspective and characterizations are Southern, "Flying Home" gives a hint of the variety of literary components and modes—Western mythology, Afro-American folk material, realism, surrealism—that Ellison would integrate artistically in *Invisible Man* and other fictions.)

In New York Ellison started a career as a sculptor and as a musician. He states in *Shadow and Act* that he regarded himself "in my most secret heart at least—a musician." He continued to read, and "as a reflex of reading," and influenced by Richard Wright, he began writing, at first short stories and pieces for periodicals and then pieces that would evolve into material for *Invisible Man*.

Some of the nonfiction pieces appeared later in *Shadow and Act* (1964), a collection of critical essays, interviews, illuminating reminiscences, reviews, and other short works. They are, he states in the preface, "At best . . . an embodiment of a conscious attempt to confront, to peer into, the shadow of my past and to remind myself of the complex resources for imaginative creation which are my heritage." He also says that the substantive concerns of the book are "literature and folklore; Negro musical expression—especially jazz and the blues; and the complex relationship between the Negro American subculture and North American culture as a whole."

Some seven years in the writing, Ellison's *Invisible Man* (1952) was greeted with critical praise. It received the 1953 National Book Award and in 1965 was identified in a poll conducted by the New York *Herald Tribune* as the most distinguished American novel published between

1945 and 1965. In terms of technique, *Invisible Man* is a virtuoso achievement that employs both traditional and modern modalities, particularly associational and linear narration, mythology, symbolism, stream of consciousness, dream sequences, irony, and folk elements. In the opinion of many, more than any other single modality its folk elements contribute to the artistic success of the work. Direct adaptations and transmutations of Afro-American folk forms such as "signifying," verbal riffing, storytelling-as-performed-speech-act, "worrying the line," in-group humor vehicles, virtuoso enumeration, "the dozens," word play, wry irony, aphorisms, music, and metaphorical constructs are critical components of the novel's structure and language texture. The plot contains situations and events common, both symbolically and literally, in the Afro-American continuum. The novel's characters include folkloric figures such as a "house nigger," Supercargo; an Uncle Tom, Brockway; a nationalist, Ras; a matriarch, Mary Rambo; and a trickster, Rinehart. As to ideational substance, the novel is infused with collective Afro-American folk wisdom, or mother wit. A central idea of the plot is that the protagonist will gain self-visibility and self-integration when he can "see" his heritage, that is, his humanistic, Afro-American, Southern folk-ness. In due course, by means of a reverberative, multi-associational pun, he expresses the epiphanic realization that "I yam what I am!"

THEODORE R. HUDSON

Ernest J. Gaines

T he fictions of Ernest J. Gaines reflect and refract the place, history, traditions, folklore and folkways, situations, and people of his native South. Born February 15, 1933, on a plantation near New Roads, Louisiana, Gaines left Louisiana in 1948 to join his mother and stepfather in California, where there was opportunity for him to continue his secondary education. There he began reading—first, white writers of fiction about the South, whom he admired for their evocations of physical place and mood but not for what he considered their nondimensional depictions of Afro-Americans; next, other American writers, especially those who wrote of agrarian life and common folk; and then European writers, especially Russian writers of peasant life. What Gaines apparently appreciated most in Mark Twain, Faulkner, Hemingway, Maupassant, Joyce, Chekhov, Turgenev was their styles, their craft. It was also in California that teenager Ernest began writing. A first fiction was eventually to evolve as *Catherine Carmier*, some fifteen years later. After service in the United States armed forces, Gaines enrolled in San Francisco State College with the intention of learning to be a writer. By the time he later attended Stanford University he was writing compulsively about his native Louisiana, striving to present authentic characters, settings, language, and situations.

His first published major work, *Catherine Carmier* (1964), has two principal characters, Catherine and Jackson, who, in order to confirm and demonstrate their feelings for each other, must break away. Catherine must break from an emotionally incestuous relationship with her father, Raoul, and the intraracial discrimination that he represents; and Jackson, from the expectations of his elders, personified by his Aunt Charlotte, that he remain there to be "the one," their Moses. The time of the novel is set during the stirrings of what would develop into the civil rights movement. Gaines followed this novel with *Of Love and Dust* (1967), an exploration of the protocols of interracial sex and love in a time of rigid taboos, before the social revolution in the South in the

1950s and 1960s. The novel's tensions develop as the protocols are violated or prove ineffective as lust becomes love. The result is that the delicate equilibrium that makes for overtly peaceful coexistence among the ethnic groups—black, white, and Cajun—is upset. His next book, *Bloodline* (1968), is a collection of shorter fictions, each about a black male in a conscious or subconscious movement toward identity, self-esteem, maturity, dignity.

Gaines's best-known novel, *The Autobiography of Miss Jane Pittman* (1971), portrays the life of Miss Jane from childhood during the Civil War to senior matriarchal status during the height of the civil rights movement. While he did not seek to write a historical novel, Gaines consciously wove into the fabric of this narrative the major real-life events and people that would have, at least indirectly, affected significantly the life of a real Miss Jane over her long life-span. *In My Father's House* (1978), less informed with local color and leaner in style than his previous works, has as its premise the dilemma of the Reverend Philip Martin—in the waning years of both his leadership and the methods and philosophy of Martin Luther King, Jr.—when he is passively confronted by a young man whom he had fathered out of wedlock and whom he has not seen since the son was an infant.

All of these works are set in the rural region of Gaines's boyhood. It is a physical place of cane, cotton, and corn plantations; of pecan trees; of bayous, swamps, and meandering rivers; of blistering, dusty summers and chilling winters. It is a place where people say "mon" for mother, "gallery" for porch, "fair" for a house party at which refreshments are sold, "quarters" for a black enclave on a plantation. It is also a place where customs, history, and economics can and almost do deterministically decide the lives of its socially stratified whites, Cajuns, and Negroes (who in later times are blacks), with the Negroes the most discriminated against and the most ostensibly powerless. But it is also a place where these elements cannot fully and consistently control the lives of people, a place where there is an inevitably different future as well as a past in the present.

Gaines's fictional people are generally well-realized and unfailingly human characters capable of humor and high seriousness, of foolishness and wisdom, of indifference and compassion, of jealousy and uncompromising, sustaining love. His central characters are usually Negroes. In depicting them and their conflicts and struggles, Gaines is not a hostile, combative writer; his fictions, at least on the surface, do not have as a major purpose indictment and condemnation of whites and racism. Rather, with great warmth, he celebrates the indomitable strength and resilience and moral reserve of black people. Trapped in circumstances of place and history and custom, his protagonists do not capitulate; they adapt to or deflect adversity or they bide their time or they revolt. Most importantly, they endure.

Often they triumph, in personal ways if not always in public ways. For example, Marcus Payne, the black male involved with a white female in *Of Love and Dust*, is intransigent and defiant, and though he comes to a predictable, tragic end, he earns the respect of black people who had perceived him as impractically rebellious. And in "The Sky Is Gray" there is a silently strong mother who engenders in her boy a value system, strategies, and the psychological toughness that he will need in order to live with dignity in an environment of institutionalized discrimination and attendant adversities. Generally, the older Afro-American characters in Gaines's fictions have learned to adapt to and to manipulate, in a pragmatic and honorable way, the socioeconomic system and antagonistic white people. Miss Jane Pittman is an archetype of a courageous, hardworking, selfless, moral, life-engaging, wise, and, above all, durable and spiritually triumphant Southern black.

The fiction of Ernest J. Gaines demonstrates his thorough factual and experiential knowledge of his native, regional South. More importantly, his fiction demonstrates his penetrating understanding of the complexities and subtleties of universal human nature that affect and are affected by these regional realities.

John Barth

John Barth was born May 27, 1930, in Cambridge, Maryland. He spent a conventional childhood and adolescence there, where his family had lived in moderate financial success for several generations. His conformity to the pattern of the American writer growing up in the twentieth century is so great that he must have been bored by the amount of expectedness that clogged his experience. He played in the high school band and wrote for the high school paper. One of his English teachers typically remembered that, while he was somewhat serious, he was possessed of a sardonic humor.

Most of his reading came from his father's store—those Faulkner, Hemingway, and Dos Passos paperbacks with the shiny, lurid covers designed to catch the light like Ford hoods in a used-car lot. After high school he went to Julliard for a few months, until he ran out of money. Then he returned to Maryland, to enter Johns Hopkins on an academic scholarship. He stayed at Hopkins to earn a bachelor's degree in creative writing (1951), a master's in creative writing (1952), and to begin the doctoral program in aesthetics. His interests lay in both the traditional material countenanced by the English Department and the Oriental fiction that he discovered as an assistant in the Classics Library. In 1953 he left Hopkins to become an instructor in freshman English at Pennsylvania State University. Thus he began a stay in Northeastern universities that lasted until 1973, when he returned to Hopkins as a professor in the graduate writing program.

Barth's early fictional efforts were to satisfy degree requirements; some of them were published in magazines. His first published novel was *The Floating Opera* in 1956, the story of Todd Andrews, a middle-aged Maryland lawyer who suffers from the boredom caused by the expectedness of things. Thus, while Andrews' physical surroundings reflect the specificity of Maryland, his outlook mirrors the alienated concerns of contemporary man. His chief enemy is time, and his chief weapon—and not a very good one at that—is the story, the temporary escape from time. Barth's second novel, *The End of the Road* (1958), treats another such borderland figure, Jacob Horner, who attempts to teach prescriptive grammar at a Maryland state college even as he realizes that he lives an entirely unprescriptive life. Not the least significance in the allusion to the nursery rhyme about Little Jack Horner is the fact that he *is* in a corner.

From these first two novels on, it is obvious that Barth's protagonist will be an existentialist. That is to say, the essential Barthian character is faced not with simple choice, to respond to exigency or not, but with anxiety, to choose among infinite choices. Life is truly a "fiction," made up on the spot, characterized in retrospect by the most rambling of plot lines, as we seek "story" to escape from time. Indeed, any denouement is so inconclusive that the Barthian protagonist sooner or later chooses a series of digressions as his life. In the earlier works there is still some regard for the ability of place to particularize an existence. The hot, dense, flattened-out land/sea scape of Maryland's Eastern Shore is not merely employed as a backdrop or as a reflection of mood, but is a factor that circumscribes. In time, though, place simply becomes a trifle, like Muzak in the dentist's office—an external which bores, but in no other way impinges upon consciousness.

Even *The Sot-Weed Factor* (1960), praised for its phenomenal success in rediscovering Maryland's Southern past, pays scant attention to physical detail. Despite the title, there is little description of the tobacco culture. So completely do Ebenezer Cooke, the factor, and all those people whom he meets constantly construct their lives from talk that they rarely focus on their surroundings. Not surprisingly, the Chesapeake Bay does force its beautiful or terrible presence into Eben's intense cerebration—but the rest of the "there" is rarely there.

The remarkable evocation of the Maryland past does not result from a close attention to landmark or artifact. Rather it comes from culture, from talk, which is not to say that the characters seem authentic because Barth has them use costume locution; they use diction appropriate to the time to express sentiments appropriate to the time, which are motivated by drives that are timeless. Maryland comes alive because we recognize not its quaintness, but its timelessness.

And once we have accepted the reality of Barth's Marylanders, we are well seduced into accepting the Maryland that they see, Barth's postmodernist world. An individual begins in innocence, to struggle toward experience, all the while beset by confusion. Society is no more than an accumulation of the individual experiences. History books are lies because they present a final and absolute interpretation of an event. Yet that event-in-the-making had no such universal meaning. The only genuine history, therefore, would be the full record of the confusion of one person. Such a book is *The Sot-Weed Factor*, the first book to tell the "truth" about Maryland's past.

Once Barth had revealed the past, he dismissed it. Having proved that it is only an earlier present, he has returned to the present, in *Giles Goat-Boy* (1966), *Lost in the Funhouse* (1968), *Chimera* (1972), *Letters* (1979), and *Sabbatical* (1982). In these fictions, Barth has pursued the post-modernist theme that consciousness *is* artificial, made-up, and, that being the case, the most realistic fiction is that which acknowledges that it is an artifice. His ambition is not to capture the materiality of reality; we are finally realizing that such a problem is for physics, which alternately speaks of ultimate knowledge or the inability to achieve it. Barth knows that the dilemma is false—human beings can only have a sense of reality, which is shared by talk. Our "sense"— which is literally our sense—is informed by the enduring structures of dream and myth, the archetypes of the racial consciousness. There is great consumer resistance to his recent fiction, for it is said to lack reference to the real world. But John Barth continues his steady course, arguing that in the end it is all talk, for it is the human fate to live in the borderland between materiality and the isolated self.

Reynolds Price

Two planetary influences shaped Southern writing in the latter days of the Southern Renascence, the late 1950s and early 1960s, when Reynolds Price began publishing fiction. No Southern writer escaped the gravitational pull of one, the other, or both. A look at the reviews of any work of fiction produced by a Southern writer in this period will reveal the two standards. How does this novel match Faulkner? How does this theme advance or baffle the cause of social justice for the Negro in the South? Some Southern writers won brief recognition by meeting the standards. Most of them faded into obscurity after one or two works.

Reynolds Price is still with us; his achievement as a man of letters has survived the vicissitudes of literary criticism. He was born in Macon, North Carolina, in 1933. He saw his first novel, *A Long and Happy Life* (1962), published a few months before the death of William Faulkner. The coincidence seems more auspicious as time passes, for Price's career was for a long time kept in Faulkner's shadow.

Not all effects of Price's brush with Faulkner have been salutary. *A Long and Happy Life* won the award of the William Faulkner Foundation as the best first novel of its year. Therefore, many reviewers were also on the lookout for the marks of an heir apparent. And some were bent on ambush. Whitney Balliett, with superb *New Yorker* hauteur, pronounced *A Long and Happy Life* "written in imitation Faulkner." He singled out the first sentence for special scorn; he said he found it weary. Eight years later Theodore Solotaroff would find the same sentence proof of Price's virtuosity and a sign of his detachment from the dead hand of the "Southern Pastoral Tradition."

Regardless of the narrowness with which many American critics read Price's first novel, its publication was an event. *A Long and Happy Life* was widely and favorably reviewed. *Harper's Magazine* published it in an illustrated supplement. Movie producers, according to Price, showed great interest. No screen version, however, has yet been completed. A few years after publication, *A Long and Happy Life* had been translated into at least ten languages. The future for Price, to borrow the words of one reviewer, seemed momentous. Besides the comparison with Faulkner, there were also positive comparisons with Joyce and Racine. Price, at the time, acknowledged the power of Faulkner's reputation by claiming that he was "not aiming to found a New Yoknapatawpha," and he has said since that the comparison with Joyce is the one he finds most gratifying. At the start of what has become a career of steady achievement, Price had to wrestle with the ghost of Faulkner for his own place as a writer of fiction. He had help from a relatively few critics who seemed able to steer reader attention toward the inherent features of Price's art, and away from the Faulkner sweepstakes.

The Names and Faces of Heroes (1963), a collection of short stories written for the most part before *A Long and Happy Life*, was also greeted by positive reviews. "A Chain of Love," Price's first published short story, was singled out for praise. It deals with the hospitalization of Papa Mustian and the attraction of Rosacoke (younger than she was in *A Long and Happy Life*) to a dying cancer victim and his family occupying a room across the corridor. "Uncle Grant" and "The Warrior Princess Ozimba" concern the significance of blacks in the social organization and moral imagination of Southerners. These two stories, naturally, drew sharp critical attention. As Price portrays them, Grant and Ozimba are forever beyond the reach of the white central consciousnesses. They are real as human persons, but not identifiable by any social scientist's classification.

Between the massive presence of Faulkner and the pressures to conform to the "truth" about relations between the races in the South, a Southern writer like Price had little room to maneuver. *A Generous Man* (1966) illustrates this creative bind perhaps as well as any single Southern work of the 1960s. The tendentious reception of *A Generous Man* prompted Price to a rebuttal, "Notes for the Mineshaft." *A Generous Man*, Price asserts, is the exorcism of several of the old Southern literary shibboleths: the mythic hunt, the mystique of naming, the sanctification of the family, the maturing of the hero through an ordeal. Milo Mustian, already known to Price's readers as Rosacoke's bitter older brother, is shown at his prime—age fifteen. In his first sexual triumphs (as he sees them), and in his heroic (but largely serendipitous) solving of all visible hurts and bleak outlooks (save his own), Milo is, in Price's words, a somber comic figure, an Isaac McCaslin with the great reverberations toned down to a human level. *A Generous Man*, then, is not *ersatz* Faulkner, but an ironically crafted counteroffensive against a burdensome tradition in style and material that, Price felt, confined the Southern writer and determined his achievement.

Granville Hicks said of *Love and Work* (1968), "For the sake of his development, it was something he [Price] had to do." *Love and Work* is a farewell to the Mustians, and the beginning of a new stage of stylistic and thematic growth for Price. This brief novel concerns a teacher of literature and creative writing who tries to reconcile the competing claims of love (his parents, his marriage) and work (his writing). In the highly controlled and spare narrative Price leaves the outer terrain—the North Carolina place of his earlier novels—for the inner terrain where, in the words of critic Elizabeth Janeway, "the supernatural [moves] the natural world to its own ends." The style of the prose becomes almost hieroglyphic; image, symbol, scene, dialogue, are set flush against each other with a minimum of prosaic mortar and ornament. Reading Hemingway had shown Price how writing was control—control of the writer's own "self-loathing and fear" and control of the blood and muscles of the reader. *Love and Work*, many reviewers agreed, forced the reader to grapple with blood and sinew.

Price's stylistic departure from earlier forms goes farther in *Permanent Errors* (1970), stories Guy Davenport called "elliptical and sketchy" but powerful. Theodore Solotaroff, in the *Saturday Review* (September 26, 1970), used the publication of *Permanent Errors* to announce that Price had finally broken free from the "Southern Pastoral Tradition." Solotaroff sees Price, having jettisoned that literary baggage, moving into a more modern and complex mode. "There is more than a hint of the spiritual in Price, rather like that in E. M. Forster or Rilke, which takes a psychological rather than a theological form: a powerful sense of dark unseen forces and influences that are only partly explained by the description of emotions and that require not just attention but supplication." Solotaroff goes on to speculate that *Permanent Errors* represents the end of a "long, grueling phase of Price's career." Price confirms this in his introduction to *A Palpable God* (1978). He had returned, he writes, to the origin of all our narratives, the Bible, for instruction in telling stories. Work on translations from the Old Testament and the New Testament seems to have liberated a spiritual and narrative power that sharp critics (like Janeway and Solotaroff) had sensed near the surface of Price's work.

It would not be a gross overstatement to claim that Price's longest and most complex work of fiction, *The Surface of Earth* (1975), is one of the more significant American novels of the twentieth century. Richard Gilman testifies to its stature when he uses the occasion of its publication to dismiss it and all "Southern" literature. (Like Yahweh he spares a few from destruction—Faulkner and O'Connor.) Indeed, Gilman banishes all fiction that espouses such antiquated values as self, love, family, and place, all of which are affirmed in *The Surface of Earth*. He classifies novels as mastodons if they use such narrative devices as a fixed point of view, dream visions, letters, compression of time, and adjustments to the pace of the narrative, familiar devices in all Western narrative. Two things become clear with the publication of *The Surface of Earth*: critical assessment of Price, with a few worthy exceptions, has run out of fresh responses and flexible antennae with which to feel the palpable work; and Price himself, as artist, has grown far beyond the shadow of Faulkner or any other single artist.

Price's most recent novel, *The Source of Light* (1981), continues the saga begun in *The Surface of Earth* by following Hutch Mayfield's attempt to make a useful life—useful to the demands of intellect and artistic creativity, useful to the demands of the flesh to love and to be loved. The imagery, stylistic grace, and narrative power of *The Source of Light* prove that the plateau Price had reached in *The Surface of Earth* is only an intermediate camp in an ongoing ascent.

Price's major achievement is the novel, but his talents extend to the essay, drama, and poetry. His critical essays, *Things Themselves* (1972), have won praise for their finesse and range. His translations from the Bible in *A Palpable God* Frank Kermode has called brilliant. Anthony Burgess would require the introductory essay to *A Palpable God*, "A Single Meaning: Notes on the Origin and Life of Narrative," in all courses in creative writing.

The career of Reynolds Price is the story of the growth of a great literary talent through a sluggish, if not stagnant, critical atmosphere. We have, in the history of Southern literature, only a few twentieth-century figures whose accomplishments in several fields of literary creativity have amounted to excellence. The range and quality of Reynolds Price's achievements so far admit him to this company.

M. E. BRADFORD

Madison Jones

Of the Southern novelists whose artistic careers began after 1950, Madison Jones, in his choice and treatment of subject matter, in his awareness of the human loss and dislocation entailed in the collapse of the old regime, is one of the more indelibly Southern in the traditional sense. Few Southern writers of his generation cut more sharply against the modern grain. Nor are many of his contemporaries more severe in the practice of their craft, in the relentless exposure of what happens to the members of their community when they fail, or refuse, to submit themselves to inevitable limits of the human condition. Whether his focus is on frontier settlement in his native Tennessee or race relations in a small Alabama town, the sexual temptation of a backcountry sheriff or the dispute within a family over the meaning of the Tennessee Valley Authority, he sees his world in a hard clear light. It is difficult to imagine the corpus of his achievement as appearing in any literary context other than that established by his mentors, Donald Davidson and Andrew Lytle, their friends, and their antagonists among the Southern progressives of the 1930s.

Madison Jones was born in Nashville, Tennessee, March 21, 1925. He was educated in the schools of that city and, following an interruption for service in the United States Army, took his bachelor's degree from Vanderbilt in 1949. During these years he was a student of Donald Davidson and, for a time, a farmer in Cheatham County, northwest of Nashville. From 1949 to 1951 he studied the craft of fiction with Andrew Lytle at the University of Florida. After receiving a master's degree from that institution, Jones taught briefly at Miami University of Ohio and at the University of Tennessee at Knoxville. He is presently writer-in-residence at Auburn University in Auburn, Alabama, where he has taught since 1956.

Jones's first novel, *The Innocent* (1957), establishes the motif of conflict between past and present that runs throughout his work. In the primordial gesture of rebellion, Duncan Welsh lost his place, abandoned the patrimony, and wandered away from Cheatham County to Nashville and then northward to Chicago. But as the novel opens (1935), he has returned home to reestablish himself upon inherited lands and in inherited ways after an absence of seven years. As is specified in his quarrels with his sister and liberal brother-in-law, Duncan has brought back from the North a thorough contempt for the abstract meliorism proposed by rootless intellectuals of that era as a correction for the tradition of his fathers. But Duncan's enterprise is compromised by a weakness of character even more serious than his brother-in-law's wooden social gospel. His deracinated preconception of the process of restoration makes his version of it a failure. Of whatever he attempts he finally complains, "the thing itself had not lived up to the anticipation of it." The traditionalism of his talk of loyalty and community does not fit his conduct because he has imagined the business of reaction in almost private terms. More and more isolated by the collapse of his second marriage and of his effort to breed an old-fashioned kind of horse, he falls under the sway of a tempter, the moonshiner Aaron McCool, who represents the darker side of Duncan's own nature. Welsh becomes a law unto himself—what Aaron has always been. The final consequences of this association are murder and death for both Duncan and his alter ego. Near the end of his life the protagonist of *The Innocent* draws back from the predatory savagery of his accomplice. But this turning comes too late. In the novelist's phrase, "The 'Innocent' who reenters the garden is destined to find that it is not God but Satan who walks there now." His mistake is repeated by many characters in Madison Jones's subsequent fiction.

Jonathan Cannon, the central figure in *Forest of the Night* (1960), is if anything more sanguine and innocent than Duncan Welsh. In 1802 this young Virginian journeys westward full of the doctrines of Jean Jacques Rousseau, hoping there, along the Natchez Trace, to recover a lost Golden Age. Jonathan believes that "man in a state of nature is good, that evil is not a positive thing or force but simply a negation of good caused by the corrupt institutions of civilization and the dead hand of the past." Influenced by his ideology, he throws away his place in the world. To disabuse him of his folly, the notorious Harpe brothers and their associates await him out along the frontier—they or the memory of them. In the end, Cannon repeats so completely the transformation which had made the outlaws what they were that people who had known the Harpes (including Jonathan's woman) confuse him with one of them. Finally Jonathan recognizes what living outside of civilized restraints has done to his soul and resolves to return to the settlement out from Nashville and forego wandering about as a "natural man." There is no more powerful exposé of the myth of the New Eden in our literature. The language, the texture of this novel are, however, not so rich as what we find in its predecessor, or in its successor, *A Buried Land* (1963).

Madison Jones's third novel is set in the valley of the Tennessee River during the time of its metamorphosis. Percy Youngblood, the son of a stern hill farmer (and a central character who could be any young Southerner of this century), embraces all of the progressive formulas that are the basis of the futurist dispensation. In the process, he alienates himself from his own place and family, abandoning with his heritage the sense of personal responsibility that was its foundation. Percy attempts to bury the world of his past (represented by the girl who dies aborting his child) under the waters of the TVA; but its truths (and their symbol) rise to haunt him into murder and confession and a return to abandoned modes of thought and feeling. In terms of the book's governing metaphor, nature and human nature join to collapse the utopian fantasy that man can live by will and cunning alone—that there are no Eumenides who will "assert the great laws of old" upon those who offend against the blood. The conclusion of the novel, rendering the truth of our limitations as contingent beings, is powerful indeed, reminiscent of Dostoevsky's masterpiece, *Crime and Punishment*. It is, with *The Innocent*, Madison Jones's work at its best.

After *A Buried Land* Jones published the short novel *An Exile* (1970), the story of a rural sheriff who, on an impulse to recover his youth, loses his place and life out of a passion for a rustic Circe, a bootlegger's daughter. Jones followed this simple and well-made narrative with his most ambitious work, *A Cry of Absence* (1971), the painful story of a middle-aged Alabama gentlewoman, Hester Glenn, who finds an excuse for her failures as wife, mother, and citizen in a self-delusive devotion to the tradition of her family. Inside a pattern of almost tragic rigor, her example, in the context of the civil rights revolution of the 1960s, is in part responsible for her younger son's sadistic murder of a Negro activist. Hester's failings and virtues are embodied for us by Ames, her older son, and are played against the self-congratulatory inhumanity and rancor of her formal adversaries, a family of conventionally liberal Northerners who have moved to her town. When she realizes what she has made of her son Cameron, Hester is driven to know herself and, after confession, to destroy that son and pay for her sins with suicide. Madison Jones has dealt masterfully with this central moment in the region's history and rendered it with remarkable balance.

Jones's two most recent books break some of the patterns set by the first five. *Passage Through Gehenna* (1978) is not so much a novel as a romance, an extended parable or morality of spiritual pride, predatory evil, unmerited grace, and redemption through the sacrifice of blood. Young Jud Rivers comes down from the hills to the river town of Halls-boro, there to encounter evil companions and a witch, Mrs. Lily Nunn, who draws him into the darkness of total cynicism. But it is only a passage *through* hell (Gehenna). Jud is redeemed through the love of Hannah, whose death breaks the power of the enchantress. He is then able to confess his sins, both legal and moral, serve out his prison sentence, and rejoice in having escaped from "the devil's daughter" without losing his soul. The reality of evil, of human malice, is here objectified with chilling and terrible authority.

Season of the Strangler (1982) is a suite of twelve short narratives whose organization recalls the design of Sherwood Anderson's *Winesburg, Ohio*. In the summer of 1969 five women are found strangled in their beds in the small town of Okaloosa, Alabama. The lives of men and women caught up in the ambiance of fear engendered by these murders and by related family and racial tensions explode in unexpected ways, but most often with a consequence of separation or death. Black and white, rich and poor, young and old, these characters gesture to escape the meaninglessness of their lives. And they fail. In *Season of the Strangler* we have come some way downslope from that "crossing of the ways" described in 1935 by Allen Tate. The protagonist in Jones's concluding story, "Familiar Spirit," before he leaves home to wander the earth, points at what has changed in the intervening years. "There was something missing, something needed to focus things the way a memory did. He could not find that something."

In the course of Madison Jones's career, his vision of the Southern experience has grown darker and darker. But his artistry has remained consistent, his objective dramatizations of the emptiness of life in a South devoid of redemptive memory honest and persuasive. All of this evidence Madison Jones has perceived from inside the consciousness of individual characters, inhabitants of his region. With reference to the burden of his work, he was well described by Allen Tate as a Southern Thomas Hardy. But perhaps a better analogy is to Aeschylus—the poet who never allows us to forget that "there are times when fear is good."

Old Ways and New Ways

Many of the Southern writers who flourished from 1950 to 1981 incorporate the same basic themes and techniques of the writers of the Southern Renascence, though there is tremendous variety in that body of fiction. Others move into themes such as the existential dilemma and techniques such as surrealism. Many focus on subjects of particular importance to the modern Southerner, such as the relationships between blacks and whites. A good number continue to work in the tradition of Southwest humor and the Southern grotesque.

Mary Lee Settle (1918–) may be best known for her novel set in Turkey, *Blood Tie*, which won the National Book Award in 1978. But she has produced a significant body of fiction that explores the past and present of her native coal-mining region of West Virginia. In fictional time the earliest novel of her Beulah quintet is *Prisons*, published in 1973. Told in the first person by young Johnny Church, a soldier in Cromwell's army, this novel establishes the themes of individual freedom and the interrelatedness of past and present that run through the quintet. Johnny's descendant Johnny Lacey, with Solomon McKarkle, descendant of Church's friend Gideon, settles the valley he calls Beulah in western Virginia in the novel *O Beulah Land* (1956). Settle uses the union of the aristocratic Sara Lacey with the commoner Ezekiel Catlett, along with Johnny's election to the House of Burgesses in 1774, to emphasize her central themes. *Know Nothing* (1960) follows the Catlett descendants from the 1830s to the outbreak of the Civil War, when Johnny Catlett joins the Confederate army and his deeply religious brother Lewis sides with the Union.

Settle's *The Scapegoat*, published in 1980, picks up the story of Laceys, Catletts, and McKarkles in West Virginia in 1912. The shifting point of view puts major emphasis on Lily Lacey, who is shocked by a confrontation with the labor organizer Mother Jones and is eventually seen with the Red Cross in England during the war. The final volume of the quintet, *The Killing Ground* (1982), may prove puzzling to those who have read *Fight Night on a Sweet Saturday* (1964) but do not know that here Settle has revised and expanded that novel to restore material cut by editors and to clarify the connections with other volumes. The focus of *The Killing Ground* is on its protagonist and narrator Hannah McKarkle, author of a group of novels bearing the titles of those in the Beulah quintet; like Settle she has been seeking the meaning of the present both in memory and through historical research. In 1960 Hannah's brother Johnny is accidentally killed by a distant Catlett cousin. By 1980 she is able to find her own identity not in artifacts from the past, but by assimilating that past and using it to move into the future.

William Hoffman (1925–) comes from the same geographical background as Settle. His earlier novels are very pessimistic; for example, in despair Tod Young in *Days in the Yellow Leaf* (1959) eventually turns to murder, and Angus McCloud in *A Place for My Head* (1960) suffers tremendous personal and professional setbacks. However, *The Dark Mountains* (1963), set during the unionization of coal miners, uses a narrator who changes because of his association with the central character. Likewise, *A Walk to the River* (1970) seems even more optimistic, as Hoffman employs the river as a symbol of renewed life. In spite of its title, *A Death of Dreams* (1973) ends hopefully, as protagonist Guy Dion finds an end to his madness and begins to deal with reality. Hoffman's latest novel, *The Land That Drank the Rain*, published in 1982, achieves its power through the skillful use of a limited point of view and the effectiveness of the language. Claytor, the protagonist, flees a life of transvestism and failed suicide in California and, through a series of bizarre and violent events in the isolation of Appalachia, experiences the kind of redemption that can only come through suffering.

John Bell Clayton (1906–1955) was a newspaperman until the success of his first novel allowed him to turn to fiction. Although his titles such as *Six Angels at My Back* (1952) and *Walk Toward the Rainbow* (1954) may suggest optimism or even sentimentality, he actually deals with the harshness of life in the South at the time he was writing. The popular journalist Robert Ruark (1915–1965) also published a variety of novels, including several that focus on violence in African settings. *Grenadine Etching* (1947) and *Grenadine's Spawn* (1952) are successful parodies of sensationalized historical novels. Particularly popular are his autobiographical *The Old Man and the Boy* (1957) and *The Old Man's Boy Grows Older* (1961).

Although Elizabeth Hardwick (1916–) is better known as a critic and an editor, she has published three novels and a number of as yet uncollected short stories. Her major works explore the consciousness of the Southern woman, such as Marian Coleman in *The Ghostly Lover* (1945), who leaves her home to study music in New York, and the narrator of *Sleepless Nights* (1979), the old woman Elizabeth whose memories control the structure and theme of the novel, an exploration of the meaning of the past. The past is likewise a strong theme in the small body of fiction by Max Steele (1922–), who has had a long career as a teacher; his most recent book-length work is the volume of stories *Where She Brushed Her Hair* (1968).

Harris Downey (1907–) moved from teaching to writing fiction in the 1950s, choosing primarily contemporary subjects such as the plans of Delia Wright for suicide in *The Key to My Prison* (1964), part of a Southern fictional tradition focusing on the decay of a family through time. Likewise using contemporary settings, Hollis Summers (1916–) in his novels of his native Kentucky, *City Limit* (1948), *Brighten the Corner* (1952), and *The Day After Sunday* (1968), has explored the sometimes nurturing, sometimes stifling roles of family and community. LeRoy Leatherman (1922–) focuses mainly on the family in his two novels, *The Caged Birds* (1950), associated with the tradition of the bizarre, and *The Other Side of the Tree* (1954), in which a seventeen-year-old boy learns about the past. The fiction of William Humphrey (1924–) consists of large family sagas set in his native northeast Texas, focusing on the Hunnicutts, dominated by larger-than-life Captain Wade, in *Home From the Hill* (1958); four generations of Ordways, from the Civil War to the 1920s, in *The Ordways* (1965); and the Renshaws in *Proud Flesh* (1973), which demonstrates Humphrey's increasing interest in the grotesque.

Of the writers focusing on racial tension and violence, none has achieved more recognition and respect than Harper Lee (1926–) for her single novel *To Kill a Mockingbird*, winner of the Pulitzer Prize for fiction in 1961. Covering three years of life in Maycomb County, Alabama, during the depression, Lee skillfully uses the point of view of the child Scout to develop two powerful and related episodes: Atticus Finch's eloquent but unsuccessful defense of black Tom Robinson, wrongly accused of raping a low-class white woman, Mayella Ewell; and the appearance of the ghostlike Boo Radley, who saves Scout and Jem Finch from the revengeful Bob Ewell. After Tom is found guilty, he is shot trying to escape; when Boo is forced to kill Ewell, the sheriff declares that Ewell accidentally fell on his knife. In both cases Lee draws the analogy of the senseless shooting of a songbird. *To Kill a Mockingbird* is most successful in its unsentimental portrayal of enlightened views on the rights of blacks.

Shirley Ann Grau (1929–   ), another woman writer of Lee's generation, was also a Pulitzer Prize winner for her 1964 novel *The Keepers of the House*. Moving from the present to the past through the point of view of Abigail Tolliver, Grau reveals how William Howland secretly married a black woman, Margaret, by whom he had three children. His white granddaughter marries John Tolliver, a bright young lawyer who seeks to further his political career both through the respectability of the Howland family and through blatant political racism. Margaret and William's son Robert, living as a white man in California, returns to Alabama after his mother's death to seek revenge by revealing William's past. Abigail, rather than give in, threatens to expose Robert's own past. She also faces the violence of the townspeople with violence of her own and strikes further by wielding her considerable economic power. Because neither Grau's black characters nor her white characters are one-dimensional, *The Keepers of the House* is a splendid study of the difficulty of interpreting the meaning of the past for the present.

Grau began her career in 1955 with a volume of short stories, *The Black Prince*; some of these, like her first novel, *The Hard Blue Sky* (1958), deal with primitive rural folk of south Louisiana. Other works, like her second novel, *The House on Coliseum Street* (1961), focus on the sterile lives of city-dwelling Southerners. Since *The Keepers of the House*, Grau has published another volume of stories, *The Wind Shifting West* (1973), and two novels, *The Condor Passes* (1971) and *Evidence of Love* (1977), which use the past to develop existential themes, primarily the difficulty of living a meaningful life.

Hubert Creekmore (1907–1966) in his most important novel, *The Chain in the Heart* (1953), follows three generations of a black family from post–Civil War to the 1930s. Moving from his early historical novels, Ovid Williams Pierce (1910–   ) in his most recent work, *The Wedding Guest* (1974), utilizes a first-person narrator, historian Kirby Wilson, to try to understand the present, especially the relationships between blacks and whites, in terms of the past. Before his early death Byron Herbert Reece (1917–1958) published several well-received novels, including *Better a Dinner of Herbs* (1950), which has been compared in mood to the literary ballads for which he is better known. *The Hawk and the Sun* (1955) reflects Reece's concern with the violent effects of prejudice in his native region. Thomas Hal Phillips (1922–   ) focuses in his fiction on masculine relationships; he moves from overt homosexual themes in *The Bitterweed Path* (1950) to universal questions of identity in *The Golden Lie* (1951), which includes an interracial friendship. A distinguished teacher and literary critic, Walter Sullivan (1924–   ) published two early novels, *Sojourn of a Stranger* (1957), which tells the story of a young man of mixed blood in antebellum Tennessee, and *The Long, Long Love* (1959). Sullivan has recently begun publishing short fiction.

Although Peter Feibleman (1930–) was born in New York, his first two novels, *A Place Without Twilight* (1958) and *The Daughters of Necessity* (1959), reflect the Deep South where he grew up in their concern with family relationships and racial identity. The most important fiction of Jesse Hill Ford (1928–) explores the effects of racial tension in the contemporary South. He is best known for the ironically titled *The Liberation of Lord Byron Jones* (1965), notable for the characters of the black undertaker Jones, who appears briefly in Ford's first novel *Mountains of Gilead* (1961), and the white attorney Oman Hedgepath. Ford emphasizes in this novel and in *The Feast of Saint Barnabas* (1969) the violence that he sees as an unfortunate but inevitable consequence of the rapid social changes occurring in the South. Ellen Douglas (1921–) has been successful at portraying relationships between blacks and whites in the contemporary South in the short works collected under the title *Black Cloud, White Cloud* (1964) and the novel *The Rock Cried Out* (1979). *Apostles of Light* (1973), set in Mississippi, has been praised as a perceptive treatment of the universal problem of aging and of the theme of the deceptive character of evil.

The mountain fiction of Wilma Dykeman (1920–) also reflects her strong interest in civil rights. In *The Tall Woman* (1962) she portrays the mountain woman's strength through adversity, following Lydia McQueen from her marriage in 1864 to her death from typhoid in 1896. *The Far Family* (1966) follows the lives of Lydia's descendants, focusing on the central episode of a white man wrongly accused of killing a black. Chapters alternate between the present and the past; only when Dykeman's characters come to understand the past are they able to move into the future. The narrative voice of the mountain woman in the fiction of Mildred Haun (1911–1966), collected in *The Hawk's Done Gone and Other Stories* (1968), is used to make the supernatural element believable.

One of the strongest continuing traditions in Southern literature is that of Southwest humor and what is often labeled the Southern grotesque. The fiction of William Goyen (1915–1983) is traditionally Southern not only because of his use of grotesque or bizarre characters and situations, but also because of his thematic emphasis on the interrelatedness of place, family, and past; however, his style and technique are unusual if not unique. His critical reputation is based primarily on his short fiction, especially the volumes *Ghost and Flesh* (1952) and *The Faces of Blood Kindred* (1960). Some stories are essentially real-

531

istic, while others have a mythic dimension, such as "A Tale of Inheritance," which develops the theme of family separation and reunion through the characters of the three bearded Lester sisters.

Goyen's first novel, *The House of Breath* (1950), was seen by reviewers as Southern in theme and technique; yet *In a Farther Country* (1955), which followed, is set in New York and involves a surreal vision of a new world. Goyen's *Come, the Restorer* (1974), also surreal in technique, portrays a group of unfulfilled characters, confused in their identity and sexuality. Mr. de Persia, the original restorer of the title, is seen in the present time of the novel in a catatonic state only. By Selina Rosheen he unknowingly fathers a son Addis, later adopted by Ace and Jewel Adair. Eventually Addis, a high-wire walker, becomes the restorer of sexual vitality for Jewel, though neither is aware of the other's identity. Addis dies in the Thicket; but Wylie Prescott, involved in a sterile relationship with Selina, continues to seek Addis to restore life to his house and land, which have been destroyed by lovelessness and greed. For Goyen, sex is frequently a thematic device to emphasize waste and sterility, often a source of humor, but rarely a natural joyous aspect of life.

From the publication of *End as a Man* (1947), set in a fictionalized version of the Citadel, the best novels of Calder Willingham (1922–) have been those set in the South. *Eternal Fire* (1963) achieves earthy humor as Willingham employs every possible convention of the Southern Gothic novel, yet gives his star-crossed lovers a happy ending. In *Rambling Rose* (1972) the narrator tells a warmly comic story of his sexual initiation. The humorous fiction of William Price Fox (1926–), optimistic but never sentimental, has been praised for carrying on the tradition of Mark Twain, though Fox claims never even to have read *Huckleberry Finn*. Fox explores a naïveté to be found even in teenage con artists like LeRoy Edge and Coley Simms, dual protagonists of *Moonshine Light, Moonshine Bright* (1967), and in the delightfully promiscuous title character of *Ruby Red* (1971), who leaves home to seek a career as a country music singer in Nashville.

Guy Owen (1925–1981), distinguished teacher, editor, and poet, is probably best known for his almost mythical comic hero Mordecai Jones, featured in *The Ballad of the Flim-Flam Man* (1965), another novel, and a collection of stories. Owen shows the influence of the Southwest humorists and directly acknowledges his debt to Mark Twain. Owen has also published two fine novels set in his fictional Cape Fear County, *Season of Fear* (1960) and *Journey for Joedel* (1970), the latter particularly notable for the realistic portrait of a thirteen-year-old protagonist who is part Lumbee, a tribe thought by Owen and others to be descended from the Lost Colonists.

Like Owen, George Garrett (1929–) has achieved a reputation as poet, editor, and fiction writer. In his fiction he has explored conflicts between individuals, between individual and society, and between societies in the context of war. He often uses techniques of humor such as the grotesque. In the title stories of *King of the Mountain* (1957) and *In the Briar Patch* (1961), Garrett invokes the memory of childhood games and stories. His most recent short fiction is found in the volume *The Magic Striptease*, published in 1973. In the novella *The Satyr Shall Cry* he employs the technique of a pseudoscreenplay to present the story of a double murder at a Southern tent revival.

In his novels as well as his short fiction, Garrett has explored a variety of situations and settings. His first long work of fiction is a political novel set in contemporary Florida. *The Finished Man* (1959) has been compared to *All the King's Men* in surface details, the single narrative voice, and the theme of the influence of the past on the present. One of Garrett's strongest themes is religion; one of his favorite subjects, the tent revival; one of his typical techniques, multiple narrators. He combines these in *Do, Lord, Remember Me* (1965) to portray the complex character of revivalist Red Smalley.

Garrett's major achievement in fiction is the novel *Death of the Fox* (1971), which tells through multiple points of view of the last two days in the life of Sir Walter Ralegh. Garrett sees him as a man who can live only in the present, without understanding the past or moving into the future; it has even been said of *Death of the Fox* that it bears obliquely on the history of the South.

Much of the fiction of John William Corrington (1932–) is concerned with religious themes, as in the highly praised novel *The Upper Hand* (1967) and many of the stories in *The Actes and Monuments* (1978), both of which bear on the tradition of the grotesque in Southern literature. David Madden (1933–) may be best known for his least Southern work, *The Suicide's Wife* (1978). However, his best fiction is that which grows out of the Southern storytelling tradition, including one collection of short stories, *The Shadow Knows* (1970), many uncollected stories, and his novels *Bijou* (1974) and *Pleasure-Dome* (1979), which explore the theme of nostalgia in portraying the growth of the boy Lucius Hutchfield into a responsible artist. These novels, like *On the Big Wind* (1980), which grew out of the long story "The Singer," are rich in humor, occasionally grotesque or absurd. *A Confederacy of Dunces*, the posthumously published novel by John Kennedy

Toole (1937–1969), was awarded the Pulitzer Prize for fiction in 1981. This comic best seller develops the theme of isolation through its protagonist, the pseudophilosopher Ignatius Reilly, and a splendid cast of minor characters such as the delightfully senile Miss Trixie. Toole's satire on contemporary taste and thought ends optimistically, with Ignatius' fleeing New Orleans with the New York intellectual Myrna Minkoff.

Southern fiction from 1950 to 1981 is tremendously varied; however, it seems that in this group of writers one sees more concern in significant thematic ways with place, family, and past than one might find in contemporary fiction by writers from any other region, and there seems to be a stronger continuing tradition of a particular kind of humor. In several instances, such as that of Shirley Ann Grau, there has been a development away from Southern settings and toward existential themes. Other writers, especially William Goyen, have become increasingly surreal in style and technique. Mary Lee Settle and others have moved from historical fiction to works set in their own time, while in his latest work George Garrett has turned from the contemporary South to Elizabethan England. Southern fiction may not be as distinctive as it was during the Renascence, yet one does not confuse writers of this generation with John Updike or Norman Mailer.

JAMES H. JUSTUS

Poets After Midcentury

In the 1960s observers of the Southern literary scene began their serious engagement with the question that few had bothered to ask
earlier: does the flowering known as the Southern Renascence still continue? That the question was even being asked suggested that the phenomenon had indeed spent itself or was taking directions that would
stamp the literature as less regional and more mainstream American
than its immediate predecessor. Unlike the fiction, poetry in the South
tended to reflect the impact of modernism as much as it celebrated its
regionalism; the early poetry of John Crowe Ransom, Allen Tate, Donald Davidson, and Robert Penn Warren was neither obviously nor consciously Southern. But if the Nashville Fugitives rarely thought of their
work as expressions of a regional sensibility, it is no longer possible for
us to read it or that of their successors without probing for evidence of
that sensibility. Because the achievements of James Dickey, A. R. Ammons, and Randall Jarrell coincided with the perceived winding down
of the Southern Renascence, a newer question, more frequently asked
since the 1960s—Is there such a thing as a distinctly Southern poetry?—reflects a regional sensibility that has been educated into self-
consciousness through the efforts not only of Southern writers but also
Southern critics, classroom teachers, anthologists, and editors. Even in
the verse of the best Southern poets whose recognition came in the
1960s and 1970s, when commitment to the art of poetry far outstripped
any commitment to the region of their birth, certain distinguishing
characteristics emerge: a recurrence of rural subjects; a residual fondness for conservative forms and techniques; an easy habit of incorporating regional diction and syntax into a poetic discourse that is otherwise
Received Standard; a penchant for order and control even in experimental efforts; a preference for the visually concrete and aurally sensuous
image over abstract meditation; the importance of memory in altering,
deepening, and extending compulsive scenic recall; and, unlike more
aggressive postmodernists of their generation, a lingering reliance upon

535

pattern, design, and wholeness despite a resigned recognition that both life and art are resolutely fragmented, disjunctive, and discontinuous.

Perhaps no two poets represent the diversity of the contemporary Southern aesthetic sensibility than Donald Justice, whose mode is serene, severe, and restrained, and Jonathan Williams, whose mode is explosive, assertive, and experimental. Yet the work of both men reveals a temperamental respect for the forms of an earlier way of life and an urgency, both cultural and personal, that images of that life be preserved and commemorated before they pass from memory. Both men celebrate the poem as artifact and the poet's voice as controlling mediator between the rawness of experience and its suggested meaning. Both Justice the academic and Williams the publicist are rigorously professional, "makers" whose careers have been honored for their dedication to the craft of poetry and their interest in the work of others.

The poems in Justice's first volume, *Summer Anniversaries* (1960; rev. ed., 1981) are among the most elegant of what was once called academic, a term from the late 1950s used to distinguish the verse of traditional practitioners from the more open, oratorical, visceral poetry spawned by the beat school. Justice's graceful and lucid gifts here are for the sonnet, the terza rima, and especially the sestina; and many of his poems are bathed in a surreal glow suggesting frozen or slow-motion situations in dreams. "Early Poems," from *Night Light* (1967), is a wry act of self-criticism of those "fashionably sad" poems: "the rhymes, the meters, how they paralyze." This judgment is followed by "Now the long silence. Now the beginning again." The new beginning here with its continuation in *Departures* (1973) means simultaneously a release from paralyzing rhymes (though more supple ones are not entirely sacrificed), toward freer, shorter lines (usually irregular trimeters and tetrameters), and a frank admission of indebtedness to and respect for other writers, suggested by such titles as "Riddle" (after the Old English form), "Homage to the Memory of Wallace Stevens," "Lorcaesques," "After the Chinese," and "Variations on a Text by Vallejo." "Poem" even manages to combine a favorite Renascence convention and a poststructuralist sentiment.

> You will forget the poem, but not before
> It has forgotten you. And it does not matter.
> It has been most beautiful in its erasures.

The most memorable of his poems, however, are those in which people, places, and events, some from his Florida boyhood, emerge fitfully as images that stimulate meditations on loss in textures artfully reflecting what Justice calls in one of his early poems "the classic landscape of dreams." Childhood experiences, awash in mysterious lights that illuminate their meanings while leaving motivation, rational sequence, and context in shadows, are perhaps the most delicately handled of his subjects; but poems on the loneliness of the poet, dying relatives, decaying mansions, geriatric men and women declining by windows and on ruined porches, are also typically removed from the rawness of setting by a precision and overt calculation of craft, often a Ransomian device: subjecting potentially sentimental situations to the restraint of traditional metrics and lines by a coolly detached speaker. "Southern Gothic," "Women in Love," and "Tales from a Family Album" are all built around the fleeting insight or the casually observed moment stripped of the heated immediacy of involvement. "The Grandfathers" is a generic portrait of ancestors as "Peevish, discredited gods" in which the vigor of the naturalistically observed gesture—hawking and spitting—is bound by their static immobilization, their "blank, oracular / Headshakes or headnods" that suggest a residual authority rendered as ineffectual as the assertions of their female counterparts in "Ladies by Their Windows." Preferring understatement to energy, Justice writes a poetry of measure, boundaries, control. Individual poems tend to be short, and there are no excursions into poetic suites and only occasionally paired poems (as in "Absences" and "Presences") or brief linked sequences (as in "Things"). Tonally the verse is dry, muted; the characteristic voice we hear is a refusal to be intense even when meditating on the loss of certitude. It is the most civilized poetry of his Southern contemporaries.

As Justice is the poet of restraint, Jonathan Williams is the poet of excess. Irreverent, prankish, cantankerous, eccentric, Williams writes poetry that owes little to either the theories or practice of earlier Southern poets. The wild civility of *An Ear in Bartram's Tree: Selected Poems 1957–1967* (1969) is announced by the transformation of the elegant convention of the epigraph into "In Lieu of a Preface: The Poet's Emblems to be Writ Large Across the Broad, Vacant Skies Every Dawn," a sequence of thirty-nine epigraphs ranging from Goethe, Blake, and Cézanne to Groucho Marx, Kenneth Patchen, and Bunk Johnson. North Carolinian Williams writes out of a tradition now associated with Black Mountain College, that un-Carolinian school whose heroes were Walt Whitman, Ezra Pound, William Carlos Williams, Louis Zukofsky, and Charles Olson. And like a Southern Pound, Williams has been unstinting in championing other writers, primarily by publishing their works through his own Jargon Press.

It is not surprising that for Williams, writing in a tradition in which the avant-garde persistently shifts ground, visual shapes become as integral as verbal harmony. Desentimentalizing E. E. Cummings, the poet

537

seizes upon slang, argot, and phonetic dialect only to rearrange them according to his own linear order and respect for white space and the juxtaposed shapes of individual words and letters. As a mountaineer, Williams describes himself as both laconic and garrulous; some of his favorite forms are epitaphs and epigrams, and even his longer works, such as "Mahler" and "Five Trail-Shelters from the Big Pigeon to the Little Tennessee," are verbal tone poems of economic intensities. In his ongoing "Garland for the Appalachians," the poems are both found and made: Williams calls his poems on the sayings of mountain people and their carved and painted signs "common words in uncommon orders." In "The Ancient of Days," he pays tribute to an old woman whom he knows only from photographs; in "Lee Ogle Ties a Broom & Ponders Cures for Arthuristis," he celebrates both the precision of following folk nostrums and the muted pride in finding modest ways to stave off the ultimate decline to which the stoic mountaineer is resigned; and in "Mrs. Sadie Grindstaff, Weaver & Factotum, Explains the Work-Principle to the Modern World," Williams repeats verbatim but transforms linearly not merely a saying but a vision that connotes both the laconic and the garrulous.

> I figured
> anything anybody
> could do a lot of I
> could do a little
> of
>
> mebby

Williams' rich profusion of influences—his mentors at Black Mountain, Edith Sitwell, Blake, the native poets of Wales and Scotland—is more than matched by the varied and magic transformation of the seen and heard of this world. Not only the Appalachian dialects but the harmonics, dissonances, and pauses of Carl Nielsen, Charlie Parker, Charles Ives, and Maurice Ravel are transferred truly but imaginatively from his ear to type; stories out of Ovid, Robert Graves, and Jane Harrison are metamorphosed into such icons as Helen Trent, Snow White, and space cadets; his concrete poems claim kin to and borrow authority from puns, anagrams, and other played-through declensions of sights and sounds. Williams once referred to some of his poems as "Southern-Fried Dada," but his inventive combinations never incorporate the purely absurd or the trivial; juxtapositions and transformations are meaningful, not merely in what he by art does to his materials but in the intrinsic value of things, the materials prior to his shaping. The least interesting products of Williams' genius are his topical satires, mostly on the

Wallace-Faubus era of racial disharmony, but even these succinct commentaries are invigorated by a remarkable adaptation of mountain songs, proverbs, nursery rhymes, and the comic valentine, that cheap-paper insult combining blunt language and vividly ugly graphics, into forms that Williams calls "Lullabies Twisters Gibbers Drags" (1963). Another group, the early "Jammin' the Greek Scene" (1959), is a self-conscious updating of legends and myths in the idiom of jazz musicians. In these, as in other clusters, the emphasis is on the nearly infinite possibilities by which language can be fixed to forms. To that end Williams has produced mostly short poems in mostly short lines: epitaphs, epigrams, mazes, concrete poems, rebuses, anagrams, riffs, pastorals, lullabies, blues lyrics, elegies, tavern songs, and mathoms (the latter, from Tolkien, identified as harmless trifles that no one would want to throw away). None of his contemporaries has matched Williams in the high-spirited act of manipulation and invention.

Although Williams' Appalachian poems are only a fraction of his output, like his poems on musicians and obscure British painters, they are acts of commemoration. To preserve the sayings, folkways, and humanity of Granny Donaldson, Uncle Jake Carpenter, and Uncle Iv is not the archivist's impulse but the human need to celebrate the increasingly rare instances of individuality, even cranky self-reliance, in a homogeneous world. For many of Williams' contemporaries, the act of commemorating people and their acts from the recent Southern past is a personal investment at least as strong as an aesthetic commitment. The Southern landscape in these poets is often a dreamscape because memory is a stronger source of poetic energy for James Applewhite, James Seay, George Scarbrough, and Dabney Stuart than it was for those poets of the Fugitive generation or even, except for the traumas of war, for Dickey or Jarrell. The reality of an older Southern scene is not wholly accessible to these younger poets, a sociological fact that requires an imaginative melding of landscape and dream, actual kin and hieratic representations of fathers, mothers, and grandparents. And since so much of their South is memory, grandparents are even more frequently invoked than fathers and mothers, a tactic for memorializing time as well as place: seizing a slightly older South in images of representative life that has already passed into the something different of the present. Old people frozen in stances of individual acts that symbolize immemorial traits of the race, or dispensing wisdom drawn from the reservoir of the agrarian occult, become talismanic figures preserving the integrity of the South *then* in the wasting homogeneous flow of the South *now*. These younger poets insist upon a circumstantial present, a gritty reality that is fully available, in part as compensation for that earlier scene when vague intimations of person and event from the past often dissipate rather than concentrate meaning. This contemporary landscape is a richly tangible world dense with cow trails, fencerows, weathered farmhouses, outdoor toilets perched on stilts over creek beds, pastures, kudzu vines smothering abandoned cars, wells, springs, cisterns, cultivators, feedstores, truckstops, revival meetings, outdoor baptisms, and hardscrabble fields choked with briars and scrub pine. But even the compulsive evoking of these items often assumes the same elegiac coloration common to the fierce summoning up of images from an earlier South.

When in one poem Dabney Stuart thinks to himself, "*Everything / Diminishes / Except loss,*" the proverblike sentiment captures a general spirit felt among those of his generation. The decline of fathers, the gradual subtraction of childhood friends, the passing of lovers, the estrangement of wives, the memory of adolescent heroes, all suggest domestic, personal, familial versions of an earlier memorializing impulse that is cultural, political, and religious in the work of Tate and Davidson. If death dominates the available topics in these poets, it serves largely as the most obvious fact of loss, and the appropriate mood for its contemplation is its elusive lesson for survivors. If the abandoned farm and the decaying homestead are the concrete images embodying the inevitable ruins of time, the rural cemetery becomes an equally forceful image of that theme placed within an ordered scheme that at once depersonalizes the loss and formalizes despair, and it also serves as the single most effective symbol of continuities between the then and the now. The stately cadences and Eliotic ruminations that we find in the South's most famous graveyard poem, Tate's "Ode to the Confederate Dead," invoke a regional pietàs, in which the fathers' culture, defined by a heritage of communal integrity, abstract honor, and generosity toward the public weal, imposes its responsibilities upon the sons. That kind of memorializing space is rare in the younger poets. Van K. Brock celebrates a less momentous piety of a summer ceremony in which far-flung aunts, uncles, and cousins gather to clean the family cemetery; Edgar Bowers writes of mountain cemeteries where the roots of pine trees replace the bones of the dead; Alice Walker writes of country graveyards where "the graves soon grow back into the land"; for Wendell Berry, the very furrowing of the ground opens up the bones of "dead tribesmen buried here / a thousand years ago"; and for William Matthews, family burial space is transmuted into a psychological state with which father and son must come to terms: "To help his sons live easily / among the dead is a father's great work."

If the symbiosis between history and memory is one of the characteristics in the writings of the Southern Renascence, contemporary poets would seem to be more national than regional. A larger history, though it flickers occasionally as a generic given, has mostly been quietly absorbed into the more immediate past of a personal history. Childhood events, initiatory experiences, early loves and lusts, summer jobs and summer camps, and marriages and divorces are alluded to regularly as monitory images whose lessons may not be perfectly clear. Their very facticity is an engagement of sorts with history, but the characteristic strategy is that such moments of the past exist more as opportunities for memory to work upon—and therefore distort—than as moments to be preserved in their integrity. The movement from actuality, activated by memory, to the kind of fantasy that extends both fact and memory can best be seen in the work of William Mills and Dabney Stuart.

In his first volume, *Watch for the Fox* (1974), Mills achieves a resonance of both the natural and human worlds by the sparest of language. The approach is direct; without conventional description or meditation, the typical movement of the poems is from the terse recounting of an experience in simple diction to its potential implications: a woman whose dead lover's shoes are worn by her present lover; cleaning a catfish in the cruel but proper manner; watching a hawk hunt food during a human lunch-break at a refinery. In Mills's disciplined severity of form and language, lines never exceed four feet—often they consist of a single word—and the syntax is prosaic, unmetaphoric. A plain-style sensitivity to the creature world, of ducks, hounds, hawks, woodlands, is matched by a sharply focused attentiveness to the world in which man most decisively lives: participating in "jukeboxbeer moments" in bars, observing random river debris, watching late-evening television, celebrating and lamenting love and other casual affairs.

In their direct apprehension of experience, Mills's earlier poems are considerably more severe than those in *Stained Glass* (1979) and *The Meaning of Coyotes* (1984), in which the subjects—the poet's aging, his lust, his hunting and fishing pleasures, his tribute to ancestors—contract as the poetic style broadens. Less staccato and more leisurely in syntax, most of these poems are still written in short lines; and the implied resonances of the earlier verse are more often made explicit. In "Rituals Along the Arkansas," a joyous celebration of a fishing trip, the cleaning of bass beneath thermal-riding pelicans becomes the focal act joining fish, man, and bird: "We are wedded to what we use, / What we love, what we find beautiful." In "Silhouette," the poet remembers his child's image scissored from construction paper: "No one could read my eyes, a statue's eyes, / And I have not since seen so clearly what I am." In both of his recent volumes are poems of cultural contrasts (a Mississippian in eastern Europe) and cultural continuities (a Mississippian in Louisiana and Arkansas). The perspectives, even in such brief pieces as "Southern Vortex" or "The Necessity of Falling," are consistently closer to the objects summoned up or experienced, and the warmer tones finally make the later verse more accessible. Emotional vulnerabilities, always more exposed in love lyrics, are also more apparent in those poems capturing important moments other than lovemaking: the "beautiful" sound of hammering as a neighbor next door, building a barn, breaks "the old terror" of silence; a squirrel hunter patiently waiting for his quarry beneath a live oak; a resident waiting out a tornado, imagining the "last ellipsis" in his trailer, the "overture to the dread rectangle." Mills's two virtuoso pieces are longer and more ambitious than his usual vignettes. "Wedington Woods" is a festive fertility hymn to a lunch-hour tryst in which the speaker's seed and his lover's Dior panties are ceremonially buried in an armadillo hole: in the speaker's dreams "an armadillo dressed strangely human" trudges home in the dark. "Our Fathers at Corinth" is an ode to the poet's great-grandfather, whose unknown soldier's grave is finally located by his descendants; it ends in the poet's vision of his ancestor's blood leeching out to "salt seas / Embracing the earth, holding us all." With the final words, "You rest in your sons / Who must keep you to keep themselves," Mills allies himself firmly with a Southern theme boasting a long history: the sanctity of family ties and the near-mythical pull of ancestral blood. That part of the Southern sensibility that fears abstractions joins with the poet's traditional skepticism of the scientific enterprise in Mills's powerful "Lords," in which an arctic bear, majestic in his "simple telemetry of grandeur," is momentarily stunned by a "dose of angel dust" and examined by the quantifying instruments of an expedition that intends "to leave no mystery unturned."

Like Mills's, Dabney Stuart's is a spare, almost severe poetry of formal rigor in which the integrity of the line, rather than metaphor, is the major shaping force. His first volume, *The Diving Bell* (1966), is a stunning display of forms and metrics in which performance almost eclipses the familiar and familial subjects. But unlike Mills, Stuart typically withholds from the chosen poetic object—old houses, a pencil ("Venus 2"), the Charles River in Boston, a fisherman—distinctness of form, and consciously infuses the object with the swirling impressions of dream and fantasy. In "To His Father, Dying," Stuart deliberately smudges fact—the most verifiable part of the situation is the title itself—by announcing "It is not necessary to remember" event either in "bright sun or in darkness" since "it is all the same / In this phase of the dream." The poem is bathed in indeterminate blurring: moments from the ancestors' pioneering past and from the son's experience with the father on a beach in the long ago are both not so much recalled as dramatized in merging spaces of dream suggestive of generalized historical images found in dusky historical paintings.

Even when Stuart writes about the same things as other younger Southern poets—love, marriage, children, separation, hero figures from adolescence—the logic of narrative or even sequential observation must be inferred because of the weight of his emphasis—the creating, brooding power of imagination. The recurring words and phrases are *dream*; *The thick dark flows around me half asleep*; *submerge*; *shadows*; *silence*; *moving stream*; *a layer beneath*; *sinking*; *stillness*. Stuart celebrates his Virginia in the Rockbridge poems from *A Particular Place* (1969), but even though the highways, rivers, baths, and mountains are the generating impulse, the geography is as much psychological as cartographical. A typical movement is the felt need to plunge beneath or behind surfaces. "His Third Decade," on death and natural transfiguration, and "The Drowning," on imaginative rehabilitation through water, are only two instances in which the poet grapples with the powerful compulsion to descend. In "Power Failure" the compulsion is in a vaguely reawakened need for mystic communication with his own psychic depths. In the best of these poems of descent, "The Real World," from *The Other Hand* (1974), Stuart combines the incantatory pull of depths through his distinct diction with a technical finish typical of much of his later verse—linear arrangement of short lines with typographical caesuras.

> When I descend
> Into the pool of sleep   suspended from the line
> Of myself lowering into myself   I am learning
> The buried words   I am dancing among the stones
> Darkening. . . .

Despite his adaptation of surrealistic techniques of various postmodernist poets and lightly echoing cadences and images out of Poe, Rilke, and St.-John Perse, Stuart achieves a distinctive line and voice. If making-do with ruin and rot is the predictable theme of "The Broken City," a Phi Beta Kappa ceremonial poem of 1967, the shrewd language of archaeology, with its urns and shards, softens the apocalyptic tone with a cultural and human perspective. In "A Gesture," a poem for his grandmother, the intricacies of two words, *bow* and *grace*, in their multiple meanings transform simple homage into complex art. In "The Fit," a spectator is convulsed at a stage show: with her arm, hand, and fingers becoming both charmed and charmer, cobra and owner, flutist and snake, she enacts a cruel physiological parody of the hundred girls on stage who sway and whirl to "the ancient music" heard on their nerve ends. In his best work Dabney Stuart retrieves the gimmickery of the surrealists for serious art, validating its harsh juxtapositions and alogical sequences by returning them to the maker's control of language and thereby making the language of dream as comprehensible as the language of consciousness.

A less portentous kind of surrealism dominates the poetry of George Garrett. Like many of his contemporaries, Garrett writes frequently of family and kin not only as stable knowns in a world that most often resists human familiarization, but also as enabling symbols of generational continuity. But the Christian base of his vision, invoked unironically, makes him virtually unique among his peers; and coupled with the persistent adaptation of classical myth, his acknowledgment of such religious and cultural legacies also links Garrett to an older generation of Southern poets. What makes his voice distinctly his own, however, is the felt tension between the stabilizing fixities of religion and culture, the time and place of a familial South, and the motif of transformation, his most obsessive trope. "It takes faith to be fixed, to live / with so much happening," he writes in "In North Carolina," but his imagination clearly responds most productively when he turns to what he calls, in "Virtuosity," the "richness of change and becoming." A camera-minded tourist may try to freeze the motion of the natural world, but its "languid chaos" resists all effort to fix its perpetual movement ("Percé Rock"). Unlike his tourist, Garrett immerses his own fancy in that "unfixed joy" with a kind of benevolent countercreation. In "Rugby Road" songs become birds flying over garden walls, where trees dream, fountains play "a bloodless, sweatless game of light and air," and falling leaves are turned into smoke. "Come as You Are" concerns a masquerade party imagined by a sensibility quivering with "the joys of Proteus."

Many of the early poems, mostly in rhymed quatrains, are witty redactions of fables, myths, and fairy tales compressed with adagelike precision but rendered in an idiom that manages to be both learned and colloquial. The later poetry shows some loosening of formal restraints— a more casual line, more flexible rhythms, even a prosy syntax. The range of Garrett's work is represented by *For a Bitter Season: New and Selected Poems* (1967), which incorporates the most skillful of both the early and later verse. The poet's imaginative indulgence in his characteristic Protean joys gives Garrett's poetry its distinctive flavor. "In Tuscany," against a backdrop of orderly Italian vineyards, the grapes spill over from their well-tended regularity, reaching out to overwhelm objects of recent war,

> flooding pillboxes, foxholes, and minefields,
> stalling tanks and trucks,
> disrupting wire communications,

like a time-lapsed scene of kudzu enveloping a Southern hillside. In an updated linkage out of the religious history of the frontier—camp meetings and uninhibited sexual coupling—Garrett notes

> bushes crawling with couples.
> I see one girl so leafy that
> she might be Daphne herself.

A mad young woman who in her dreams was a willow tree is juxtaposed to a speaker who pinches himself to see if he has "turned to stone." In "General Prologue," a poem about teaching Chaucer in late winter, the speaker notes that a robin on the path outside the classroom window is being readied "to be transformed into" the Wife of Bath.

Knowing that "truth is the center / of all fables," Garrett writes lyrics in praise of Narcissus, Tiresias, Aesop, Midas, Jacob and the Angel, Diana, all those like Orpheus, Virgil, Dante, and Christ who "descended in the dark and stirred / the troubled bones," signaling the change of eras as well as seasons, mankind as well as men. But perhaps no poem captures the interplay between the values of fixity, the domestic security of family and kin, and the values of transformation, the magic creativity of change that ratifies the primacy of the imagination, than "Child Among Ancestors," Garrett's most affecting statement on the ambivalent nourishing of love, respect, and blood identification among generations. Family legends fall lightly on the dutiful and skeptical ears of a child; because the marvels among the ancestors—a magnificent tamer of horses, one who met a dragon, another who because of lust was "changed into a pig with a ring tail"—are remote, they are uncherished, and the child retires to his own childish games as a warrior among the chickens. The final scene is framed by the father, brooding on the links between adult escapades and children's games, lessons that must be learned but that can never be taught.

If Garrett's use of myth and legend reaffirms the continuance of vitality, even in a spiritually diminished age, the mythical heightening seen in Miller Williams is both ambiguous and oblique, especially in his early work. The most successful poems in A Circle of Stone (1964) are those that go decisively beyond mere transcription of observed or remembered scenes. The threat of retribution for killing a music student is transposed into a softer key of childhood games of cowboys and Indians. A personal tribute, "For JW, on his marriage in the faith," becomes something more than a poem for an occasion through its elevation by religious allusion. "Depot in a River Town," which begins as a deceptively straight-forward account of a speaker observing other passengers on depot benches, slowly turns into a vision of modern man waiting for Charon's boat. The domestic setting of "For Robert, Son of Man," focuses on a five-year-old who points to his genitals with the question, "*What are these for?*" And in the father's imagination the fleshly stones become boulders "tumbling from some cold and holy place," as the familiarity of his son's "Roy Rogers room" turns into a strangely familiar site evoking the ancient burdens of initiation rites, ritual sacrifice, and circumcision from Jewish, Christian, and Druidic pasts.

> the answer comes ochre and swelling of earth
> and we are together
> in a circle of stone
> where the sun slips red and new
> to a stand of oak.

In his later verse Williams strips away such mythical heightening along with the graceful rhetorical modulations of his Audenesque tributes in songs of benediction and praise. By the time of *Why God Permits Evil* (1977) the emphasis is upon the harsh deprivations and thinned-out possibilities of the present: bad sex, the gloomy slide to middle age, disappointments in love, the loss of old friends, automobile accidents, prisoners, Southern interstates, and country musicians. Depite their harder, more relentlessly contemporary feel, many of these later poems are portentously informed by a residual Calvinism, as in "Everyone Dies in a Light Rain" and "Where to Turn When Sorrow Comes"; a disquieting number of poems are epitaphs—some laced with irony, others conventionally ceremonial; and there is a thread of anguish running through even those poems that traditionally bolster human failures by reliance upon human making.

> We have failed at what makers of poems do,
> which was never to save the world from the world
> but to save the world from the failure of poetry.

In *The Boys on Their Bony Mules* (1983), Williams more often manages to infuse a poignant but unsentimental concern into that characteristically cool hardness, as in "A Newspaper Picture of Spectators at a Hotel Fire" and "Wiedersehen." In "Notes from the Agent on Earth: How to Be Human," his most ambitious poem from the 1970s, Williams constructs a dark meditation on "what we have in common," ringing the changes on all the significant abstractions that challenge complacent spiritual health—"Love, Ambition, Faith, the Sense of Death." But here, as in his other poems, such abstractions are nailed down to tangible referents, and what is summoned up is the often inevitable manifestation of terror lurking within ordinary experience. The frequency with which certain ordinary subjects appear in his work—games and anxieties of childhood, sexual rivalries, funerals, Saturday afternoon preachers—suggests an important link among most of the Southern poets of Williams' generation: the persistent pull of the village South, even in the standardized nationalism of the present, the South of small-town habits, obscure domestic rituals, and the leftover nourishments of country life. "Running into Things" is Williams' eight-line elegy for twelve farmers killed coming to town in their pickup trucks "Because they couldn't remember the bypass / that cut across their roads"; and in "Coming to Town," William Mills illuminates the close links between country and town, past and present, through visual and aural "carryover" images.

> Coming to town hasn't been as bad
> as I thought.
> There are two old trees on the block
> and a church bell reminds me of bells
> I have heard before.
> . . . .
> An occasional silence
> brings back the bells,
> borders a world I have complained in,
> of cawing crows and cows,
> and been inattentive to the baying hounds.

None of the poets of this generation has done better than James Seay in not only evoking the village culture of the contemporary South but also transforming its commonplaces into objects and events of talismanic significance. A high school athlete sent to a state prison for cattle rustling is himself drowned trying to recover a body from a lake; a billboard majorette behind a local practice field imaginatively takes on life as a tattered tart "again full-fleshed / In these half-times of our lives"; the magic pull of carnivals on the small-town circuit is enhanced rather than supplanted by the newer charms of transistor radios. Acknowledging the totems and detritus of village life—mobile homes on concrete blocks, rotgut whiskey in Clorox bottles, Kotex boxes used by children to trap starlings, abandoned cars—Seay tends to invest such phenomena with mysterious potentiality that transforms them into the stuff of legend. Making a bottle tree, a detail out of Eudora Welty's Mississippi, is an act of both creation and propitiation: a natural bay tree must be cruelly sheared, pruned, and stripped in order to receive its human offering of blue bottles that will make it "fit for a golden bird."

When a veterinarian relieves a bloated bull by inserting "a trocar be-tween his ribs" and puts a match to the valve of the escaping gas, a blue flame spurts and the animal bolts, but the clinically precise and unique event modulates into mythic recurrence in which the godlike bull flames blue and soft in the pasture each night.

The resonances of change in "The Bluebottle Tree," "The Majorette on the Self-Rising Flour Sign," and "No Man's Good Bull" occur through an often whimsical process of wordplay in casual idioms and the imaginative literalizing of pun, metaphor, and cliché. Seay playfully speculates on the alteration of personality occasioned by wearing home a mariner's glove that washes up on the beach by playing on such phrases as "caught short-handed" and "willing to give a helping hand." Some poems escalate a physical fact—the poet's "lost right eye"—into a rich source of metaphorizing on the theme of insight. Only occasionally does Seay make merely literal use of the contemporary Southern town; he describes in one poem how a hometown industry, heretofore geared to turning out ice buckets and camp stoves, retools in order to make bomb fins for the Defense Department. Both in the early poems of *Let Not Your Hart* (1970) and in later verse, where Seay's Southern settings are used more sensitively, the familiar locales of an older South (a coun-try graveyard, a Southern beach) and those of a newer (the restroom of a gas station, a tourist home in Nashville) typically carry a weight dis-proportionate to their modest actuality. Seay's water imagery in *Water Tables* (1974) and his invocations of the green world are thoroughly modern pastoral. The dominant structural metaphor in "The Green World" is a house, at once sinister and inviting. Its thesis—that "the great bodies of water" are less than salutary because they attract the hurt and bewildered—makes "Patching Up the Past" an ironic hymn to the pain that humans inevitably visit upon one another.

When Seay expresses his wariness of surrealist techniques—"images coming at random as in a dream, in no logical manner"—his view would seem to be shared by most of his Southern peers, whose verse is generally stamped by a respect for the communicable image and the values of the rational crafting of language. But as Seay's own verse demon-strates, as well as that of Miller Williams and William Mills, the metaphy-sical imagination is an enabling instrument that probes for continuities in Southern life that, like present life anywhere, suffers discontinuities. For those who write fully out of a tradition of the rural South their art is frankly shaped by the pressures of life-fronting actualities: sowing, ploughing, harvesting, sawing, fence mending, soil saving. The work of James Applewhite, Fred Chappell, Jim Wayne Miller, Van K. Brock, Jeff Daniel Marion, and others owes nothing to the patrician Vergilian vision of the Fugitives before them and little to the nineteenth-century philosophical belief in the unity of all being in which God, Man, and Nature fell into a shapely alternative Trinity. Rather, their work recalls the life on the old lands in synecdochic images: a grandmother sifting flour, the poet-as-child looking for arrowheads, the visceral experience of cleaning the family well or facing the annual slaughter of hogs for the family smokehouse, all assume iconographic importance for lives lived according to ancient patterns of submission and dependency, in cyclic rituals performed as practical folkways.

Perhaps the most striking of these poets is Fred Chappell, whose earlier talents as a novelist serve him well in the vivid geography and characterization of his poetry. Traces of his contemporaries—A. R. Ammons, George Garrett, perhaps Miller Williams—flash too often through *The World Between the Eyes* (1971). The weaker poems suffer from a dispersed, unanchored point of view; the strongest are those firmly fixed by a persona—the poet himself surveying his family, addressing his cough, sizing up other poets; and the poet's persona as the bookish, imaginative child ("lonely in the house of his fathers") in unpoetic Canton, North Carolina, especially "The Mother," "Sunday," and the title poem.

For *Midquest* (1981) Chappell constructs "Old Fred," not a literal autobiographical persona but a kind of "demographic example" in the manner of Jim Wayne Miller's "Brier," whose memory of the papermill-railroad town and its hardscrabble outlying hill farms is counterpointed by experience in the modern Southern city and the academy. In his uncut introduction to *Midquest* (in *The Small Farm* [1980]), Chappell notes that his long poem can incorporate some of the opportunities lost to the lyric of revelation that has so dominated twentieth-century poetry—"detachment, social scope, humor, reportage, discursiveness, portrayal of character and background, wide range of subject matter"—while simultaneously trying to preserve the crucial advantages of that kind of lyric—"intensity, urgency, metaphysical import, emotional authenticity." One of the most ambitious poems since *Paterson, Midquest* is a four-part meditation on time and place by Old Fred on his thirty-fifth birthday, May 28, 1971. The first part, *River*, takes its shaping motif from the enduring power of one element, water, the countervailing force against which this temporal mortal assesses his being; the succeeding parts—*Bloodfire, Wind Mountain,* and *Earthsleep,* centering on fire, air, and earth—build on the accrued implications of the elements in the ongoing tensions between the temporary and the permanent. Chappell avoids the dangers of rigid predictability inherent in his formal organization in at least two ways: he so manipulates his persona that Old Fred becomes not merely a shrewd "Haywood County hill-billy" but a deft Odysseus, a faith-seeking Dante, a sensual Leopold Bloom on a wide-ranging journey through the mysteries of self, family, friends, and society; and he articulates his midlife journey in a bravura profusion of verse forms—rhyming couplets, terza rima, blank verse, free verse, Old English alliterative verse, traditional stanzas of varying rhyme schemes, verse epistles, even that most treacherous of forms, the prose poem. In Chappell's virtuoso quest, the wisdom of the ancients is invoked, dickered with, placed in perspective along with the Appala-chian wisdom of grandparents, parents, and an eccentric codger with the happy name of Virgil Campbell. Old Fred debates Big Issues with his fellow writers, and he begins and ends his meditations, both fleshly and spiritual, in bed with his wife Susan.

What lends coherence to *Midquest*, even more than the organizing scheme, is the verbal energy that informs every poetic mode within the sequence. Like Robert Penn Warren's impure poet, Chappell taps every level of discourse, both high and low, each one with equal facility emerging from the detail of a local situation: the marital bed, the burial of a mule, a panel dialogue on the literary symbol, a burning church, a baptism by immersion, the washing of milk cans, Vietnam war victims as martyrs, a "silver planet" that takes imaginative shape through a bout with fever. The idioms of Rimbaud, Louis Armstrong, the Carter family, a dozen writers ancient and modern, and the good old boy turned academic jostle each other provocatively, but all are subordinated to the intensity of a single voice, looping and circling with calculated spontaneity. Chappell's sense of improvisation reaches an efflorescence in "The Autumn Bleat of the Weathervane Trombone," in which Old Fred plays a Bach partita on the barn roof for an audience of Guern-sey cows.

> What a dazzle of driftage, what dribble of daft
> Storms the skin of the eye, I'm surfeit to bursting,
> Have mercy, October, my eyes have eaten all,
> I'm rich to the ears, my buttons are each in danger,
> O take this table away I've gluttoned on honey,
> Honey the heavy gold of time bronze bees
> Have hived in the apple belly of the sun

In the tumbling wit of wordplay, the playful allusiveness, the breathless alliterations, Chappell's music projects him, the cows, and us beyond the generating locale into an imaginative otherworld. This sense of im-provisation is paradoxically a sustaining strategy that not only brings individual poems to their natural completion but also knits up the interlinked poems into a grand whole. For all its unapologetic artifice and symmetry, Chappell's tetralogy is a raucous, buoyant, serious but unsolemn meditation on the place of the human in the natural order. In 1985 Fred Chappel was awarded the Bollingen Prize for the body of his work.

Robert Morgan is also a quintessential poet of locale, yet the literal rural landscape is more than a formative influence of what he calls his "archetypal acreage"—the North Carolina farm whose contours show up repeatedly in startling combinations. From *Zirconia Poems* (1969) to *Land Diving* (1976) he has appropriated places of water—cellars, cisterns, well houses, caverns, gullies—as ready metaphors for human functions. In this process of metaphorical transference, landscape and the human—rank vegetation and rutting sexuality—are interchangeable.

The rich variousness of these poets who write out of a rural South is perhaps best illustrated by the work of George Scarbrough, a Tennessee poet who began publishing in the early 1950s, and Wendell Berry, a Kentuckian whose writing career coincided with the rise of the ecological movement in America in the late 1960s.

Although Scarbrough no longer farms, the source of his subjects and the energy of their articulation derive from his younger days as the child of a tenant farmer. Despite their retrospective sympathy for the "easy way" of children who "put a full belly before a full barn," Scarbrough's memories of childhood are stark and fiercely ambivalent. They include the futile attempts to cultivate corn during drought times when mules drink freely of the water in the spring; abandoned orchards "that hardly remembered the apple"; lovemaking among the *disjecta membra* of a country slaughterhouse; hogpens choked with ironweed; snake-handling ceremonies conducted in single-minded ecstasy; a Cherokee father of both brutality and courage; angry instances of restrictive country manners and moralities; metaphysical anger occasioned by rural funerals, those sad reminders of "man's unsweet divinity" that insult "those who must do the work / Of cleaning up and filling the hole in after."

The tensions in Scarbrough's work stem largely from an almost primitive awe at the semiotics of nature—the message of animal tracks, ruined birds' nests, empty snake skins, torn spider webs—and the fearful suspicion that human words are forever incapable of conveying those meanings. Signs, sounds, and symbols are natural acrostics or cryptograms signifying richness that eludes mere language. Yet the poetic style that gradually evolves from the early volumes through *The Course Is Upward* (1951) to the verbal release of his later work in *New and Selected Poems* (1977) is one that comes from the caressing cultivation

551

of words for their own value and the sheer joy of indulgence in exotic diction, an indulgence that can make *intrados, wiffle,* and *riverine* as domesticated as *mule* and *plough.* One phrase—"the elegant cave / of my country mind"—from a later poem, "The House Where Rivers Join," suggests the tension that removes Scarbrough decisively from the bucolics of Jesse Stuart or the more skewed pastorals of Robert Frost, a tradition in which earlier readers were content to place him.

The couplets, sonnets, and sonnet sequences of the early volumes gradually give way to more interesting work: longer forms and variable lines of Scarbrough's own devising, some of them in free verse and some intricately stitched by assonance and eye rhymes. Noteworthy are at least three longer poems structured in unrhymed nine-line stanzas, the best of which, "The Private Papers of J. L. McDowell, M.D.," is the poet's tribute to his grandfather, incorporating the spidery words the "migratory medico" records in his daybook and a letter to his wife across the mountains urging her to join him. "Madness Maddened" is an eighteen-page poem in which the poet engages in a breathtaking stripping of the self. The domestic ordinariness of the situation—an ailing bachelor son tending to an aged mother in a dark form of house-wifery—is counterpointed by swirling half-dreams, fantasy, and erup-tive brooding. The intensity of its psychic compulsions and the speci-ficity with which the speaker faces his mortality without the falsifying guise of stoicism makes the descriptive tag *confessional poetry* ludi-crously inadequate. If "Tenantry" celebrates feats of human survival with full recognition of the emotional scars such survival incurs, "Mad-ness Maddened" is terrible and eloquent testimony to the scars themselves.

Most contemporary Southern poetry deriving from rural realities makes tentative affirmations out of the same stoic acceptance of one's "place" that Scarbrough scorns. But even rarer than Scarbrough's harsh resistances are those poets who see farming as a means of promoting insight into a grand principle of organic oneness. Wendell Berry, how-ever, boldly asserts the necessity for the accommodation of the self to the primitive gods of place. Following his return to Kentucky to live the life of a farmer, Berry so intensely shaped his work upon holistic prin-ciples that his is the only rural Southern poetry that can be termed eco-logical. Because that commitment informs everything he writes, many of Berry's poems aspire to the state of functional report, and the weaker ones bear the impress of ideology more than they do imagination. Floodtime, in which "uprooted trees, soil of squandered mountains, / the debris of kitchens, all passing seaward," triggers a strained medita-tion on "official meaningless deaths" in Vietnam. In his stronger poems, however, Berry confronts the depredations of the land out of a need to care for it, nourishing the land with assiduous labor the better to be nourished by it. In both kinds he tends to gloss his own meanings with greater explicitness than most of his contemporaries consider necessary. The too-literary effects of his early volume *The Broken Ground* (1964) disappear by the time of *Findings* (1969), in which a characteristic plain style emerges as the idiom most congenial to his gift; but the mature work begins properly in *Openings* (1968). Out of his earlier imitations of William Carlos Williams in both *Findings* and *Openings*, Berry's urgency to subordinate human rhythms to natural ones finds a technical correlative in the authoritative modulation of the line. Here also for the first time is the poet's assertion of harmony as a human necessity, a philosophical equivalent of Christian grace. Despite occasional flaccidity, these poems effectively articulate Berry's favorite theme: the busyness of man's conventional but chaotic life as opposed to the serenity with which nature conducts her business. The healing of human fragmentation and abstraction, he seems to argue, can be accomplished only through a more organic relationship between individual and place, and to that end, to counter the ongoing terrors of history and industry, his poems celebrate the liminal inspiration of soil, the almost primitive propitiating of agrarian tutelary spirits. His "Mad Farmer" poems ambivalently evoke ancient rights of behavior—the organic man as activist who disallows mere human interference and who remains innocent of the oratorical arts of persuasion. That these poems recur in both fables and dramatic monologues indicates that something of the angry ecologist in Berry has its source in an older, more primitive, almost animistic vision of man and earth.

Farming: A Hand Book (1970) incorporates the full range of Berry's interests. In addition to his antiwar, anticity verse, he exults in the more private mysteries of being. "I was born in a drouth year," begins "Water," and the poet proclaims himself a lover of wells, springs, and cisterns. "I am a dry man whose thirst is praise / of clouds, and whose mind is something of a cup." This Berry, who sings of his excitement in remaking, reworking, reanimating decayed farms, can also joyously submit to his own decay, "a patient willing descent into the grass." In "The Birth," a little Frost-like narrative, he acknowledges a darkness that is chthonic, a primordial eruption associated with "the old ground."

These and related themes reappear in *Clearing* (1977), a volume that reveals greater technical mastery of form than any of his previous volumes. Actually a suite of celebratory poems of variable measures, *Clearing* is his most integrated work. Here Berry attacks "the coming of numbers" that replace "life's history" and sings of physical labor, which

553

"clarifies / the vision of rest. In rest / the vision of rest is lost." One poem proclaims "the mystic order" to which man, beast, and earth belong. "Work Song" traces a kind of imaginative possession of the earth from "memory" to "legend" to "song" and finally to "sacrament." Constructed in short lines, usually irregular trimeter and tetrameter and with few figurative tropes, these related poems represent Berry's finest accomplishment in a stripped-down poetry of statement. In "Where," a historical survey of the deed to his own farm, Berry praises one of his predecessors with the appropriate eloquence of simplicity.

> He kept
> his place, milked and fed,
> waked and slept, helped
> his neighbors, imposed on none,
> was tolerably satisfied,
> and died.

And when he concerns himself as present keeper of his earth, his meditation becomes a prayer.

> Let
> my hands find their work
> —now there is no choice—
> in what is spoiled, and let
> my mouth find better words.

Thus, Berry effectively joins his two passions, farming and the making of art. "The farm is an infinite form," he says in a later poem, linking farm and poem through the process of active, loving cultivation. But if the family farm supplies a sense of place to a creating imagination that equates the process of farming to the making of poems, Berry engages in that process without the exaggerated elevation of the latter often seen in modern pastorals; such activities as putting on a new roof, sowing clover, or unloading cut timothy never function as mere metonymy for the poetic enterprise. As poet and farmer, Berry celebrates both terms of the equation.

The work of few poets in this generation—those like Scarbrough and Berry who literally write out of their ancestral soil, or those like Mills and Seay who respond to the humdrum culture of a contemporary village South—can be said to resemble that of such spiritual fathers as John Crowe Ransom, Allen Tate, Donald Davidson, or Robert Penn Warren. If the Nashville Fugitives were the first professional poets of the modern South, they were notably conspicuous because of not only their quality but also their sheer rarity. The later Renascence which they largely initiated was marked by a proliferation of poets from every state in the South, some working in isolation but many in the same inspiriting collegiality enjoyed by their counterparts in the Northeast and the Pacific Northwest. In subject, tone, and form, the generation of poets born in the years just following the publication of the Fugitive anthology (1928) consciously eschewed the practice of their elders, for whom regionalism was a quality to be refined out of poetry through the vigorous application of modernist principles. Contemporary Southern poets are self-conscious about neither regionalism nor modernism; both have been quietly absorbed as givens in their work. Their careers, however, often bear fruitful resemblances to those of their predecessors. Usually the products of colleges and universities, most of them are academics teaching creative writing or traditional courses in literature—many of them in institutions outside the South. Some—Dabney Stuart, Miller Williams, William Mills—are scholar-critics as well as poets. The fact that some, like Donald Justice and Jonathan Williams, are musicians as well as poets has had an important bearing on their aesthetics, their subjects, and often the forms of their characteristic poems. George Garrett and Wendell Berry are comfortable in writing fiction and poetry alike. Such widespread versatility among this generation has not diminished either its productivity or its commitment to poetry as a making art; indeed, much of the poetry resulting from such collateral interests can boast visible strengths that it would otherwise lack.

Randall Jarrell

Like several other twentieth-century Southern writers (John Crowe Ransom, John Peale Bishop, Allen Tate, and Robert Penn Warren, to name just the best known), Randall Jarrell could be called a "hyphenated" man of letters: poet-critic-novelist-teacher. Since his fiction and teaching are less important, we shall concentrate here on his career as poet and critic.

Jarrell was born in Nashville, Tennessee, May 6, 1914. He was raised there and, for a period, in California, where he lived with his mother and some of her people after his parents were divorced. He attended Vanderbilt University and then taught at Kenyon College for a few years before World War II. During the war he served in the Army Air Corps in Europe and afterward taught at Sarah Lawrence College and the Women's College of the University of North Carolina (now UNC-Greensboro). He died after being hit by a car October 14, 1965.

Jarrell's poetry resembles that of his most illustrious American contemporaries—Delmore Schwartz (1913–1966), John Berryman (1914–1972), and Robert Lowell (1917–1977)—whose work can be learned, innocent, anguished, and poised all at once. In some respects—such as attention to minute detail, awareness of mythic overtones, and sympathy for the "bottom dogs" of the world—they continued a shift of focus inaugurated by their great modernist precursors, preeminently Williams, Pound, and Eliot. But in some other respects, particularly a retreat from extreme technical innovations and an avoidance of obscurity, they were more staid than their ancestors. Most of them relaxed the discipline that had constricted the poetry of their youth, but they never achieved the rare heights of invention explored by Williams, Pound, and Eliot. The later generation inhabited an age of contraction and consolidation.

Jarrell specialized in a poetry indebted to earlier modern masters. His typical subject matter can be traced to Thomas Hardy, and his typical treatment, rather loose iambic lines with some rhyme, seems to owe a good deal to Robert Frost (though Jarrell uses urban or suburban gestures in the place of Frost's rural manner). More faintly, Jarrell's verses also display the influence of Rainer Maria Rilke, not only in their persistent tropism toward Germanic words and lore but also in a suave, precariously sophisticated verse-surface that seems always on the brink of failing to conceal great wounds of the spirit. In Jarrell's poems, the upper lip is never quite stiff.

Probably Jarrell's best, and certainly his best-known, poem is the five-line "Death of the Ball Turret Gunner," with its stark beginning line, "From my mother's sleep I fell into the State," and brutal close, "When I died they washed me out of the turret with a hose." This account of the death and disposal of a young victim of war seems related to Hardy's great poem of the Boer War, "Drummer Hodge," and ends with a reference to the same impersonal "they" that appear at the beginning of Hardy's poem: "They throw in Drummer Hodge to rest." The main difference between the poems is that Hardy maintains a cool third-person viewpoint that permits easy shifts from the particular victim to the alien landscape of Africa and on to a celestial, eternal vision. As compensation for the remoteness of the third person, Hardy's poem begins in the present tense with gross physical activity. Jarrell's choice of first person and past tense seems justifiable but may introduce some difficulties. The reader must wonder who is speaking in what sort of afterlife condition. There is also a problem with a pathetic victim who, from whatever perspective, seems all-too-ready to convert certain details of his own history into analytical myth with neat paradoxes that reverse the senses of sleep and waking, dream and nightmare, birth and death. Capitalized, "State" too easily migrates upward from a political condition to the condition of man. Even so, the poem remains powerful, dramatic, and perfectly articulated, especially the explosive "black flak" and the final rhyme. And the poem is the most compact evidence of Jarrell's sympathy for victims, losers, and other suffering people.

In most of Jarrell's best poems, the central figure is either a woman or a child (or himself as a child). As in the work of another Tennessean with Hollywood connections and a big heart—James Agee—the meaning of all the pain in a world of patriarchal adults is best distilled by the voice of a child or a woman. (It is probable that the ball turret gunner was an undersized person who had not even reached voting age.) The finest poems about women in Jarrell's work are "A Girl in a Library," "Next Day," "Woman," and "The Woman in the Washington Zoo."

Jarrell's most memorable criticism is to be found in his enthusiastic essays on Whitman, Frost, Stevens, Williams, Ransom, and Marianne Moore. About these precursors, Jarrell found a treasury of things to say

557

that are permanently sympathetic, useful, and refreshing. Loftier topics, such as those discussed in "The Obscurity of the Poet" and "The Age of Criticism," furnished a show of wit and erudition but not much in the way of sound general theory. Immediate challenges, such as writing quick book reviews, exploited Jarrell's unparalleled talents in a species of journalism almost never distinguished by talent. Here, for example, is part of a paragraph that Jarrell wrote in a review of Richard Wilbur's second book.

> Most of his poetry consents too easily to its own unnecessary limitations. An unusually reflective halfback told me that as a run develops there is sometimes a moment when you can "settle for six or eight yards, or else take a chance and get stopped cold or, if you're lucky, go the whole way." Mr. Wilbur almost always settles for six or eight yards; and so many reviewers have praised him for this that in his second book he takes fewer risks than in his first. (He is like one of those Southern girls to whom everybody north of Baltimore has said, "Whatever you do, *don't* lose that lovely Southern accent of yours"; after a few years they sound like Amos and Andy.)

This, a condign and accurate appraisal, is a prismatic example of Jarrell's characteristic humor. He brings in types from current lore—the halfback, Southern girls, everybody north of Baltimore—and makes up two authentic-sounding speeches for them. And in the sentence that follows the evocation of Amos and Andy, Jarrell quotes William Blake. Anybody with acute critical vision could size up a volume of poems, but Jarrell's amusing and dramatic presentation of his verdict shows much besides critical acuity. It shows that Jarrell had a heart and that it was in the right place. The heart with room for a reflective halfback and a harassed Southern girl could also contain a doomed gunner.

James Dickey

J ames Dickey burst rather belatedly (in his late thirties and early forties) into literary prominence as a result of a decade (1957–1967) of exceptional literary achievements. In 1957 he was a successful advertising copywriter by day and aspiring poet by night and on weekends. He was known to a few literati as a lively and often controversial reviewer of contemporary poetry for the *Sewanee Review* who made clear his disapproval in the 1950s and 1960s of the academic tameness of recent modernist poetry as well as the alternatives—beat poets with their practice of spontaneity as an end in itself, and confessional poets with their attempts to be both literal and pretentiously shocking.

By 1967 Dickey had published five volumes of poetry, climaxed by the National Book Award and the publication of his collected poems thus far, *Poems: 1957–1967*, documenting his ten-year accomplishments. The critical success of his poetry was more than matched by the popular reception of his novel, *Deliverance* (1970). Reinforced by the popularity of the movie version, it attracted a cult following among white-water devotees.

James Dickey has such a strong reputation for egocentricity that it is difficult to think of him in terms of influences. He is Southern born (in Atlanta, Georgia, February 2, 1923) and Southern bred (North Fulton High, Clemson, and Vanderbilt), but as a writer he is seldom regarded as particularly Southern. He admits to having "read a good deal" in the works of the Vanderbilt Agrarians and the New Critics, but has never regarded himself as "a latter-day Agrarian," and he has discernibly never been a modernist poet, writing strictly according to new critical formalist prescriptions. His affinities are with the neoromanticism of Theodore Roethke, that poet's celebrations of life while confronting the dark, and his ability, Dickey notes, to place "the body in an environment," a capsule description of what Dickey does well himself. Nevertheless, if not influences, analogies with Ransom, Tate, and Warren are at least arguable. Like the Agrarians, Dickey has his own forebodings regarding debilitating effects of urbanization and technology on the possibilities of a unified sensibility and on the perceived value of literature. Like the New Critics he has exhibited a strong conviction that not only content but also technique and form matter.

In *Self-Interviews* (1970) Dickey asserts believably that his readings at Vanderbilt in astronomy and in anthropology were influences on his poetry. From astrology he derived "a feeling of intimacy with the cosmos" and from anthropology a fascination with the perspectives on life of primitive peoples. Dickey sees modern man as deprived of instinctual life, laments its loss, and dramatizes the enhancing effects of its temporary restoration. What he very early identified as the "suspect" in poetry is a consequence of this loss—a modern literature produced with a dazzling technical virtuosity but with little or no *virtual* life. It was Monroe Spears who alerted Dickey to the possibilities inherent in the poet's expansive imagination for transcending the literal and the ordinary by "lying creatively."

In the early poem "The Performance" (1959) Dickey knew only the barest of facts, that Donald Armstrong was shot down in the Philippines and beheaded by his Japanese captors. Dickey transcends this horror by imagining Armstrong, at the exact moment his executioner's sword was set to strike, performing the perfect handstand that had always eluded him back at the base. In the poem "Falling" (published in *Mademoiselle* under the significant title "The Poet Tries to Make a Kind of Order"), Dickey imagines the falling stewardess surrendering her fantasies of rescue by sky divers or by diving into water and emerging miraculously. She makes "a kind of order" by achieving some aerodynamic control over her falling flight and even transcending the loneliness and absurdity of her death by ritualistic preparation for impact with earth. In *Drowning with Others* (1962), Dickey discovered his most highly touted means of transcendence, his "way of exchange," an empathetic identification permitting him imaginatively to become something more attuned to the processes of nature. In "A Dog Sleeping on my Feet" (1962), he observes his dog presumably dreaming of a fox hunt, and he imaginatively regains the animal excitement of a chase.

Dickey also relishes "the big forms" of nature, which permit him to import archetypal and mythological implications into his poems. In "The Vegetable King" (1959) an ordinary householder's dream, outside in early spring, is endowed with qualities of the mystery associated with the sacrifice of the Vegetable King, whose orphic dismemberment is necessary for the creation of spring. In "The Owl King" (1961) a blind child is taken up into the tree of the mythical Owl King and "metamorphosized," though blind, taught to see. The love of the young lovers, reported ambivalently by the woman preacher in "May Day Sermon" (1967), survives because Dickey is able to associate it inseparably with the resurrection of nature each spring.

Dickey's novel *Deliverance* offers its own version of transcendence. It dramatizes the deliverance of Ed Gentry and a trio of urbanized wastelanders from the ennui of modern living through entrance into the woods; then the survival of all but one in the deadly game of hunter and hunted enacted between city dwellers and backwoodsmen; finally, Ed Gentry's deliverance from his reawakened readiness to kill. In the poetry and in the novel, reconnecting with instinctual life is short-lived. The poet reverts to the human after imaginatively sharing the chase of his dog; Ed Gentry reenters normal living after killing amorally.

Dickey has been accused of writing in a social vacuum, of a gross insensitivity to social and political problems. He does demand for the poet the freedom to go beyond current issues, even to stand apart from society momentarily in order to "reconnect" with nature. Just before the war in Vietnam he wrote a poem, "The Firebombing" (1964), in which he tries to experience guilt for the Japanese slain in the firebombing of Tokyo; but he recalls the distance between the pilot in his plane above and the havoc below, and he cannot now cross the distance that time and a life of suburban comforts have forged. More damaging to his reputation was the comparatively unenthusiastic critical reception of much of his poetry published in the 1970s. His poems seemed to lack the strong narrative base, the felt presence of the persona as grateful survivor so essential to the earlier poems. Instead there was a much looser associational poetic structure, and (apparently) a much less affirmative attitude, as the middle-aged poet became more preoccupied with physical decline, madness, and death. He did write good poems during the second decade of his career—"The Eye-Beaters," "Apollo," "Pine," and "Madness," all in *The Eye-Beaters, Blood, Victory, Madness, Buckhead and Mercy* (1970). There are moments of the old poetic power in his long imitation, *The Zodiac* (1976), based on a poem by the Dutch poet Hendrik Marsman. Most promising are signs in *Puella* (1982), his tribute to femininity, of a return to the lyric grace amply evident in early poems like the much anthologized "The Lifeguard" (1961).

Dickey's total output, poetry and prose, is impressive. A second novel, *Alnilam*, is expected in the near future. There are four books of literary criticism, *The Suspect in Poetry* (1964), *Babel to Byzantium* (1968, reissued in 1983), *Self-Interviews* (1970), *Sorties* (1971); two illustrated books of poetic prose, *Jericho: The South Beheld* (1974) and *God's Images* (1977); a screenplay; and television adaptations. To

Dickey, poetry is "the center of the creative wheel." Nevertheless his work, prose and poetry, is tightly unified. The themes of the poetry are evident in the fiction; his criticism expounds on his poetic practice. What Dickey champions is a more intensified life, moments of beholding the world with a more totally responsive vision than modern urbanized life ordinarily allows. His version of "the body in an environment" is a ministry "fostered alike by beauty and by fear," with more fear than in Wordsworth's brand of romanticism. Reconnecting to the dynamic processes of nature cannot be retained too long without dire consequences for human nature. Dickey's themes may be neoromantic, and like current postmodernists he proposes the opposite of Eliot's modernist dictum that poetry "is not the expression of personality, but an escape from personality." Still, whether it is with the directness of the declarative sentences of his early poems or with the rhetorical power often conveyed by his later "split line," Dickey at his best displays the formal control of a superb craftsman.

WILLIAM HARMON

Archie Randolph Ammons

ittle in the ample work of A. R. Ammons displays his Southern identity in any overt detail. His first book, *Ommateum*, was published
in 1955 by a Philadelphia firm (which, like the first publishers of books
by E. A. Robinson and Gertrude Stein, is a trade house of what is po-
litely called the subsidy type). All his subsequent books have been published by presses in the Midwest and Northeast, and for most of the
time since 1952 he has made his home away from the South. Except for
such variants as "anch" and "sprankled" for "inch" and "sprinkled" (in
rather uncharacteristic poems called "Carolina Said-Songs"), Southern
vernacular plays very little part in his poetry. He could be called local,
since he has a potent sense of place; the titles of some of his poems and
books are place-names (*Corsons Inlet, Northfield Poems,* "Triphammer
Bridge"), but the places are mostly in New Jersey and New York.

Even so, much that distinguishes Ammons' poetry could be traced to
the pervasive, persistent influences of his native North Carolina. He was
born near Whiteville, in Columbus County, which remains today much
as it was when he was born there in 1926: flat, poor, parched, and
sparsely populated. It is in the "Sandhills" of North Carolina, close
enough to the Atlantic to keep the soil and terrain of the shore but too
far away to enjoy many of the shore's occupational and recreational
benefits. Ammons served in the United States Navy during World War II,
received a bachelor's degree from Wake Forest College in 1949, worked
as a businessman in New Jersey from 1952 to 1964, then joined the
faculty of Cornell University where he has been ever since.

Beginning in an austere environment, Ammons developed into a
rustic poet with elemental vision registered by a correspondingly elemental voice. His is a compound eye like that of an insect ("ommateum") that breaks up the world into a mosaic of manifold atoms of
sight provisionally summed up into a sort of mobile cubist unity that
preserves the multitudinousness of the world but at the same time honors its general language. Language itself—especially written language

and most especially written language in the emphatic form of poetry—encompasses both the multiplicity of the many (by foregrounding the physical anatomy of utterance) and the unity of the one (by having to stay forever at least one semantic remove from things). Ammons' is an eccentric poetry poised delicately between centripetal and centrifugal impulses, so that one can say that Ammons is both peculiarly Southern (plain, modest, humble, country-courtly, reverent, eloquent, stubborn, humorous, somatic, idiosyncratic) and not particularly of any region or period. The earliest important critical appreciation of his work came from the likes of Harold Bloom and Richard Howard, neither of whom is at all Southern, so that, whatever his origins, pedigree, or accent, Ammons' appeal is broadly and even patriotically American. (Not that he is ecumenical, either; even with his current celebrity, he has received little notice from British critics.)

Fully nine years after *Ommateum*, Ammons published *Expressions of Sea Level* (1964), and a steady stream has flowed ever since: *Corsons Inlet* (1965), *Tape for the Turn of the Year* (1965), *Northfield Poems* (1966), *Selected Poems* (1968), *Uplands* (1970), *Briefings* (1971), *Collected Poems 1951–1971* (1972), *Sphere: The Form of a Motion* (1974), *Diversifications* (1975), *The Snow Poems* (1977), *The Selected Poems: 1951–1977* (1978), *Selected Longer Poems* (1980), *A Coast of Trees* (1981), and *Worldly Hopes* (1982). Beginning with a Guggenheim Fellowship in 1968, Ammons and his work have been heavily rewarded: a National Book Award, a Bollingen Prize, a National Book Critics Circle Award, an award from the American Academy of Arts and Letters, and beginning in 1981, a five-year bestowal of extraordinary generosity from the MacArthur Foundation.

Some of Ammons' poems are tiny. "Coward" consists of one line only. Some are long but thin. *Tape for the Turn of the Year*, though printed as an orthodox book, was written originally on a roll of adding machine tape. And some of the poems are long and wide, secreted in solid stanzas of three or four lines. In an enterprising group of experiments—*Essay on Poetics, Extremes and Moderations, Hibernaculum*, and *Sphere*, dating mostly from the late 1960s and early 1970s—Ammons set up as a signally successful broker of a happy marriage between two complementary domestic American poetries: William Carlos Williams' inclusive passion for unruly things and Wallace Stevens' exclusive rage for ordered ideas. Ammons, a fine painter and musician as well as a poet, has devised a unique idiom that robustly asserts a nearly absolute graphic order inside of which, however, anything can happen. The visual regularity is not matched by any logical, narrative, grammatical, or rhythmic regularity. In the finest of these long poems (*Hibernaculum* and *Sphere*) the equilibrium between regularity and chaos is chastely conceived and perfectly executed. Here, with a subtle allusion to Keats and a blatant paroxysm of neologism, is a wholly characteristic passage from *Hibernaculum*:

54

much have I studied, trashcanology, cheesespreadology,
laboratorydoorology, and become much enlightened and
dismayed: have, sad to some, come to care as much for

a fluted trashcan as a fluted Roman column: flutes are
flutes and the matter is a mere substance design takes
its shape in: take any subject, everything gathers up

around it: friend of mine is studying barbedwireology
and he finds you can marshal up much world and history
around the discipline: barbedwire limitations and

55

intellectual definitions produce about the same
securities and disasters: I think a lot about meter and
right away it becomes the mirror in which I see the face

of the times . . .

The poem is in 112 such stanzas—three 3-line groups about 60 typed characters across. Although not strictly justified, the right-hand margin is about as regular as it is in ordinary typed prose. But that rigid graphic discipline is the only rule in the poem. However much he may think about meter, Ammons rarely employs it. The vocabulary and syntax both seem open-ended, and the reliance on the colon suggests a fluid continuity at odds with the boxy discreteness of the printed stanzas.

Here Ammons is improvising and experimenting with what, in the jargon of these high-tech times, might be called "digital prosody." In normal "analogue" prosody, the printed line is an analogue to a spoken line—further zoned by rhymes, punctuation, and spaces—which, in turn, is a fortified acoustic analogue to the semantic line. In digital prosody, however, the printed line is just that: an adherence to an arbitrary convention dictating *that* the lines end but not at all dictating *how* they should end. Likewise, a stanza may end *and, the,* or *of.* In *The Snow Poems*, Ammons adds yet another digital dimension to such dynamic play between order and disorder. Each of these 120 poems has a title, but in each case the title is merely the same as the first line. A poem may, for example, be called "My Father Used to Tell of an." There is plenty new under the sun, and poets like Ammons offer eloquent and convincing testimony to that fact.

Black Writers in a Changed Landscape, Since 1950

The history of black writers and black writing in the South since 1950 is the history of a group of relatively young individuals who struggled to find means of expressing their literary responses to the civil rights movement and who chose to retain distinctive voices against the rhetorical onslaught of other young black writers, primarily located in the northern United States, who were identified with the black arts movement of the 1960s. The changes in the political and social climate in the 1950s gave these writers license to explore in greater detail many of the themes and subjects generally ignored or merely touched upon by earlier generations of Southern black writers. The changes also gave them the inspiration to form support groups and publishing outlets in the South instead of migrating North to the traditional publishing centers.

It is increasingly difficult to isolate all the criteria that would identify a writer as "Southern." For the sake of bolstering a literature and cleansing the literary reputation of the part of the country most frequently maligned, scholars and critics have been broad in the definitions that would allow them to claim a number of writers who reside both within and outside the southern United States. No less is this true of black American writers. Clearly Richard Wright was born and raised in Mississippi, but Maya Angelou barely passed through Arkansas before moving on to California; yet both are claimed as Southern. And a more problematic case is that of Sonia Sanchez; though born in Birmingham, Alabama, Sanchez has pursued her work so that it is neither as geographically nor as thematically tied to the South as that of other black writers. For the purpose of this essay, which is designed to treat black writers in the South since 1950, I have chosen to focus on writers who were born and raised in the South *and* whose primary works are set in the South, or whose works raise issues peculiarly deriving from the political and social climate of the South.

Some of the writers who experienced the changes brought about by the civil rights activity of the 1950s and the black aesthetic and the black arts movement of the 1960s bridge the gap between older and younger writers. These include Margaret Walker, born in Birmingham, Alabama, in 1915, Albert Murray, born in Nokomis, Alabama, in 1916, and Robert Deane Pharr, born in Richmond, Virginia, in 1916. It is Walker, however, whose publications extend from the Second World War into the 1960s and 1970s. In 1942, Walker won the Yale University Younger Poets Competition with *For My People*, a volume originally submitted in completion of her master's thesis in 1940 at the University of Iowa; the book established her reputation as a poet who reflected the struggles of black people and the hope that social conditions would improve. The title poem of the volume has been anthologized many times.

Few writers are able to change with the times, to redirect their creations into the dominant modes that political and social realities might encourage. Gwendolyn Brooks is an exception in that she transcended her 1940s beginnings and became a model of inspiration to many of the younger, militant writers of the activist, nationalistic 1960s. By contrast, Margaret Walker, whose novel *Jubilee* appeared in 1966 and won the Houghton Mifflin Literary Award, was not similarly able to inspire younger writers on such a broad scale. Walker's historical novel, which she had begun many years before, perhaps smacked too much of the social circumstances that the aesthetic of the 1960s worked to push into the background. None of the younger writers had time for a black woman who remained loyal to a slave heritage that blacks were still struggling to overcome in the 1960s. Thus Walker's work, despite its artistic accomplishments, was outdated from the date of its publication. It would be the late 1970s and early 1980s before scholars began to look at the novel for the good things it accomplished and for the solidness of its creations. But the approach to the novel was still not holistic; for example, a critic could praise Walker's use of the folk tradition, especially her use of music, without making reference to the many objectionable aspects of the novel, such as Vyry's loyalty to her white mistress.

Walker did receive praise for the litanylike fervor of the title poem in *For My People* as well as for the use of folk materials in such poems as "Molly Means." Although Walker remained on the scene in the late 1960s and 1970s as a teacher (primarily at Jackson State University in Mississippi), lecturer, and frequenter of conventions, she was looked upon as one whose achievements were in the past, someone who had earned respect but to whom no undue attention need be given. Her *Prophets for a New Day* (1970) and *October Journey* (1973), though praised, did not bring the same critical acclaim as *For My People*. Although her younger contemporaries might have been reluctant to praise, they nevertheless share with Walker an optimistic outlook for the political and social future of black people in the United States. She is spiritual if not designated godmother to them.

Walker's "Let a new earth rise" stanza of "For My People" resounded the hopeful tone for the 1960s and 1970s. Hope has always been an undercurrent in the writings of black Americans, no matter what part of the country they called home. In the works of Alice Walker and Ernest Gaines, two of the prominent Southern black writers since 1950, hope becomes almost a tangible symbol. In *The Autobiography of Miss Jane Pittman* (1971), Gaines may properly be said to be "preaching the great sermon" inspired by the activities of Martin Luther King, Jr. In the world in which Miss Jane lives, the search for a savior began in the days of slavery and continued in each new boy child born in the quarters and the shacks which marked the transition to freedom. The longing, the waiting, the constant hoping for better things that define the tone of Gaines's novel also define the climate in the South and throughout the black national community in the years immediately preceding Gaines's writing of the novel. Echoing the words of the song, "How long, O God, how long?," the novel essentially asks the same question. For black people who waited through slavery for deliverance, and waited through sharecropping for freedom, the first two quarters of the twentieth century had not offered very much more. The conditions under which Miss Jane and her fellow blacks reside on that Louisiana plantation in the early 1960s are not substantially different from those during Gaines's birth in 1933 and the years of his growth, or from those during Reconstruction. And just as they hoped for change then—in spite of suffering, pain, and death—so they continued to hope for change through the integration and voting rights of the 1960s.

That element of hope is no less manifested in Alice Walker's picture of the sharecropping conditions in Georgia, where she was born in 1944. Her novel, *The Third Life of Grange Copeland* (1970), complements Gaines's in its depiction of the dehumanizing, brutal effects of not owning oneself even after being freed from slavery. But it also depicts the painfully destructive consequences the owned individuals heap upon themselves. Grange can be forced into sharecropping, but he makes the choice to beat his wife. His son Brownfield may be similarly forced into that sharecropping syndrome, but he makes the decision to abuse his wife and children, to poison animals for the fun of it, and finally to blow off his wife's head with a shotgun. The novel paints blacks not only as victims, but as victimizers. Against that kind of twofold dehumanization, then, one has to be especially vigilant in maintaining an ounce of hope. Grange, who has indirectly caused his wife to poison herself and her child by walking out on them, manages to retain an element of hope in the face of all the brutal experiences that he initiates and that are initiated against him. Like Miss Jane, he finds himself putting his last ounce of hope in the civil rights movement in the South. Miss Jane never made it to the North after emancipation; Grange has gone and found it to be more dehumanizing than his experiences in the South. His conscious decision to return to the South is a literary manifestation of a phenomenon that would become widespread in the late 1960s and after. Grange's movement reverses the traditional pattern of escape envisioned for black people in America, and it reflects the tone of the political: yes, things could work out in the South; yes, it was better to take a stand where one had roots than to die on the cold, forbidding streets of the North; yes, there was a future south of the Mason-Dixon Line.

The tone of these works, in spite of all the suffering, pain, and death strewn through their pages, is the possibility for something better. In contrast to the rounds of dehumanization and despair that characterize the stories in Richard Wright's *Uncle Tom's Children*, the writers in this changed landscape after 1954 could envision something beyond the endless cotton rows and the forged debts. They espoused hope in the same way that Richard Wright espoused the primitive instinct to go on without hope, even in the face of despair.

Walker ends *The Third Life of Grange Copeland* with a focus on the voting-rights marches in Grange's town, but in *Meridian* (1976) she joins some of the younger black writers who came to prominence in the 1960s and who participated in the civil rights movement; she makes the movement her primary subject. *Meridian* is perhaps the most memorable of the works in this vein; it depicts the involvement of the title character in civil rights activity both during the heyday of the movement and when it was no longer fashionable. Walker draws upon her own experiences as a worker in voter registration and other activities in Mississippi and Georgia in the 1960s to portray Meridian's intense involvement in marches, voter registration, and desegregation of public facilities. Having deserted her child and husband to commit herself, paradoxically, to a life of improving conditions for black people, Meridian finds it hard to give up that pledge once the fervor of the movement has subsided. She therefore continues her solitary crusade against white Southern sheriffs and others who would stand in the way of progress. Strangely effective, indeed almost "touched in the head" in the manner of Harriet Tubman, Meridian not only has her small triumphs but succeeds in inspiring those who would prefer not to be inspired to follow in her footsteps. An exploration of the dissolution of the civil rights movement, the novel is no less an exploration of its psychological impact upon a particular kind of committed individual. The movement, from one perspective, may have destroyed Meridian's homelife, but it represents the only fulfillment she finds in life; when it slows down, her dogged continuance successfully conveys Walker's point that the future in the South is possible only through constant vigilance.

The changes the civil rights movement brought about in the Southern black writer's conception of character can also be seen in Ted Shine's one-act play, *Contribution* (1969). In it, Shine, who currently teaches in Texas, depicts confrontations between a white Southern sheriff and the blacks who want to integrate a lunch counter in his town, and between one of the demonstrators, a Northern-born young black man, and his Southern grandmother. Mrs. Love, the grandmother, accuses her Northern relative of being misguided, in the sense that he has come South hoping to help the needy blacks there. Southern blacks have managed very well, she maintains, and it is outsiders like her grandson who are literally shaking in their shoes when they tread upon Southern soil. While Southern blacks may appreciate their help, they are not in desperate need of it.

Mrs. Love, a servant to the sheriff, has managed to make her "contribution" to the civil rights movement by using her invisible position as a servant to poison all of her masters. Her role enabled her to come into close enough contact with them to accomplish her objective, and similarly, through its acquiescent nature, saved her from suspicion when the deaths were discovered. Clearly a post-1963 character, Mrs. Love also shows how Southern black writers became more willing after the movement to defy some of the unspoken and unwritten taboos that characterized their writing prior to the movement. If militancy, even through indirection, could come to Southern soil, then that presaged a different kind of hope for the black population in general as well as for black writers.

Black readers and critics have not been especially tolerant of writers who broached subjects that reflected, from the evaluators' points of view, negatively upon the black community. Therefore, some topics have been consistently ignored by black writers. It has only been in recent years that these writers have been willing to treat subjects such as incest, lesbianism, and homosexuality. Northerner James Baldwin was early in the treatment of homosexuality, and in his most recent novel, *Just Above My Head* (1980), he treats the subject of incest. Ralph Ellison in *Invisible Man* (1952) offered a near-surrealistic approach to incest, as did Toni Morrison in *The Bluest Eye* (1970). For Southern black writers, however, explicit treatment of such topics has lingered behind their non-

Southern counterparts. Notable exceptions are the lesbian relationship portrayed by Ann Allen Shockley in *Loving Her* (1974) and the incestuous and lesbian relationships Alice Walker describes in *The Color Purple* (1982). Shockley's novel is Southern more in its writer's origins than in its development of theme or in its scenery, for it focuses upon a middle- to upper-class interracial bohemian community, the likes of which are rare in the South. Walker's novel, on the other hand, concentrates upon a black woman "born and bred" in the South. Celie, the main character, is raped repeatedly by her stepfather and bears two children as a result of those violations; he passes the children along to a neighboring childless couple. When Celie is shunted off like chattel and married to a man twenty years her senior, her opinion of herself is so low that she acquiesces to wife-beating for the twenty years of her married life. It is only through involvement in a lesbian relationship with the woman who has borne two children for Celie's husband that Celie finds the wholeness that has been missing from her life. Yet Walker's treatment of the lesbian relationship is wrought with the fairy-tale, school-girl discovery of sexuality by two women who are well into their forties. No matter how unrealistic the treatment of the two characters, though, Walker nevertheless moves the literary portrayal of Southern black women to another level of conception in this Pulitzer Prize–winning novel.

One culmination of the changed landscape in the third quarter of the twentieth century for Southern black American writers came in the publication of Alex Haley's *Roots* (1978). Advocating a spirit of celebration, triumph, endurance combined with unity, and a certain degree of militancy, this novel of family and racial history differed substantially in tone from other historical novels that had treated the slave experience in the United States. Beginning with the publication of excerpts from the work in *Reader's Digest*, Haley's story became a media phenomenon. Nor was the attention without justification; for many who had seen the changes of the 1960s, Haley's work captured the possibilities that existed for black writers with the necessary talent and imagination.

Haley's story of his search for his African family, through the tidbits of information provided by his American ancestors and passed down through each generation, conveyed to black Americans in general that the slave heritage was not their only tangible source of ethnic identification. If Haley could plow his way through that tangled field to a stronger heritage, then others could as well. Haley moved the depiction of the slave background beyond that of Margaret Walker in *Jubilee* by portraying a broader cast of defiant slaves, ones who ran away or fought back even if it meant losing a limb or being raped in punishment. The media images that brought the characters to life solidified the pride and defiance that progressive blacks felt in reading the novel; viewers will long remember the graceful maneuverings of Lou Gossett as Fiddler and the antics of Ben Vereen as Chicken George, and LeVar Burton as the wide-eyed, innocent Kunta Kinte who is slowly transformed from enthusiastic African to somber slave. The time was right for Haley's work; the changed landscape made a celebration of slave ancestors and African forebears a source of pride. In a land where many blacks adopted Xs because they did not know the names of their ancestors, Haley's roots made them know that the Xs could, with diligence, be replaced with meaningful surnames.

Albert Murray, steeped in the culture of southern Alabama and in the folk tradition so central to it, drew upon both those traditions in the works that brought recognition to him in the late 1960s and early 1970s. He celebrated at home what Haley's work would do later with the return to Africa. Murray's *Trainwhistle Guitar* (1974) depicts growing up in rural Alabama in the first half of the twentieth century. His characters may be broke, but they are not poor; their richness comes in the heroes they make of the commoners among them and in the intrinsic qualities of the life and land they share. "The Man" and "Little Buddy," the adolescents, admire Luzana Cholly (old Luze) precisely because he is a traveling bluesman who has earned respect from those who would usually not give such largesse to a black man. Although his world may be right for him, he recognizes that the boys in the community who admire him must find a different way to make their way in the world. He adapted to his times, and they must adapt to theirs; travel was his mode of adaptation, but education must be theirs. A part of old Luze's stance in the story is to see himself as guide, a role model in spite of his material poverty. The spirit he passes along to the boys is one that has been tested in the fire of change.

Throughout his novel, Murray celebrates the cultural forms that are intrinsic to the black community. His characters listen to jazz and to the blues, go to traditional churches, play their rhymes and games, and bask in the poetic language characteristic of their environment. Murray explored that richness of culture in *The Hero and the Blues* (1973) and again in *Stomping the Blues* (1976), which posits the theory that the blues were made for dancing, not just for listening.

Other writers joined Murray in focusing upon themes that emanated from within and were peculiar to the black community. Thus one trend of the literature of this period is that it is less directly reactive to the larger white community. Robert Deane Pharr, for example, in *The Book of Numbers* (1969) created a work in which the action is exclusively centered upon black people within a black community. Pharr sets his novel in a Southern city in the 1930s where blacks own a numbers bank with assets of over a million dollars. Usually treated as an urban, Northern phenomenon, the numbers game is shown on Southern soil and developed within the context of the impact it has upon characters drawn from all levels of the black community. Whites are not only absent from this world; they are barely mentioned. Pharr was born in Richmond in 1916 and, like Margaret Walker, is therefore older than most of the writers of this period, yet his work reflects the legacy of the black arts movement in its emphasis upon a black community defined by the features that are an integral part of it.

Three other writers, representing different generations but all influenced by the desire to reflect black culture in their works, are James Alan McPherson, Arthenia J. Bates Millican, and Julia Fields. A native Georgian, James Alan McPherson has published two critically acclaimed collections of short stories. The first, *Hue and Cry*, appeared in 1969. The second, *Elbow Room*, won the Pulitzer Prize for fiction in 1978. Although McPherson is a graduate of the Law School of Harvard University, he has been employed fulltime as a teacher of creative writing. The last post he held was at the University of Virginia, from which he resigned upon being awarded one of the prestigious MacArthur fellowships. Arthenia J. Bates Millican, native South Carolinian and professor of English at various universities, has published *Seeds Beneath the Snow* (1969), a collection of short stories, and *The Deity Nodded*, a novel. She focuses upon the rural South and how black people there deal with the changes they must face. She is especially adept at capturing the speech of her characters and in keeping them within the environments from which that rich speech derives. Julia Fields, born in Uniontown, Alabama, in 1938, has published two collections of poetry, *East of Moonlight* (1973) and *A Summoning A Shining* (1976). The second volume illustrates Fields's kinship to Gayl Jones in its concern with the past, the present, and the future. Fields's creation of characters such as "Big Un," the grandfather whose heroic stature overshadows the present, and her depiction in "Legacies" of children who are named for past heroes connect her concerns with time and history. But Fields is also concerned with racial injustice and the oppression that weighs black people down in the South as well as in the urban areas of the North. Fields has also written fiction. One of her stories, "Not Your Singing, Dancing Spade," which deals with an interracial marriage, appeared in *Black Fire* (1968) and another, "August Heat," which deals with salvation in a traditional black church, in *Callaloo* (October, 1978).

Some of the writers of this period, though Southern in origin, have been identified more with the North than with the South. Sonia Sanchez, though born in Birmingham, Alabama, in 1939, is a New Yorker by schooling and experience, and most of her writing career has been spent in the North. She became one of the most important spokespersons for the black arts movement of the 1960s, voicing nationalistic concerns more than regional ones. Her works reflect that nationalistic bent as well as the urban, Northern experiences with which she is most familiar. She has published several volumes of poetry, including *Homecoming* (1968), *We a BadddDDDD People* (1970), *Love Poems* (1973), *Blues Book for Blue Black Magical Women* (1974), and *I've Been a Woman* (1978).

The pattern of Sanchez' life is similar to that of A. B. Spellman and Nikki Giovanni, both Southerners by birth. Spellman, born in Elizabeth City, North Carolina, in 1934, moved to New York in 1959 and has remained there since. He published *The Beautiful Days*, a collection of poetry, in 1965, and *Four Lives in the Bebop Business*, a study of four jazz personalities, in 1966. Again, his concerns are more nationalistic than Southern, though certainly the two are not mutually exclusive. Giovanni, like Sanchez and Spellman, was born in the South (in Knoxville, Tennessee, in 1943). Her autobiography, *Gemini* (1971), comes closer to capturing her roots in Southern soil than any of her other works. A few of the poems paint scenes of visiting in or remembering the South, such as "Knoxville, Tennessee," but the majority of them from this period focus on the larger themes of bringing about change in American society and inspiring black people to relish their blackness.

Also like Sanchez, Giovanni found herself at the heart of the black arts movement and became, perhaps more than any other female writer, the household name for a generation of black students. Her no-nonsense poems in *Black Feeling Black Thought Black Judgment* (1970) inspired younger blacks to examine their individual blackness in relation to the larger population and to take up their symbolic guns when necessary to further the moral, political, and social revolution in the United States. Giovanni was one of the first to signal the commercial value of the movement of the 1960s when she recorded many of her poems, such as "Ego Tripping." Black people, especially students, bought the records, listened, and imitated the style of poetry reading that Giovanni, Don L. Lee (Haki Mahabuti), and others made standard in the 1960s.

Sanchez, Spellman, and Giovanni are all known for the stylistic experimentation that characterized much of the poetry of the black arts movement. Unusual typography, lowercase letters, sentenceless clusters of ideas, black street dialect, use of profanity, and harsh, realistic confrontations between blacks and whites are all a part of their works. In

"The True Import of the Present Dialogue, Black vs. Negro," Giovanni asks, "Nigger, can you kill? . . . Can a nigger kill a honkie? . . . Can you kill the nigger in you?" Or consider how Spellman sets up the first couple of lines of one of his poems.

> friends i am   like you   tied
> to you & the delicate chain   knots

Or Sanchez these lines in "summary."

>   fool
> black
>   bitch
> of fantasy. life
> is no more than
>   gents
>   and
>   gigolos (99% *american*)
> *liars*
> *and*
> *killers* (*99%* american)
>   dreamers
>   and drunks (99% *american*)
> (*ONLY GOD IS 100%* AMERICAN)

Typographically reminiscent of E. E. Cummings, the writers of the sixties nonetheless added their own distinctive features to this visual break with tradition.

Many of the writers of this period also wrote in more than one genre, frequently with equal dexterity. Alice Walker, for instance, has been nominated for awards in both fiction and poetry, culminating in the Pulitzer Prize for fiction with *The Color Purple* (1982). Walker has also written criticism and essays of an autobiographical and lyrical nature. Likewise, Julia Fields has written both fiction and poetry, as has Margaret Walker. Albert Murray is not only adept at fiction, but also at cultural history, particularly evaluation of the blues genre. Tom Dent of New Orleans has written criticism, poetry, and plays, thus joining Sonia Sanchez in these combinations of creativity (Dent has also written fiction).

There have been a few instances of young black writers in the South trying to find their own outlets for literary expression. One of these efforts, headed by John O'Neal and supported by writers like Tom Dent, culminated in the formation of the Free Southern Theatre. Established in 1963 as a part of the Student Non-Violent Coordinating Committee and viable through 1978, the Free Southern Theatre traveled throughout the South producing shows written by members of the group as well as those by better-known black American writers.

Another regional effort to bring writers and other artists together prompted the formation of the Southern Black Cultural Alliance. Formed in 1972 and still thriving in the mid- to late-1970s, this group met semi-annually in cities throughout the South. Although it professed to be "a loose regional association encompassing groups from Miami to Austin," the organization was hampered by the great distances between its member units. Still, at the semiannual meeting at Tougaloo College in May of 1978, several artistic groups affiliated with the larger one were reported to be thriving; they were Black Fire Company in Birmingham, Theater of Afro-Arts and M Ensemble in Miami, Beale Street Repertory Company in Memphis, Ethiopian Theatre and Free Southern Theatre and Congo Square Writers Union in New Orleans, Urban Theater in Houston, and the Afro-American Players in Austin.

The Congo Square Writers Workshop in New Orleans introduced many young black writers in its first anthology of poems, *Bamboula*, which appeared in 1976. Although no writer included in that volume has become well known, the volume was nevertheless significant in marking a time in history when black writers once again found their own outlets for publication, as they had done in the 1920s. Tom Dent, a member of that workshop, is perhaps the best known of its participants. His *Magnolia Street* (1976), poems focusing on black New Orleans, received favorable reviews, and his play, *Ritual Murder*, was performed in 1978 by the Ethiopian Theatre in New Orleans.

One of the publishing outlets begun in the South during this period has become a major force in publishing works by established authors such as Alice Walker, Gayl Jones, and Ernest Gaines, and by the up-and-coming writers such as Tom Dent, Lorenzo Thomas, Pinkie Gordon Lane, Patricia Jones, and Brenda Marie Osbey. *Callaloo*, founded and edited by Charles H. Rowell, and produced by the English Department of Southern University in Baton Rouge, first appeared in 1976 primarily as a result of contributions solicited from supportive individuals. Subtitled *A Black South Journal of Arts and Letters*, *Callaloo* is "devoted largely to the creative and critical writings, visual arts, culture and life of the Black South." Relocated to the University of Kentucky at Lexington in 1977, when Rowell joined the English faculty there, the journal is now thriving and appearing regularly after a period of intermittent publication. Rowell has managed to assemble an impressive editorial board and to devote special issues of *Callaloo* to individuals and to groups of writers from the South. One issue focuses on Ernest Gaines (May, 1978); another is a special number on women poets (February, 1979); and yet another, in a section called "South of the South," focuses on Caribbean and Latin writers of African descent (February—October, 1980). The February—May, 1982, issue is devoted almost exclusively to Sterling Brown; the October, 1982, issue has a special section on Gayl Jones; and the February, 1983, issue is devoted almost exclusively to Aimé Céaire. The journal has become one of the most significant voices reflecting the changed landscape for black writers in the South.

DONALD R. NOBLE

The Future of Southern Writing

D iscussions of the future of Southern writing rarely occur. Such discussions as do take place are not really about the future at all; they instead take the form of debate over two already shopworn questions. First, is there still such a thing, an entity, that one can call the South, which might reasonably be expected to produce a kind of writing called "Southern literature"? If the answer is no, if it is concluded that the South is now culturally one with the rest of the country in faith, fashion, accent, occupations, preoccupations, economics, and so on, then there is little point in talking any longer about a distinctive literature from this region. Yet, for every sign of homogenization there is equal evidence that Southern life retains traditions and values, attitudes and accents that will be a very long time in the erasing. For the foreseeable future there is a South, therefore a Southern literature.

A corollary to this question, which also gives rise to some sprightly debate, concerns just who is or is not a Southern writer. It has some parallels in the debate over how to determine who is Jewish ("Funny, you don't sound Southern"). Must a Southern writer have been born and have spent his formative years in the South? Is it the subject matter that defines Southern writing, and not the author? Could a Yankee of long residence be considered a Southern writer? What about novels by Southerners that take place in New York City or Paris? It is clear that there is no particular litmus test for literary Southernness, and that a Southerner is probably someone who has spent his childhood in the South and conceives of himself as Southern, even if he resides in Connecticut now.

The second question often debated concerns whether the Southern Renascence is still going on. If we define the Renascence closely, in terms of the historical and cultural forces that gave rise to the flowering of letters between 1925 and 1955, then one must suppose that by definition it is over. But this is of itself a useless conclusion. There is no point

578

in expecting writers raised in the fifties and sixties to write in the mode of Faulkner, Caldwell, Wolfe, or Warren. These writers came of age in a different South, so their subjects, characters, and concerns and the voices they use to express them will of necessity be different. The ways in which this new writing will partake of the new and the old together may be seen in the work of all the writers under discussion here, but particularly in the work of two of the younger writers. These two, Beth Henley and Barry Hannah, both of Mississippi, a playwright and a fiction writer respectively, won praise and attention with their first attempts. Henley, who won the Pulitzer Prize with her comedy *Crimes of the Heart* in the 1980–1981 season, when she was only twenty-nine, bids fair to be the premier Southern playwright of the 1980s. Her first play chronicles two days in the lives of the MaGrath sisters of Hazelhurst, Mississippi. The youngest of the three, Babe, has just shot her husband for being mean and "because I didn't like his stinking looks." The other two sisters face crises, too. Lenny, thirty, is celebrating her birthday when she learns her horse has been struck by lightning. Meg, the middle sister, has just given up on a career as a singer to take a job in a dog food factory. The three are having trouble finding Babe a good lawyer because, as it happens, her husband was the best lawyer in Hazelhurst. This play takes place entirely in the MaGrath kitchen, and is propelled almost entirely by witty, anecdote-filled dialogue. Henley's characters are modern young women, but the stuff of this play is the gossip and stories Henley asserts she can hear in abundance any day in her childhood home in Jackson.

Barry Hannah is a different kind of writer. His first novel was conventional enough: *Geronimo Rex* (1972) is a longish book about the growing up of Harry Monroe, through high school and college in Mississippi. *Geronimo Rex* was nominated for the National Book Award and Hannah seemed assured of a career as a storyteller. But the writing took another direction. After *Nightwatchmen*, a kind of murder mystery using multiple points of view in 1973, Hannah moved away from conventional narrative. His next three works, the story collection *Airships* (1978), the short novel *Ray* (1980), and more recently the novel-connected stories *The Tennis Handsome* (1983), all present a fragmented vision, told by a "voice" that seems to have lost all faith in order. In *Ray*, for example, the protagonist, a Vietnam veteran and former carrier pilot/physician, is also a drug abuser, alcoholic, and unsuccessful husband. His life is a violent shambles by any standard, yet he perseveres. A believer in reincarnation, Ray recounts his adventures from the Civil War as well as the Vietnam War. He stands in no awe of mutability, asserting that he has lived in many centuries. Perhaps because of this belief, *Ray*, and *Airships* also, to a lesser extent, contain what would otherwise appear to be an unwarranted optimism.

There is none of this unwarranted optimism in the novels of Harry Crews. From the first of his eight novels, *The Gospel Singer* (1968), to the most recent, *A Feast of Snakes* (1976), Crews writes powerfully of the impossibility of love. Crews's novels usually end in violence, death, and disorder. Although they are often set in rural Georgia, among people who would be at home in a Caldwell novel, there is a nihilism and despair to his fiction that transcends the simple ignorance and misery of Southern depression-era literature. Like Caldwell and others, Crews uses grotesques in his novels, but in Crews even more than in the Southern writers of the past, the point is that the dwarves, the mutilated characters like the legless deaf-mute, Marvin Molar, in *The Gypsy's Curse* (1974) are different from the rest of us only in that their deformities are visible; to Crews, we are all freaks.

As strong as many of his novels are, it may be that Crews's best work is in his nonfiction collection, *Blood and Grits* (1979), and his memoir of rural southwest Georgia, *A Childhood: A biography of a place* (1978). This last is a beautifully written memoir and may serve Bacon County, Georgia, in the way Isaac Bashevis Singer's writings have served the shtetlach of Poland: by preserving in literature a way of life that has nearly disappeared.

Cormac McCarthy, who has staked out Knoxville, Tennessee, and the mountains to the east of it as his literary territory, also sprinkles his novels with grotesques, but the effect is far less cynical than in Crews's work. Even when McCarthy creates a murderer-necrophile in *Child of God* (1974) or a character in *Suttree* (1979) who sneaks into farmers' gardens at night to rape their watermelons, there is a certain amount of sympathy for these demented souls. They often live lives close to nature in the Smokies and have a certain outlaw quality about them. (McCarthy has a capacity to describe nature with such a sharp and fresh eye that nature itself becomes a character in the fiction, not merely a setting or two-dimensional backdrop.) The outlaw quality takes its most distinct form in the protagonist of McCarthy's first and perhaps best novel, *The Orchard Keeper* (1965). Here Marion Sylder, moonshine runner, is forced to kill Kenneth Rattner, a despicable little man, in self-defense. Later Sylder is pulled out of a car wreck by young John Wesley Rattner and the two establish a kind of father-son relationship, neither knowing that it was Sylder who orphaned John Wesley. The novel is rendered in a poetic sophisticated prose style, astonishing in a first novel, and though many reviewers took McCarthy to task for what they saw as Faulknerian imitation, other readers, like Ralph Ellison, found its prose of "great beauty and hallucinating vividness." This first novel won the Faulkner Foundation Award and McCarthy has recently been awarded the lucrative MacArthur prize.

Two other male writers who have made important contributions to contemporary fiction and show promise of more are Fred Chappell and James Whitehead. Chappell and Whitehead have both published their best work in the 1960s and 1970s and are thus "new" writers.

Chappell, a native North Carolinian and the author of several volumes of verse, has written several novels of boyhood and the North Carolina mountains. The first of these, *It Is Time, Lord* (1963), is perhaps the best. The protagonist is married to a good woman, has two healthy children, but like a Walker Percy hero is suffering badly from "Everydayness," the "unhappiness for no reason." Unlike a Percy hero, James Christopher does not philosophize, he excavates. Christopher searches through his past, his boyhood, especially his relationships to his rural grandparents and his country schoolteacher father, to discover what useful values they passed on to him, who he is, and how he can be happy again with his job at the press and with his rather patient family. *The Inkling* (1965) is a more straightforward account of growing up in the North Carolina mountains, while *Dagon* (1968) handles the same material in a more experimental, even surrealistic manner. In Chappell's fourth novel he has exercised his comic vision. *The Gaudy Place* (1973) is the story of the confusion that erupts when the son of a conventional college professor becomes involved with a teenage prostitute.

James Whitehead has written poetry and fiction. His two volumes of verse, *Domains: Poems* (1966) and *Local Men* (1978), embody many of his concerns. Not particularly avant-garde in language or style, these poems are noteworthy for their treatment of subjects that Whitehead knows and feels strongly about. The first contains poems about the civil rights movement and Whitehead's boyhood in Mississippi, while the second is more concerned with men at work, in the lumber mills and construction crews Whitehead experienced as a young man.

As readable as these poems are, however, it is another novel his readers are waiting for, since the publication of *Joiner* in 1971. Sonny Joiner, the protagonist, is a six-foot-seven-inch tackle who plays high school and college ball, gets into the NFL, and then is knocked out because of an injury. Reading the sections of this novel having to do with Southern football, one is astonished: why hadn't anyone done this before? (Charles Gaines's novel, *Stay Hungry* [1972], about weight lifters and bodybuilders in a Birmingham gym gave the same feeling. Here was material no one had thought to use before.) But *Joiner* is more than a violent giant. He is also a committed believer in the civil rights movement and an intellectual with a specialty in the leveling and egalitarian revolutions of the Reformation era in Germany. He sees the application of those sixteenth-century theories to the Mississippi of the 1960s. Joiner is a man of large appetites and passions. His sins are sins of excess, up to and including violence and manslaughter, but he is a decent and likable person, a memorable fictional creation. Whitehead arrived convincingly with this first novel.

Among the best of the women writers today, several, like Anne Tyler, Doris Betts, Lee Smith, Sylvia Wilkinson, Gail Godwin, and Alice Walker, have produced a number of novels each, while Lisa Alther, Mary Mebane, and Gayl Jones are relative newcomers. Anne Tyler, who is also establishing a national reputation as book reviewer for the Sunday *New York Times,* is the author of nine novels, the first having appeared in 1964. These books, set mainly in Baltimore but sometimes in Virginia or North Carolina, have earned her a wide readership and, with *Dinner at the Homesick Restaurant* (1982), a growing critical response. Tyler has always been a whimsical and delighting writer. In *Searching for Caleb* (1976) her protagonists Justine and Duncan are wonderful eccentrics. Justine is a fortune-teller and Duncan is a genius-tinkerer who can become passionately interested in, accomplished at, and bored with almost anything in the span of two years. They lead a zany life, but Tyler tells us of it in such an affectionate and matter-of-fact tone that one accepts without question such information as Duncan's putting all their organic garbage through the blender and then spreading it on the front lawn. Why not? It might be a good idea. Morgan, of *Morgan's Passing* (1980), dresses in a different costume each day to relieve his tedium. One day, while impersonating a doctor, he delivers a baby and falls in love with the mother.

Tyler is not always so effervescent. Jeremy Pauling of *Celestial Navigation* (1974) loses the only woman he has ever or could conceivably ever love because he simply does not know how to tell her what he is thinking and feeling. The reader is in agony but cannot help. Change is inevitable; people will drift together and apart. In *Dinner at the Homesick Restaurant,* Tyler explores the implications of family. Despite being bound by blood and experience, families fall apart. Tyler is not sentimental about this, but is, perhaps, optimistic. Maybe the deserting father or the brother who rejects the whole idea of family is simply mistaken. He has never really left; the family is still intact. A fine storyteller and an astonishingly productive writer, Tyler is certainly one to watch as she matures and expands into increasingly important themes.

Much the same might be said for Doris Betts, whose career began with a collection of stories, *The Gentle Insurrection* (1954), but who has only recently achieved attention with *Heading West* (1981). Her stories and novels have often been tales of planned, if not executed, escapes. Her female protagonists, often young girls, feel trapped and thwarted by the role of the Southern female but cannot see the way out. Sometimes the protagonist is male, suffering from an inability to communicate, as with the title character of "The Astronomer" from *The Astronomer and Other Stories* (1973). A widower, he is alone and interested in nothing at all until he begins to study the stars and then the myths behind the constellations' names, and then learns to care about a young couple who have rented rooms in his house. He is saved from his alienation as his interest in stars, then stories, leads him to take an interest in other people.

Betts's latest work is probably her best. In *Heading West* Nancy Finch, a small-town librarian, single and in her thirties, is kidnapped by a madman who insists that she accompany him. After the first few days, she realizes that she has stopped actively trying to escape back to the narrow life she has been snatched from. She finally gets away unharmed from her kidnapper, but is permanently changed by the experience. Now, perhaps, she can respond to the love of a man she has met and make good the escape that Betts's younger heroines only dreamed of.

To an even greater extent than Doris Betts, Sylvia Wilkinson is the chronicler of the developing female psyche. Although her five novels are fully set in time and place, the focus is on the inner life of the intelligent young woman trying to fulfill herself and avoid the cramped half-life she sees many of the older women around her leading. Cary, the young heroine of *Moss on the North Side* (1966), hates her slatternly mother and feels close to her father, though like many Wilkinson heroines she wishes he were stronger. Ramy of *A Killing Frost* (1967) is searching for a role model but cannot find it in her loving but old-fashioned grandmother. *Cale* (1970) is a novel of childhood with a male as protagonist, but the real interest lies in the plight of Cale's mother, who was relieved to find herself raising a boy instead of a girl, but then feels trapped and unappreciated. Jean of *Shadow of the Mountain* (1977) differs from the earlier heroines in that she is upper-class and educated, but she is a failure as an Appalachian social worker and is finally killed by the people she is trying to help.

As with the work of Doris Betts, in Wilkinson's more recent novel, *Bone of My Bones* (1982), the situation changes. Ella Ruth Higgins finds her way to fulfillment; she will pursue her career as writer in spite of any opposition. Instead of literally escaping her community, she escapes instead the traditional role it would impose upon her and stays to write about it.

The fourth and youngest of this group is Lee Smith, a writer who has been gaining momentum since her first novel, *The Last Day the Dogbushes Bloomed* (1968). Her female protagonists have grown increasingly older, from Susan Tobey of *Dogbushes* who encounters evil in her ninth summer, through Brooke Kincaid of *Something in the Wind* (1971), who moves through a series of meaningless college affairs hoping perhaps that one of the men would shape her, to Crystal Spangler of *Black Mountain Breakdown* (1980). Crystal is a girl in pain over her father's rejection of life and her mother's struggle to make her into the perfect little girl: cheerleader, born-again Christian, beauty queen, finally Junior Woman in good standing. Like the other Smith heroines, Crystal lacks a strong sense of self and finally succumbs to the cumulative traumas, including a childhood rape. Smith's rendering of Crystal's emotional disintegration is sure and strong. Since *Black Mountain* Smith has published, in short order, *Cakewalk* (1982), and *Oral History* (1983), which is by far her best book. *Oral History* takes place in the same corner of Appalachia as several of the earlier novels, but is set in the late nineteenth and early twentieth century, rather than in the present. The novel is framed by a college girl's assignment—to record her mountain relatives, get their stories, and learn why the old homestead is haunted—but the frame device is soon dropped as the voices of these mountain people take over, some living and some dead, to tell the story of the Cantrell family and the curse that lies upon it. Perhaps because this is a "researched" novel, set in the past and less directly drawn from Smith's own life, it has a more fully imagined quality. It is, in any case, a distinguished piece of work.

While it is clear that feminist concerns are implicit in the novels of the preceding four women, in the fiction of Gail Godwin and Lisa Alther these concerns become explicit. The heroine of Godwin's *Glass People* (1972) makes an attempt to gain independence from her paternalistic, rich, politician husband but is not strong enough to make the break. In *The Odd Woman* (1974), however, we have a female of much greater resources. Jane Clifford, unlike Francesca—the names tell a lot—is a college professor with a doctorate in English. She has to weather loneliness, male chauvinism, and a painful affair with a married art professor to learn finally that she can live by herself, without a man and without wasting a lot of her energy in bitterness. *A Mother and Two Daughters* (1979) is also a strong, topical work. The relationship between the female generations has recently received a lot of psychological and sociological attention and is deftly treated here in fiction.

The two novels of Lisa Alther, *Kinflicks* (1975) and *Original Sins* (1981), suffer from a variety of small flaws—some of the characters are stereotypes, and the propaganda can be quite shrill as the men all turn out to be worthless—but no one will deny one important thing: these novels, especially the first, are among the funniest produced in the South in years. *Kinflicks* follows Ginny Hull through her adolescence, college years, and young womanhood as she tries to grow up in Hullsport, Tennessee, right outside Oak Ridge. Ginny is dated by the high school football hero, has a fling with Clem, a greaser on a Harley, then heads north to school to a lesbian affair at prestigious Worthley College and a misbegotten marriage that ends, of course, in misunderstanding and divorce. The novel is told as a series of flashbacks as Ginny flies home from Vermont to see her mother through her last days. The two women reach some new understanding in these few days, but the shock for Ginny is strong. Unsuccessfully, even comically, she attempts suicide and then packs her few belongings and leaves, "to go where she had no idea."

Original Sins is not greatly inferior to *Kinflicks*; it is simply too repetitive. The most original element in *Original Sins* is the introduction of a black character, Donny, the Black Most Likely to Succeed, who becomes embittered over the racism of the bigots he meets, in the North and South, and what he sees as the hypocrisy of the white liberals. There are scenes of great comedy in this novel and some moving ones as well, but to move ahead Alther must find a new story to tell.

Of the contemporary Southern black writers, it is clear that Alice Walker leads the field. Her triumphs with the story collection *In Love and Trouble*, the novel *Meridian*, and the 1982 winner of the Pulitzer Prize and American Book Award, *The Color Purple*, have given her much deserved attention. Three other Southern black women writers, newer on the scene if not necessarily younger, have also produced some impressive writing.

Berry Morgan, born in 1919 in Port Gibson, Mississippi, may be best known to readers for her *New Yorker* stories of the late 1960s and 1970s. She is also the author of two works of fiction, the novel *Pursuit* (1966) and *The Mystic Adventures of Roxie Stoner* (1974). The first of these is a dark story; a father struggles to help his illegitimate son in his conflict between sin and faith. The second, the Roxie Stoner tales, is a delightful collection of stories, the recollections of an old Mississippi plantation black. Roxie's domestic and amorous adventures from the past are balanced by her present activities as a patient/nurse's aide at the state mental hospital.

Gayl Jones, born in 1949, is the author of *Corregidora*, *Eva's Man*, and the recently published *White Rat*. *Eva's Man* (1976) is a chilling, and at the same time, sensuous novel. Eva is a Southern black woman in prison in New York State. In the course of the action we learn why she killed her man, and we see her slowly seduced, out of despair, by her lesbian cell mate. Like *Eva's Man*, the stories in *White Rat* (1983) fit no mold. The title story has a protagonist who is so light neither blacks nor whites will believe he is black. Henry keeps to the part of the black community that knows him, but he is unable to achieve any status or to keep the affections of his wife Maggie who runs off for a spell with and becomes pregnant by the coal-black J. T.

"The Women" is an even more startling story of sexual initiation told by a young girl whose father has deserted his family. Her mother does not remarry, but instead has a series of women friends. The knowledge of her mother's lesbianism comes slowly to Winnie through the gossip of other small children who themselves only dimly understand. The other women in the neighborhood tell their children Winnie will grow up to be just like her mother, and the girl barely understands what that could mean. As Winnie moves into adolescence she loses her virginity to a young man, in a scene that is filled more with will and defiance than with tenderness, on her mother's bed.

We can hope that Mary Mebane's autobiography, *Mary* (1981), will be one of many produced by Southern blacks. Although there has been a great deal of writing from the black community, little of it has been about the black community. Too little has been written about the every-day life, food, family conversations, domestic crises, stresses, and preju-dices inside that culture. Mebane has produced a fascinating account of growing up in a small black neighborhood on the edges of Durham, North Carolina, in the 1930s and 1940s. She writes of the exhausting work of washing clothes, farming, gathering and preparing food, and so on, but more importantly Mebane writes of the flow of feelings and power in this narrow world. Mary's mother bitterly resented any at-tempts Mary made at education or culture; had it not been for support from her Aunt Jo, Mary would never have had the opportunity for col-lege. And at college, Mary learned more than what was taught in class; she learned how stratified by wealth, social class, and color the black world is, and that white prejudice was not all she had to overcome. This volume should take its place on the shelf with the major slave narratives and black autobiographies of the past. We can only hope that other blacks will be inspired by it to write of their own experiences and thus keep a portion of the American experience from being permanently lost.

Although there are many writers not considered here who might very well have been (to name some would only compound the error), from the examples at hand some predictions about the future of Southern writing can be made. First, one can assume that race will still be a major subject for Southern literature, but not in the same way. The stories of gross cruelty, lynching, and brutality will be fewer and give way to more subtle examinations of race relations in an integrated society. Southerners will continue to be a church-going people, but the role of fundamentalist religion will be diminished in the literature ahead as the influence of the church in the community diminishes. The sense of community itself, long understood as an identifying mark of Southern writing, will also be weaker. Strangers are moving in, and now probably not everyone residing in a small town was born there.

Along with this diminution in sense of community, the South seems to be joining the nation in other attitudes as well. There is more non-teleological thinking, for example, less sense of a master plan. The South will not soon be a nest of nihilists or existentialists, but concerns will move from communal to personal; and chaos and disorder that have been depicted in much Southern literature, as in Shakespearean drama, as a rending of the social fabric, a wound to the body politic, will now be seen in personal and domestic terms, not communal ones. Southerners feel increasingly isolated, alienated from their society, albeit less so than New Yorkers or Los Angelenos, perhaps, and this sense of isolation from kin and neighbors will be a theme of future writing.

As a smaller number of Southerners remain on the land, this central relationship will play a smaller part in Southern writing. The characters of the writing of the future will earn their livings not just as farmers or sheriffs or the owners of small businesses, but as professional people, executives with large corporations, as real estate and life insurance salesmen, and the literature will be set more often in offices, factories, suburbs, and country clubs and less in the fields or woods. The characters of future Southern literature will be a more diverse group. Many will have been sent by their corporations; some will have come from Germany or Japan, perhaps, but they will be making their homes in the South. Because many of them will not have Southern accents, and because radio and television are having their effects on regional speech, there will be less dialect in Southern literature. Phonetic spelling and orthographic humor are already nearly dead and will expire. There will still be Southern speech, of course, but it will be rendered more subtly, through the pronunciations of a few chosen words, through expressions and idioms, through the cadence and lilt of particular regions and groups, such as the way a sorority girl's voice rises at the end of each phrase, making it into a question and an appeal for agreement and approval.

A good portion of the Southern literature of the past has been written by women. Before 1930 or so, much of it was sentimental, popular, and second-rate, but after 1930 Welty, O'Connor, and others have stood in the first rank. But in the future an even higher percentage will be by women, and more importantly, it will be more and more about the question of being female. We can surely look for more frank and even angry writing from Southern women who see themselves as having been denied access in the past to educational opportunities, jobs, full freedom, by having been assigned narrow roles or by having been put up on a pedestal too high to jump off.

Without question, a larger share of the literature will be written by blacks. As educational opportunities for blacks continue to improve there will be more writers; as the economic situation for blacks improves there will be more readers. White readers will, of course, buy and learn from black writings, but the creation of a larger market of black readers is bound to help the black writers. There is every sign this is already underway. There are also indications that this black writing will be different in kind. Rather than focusing on the relations between the races, it will be more frank. It will be about family life, status, love, pain, prejudice, *within* the black community, a community that is still a mystery to most whites, in and out of the South.

Whether most or even some of these predictions turn out to be correct will not be known for several years. What can now be known is this: there are a great many Southern writers who have come to the fore in the last fifteen or so years, many of them have large talents that have already been or will soon be recognized, and in the writings of this group of talented men and women may be found clues to the future of Southern writing.

M. THOMAS INGE

Appendix A
The Study of Southern Literature

The concept of a distinctly Southern literature or culture seems to be as old as the development of a regional self-consciousness early in the nineteenth century. If the Confederacy had succeeded and become a separate nation, what we know as Southern literature would in effect be a national literature. Perhaps culture succeeded where men and arms failed because, whatever the reasons, the development of Southern writing has been insistent and inevitable, and along with the writing there has been a parallel effort to come to critical terms with it as a regional phenomenon. Early commentators and anthologists were soon joined by literary historians and modern critics, who in turn established scholarly journals and university courses and finally created associations and institutions, all basically united in their focus on the study of Southern literature.

As early as 1816 in *Letters from Virginia, Translated from the French*, George Tucker complained about the backwardness of Virginia in its cultural development and urged young people to forego law and medicine for the nobler pursuit of literature and the arts. Intellectuals in other Southern states voiced similar complaints in the 1820s and 1830s, and in letters to Philip C. Pendleton in 1840, William Gilmore Simms voiced his regret that the South was unwilling to support a literary magazine of high quality. Simms recognized the potential for a Southern literature through his several efforts to found a magazine, and his comments on the matter, along with those of many of his contemporaries, constitute the beginnings of a critical awareness. By 1859, for example, in his essay "Literature in the South" for *Russell's Magazine*, Henry Timrod continued to lament the shabby way the South supported its writers, but he went on to state his belief that Southern writing should rise above its use of regional material to a universal level in artistry and theme, and to note that "the South already possesses a literature which calls for its patronage and applause," particularly the work of Poe and Simms.

589

The differences between Northern and Southern culture were encouraged by those who wished to fan the fires of sectionalism and encourage the formation of the Confederacy, and the Civil War would make definitive in the popular mind the concept of a solid, culturally distinct South. That this understanding had entered the college classroom not too long after the end of the war is indicated by the publication in 1879 of *The Southern Student's Hand-Book of Selections for Reading and Oratory*, edited by John G. James, superintendent of the Texas Military Institute in Austin. His selection of 220 speeches, essays, excerpts, and poems on Southern topics was designed to support the notions that the antebellum South was an ideal society and a center of classical culture and that the Civil War was merely the result of an unfortunate misunderstanding.

The anthology, whether intended for the student or the general reader, has been an early and significant force in shaping our perceptions of the development of Southern literature and who the important writers are. The late nineteenth- and early twentieth-century collections in their introductions and biographical headnotes tended to be more laudatory than critical, and careless in their research. This was less true of Louise Manly's 1895 textbook *Southern Literature from 1579 – 1895*, a conscientious and thorough selection designed to place literature in its historic context on the theory that literary works reflect on and elucidate each other (an anticipation of the modern American Studies approach). Selections from eighty-nine authors are arranged in four chronological units with an additional list of thirty-nine recommended writers and a comprehensive appendix of about fourteen hundred other writers deserving attention. The appendix is characteristic of the overstatement found in most of the turn-of-the-century anthologies intended as a retort to the exclusion of Southern authors from the major American literary reference books and encyclopedias published in New York.

Other textbooks widely used in Southern schools were Jennie Thornley Clarke's *Songs of the South* (1896), a generous but mundane selection from the work of over 120 poets; Ross D. Barton's *A Southern Speaker Containing Selections from the Orations, Addresses and Writings of the Best-Known Southern Orators, Southern Statesmen and Southern Authors* (1902), a work defensive of the Old South but accommodationist in its stance; William Lander Weber's *Selections from the Southern Poets* (1901), designed to meet a requirement that all freshmen in Georgia colleges pass an examination on Southern poetry; F. V. N. Painter's *Poets of the South* (1903), pietistic in its selections and editorial opinions; W. P. Trent's *Southern Writers: Selections in Prose and Verse* (1905), a wide-ranging and historically oriented compilation by a distinguished scholar of American literature and biographer of Simms;

Charles William Hubner's *Representative Southern Poets* (1906), a set of biographical sketches of ten poets with the poems interspersed among the jejune prose; Kate Alma Orgain's *Southern Authors in Poetry and Prose* (1908), with twenty-six biographical profiles uniformly superficial, defensive, and laudatory, and probably intended for the general market rather than the classroom; Edwin Mims and Bruce R. Payne's *Southern Prose and Poetry for Schools* (1910), a cooperative venture between the head of the English Department at Vanderbilt University and the president of Peabody College for Teachers, strongly oriented toward the New South movement but critically respectable in its selections; Henry Jerome Stockard's *A Study in Southern Poetry For Use in Schools, Colleges and the Library* (1911), which is less a study than a celebration of the sentimental and romantic by fifty poets; Leonidas Warren Payne's *Southern Literary Readings* (1913), an eclectic selection of more poetry than prose and fiction and with study questions at the back of the book, which demonstrate a distinct approach to the analysis of poetry that would soon be defined as New Criticism (one wonders if any of the New Critics used this textbook in school); and Maurice Garland Fulton's *Southern Life in Southern Literature* (1917), another conventional collection of fiction, poetry, and essays.

A large-scale but monumentally inconsequential effort to document Southern literature in an anthology form was the seventeen-volume *Library of Southern Literature* (1907–1923), edited by Edwin Anderson Alderman, Joel Chandler Harris, and Charles William Kent. In direct reply to numerous Northern anthologies, which neglected Southern writers, especially the eleven-volume *A Library of American Literature* (1889–1890) edited by E. C. Stedman and E. M. Hutchinson, this effort was undertaken to "induce those who write of our American literature to revise their perspective and do ampler justice to a part of our Union too little given to exploiting its own achievements." The publishers assembled an eight-man editorial board, a seventeen-member group of consulting editors (mostly presidents of Southern universities), a nineteen-man advisory council, and a corps of contributing writers (including a few women, unlike the above groups) to produce a thirteen-volume collection of writings in 6,080 pages by 278 writers, with separate essays surveying literature in the South and the French literature of Louisiana. Volume fourteen is a miscellaneous collection of anonymous and fugitive poems, letters, anecdotes, epitaphs, and quotations; volume fifteen is a biographical dictionary of almost 3,800 sketches of writers; and volume sixteen contains seventy-nine essays and poems on various subjects, fifty reading lists for systematic study, a historical chart, bibliographies for individual authors, and an analytical index.

The final volume is an additional collection of works by thirty-three authors not included in the earlier volumes, apparently intended to be the first of a series, as it is titled *Supplement No. 1*, which was not continued. Despite the impressive size and range of this project, still handsome today in the deluxe edition bound in red leather with a seal of a Southern state stamped in gold on each volume, the state of scholarship was so inadequate when it was completed, and the editorial control so given to enthusiasm rather than critical judgment, that the library did little to change national attitudes toward Southern writers. In many cases it does contain, however, the first and last word on a host of minor figures.

The earliest effort to deal with Southern literature in a comprehensive fashion is James Wood Davidson's *The Living Writers of the South* (1869), a survey of some two hundred writers with entries arranged alphabetically and including a biographical sketch and a brief excerpt. Comprehensiveness rather than literary value seemed to be Wood's working principle. The two-volume *Pioneers of Southern Literature* (1896) by Samuel Albert Link is a collection of selective essays on Southern poets, fiction writers (including Simms and Poe), humorists, historians, and political writers. Largely derivative and relying more on quotation than original thought, it is written in a straightforward style and unusually free of the sentimental and provincial. A selection of six essays on Irwin Russell, J. C. Harris, Maurice Thompson, Sidney Lanier, G. W. Cable, and M. N. Murfree constitutes *Southern Writers: Biographical and Critical Studies* (1897) by William Malone Baskervill, a pioneer teacher-scholar in Southern studies (Baskervill's "Southern Literature," *PMLA*, 7 [1892], 89–100, was probably the first article on the subject in a scholarly journal). Although trained in German scholarship at Leipzig and independent in his critical judgment, Baskervill was not entirely free of the prejudices of his age. His intention to publish a second collection of essays, prevented by his death, was fulfilled by his students who contributed another eleven essays largely on local-color writers to *Southern Writers: Biographical and Critical Studies* (Volume II, 1903), a collection uneven in quality and usefulness.

The turn of the century brought a host of new efforts to assess and survey Southern writing, nearly all marred by derivative research, commonplace opinion, and sectional piety: Carl Holliday's *A History of Southern Literature* (1906), noteworthy mainly as the first effort to produce a comprehensive history in chronological chapters; F. V. N. Painter's *Poets of Virginia* (1907), a relentless description of seemingly every poet who ever published a volume of verse in Virginia (over one hundred, plus seven from West Virginia); Caroline M. Brevard's *Literature of the South* (1908), a superficial secondary school survey from Thomas Hariot to Sidney Lanier with more history than literary comment; and La Salle Corbell Pickett's *Literary Hearthstones of Dixie* (1912), an early example of the literary guide to the homes of famous authors, cloying in its sentimentality and purple prose. The best of the lot is Montrose J. Moses' sensible and comprehensive survey *The Literature of the South* (1910), which begins by condemning the tendency of Southerners to overpraise local minor talents and determines to dwell "only upon that writing which affects or has influenced Southern thought and culture." Although given to careless error and generalization, the book remained the standard survey for a long time.

In 1927, in the second volume of his monumental *Main Currents in American Thought*, Vernon Louis Parrington brought Southern writing of 1800 to 1860 into conjunction with the liberal tradition in American letters. With no interest in aesthetics, he found the material rich in information about politics and social thought. Also in 1927, the widow of university professor C. Alphonso Smith collected some of his popular lectures on literature and oratory in the South, including lectures on Jefferson, Poe, J. C. Harris, and O. Henry, in the memorial volume *Southern Literary Studies*, which still has its charm.

The most influential book of the 1930s was the collaborative effort edited by W. T. Couch, *Culture in the South* (1934), in which over thirty writers and scholars—including Donald Davidson ("The Trend of Literature") and John Donald Wade ("Southern Humor")—examine every conceivable aspect of Southern life, character, and culture in many surprisingly durable essays. Also still useful are the fifteen fine essays on general trends and writers in Southern literature and culture written and collected by Edd Winfield Parks in his *Segments of Southern Thought* (1938). While it dealt with literature only indirectly, W. J. Cash's *Mind of the South* (1941) should be noted for the debate it generated on all things Southern and its ultimate value less as sociology than as the creative act of a brilliant but troubled imagination.

In Southern literary and cultural studies, the publication of Jay B. Hubbell's *The South in American Literature: 1607–1900* (1954) was a momentous event. Twenty years in the making, exhaustively researched, and gracefully written, the book is an encyclopedic compendium of little-known and fascinating information. Its suggestions for further research have fed several generations of graduate students and scholars. It lacks a central focus, and barely steps into the twentieth century, yet it remains the only comprehensive study of its kind by a single author.

Further scholarly excursions into the material by Hubbell are found in his lectures, *Southern Life in Literature* (1960), and most of the collected essays in *South and Southwest* (1965).

Among the general studies after Hubbell worth mentioning, but each specialized in its scope, are Edmund Wilson's provocative but always engaging essays in *Patriotic Gore: Studies in the Literature of the Civil War* (1962); J. V. Ridgely's concise and accurate overview, *Nineteenth-Century Southern Literature* (1980); and Anne Goodwyn Jones's judicious study, *Tomorrow is Another Day: The Woman Writer in the South, 1859–1936* (1981). Many areas of Southern literature and culture are also well handled in a collection of essays *The American South: Portrait of a Culture* (1980), edited by Louis D. Rubin, Jr.

Twentieth-century scholarship, as well as the literary Renascence itself, encouraged a whole new generation of anthologies and textbooks. Both Addison Givvard's trade anthology, *The Lyric South* (1928), and William T. Wynn's textbook, *Southern Literature* (1932), highlighted the work of recently arrived writers like John Crowe Ransom and John Donald Wade. Two volumes in the American Writers Series, Edd Winfield Parks's *Southern Poets* (1936) and Gregory Paine's *Southern Prose Writers* (1947), were the first to incorporate modern critical scholarship in their textual apparatuses and thorough introductions. Other collections, compiled primarily by the writers themselves, included Robert Penn Warren's *A Southern Harvest: Short Stories by Southern Writers* (1937), Stark Young's *Southern Treasury of Life and Literature* (1937), *Contemporary Southern Prose* (1940) compiled by Richmond Croom Beatty and William Perry Fidler, Allen Tate's collection of stories, poems, and essays in memory of John Peale Bishop, *A Southern Vanguard* (1947), and Willard Thorp's topically arranged *A Southern Reader* (1955).

Under the editorial supervision of Randall Stewart, three scholars—Richmond Croom Beatty, Floyd C. Watkins, and Thomas Daniel Young—edited the textbook that largely shaped the teaching of Southern literature for over two decades, *The Literature of the South* (1952, revised 1968). A useful collection that excluded contemporary writing was *Southern Writing, 1585–1920* (1970), edited by Richard Beale Davis, C. Hugh Holman, and Louis D. Rubin, Jr. The only other major textbook is Rubin's *The Literary South* (1979), a less historical and more broadly cultural approach to the study of Southern letters.

Some of the useful specialized anthologies include Arlin Turner's *Southern Stories* (1960); *Southern Writing in the Sixties: Fiction* (1966), and *Southern Writing in the Sixties: Poetry* (1967), both edited by John William Corrington and Miller Williams; John C. Guilds's *Nineteenth-*

Century Southern Fiction (1970); The Southern Experience in Short Fiction (1971) by Allen F. Stein and Thomas N. Walters; and Stories of the Modern South (1977) by Benjamin Forkner and Patrick Samway, S.J. Well-edited state-oriented anthologies are A Tricentennial Anthology of South Carolina Literature, 1670–1970 (1971) by Richard J. Calhoun and John C. Guilds, New Writing in South Carolina (1971) by William Peden and George Garrett, and An Anthology of Mississippi Writers (1979) by Noel E. Polk and James R. Scafidel. Southern literary humor has been well served by five anthologies: Franklin J. Meine's Tall Tales of the Southwest (1930), Arthur Palmer Hudson's Humor of the Old Deep South (1936), Walter Blair's Native American Humor (1937), Hennig Cohen and William B. Dillingham's Humor of the Old Southwest (1964), and John Q. Anderson's With the Bark On (1967).

What we have come to call the Southern literary Renascence, the remarkable flowering of writing by Southern authors since 1920, was first surveyed in two excellent collections of essays edited by Louis D. Rubin, Jr., and Robert D. Jacobs—Southern Renascence: The Literature of the Modern South (1953) and South: Modern Southern Literature in Its Cultural Setting (1961). More distinguished for its comprehensiveness (over seven hundred writers are discussed in two hundred pages) than its critical perception is John M. Bradbury's Renaissance in the South: A Critical History of the Literature, 1920–1960 (1963). In The Literature of Memory: Modern Writers of the American South (1977), Richard Gray examines the literature within the social and historical contexts of Southern tradition and identity, an approach which often threatens to distort the literature but which is applied with more satisfactory results by Michael O'Brien in his study of such intellectuals as Howard Odum, John Donald Wade, John Crowe Ransom, Allen Tate, Frank Owsley, and Donald Davidson and their interpretations of the "Southern consciousness" in The Idea of the American South, 1920–1941 (1979). Richard H. King's A Southern Renaissance: The Cultural Awakening of the American South, 1930–1955 (1980), moves beyond history and sociology into cultural anthropology and psychoanalysis, which in conjunction with his sympathy for the liberal tradition makes a balanced treatment of the literature impossible. A full critically balanced survey of the Renascence remains to be written, but there are several studies of the fiction that have been influential: Louise Y. Gossett's Violence in Recent Southern Fiction (1965), Frederick J. Hoffman's The Art of Southern Fiction (1967), and the symposium of papers and conversations among Walter Sullivan, C. Hugh Holman, and Louis D. Rubin, Jr., in Southern Fiction Today: Renascence and Beyond (1969), edited by George Core. The knell of doom and case for the conclusion of the Renascence has been argued in brilliant style by Walter Sullivan in two brief volumes, *Death by Melancholy: Essays in Modern Southern Fiction* (1972), and *A Requiem for the Renascence: The State of Fiction in the Modern South* (1976).

The specific movements in modern Southern letters most written about are the separate but related Fugitive and Agrarian movements (separate in purpose and ideology but related in that the leaders of both were the same—Ransom, Davidson, Tate, and Warren). The best background statements for both are found in the lectures of one of the participants—Donald Davidson's *Southern Writers in the Modern World* (1958). While John M. Bradbury's *The Fugitives: A Critical Account* (1958) was the first history of the poetry movement, it is neither as well researched nor as critically sound as Louise Cowan's *The Fugitive Group* (1959), which was written with full access to the writers and their papers. Also useful are the transcriptions of conversations held at Vanderbilt in 1956 among the writers and published by Rob Roy Purdy in *Fugitives' Reunion* (1959). William Pratt's anthology, *The Fugitive Poets* (1965), is an extremely useful adjunct to the study of the group.

The most comprehensive and exhaustively thorough history of the Agrarian movement is found in Virginia Rock's 1961 dissertation "The Making and Meaning of *I'll Take My Stand*: A Study in Utopian-Conservatism, 1925–1939" (published on microfilm in 1964). John L. Stewart's weighty *The Burden of Time: The Fugitives and Agrarians* (1965) attempts history and criticism, both unsatisfactorily because the research was not extensive enough and the analyses the result of a biased and narrow critical vision. Also inadequately researched and derivative is *Tillers of a Myth: Southern Agrarians as Social and Literary Critics* (1966) by Alexander Karanikas, who attempts to place the group in its social and intellectual context. By far the richest and most critically balanced assessment of the four major figures (Ransom, Davidson, Tate, and Warren) and their relationships to both movements is *The Wary Fugitives: Four Poets and the South* (1978) by Louis D. Rubin, Jr. The fiftieth anniversary of the publication of the Agrarian symposium *I'll Take My Stand* brought forth a collection of interesting retrospective essays in *A Band of Prophets: The Vanderbilt Agrarians After Fifty Years* (1982), edited by William C. Havard and Walter Sullivan, and a set of perceptive lectures examining the continuing relevance of the book in Thomas Daniel Young's *Waking Their Neighbors Up: The Nashville Agrarians Reconsidered* (1982). A selection of primary materials are reprinted in *Agrarianism in American Literature* (1969), edited by M. Thomas Inge. A liberal response to *I'll Take My Stand* was framed by members of the moderate L. Q. C. Lamar Society in *You*

Can't Eat Magnolias (1972), edited by H. Brandt Ayers and Thomas H. Naylor, and a reaffirmation of its principles by a new generation of Fifteen Southerners is found in *Why the South Will Survive* (1981).

While it will be impossible here to provide a detailed overview of the work of the numerous modern critics who have established and clarified the aesthetic principles and social forces at work in Southern literature, it is essential to mention just a few of the most influential (in the order of their chronological seniority). While Cleanth Brooks has achieved major distinction for his work on the entire range of English and American literature, his work on Faulkner in *William Faulkner: The Yoknapatawpha Country* (1963) and *William Faulkner: Toward Yoknapatawpha and Beyond* (1978) may well be definitive in its rich use of Southern history and culture and its clear grasp of Faulkner's aesthetic intent. Lewis Leary has taken the entire body of American literature as his province, but his works on Mark Twain, Faulkner, and Nathaniel Tucker have been of particular importance. Many of Leary's best essays on Southern writers are collected in his book *Southern Excursions* (1971).

Few scholars have been so scrupulously thorough and exhaustive in their research as Richard Beale Davis, who refused to accept the easy generalizations about the lack of culture in the colonial South and turned up through his persistence a seemingly inexhaustible supply of information to prove the richness of early intellectual life, as documented in such works as *Intellectual Life in Jefferson's Virginia, 1790–1830* (1964) and *Literature and Society in Early Virginia, 1608–1840* (1973), all capped by his impressive magnum opus, published before his death, the three-volume *Intellectual Life in the Colonial South, 1585–1763* (1978). If a scholar may be known by his students and the other scholars inspired by his example, Davis is well served by such works as J. A. Leo Lemay's *Men of Letters in Colonial Maryland* (1972) or the essays contributed by fourteen hands in *Essays in Early Virginia Literature Honoring Richard Beale Davis* (1977), edited by Lemay.

C. Hugh Holman believed that Southern literature was best understood in the historic, social, and moral environment out of which it came, and he approached his critical work after a scrupulous study of the past and with a refined moral sensibility that both condemned and praised the South for its vices and victories. His exact prose style and keen intellect abound in such books as *Three Modes of Southern Fiction* (1966), *The Roots of Southern Writing* (1972), *The Immoderate Past: The Southern Writer and History* (1977), and *Windows on the World: Essays on American Social Fiction* (1979). Holman's concerns over the influence of the past on the present, and the presence of a moral sensibility in life and out, are shared by several other critics, such as Lewis P. Simpson, as seen in *The Man of Letters in New England and the South* (1973) and *The Dispossessed Garden: Pastoral and History in Southern Literature* (1975); Thomas Daniel Young, whose *Gentleman in a Dustcoat: A Biography of John Crowe Ransom* (1976) and *The Past in the Present: A Thematic Study of Modern Southern Fiction* (1981) have been praised for their grasp of the main currents in Southern thought; and Floyd C. Watkins, whose independence of mind and trenchant opinions can be seen in such books as *The Death of Art: Black and White in the Recent Southern Novel* (1970) and *In Time and Place: Some Origins of American Fiction* (1977).

Among the more productive and influential of the modern critics is Louis D. Rubin, Jr. In addition to the books mentioned elsewhere in this essay, as well as studies of Thomas Wolfe and George W. Cable, he has written a veritable bookshelf of criticism that leaves few corners of Southern literature unexplored, a partial list of which would include *The Faraway Country: Writers of the Modern South* (1963), *The Curious Death of the Novel: Essays in American Literature* (1967), *The Writer in the South* (1972), *William Elliott Shoots a Bear: Essays in the Southern Literary Imagination* (1975), and *A Gallery of Southerners* (1982).

The work of a host of other critics, literary historians, and bibliographers should be discussed in any survey of Southern studies. At a minimum, a list of names would include (in alphabetical order and omitting any names mentioned elsewhere in this essay) Joseph Blotner, M. E. Bradford, Panthea Reid Broughton, Jackson R. Bryer, Louis J. Budd, James R. Colvert, Martha E. Cook, Eugene Current-Garcia, Charles T. Davis, Cecil D. Eby, Ruel E. Foster, Melvin J. Friedman, Richard Harwell, Blyden Jackson, James H. Justus, Richard S. Kennedy, Kimball King, Lewis A. Lawson, Edgar E. MacDonald, Julian D. Mason, Jr., James B. Meriwether, Rayburn S. Moore, Guy Owen, Ladell Payne, Noel Polk, J. R. Raper, Saunders Redding, Paschal Reeves, Milton Rickels, Blair Rouse, Dorothy M. Scura, L. Moody Simms, Lawrence S. Thompson, Darwin T. Turner, Ruth M. Vande Kieft, Richard Walser, Charles S. Watson, Robert L. White, Mary Ann Wimsatt, and Louis B. Wright. This inventory is far from exhaustive.

The Society for the Study of Southern Literature (SSSL), founded in 1968, is an organization of scholars devoted to the mission stated in its name. In addition to providing programs for major professional conventions, the SSSL has supported a series of bibliographic and reference works that are the beginning points for further research: *A Bibliographical Guide to the Study of Southern Literature* (1969), edited by

Louis D. Rubin, Jr.; *Southern Literary Study: Problems and Possibilities* (1975), edited by Rubin and C. Hugh Holman; *Southern Writers: A Biographical Dictionary* (1979), edited by Robert Bain, Joseph M. Flora, and Rubin; *Southern Literary Culture: A Bibliography of Masters' and Doctors' Theses* (1979), edited by O. B. Emerson and Marion C. Michael; and *Southern Literary Culture, 1969–1975: A Checklist of Theses and Dissertations: A Supplement*, a special issue of *Mississippi Quarterly* (Winter, 1978–1979). The Bibliography Committee of the SSSL since 1969 has produced an annual annotated checklist of scholarship on Southern literature published in the spring issues of the *Mississippi Quarterly*, an eight-year conflation of which was edited by Jerry T. Williams as *Southern Literature, 1968–1975* (1978).

While several of the major literary quarterlies—such as *Sewanee Review* (1892–), *Virginia Quarterly Review* (1925–), *Southern Review* (1935–1942, 1965–), and *Georgia Review* (1947–)—have always been hospitable to essays about Southern writers, those which specialize in Southern literature and culture are *Mississippi Quarterly* (1948–), *Southern Studies* (1961–), *Southern Quarterly* (1962–), and *Southern Literary Journal* (1968–). Bibliographic guides to the periodical criticism are mentioned in the preceding paragraph.

An encouraging sign of the permanency of the study of Southern literature is the establishment in recent years of institutes devoted to gathering research materials and promoting special programs and projects in the field—the Institute for Southern Studies at the University of South Carolina and the Center for the Study of Southern Culture at the University of Mississippi are two major examples. There is, unfortunately, no guide to Southern manuscript materials and archival resources, such as the Fugitive and Agrarian collections at Vanderbilt University or the Weatherford-Hammond Appalachian Collection at Berea College, but a little information can be gleaned from Margaret L. Young's *Directory of Special Libraries and Information Centers* (1981) and the second edition of *American Literary Manuscripts* (1977) edited by J. Albert Robbins.

Even more encouraging is the fact that a large number of universities and colleges have in their catalogs courses in Southern literature, Faulkner, or selected Southern writers, which are taught frequently to meet the student demand. A great many of these institutions are outside the South, a clear sign that the study of Southern literature is entirely free of its provincial beginnings and has become a part of the mainstream of American scholarship and criticism. Given the hands at work and the tools available, the time was never brighter for coming to terms with the history, life, and culture of this major American region.

BLYDEN JACKSON

Appendix B
The Black Academy and
Southern Literature

Colleges for the slaves would have been, of course, an anomaly of the first magnitude in the antebellum South. Even so, the last guns of the Civil War were hardly stilled before black Shaw University in Raleigh admitted its first student. Twenty more black colleges were started in the South before the end of 1870. Perhaps four times as many other black colleges (some of which have long been closed) were added to these first twenty by 1900. Another thirteen, one as late as 1977, have been added in the South since 1900. As of the 1980s about eighty-five predominantly black colleges survive within the region. Of this eighty-five, Howard University and the Southern University System (in Louisiana) each annually enrolls slightly more than ten thousand students. Nevertheless, even in the late twentieth century the typical black college is a relatively small institution with less than two thousand students, where everybody tends to know everybody else and the directly personal influence of one professor throughout an entire school may be pervasive as it never could be in a truly populous center of learning.

The black college in the South, then, before desegregation (as largely after) was intimate, isolated, and—especially as long as it prudently avoided any attacks upon the status quo—something of an oasis of middle-class respectability and comfort. At one level of its apparent self-expression, it was a virtual antithesis of the black folk culture on which many of its students and faculty members had been weaned.

Late in the sixteenth chapter of *Invisible Man* the anonymous protagonist of the novel, who has just delivered his first speech for the Brotherhood (clearly the Communist party under another name) and is still in a state of heightened activity of all of his powers, recalls one of his teachers in the Southern black college he has recently left. The teacher's name is Woodridge and the protagonist envisions Woodridge, in the mirror of reminiscence, "half-drunk on words and full of contempt and exaltation, pacing before the blackboard chalked with quotations from

Joyce and Yeats and Sean O'Casey." It seems unquestionable that the college in *Invisible Man* is a very thinly disguised version of the Tuskegee Institute, which Ralph Ellison, the author of *Invisible Man*, actually did attend. There was at Ellison's Tuskegee an English professor named Saunders Walker who fits the image of Woodridge in every significant detail. Ellison makes easily evident his protagonist's accurate perception that Woodridge, whatever else might be said of him, was genuinely attracted to Joyce and Yeats and O'Casey simply because they were artists worthy of anyone's serious attention. Woodridge is no parochial and no pretender as a patron of the arts.

But Ellison also makes it clear that the protagonist of *Invisible Man*, even as he remembers the empirical reality of Woodridge's concern for art as art, remembers as an equally empirical reality Woodridge's interest in Joyce and Yeats and Sean O'Casey because they were Irish. As Irish they had their own consciousness of what it meant to be a member of a minority group and to try to accommodate that when they wrote. Woodridge, or Saunders Walker, aptly symbolizes one aspect of the black academy, particularly in its humanist contingent. Throughout the South since Appomattox on the faculties of black colleges there have been teachers like Woodridge, benignly enchanted with literature, full of a missionary spirit to infect their students with a similar enchantment, and troubled lest that very enchantment should occasion, on their part, any treachery to their race. Such teachers, however tenuously in some respects, have played a role in Southern literature.

In one way the role of these teachers in Southern literature has not been tenuous, for some teachers have been writers—most notably, perhaps, Melvin Tolson, Saunders Redding, Sterling Brown, Margaret Walker and, until he abandoned college teaching to become, eventually, a great public figure as the president of the National Urban Coalition, M. Carl Holman. But mainly Southern literature has benefited indirectly from these teachers. A few of their students, like Ellison or Alvin Aubert or Alice Walker, for instance, have matured into writers themselves. But the major service of these teachers to Southern literature has been to create and sustain in their constituency an audience for written literature. They have obviously performed this service in their classrooms. But they have performed it also through students of theirs who were once virtually the only teachers of black high school students in the South.

It is true that for more than a generation after the Civil War many of the teachers in the private colleges for blacks in the South (though never in any state-supported schools) were white. The men who molded James Weldon Johnson, for instance, at the old Atlanta University were New

Englanders of the abolitionist strain, and Fisk University's last white president, a Quaker, did not quit his office until 1946. Nevertheless, from the beginnings of the black college, black teachers were employed there. Black high schools did not flourish in the South until after World War I. Some of them, incidentally, disappeared after desegregation, having experienced a life shorter than the lives of most of their students. In any case, however, these high schools lasted long enough for the evangelism of teachers taught by the black teachers of college literature to exercise itself within them. It was largely thus that an awareness, and some love, of written literature was imparted to descendants of a people to whom, for more than two hundred American years, the world of recorded communication had been a phenomenon occurring on another planet.

Perhaps no single individual provides a more striking illustration of the black teacher of literature in the black college during the difficult years between 1880 and 1940 than Benjamin Griffiths Brawley—born in South Carolina in 1882, dead in 1939, son of the president of a black college, educated at Morehouse, Chicago, and Harvard, once an academic dean at Morehouse and, for perhaps some twenty years, probably the best-known and most respected of all black publishing scholars in literature in the entire black college world. Connoisseurs of black scholarship tend to venerate as classics Brawley's *The Negro in Literature and Art, A Social History of the American Negro, Early Negro American Writers* and *The Negro Genius*. But Brawley may have rendered no greater service to the Southern black college and Southern literature than the instruction he provided in the classroom to black students at Morehouse, Shaw, and Howard, the three colleges at which he taught. A decided mulatto, Brawley was also, in tastes, a Boston Brahmin. He could not reconcile himself to what he perceived as the coarser (where some undoubtedly would have said, instead, the black-folk) elements in luminaries of the Harlem Renaissance like Langston Hughes. But this is not a simple world. Du Bois, in his famous essay "Of Mr. Booker T. Washington and Others," reminded Washington that, had there not been liberal arts colleges for Negroes such as Fisk, there would certainly have been no institutions like Tuskegee oriented toward training black farmers and artisans. So, without Brawley and his kind there may well not have been some of the very black artists, and critics, of whom Brawley disapproved, or would have disapproved, as well as black followers of the genteel tradition who were very much in Brawley's own vein.

Brawley worked largely alone. So, to some extent, did every black teacher of literature in a Southern black college. Yet, associations of teachers of literature in black colleges did occur. The most important of them for Southern literature certainly has been the one conceived by Hugh Gloster and founded in 1937 at then LeMoyne College in Memphis as the Association of Teachers of English in Negro Colleges which became, in 1941, the College Language Association. The CLA, as it now is usually called, has not been a mere shadow of a substance. A major reason for its formation was the feeling universally shared by black college teachers for many years that they were not truly included in the deliberations, and especially in the conviviality, supposedly available to them at meetings of the Modern Language Association or its regional subaffiliates in the South. Moreover, in the South black college teachers once wondered how much they would be segregated, not necessarily by the regional subaffiliates, but by the hotels at which the subaffiliates tended to meet.

Hence, as well as because of its compactness in size, the College Language Association has elicited, and elicits, from its members a perhaps unusually intense measure of loyalty and support. Its presidents and vice-presidents (who automatically succeed to the presidency) serve two-year terms but come and go and are not reelected. Still, the College Language Association tends to be a very stable organization. Its secretary and treasurer rarely change. One of its treasurers, John Matheus (who wrote poetry and short stories before and during the Harlem Renaissance, in addition to teaching French) served in that capacity for more than thirty years before retiring from office in his nineties.

A prominent function of the CLA, as of all organizations of its kind, has been its annual meetings where scholarly papers are read. Within a few years of its founding the CLA began to issue, in mimeographed form, the *CLA Bulletin*. But in 1957 the *CLA Bulletin* was discontinued and a printed periodical, the *CLA Journal*, under the editorship of Therman O'Daniel, a professor of English at what is now Morgan State University, made its first appearance. During its first year the *CLA Journal* was issued twice. For the next eight years it appeared three times annually. In its tenth year of operation it became a quarterly. O'Daniel, the epitome of the dedicated and competent, though modest, servant of a cause, without a subsidy, had transformed it from the subject of a piece of legislation into a respectable periodical. The black scholar A. Russell Brooks, once an editor of the *CLA Bulletin*, in 1982 studied the *CLA Journal*. He was struck by the insights the *Journal* provided into black attitudes. For the first decade of the periodical less than half of the articles it published were racially oriented. In its second decade for every article it published that was not racially oriented the *Journal* published three that were. Seventeen special issues of the *Jour-*

nal between 1969 and 1976 each dealt with some aspect of black studies. The scholarship represented in the papers read at the CLA annual meetings also became more racially oriented by much the same percentages and over precisely the same decades as the articles in the *Journal*. The way of the CLA *Journal* attitudinally was the way of the CLA, and both were the way of the black writer, and perhaps of black people everywhere, in the South of desegregation.

An organization that to some extent parallels the CLA was established in 1930 when representatives from five black schools, led by Randolph Edmonds of the then Morgan College, formed the Negro Intercollegiate Dramatic Association. By 1936 Edmonds had moved to, Dillard University. In that year he largely engineered the establishment of the Southern Association of Dramatic and Speech Arts, which came to be known as SADSA and, in effect, superseded the Negro Intercollegiate Dramatic Association. Over Edmonds' objections, SADSA became, in 1951, NADSA, the National Association of Dramatic and Speech Arts. Under both its names, the association has encouraged the writing and the staging of plays on Negro campuses, collegiate and otherwise. For years Melvin Tolson was one of its most active members.

Edmonds himself was an indefatigable writer of plays. Annual meetings of NADSA (or SADSA) were unfailingly occasions for the presentation of many original works by black writers, including one-act plays. Before the 1960s, Negroes wrote relatively few plays. Since that time, on and off Broadway and in such ventures as the Free Southern Negro Theater, Negro playwrights have become more active, as have blacks in every phase of serious theater. To some extent the black dramatist of the 1960s and afterward and other blacks professionally connected with the same theater are creatures of NADSA. William Wellington Mackey whose one-act play *Family Meeting* is included in William Couch's anthology *New Black Playwrights*, had seen the one-act plays of NADSA members and had been engaged in their production while he was a student at Southern University.

Since the 1950s, in all forms of literature American blacks have been active as never before. Not only the children from the Northern black ghettos, but also their counterparts in the South, have grown up under conditions that have permitted an increase in formal education. And so there have been more Woodridges. In the works of the Woodridges have come enterprises like the no longer extant little magazines primarily for student writers, *Dassein* at Howard and *Ex Umbra* at North Carolina Central University, or the journals for both critics and creative writers, *Obsidian*, edited by Alvin Aubert, and *Callaloo*, edited by Charles Rowell, former members of black faculties who now teach at white universities. Strong centers of interest in literature, especially black, exist on black campuses, as at Howard, where the apostle of a black aesthetic, Stephen Henderson, succeeds Arthur Davis and Sterling Brown, or in the Atlanta University System, domicile of, among others, the extremely able and erudite observer of black literature and culture, Richard Long. Some of the latterly increasing ferment in black literature is certainly occasioned by powerful, almost ubiquitous forces in our social order, such as the civil rights activism of the 1960s. But some of it, too, is occasioned by the presence and the work of the black academy. The Woodridges have had their day. Even in schools designed to fit Booker T. Washington's philosophy of education for the Southern Negro, their doctrine has established a chain of converts, of black Southerners to whom literature is real as it never would have been had not the Woodridges been part of these converts' experiences in school.

Index